The Divine Names

A Mystical Theology of the Names of God in the Qur'an

Letter from the General Editor

The Library of Arabic Literature makes available Arabic editions and English translations of significant works of Arabic literature, with an emphasis on the seventh to nineteenth centuries. The Library of Arabic Literature thus includes texts from the pre-Islamic era to the cusp of the modern period, and encompasses a wide range of genres, including poetry, poetics, fiction, religion, philosophy, law, science, travel writing, history, and historiography.

Books in the series are edited and translated by internationally recognized scholars. They are published as hardcovers in parallel-text format with Arabic and English on facing pages, as English-only paperbacks, and as downloadable Arabic editions. For some texts, the series also publishes separate scholarly editions with full critical apparatus.

The Library encourages scholars to produce authoritative Arabic editions, accompanied by modern, lucid English translations, with the ultimate goal of introducing Arabic's rich literary heritage to a general audience of readers as well as to scholars and students.

The publications of the Library of Arabic Literature are generously supported by Tamkeen under the NYU Abu Dhabi Research Institute Award G1003 and are published by NYU Press.

Philip F. Kennedy
General Editor, Library of Arabic Literature

معاني الأسماء الإلهيّة

الشيخ الإمام عفيف الدين سليمان التلمسانيّ

LIBRARY OF
المكتبة
ARABIC
العربية
LITERATURE

The Divine Names

A Mystical Theology of the Names of God in the Qur'an

ʿAfīf al-Dīn al-Tilimsānī

Edited and translated by
Yousef Casewit

Volume editor
Mohammed Rustom

NEW YORK UNIVERSITY PRESS
New York

NEW YORK UNIVERSITY PRESS
New York

Library of Congress Cataloging-in-Publication Data

Names: Tilimsānī, ʿAfīf al-Dīn Sulaymān ibn ʿAlī, -1291, author. | Casewit, Yousef, translator. | Tilimsānī, ʿAfīf al-Dīn Sulaymān ibn ʿAlī, -1291. Maʿānī al-asmāʾ al-ilāhīyah. English. | Tilimsānī, ʿAfīf al-Dīn Sulaymān ibn ʿAlī, -1291. Maʿānī al-asmāʾ al-ilāhīyah.
Title: The divine names : a mystical theology of the names of God in the Qur'an / ʿAfīf al-Dīn al-Tilimsānī ; edited and translated by Yousef Casewit.
Description: New York : New York University Press, 2024. | Includes bibliographical references and index. | In English and Arabic; includes original Arabic and English translation. | Summary: "A Sufi scholar's philosophical interpretation of the names of God"-- Provided by publisher.
Identifiers: LCCN 2023012388 | ISBN 9781479826124 (cloth) | ISBN 9781479826131 (ebook) | ISBN 9781479826148 (ebook)
Subjects: LCSH: God (Islam)--Name. | Muslims--Prayers and devotions.
Classification: LCC BP166.2 .T5513 2024 | DDC 297.2/112--dc23/eng/20230508

LC record available at https://lccn.loc.gov/2023012388

New York University Press books are printed on acid-free paper, and their binding materials are chosen for strength and durability.

Series design by Titus Nemeth.

Typeset in Tasmeem, using DecoType Naskh and Emiri.

Typesetting and digitization by Stuart Brown.

Manufactured in the United States of America
c10 9 8 7 6 5 4 3 2 1

Table of Contents

بِسْمِ ٱللَّهِ ٱلرَّحْمَٰنِ ٱلرَّحِيمِ

ٱللَّهُ وَلِيُّ ٱلَّذِينَ آمَنُوا يُخْرِجُهُم مِّنَ ٱلظُّلُمَاتِ إِلَى ٱلنُّورِ

To Sidi Shaykh Mohamed Faouzi al-Karkari
quddisa sirruh

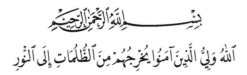

Acknowledgments

I am immensely grateful to Seyyed Hossein Nasr, who inspired me to pursue Islamic Studies, and to William Chittick, who taught me to read Arabic Sufi texts. I also wish to express my profound gratitude to my volume editor, Mohammed Rustom, for his meticulous help and generous support. My dear parents, Daoud and Fatima, read early drafts of my translation and I remain in their debt, both in this world and in the hereafter. A special thanks to Khalid Williams for his careful reading of the text, to my dear brother Faris Casewit for his insightful suggestions, and to the external reviewers and the Library of Arabic Literature's outstanding editorial board. I greatly appreciate the insights of my learned friend Saad Ansari, as well as those of my esteemed colleagues ʿAbd al-Rahim al-ʿAlami, Oludamini Ogunnaike, and Dina Ibrahim Rashed. I am also grateful to several graduate students at the University of Chicago for looking over parts of the text: Elon Harvey, Sarah Aziz, Wayel Azmeh, Hamza Dudgeon, Susan Lee, Zahra Moeini Meybodi, Chad Mowbray, Samantha Pellegrino, Kyle Wynter-Stoner, Grace Brody, Allison Kanner, Clay Lemar, Scott Doolin, Lien Fina, Arthur Schechter, Saleem Ariz, Jeson Ng, and Daniel Morgan. Last but not least, I wish to express my love and gratitude to the *basmalah* of my life: my beloved and patient wife, Maliha Chishti, for her unfailing support and encouragement throughout the years, and my two loving daughters, Ayla and Hanan.

Introduction

I. The Author

ʿAfīf al-Dīn al-Tilimsānī (d. 690/1291) was a product of the full flowering of the seventh-/thirteenth-century Islamic mystical tradition. The list of Sufis whom he trained under and encountered during his life is extraordinary. His teachers include the Andalusī "greatest master" (*al-shaykh al-akbar*), Muḥyī l-Dīn ibn al-ʿArabī (d. 638/1240). He was also the closest friend and foremost disciple of the latter's top pupil and stepson, Ṣadr al-Dīn al-Qūnawī (d. 673/1274). Al-Tilimsānī met the great eponymous founder of the Shādhilī order, Abū l-Ḥasan al-Shādhilī (d. 656/1258), married the daughter of the outspoken Andalusī nondualist mystic Ibn Sabʿīn (d. 669/1258), and witnessed the beloved Persian Sufi poet Jalāl al-Dīn al-Rūmī (d. 672/1273) at the height of his career in Konya. His classmates went on to become influential masters, including such renowned figures as Saʿīd al-Dīn al-Farghānī (d. 699/1300), Fakhr al-Dīn al-ʿIrāqī (d. 688/1289), and Muʾayyid al-Dīn al-Jandī (d. 700/1300).[1]

The late Ayyubid and early Mamluk period in which al-Tilimsānī lived saw the rise of state-sponsored Sufi hospices (Per. *khānqah*s; Ar. *zāwiyah*s), the institutionalization of formal Sufi orders from the Islamic East, and important doctrinal formulations of Sufism in Arabic and Persian. The mystical poems of Farīd al-Dīn ʿAṭṭār (d. 627/1230) and ʿUmar ibn al-Fāriḍ (d. 632/1234) were popularized at this time.[2] The emergence of the late Ashʿarī school of philosophical theology was also a noteworthy feature of this period.[3] Finally, Naṣīr al-Dīn al-Ṭūsī (d. 672/1274) and his students were responsible for further developing the Avicennian tradition in Iran.[4] These various strands of Islamic thought all find expression in al-Tilimsānī's life and thought.

The full name of our author is Abū l-Rabīʿ ʿAfīf al-Dīn Sulaymān ibn ʿAlī ibn ʿAbd Allāh ibn ʿAlī ibn Yāsīn al-ʿĀbidī al-Kūmī al-Tilimsānī. His paternal tribal designation (*nisbah*), al-ʿAbidī al-Kūmī, is a reference to the Banū ʿĀbid, a clan of the small Berber tribe of Kūmah residing on the seacoast of the provinces of Tlemcen in present-day northwestern Algeria.[5] According to the most reliable sources, the shaykh was most likely born in the city of Tlemcen in 610/1213, although he spent most of his life in Cairo, Damascus, and Konya. He died and was buried in Damascus in 690/1291 at the age of eighty.[6]

Al-Tilimsānī's writings consist mostly of commentaries on important works. His commentary on the divine names bears the mark of not only a fully realized Sufi, but also the clarity of a highly trained and keen philosophical mind, and the eloquence of an accomplished poet. In addition to possessing depth and originality, al-Tilimsānī was a highly independent thinker who engaged critically with the authors and texts upon which he commented. His writings, moreover, represent the cosmopolitan nature of Islamic civilization in the seventh/thirteenth century. He was conversant in Persian, and studied with al-Qūnawī in Persian and Arabic. For thirty years he made his home in Egypt, a melting pot of Persian, Central Asian, and North African Sufis.

Little is known about al-Tilimsānī's early youth, and his writings contain little historical and biographical information. The medieval biographers affirm that he inhabited many roles throughout his life, including that of Sufi shaykh, author, renunciant, and government bureaucrat. They describe him as amiable, magnanimous, and characterized by sanctity (*ḥurmah*) and authority (*wajāhah*). He appears to have moved to Egypt at a young age, perhaps with his family, although it is possible that he was born in Egypt to a family that had recently settled there from the Maghrib. The early seventh/thirteenth century witnessed an increase in migration from al-Andalus and the Maghrib to the Islamic East for several reasons, including the Christian Reconquista, a stifling intellectual atmosphere created by the Almohad regime, and the prospect of more easily performing the pilgrimage to Mecca. Many of the scholars and Sufis who moved to the east never returned to their homelands. They settled in Egypt between Cairo and Alexandria, where they were provided for under the reign of Ṣalāḥ al-Dīn al-Ayyūbī (r. 570–89/1174–93), known in the West as Saladin.

Al-Tilimsānī was a seeker for spiritual guidance and a poet from a young age. The first account we have of him is from when he was in Cairo, at the age of twenty, a resident in Cairo's largest Sufi hospice, Saʿīd al-Suʿadāʾ, "The Most Felicitous of the Felicitous." According to one of his poems, it appears that he began searching for spiritual guidance in his teens. In a rare autobiographical anecdote, al-Tilimsānī notes the resolve with which he joined the Sufi Path. Despite having been warned that "in the path of the Sufis there are places where feet stumble," al-Tilimsānī notes:

> I looked into my heart, and made sure that my bonds of contentment with my Lord were strong, and I said, "Would I turn away after seeking? Would I fear being misguided despite my genuine love of God?" My eyes then swelled with tears, and the invigorating force of reverential fear and humility flowed through my being. I was taken by such a state of ecstasy that I nearly passed out and lost all sense of myself. When I returned from this state, I improvised these verses:
>
> My reins are held by the Beloved's will—I will run my inevitable course,
> be it willingly to pure guidance or to misguidance;
> I love Him, as long as He loves me—I am His servant, no matter what.[7]

The Saʿīd al-Suʿadāʾ where al-Tilimsānī resided had been a mansion for former Fatimid courtiers and was converted into a Sufi hospice during the Ayyubid sultanate. This hospice, which is located on present-day Jamāliyyah Street, was founded by Saladin in 569/1173–74 as part of his policy of restoring Sunnism in the wake of the Fatimid Shiʿi rule over Egypt. Saladin established the hospice in Cairo, in addition to four legal colleges (sing. *madrasah*), each representing one of the main Sunni schools of law (sing. *madhhab*). Being Egypt's first state-sponsored and formally organized *khānqah*, it hosted immigrant Sufis displaced by the encroaching Mongol threat from the east and the Christian Reconquista in the west. A salaried shaykh presided over the hospice, and he was given the political and diplomatic title of "chief shaykh" (*shaykh al-shuyūkh*) to serve as the representative of official Sufism. The resident Sufis (sing. *mutajarrid*) received a daily allowance of bread, meat, and provisions from the revenues of the endowment (*waqf*) instituted for the hospice. They had access to a nearby public bath, Ḥammām al-Jāmāliyyah, founded for Sufis—it continued to function until the thirteenth/nineteenth century. The resident Sufis devoted themselves to worship, study, copying manuscripts, training disciples, and teaching a variety of subjects, including Sufism and Islamic law.[8] They were also given time away to perform the pilgrimage to Mecca.

Meeting with al-Qūnawī in Cairo

Al-Tilimsānī's prayers for guidance were answered in 630/1232–33 when, at the age of twenty, he had a decisive encounter with Ṣadr al-Dīn al-Qūnawī. This accomplished young scholar and mystic, then in his mid-twenties, changed the course of al-Tilimsānī's life and was to become his closest friend, lifelong master, and spiritual companion. Al-Qūnawī had studied with Ibn al-ʿArabī and hailed from a prominent family of scholars. His father, Majd al-Dīn Isḥāq ibn Yūsuf al-Rūmī (d. 618/1221), was the "shaykh of Islam," which means he was the head of the religious establishment of the Saljūq court. Majd al-Dīn befriended Ibn al-ʿArabī and hosted him for several years in Rūm, present-day eastern Anatolia, a remnant of the once much larger Saljūq Empire. After the death of Majd al-Dīn, Ibn al-ʿArabī married Ṣadr al-Dīn's widowed mother, and in 620/1223 the family settled in northern Damascus, where Ibn al-ʿArabī enjoyed the patronage of the Banū Zakī, a prominent family of judges. Al-Qūnawī likely spent at least part of his teens in Ibn al-ʿArabī's household in Ayyubid Damascus, where he studied Hadith and the Sufi sciences. His reading sessions attracted large numbers of attendees, including individuals of high social standing, scholars, judges, preachers, imams, and Hadith experts. By the time the young al-Qūnawī met al-Tilimsānī, he had already received permission to teach and transmit all the works of Ibn al-ʿArabī, including the first redaction of the monumental *Meccan Openings* (*al-Futūḥāt al-Makkiyyah*), one of the most important works in Islamic mysticism, which Ibn al-ʿArabī read to al-Qūnawī from beginning to end.[9] After completing his studies with Ibn al-ʿArabī, al-Qūnawī accompanied the Persian Sufi Awḥad al-Dīn al-Kirmānī (d. 636/1238) to Egypt. The latter was affiliated with the Suhrawardī order and had initiated al-Qūnawī into Sufism at a young age. Al-Qūnawī had hoped to meet the elderly Sufi poet Ibn al-Fāriḍ (d. 632/1234), whose poems would play an important role in his own spiritual development as well as that of al-Tilimsānī and his students, but the poet died before they had a chance to meet.

Study with Ibn al-ʿArabī in Damascus

It appears that al-Tilimsānī dedicated himself to Sufi practice and study under al-Qūnawī's supervision at the Saʿīd al-Suʿadāʾ hospice for the next three years. He also studied Hadith, especially the *Ṣaḥīḥ* of Muslim, with prominent scholars in Cairo, including the Kurdish Shāfiʿī Hadith expert Ibn al-Ṣalāḥ (d. 643/1245). Al-Qūnawī and al-Tilimsānī headed for Damascus in 634/1236–37 to study with Ibn al-ʿArabī, where they attended the official reading sessions (*samāʿ*) of the second redaction of Ibn al-ʿArabī's *Futūḥāt* in the author's home and in his presence four years before his death in 638/1240. The name of al-Tilimsānī, then twenty-four years old, is written on the attendance sheet of the *Futūḥāt* reading session (*majlis al-samāʿ*). The copyist who took a note of attendance was none other than his close friend Ṣadr al-Dīn al-Qūnawī.[10]

In Anatolia with al-Qūnawī

While in Syria, al-Tilimsānī probably also accompanied al-Qūnawī to other cities, including Aleppo, to meet notable scholars and saints. Although he benefited enormously from his time in Damascus with Ibn al-ʿArabī, his most formative and longest period of training and personal mentorship was under the supervision of al-Qūnawī in his hometown, Konya, and in Cairo. It was probably in 636/1238, when Ibn al-ʿArabī completed the second redaction of the *Futūḥāt,* that al-Tilimsānī accompanied al-Qūnawī back to Konya. Al-Tilimsānī spent his formative mid-twenties and early thirties (that is, mid-630s/1230s until 643/1245) in rigorous spiritual training and study under al-Qūnawī. Much of this was spent in long spiritual retreats (*khulwah*). According to the Syrian historian Shams al-Dīn al-Jazarī (d. 739/1338), al-Tilimsānī made the forty-day retreat forty times in various parts of Rūm. However, one of al-Qūnawī's students, Shams al-Dīn Muḥammad al-Īkī (d. 697/1298), insists that this statement is not to be taken literally, given the vast amount of time it implies.[11]

Al-Tilimsānī usually refers to al-Qūnawī in his writings simply as "the shaykh."[12] He rarely makes reference to the time spent in spiritual training under him in Rūm. While in Rūm, al-Tilimsānī likely became conversant in Persian. He spent time with Persian Sufis, and in his works he quotes Persian words, as well as the *rubāʿiyāt* of Omar Khayyām, which he heard orally.[13] He almost certainly met al-Qūnawī's close friend, the celebrated Persian Sufi poet Rumi (Jalāl al-Dīn al-Rūmī), in Anatolia. At the time, Rumi was head of the Bahāʾ al-Dīn School.

Al-Qūnawī Moves to Cairo

In 641/1243, the Mongol victory over the Saljūq in the battle of Köse Dağ likely affected al-Qūnawī's plans to settle in his homeland. Seeking a safe and peaceful environment, he left for Egypt a second time, this time as an emissary for the Rūm government. During this second move to Egypt, al-Qūnawī was accompanied from Anatolia not only by al-Tilimsānī but also by a circle of Persian disciples, including Saʿīd al-Dīn al-Farghānī, and possibly Fakhr al-Dīn al-ʿIrāqī. On his way to Egypt, al-Qūnawī commented on *The Poem on Wayfaring* (*Naẓm al-sulūk*), a 750-verse Sufi poem by Ibn al-Fāriḍ.[14] Al-Tilimsānī and his classmate al-Farghānī attended those lessons, which were taught at least partly in Persian. Both pupils took notes and subsequently wrote their own commentaries on the poem.[15] In Cairo, they settled once again in the Saʿīd al-Suʿadāʾ hospice, and one of its Sufi residents, al-Īkī, joined their circle. A few decades later, in 684/1284, al-Īkī would go on to become Egypt's "chief shaykh," (*shaykh al-shuyūkh*)—that is, the formal head of all Sufis in the Mamluk kingdom, and the head of Saʿīd al-Suʿadāʾ, as well as the al-Fayyūm hospice and the al-Mashṭūb hospice.[16] Looking back on his days with al-Qūnawī at the hospice, Shams al-Dīn al-Īkī describes his remarkable lessons as follows:

> Both students and scholars would attend the gathering of our master [Shaykh Ṣadr al-Dīn], and the talk would range across various sciences, but such sessions would always come to a close with a line from Ibn al-Fāriḍ's ode, the *Naẓm al-sulūk*, about which the shaykh would then speak in Persian, expounding such mysteries and esoteric meanings as may be grasped by the initiated alone. Sometimes it would happen that, at the following session, he would tell us that another of the verse's meanings had become apparent to him, and then he would reveal to us a meaning even more wondrous and profound than the previous one. Indeed, he often used to say that the Sufi should memorize this ode and seek to elucidate its meanings with the help of someone who understands it. In this respect, Shaykh Shams al-Dīn tells us that "Shaykh Saʿīd al-Farghānī used to bring all his concentration to bear on understanding what the shaykh was expounding regarding the *Naẓm al-sulūk*, while at the same time making notes. Whereafter, he produced a commentary on the poem, first in Persian and then in Arabic; all of which derived from the blessings contained in every breath of our venerable master, Shaykh Ṣadr al-Dīn."[17]

The hospice served as the place of residence, worship, study, and instruction for al-Qūnawī and his students, including al-Tilimsānī, for nearly ten years.[18] It is likely that during this period al-Tilimsānī made his pilgrimage to Mecca, and visited the tomb of Abraham in Hebron, which he refers to in his commentary on the divine names (§83.5). It is also likely that around this period al-Tilimsānī participated in a battle against the Crusaders. In a discussion of the station of contentment with God's decree (*riḍā*) and experiencing genuine servanthood vis-à-vis the Lord, which is attained by the true lovers of God, al-Tilimsānī thanks God for having experienced this station, specifically:

> When I faced death at the swords of the Franks, may God forsake them, I looked into my heart and found no preference for life over death, but only contentment with God's decree owing to the overwhelming power of love.[19]

Like many other Western Sufis who fled the Reconquista, al-Tilimsānī was probably in part attracted to Egypt for the pious duty of defending the faith in jihad against the Franks. In a similar vein, the renowned Sufi Abū l-Ḥasan al-Shādhilī fought alongside his disciples against the Crusaders in the battle of Manṣūrah (648/1250), despite his advanced age and blindness.[20] It is also likely that the famous Andalusī Sufi poet Abū l-Ḥasan al-Shushtarī had fought against the Crusaders around the same period.[21]

Al-Tilimsānī made frequent trips to meet holy men around Egypt and the Levant during these years. He occasionally refers to the personal encounters he had with various shaykhs, citing them as cases in point to illustrate various spiritual stations.[22] In 643/1245, the year of his arrival in Cairo at the age of thirty-three, al-Tilimsānī had an important encounter with the nondualist Andalusī Hermeticist, philosopher, and mystic Ibn Sabʿīn (d. 669/1258). Their encounter, which occurred through al-Qūnawī, must have led to successive meetings, and Ibn Sabʿīn was evidently impressed by al-Tilimsānī's acumen. To this effect, the historian al-Munāwī relates that after Ibn Sabʿīn met al-Qūnawī, he was asked for his impressions of al-Qūnawī and replied that he was a truth-realizer (*muḥaqqiq*), "but with him is a young man who is sharper than him (*aḥdhaq minhu*)"[23]—namely, al-Tilimsānī. Our author, who only mentions Ibn Sabʿīn once in his works,[24] later married one of Ibn Sabʿīn's daughters, who gave birth to his son Shams al-Dīn Muḥammad in 661/1262 in Cairo. The son, known as "the Charming Youth" (al-Shābb al-Ẓarīf), would become renowned as a young poet in Damascus.

Another holy man who left a deep impression on him was the aforementioned Sufi from northern Morocco, Imam Abū l-Ḥasan al-Shādhilī (d. 656/1258), who established the vibrant Shādhilī order, which has continued to thrive to the present day. Imam al-Shādhilī had suffered persecution in Tunis before settling in Alexandria in 642/1244, only a year prior to al-Qūnawī's arrival in Cairo. The city of Alexandria was an important religious and political frontier city for the Ayyubid and later Mamluk sultans, and had a strong presence of the Mālikī and Shāfiʿī legal schools, as well as Ashʿarī theologians. As one of the principal maritime points of access into the Muslim world from Europe, it was where Saladin confronted European Crusader sieges, and he reconstructed its walls and towers. Despite the threat from Mongol invaders and Crusaders, the second half of the seventh/thirteenth century was a period of stability for Alexandria.[25] As a city that lies on the pilgrimage route between the Muslim West and Mecca, it was an important route for Hajj pilgrims from the Muslim West and became an important Sufi center in the seventh/thirteenth century from the Ayyubid period into the Mamluk period. Saladin had promoted Sunni religious institutions in this city just as he had done in Cairo. These state endeavors included Sufi convents and organized Sufi brotherhoods, law colleges, and mosques. The Sufi convents were located in the northern quarter of the city, outside the walls near the "Gate of the Ocean" (Bāb al-Baḥr). Alexandria was also home to independent Sufi convents that did not receive state patronage. Prior to Imam al-Shādhilī's arrival, North African and Iraqi Sufis had already settled in Alexandria.

Early Polemics between Akbarī Sufis and Ahl al-Ḥadīth Traditionists

Al-Tilimsānī's time in Cairo was not without controversy. Traditionist opponents of Ibn al-ʿArabī and his followers, the Akbarīs, branded al-Tilimsānī a heretic "monist" (*ittiḥādī*) Sufi, and viewed him as a personification of everything they considered to be wrong with Sufism. Although these scathing criticisms of al-Tilimsānī are repetitive and lack depth, they show that he earned a reputation of being more overt in his nondualist doctrine than Ibn al-ʿArabī. Ibn Taymiyyah calls al-Tilimsānī among the most intelligent and eloquent of the monist heretics (*ittiḥādiyyah*), reserving much of his criticism for his poetry, which he likens to "pork on a silver platter."[26] According to Ibn Taymiyyah, al-Tilimsānī fails to differentiate between the essence of a thing and its existence, and thus between absolute and delimited existence, and ultimately denies God's role as Creator and Sustainer of the universe. It could well be that it was al-Tilimsānī's open and forthright adherence to the nondualistic perspective that made him the target of particularly harsh criticism among his peers. In his writings, al-Tilimsānī rarely speaks at the level of the ordinary believer or formal Islamic theological discourse, in contrast to Ibn al-ʿArabī, who "descends to the level of the veil," as al-Tilimsānī would have put it. Moreover, it is telling that Ibn Sabʿīn and al-Tilimsānī are perhaps the only Sufis of this period who employed the term "oneness of existence" (*waḥdat al-wujūd*). This term became a catchphrase for monism in polemical literature against the Akbarī tradition and is used by al-Tilimsānī once, in passing, in his commentary on the *Manāzil al-sāʾirīn*, where he describes the manifestation of the oneness of existence as "the disclosure of the Essence" (*tajallī dhātī*).[27]

Early challenges to Akbarī "monist" Sufis, including Ibn Sab'īn, al-Tilimsānī, and al-Ḥarrālī, were launched by Ibn 'Abd al-Salām, who arrived in Cairo in 639/1241, four years prior to the arrival of al-Qūnawī and al-Tilimsānī, where he assumed the post of chief judge (*qāḍī l-quḍāt*), a counterpart to the Sufi position of chief shaykh (*shaykh al-shuyūkh*). There were also contentious exchanges between these Sufis and Quṭb al-Dīn al-Qasṭallānī (d. 686/1287), who became head of Cairo's Hadith College, known as Dār al-Ḥadīth al-Kāmiliyyah.[28] There were also tensions among Sufis of various outlooks within the *khānqah*, and some of these were ad hominem attacks on al-Tilimsānī's character or accusations of impiety and violating the Shariah.[29] The writings of Ibn al-'Arabī and his followers continued to generate debate throughout the centuries. One of the great defenders of al-Tilimsānī in the Ottoman period was 'Abd al-Ghanī l-Nābulusī (d. 1143/1731), who describes himself as having benefited greatly from the blessings of his works, and wrote passionate defenses of his writings, as well as those of Ibn Sab'īn and Ibn al-'Arabī.[30]

Al-Qūnawī Returns to Konya

After nearly a decade in Egypt, al-Qūnawī returned to Konya sometime before 652/1254, and there he spent the last twenty years of his life writing his major works. He was appointed to his father's prestigious position, the "shaykh of Islam" (*shaykh al-Islām*) of the Saljūq state. Al-Qūnawī was also given a sizeable Sufi lodge, where he continued to teach and train resident disciples, including Mu'ayyid al-Dīn al-Jandī and others who would become important transmitters of their master's philosophical exposition of Ibn al-'Arabī's teachings. Al-Tilimsānī, for his part, stayed on in Egypt at the *khānqah* of Sa'īd al-Su'adā', where he began putting pen to paper. Sometime in the mid- to late 650s/late 1250s, in his forties, he married Ibn Sab'īn's daughter, who gave birth to his son Shams al-Dīn Muḥammad in 661/1263.[31]

Al-Tilimsānī Moves to Damascus

A few years after al-Qūnawī's appointment as *shaykh al-Islām* in Konya, al-Tilimsānī also landed an important position in Damascus. He moved back to Damascus in the 660s/1260s and spent the last twenty to thirty years of his life there.[32] He took up residence in Ṣāliḥiyyah, on the lower slopes of Mount Qāsiyūn overlooking the city. He enjoyed a close relationship to the ruling Mamluk authorities in Damascus. In an account related by Jamāl al-Dīn Maḥmūd ibn Ṭayy al-Ḥāfī, a deputy accompanying al-Malik al-Manṣūr (r. 587–617/1191–1220) to Damascus acted insolently toward al-Tilimsānī, prompting the people to upbraid him, saying, "This is not a secretary; this is Shaykh ʿAfīf al-Dīn al-Tilimsānī. He is well known among the people for his augustness and generosity. Were he to raise this with the sultan, the sultan would harm you."

Al-Tilimsānī served in several roles in Damascus, including inspector of market dues (*jibāyat al-ḍarāʾib*) and treasurer for the region of Shām (*amīn al-khizānah*), until his death. He enjoyed a luxurious life under the reign of the Mamluk sultan al-Malik al-Manṣūr Sayf al-Dīn Qālawūn (r. 678–89/1279–90). Muḥammad, his son, spent his childhood and early education in Damascus, where he studied with his father and other scholars. Al-Tilimsānī continued to study Hadith, in typical Akbarī fashion. In 670/1271, the sixty-year-old al-Tilimsānī and, apparently, his brilliant nine-year-old son Muḥammad, received authorization from the great Hadith scholar Abū Zakariyyā l-Nawawī (d. 676/1277) to transmit the book *al-Minhāj bi-sharḥ Ṣaḥīḥ Muslim ibn al-Ḥajjāj*.[33] Al-Nawawī had assumed the prestigious position of head of the Ashrafiyyah Hadith College (Dār al-Ḥadīth al-Ashrafiyyah) in Damascus in 665/1266, and it was during his tenure there that he wrote his major works.[34] *Al-Minhāj*, which spans eight volumes in modern print, was completed by al-Nawawī in 669/1270–71, and is the central commentary on Muslim's *Ṣaḥīḥ* collection of authenticated hadith reports. The collection covers major topics of Islamic law, and combines chains of transmitters (sing. *isnād*), grammatical explanations of the hadith text, and a theological and legal Shāfiʿī commentary. Al-Tilimsānī would have studied this text with al-Nawawī in the mid-660s after al-Nawawī began to write and teach. Moreover, the son's poetry quickly gained popularity in the literary and political circles of Damascus. He dedicated his poems to praising the Prophet and local rulers. He was also a calligrapher, as mentioned by al-Tilimsānī in a lamentation (*rithāʾ*) for his son.

According to al-Dhahabī, our author also received permission to transmit Muslim's *Ṣaḥīḥ* from a number of scholars. It is reported that during one lecture, Shams al-Dīn al-Iṣfahānī asked who the son Muḥammad was, to which he responded, "I am the son of your servant al-ʿAfīf al-Tilimsānī," whereupon the shaykh smiled and said, "You are steeped in godliness! (*anta ʿarīq fī l-ulūhiyyah*). Your mother is the daughter of Ibn Sabʿīn and your father is al-ʿAfīf al-Tilimsānī."[35] The master's humor here lies in the fact that his student had been born into a family of monist Sufis.

Death of al-Qūnawī and al-Tilimsānī

Al-Qūnawī died in Konya in 673/1274. It is telling that he instructed in his last will and testament that his own writings should be sent to al-Tilimsānī alone, to distribute them to whomever he deemed worthy of reading them.[36] Another major event in al-Tilimsānī's life in Damascus was the death of his beloved son in 688/1289.[37] Afflicted by bereavement, al-Tilimsānī died at the age of eighty on Wednesday, 5 Rajab 690/1291, in his home in Ṣāliḥiyyah in Damascus. He was buried in the Sufi cemetery on Mount Qāsiyūn. His funeral prayers were performed in the Umayyad Mosque after the ʿAṣr prayer. Shortly before his death, the shaykh was asked how he was and he replied, "I am well! How can someone who knows God have any fear? By God! From the time I came to know Him, I have not feared Him, but rather I long for Him, and I am joyful to meet Him!"[38]

II. Situating al-Tilimsānī's *The Divine Names*

The *Maʿānī l-asmāʾ al-ilāhiyyah* builds upon commentaries by earlier lexicographers, late Ashʿarī theologians, Sufi ethicists, and the teachings of Ibn al-ʿArabī and al-Qūnawī. The first major Sufi ethical commentary on the divine names was written by the renowned Sufi-Ashʿarī theologian Abū l-Qāsim al-Qushayrī (d. 465/1074). His groundbreaking commentary, *The Adornment of the Science of Exhortation* (*al-Taḥbīr fī ʿilm al-tadhkīr*), is a synthesis of at least three major interpretive vectors: philological, theological, and Sufi. The first vector is exemplified in philological commentaries (*shurūḥ lughawiyyah*), such as *Matters Concerning Supplication* (*Shaʾn al-duʿāʾ*) by the Shāfiʿī scholar al-Khaṭṭābī (d. 388/998). Such works are predominantly lexicographic exercises in uncovering the variety of meanings of each divine name. They function as precursors to the second vector seen in theological texts, such as al-Bayhaqī's (d. 458/1065) Ashʿarī classic, *The Names and Attributes* (*al-Asmāʾ wa-l-ṣifāt*), which al-Tilimsānī cites in his commentary. This work takes the earlier philological discussions as its starting point and explores the scriptural foundations and theological dimensions of the divine names. The theological texts, for their part, were often penned by Sufi-inclined theologians who were attentive to analyzing the intimate connection a human being can have to a name of God through embodying its properties and living according to its dictates. Thus, al-Qushayrī's *The Adornment of the Science of Exhortation*, al-Ghazālī's *The Highest Aim in Explaining the Meanings of God's Beautiful Names* (*al-Maqṣad al-asnā fī sharḥ maʿānī asmāʾ Allāh al-ḥusnā*), and Ibn Barrajān's *Commentary on the Beautiful Names of God* (*Sharḥ asmāʾ Allāh al-ḥusnā*)[39] exemplify the third vector in bringing their expertise in Sufism to bear upon the divine names tradition.

Ibn al-ʿArabī's (637/1240) writings mark an ontological turn in the divine names tradition, which was elaborated upon by his students al-Qūnawī and al-Tilimsānī, and by their students in turn. Authors who write within the Akbarī tradition tend not to engage with the divine names from an Ashʿarī voluntarist perspective. That is, they do not tend to reflect on the names in relation to God's will. Rather, they conceive of the names as ontological relationships between God and creation. This ontological turn raises a host of new questions and debates, and solves some of the theological tensions in earlier Ashʿarī treatments of the divine names.[40]

For example, Ashʿarī Sufis treat names like the Ever-Merciful (*al-Raḥīm*) or the Harmer (*al-Ḍārr*) as aspects of God's will. Mercy is His will to bless a servant, and harm is His will to punish. Ashʿarīs tend to define mercy in these terms in order to avoid anthropopathic implications entailed by human mercy, such as hurt and relief, that would ascribe imperfect human emotions and psychological states to God. In contrast, Ibn al-ʿArabī and his followers understand divine mercy and pure existence to be synonymous. Instead of conceiving of mercy as God's will to bless, they prioritize the servant's subjective response to God's singular reality. The experience of bliss is thus the capacity, or "preparedness" (*istiʿdād*), of the servant for the encounter with the unique divine reality. The servant responds to the disclosed properties of the names, displaying "agreeability" (*mulāʾamah*), "disagreeability" (*munāfarah*), "readiness" (*tahayyuʾ*), or "preparedness" (*istiʿdād*) for the divine self-disclosure. As such, names like the Harmer are not aspects of God's will to punish, but the manifestation of a relationship that obtains with respect to God's self-disclosure and the servant's degree of readiness, or lack thereof, to receive it.

It is notable that, in contrast to earlier Sufi-Ashʿarī commentaries on the names by Qushayrī and al-Ghazālī, al-Tilimsānī's text does not emphasize the ethical dictates of the divine names. For instance, his commentary on the divine name the Giver (*al-Muʿṭī*) does not end with an exhortation to practice the virtue of generosity. Instead, he emphasizes the occult powers, talismanic functions, and healing properties of the names, which can be used as remedies for ailments in the soul when invoked under the supervision of a spiritual teacher. These remedies are a common feature of divine names commentaries in the later Islamic Middle Period. Traces of this discourse are found in earlier Sufi and Shiʿi texts, and are featured prominently in the writings of al-Būnī (d. 622/1225).

III. Spiritual Training

There seem to be clear similarities between al-Tilimsānī's method of spiritual training and that of al-Qūnawī,[41] although our author's approach retains its unique flavor and is deeply informed by his own realization of the divine names and his emphasis on the Akbarī schematization of the Sufi path into four journeys: the journey toward annihilation in God, the journey of subsistence in God, the journey of the spiritual traveler back to the world, and the final journey back to the divine. Based on the biographical sources as well as al-Tilimsānī's own writings, it is possible to sketch a general outline of the spiritual practice of al-Tilimsānī and the inner circle of Ibn al-ʿArabī's disciples. Three aspects stand out in this regard: the spiritual master, the spiritual retreat, and the invocation of specific divine names prescribed by the master.

The Spiritual Master

Al-Tilimsānī considered the companionship of a master to be indispensable for spiritual growth. He holds that the disciple must surrender to the shaykh (§69.6), although he himself sometimes engages critically with his own masters' teachings and instructions. He occasionally refers to fake masters or charlatans who falsely claim to be spiritual guides (*mashāyikh kādhibīn*), and seeks refuge in God from them. He insists that advanced and genuine masters of the Sufi path tend to be nondescript and rather unimpressive to the untrained eye, being veiled from the perception of common people. One reason for this is that such shaykhs are bearing witness to the divine name, the Manifest, in all things, places, schools of thought, and levels of political power, and they honor all things. In so doing, they themselves become nonmanifest for others (§36.4).

In §83.5, al-Tilimsānī tells of how he became the spiritual guide for another guide during a visit to Abraham's tomb in Hebron. His account sheds light on the master-disciple relationship, and indicates that for al-Tilimsānī, a genuine spiritual seeker is willing to take from any master who can teach him more about God. In this case, a spiritual teacher recognizes that he still has much to learn from al-Tilimsānī and thus surrenders to his guidance.

Al-Tilimsānī's mystical theology forms the basis for the relationship between the master and the disciple. The function of the master is to help the disciple see things for what they are: traces of God's names. It goes without saying that al-Tilimsānī considers full adherence to the revealed Law to be essential to the Sufi path. However, the rituals that are performed by the body are experienced at a supersensory level by the heart. For instance, the performance of the ritual ablutions (*wuḍūʾ*) is experienced by the spiritual traveler not simply as a physical cleansing but also as a practice of discarding impurities of temporality (§61.4).

The shaykh closely monitors the disciple's state to help him attain his full spiritual potential. He begins by identifying illnesses in the disciple's soul and prescribes the correct medication to treat him. When a shaykh is unsure about the disciple's preparedness for the path, he instructs the disciple to invoke the name the Setter of Trials (*al-Mumtaḥin*) "in order to know which path to guide them along toward God" (§116.2).

The Spiritual Retreat

An integral aspect of the training, according to al-Tilimsānī, is the spiritual retreat (*khulwah*). Al-Tilimsānī himself performed many long retreats throughout his life. During these retreats, he presumably invoked names of God under al-Qūnawī's supervision, and was attentive to the disclosures of the divine names that he experienced. Through his practice of the spiritual retreat under al-Qūnawī, al-Tilimsānī gained intimate knowledge of the divine names, as well as the "fruits" they bear when invoked methodically.

Al-Tilimsānī thus speaks in almost medical terms of how the names can heal illnesses of the soul. He holds that the divine names, which can be invoked in pairs or combinations, contain beneficial properties as well as possible adverse side effects. A shaykh prescribes names as medications to treat specific vices or illnesses in the disciple's soul. Al-Tilimsānī insists that disciples are to take these spiritual medications as directed, in order to avoid substance-abuse disorders, for the soul's exposure to the properties of the divine names can have adverse effects if they are invoked at an inappropriate stage of spiritual development or without adequate preparedness. Given these potential dangers, the author insists that it is vital to learn from a qualified master who has experience in training and nurturing disciples (*al-shaykh al-murabbī*, §50.7).

Invocation of Specific Divine Names

Broadly speaking, al-Tilimsānī's apothecary of the divine names can be divided into five categories of names that can be invoked during the retreat: (1) universal names that are suitable for all believers and wayfarers, (2) names for beginner wayfarers, (3) names for intermediate wayfarers, (4) names for advanced wayfarers, and (5) names that are only invoked in rare cases.

Among the names that are beneficial to all types of wayfarers in the retreat are the names the Provider (*al-Razzāq*) and the Guide (*al-Hādī*). Invoking these names is suitable for all groups because the former attracts divine provision and the latter attracts guidance. Beginners on the Sufi path, moreover, suffer from a variety of ailments that the shaykh must diagnose and treat. For those who lack concentration and are heedless, he recommends invoking the Knowing (*al-ʿAlīm*) to inspire fear and hope in them. For the absentminded, he recommends the Possessor of Majesty (*Dhū l-Jalāl*). For those who experience a distance from God or aridity in their wayfaring, he recommends names of intimacy such as the Loving (*al-Wadūd*), the Tender (*al-Ḥannān*), and the Peace (*al-Salām*).

Certain disciples are excessively fearful of divine punishment and should invoke the name the Concealer (*al-Ghāfir*). However, seekers who are suitable for the divine presence are discouraged from invoking this name because their goal is to pass away from themselves, whereas the Concealer recalls one's deeds and misdeeds. There are also disciples who tend to relate to God merely as an abstract and transcendent reality. Al-Tilimsānī recommends that they invoke the name the Possessor of the Throne (*Dhū l-ʿArsh*) in order to regain intimacy with God and visionary disclosures of the names. In contrast, those who are obsessed with creedal belief are recommended to invoke the Pure (*al-Ṭāhir*), and those who tend to become confused by the discourse of anthropomorphists are recommended to invoke the Holy (*al-Quddūs*).

There are also names that are suitable for disciples who are overwhelmed by worldly distractions and unable to keep up with their rigorous spiritual practices. For such cases, al-Tilimsānī recommends the name the Assister (*al-Naṣīr*). Likewise, the Watchful (*al-Raqīb*) is appropriate for those who are heedless of God, in order to help them "awaken from their stupor" (§51.11). Finally, al-Tilimsānī recommends the names the Uplifter (*al-Rāfiʿ*) and the Ennobler (*al-Mukarrim*) for those who suffer from a lack of self-esteem and are dominated by humility to the point that they underestimate themselves and lose spiritual intimacy with God.

Withdrawing from workaday life (*tajrīd*) is often seen as a necessary, albeit temporary, phase in the spiritual path, as exemplified by the life of al-Tilimsānī himself, who returned to daily life in Cairo and Damascus after his time in the *khānqah*, his retreats in Konya, and his completion of the Sufi path under the supervision of his master al-Qūnawī. In preparing the disciple to transition into this mode of life in which he earns a living by begging for pieces of bread, the shaykh will often recommend invocation of the name the Nourisher (*al-Muqīt*) so that he can begin to cultivate genuine trust in God.

For those who struggle to overcome their dependence on secondary causes, al-Tilimsānī recommends invoking the name the Reckoner (*al-Ḥasīb*), the Enricher (*al-Mughnī*), or the Guarantor (*al-Kafīl*), so that the disciple's heart becomes attached to God. In addition to cultivating trust in God, the disciple must learn to give himself up to God and renounce everything apart from Him. To this end, he is recommended to invoke names such as the Everlasting (*al-Bāqī*), the First (*al-Awwal*), and the Last (*al-Ākhir*).

Once a disciple withdraws from the world and enters into the spiritual retreat, the shaykh instructs him to invoke names for spiritual opening (*fatḥ*). He begins his retreat with the name the Originator (*al-Mubdiʾ*). Thereafter, beginners who have little experience with visionary disclosures of the divine names are discouraged from invoking names of glory and transcendence because they have not yet cultivated intimacy with God. However, for intermediates who have experience with divine disclosure, he recommends invoking the Glorious (*al-Majīd*, §73.5).

For beginners in the retreat, al-Tilimsānī recommends names that yield weaker spiritual openings, such as the Giver (*al-Muʿṭī*). Likewise, the Clement (*al-Barr*) gives intimacy and hastens the partial spiritual opening, and the Light (*al-Nūr*) "hastens the spiritual opening of those who practice the spiritual retreat. But the opening comes in degrees, and it rarely bestows it in full" (§100.4). Similarly, invoking the Opener (*al-Fattāḥ*) and the Abundant (*Dhū l-Ṭawl*) hastens the spiritual opening.

Sometimes the intensity of the divine disclosures during the retreat can be overwhelming. To offset their intensity, al-Tilimsānī recommends names that can strengthen the disciple's preparedness. For instance, a disciple who is agitated or whose preparedness is mixed is instructed to invoke the Clarifier (*al-Mubīn*). Likewise, the Fulfiller (*al-Wafī*) gives the most preparedness that one is able to receive and is an invocation for the intermediate stages of the spiritual path. Sometimes a disclosure can be overwhelming and may cause mental imbalance. Disciples who risk losing their sanity are recommended to invoke the Faithful (*al-Muʾmin*) to heal from the shock of experiencing the world of divine majesty. There are also names that can help disciples counterbalance the experience of divine proximity and recover from its intense disclosures. For instance, the disciple is told by the shaykh to invoke the name the Stitcher (*al-Rātiq*) to veil the visionary disclosure of God's light. Moreover, the Restorer (*al-Muʿīd*), the Nonmanifest (*al-Bāṭin*), the Great (*al-Kabīr*), and the Transcendent (*al-Mutaʿālī*) help disciples who are overwhelmed by the experience of divine proximity to return to their senses.

Al-Tilimsānī prescribes a number of names for advanced seekers. For "recognizers" who have witnessed name disclosures firsthand and are journeying toward annihilation in God, the name the Inheritor (*al-Wārith*) draws them toward total annihilation in God and enables them to arrive at the "station of halting" (*maqām al-waqfah*) beyond all names. Disciples who have passed away in the divine presence and embarked upon the second journey of subsistence in God are recommended to invoke names such as the Cleaver (*al-Fāṭir*), the Manifest (*al-Ẓāhir*), and the Thankful (*al-Shakūr*), which help them recognize God's presence within the forms of this world. While invoking such names would be inappropriate for disciples on the first journey to God because they would create distance from Him, they are suitable for spiritual travelers on the second journey in God.

Finally, there are names that are appropriate for certain kinds of souls. These include the Harmer (*al-Ḍārr*), the Painful in Retribution (*al-Alīm al-Akhdh*), and the Misguider (*al-Muḍill*), which were invoked by the early ecstatic Sufi Abū Yazīd, who famously proclaimed:

> I love You. I love You not for the recompense,
> but rather I love You for the chastisement.
> For I have attained all I need from the recompense,
> but my pleasure in the ecstasy of chastisement![42]

Al-Tilimsānī also mentions certain names that are suitable only for particular situations. For instance, the name the Setter of Trials (*al-Mumtaḥin*) is recommended for disciples in the retreat who are afflicted by a trial, because it reminds them of God. Moreover, if shaykhs have disciples who are kings or tyrants, the name the All-Subjugating (*al-Qahhār*) reminds them of the One who is truly in charge, and thus brings them back to God. Finally, the Potent (*al-Muqtadir*) and the Fully Active (*al-Faʿʿāl*) benefit those who wish to work miracles.

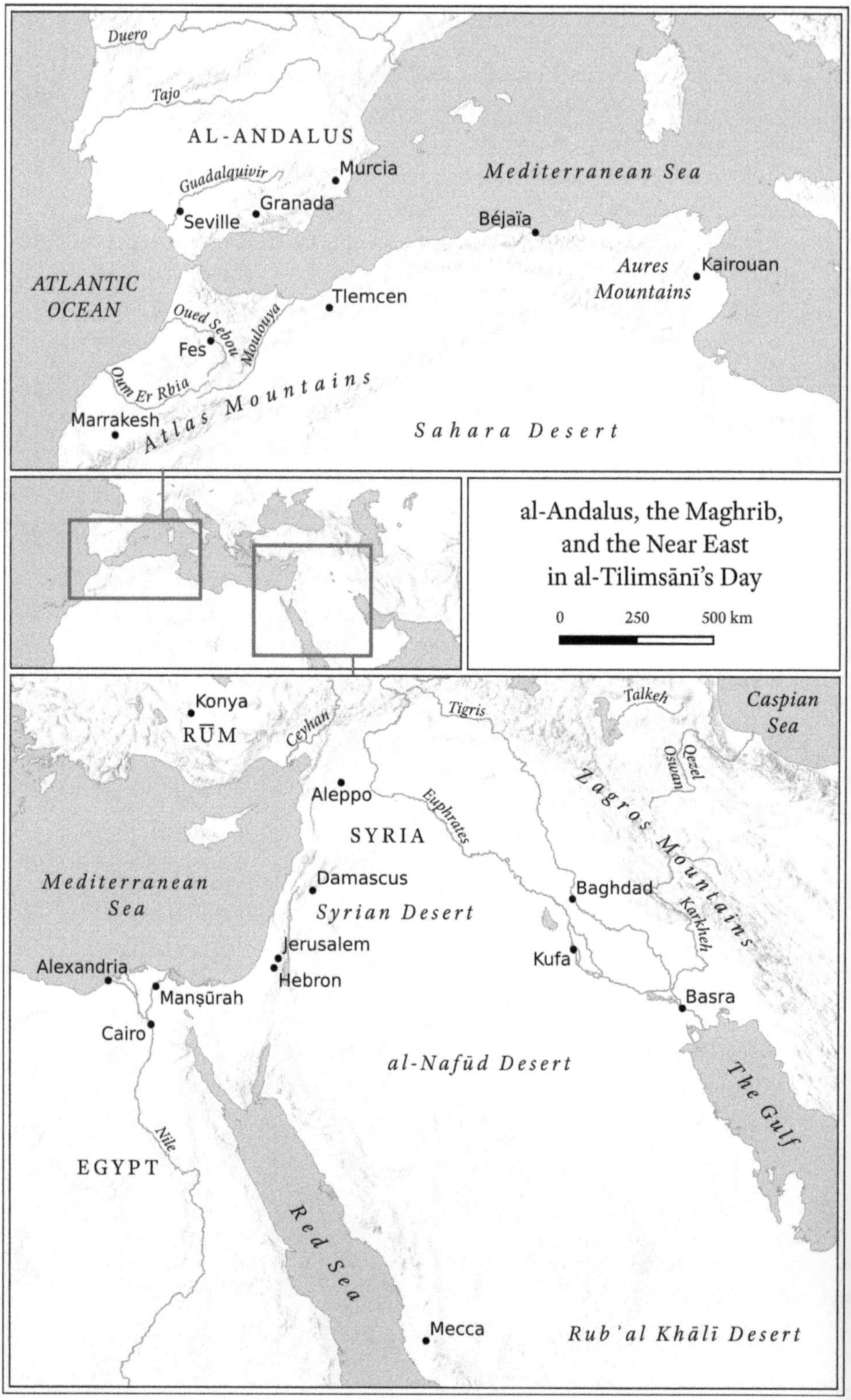
al-Andalus, the Maghrib, and the Near East in al-Tilimsānī's Day
0
250
500 km
Duero
Tajo
AL-ANDALUS
Guadalquivir
Murcia
Granada
Seville
Mediterranean Sea
Béjaïa
Aures Mountains
Kairouan
ATLANTIC OCEAN
Oued Sebou
Moulouya
Tlemcen
Fes
Oum Er Rbia
Atlas Mountains
Marrakesh
Sahara Desert
Konya
RŪM
Ceyhan
Tigris
Talkeh
Caspian Sea
Oswan
Qezel
Aleppo
Euphrates
Zagros Mountains
SYRIA
Mediterranean Sea
Damascus
Syrian Desert
Baghdad
Karkheh
Jerusalem
Hebron
Kufa
Alexandria
Manṣūrah
Basra
Cairo
al-Nafūd Desert
The Gulf
Nile
EGYPT
Red Sea
Mecca
Rub 'al Khālī Desert

Note on the Text

Arabic Edition

In establishing my Arabic text of al-Tilimsānī's *Maʿānī l-asmāʾ al-ilāhiyyah,* I relied on three excellent manuscripts and one recent printed edition.

1. Laleli MS 1556 = آ

The primary manuscript was copied in 794/1392, about one hundred years after the author's death. It is a reliable witness, despite occasional scribal and orthographical deficiencies. This primary manuscript contains sixty-five folios (1b–67b), with twenty-five lines per folio. It is held in the Süleymaniye Manuscript Library in Istanbul, and is a single miscellany codex preserved in the library of the Ottoman sultan Muṣṭafā III (r. 1171–87/1757–74). The manuscript's colophon indicates that it was completed on Thursday, 13 Rabi al-Awwal, 794/1392 by Muḥammad ibn Yūsuf ibn Ibrāhīm al-Maghlūṭī.

2. Bayezit MS 8011 = ب

The second witness is also from Istanbul. It is undated, and was endowed in 1266/1850 by the mother of Sultan ʿAbd al-Majīd Khān (r. 1255–77/1839–61). The manuscript in question, the Bayezit MS 8011, is the eleventh of twenty treatises found in a single codex (*majmūʿah*) that brings together al-Tilimsānī's commentary and the works of other major Sufi figures, including ʿAbd al-Karīm al-Jīlī and Ibn al-ʿArabī. The MS of al-Tilimsani's text covers eighty-seven folios (192a–279b), with twenty-three lines per folio.

3. Khuda Bakhsh MS 2789/16 = ج

The third witness is from the Khuda Bakhsh Library from northeast India. It was copied in 1100/1689 and covers eighty-four folios, with twenty-seven lines per folio. Some of the folios are misbound and do not belong to al-Tilimsānī's commentary. I discovered this manuscript in a larger codex that comprises al-Tilimsānī's commentary on the *Fuṣūṣ al-ḥikam.* I was unable to obtain the colophon, but based on codicological evidence, it was probably copied after the eighth/fourteenth century. MSS ب and ج share common errors almost consistently, and thus pertain to the same manuscript family.

4. *Musakhanov's edition* = و

In 2018, the erudite Turkish scholar and editor Orkhan Musakhanov published an excellent critical edition of this text, which used a Konya MS (695) as its base. This MS, copied in 695/1295, only five years after the author's death, was copied from the original manuscript in al-Tilimsānī's handwriting.[43] After completing my own critical edition based on MSS آ, ب, and ج, I collated it against Musakhanov's recent edition (و). This led to a few corrections and minor variants in the textual reception of the commentary that are noted in the Arabic text. I have indicated only places where و offered a more plausible reading than that provided by آ, ب, or ج, or where it included an interesting or probable variant. I relied extensively on the Hadith and poetry citations in Musakhanov's edition for my English translation. The editor describes Konya MS 695 as a well-preserved single volume, spanning 176 folios (1b–167b), with fifteen lines per folio, written in clear, professional, vocalized *naskhī* script. The MS also has an ownership mark dated 796/1394 for Muqayyad ibn ʿAbd Allāh, and on the title page, the manuscript was endowed in 1137/1725 by Ḥusayn Katakhda ibn Yūsuf al-Dīrūzī. The copyist is Maḥmūd ibn Ismāʿīl ibn Jaysh al-Rubaʿī, known as Ibn Dabūqā, and he completed the copy in Rabi al-Awwal 695/1295.

Generally speaking, the textual differences between the three manuscripts and the Turkish edition are minor, and these four texts provide an excellent basis for the present edition. MSS ج and ب share consistent grammatical errors and scribal omissions, indicating that they pertain to the same manuscript family. The three witnesses are written in regular *naskh* and can be read, for the most part, without much difficulty. Diacritical points are included fairly regularly. MS آ is generously vocalized. I have encountered several sentence-long scribal omissions, which are filled by ب and ج. MS ج occasionally drops the definite article. MSS آ, ب, and ج contain few marginal notes and glosses, and show minimum signs of collation. The subheadings that demarcate a new discussion of a divine name are either written in red ink or underlined in bold strokes. Minor differences in orthography are not noted in the footnotes. I follow modern standard orthographic conventions for the hamzahs, which are either omitted from the manuscripts or inserted incorrectly.

English Translation

The English translation was completed over the course of ten years. In translating al-Tilimsānī's text, I try to strike a balance between the scientific, the pietist, the literary, and the aesthetic. In order to render the commentary maximally intelligible to nonspecialists, I try to be as consistent as possible in translating technical terms while retaining the author's metaphysical vocabulary. I have avoided awkward stylistic constructions and excessive literalism to the best of my ability. If two words or expressions carry the same meaning, I have tended to opt for the less literal but more readable and idiomatic, bearing in mind the importance of consistency. Nonetheless, there are certain words and technical terms in al-Tilimsānī's Arabic that are difficult to translate without recourse to unwieldy English equivalents. Likewise, certain divine names, such as the Reckoner (*al-Ḥasīb*) and the Mighty (*al-ʿAzīz*), carry more than one meaning and one term is not enough to translate them. Finally, I tend to leave out pious standard phrases that hinder the flow of the text. However, references to Muḥammad are usually translated as "blessed Messenger" as a way of highlighting that the Prophet is being quoted and to preserve some of the pietist language of the original Arabic without encumbering the English translation with long optative prayers and pietist formulations. I also include some pious formulas, such as the occasional "God be pleased with them," in reference to Ibn al-ʿArabī, Ibn Barrajān, al-Ghazālī, and al-Bayhaqī. For the Qur'an, I primarily consulted *The Study Quran* translation, although Arberry, Pickthall, and Asad have been useful as well. Occasionally, the Arabic text assumes knowledge of Arabic, or of a Prophetic saying, and the translation had to be spelled out more fully for the reader. Similarly, al-Tilimsānī assumes that his reader is familiar with the Qur'an and often quotes only parts of verses. Often, only the opening words of Qur'anic verses are cited; for the sake of clarity, I quote the verse in full.

Notes to the Introduction

1 For a study of the school of Ibn al-ʿArabī, see Dagli, *Ibn al-ʿArabī and Islamic Intellectual Culture.*

2 For an overview, see Knysh, *Islamic Mysticism,* 172–218.

3 See Shihadeh and Thiele, *Philosophical Theology in Islam: Later Ashʿarism East and West.*

4 See Meisami, *Naṣīr al-Dīn al-Ṭūsī.*

5 See al-Ṣafadī, *al-Wāfī bi-l-wafayāt,* 15:250; al-Jazarī, *Tārīkh ḥawādith al-zamān wa-anbāʾih wa-wafayāt al-akābir wa-l-aʿyān min abnāʾih,* 1:80–96; al-Sakhāwī, *al-Qawl al-munbī ʿan tarjamat Ibn al-ʿArabī,* 2:293–94; and al-Kutubī, *Fawāt al-wafayāt,* 2:72–76.

6 Al-Dhahabī, *Tārīkh al-Islām wa-wafayāt al-mashāhīr wa-l-aʿlām,* 51, no. 627, 406–12; al-Dhahabī, *al-ʿIbar fī khabar man ghabar,* 3:372–73. Al-Dhahabī confirms that he saw the birthdate written in al-Tilimsānī's hand.

7 Al-Tilimsānī, *Sharḥ Manāzil al-sāʾirīn,* 134. Al-Kayyālī's edition cited henceforth.

8 Geoffroy, "Les milieux de la mystique musulmane à Alexandrie aux XIIIe et XIVe siècles."

9 On the life of al-Qūnawī, see Todd, *The Sufi Doctrine of Man: Ṣadr al-Dīn al-Qūnawī's Metaphysical Anthropology,* 13–27.

10 Yaḥyā, *Muʾallafāt Ibn ʿArabī,* 440; Addas, *Quest for the Red Sulphur: The Life of Ibn ʿArabī,* 265; Chittick, "The Last Will and Testament of Ibn ʿArabī's Foremost Disciple and Some Notes on Its Author."

11 Al-Ṣafadī, *al-Wāfī bi-l-wafayāt,* 15:250.

12 See al-Tilimsānī's commentary on the *Manāzil,* e.g., *Sharḥ Manāzil al-sāʾirīn,* 299, 309.

13 E.g., al-Tilimsānī, *Sharḥ Mawāqif al-Niffarī,* 121, 133, 264, 282 (Marzūqī's edition cited henceforth); *Sharḥ Manāzil al-sāʾirīn,* 344.

14 See Ibn al-Fāriḍ, *Dīwān,* 46–143.

15 Khalīfah, *Kashf al-ẓunūn,* 1:266.

16 Fernandes, *The Evolution of a Sufi Institution in Mamluk Egypt: The Khanqat,* 52.

17 Translation by Richard Todd, with some modifications. Jāmī, *Nafaḥāt,* 541–42; see Todd, *The Sufi Doctrine of Man,* 19.

18 Geoffroy, *Le soufisme: Histoire, pratiques, et spiritualité,* 168.

19 *Sharḥ Manāzil al-sāʾirīn,* 134. See also 196, where he mentions that warfare is prohibited in Christianity because Jesus occupied the station of beauty (*jamāl*), and that

Christians launched the Crusades on the pretense of recovering their lost Holy Land of Jerusalem.

20 Post, *The Journeys of a Taymiyyan Sufi*, 70–117.

21 Al-Shushtarī participated in a battle against the Crusaders in the fortified outpost (*ribāṭ*) of the port city of Damietta in the early seventh/thirteenth century. He would have been too young to participate in the fight against the Fifth Crusade (613–18/1217–21) when the Crusaders laid siege to the city for several months, as a first step toward conquering Egypt and reinforcing Christian conquest of the Holy Land. See Casewit, "Shushtarī's Treatise *On the Limits of Theology and Sufism*," 8.

22 Given the extensive travels, shared spaces, and mutual interests of seventh/thirteenth century Sufis who roamed between the cities of Damascus, Cairo, Alexandria, Mecca, Medina, and Konya, it can be safely assumed that most of the seventh-/thirteenth-century Maghribī mystics who settled in the East knew each other either directly or indirectly. Al-Tilimsānī tends to mention his encounters in passing: they include Ibn Sabʿīn, his Andalusī disciple Ibn Hūd, the Alexandrian Sufi Abū l-Qāsim al-Qabbārī, and Abū Bakr al-Mustawfī. Al-Tilimsānī may have met al-Shushtarī in Cairo. See Casewit, "Shushtarī's Treatise *On the Limits of Theology and Sufism*" and "The Treatise on the Ascension (*al-Risāla al-miʿrājiyya*): Cosmology and Time in the Writings of Abū l-Ḥasan al-Shushtarī (d. 668/1269)."

23 Ibn al-ʿImād, *Shadharāt al-dhahab fī akhbār man dhahab*, 7:720.

24 See al-Tilimsānī, *Sharḥ Mawāqif al-Niffarī*, 353.

25 Fernandes, *The Evolution*, 75.

26 See Ibn Taymiyyah's scathing critique in *Majmūʿat al-rasāʾil wa-l-masāʾil*, 1:176–77; 4:74–75. For a close study of the polemics against the Akbarian tradition in Arabic-speaking contexts during this period, see Knysh, *Ibn ʿArabī in the Later Islamic Tradition.*

27 Al-Tilimsānī, *Sharḥ Manāzil al-sāʾirīn*, 245.

28 Knysh, *Ibn ʿArabi in the Later Islamic Tradition*, 61–85; Chodkiewicz, "Le procès posthume d'Ibn ʿArabī," 98–99; Homerin, "Sufis and Their Detractors in Mamluk Egypt."

29 Ibn Taymiyyah regards al-Tilimsānī with great disdain, calling him the most pernicious of the lot, and the most excessive in his impiety, and referring to his eloquent writings and poems as "pork on a silver platter." See al-Dimashqī, *Tawḍīḥ al-mushtabih*, 1:138, and Hofer, *The Popularisation of Sufism in Ayyubid and Mamluk Egypt, 1173–1325*, Chapter 2.

30 On al-Nābulusī, see Sirriyeh, *Sufi Visionary of Ottoman Damascus: ʿAbd al-Ghani al-Nabulusi, 1641–1731.*

31 Al-Ṣafadī mentions that the son was born while the father was a Sufi living in the *Khānqah*. See *al-Wāfī bi-l-wafayāt*, 3:109.

32 Some sources say that he moved to Damascus between 670/1267 and 675/1271, which is unlikely because in 670/1267 he received authorization from al-Nawawī to transmit (*ijāzah*) *al-Minhāj bi-sharḥ Ṣaḥīḥ Muslim ibn al-Ḥajjāj*, a text that would take approximately two to four years to study cover to cover.

33 Al-Ṣafadī, *al-Wāfī bi-l-wafayāt*, 3:109.

34 Halim, *Legal Authority in Premodern Islam*, 22–24.

35 Ibn al-ʿImād, *Shadharāt al-dhahab*, 7:720–21; al-Dhahabī, *Tārīkh al-Islām*, 51, no. 627, 406–12; al-Sakhāwī, *al-Qawl al-munbī ʿan tarjamat Ibn al-ʿArabī*, 2:293–94.

36 Chittick, "Last Will and Testament."

37 Al-Ṣafadī, *al-Wāfī bi-l-wafayāt*, 3:113.

38 Al-Jazarī, *Tārīkh ḥawādith al-zamān*, 1:81.

39 On Ibn Barrajān, see Casewit, *The Mystics of al-Andalus: Ibn Barrajān and Islamic Thought in the Twelfth Century*, 136–56.

40 Casewit, "Al-Ghazālī's Virtue Ethical Theory of the Divine Names."

41 On al-Qūnawī's spiritual practices, method, and conception of the Path, see Todd, *The Sufi Doctrine of Man*, 141–69.

42 Ibn al-ʿArīf and Ibn al-ʿArabī ascribe this verse to Abū Yazīd al-Basṭāmī. See Ibn al-ʿArīf, *Maḥāsin al-majālis*, 83; Ibn al-ʿArabī, *Futūḥāt*, 1:745–46.

43 Under the name al-Fāliq, the scribe states that he copied the manuscript from the archetype written in the hand of the author (*bi-khaṭṭ al-muṣannif*, fl. 122b). See Musakhanov's edition of al-Tilimsānī's *Maʿānī l-asmāʾ*, 64.

معاني الأسماء الإلٰهيّة

The Divine Names

مَعـاني الأسـمـاء الإلـهيّـة
للشيخ الإمام عفيف الدين سليمان التلمسانيّ
قدّس الله روحه ونوّر ضريحه آمين آمين

بِسْمِ اللَّهِ الرَّحْمَنِ الرَّحِيمِ وبهِ تَوْفِيقي

١.٠   الحـمــد لله الأحَد ذاتًا وصفات وأفعالاً المنفرد وحده بالديمومية كمالاً الواجب الذي لولاه لكان كلّ ممكن محالاً أحمده حمده نفسه فاستوعب الحد تفصيلاً وإجمالاً وأصلّي على سمة حضرته وحضرة اسمه الذي أنقذ الأنام بالاسم الهادي بعد أن جعلهم الاسم المضلّ ضُلَّالاً صلّى الله عليه وآله وصحبه ما تناوحت جنوبًا وشمالاً وتقاوحت غدايًا وآصالاً وشَرُف وكَرُم.

٢.٠   وبعد فقد استخرتُ الله تبارك وتعالى في ذكر شيء من معاني الأسماء الإلهيّة الواردة في الكتاب العزيز مرتّبًا لها على حكم ما وردت فيه من أوّل الفاتحة إلى سورة الناس وأذكر الاسم ثمّ أذكر الآية التي وردت فيه ولا أذكر اسمًا من سورة وقد بقي في السورة التي قبلها اسم لم أذكره وأذكر السورة بعد السورة مرتّبًا ثمّ أذكر في كلّ اسم من ذكره من الأئمّة الثلاثة رضوان الله عليهم وهم الإمام أبو بكر محمّد البيهقيّ والإمام أبو حامد الغزاليّ والإمام أبو الحَكَم بن بَرَّجان الأندلسيّ وما انفرد به كلّ واحد منهم وما اتّفق عليه اثنان منهم.

٣.٠   وأعتصم بالله من قولي حتّى يكون هو القائل فليتعصم سامعه بالله حتّى يكون في قبول ما يسمعه هو القائل فإنّ هذا الكلام صادر من حضرة غاب الاسم بها في مسمّاه واشتمل فيها المعنى على لفظه لا اللفظ على معناه وهذا النفَس مبدؤه التصوّف ومنتهاه فوق التعرّف وها أنا أبتدئ ذلك والعصمة له به منه تقدّس اسمـه.

The Divine Names
A Mystical Theology of the Names of God in the Qur'an
By the Master and Eminent Scholar
ʿAfīf al-Dīn al-Tilimsānī
God sanctify his spirit and illumine his tomb

In the name of God, the All-Merciful, the Ever-Merciful, from Whom comes my success

Praise be to God, the One in Essence, qualities, and acts; the exclusively unique in everlasting perfection; the Necessary, if not for Whom every possible thing would be impossible. I praise Him as He praises Himself, with praise that embraces every particular and universal. And I send blessings upon Muḥammad, the mark of His presence and the presence of His name, who delivered humanity through His name the Guide, after His name the Misguider had led them into error. God bless, honor, and ennoble him, his family, and his Companions so long as the winds waft from north to south, spreading their sweet fragrance day and night. 0.1

I asked God to guide me in my treatment of the meanings of the divine names revealed in the Exalted Book. These I have arranged in the order they occur therein, from the start of the Opening Surah to the final surah, Mankind. I first discuss the divine name in question, then cite the verse in which it is revealed. I do not proceed to discuss another name from a subsequent surah until all the divine names in the previous surah have been treated. I proceed from surah to surah sequentially. For each divine name, I specify which of the three eminent scholars discussed it: Abū Bakr Muḥammad al-Bayhaqī, Abū Ḥāmid al-Ghazālī, and Abū l-Ḥakam ibn Barrajān al-Andalusī. I indicate the names that are singled out by only one scholar, and those about which two of them are in agreement. 0.2

I seek protection from God from my own statements in order that He be the Speaker, so let all who hear my words also seek protection from God, so that they receive them as though spoken by Him. These words issue from a presence through which the divine name is concealed in what it names, and in which the meaning encompasses its word, not the word its meaning. The starting point of this breath is Sufism, and its end point is beyond recognition. So let me begin, with the protection of the One Whose name is holy. 0.3

سورة الفاتحة

وفيها خمسة أسماء وهي الله الربّ الرحمٰن الرحيم الملك وهذه الخمسة في قوله تعالى ﴿ٱلْحَمْدُ لِلَّهِ رَبِّ ٱلْعَالَمِينَ ٱلرَّحْمَٰنِ ٱلرَّحِيمِ مَٰلِكِ يَوْمِ ٱلدِّينِ﴾ فالأوّل منها هو الاسم الله وآخرها ينتهي إلى مائة وستّة وأربعين اسماً.

اسمه الله تبارك وتعالى

١،١ هذا الاسم العظيم هو ممّا اتّفق عليه الأئمّة الثلاثة رضوان الله عليهم وقد اختُلف في أنّه مشتقّ أو ليس بمشتقّ فقال قوم نعم وقال قوم لا وبعض من قال نعم يرى أنّه مشتقّ من مصدر أَلِهَ يَأْلَهُ إِلَاهَةً أي عَبَدَ يَعْبُدُ عِبَادَةً فكأنّهم قالوا إلاه أي عبادة والمراد ذو العبادة أي الذي يعبَد فهو اسم مصدر كقولهم هو رجل عدل ورِضاً فهو من التسمية بالمصدر وقوم قالوا اشتقاقه من الوله أي الذي تتولّه فيه العقول وأصله أله ثمّ دخلت عليه الألف واللام بدلاً من الهمزة التي كانت في أله حُذفت فبقي ال لاه مرقّق اللامين ثمّ وُصلت اللام باللام في الخطّ وفُخّمتا للتعظيم فقيل الله.

٢،١ وأمّا من قال إنّه ليس بمشتقّ فلم يلحظ فيه الصفة بل جعله لمجرّد الذات المقدّسة التي لا يدرَك كنهها وإنّما تقع التسمية منها على ما يتعلّق به الإيمان لا العيان فإنّ العيان

The Opening Surah

This surah contains five names: Allāh, the Lord, the All-Merciful, the Ever-Merciful, and the King. These five are found in the verses: «Praise be to God, Lord of the worlds, the All-Merciful, the Ever-Merciful, King of the Day of Judgment».[1] Hence, the first name in this treatise is Allāh, and the final name ends at the number 146.[2]

Allāh

1.1 The three eminent scholars agree that this august name is a divine name. But there is disagreement over whether or not it is etymologically derived from a root, with one group affirming it and the other denying it. Among the former are those who consider it to derive from the verbal noun *aliha, ya'lahu, ilāhatan*, which means the same as "to worship," *ʿabada, yaʿbudu, ʿibādatan*.[3] In essence, they maintain that god, *ilāh*, means "worship," *ʿibādah*, and that the name means "possessor of worship," *dhū ʿibādah*—that is, the one who is worshipped. Thus, it is a verbal noun. Similarly, in Arabic one says, for instance, "he is justice and goodwill," which are designations in the form of verbal nouns. Others say that *Allāh* derives from the word for "ecstatic craze," *walah* (from the root *aliha*)—that is, "that by which intellects become ecstatically crazed." Then the definite article *al-* preceding *ilāh* was merged with it and the initial vowel was dropped, forming *al-lāh* with two soft *l*s. The two *l*s then came to be connected orthographically and emphatically pronounced out of reverence, hence "Allāh."

1.2 Those who say that Allāh is not derivative do not consider it to designate a quality, but only the Holy Essence itself, whose true nature cannot be

إن كان بعين العقل فما يقع عليه عيان العقل فهو محصور والذات منزّهة عن الحصر وإن كان العيان بعين الشهود والكشف الذاتيّ فلا اسم للذات من هذه الحضرة فإنّ شهودها يمحو الأسماء والصفات والمسمّيات ويطمس أعلام الصفات والأفعال والذوات فعلى كلا التقديرين لا يتعيّن للذات المقدّسة اسم إلّا من حضرة الإيمان فقط ومن حاول أن يعلو إلى غير ذلك سقط.

٣،١ ثمّ هذا الاسم لم يتسمّ به غيره تعالى وأين غيره تعالى فلمّا حمته عزّته عن المشاركة علمنا أنّ الذات المقدّسة أولى بعدم الشركة ألا ترى أنّه ما كان يمتنع في العقل أن يتسمّى بهذا الاسم بعض الموجودات فيقع هذا الاسم باشتراك على الله تعالى وعلى ذلك الموجود لكن حمته العزّة وظهرت بذلك المعجزة.

٤،١ واعلم أنّ الذات المقدّسة غنيّة عن الأسماء وليست أفعالها الذين هم العقلاء غنيّين عن أن يكون لها أسماء لأنّهم يتخاطبون فيها فيحتاجون إلى الأسماء الدالّة على معانيها المتناسبة والمتخالفة فجعلوا للذات المقدّسة أسماء على قدر حاجتهم.

٥،١ وقد علمتَ أنّ الأسماء متداخلة يدخل معنى بعضها في معنى بعض حتّى يكون كلّ اسم فيه بالقوّة كلّ اسم لكنّ بعضها أحقّ بأن يكون مجمعاً للأسماء من بعض لأنّ الأسماء الأصول هي أولى بدخول الأسماء تحتها من الأسماء الفروع وللأسماء الأصول أسماء هي أصول الأصول حتّى تنتهي إلى أصلين أحدهما الاسم الله وهو أوّلها ومبدؤها والثاني الاسم الرحمٰن وهو في ثاني رتبة عنه ولكنّ كلّاً منهما مشتمل على الأسماء كلّها وإن لم يكن لها كلّ إذ هي غير متناهية العدد ولكون كلّ منهما مشتمل على الأسماء ورد قوله تعالى ﴿قُلِ ٱدْعُواْ ٱللَّهَ أَوِ ٱدْعُواْ ٱلرَّحْمَٰنَ أَيًّا مَّا تَدْعُواْ فَلَهُ ٱلْأَسْمَآءُ ٱلْحُسْنَىٰ﴾ إلّا أنّ اشتمال الاسم الله هو أقعد بالتقدّم من الاسم الرحمٰن والاسم الرحمٰن يليه.

perceived. For the naming of the Essence only occurs on the basis of belief, not vision. If this vision occurs with the eye of the intellect, then that which the eye of the intellect falls upon is constrained. But the Essence is beyond all constraint. And if this vision occurs with the eye of witnessing and the unveiling of the Essence,[4] then there is no name for the Essence from this presence, for witnessing It effaces all names, qualities, and named things, and erases all signs of the qualities, acts, and essences.[5] Thus, in either case, no name can be designated for the Holy Essence except from the presence of belief alone, and to try to progress further is to meet with failure.

Only He is named by the name Allāh—and is there anything other than He? 1.3
Moreover, the fact that the name's majesty prevents it from being shared with anything else serves to show us that it is all the more impossible for the Holy Essence to be associated with anything. Note that it is not rationally impossible for some existents to assume this name, which would cause Allāh to be shared by God as well as that thing. Yet this name is protected by His might in such a way that a miracle is manifested through the name.[6]

The Holy Essence has no need of the names, but Its acts—which are the 1.4
Intellects—are not free from having names, for the Intellects converse with each other about the Essence and therefore need the names to designate Its corresponding and contrasting meanings. Thus they give the Holy Essence names according to the requirements of those names.

As you know, the names are interpenetrative. The meaning of some pertain 1.5
to others, such that each name potentially contains all the names. However, some names have a greater claim to being a gathering place for the names than others. The root names are more worthy of having the names included within them than the branch names. Moreover, the root names themselves pertain to other root names, which are the roots of the roots. Ultimately, all names end at two roots. The first is Allāh, which is their beginning and starting point, and the second is the All-Merciful, which is at a second level below Allāh. However, Allāh and the All-Merciful envelop all the names, even though the names have no totality because they are infinite in number. It is on account of the fact that both root names envelop all the names that God says: «Say: Call upon Allāh, or call upon the All-Merciful; whichever you call upon, His are the most beautiful names».[7] However, the inclusiveness of Allāh is more fundamental in precedence than the All-Merciful, and so the All-Merciful comes after it.

هذا في تقدير الأصالة ثمّ هنالك اعتبارات تجعل الاسم الرحمٰن متقدّماً على الاسم ٦،١
الله وذلك لأنّ الرحمٰن مشتقّ من الرحمة والرحمة هي وجود ما بدا إذ ظهور ما ظهر إنّما كان بالرحمة فللرحمن السبق بالنسبة إلى ما بدا ولذلك ورد قوله عليه السلام مخبرًا عن ربّه عزّ وجلّ أنّه قال سبقت رحمتي غضبي فللاسم الرحمٰن سبق بوجه حقّ وبالوجه الآخر هو مسبوق بوجه حقّ إلّا أنّ الأسماء كلّها تدخل تحت الاسمين الاسم الله والاسم الرحمٰن دخولاً تامّاً وإن كانت تدخل تحت كلّ اسم اسم دخولاً باعتبارات سوف نذكر بعضها إن شاء الله تعالى.

وإذا علمتَ دخول الأسماء كلّها تحت الاسمين المذكورين بل تحت كلّ اسم منهما ٧،١
دخولاً تامّاً فاعلم أنّ كلاً منهما يختصّ من الأسماء ببعضها اختصاصاً خاصّاً لا تكون الأسماء كلّها بذلك الاعتبار الخاصّ تدخل تحت كلّ اسم منهما فالواجب أن نبيّن ما الاعتبار الخاصّ بكلّ منهما فنقول أمّا الاسم الله فيختصّ بدخول الأسماء المرتبيّة التي ليس الوجود لها إلّا في ثاني رتبة مثل الأعدام الإضافيّة التي ليست أعداماً صرفاً ولا هي وجودات صرفاً ولهذه أسماء خاصّة وللوجودات الصرفة أسماء خاصّة فأمّا أسماء الأعدام فمثل الاسم المانع والقابض والمميت والعليم والباطن والمبتلي والسميع والعزيز والغنيّ والمذلّ والعفوّ بوجه ما والكبير والمتعال والإلٰه والوارث والواقي بوجه ما والراتق والرفيع وذو العرش بوجه ما والممتحن بوجه ما وذو الجلال والعفوّ بوجه ما والقدّوس والجبّار بوجه ما والمتكبّر والأحد والصمد بوجه ما فهذه كلّها من خواصّ الاسم الله ولا تدخل في الاسم الرحمٰن إلّا باعتبارات هي في ثاني رتبة من الوجود وتدخل في الاسم الله تعالى في الاعتبار الأوّل من الوجود.

وأمّا الاسم الرحمٰن فيختصّ بدخول الأسماء الوجوديّة التي الوجود لها في أوّل رتبة ٨،١
وذلك مثل الاسم الربّ الرحمٰن الرحيم الملك بوجه ما والمحيط بوجه ما والقدير والحكيم بوجه ما والتوّاب والمفضل والبصير وذو الفضل والوليّ والنصير والواسع والبديع والكافي والرؤوف والشديد العذاب بوجه ما والقريب والمجيب والسريع الحساب

This precedence is the case if we suppose there is a primacy. From other perspectives, however, it is the All-Merciful that precedes Allāh. For the All-Merciful is derived from mercy, and mercy is the existence of all that appears, since all that manifests only becomes manifest through mercy. Thus the All-Merciful has precedence over Allāh in relation to all that appears, which is why the blessed Prophet quoted God as saying, "My mercy precedes My wrath."[8] Thus, the All-Merciful is precedent in one respect, while in another respect it is preceded by Allāh. In any case, all the names are included within these two names, Allāh and the All-Merciful, even though in a certain sense it is true that all the names are included within every other name as well. We shall discuss some of this below, God willing. 1.6

Since you know that the totality of the names are included within Allāh and the All-Merciful—and indeed within each of them individually—you should understand also that Allāh and the All-Merciful lay special claim to certain names in particular ways; from this specific perspective, not all the names are included within them both. Therefore, it is necessary to clarify the specific considerations that cause each name to pertain to Allāh or to the All-Merciful. So we say: Allāh lays special claim to the names of rank. These are the names that only exist in a secondary rank. Consider, for instance, the relative nonexistents, which are neither absolute nonexistents nor pure existents. These have specific names, just as pure existents have specific names. As for the names of nonexistents, they are, in a certain sense, names such as the Preventer, the Withholder, the Death-Giver, the Knowing, the Nonmanifest, the Tester, the Hearing, the Mighty, the Independent, the Abaser, the Forgiver, the Great, the Transcendent, the God, the Inheritor, the Protector (from a certain perspective), the Stitcher, the Uplifter, the Possessor of the Throne, the Setter of Trials, the Possessor of Majesty, the Forgiver, the Holy, the All-Dominating, the Proud, the Only, and the Self-Sufficient. These are all included among the names specific to Allāh. They are included within the All-Merciful only from the standpoint that they exist in a secondary rank, whereas they pertain to Allāh from the standpoint that they exist in a primary rank. 1.7

As for the All-Merciful, it lays special claim to the names of existence, which possess existence in a primary respect. In a certain sense, these are names such as the Lord, the All-Merciful, the Ever-Merciful, the King, the Encompassing, the Powerful, the Wise, the Ever-Turning, the One Who Favors, the Seeing, the Bountiful, the Overseer, the Guardian, the Helper, the All-Embracing, the 1.8

والخبير بوجه ما والباسط والحيّ والقيّوم وهما أعظمهما اختصاصاً بالاسم الرحمٰن الحميد بوجه ما والمنتقم بوجه ما والوهّاب والجامع والمقسط بوجه ما ومالك الملك والمعزّ بوجه بعيد والحكم بوجه ما والناصر والحيّ والوكيل بوجه ما والمرسل بوجه والصادق والشاكر والفاطر والقاهر والقاضي والقادر والفالق واللطيف والبادئ والهادي والمغيث والضارّ بوجه ما والنافع بوجه والقويّ والحفيظ والمجيد والودود والفعّال والخافض والرافع والمدبّر والقهّار والواقي والولي والمنّان والكفيل بوجه ما والمكرّم والمقتدر بوجه ما والحنّان والباقي بوجه ما والمعطي والفاتق والباعث والحقّ بوجه ما والمولى بوجه ما والمزكّي والوفيّ والنور والمبين والشافي والكريم والمحسن والمبدئ والطاهر والفتّاح والعلاّم بوجه ما والشكور وذو الطول والممتحن بوجه ما والرازق والمتين والبرّ والمغني وذو الجلال والإكرام بوجه ما والظاهر والمهيمن والجبّار بوجه ما والخالق والبارئ والمصوّر وهو أعظم حكماً والذارئ وذو المعارج والشديد البطش بوجه ما.

٩،١ فهذه الأسماء التي تقدّم ذكرها هي أكثر عدداً من الأسماء المختصَة التي تُنسب للاسم الله وما ذاك إلّا أنّ الرحمة غلبت الغضب والغضب في الأسماء المختصّة بالاسم الرحمٰن قليل ولا يكون إلّا بطريق اللحوق لا بالأصالة وأمّا في الاسم الله فهو بطريق الأصالة لأجل أنّ أحكام المراتب عدميّة والعدم عذاب والوجود نعيم ثمّ قد يقع النعيم بأحكام المراتب بطريق العرض أيضاً كما كان الغضب في الأسماء الوجوديّة بطريق العرض.

١٠،١ وقد علمتَ أنّ ما ثَمّ إلّا الوجود ومراتبه وقد اقتسم هاذان الاسمان فأخذ الاسم الله المراتب وأخذ الاسم الرحمٰن الوجود واشتملت حقيقة الحقائق على الاسمين المذكورين بما تحتهما من الأسماء في أحد شطريها وبقي الشطر الآخر لأسماء العبد فإنّ العبد المطلق الذي هو الإنسان باعتبار عبوديّته وألوهيّته هو في مقابل حضرة جامعة

Innovative, the Sufficer, the Kind, the Severe in Chastisement, the Near, the Responder, the Swift in Reckoning, the Aware, the Lavisher, the Living, and the Self-Subsisting—and of them all these last two are the most closely associated with the All-Merciful—the Praiseworthy, the Avenger, the Bestower, the Gatherer, the Impartial, the Owner of the Kingdom, the Exalter (in a very limited sense), the Ruler, the Assister, the Living, the Trustee, the Sender, the Truthful, the Grateful, the Cleaver, the Triumphant, the Judge, the Able, the Splitter, the Subtle, the One Who Originates, the Guide, the Deliverer, the Harmer, the Benefiter, the Strong, the Preserving, the Glorious, the Lover, the Fully Active, the Lowerer, the Uplifter, the Governing, the All-Subjugating, the Protector, the Guardian, the Gracious, the Sponsor, the Ennobler, the Potent, the Tender, the Everlasting, the Giver, the Unstitcher, the Resurrector, the Real, the Patron, the Purifier, the Fulfiller, the Light, the Clarifier, the Healer, the Noble, the Benevolent, the Originator, the Pure, the Opener, the Ever-Knowing, the Thankful, the Abundant, the Setter of Trials, the All-Provider, the Firm, the Clement, the Enricher, the Possessor of Majesty, the Honorer, the Manifest, the Overseer, the All-Dominating, the Creator, the Maker, the Form-Giver—whose properties are most prominent—the Multiplier, the Lord of the Ascending Pathways, and the Severe in Assault.

The names of existence that we have listed are greater in number than 1.9 the names of rank that are specifically ascribed to Allāh. The reason for this is that mercy takes precedence over wrath,[9] and wrath in the names that belong specifically to the All-Merciful is rare, and comes only through association, not fundamentally. But in Allāh, wrath is fundamental, because the properties of the ranks pertain to nonexistence, and nonexistence is chastisement, while existence is bliss. Moreover, bliss may occur in the properties of the levels accidentally, just as wrath may occur in the names of existence accidentally.

As you know, there is only existence and its levels. The two names Allāh 1.10 and the All-Merciful divide this among themselves: Allāh takes the levels, and the All-Merciful takes existence. For its part, the Reality of Realities encloses in one of its two halves the names Allāh and the All-Merciful, and all the names derived from them. The other half of the Reality of Realities remains for the names of the servant. For the nondelimited servant, who is man from the standpoint of his servanthood and his divinity, is the counterpart of the comprehensive presence of the divine names and the presence of the cosmic

للأسماء الإلٰهيّة وحضرة الأسماء الكونيّة وهما أعني الحضرتين متقابلتان أزلاً وأبداً لا من بداية ولا إلى نهاية.

١١،١ فأمّا الإنسانيّة التي لا اسم لها فهي بإزاء الذات التي لا اسم لها ولا مقابل لها ولا عبارة عنها ونسبة الدهر إلى بقائها كنسبة الزمان إلى الدهر وأكثر من يجعل الاسم الله للذات المقدّسة وأنّه غير مشتقّ يظنّ أنّه لهذه الذات فقط وإن لم يشهدها وليس الأمر كذلك لأنّ القائلين المذكورين لا شعور لهم بهذه الإنسانيّة وقد غرق علم الأوّلين والآخرين في أيسر بحر من هذه البحار فلا تجري العقول هنا في مضمار فلنقبض عنان القلم في هذا الاسم المعظّم حيث انتهينا.

اسمه الرحمٰن عزّ وجلّ

١،٢ هذا الاسم منه الرحمة ممّا أجمع عليه الأئمّة الثلاثة رضوان الله عليهم ومحلّ ذكره من الفاتحة هو في قوله تعالى ﴿ٱلْحَمْدُ لِلَّهِ رَبِّ ٱلْعَٰلَمِينَ ٱلرَّحْمَٰنِ﴾ ولم ينقل أيضاً أنّه يسمّى به غير الذات المقدّسة لكن قالوا رحمٰن اليمامة يعنون مسيلمة الكذّاب لكن قيل ذلك بالإضافة إلى اليمامة فالاسم الرحمٰن منزّه عن القول بالاشتراك أيضاً كما كان ذلك في الاسم الله عزّ وجلّ وقد تقدّم ذكر أنّ الأسماء أكثرها تدخل تحت حيطة الاسم الرحمٰن فإذا ذُكرت تلك الأسماء بيّنّا إن شاء الله تعالى كيفيّة دخولها وبأيّ اعتبار دخلت فيكون ذلك كالشرح لهذا الاسم أيضاً.

٢،٢ وأمّا ما يختصّ بهذا الاسم لا باعتبار الأسماء الداخلة تحته فهو أنّه المتحرّك بحركة له أزليّة أبديّة ديموميّة تعطي الصور المعنويّة والروحانيّة والمثاليّة والخياليّة والحسّيّة في أنواع غير متناهية العدد وإذا كانت أنواعه غير متناهية العدد فلأن تكون أشخاصه

names. These two presences are counterparts eternally and forever, without beginning and without end.[10]

The human presence, which has no name, stands face-to-face with the Essence, which has no name, no counterpart, and no mode of expression. The relationship of the aeon to the subsistence of this human presence is like the relationship of time to the aeon.[11] Most of those who ascribe Allāh to the Holy Essence, claiming that it is not derived, surmise that Allāh is for the Essence alone even though they have not witnessed It. But such is not the case, and therefore those who make such claims have no awareness of this human presence. For all their knowledge, previous and later scholars would drown in the least of these oceans, for intellects cannot operate in this arena. At this point, let me rein in my pen on the subject of this magnificent name. 1.11

Al-Raḥmān: The All-Merciful

The three eminent scholars agree that this name, from which mercy is derived, is a divine name. Its place of occurrence in the Opening Surah is: «Praise be to God, Lord of the worlds, the All-Merciful».[12] Like Allāh, only the Holy Essence has been reported as being called by this name. Even though it is said that the false prophet Musaylimah was known as the all-merciful of Yamāmah, this was expressed in the genitive construction with the word al-Yamāmah. Thus, the All-Merciful is, like Allāh, far above any equivocation. We have also noted previously that the majority of the names are included within the scope of the All-Merciful. Therefore, when those names are referred to below we shall clarify how and in what respect they are included within it, and this will serve as further commentary on the name. 2.1

What is particular to this name and not to the other names that enter its purview is that it moves with a movement that is beginningless, endless, and continuous. This movement gives rise to the supersensory, spiritual, imaginal, imaginative, and sensory forms in all their infinite species. Now, if its species are infinite in number, it is because the engendering of its individuations is 2.2

غير متناهية العدد من باب الأولى وليست هذه الحركة له من محرّك غير ذاته فتثبت له الحركة من حيث تثبت ذاته وتخصّه من كلّ صورة تحقّقها بما هي وتمامها بنسب ما كانت إذ هو من جانب وجودها فإنّ الأعدام الإضافيّة لاحقة للاسم الله وجانب وجودها للاسم الرحمٰن.

٣،٢ وأقرب ما ينسَب إلى الاسم الرحمٰن النفَس وهو الذي سمّاه عليه السلام النفَس الرحمانيّ فإنّه حركة وجود تتعيّن به ومنه وفيه الموجودات كلّها ولا كلّ لها إذ لا يتناهى الكلّ والكرة التاسعة بما حوت من الأفلاك والسماوات والأرضين شخص واحد من هذه الموجودات التي لا تتناهى لحركة الوجود فيما لا يتناهى هي حركة إيجاد وإعطاء فإذا انتهى موجود من الموجودات إلى حدّ طوره وطور حدّه صار القهقرى إلى الاسم الله ﴿أَلَآ إِلَى ٱللَّهِ تَصِيرُ ٱلْأُمُورُ﴾ فيكون على هذا التقدير الاسم الباسط هو صاحب العطاء الصادر عن النفَس الرحمانيّ والاسم القابض هو صاحب الردّ إلى الاسم الله عزّ وجلّ لكنّ بعض الموجودات الراجعة إلى الاسم الله تبقى أبدًا وهي النفوس السعيدة من البشر فإذا قبضها الاسم القابض لم يعدم حقائقها بل ينقلها نقلًا إلى عالَمها المناسب لاستعدادها ثمّ يستمرّ البسط والقبض فيما بين هاتين المرتبتين استمرارًا لم يكن عن أوّل ولا هو إلى آخر لِعدم تناهي القدرة ولسعة الحضرات الصفاتيّة.

٤،٢ وتلحق هذه الموجودات لحوقًا واجبًا أسماء العبوديّة لا بالقصد الأوّل وأسماء العبوديّة وإن كانت تابعة فإنّ بعضها يكون عليه ينبني بعض الأسماء الإلٰهيّة ويتحقّق أثره في الوجود فإنّ الحقّ تعالى من جهة رحمانيّته معط للوجود ومن جملته وجود الرزق فهو رزّاق يتحقّق بالمرزوق وهو خلّاق يتحقّق بالمخلوق ووهّاب يتحقّق بالموهوب ولمّا كانت الوحدانيّة ثابتة كانت هباته واصلة إلى يده ورزقه كذلك وتحقّق ما تحقّق من الأسماء لم يكن إلّا بتحقّقه تعالى من أطوار عباده وأطوار عباده منه فتحقّق ما تحقّق هو به له

infinite from the beginning. And the All-Merciful only moves by virtue of its own essence. Thus, its movement is constant inasmuch as its essence is constant. The movement, moreover, is specific for each form by virtue of the realization of what it is, and the form's perfection is in relation to what it is, pertaining as it does to its existence. For the relative nonexistents attach to Allāh, but their actual existence attaches to the All-Merciful.

The closest thing that is ascribed to the All-Merciful is the Breath, which 2.3
the blessed Prophet called the "Breath of the All-Merciful,"[13] for it is a movement of being through which, from which, and in which all existent things are determined, keeping in mind that "all" does not really pertain to existents, since "all" denotes infinity. For among "all" these existents that are infinite, the ninth sphere, together with the spheres, heavens, and earths it encompasses, is a single individuation. The movement of existence within this infinity is a movement of existentiation and bestowal. When the motion of an existent reaches the limit of its scope and the scope of its limit, it then moves back to Allāh: «Do not all affairs end up with Allāh?»[14] Thus, the Lavisher is responsible for the bestowal that issues from the All-Merciful Breath, while the Withholder is responsible for returning the existents back to Allāh. However, some existents that go back to Allāh subsist forever; namely, felicitous human souls. When the Withholder seizes them, it does not nullify their realities—rather, it moves them to the world that is appropriate to their level of preparedness.[15] This expansion and contraction continues ceaselessly between these two levels because of the infinity of God's power and the expanse of the presences of the divine qualities.

These existents, moreover, join to the names of servanthood[16] by necessity, 2.4
not by way of primary intention. For although the names of servanthood are subordinate, some divine names are constructed upon them, and thus their traces become actualized in existence. With respect to His all-mercifulness, the Real is the bestower of existence, and this includes the existence of provision. Therefore, He is the Provider, which is actualized through the one who is provided for. Likewise, He is the Ever-Creating, and this is actualized through that which is created; He is the Bestowing, and this is actualized through the one bestowed upon. And since His oneness is affirmed, His bestowals reach His own hand, as do His provisions.[17] What is realized of the names can only come to be through His actualization of the various stages of His servants, which come from Him. Thus, the actualization of what is actualized is through, for, and from Him; and divine transcendence remains His alone, while the stages

منه فبقيت النزاهة له حاصلة وأطوار موجوداته متيقّنة ومعطية لمعطيها ومن جملة ما أعطاها ما أعطته فصار العطاء منه فقط.

٥،٢ وبسط حقائق الاسم الرحمٰن مساوق لما لا يتناهى فهو لا يتناهى فلنكتف بذلك على ما يتفصّل عند ذكر الأسماء من تعلّق كلّ اسم بالاسم الرحمٰن وقد قدّمتُ ذكر الاسم الرحمٰن على الاسم الربّ لتآخي معنى اسمه مع اسم الله في جمعها لحقائق الأسماء وترتيب الأسماء على صورة ورودها في الفاتحة هو بتقديم الاسم الله الربّ فافهم.

اسمه الربّ تبارك وتعالى

١،٣ هذا الاسم اتّفق على إيراده أبو بكر البيهقيّ وأبو الحكم الأندلسيّ ولم يذكره الإمام الغزاليّ رضوان الله عليه واشتقاقه من الربّ الذي هو الإصلاح والتربية قريبة من معناه وهو من التسمية بالمصدر كعدل ورضاً ووروده في الفاتحة في قوله تعالى ﴿لِلَّهِ رَبِّ ٱلْعَـٰلَمِينَ﴾.

٢،٣ وهو من الأسماء الوجوديّة التي اختصاصها بالاسم الرحمٰن من جهة وجود التربية فإنّها نفع وجوديّ يصل إلى المربوب فالرحمٰن من طور التربية هو ربّ في التدلّي وهذا الكلام باعتبار مراتب الأسماء وأمّا الذات الموصوفة بهذه الأسماء فهي حيث وُجدت الأسماء وحيث لم توجد ولا يقع فيها اختلاف الاعتبارات بل إنّما تلحق الاعتبارات أسماءها فعلى هذا يكون الربّ صفة تجلّ من الاسم الرحمٰن يتفصّل في محالّ التربية في جميع أطوار الوجود ظاهره وباطنه.

٣،٣ وهذا الاسم وإن ذكرنا اختصاصه بالاسم الرحمٰن من جهة وجوديّته فله نسبة أيضاً إلى الاسم الله من جهة عدميّة إضافيّة ومثاله أنّ التربية بحسب كلّ موجود

of His existents are most certainly bestowed by their Bestower. The existents can only give what they are given, so bestowal comes from Him alone.

An expanded commentary on the realities of the All-Merciful would extend to infinity, because this name is infinite. Let this much suffice for now, and more will unfold from our discussion of how the other names are attached to the All-Merciful. Note that I mentioned the All-Merciful before the Lord because of the correspondence between the meanings of the All-Merciful and Allāh in how they bring together the realities of the names. According to the sequential order of the names that are mentioned in the Opening Surah, the divine name the Lord comes before the All-Merciful. 2.5

Al-Rabb: The Lord

3.1 Al-Bayhaqī and Ibn Barrajān both consider this to be a divine name, while al-Ghazālī, may God be pleased with him, makes no mention of it. It is etymologically derived from the Arabic word *rabb*, which means "to make wholesome." It is also closely related to "nurturing" (*tarbiyah*). This is another example of using a verbal noun to denote a name, as when one refers to a just person or a person of goodwill by saying, "he is justice" or "he is goodwill." This name is mentioned in the Opening Surah in the verse: «Praise be to God, Lord of the Worlds».[18]

3.2 This is one of the names of existence that through the aspect of nurturing especially pertain to the All-Merciful. Nurturing is an existential benefit that reaches the Lord's servant, and thus the All-Merciful in the stage of nurturing is the Lord in the stage of descent. All of this applies to the perspective of the ranks of the names; the Essence described by these names is both where the names are and where they are not, and different perspectives do not apply to It, but only to Its names. Accordingly, the Lord is a quality of disclosure from the All-Merciful, differentiated within the loci of nurturing throughout all the stages of existence, outward and inward.

3.3 Although we said that with regard to its existential status this name pertains especially to the All-Merciful, it is also ascribed to Allāh with regard to relative

إنّما هي بقدر ما يحتاج إليه ذلك الموجود فلو زادت عن قدر حاجته انعكس معنى التربية إلى ضدّه فيصير زيادةُ وجود التربية عدمَ تربية في حقّ ذلك المربوب وهذا الأثر المذكور وإن كان صفة وجوديّة وحقّ كلّ صفة وجوديّة في الأصل أن ترجع إلى الاسم الرحمٰن إلّا أنّ رجوعها هنا إلى اسم الله لفوات التربية المصلحة لهذا الموجود الخاصّ ولفوات صفة الرحمانيّة التي هي هنا إيجاد التربية لهذا الموجود وفي الحقيقة ليس هذا من الاسم الربّ إلّا بالعرض من كون مبدأ ذلك كان تربية ثمّ خرج.

٤٫٣ واعلم أنّ التربية الوجوديّة ربّما ظنّ المحجوب أنّها صفة فعل حقيقيّ في غيرٍ فرقيّ فيقع في الشرك ولم يعلم أنّها صفة من الصفات ترجع إلى الاسم الظاهر من حيث هو ثابت للاسم الرحمٰن فالتربية إذاً تجلّيات متتابعة ما الظاهر بها غير الرحمٰن عزّ وجلّ فلا تأخذك معاني الأسماء فتغيب عن المسمّى فقد دخل الاسم الربّ في معنى الاسم الظاهر وهما معاً في ضمن الاسم الرحمٰن ويدخل في الاسم الربّ الاسم المعطي من جهة ما في التربية من العطاء وفيه الاسم الودود وفيه المحسن والمنعم والجواد وغير ذلك ويتفاوت دخول هذه الأسماء في الاسم الربّ على قدر قسط كلّ منهم.

٥٫٣ فصل لا يجوز أن تكون تربية في الموجودات بعضها لبعض إلّا وهي قوًى من سريان قوّة التربية الإلٰهيّة ولو بقدر ما ينسَب إلى القيّوميّة الإلٰهيّة التي قام بها كلّ شيء وكلّ تربيـة هي من قيّوميّـة القيّوم تعالى وإن شئتَ نسبتها إلى الاسم القادر فإنّ كلّ مقدور فرضتَه هو بالقدرة الإلٰهيّة و﴿ٱلْقُوَّةَ لِلَّهِ جَمِيعًا﴾ وهو توحيد الأفعال فالقادر داخل في الاسم الربّ بهذا الاعتبار وقِسْ على هذا المعنى جميع معاني الأسماء الإلٰهيّة.

٦٫٣ واعلم أنّ التربية أعمّ ممّا يُفهم منها في العرف فإنّ تربية الحقّ تعالى من حيث ما هو ربّ للعالمين هي سرّ الحياة في كلّ موجود من العالمين فالحياة في البسائط حركة

nonexistence. For example, each existent is nurtured precisely in proportion to its own needs. Were the nurturing to surpass the measure of the existent's needs, it would no longer be nurturing, but the opposite: an excess in nurturing would entail the absence of nurturing with respect to the individual. Now, although the effect we have described is an existential quality, and every existential quality must fundamentally trace back to the All-Merciful, in such a case of excess it traces back to Allāh due to the absence of wholesome nurturing for that specific existent, and due to the absence of the quality of all-mercifulness, which in this case is the existentiation of nurturing for that existent. In reality, this only comes accidentally from the Lord insofar as it originated as nurturing and then ceased to be so.

A thinker whose mind is veiled might suppose that existential nurturing 3.4
is a quality of a real act within a separative entity, and would thus fall into polytheism. Such a person does not know that existential nurturing is among the qualities that derive from the Manifest, inasmuch as the Manifest is firmly affixed to the All-Merciful. Nurturing is therefore a sequence of disclosures, and it manifests through none other than the All-Merciful. Therefore, do not become so engrossed in the meanings of the names that you become absent from the Named. For the Lord is included within the meaning of the Manifest, and both of them are embraced by the All-Merciful. Moreover, the Giver is included within the Lord due to the fact that nurturing involves giving. The Lord also contains the Lover, the Beneficent, the Benefactor, the Munificent, and others. The ways in which these are included within the Lord differ according to the appropriate measure of each of them.

It is not permissible for one existent to nurture another unless it acts as 3.5
a faculty of the permeating force of divine nurturing, if only in the measure by which it is ascribed to the divine quality of self-subsistence by which all things subsist. For every type of nurturing comes from the self-subsistence of the Self-Subsisting. You may also ascribe it to the Powerful, for every imaginable object of power comes from the divine power, and «all power belongs to God».[19] This is the oneness of divine acts. Thus, from this standpoint the Powerful is included within the Lord, and you can extend this by analogy to all the meanings of the divine names.

Moreover, nurturing is broader than is commonly understood. For divine 3.6
nurturing, inasmuch as God is «Lord of the worlds»,[20] is the secret of life that exists within each inhabitant of the cosmos. The life of simple forms is

ذاتيّة تنشئ التراكيب فهي حياة للتركيب ثمّ لأجزاء المركّب ثمّ للمركّب ثمّ لبقاء المركّب ثمّ لكونه قد يكون جزءًا لمركّب آخر فتصير المركّبات في الطور الأوّل أجزاءً للمركّب في الطور الثاني ويستمرّ إلى حيث تقف فهذه حياة بها يدخل الاسم الحيّ في الاسم الربّ بهذه التربية المذكورة.

وأمّا مفهوم العوامّ من التربية فهو ما يشبه تربية الطفل فقط ولو كان كذلك لخرج ٧،٣
بعض العالمين من حيطة تربية اسم الربّ له وكيف وهو ﴿رَبِّ ٱلْعَالَمِينَ﴾ بالعموم وذلك يقتضي العوالم كلّها ظاهرها وباطنها أوّلها الإضافيّ وآخرها ولو جرى القلم بما يقتضي معنى الربوبيّة لم يقف عند حدّ أبد الآبدين ﴿وَٱللَّهُ وَٰسِعٌ عَلِيمٌ﴾.

اسمه الرحيم تبارك وتعالى

هذا الاسم العظيم ممّا اتّفق عليه الأئمّة الثلاثة رضوان الله عليهم البيهقيّ والغزاليّ ١،٤
وابن برّجان وَوروده في الفاتحة في قوله تعالى ﴿ٱلْحَمْدُ لِلَّهِ رَبِّ ٱلْعَٰلَمِينَ ٱلرَّحْمَٰنِ ٱلرَّحِيمِ﴾ وهو مشتقّ من الرحمة وصيغة فعيل فيه للمبالغة والفرق بينه وبين الاسم الرحمٰن أنّ الاسم الرحمٰن لكمال الرحمة والرحيم للأكمليّة فكلّ رحمة ظهرت في الوجود فيقال لها الرحمة ما بقي للخلاف أثر في نظر الناظر وإن لم يبق للخلاف أثر فهو رحمانيّة في فناء الشاهد بالمشهود وإن زاد على ذلك زيادة بعد التمام فهي رحيميّة والرحيميّة هي مقام التحقيق والرحمانيّة من مقام الوقفة والرحمة من مقام العلم.

an essential motion that brings about composites. It is the life of the composition, then of the composited parts, then of the composite entity itself, then of the subsistence of the composite entity, then of the fact that it may be a part of another composite entity. Thus, the composite entities in the first stage become parts of a composite entity at a second stage, and this process continues until it comes to a halt. This, then, is a type of life that brings the Living within the Lord, through this aforementioned nurturing.

The concept of nurturing as it is understood by ordinary believers is limited 3.7
to the raising of children and the like. But if this were the case, then parts of the worlds would be excluded from the scope of the Lord—and how could this be, when He is «the Lord of the worlds»[21] in the most universal sense? This entails the worlds in their entirety, both inwardly and outwardly, and both in the sense of their relative beginning and end. For once the Pen proceeds in accordance with the dictates of lordship's meaning, it will never stop at any limit: «God is All-Embracing, Knowing».[22]

Al-Raḥīm: The Ever-Merciful

The three eminent scholars al-Bayhaqī, al-Ghazālī, and Ibn Barrajān agree 4.1
that this is a divine name. It is mentioned in the Opening Surah in the verse: «Praise be to God, Lord of the worlds, the All-Merciful, the Ever-Merciful»,[23] and it derives from mercy, *raḥmah*. The form of the word in Arabic (*faʿīl*) denotes intense emphasis. The difference between this name and the All-Merciful is that the All-Merciful denotes the perfection of mercy, whereas the Ever-Merciful denotes the superlative perfection of mercy. Every mercy that manifests in existence is called mercy as long as there is a trace of opposition in the beholder. But if there is no trace of opposition, then it is all-mercifulness in that the witness is annihilated in what is witnessed. If all-mercifulness is surpassed with an even more complete mercy, then it is ever-mercifulness. Ever-mercifulness is the station of realization, while all-mercifulness belongs to the station of halting, and mercy belongs to the station of knowledge.

واعلم أنّ كلّ اسم من أسمائه تعالى فيه مبالغة على صيغة فعيل فهو داخل في الاسم ٢،٤
الرحيم لا من كلّ وجه بل من الوجه الذي يدخل به الرحيم في الاسم الرحمٰن وهو جانب الوجود الذي هو نَفَس الرحمٰن في كلّ مرتبة وذلك مثل العليم والقدير والسميع من وجه والبصير من وجه آخر أيضاً وأشباه ذلك من الأسماء.

اسمه الملك تبارك وتعالى

هذا الاسم الكريم هو ممّا اتّفق عليه الأئمّة الثلاثة رضوان الله عليهم وأوّل وروده ١،٥
في الكتاب العزيز هو في قوله تعالى ﴿مَلِكِ يَوۡمِ ٱلدِّينِ﴾ وهو وإن ورد هنا مضافاً فهو مطلق في المعنى بدليل وروده خالياً عن الإضافة في قوله ﴿هُوَ ٱللَّهُ ٱلَّذِى لَآ إِلَٰهَ إِلَّا هُوَ ٱلۡمَلِكُ﴾ واشتقاقه من المُلك ومن قرأ ﴿مَٰلِكِ يَوۡمِ ٱلدِّينِ﴾ فهو مشتقّ من المِلك بكسر الميم وهما اسمان مختلفان في المعنى وفي مصنّف أبي جعفر أحمد بن محمّد بن إسماعيل البغويّ قال سمعتُ محمّد بن الوليد يحكي عن محمّد بن يزيد أنّه كان يستحسن أن يقرأ ﴿مَلِكِ يَوۡمِ ٱلدِّينِ﴾ ويستدلّ على ذلك بقوله ﴿لِّمَنِ ٱلۡمُلۡكُ﴾.

ومرتبة ﴿مَٰلِكِ يَوۡمِ ٱلدِّينِ﴾ في الأسماء الإلٰهيّة تدخل تحت حيطة الاسم الباطن ٢،٥
من حيث أنّ الآخرة غيب الآن وعند تعيّن يَوۡمِ ٱلدِّينِ وهو القيامة تدخل في حيطة الاسم الظاهر وتبعد نسبة الاسم الملك عزّ وجلّ من الاسم الأوّل لأنّ الأوّليّة سابقة و﴿مَٰلِكِ يَوۡمِ ٱلدِّينِ﴾ لاحق لتأخّر ظهور حكمه إلى ﴿يَوۡمِ ٱلدِّينِ﴾ أمّا من حيث قدم الأسماء بقدم المسمّى فذلك لا يختلف لكن لا تنقطع النسبة بينه وبين الاسم

Every emphatic divine name that appears in Arabic with the same form (*faʿīl*) is included within the Ever-Merciful, not in every aspect, but in the same way that the Ever-Merciful is included within the All-Merciful, which is the aspect of existence, the Breath of the All-Merciful at every level of being. Names such as the Knowing, the Powerful, and the Hearing are also included within the Ever-Merciful in a certain sense, as in another sense is the Seeing, and so too for other similar names. 4.2

Al-Malik: The King

This noble name is considered to be a divine name by the three eminent scholars. Its first occurrence in the Holy Book is in the verse: «King of the Day of Judgment».[24] Although "King" occurs here in a possessive construction, its meaning is without condition, as indicated by another verse in which it is not mentioned in a possessive construction: «He is God; there is no god but He. He is the King».[25] "King" (*malik*) is derived from the word kingship (*mulk*). Those who read verse 1:3 as «Owner (*mālik*) of the Day of Judgment» consider the word to derive from ownership (*milk*); the King and the Owner have different meanings. Abū Jaʿfar Aḥmad ibn Muḥammad ibn Ismāʿīl al-Baghawī[26] says in his anthology of Prophetic Traditions: "I heard Muḥammad ibn al-Walīd say that Muḥammad ibn Yazīd preferred to read it as «King of the Day of Judgment», citing in support of this the verse «Whose is the kingship today?»"[27] 5.1

The rank of «King of the Day of Judgment» among the divine names falls within the scope of the Nonmanifest, inasmuch as the next world is now unseen; but, at the time of the Day of Judgment—namely, the resurrection—it will fall within the scope of the Manifest. The King has a distant relation to the First, because "first" denotes precedence while «King of the Day of Judgment» denotes subsequence because its manifestation is delayed until the day of resurrection. However, there is no precedence of one name over another from the perspective of the eternity of the names through the Named Essence. At the same time, the relationship between the King and the First is 5.2

الأوّل بالكلّيّة فإنّ يوم الآخرة بالنسبة إلى الله تعالى هو الآن حاضر لأنّه تعالى لا تختلف في حقّه الأزمنة ولا هو زمانيّ فالماضي والمستقبل عنده حاضر وهذا المعنى يفهمه أهل الله تعالى فهماً يستند إلى المشاهدة فلا يعترضهم[1] فيه الشكّ ولا الظنّ ولا الوهم.

٣،٥ والمملكة ﴿يَوْمِ ٱلدِّينِ﴾ تنقسم إلى قسمين أحدهما للرحمٰن قال الله تعالى ﴿ٱلْمُلْكُ يَوْمَئِذٍ ٱلْحَقُّ لِلرَّحْمَٰنِ﴾ والقسم الآخر للمنتقم وكذٰلك هو الملك ينعم على قوم وينتقم من آخرين قال الله تعالى ﴿وَكَانَ يَوْمًا عَلَى ٱلْكَٰفِرِينَ عَسِيرًا﴾ فيَوْمُ ٱلدِّينِ هو يوم الجزاء والجزاء إمّا بالرحمة وإمّا بالانتقام وحقيقة الرحمة ظهور حكم الملاءمة وذلك هو النعيم وحقيقة الانتقام ضدّه وهو إدراك المنافر وحقيقة ظهور الملاءمة والمنافرة المذكورين هنا أن يتجلّى الاسم الباطن بأحكام الاسم الآخر فإنّها الآخرة فيراه أهل الموقف على قدر استعداداتهم في رؤيته فمن لاءم ما رآه تنعّم ومن نافره تألّم وذلك لأنّ الاسم الباطن معنويّته الأحديّة وأهل الموقف جاؤوا من الدنيا وهم لا يعرفونها حقيقة فإن كان أحد منهم في الدنيا معترفاً بالوحدانيّة فاعترافه إيماناً لا عياناً.

٤،٥ وأمّا أهل التوحيد الذاتيّ فلا ينافرهم تجلّي الوحدانيّة بوجه من الوجوه فيكون نعيمهم ذاتيّاً مساوياً لتنعّم أهل الدنيا والآخرة كلّه محسوسه ومتخيّله وموهومه ومعلومه بسائر اعتبارات النعيم ويليهم في المرتبة أهل المعرفة وهم عرفوه تعالى من حضرة اسم من أسمائه أو اسم على قدر مرتبتهم في المعرفة فتنعّم هذه الطائفة ببعض نعيم الطائفة الأولى ويفوتهم من النعيم بقدر ما فاتهم من الشهود الذاتيّ.

٥،٥ ويلي هذه الطائفة المؤمنون وهم على قسمين منهم ﴿يُؤْمِنُونَ بِٱلْغَيْبِ﴾ ومنهم من ﴿أَلْقَى ٱلسَّمْعَ وَهُوَ شَهِيدٌ﴾ فيكون نعيم هذا القسم الثاني أقوى من نعيم قسيمه

---

[1] و: يعتريهم.

not entirely severed, because the day of resurrection is present right now for God. After all, there are no differentiations of time with Him, nor is He temporal, and so past and future for Him are present. This concept is understood by God's folk in a manner that depends upon direct witnessing, so they experience no doubt, conjecture, or illusion concerning it.

The Kingdom on «the Day of Judgment» is divided into two sorts. One belongs to the All-Merciful, for God says: «True kingship on that day belongs to the All-Merciful».[28] The other sort belongs to the Avenger for, as the King, He grants blessings to some and exacts vengeance on others. God says: «For the unbelievers it is a difficult day».[29] The «Day of Judgment» is the day of recompense, and recompense occurs either by way of mercy or vengeance. The reality of mercy is the manifestation of agreeableness, which is bliss; whereas the reality of vengeance is its opposite—namely, the perception of what is disagreeable. The reality of the manifestation of this agreeableness and disagreeableness is that the Nonmanifest discloses itself through the properties of the Last, for it takes place in the hereafter. The people at the plane of resurrection thus see the Nonmanifest disclosing itself through the properties of the Last, to the degree of their preparedness for seeing It. Whoever finds what he sees agreeable experiences bliss, and whoever is repulsed by what he sees experiences pain. This is because the supersensory reality of the Nonmanifest is unity, and the people at the plane of resurrection come from the world but do not truly recognize it. If God's oneness in the world was recognized by any of them, such acknowledgment was through belief, not direct vision. 5.3

As for those who realize the oneness of the Essence, they are not repelled by the disclosure of divine oneness in any respect. Their bliss is inherent to their essence. It is equivalent to the totality of the bliss of the people of the here below and the hereafter, including its sensorial, imaginal, illusory, and cognitive aspects, and in respect to all considerations of bliss. Those who realize the unity of the Essence are followed in rank by the recognizers—namely, those who recognize God from the presence of one of His names, or from the presence of a name that corresponds to their level of recognition. This group enjoys some of the bliss enjoyed by the first group, but the bliss of the former falls short of the bliss of the latter to the same extent as the direct witnessing of the Essence by the former fell short of the direct witnessing of the Essence by the latter. 5.4

After this group come a first group of believers, who are of two sorts: Some are «believers in the unseen»,[30] and others are those who «hearken and are witnessing».[31] The bliss of the latter is more intense than the bliss of the 5.5

ومقام هؤلاء هو مقام السكينة ويبقى القسم الآخر من المؤمنين فينقسم قسمين أحدهما أهل مقام الإحسان وهو مقام أن تعبد الله كأنّك تراه وهم أشرف نعيماً من الذين في مقام فإن لم تكن تراه فإنّه يراك وكلا هذين في مقام الإحسان.

٦،٥ والقسم الآخر من المؤمنين هم الذين لم يصلوا إلى مقام الإحسان فهم ﴿ٱلَّذِينَ يُؤْمِنُونَ بِٱلْغَيْبِ وَيُقِيمُونَ ٱلصَّلَوٰةَ﴾ الآية فهؤلاء يتنعّمون نعيماً أضعف من نعيم من ذُكر قبلهم وإن كان نعيمهم لو فُرّق على الناس أجمعين لوسعهم لكنّ بعض هذه الطائفة اعتقدوا عقائد غير مناسبة فيلحقهم من العذاب ما يطهّرهم من دنس كفر باطن كان فيهم وشرك خفيّ كان في ذواتهم وذلك العذاب متفاوت على مقدار انحرافهم عن الاعتدال الإيمانيّ فهذه الطائفة أهل السعادة التي تظهر عليهم أحكام ﴿مَٰلِكِ يَوْمِ ٱلدِّينِ﴾.

٧،٥ وأمّا الطائفة الأخرى وهم أهل نسبة الاسم المنتقم فإذا تجلّى عليهم الاسم الباطن بظهور أحكام الاسم الآخِر وبمقتضى معنويّة الوحدانيّة لم يجد التجلّي فيهم موضعاً للقبول وأمر هذا التجلّي إذ ذاك لا يزداد كذلك تكون أحكام الملك المطاع طوعاً وكرهاً فأمّا أهل النعيم فطوعاً وأمّا هؤلاء فكرهاً وحينئذ تنفذ أشعّة التجلّي فيهم كرهاً فلا يبقى منهم رسم مع رسم بل يتمزّقون لظهور أشعّة الوحدانيّة فيهم وذلك هو عذاب النار فالذي به ينعَّم أهل النعيم هو الذي به يعذَّب أهل العذاب قال الواقف أوقفني في النار فرأيتُ جيم الجنّة جيم جهنّم ورأيتُ ما به يعذّب عين ما به ينعّم.

٨،٥ فإذا نفذ حكم الملك فيهم ومَزَّقهُمۡ كُلَّ مُمَزَّقٍ بحكم ظهوره لهم بالصورة التي لا يعرفونه بها وذلك قولهم نعوذ بالله منك نحن هنا حتّى يأتينا ربّنا فبعد تمزّقهم يتحوّل لهم في الصورة التي يعرفونه فيها فيقولون نعم أنت ربّنا وذلك في أحقاب من العذاب.

former, and their station is the station of tranquility. Then there is a second group of believers, who are also of two sorts: Those who attain the station of spiritual excellence, which is the station of "worshipping God as though you see Him," and they enjoy a nobler bliss than the second sort, those who are in the station of "and if you do not see Him, He nonetheless sees you."[32] And both of these are in the station of spiritual excellence.

5.6 Yet another group of believers are those who have not attained the station of spiritual excellence. They are those who «believe in the unseen and establish the prayer».[33] They experience a bliss that is weaker than the bliss of those mentioned before them, though their bliss would be sufficient were it to be distributed among all humankind. However, some among this group hold inappropriate beliefs and so are met with a punishment that purifies them from the filth of their inner disbelief, and from the hidden idolatry of their inner selves. This punishment differs according to the measure of their deviation from the proper equilibrium of faith. This group consists of those who attain happiness, upon whom the properties of «the King of the Day of Judgment» become manifest.

5.7 When the Nonmanifest discloses itself upon those who are ascribed to the Avenger—by manifesting the properties of the Last, and by the supersensory dictates of God's oneness—the disclosure does not find in them a site of receptivity, and so at that particular moment the disclosure does not increase. The same is true for the properties of the King, who is obeyed both voluntarily and involuntarily: for the blissful, it is voluntary; and for those ascribed to the Avenger, it is involuntary. At that moment, the rays of the disclosure penetrate them by compulsion, and no trace remains. Instead, they are torn to pieces because of the manifestation of the rays of God's oneness in them, and that is the punishment of the Fire. Thus, the very thing that is bliss for the blissful is punishment for those who are punished. Al-Niffarī says: "God brought me to a halt at the Fire, and I saw that the *G* of Gehenna is the same as the *G* of the Garden, and I saw that the instrument of punishment is none other than the instrument of bliss."[34]

5.8 When the property of the King penetrates into them and «utterly tears them apart»,[35] it is by virtue of His manifesting to them in a form they do not recognize Him by—whence their saying, "We seek refuge in God from you; we shall remain here until our Lord comes to us."[36] Once they are torn apart, He transforms into the form that they recognize Him by, and they say, "Yes, You are our Lord." That, however, occurs over a very long period of punishment.

ومعنى هذا التحوّل لا يعود إلى تغيّر في المتجلّي الذي هو الباطن بإذن الملك بل إنّما ٩،٥
يعود إلى قوابل المعذّبين فكأنّه قال إنّهم عند بلوغ غاية العذاب ترجع قوابلهم مناسبة للمتجلّي لا بمعنى أنّها تغيّرت عمّا كانت عليه بل لِسعة معاني المتجلّي لهم وحيطتها فإذًا إنّما يتحوّل حالهم بالنسبة إلى التجلّي فيشهدون منه ثانيًا ما لم يشهدوه منه أوّلًا وذلك لأنّهم بالعذاب استعدّوا استعدادًا تامًّا لأنّ بعض استعداداتهم كان مغمورًا في الحجاب فعندما كشف حجابَهم العذابُ رأوا فاعترفوا بما أنكروا فذلك هو حين ظهور حكم الاسم الرحمٰن فيهم فيُلحقون بالنعيم ويبقى أهل الجحيم الذين هم أهلها فقال أهل الله إنّهم بعد أن يجري العذاب فيهم مدى علمه ينعطف عليهم بالرحمة فينعّمهم في النار بها حتّى لو خُيّروا لاختاروها على الجنّة وهنا يتحقّق أنّ أسماء النقمة قد تعود إلى الرحمٰن قال الله تعالى ﴿قُلِ ٱدْعُوا۟ ٱللَّهَ أَوِ ٱدْعُوا۟ ٱلرَّحْمَٰنَ أَيًّا مَّا تَدْعُوا۟ فَلَهُ ٱلْأَسْمَآءُ ٱلْحُسْنَىٰ﴾ ومن جملة الأسماء الحسنى أسماء النقمة فهي للاسم الرحمٰن أيضًا.

Now, this transformation does not mean that a change has occurred in the Self-Discloser—that is, in the Nonmanifest by the permission of the King. Rather, the transformation goes back to the receptacles of those who are being punished. Al-Niffarī was saying in essence that when the punishment reaches its ultimate end, their receptacles become suitable for the Self-Discloser. This is not in the sense that the receptacles become something different, but because the scope of the meanings of the Self-Discloser embraces them, and their state transforms itself only in relation to the disclosure. As such, what they witness in the second disclosure is not what they witnessed in the first, and through the punishment they have become completely prepared. Some of their preparedness will be covered by the veil, and when the punishment removes the veil, they will see and acknowledge what they had previously denied. This is the moment when the properties of the All-Merciful manifest in them, and they will be granted bliss, while the People of the Blaze remain there, "for they belong to it."[37] To this effect, God's folk say, "After the punishment grips them for as long as God determines, God inclines toward them in mercy and bestows them with bliss in the Fire, such that if they were given the choice they would choose it over the Garden." This shows how even the names of vengeance can trace back to the All-Merciful. God says: «Say: Call upon Allāh, or call upon the All-Merciful; whichever you call upon, His are the most beautiful names».[38] And among the most beautiful names are the names of vengeance, for they too belong to the All-Merciful. 5.9

سورة البقرة

اسمه المحيط تبارك وتعالى

هذا الاسم الكريم يلي الاسم الملك في وروده في الكتاب العزيز في ترتيب سوره ١،٦
وهو قوله تعالى في سورة البقرة ﴿وَٱللَّهُ مُحِيطُۢ بِٱلۡكَٰفِرِينَ﴾ وهو ممّا انفرد به الإمام أبو الحكم بن برّجان فلم يذكره الإمامان البيهقيّ والغزاليّ وورد في الحديث النبويّ قال النحّاس وممّن كتبنا عنه محمّد بن إبراهيم عن أحمد بن محمّد ابن غالب قال حدّثنا خالد ابن محمّد قال حدّثني عبد العزيز بن حُصين قال حدّثني ثابت بن هشام بن حسّان عن محمّد بن سيرين عن أبي هريرة عن النبيّ صلّى الله عليه وسلّم وذكر الأسماء وذكر فيها المحيط.

وإحاطته قال العلماء إنّه بمعنى قوله تعالى ﴿أَحَاطَ بِكُلِّ شَيۡءٍ عِلۡمَۢا﴾ فخصّوا ٢،٦
الإحاطة بالعلم ومعلوم أنّ قوله تعالى ﴿وَٱللَّهُ مُحِيطُۢ بِٱلۡكَٰفِرِينَ﴾ أنّه لم يرد علماً ولئن قلنا إنّ المراد العلم فالموصوف لا يغاير صفته بل هو هي وليس هي هو فهو هي وغيرها وهي هي لا غير مع أنّنا لا ننكر أنّ قوله ﴿أَحَاطَ بِكُلِّ شَيۡءٍ عِلۡمَۢا﴾ أنّه أراد إحاطة اسمه العليم بالمعلومات كلّها ولا أنّ قوله ﴿وَٱللَّهُ مُحِيطُۢ بِٱلۡكَٰفِرِينَ﴾ أنّه أراد إحاطة انتقامه ﴿بِٱلۡكَٰفِرِينَ﴾ لكنّ إحاطته الذاتيّة أعمّ وبعدها إحاطته بالقيّوميّة إحاطة بكلّ شيء فإنّ به قام كلّ شيء وهو معنى القيّوم سبحانه فهو محيط.

The Surah of the Cow

Al-Muḥīṭ: The Encompassing

This noble name comes after the King, in accordance with the order in which the names occur in the surahs of the Holy Book. It appears in the Surah of the Cow in the verse: «God encompasses the disbelievers».[39] Only the eminent scholar Ibn Barrajān cites *al-Muḥīṭ* as a divine name, whereas the other two, al-Bayhaqī and al-Ghazālī, do not. This name is also mentioned in a prophetic report transmitted by al-Naḥḥās—as well as by other transmitters from whom I copied Prophetic Tradition—who narrates from Muḥammad ibn Ibrāhīm; who cites Aḥmad ibn Muḥammad ibn Ghālib; who cites Khālid ibn Muḥammad; who cites ʿAbd al-ʿAzīz ibn Ḥuṣayn; who cites Thābit ibn Hishām ibn Ḥassān, from Muḥammad ibn Sīrīn, from Abū Hurayrah, from the blessed Prophet, who listed the names and included the Encompassing among them.[40] 6.1

The scholars say that God's encompassing ought to be understood in the sense of Him «encompassing all things in knowledge».[41] They thus qualify God's encompassing by knowledge. But it is well known that the verse «God encompasses the disbelievers» does not imply that He encompasses them by His knowledge alone. Even if we were to accept that the intended meaning is divine knowledge, the possessor of a quality cannot be at odds with his own quality; the possessor of a quality *is* the quality. Yet the latter is not the former, since the qualified is the quality and other than the quality; whereas the quality is nothing but the quality.[42] Thus, we agree and do not deny that the verse «He encompasses all things in knowledge» means that the Knowing encompasses every object of knowledge; nor do we deny that the verse «God encompasses the disbelievers» denotes that God's vengeance encompasses the disbelievers. However, the encompassing of His Essence is more inclusive, and this encompassing is followed by His encompassing of all things through His quality of self-subsistence, because all things subsist through Him, whence the meaning of the Self-Subsisting. Thus He is the Encompassing. 6.2

٣،٦ وينبغي أن تعلم أنّ إحاطته الذاتيّة ليست كإحاطة الشيء بظاهر الشيء فقط أو بباطنه فقط بل إحاطة تستغرق ما أحيط به حتّى إذا شهد الشاهد هذه الإحاطة لم يجد للمحاط به وجوداً غير وجود المحيط به ويرجع معنى ذلك إلى شهود الوحدانيّة وذلك لدخول كلّ موجود في وجوده عزّ وجلّ لأنّ وجوده عزّ وجلّ ظهر باختصاصات ظهوره فلم يكن غيره وهذا نفَس يعرفه أهله وهذه الإحاطة إلغائيّة.

٤،٦ وأمّا إحاطته ﴿ بِٱلْكَٰفِرِينَ ﴾ فبطريق ظهور أحكام اسمه المنتقم من حيث ما يدخل المنتقم في الاسم المحيط وهذا الانتقام إذا بلغ الغاية انتقل رحمة فدخل الاسم المنتقم في الاسم الرحمٰن حين لا يبقى للكافرين أثر للخلاف فإن بقي أثر ما رجع إلى الاسم الرحيم.

٥،٦ وهذا الكلام في قوّة قوله غلبت رحمتي غضبي وكذلك ما ورد أنّه تعالى قال سبقت رحمتي غضبي أي إلى الغاية فعمّت الرحمة أخيراً ومن هنا يدخل الاسم المحيط في الرحمٰن وسرّ ذلك في الوحدانيّة وبها قيل إنّ وجود كلّ شيء فيه كلّ شيء.

٦،٦ ومن هنا قال الشيخ أبو مدين رضي الله عنه من قال التمر ولم يجد حلاوته في فمه فما قال التمر وذلك أنّ حالة الشهود يتّحد الوجود في شهود الشاهد بكلّ موجود فيرى كلّ شيء في كلّ شيء رؤية ذوق فيكون كأهل الجنّة في كونهم يذكرون مطعومات الجنّة فيجدون أذواقها وتغذيتها في ذواتهم تماماً وهذا هو أخصّ مطعومات أهل الجنّة فافهمه تجد معنى المآل بالذوق والحال لا بالنقل والقال.

You must understand that His Essence's encompassing is not like the encompassing of one thing by something else, be it outwardly or inwardly. Rather, the encompassing of the Essence completely engulfs that which is encompassed. If someone were to witness this encompassing, he would be unable to find an existence for the encompassed object other than the existence of the encompassing Subject. The meaning of this encompassing goes back to the witnessing of God's oneness, because every existent is included within God's existence since His existence becomes manifest through the specifications of His manifestation. Thus, there is nothing other than Him. This subtle point is only known by those who are qualified to know it, and this encompassing excludes all duality. 6.3

As for His encompassing of «the disbelievers», it is by way of the manifestation of the properties of the Avenger, insofar as the Avenger is included within the Encompassing. When this vengeance reaches its fullest extent, it becomes divine mercy, so that the Avenger becomes included within the All-Merciful once the disbelievers lose all traces of opposition. However, if a trace of opposition remains, then the Avenger goes back to the Ever-Merciful. 6.4

This discussion is implied in God's saying, "My mercy triumphs over My wrath,"[43] as well as the transmitted saying, "My mercy outstrips my wrath";[44] that is, to the fullest extent, so mercy finally prevails. It is from here that the Encompassing is included within the All-Merciful. The secret behind this lies in God's oneness, by which it is said that "the existence of each thing contains all things." 6.5

Along similar lines, Abū Madyan said, "Whoever speaks of dates without tasting their sweetness in his mouth has not spoken of dates!" For in the state of witnessing, existence and existents become unified in the eye of the witness, such that by means of his visionary taste he sees all things within all things. Thus he resembles the people of the Garden who, upon the mere mention of foods of the Garden, discover those tastes and nourishments in their essences, in the most complete way. This is the most special food in the Garden. So understand this, and you will understand the deepest meanings of the final end through your own tasting and state, not through transmitted reports and hearsay! 6.6

اسمه القـدير تبارك وتعالى

١٠٧ هـذا الاسم الكريم ممّا اتّفق على إيراده الإمامان أبو بكر البيهقيّ والإمام أبو الحكم الأندلسي ولم يذكره الإمام الغزاليّ وورد أوّل وروده في ترتيب سور القرآن في قوله تعالى ﴿ وَلَوْ شَآءَ ٱللَّهُ لَذَهَبَ بِسَمْعِهِمْ وَأَبْصَٰرِهِمْ إِنَّ ٱللَّهَ عَلَىٰ كُلِّ شَىْءٍ قَدِيرٌ ﴾ وهو ثاني اسم ورد في سورة البقرة وهو مشتقّ من القدرة بمعنى التمكّن من الفعل والترك بالنسبة إلى كلّ مقدور.

٢٠٧ ومن هنا يدخل الاسم القدير في الاسم المحيط وإن شئت قلت يدخل الاسم المحيط في الاسم القدير وهو الأولى لأنّ الاسم في حضرة تصرّفه هو الذي يرجع إليه غيره فيدخل القدير في المحيط عند ذكر أحكام الاسم المحيط ويدخل المحيط في الاسم القدير عند ذكر أحكام الاسم القدير.

٣٠٧ وإذا كانت الأسماء الأضداد تصير عيناً واحدة فلأن تصير كذلك الأسماء الأغيار من باب الأَولى وذلك لأنّ الغيريّة في القبيلين إنّما هي مغايرة نسبيّة والنّسب أعدام إضافيّة تثبتها الأذهان وتنكرها الأعيان فوجودها ذهنيّ لا عينيّ وهذه المسألة تدقّ عن أفكار المحجوبين.

٤٠٧ ثمّ إنّه إن ظهر لك الوحدانيّة رأيت القادر حيث القدرة فالأرض تحمل ترابها وحجارتها وغير ذلك بالقدرة والقدرة حيث القادر الحقّ والمولّدات كذلك والأركان وما فوقها كذلك فكلّ فعل رأيته من فاعل طبيعيّاً كان الفعل أو إراديّاً جسمانيّاً كان أو روحانيّاً أو عقليّاً أو خياليّاً أو وهميّاً أو شكّيّاً أو ظنّيّاً أو علميّاً أو غير ذلك فكلّ تلك القدر قدرته تعالى وهو حيث وُجدت قدرته.

٥٠٧ وهذا الكلام فوق طور العلم الرسميّ وتحت طور العلم الحقيقيّ وفي وسط دائرة العلم العرفانيّ فمن عرّف القدير سبحانه هذه المعرفة سلم لكلّ قادر وعذر كلّ عاذل وجائر

Al-Qadīr: The Powerful

The two eminent scholars al-Bayhaqī and Ibn Barrajān agree that it is a divine name, though the eminent scholar al-Ghazālī does not mention it in his commentary. Its first place of occurrence in accordance with the order of the surahs of the Qur'an is: «had God willed, He would have taken away their hearing and their sight. Truly, God is Powerful over everything».[45] The Powerful is the second name that is mentioned in the Surah of the Cow, and it derives from power; that is, the masterful ability to act or refrain with respect to every object of power. 7.1

The Powerful is included within the Encompassing in this respect. You could also say that the Encompassing is included within the Powerful, which in fact would be the more obvious way of viewing it, since the name that exercises control is the one to which the other names trace back. Accordingly, the Powerful is included within the Encompassing when one speaks of the properties of the Encompassing, while the Encompassing is included within the Powerful when one speaks of the properties of the Powerful. 7.2

Furthermore, if the names with an opposing counterpart can become a single entity, then this is all the more so for the lone names of contrast that have no opposing counterpart. For, unlike the opposition of pairs, contrast between two different names is only relational, and relations are relative nonexistents that the mind affirms but the entities themselves deny. Hence, the existence of these relations is mental, not entitative, but this matter is too subtle to be grasped by veiled intellects. 7.3

If God's oneness becomes manifest for you, you will see the Powerful wherever there is power. The earth supports its soil and rocks and other things through power, and power is where the truly Powerful is. The same goes for minerals, plants, and animals, as well as the four elements and what is above them.[46] For every action that issues from an active agent, whether that act be natural, volitional, corporeal, spiritual, intellective, imaginal, imaginary, skeptical, conjectural, cognitive, or otherwise, all these powers are His power, and He is wherever His power is found. 7.4

This discourse lies beyond the stage of exoteric knowledge, beneath the stage of real knowledge, and at the center of the circle of the science of recognition. 7.5

ومن هذه الحقيقة قال السيّد المسيح من لطمك على خدّك فأدر له الخدّ الآخر ومن سلب رداءك فردّه قميصك ومن سخّرك ميلاً فامض معه ميلين وكان بعضهم إذا علق في مرقّعته عود شجرة وقف معه حتّى يحقّق معنى هذا الشهود ثمّ ينفصل بنسبة اسم آخر من أسماء الوجود الحقّ.

٦،٧ والقدرة منها معتادة تجري على منهج معلوم بحسب أطوارها ومنها خارقة للعادة والخارقة للعادة منها ما وقع بها التحدّي ومنها ما لم يقع به التحدّي والذي يخصّ الناطق بالوحدانيّة في مقام التحقيق أن يشهد ﴿أَنَّ ٱلْقُوَّةَ لِلَّهِ جَمِيعًا﴾ فافطن لهذا المعنى فإن ضعفت عن إدراك هذا فاعلم أنّه ﴿لَا قُوَّةَ إِلَّا بِٱللَّهِ﴾ وإذا علمت أنّه ﴿لَا قُوَّةَ إِلَّا بِٱللَّهِ﴾ فهل الباء ممّا يعلم بماذا تعلّقت أبقدرة الله أم بالله وبين إدراكهما مجال رحب.

٧،٧ واعلم أنّ القدرة خصوص وصف في القوّة والقوّة خصوص وصف في القيّوميّة والقيّوميّة خصوص وصف في الوجود والوجود هو الذي أقام الموجود بالقيّوميّة والموجود حقيقة هو حقّ بخصوص وصف فعُلم من هذا أنّ الموجود يغاير الوجود لا بالحقيقة والوجود لا يغاير الموجود لا بالحقيقة ولا بالمجاز.

٨،٧ وهذا الكلام يبعد عن حقيقة الاسم القدير بقدر ما بين الاسم القدير والاسم الرحمٰن من المراتب الاعتباريّة ولولا الاعتبارات لما فُضّل الاسم الرحمٰن على اسم غيره ولو كان أبعد الأسماء في الاعتبار. فإذاً بُعد القدير لولا الاعتبار ما بُعد من حضرة الاسم الرحمٰن. ألا ترى أنّ الاسم الرحمٰن محتاج إلى كلّ اسم في تحقّق وجود معنى الرحمة في طور طور من أطوار الأسماء فعُلم بهذا أنّ أعلى الأسماء يعود أنزل الأسماء وأنزل الأسماء يعود أعلى الأسماء وتتعارض الأسماء الإلٰهيّة في المراتب حتّى يصبح وجود كلّ اسم في كلّ حضرة اسم غيره.

Therefore, whomever the Powerful enables to recognize this knowledge will yield before powerful figures and excuse censurers and oppressors. It is in view of this reality that the Messiah said: "When someone slaps you on the cheek, turn the other cheek; and when someone takes your tunic, let him have your cloak as well; and when someone forces you to walk for a mile, walk two miles with him."[47] Thus, if the patched cloak of a Sufi got caught on a twig, he would stand still until he apprehended the meaning of what he was witnessing, and then would extract himself from the twig by means of a relation to another name of the True Being.

Power is either ordinary in that it follows well-known patterns according to its stages, or extraordinary in that it disrupts the habitual course of nature. The one that disrupts the habitual course of nature sometimes occurs as a challenge to unbelievers, and other times does not.[48] Moreover, what distinguishes the one who speaks of unity in the station of realization is that he bears witness that «all power belongs to God».[49] So comprehend this meaning! But if you are too weak to perceive it, then know that «there is no power except through God»;[50] and when you know that «there is no power except through God», then ponder what the «through» attaches itself to: God's power or God? These two perceptions are separated by a vast distance! 7.6

Power is a specific quality of strength, and strength is a specific quality of self-subsistence, and self-subsistence is a specific quality of existence, and existence is that which sustains an existent through self-subsistence. The existent's true nature is reality when it assumes a specific quality. From this we know that an existent does not differ from existence in the true sense, while existence differs from an existent neither in the true sense nor in metaphor. 7.7

This discussion is as removed from the true nature of the Powerful as the Powerful is separated by levels of perspective from the All-Merciful. Moreover, were it not for such levels of consideration, the All-Merciful would not have precedence over the other names, not even those that are most distant when considered in terms of perspectives. Therefore, the distance of the Powerful is only perspectival, otherwise it would not be distant from the presence of the All-Merciful. Do you not see that the All-Merciful is in need of all the names in order to realize the existence of the meaning of mercy at every stage of the names? From this it is known that the highest names become the lowest names, and the lowest names become the highest names, and the divine names clash at the cosmic levels until the existence of each name is within the presence of every other name. 7.8

٩.٧ ويشهد الشهود الذاتيّ فلا يرى من الأسماء شيئاً بل تكون الذات فقط ولا عبارة عن هذه الحضرة لأنّ الأسماء تكون فيها من عين المسمّى وتدخل العبارات معها فيما دخلت فيه فتقوم الصمدانيّة بذاتها وهي أحديّة الجمع وهي مشهودة في كلّ متفرّق ومجتمع غير أنّ تمايز الأسماء في الاعتبارات المذكورة تعطي العبارة وتثبت الإشارة وإذا سمعت أهل العرفان يقولون من عرف الله كلّ لسانه فإنّما يعنون شهوده تعالى من حضرة الصمدانيّة فقط.

اسمه العليم تبارك وتعالى

١.٨ هذا الاسم الكريم ورد في سورة البقرة في قوله تعالى ﴿ إِنَّكَ أَنتَ ٱلۡعَلِيمُ ﴾ وهو ممّا اتّفق عليه الأئمّة الثلاثة البيهقيّ والغزاليّ وابن برّجان الأندلسيّ واشتقاقه من العلم وهو تكثير العلم للمبالغة على صيغة فعيل وفي الحقيقة العالم لا ينقص عن درجة العليم بمعنى أنّ صيغة العليم للمبالغة فإنّ علم الله تعالى لا يتكثّر ولا يقلّ لاستيعاب علمه كلّ معلوم في كلّ آن لا ينقسم وإنّما المبالغة من باب التنزّل إلى أفهام المحجوبين وعلى عادتهم أنّ الموصوف بصيغة الفعيل يكون مراداً به المبالغة فهو نوع من إيناس الناس بمخاطبتهم بما يألفون.

٢.٨ واعلم أنّ حقيقة العلم بالنسبة إلى الذات المقدّسة هي أقرب من حقيقة الاسم القدير بمقدار ما بين مقام العلم إلى مقام القدرة فإنّ الاعتبار في ذلك يقتضي في العادة أن يعلم ثمّ يريد ثمّ يقدر فالعلم فوق الإرادة التي هي فوق القدرة وليس فوق العلم

However, those who witness the Essence do not see any of the names; indeed, there is only the Essence. There is no way of expressing this presence because the names therein are from the Named Itself, and all expressions pertain to the names insofar as they pertain to the Named. Thus, the divine quality of self-sufficiency subsists by itself, and that is the unity of the all, and it is witnessed through every entity of separation and union. However, the contrast of the names in these considerations serves to make expression possible and corroborate allusions; and when you hear the recognizers say, "Whoever recognizes God becomes speechless,"[51] what they mean is that witnessing God is only from the presence of His self-sufficiency. 7.9

Al-ʿAlīm: The Knowing

This noble name is mentioned in the Surah of the Cow in the verse: «Truly, You are the Knowing».[52] It is among the names that the three eminent scholars al-Bayhaqī, al-Ghazālī, and Ibn Barrajān of al-Andalus agree upon as being a name of God. Its etymological derivation is from knowledge, and the emphatic form (*faʿīl*) means an increase in knowledge. But in reality, the level of the Knower is not less than that of the Knowing, even though the active form of the Knowing denotes emphasis. For God's knowledge neither increases nor decreases, since His knowledge subsumes all objects of knowledge in every instant and without division. The emphasis is only a means of descending to the comprehension of veiled intellects for whom it is customary to apply the active form to an object to denote emphasis. This is therefore a way to comfort people by addressing them in a manner they are accustomed to. 8.1

The reality of knowledge in relation to the Holy Essence is closer than the reality of the Powerful, according to the measure that separates the stations of knowledge and power. For such a perspective would usually require that He knows, then wills, then exerts power. Knowledge is therefore above will, which is above power; and nothing is above knowledge except life. This entails that His name the Living is more eminent in status than the Knowing. 8.2

إلّا الحياة فيلزم أن يكون اسمه الحيّ تبارك وتعالى أشرف مقاماً من الاسم العليم شرفاً هو القرب والقرب هنا اعتباريّ كما هو في الأسماء كلّها.

٣،٨ ثمّ اعلم أنّ حقيقة علمه تبارك وتعالى شاملة فكلّ علم عالم هو خصوص وصف في علمه المطلق فإذاً علم الله تبارك وتعالى محيط بكلّ علم إحاطة الكلّ بأجزائه في الخارج فيعلم كلّ علم بعين علم كلّ عالم حتّى يكون علمه بالجزئيّات من نفس علم العالمين بالجزئيّات ويعلم العلم الكلّيّ بعين علم كلّ عالم بالكلّيّات من نفس علم ذلك العالم بالكلّيّات ويكون علمه في علم من يعلم العلم بالتصوّر والتصديق تصوّراً وتصديقاً وفي علم من يعلم العلم بالحال علماً بالحال وفي علم من يعلم العلم بالذوق علماً بالذوق.

٤،٨ ويعلم علم كلّ طور بعين علم العالم بعلم ذلك الطور حتّى يعلم علم الموجودات التي تسمّى في العرف غير عالمة بعلم حاليّ يليق بتلك الأطوار وذلك أنّه ليس في الوجود شيء عار من العلم غير أنّ العلم ينقسم إلى ما اصطلح الناس عليه أنّه علم وإلى ما اصطلح الناس عليه أنّه ليس بعلم وهو كلّه أعني العلم عند أرباب هذه الحقيقة علم وذلك أنّ أهل هذه الحقيقة يشهدون علم الحقّ الذاتيّ فيجدون العلم في كلّ ذات.

٥،٨ ومن أمثلة هذا أنّ الماء عندهم لا يعقل ونحن نراه إذا جرى طلب الانحدار وعدل عن الصعود وإذا وجد متخلّلاً داخله وإذا وجد متلزّزاً تعدّاه وبلّ سطحه ورطّب ما يقبل الترطيب وربّما يبّس ما يقبل التيبيس وفعل أفاعيل فيما يتّصل به لا يتجاوزها ولا تختلف حاله فيما هو فيه بالذات من أفاعيله. فإن قيل إنّ القائل ربّما نقل الفاعل عن مقتضى طبيعته قلنا ومن جملة علم ذلك الفاعل كان ما كان أنّه لا يخالف في فعله ما يقتضيه القابل له وهذه الهدايات إلى طرق أفاعيل الموجودات بالذات كلّها علوم بحسب أطوار تلك الموجودات.

٦،٨ واعلم أنّ من شهد هذا المشهد لم يجد شيئاً من الموجودات جاهلاً ولم يجد حسّاً من الحواسّ حالة الإحساس كاذباً حتّى إنّه لو صحّ أنّ الأحول يرى الواحد

"Eminence" here means proximity, and this proximity is perspectival, as with all the names.

The reality of His knowledge is exhaustive; the knowledge of each knower is a specific quality of His unconditioned knowledge. Hence, the knowledge of God encompasses all knowledge, just as universals encompass particulars in the external realm. He therefore knows every form of knowledge by the very knowledge of every knower. His knowledge of particulars is identical to the knowers' knowledge of those very particulars, just as His knowledge of universals is identical to their knowledge of those very universals. His knowledge through those who know by means of concept and affirmation is conceptual and affirmative, and His knowledge through those who know experientially is likewise experiential, and His knowledge through those who know by tasting is likewise by taste. 8.3

He also knows the knowledge of each stage by the very knowledge that the knower has of that stage. He even knows the knowledge of existents that are commonly called "non-knowing things" through an experiential knowledge that is appropriate to those stages. This is because nothing in existence is devoid of knowledge, except that "knowledge" is divided into what people commonly refer to as "knowledge" and into what people do not commonly refer to as "knowledge." But all of it—I mean "knowledge" as understood by the masters of this reality—is knowledge. For the people of this reality witness the Real's essential knowledge, and therefore find knowledge in every essence. 8.4

For example, according to most people water is not intellective. Yet we observe that when it runs, it seeks to flow downward and avoids flowing upward. When it finds a fissure it penetrates it, and when it encounters an impermeable surface it flows over it and wets it. It wets what is receptive to wetness, and sometimes dries what is receptive to dryness. Within its own limits it interacts with all it comes into contact with, and its essential state is never at variance with its actions. If someone objects, saying: such a statement displaces the agent beyond the confines of its nature, we would reply that part of the knowledge of the agent, whatever it may be, is that its actions do not contradict the requirements of its recipient. These hints toward the modes of action of existents describe forms of knowledge in keeping with the stages of those existents. 8.5

You should also know that anyone who witnesses this contemplative station will not find any existent to be devoid of knowledge, nor will he find any of his senses in its state of sensory perception to be untruthful: So, when a cross-eyed 8.6

اثنين لم يكن ذلك الإدراك كذبًا وذلك لأنّه لو رآه واحدًا لم يكن أحول فرؤية الأحول لمرئيّه إنّما هو كذلك ولو رآه الذي ليس بأحول اثنين لكان كذبًا لكنّه لا يراه إلّا واحدًا فهو أيضًا صادق وكلاهما إذًا صادق كلّ منهما في طوره بحسب ما يخصّه من طوره وما طلب النار بالطبع العلوّ إلّا لعلم ذاتيّ عرف به جهة طبعه فقصده وكذلك الهواء فيما هو طبيعيّ له والأرض والماء وما تولّد من هذه كلّ موجود أعطاه الحقّ تعالى ﴿خَلْقَهُۥ ثُمَّ هَدَىٰ﴾ أي هداه حتّى استولى بعلمه الخاصّ به حقّه.

وإذا شهدت بأنّ الإحاطة هيمنة علم الله تعالى من قيّوميّته أو أعلى من ذلك بأن يكون من حيث وجوده علمت أنّ لا علم إلّا لله تعالى وعلمت أنّ كلّ شيء عالم وعلمت أنّ كلّ علم حقّ لا جهل فيه ولو فرضنا جاهلاً في العرف يحكم بحكم هو جهل عند المحجوبين رآه المحقّق علمًا لأنّه لو حكم حكمًا حقًّا لم يكن في طور غير طور الذي يسمّى في العادة عالمًا لكنّه قام بحقّ المرتبة التي هو فيها لا يتجاوزها ﴿مَا تَرَىٰ فِى خَلْقِ ٱلرَّحْمَٰنِ مِن تَفَٰوُتٍ فَٱرْجِعِ ٱلْبَصَرَ هَلْ تَرَىٰ مِن فُطُورٍ ثُمَّ ٱرْجِعِ ٱلْبَصَرَ كَرَّتَيْنِ يَنقَلِبْ إِلَيْكَ ٱلْبَصَرُ خَاسِئًا﴾ في زعمه أنّه رأى التّفاوت ﴿وَهُوَ حَسِيرٌ﴾ عن إدراك أنّ هناك تفاوتًا هذا إذا رآه بعين حقّ في حضرة حقّ يكون الباطل فيها من جملة الحقّ كما قلتُ ٧،٨

لَا تُنْكِرُوا ٱلْبَاطِلَ فِي طَوْرِهِ   فَإِنَّهُ بَعْضُ ظُهُورَاتِهِ
وَأَعْطِهِ مِنْكَ بِمِقْدَارِهِ   حَتَّى تُوَفِّيَ حَقَّ إِثْبَاتِهِ
أَظْهِرْهُ فِي ذَاتِكَ فِي طَوْرِهِ   خَشْيَةَ أَنْ تَظْهَرَ فِي ذَاتِهِ

person sees a single object as two, that perception is not untrue because if he were to see the object as one, he would not be cross-eyed. Thus, the cross-eyed person's object of vision is precisely what he sees. Were the person who is not cross-eyed to see the same object as two, then that would be untrue; but he only sees the object as one and is thus truthful. Both are truthful, each in his own manner and according to what specifically pertains to each. Similarly, fire only rises on account of an essential knowledge by which it recognizes how its nature operates and advances toward it. So also is it the case with air in terms of its nature, and with earth and water and what is produced by their admixture: to each existent God «gave its creation, then guided»;[53] that is, He guided it until it presided through its own specific knowledge over its rightful due.

If you witness that the encompassment amounts to the supremacy of God's 8.7
knowledge by way of His self-subsistence, or, in a more exalted sense, if you witness that it pertains to His very existence, you will then come to know that knowledge only belongs to God. You will also come to know that all things are knowing, that every form of knowledge is true, and that no form of knowledge is baseless. Suppose, for example, that someone expresses opinions that are commonly deemed by those with veiled intellects to be "baseless." In the eyes of those who have realized the truth, these baseless opinions are in fact forms of knowledge; for if the same person held opinions that happened to be true, he would have been generically described by veiled thinkers as "knowledgeable." In fact, in expressing his opinions he merely satisfies the requirements of the stage he occupies but does not surpass it: «You will see no disproportion in the All-Merciful's creation. Cast your sight again; do you see any flaw? Then cast your sight twice again; your sight will return to you humbled»—by the claim of having spotted a flaw—«and wearied»[54] of trying to perceive any flaw. All this is if one sees creation with the eye of truth and with the presence of truth that subsumes all falsehood, as I once expressed in verse:

Do not deny falsehood at its own stage,
  for it is a part of His self-manifestation,
And give it its measure of yourself
  in order to fulfill its due in affirming it.
Manifest it in your essence at its stage
  for fear of manifesting yourself in its stage.[55]

١٠٨ وقد يقول بعض المحجوبين كيف يكون ما هو علم لمخلوق هو علم لخالق فنقول ليس هو علماً لخالق من هذه الجهة بل من جهة تكون القدرة فيها تقتضي ظهور القادر بالعجز ظهوراً يشهد أنّ القادر قادر على أن يظهر بالعجز ولو كان المنزّه عندنا غير متمكّن من الظهور بالعجز لم يكن قادراً من حيث الظهور بالعجز فما كان يكون قادراً من هذه الجهة[١] ولو كان يكفي القادر في ثبوت القدرة له أنّه قادر بالقوّة لا بالفعل على بعض المقدورات لكانت قدرته في بعض المراتب ليست بالفعل هذا إذا استمرّ على أن تكون قدرته على ذلك الظهور الذي نُزّه عنه قدرة بالقوّة أبداً لكنّه يسوق ما وُقّت إلى ما قدّر فيعطي الأشياء وأوقات الأشياء ويظهر بالقدرة وبالعجز ويتفصّل ذلك فيما لا يتناهى تفصيلاً غير متناه ويلزم من هذا أن يكون علمه بحسب الأطوار موصوفاً بكلّ شأن من شؤون الآثار فهوَ ﴿بِكُلِّ شَيْءٍ عَلِيمٌ﴾ وكُلّ شَيْءٍ عَلِيمٌ إذا شهد رجوع الحرف إلى وصفه والوصف إلى صرف الكنه بعد صرفه فيكون ولا شيء معه كما لم يزل في أحديّة ما صرّفه وجوده ﴿وَٱللَّهُ يَقُولُ ٱلْحَقَّ﴾ ويحقّق القولـــــ.

اسمه الحكيم سبحانه وتعالى

١٠٩ هـذا الاسم الكريم ممّا اتّفق على إيراده الأئمّة الثلاثة البيهقيّ والغزاليّ وابن برّجان ومحلّه من الذكر العزيز قوله ﴿إِنَّكَ أَنتَ ٱلْعَلِيمُ ٱلْحَكِيمُ قَالَ يَٰٓـَٔادَمُ﴾ في سورة البقرة قال ابن عبّاس رضي الله عنه الحكيم هو الذي قد كمُل في حكمته والعليم الذي قد كمُل

١ ب: (ومن كمال الوجود وجود النقص فيه وشبه) وردت في الهامش بخطّ آخر.

Now, a veiled thinker might say: how could the knowledge of a created existent be the knowledge of the Creator? Our answer is that the existent's knowledge is not the knowledge of the Creator from this respect, but in respect to the fact that His power dictates the manifestation of the Powerful as powerless, and this manifestation bears witness that the Powerful has the power to manifest as powerless. For if the Transcendent were unable to manifest as powerless, then He would not be Powerful with respect to manifesting as powerless, and so in this regard He would not be Powerful. Moreover, if it were sufficient for the Powerful to affirm His possession of power by being powerful over some objects of power only in potentiality, not in actuality, then His power at certain stages would be merely potential, not actual. This would be the case if He persisted in having power over that level of manifestation that He transcends only in everlasting potentiality. Rather, He impels that which has been created in time toward that which has been predestined to exist, and so provides things and the times of things, and He manifests in powerfulness and powerlessness, and these differentiate infinitely and without end. From this it follows that His knowledge in relation to the stages is conditioned by all the workings of the traces, for «He is Knowing of all things»,[56] and all things are knowing inasmuch as they witness the return of the form to its quality, and the quality to its absolute core after its activity ends, such that He is, "and nothing is with Him,"[57] just as He remains in the unity of that whose existence He activated. «And God speaks the truth»[58] and makes His speech true. 8.8

Al-Ḥakīm: The Wise

This is one of the noble names that the three eminent scholars al-Bayhaqī, al-Ghazālī, and Ibn Barrajān agree upon as being a name of God. In the holy revelation, it is mentioned in the verse from the Surah of the Cow: «Truly, You are the Knowing, the Wise».[59] Ibn ʿAbbās said: "The Wise is He whose wisdom is perfect, and the Knowing is He whose knowledge is perfect." It has also been said that the Wise (*al-ḥakīm*) means the same as the Ruler (*al-ḥākim*). Another 9.1

في علمه وقيل إنّ الحكيم هو الحاكم وقال قوم إنّ الحكيم هو الذي أحكم بمعنى أحكم ما خلق مشتقٌّ من أحكمتُ الشيء إذا استوثقت منه ومنعته أن يفسد وحكى ابن الأعرابي أنّ الحكيم مشتقٌّ من قولك أحكمت الرجل أي رددته عن رأيه الخطأ كأنّه الذي يردّه إلى الصواب.

٢،٩ أمّا أنّه كامل الحكمة تعالى فمنه يستفاد الكمالات لكنّ كمال ما هو منه هو بأن يعطي كلّ موجود على قدر استعداده فكمال حكمة كلّ كامل الحكمة على قدر كمال استعداده ونقصه فالاستعداد هو سرّ القدر الإلٰهيّ.

٣،٩ واعلم أنّ الاستعداد قد يكون مركّباً من ذات المستعدّ ومن عوارض وجوده ومن عوارض زمانه ومكانه فالاستعداد هو هيئة اجتماعيّة تحصل من مجموع ما ذُكر فإنّ المسبّب حيث الأسباب والقدرة بحيث المقدور وحيث رأيت القدرة فثَمّ القادر فإذاً كمال الحكمة التي بها يسمّى الحكيم حكيماً هو فرع عن القدر الجاري على وفق الاستعداد المذكور وهذا الكلام من عالَم الفرق وأمّا عالم الجمع فهو فوق هذا النفَس.

٤،٩ ومن جعل الحكيم بمعنى الحاكم فإمّا بمعنى أن يحكم بين عباده وإمّا بمعنى أن يحكم عليهم بقدرته أو غير ذلك ومن جعل الحكيم مشتقّاً من أحكمت الشيء ومنه الحكمة للبعير وغيره فمعناه المتقن المانع من فساد ما أتقنه. ويتصرّف هذا الاسم في معانيه كلّها في نسب الحقيقة على مقتضى الاعتبارات المذكورة.

٥،٩ فأمّا دخول الاسم الحكيم في الأسماء الإلٰهيّة فباعتبارات منها أنّ من ظهرت حكمته فقد دخل الحكيم في الاسم الظاهر ومن بطنت حكمته فقد دخل في الاسم الباطن ومن عظمت حكمته فقد دخل الاسم الحكيم في العظيم ويدخل في الخبير بالخبرة المختصّة بالحكمة ويدخل في المعطي إذا أعطى الحكمة غيره ويدخل في المانع إذا

group says that the Wise is the One Who makes firm (*aḥkama*) in the sense of making firm that which He creates, in the sense of securing something and preventing it from being corrupted. Ibn al-ʿArābī, for his part, says: "The Wise derives from the expression 'I rectified (*aḥkamtu*) the man'—that is, I turned him away from his errant opinion, as if one were turning an errant person back to what is correct."[60]

The meaning of His possessing perfect wisdom is that all perfections are gained from Him. However, the perfection that comes from Him is that which He bestows upon each existent according to the measure of its preparedness. Therefore, the perfection of the wisdom of every possessor of wisdom depends on his preparedness and the extent to which it is perfect. Preparedness is therefore the secret of divine pre-apportioning. 9.2

Preparedness may be composed of the essence of the prepared one, or from the accidental qualities of his existence, or from the accidental qualities of his time and place. For preparedness is a holistic condition resulting from the combination of these variables. The Causer is wherever the secondary causes are, and the divine power is wherever its object is, and the Powerful is wherever you see power. Therefore, the perfected wisdom by which a wise one is named "wise" derives from the proportion that conforms to preparedness. This discussion pertains to the realm of separation. As for the realm of union, it pertains to a higher register.[61] 9.3

For those who take the Wise (*al-ḥakīm*) to mean the Ruler (*al-ḥākim*), it means either that He judges between His servants, or that He rules over them by His power or by another manner. For those who consider the Wise to derive from "I secured something" (*aḥkamtu*), whence the bridle (*ḥikmah*) that secures camels and other animals, it means the meticulous perfectionist who prevents the corruption of what He has perfected so meticulously. This name, moreover, operates freely in all of its meanings through the existential relations and in accordance with the dictates of the aforementioned perspectives. 9.4

The Wise is included within the other divine names from several perspectives. An example is that when someone's wisdom becomes manifest the Wise is included within the Manifest. Conversely, when someone's wisdom is hidden, the Wise is included within the Nonmanifest. Likewise, when someone's wisdom is magnificent, the Wise is included within the Magnificent. The Wise is also included within the Aware through the awareness specific to wisdom; and it is included within the Bestower when He bestows wisdom 9.5

منع الحكمة غيره ويجوز أن تقول دخلت هذه الأسماء المذكورة في الاسم الحكيم وهذا أنموذج إذا اعتبرته وجدت دخول الأسماء بعضها في أحكام بعض.

وقد تحقّقنا انتساب الحكمة إلى غير الآدميّين والملائكة إذ قد يقولون إنّ الطبيعة حكيمة وهي قسط من حكمة الحكيم سبحانه ظهرت فسُمّيت طبيعة بالانتساب إلى مرتبة وجودها وإلا فهي حكمة الحكيم سبحانه وتعالى وكلّ من حكم أو أحكم أو نال الحكمة فإنّما نال صفة من صفات الحكيم سبحانه وتعالى. ٦،٩

والصفة لا تقوم إلا بالموصوف الحقّ[١] فإن وجدت حكيماً فقد وجدت الحكيم الحقّ وذلك لأنّ القيّوميّة التي قام بها ذلك الحكيم متّصلة غير منفصلة والقيّوم تعالى به قام كلّ موجود فليس يفقده شيء والقيّوميّة هي التي ﴿يُمۡسِكُ ٱلسَّمَٰوَٰتِ وَٱلۡأَرۡضَ أَن تَزُولَاۚ وَلَئِن زَالَتَآ إِنۡ أَمۡسَكَهُمَا مِنۡ أَحَدٖ مِّنۢ بَعۡدِهِۦٓۚ﴾ فإذا رأيت الحكمة فهناك الحكيم الحقّ فلا تستوحش واستأنس فإنّك بحضرته ولمّا كان الموجود في الخارج وفي الداخل كلّه على مقتضى الحكمة كان الحكيم سبحانه غير غائب عن تلك الحضرات فإذاً جميع مراتب الموجودات هي حضرات عُلاً وإنّه ليس فيها سفليّ إلّا عند نظر أهل الحجاب وباعتبار لغة أهل الاغتراب. ٧،٩

واعلم أنّ من أراد تعظيم شعائر الله تعالى من حيث اسمه الحكيم فليعظّم الحكمة حيثما وجدها وليحبّ كلّ من تسمّى حكيماً ولو بالاسم فقط فإنّ الوصلة الإلهيّة من حيث اعتبار هذا الاسم شاملة الموجودات. ٨،٩

١ ب: (بمعنى الانطباع) وردت في الهامش.

upon others; and it is included within the Preventer when He prevents others from wisdom. One could also say that these names are included within the Wise. If you ponder this example, you will find that the names are included in one another's properties.

It is certainly true that wisdom is not only ascribed to humans and angels. 9.6
They say that nature is wise, which means that it is a portion of the wisdom of the Wise that became manifest and was called "nature" by attribution to its own level of existence. Yet it is none other than the wisdom of the Wise; and to rule (*ḥakama*) is to firmly secure (*aḥkama*); and to acquire wisdom (*ḥikmah*) is to acquire one of the qualities of the Wise.

A quality subsists only in the one who is truly qualified by it. Therefore, 9.7
when you find a wise person, you have found the truly Wise. For the quality of self-subsistence by which that possessor of wisdom subsists is connected, not disconnected. Moreover, the Self-Subsisting by Whom every existent subsists is not devoid of anything. The quality of self-subsistence is what «maintains the heavens and the earth, lest they fall apart. And were they to fall apart, none would maintain them after Him».[62] Wherever there is wisdom, there is also the truly Wise. So do not be alienated, but find His intimacy, for you are in His presence. Moreover, since existents both outwardly and inwardly conform to the dictates of wisdom, the Wise is not absent from any of these presences. All levels of existents are therefore exalted presences, and there are no base presences in them except through the gaze of the veiled intellects and the perspective of those who speak in the language of separation.

Whoever wishes to honor the signs of God with respect to His name the 9.8
Wise should honor wisdom wherever he encounters it, and should love anyone who is called wise even if only by name, for the divine connection with respect to this name embraces all existent things.

اسمه التوّاب عزّ وجلّ

١،١٠ ورد في البقرة في قوله تعالى ﴿إِنَّهُۥ هُوَ ٱلتَّوَّابُ ٱلرَّحِيمُ﴾ واتّفق على إيراده الأئمّة الثلاثة البيهقيّ والغزاليّ وابن برّجان واشتقاقه من معنى تاب أي رجع ومقصوده في لسان العلم الذي يعود إلى التائبين لأنهم عادوا إلى طاعته فأوجب على نفسه العود إليهم بالعفو ومقابلتهم بالصفح الجميل وإنّهم كلّما عادوا إليه عاد بذلك إليهم وأمّا ما في الفعّال من المبالغة فلأنّه يعود إلى كلّ عائد إليه فيكثر عوده لكثرة العائدين إليه فيناسب المبالغة.

٢،١٠ وأمّا ما يقتضيه العرفان فالمبالغة متعلّقة بكون العود من العبد في الحقيقة إنّما هو منه وقد ورد في بعض المناجاة يا عبدي أنا أشوق إليك منك إليّ تطلبني بطلبي وأنا أطلبك بطلبك وبطلبي وهذا يرجع إلى توحيد الفعل.

٣،١٠ واعلم أنّ هذا الاسم الكريم أخصّ الأسماء بأهل الترقّي في السفر الأوّل وهو سفر أهل التجلّيّات الأسمائيّة ومعنى ذلك أنّ السالك إذا حصل له تجلّ من التجلّيات الأسمائية الإلٰهيّة سمّي عارفاً فالله تعالى متجلّ من حضرة ذلك الاسم فإن اتّفق أن كان الاسم المذكور له مقابل من الأسماء مثل مقابلة المعطي للمانع أو الضارّ للنافع أو الباطن للظاهر أو الأوّل للآخر فلا شكّ أنّ حصول التجلّي من أحد أمثال هذه الأسماء هو تعرّفٌ يقتضي تنكّر الاسم المقابل له حتّى يترقّى ذلك السالك من الحدّ الذي بين ذينك الاسمين الذي هو برزخ الجمع والتفرقة بينهما فيوصل من ذلك إلى المطلع فتنكشف له حضرة الاسم المقابل للاسم الذي كان تجلّى له أوّلاً فيكون تعالى قد عاد إليه بصفة أنّه توّاب أي عوّاد فحصل له تعرّفه تعالى من حيث قد كان ينكر عليه في حضرة المقابلة بين ذينك الاسمين.

Al-Tawwāb: The Ever-Turning

This name is mentioned in the Surah of the Cow in the verse: «Indeed, He is the Ever-Turning, the Ever-Merciful».[63] The three eminent scholars al-Bayhaqī, al-Ghazālī, and Ibn Barrajān agree that it is a name of God. It derives its meaning from the verb "to turn" (*tāba*). In the language of exoteric knowledge, the name means "He who turns toward those who repent," because the latter return to Him in obedience, and He therefore obliges Himself to turn toward the repenters in forgiveness and to receive them with graceful forbearance. Each time they turn to Him, He turns to them in that manner. The emphatic form *faʿʿāl*, whence *al-Tawwāb*, implies that He turns to whomever turns to Him, and is frequently turning due to the frequency of those who turn to Him, whence the emphasis. 10.1

Esoterically, the emphatic form (*faʿʿāl*) pertains to the fact that the servant's turning is really His turning. A traditional saying attributed to God is: "My servant, I yearn more to meet you than you yearn to meet Me. You seek Me through my quest for you; and I seek you through both your quest and Mine." This discourse goes back to the oneness of God's acts. 10.2

Of all the names, this noble name pertains most specifically to those who are ascending on their first journey; that is, the journey of those who experience disclosures of the names.[64] In other words, when the wayfarer experiences a disclosure of a divine name, he is called a recognizer because God discloses Himself to him from the presence of that particular name. And if that disclosed name happens to have a counterpart—such as the Giver and the Preventer, or the Benefiter and the Harmer, or the Nonmanifest and the Manifest, or the First and the Last—then the disclosure of that name will cause the wayfarer to recognize it but be blind to its counterpart, at least until he ascends beyond the boundary between those two names—which is the isthmus of union and separation between them. From here the wayfarer will be taken to the place of ascent, where the presence of the counterpart will disclose itself to him. Thus God will turn to Him with the quality of the Ever-Turning—that is, the Ever-Returning—and he will attain recognition of Him where before he had been blind to Him in the presence of the confrontation between those two names.[65] 10.3

٤،١٠ وإن لم يكن الاسم مثلاً من الأسماء التي لها مقابل مثل الله والرحمٰن وما لعلّه كان من هذا القبيل فإنّه أيضاً عند انتقاله في الترقّي إلى حضرة اسم آخر بتجلّ آخر يكون الحقّ تعالى توّاباً إليه أي عوّاداً إليه وإن لم يكن قد تنكّر عليه قبل وذلك لأنّ هذا الاسم المتجدّد حصول تجلّيه لم يكن الحقّ سبحانه وتعالى متجلّياً منه على هذا العبد فكأنّه متنكّر عليه فإذا حصل منه التجلّي الإلٰهيّ كان كأنّه تاب إليه أي رجع وذلك لتنزّل الغيبة منزلة الذهاب وتجدّد الشهود منزلة العود ثمّ لا يزال أهل هذا الترقّي أعني السائرين في السفر الأوّل وهم الذين سافروا إلى الله تعالى ينتقلون في الترقّي والحقّ تعالى يتوب عليهم بتعرّفه إليهم حتّى تذهب نسبة عارف ومعروف وواصف وموصوف وذلك في نهاية السفر الأوّل وهو مقام قولهم وهو الآن على ما عليه كان أي ولا شيء معه وسمّاه النفري موقف الوقفة.

٥،١٠ فالاسم التوّاب جلّ وعلا في حضرات الأسماء عائد إلى أهل هذا السلوك بالتوب أي الرجوع وليس فوق مقام الوقفة التي هي نهاية السفر الأوّل نسبة للاسم التوّاب وإن كانت الأسماء كلّها تثبت في السفر الثاني الذي هو فوق هذا السفر لكنّ عودها بمعنى تحقّق تفصيل الوحدانيّة لتعيّن المراتب في شهود الشاهد فإنّه قد كان في مقام الطمس الذي الفناء بابه فعاد في الترقّي الذاتيّ يستجلي الكثرة في الوحدة بعدما كان ينكر الكثرة ويجهلها ولا يرى الأغيار ولا يعقلها ومن هذا مقامه لا يقال فيه أنّه يتوب الاسم التوّاب إليه بل كلّ اسم تائب إليه بحقيقة ظهوره في العين الواحدة وقد يصحّ أن يقال إنّ الأسماء كلّها دخلت في الاسم التوّاب في هذه الحضرة لكن لا لأنّها في الاسم التوّاب بل لأنّها عين العين فإذا علمت هذا علمت أنّه لا عود للاسم التوّاب فيما فوق مقام الوقفة من السفر الثاني.

٦،١٠ وأمّا ظهور أحكام الاسم التوّاب من حضرات أسفل من مقام السفر الأوّل فهو إن كان في حضرات حجابيّة ومقامات اغترابيّة إلّا أنّ الاسم التوّاب ظاهر بالفعل في تلك المقامات وكذلك هو في عوده علينا بالعطاء بعد المنع أو الخفض بعد الرفع أو

However, if the name does not have a counterpart, such as Allāh, the All-Merciful, or another such name, then when, through another disclosure, the wayfarer advances to the presence of another name, God will be Ever-Turning toward him—that is, Ever-Returning to him—even though God may not have disguised Himself from him previously. This is because God had not previously disclosed Himself to that particular servant through that ever-renewing name, and so it is as if it was unfamiliar to him. When he experiences the divine self-disclosure through that name, it is as though it is turning toward him—that is, returning to him. For nondisclosure is akin to a departure, and renewal of witnessing is akin to a return. Then, as the spiritual travelers—by which I mean the wayfarers on the first journey to God—continue to advance, God turns to them by making Himself known to them. This continues until the relation between knower and known, subject and object, disappears, at the end of the first journey, which is the station of their saying: "He is now as He ever was"—that is, when "nothing was with Him."[66] Al-Niffarī called this the station of halting.[67] 10.4

Therefore, the Ever-Turning, within the presences of the names, returns to these wayfarers in repentant turning, or in returning. Moreover, there is no relation to the Ever-Turning beyond the station of halting, which is the end of the first journey. For although all the names are affirmed in the second journey, which is above this journey, their return means the realization of the differentiation of oneness in order for the levels to become determined in the witnesser's witnessing. For he was in the station of obliteration whose door is annihilation, and then returned in essential ascension to manifest multiplicity in unity after having denied and ignored multiplicity, without either seeing or conceiving of separative entities. It is not said that the Ever-Turning turns to the one who is in this station. Rather, every name turns to him through the reality of His manifestation within a single entity. It would also be correct to say that all the names are included within the Ever-Turning in this presence, not because they are under the Ever-Turning, but because they are the entity of entities. If you know this, you also know that there is no return of the Ever-Turning beyond the station of halting at the second journey. 10.5

Although the manifestation of properties of the Ever-Turning at presences before the first journey occurs in presences of the veil and stations of separation, the Ever-Turning actually manifests in those stations. It is similar to His return to us in bestowal after deprivation, or in abasement after exaltation, or in expansion after contraction. In general, whenever the property of 10.6

البسط بعد القبض وبالجملة فحيث ظهر حكم وجوده في تجدّد نعمه فهو العوّاد بالخيرات أي التوّاب وحيث ظهرت نقمه فهو العوّاد في ظهور نقمه من حضرات أسماء الانتقام كالجبّار والقهّار والمنتقم والشديد البطش وخصوصاً ما كان من هذه الأسماء وجوديًّا صرفًا كالدافع لا عدميًّا كالمانع.

٧،١٠ واعلم أنّ ظهور الثمار من سائر الأشجار وظهور المطلوب من عَود عُود الحبوب في النبات بالمحبوب وبالجملة فكلّ فصل عائد في كلّ عام كالنبات على اختلاف أنواعه أو في أقلّ من عام أو أكثر بل وكلّ شيء فصلاً كان أو غيره فإنّه عَود من التوّاب سبحانه بحقائق ما يبدو وضابطه أنّ كلّ ما عاد ولو مرّة أو كرّ الكرّة بعد الكرّة فهو من الاسم التوّاب فأمّا أهل العلم فيقولون إنّ الله تعالى أنبت لهم الزرع وأدرّ لهم الضرع وأجراهم على العوائد الجميلة والمألوفات المأمولة المعلومة منها والمجهولة وأمّا أهل الشهود فيقولون إنّه تعالى ظهر باسمه التوّاب لإكمال أهل الحجاب وأظهر الإثابة من اسمه الوهّاب.

اسمه المفضل تبارك وتعالى

١،١١ هذا الاسم الكريم انفرد بإيراده أبو الحكم بن برّجان الأندلسيّ وورد في الكتاب العزيز في البقرة في قوله تعالى ﴿وَأَنِّي فَضَّلْتُكُمْ عَلَى ٱلْعَٰلَمِينَ﴾ ولا شكّ أنّ اشتقاقه من التفضيل والتفضيل معنًى مفهوم لا يشَكّ فيه فلا شكّ في الاسم منه.

٢،١١ وحقيقته أنّ الاستعدادات متفاوتة فمن كان استعداده أتمّ من سائر الاستعدادات فلا شكّ أنّ الحقّ العادل يعطيه أتمّ ممّا أعطى من هو دونَه فباب الاستحقاق هو الاستعداد فإذا فضل استعداد شخص استعدادَ غيره فهو التفضيل

His existence is manifested through the renewal of His blessings, it is He who is Returning, or Ever-Turning, with all manner of graces. And whenever His vengeful afflictions manifest, He is the Ever-Turning by manifesting His vengeful afflictions from the presences of the names of vengeance such as the All-Dominating, the Subjugating, the Avenger, and the Severe in Assault. This is especially true for the names of pure existence such as the Repeller, but not for the names of nonexistence such as the Preventer.

The appearance of fruits on the trees and the fulfillment of desires when 10.7
seeds repeatedly produce growth on the branches of plants come from the Ever-Turning. In summary, every yearly cycle, such as vegetal growth in all its variety, or cycles that last more or less than a year, and in fact all returns in all things, be they seasons or otherwise, are the Ever-Turning returning with the realities of all that becomes apparent. As a general rule, all things that return, whether only once or time and again, are from the Ever-Turning. Exoteric scholars say that God caused their crops to grow, and their livestock to give milk, and that this pleasing and wonted predictability, both known and unknown, is His doing. Those who witness, for their part, say that God manifests Himself through His name the Ever-Turning in order to bring veiled intellects to perfection, and that He manifests His reward from His name the Bestower.

Al-Mufḍil: The One Who Favors

This noble name is only considered to be a divine name by Ibn Barrajān. Its 11.1
place of occurrence in the Holy Book is in the Surah of the Cow in the verse: «I have favored you above the worlds».[68] It certainly derives from "to favor." Given that the meaning of "to favor" is well known and uncontested, there is no uncertainty about the meaning of the divine name that derives from it.

The reality of this name is that people's levels of preparedness are disparate, 11.2
and when one individual is more completely prepared than another, God in His justice undoubtedly bestows more completely upon him than He does upon an individual beneath him. For the door to worthiness is preparedness, and the

المشار إليه في قوله تعالى ﴿وَأَنِّي فَضَّلْتُكُمْ عَلَى ٱلْعَٰلَمِينَ﴾ وذلك لأنّ الاستعداد إنّما يستفاد من الحقّ تعالى فنفس كمال الاستعداد هو تفضيل الحقّ تبارك وتعالى للشخص المستعدّ لذلك الكمال وقد علمت أنّ الاستعداد لا يكون من ذات المستعدّ فقط بل ومن المكان والزمان والعوارض اللاحقة لذلك المستعدّ وأنّ مجموع ذلك هو الاستعداد الذي يقع فيه التفضيل.

٣،١١ واعلم أنّ الحقّ تعالى ﴿لَا يَظْلِمُ ٱلنَّاسَ شَيْـًٔا﴾ فمن كان استعداده للكمال ظهر كاملاً ومن دونه إمّا متوسّط وإمّا متأخّر ومن كان متوسّطاً كان متوسّطاً ومن كان متأخّراً كان متأخّراً ﴿لَا تَبْدِيلَ لِكَلِمَٰتِ ٱللَّهِ﴾ ﴿ذَٰلِكَ ٱلدِّينُ ٱلْقَيِّمُ﴾.

٤،١١ وعليك أن تنظر إلى ظاهر ما بدا فتعلم أنّه الظاهر الحقّ فمن كان أفضل كان هو الذي فضّله الحقّ تبارك وتعالى فيجب عليك أيها المؤمن أن تعترف له بالتفضيل عليك فتدخل تحت أحكامه فإنّه ربّك بمقدار ما به فضّلك فإن فضّلك من وجه وفضّلته من وجه فأنت ربّه من الوجه الذي فضّلك به وهو ربّك من الوجه الذي فَضّله[1] به فإنّ الربوبيّة لا تتقيّد بمرتبة واحدة وإنّما هي حكم دائر في الأطوار فحيث تحقّق طور من أطوارها ظهرت فيه ووجب على عبد تلك المرتبة التي ظهرت فيها الربوبيّة أن يعبدها عبادة مساوية لما ظهرت به من الربوبيّة وإن لم يفعل ذلك كان كافراً بربّه تبارك وتعالى من حيث تلك الحضرة ولا ينفعه في كفره بتلك الحضرة أنّه مؤمن بربّه تبارك تعالى من حضرة أخرى فإنّه من تلك الحضرة منعَم ومن هذه الحضرة معذّب فيجتمع في حقّه أن يكون منعّماً مُعذّباً في وقت واحد ولا تقل كيف يجتمع الضدّان فإنّا نقول إنهما اجتمعا لتخالف الاعتبارين فافهم ذلك.

٥،١١ واعلم أيّها الأخ أنّك متى فرّطت في العدل فإنّك ظالم وبقدر ما أنت به ظالم تعاقب ﴿جَزَآءً وِفَاقًا﴾ فإن كنت من أهل الوجود الحقّ من أوّل السفر رأيت كلّ شيء حسناً وإن كنت من أهل شهود الحقّ من حيث السفر الثاني كان الحسن

---

١ و: فضلك.

favoring that is alluded to in the verse: «I have favored you above the worlds» is whenever the preparedness of one individual exceeds that of another. This is because preparedness is acquired from none other than the Real, and the very perfection of an individual's preparedness is the Real's favoring of that individual who is prepared for that perfection. Moreover, you know that preparedness is premised not only on the essence of the individual, but also on the time, place, and circumstances associated with the individual. The sum total of this is the preparedness through which favoring occurs.

God «does not wrong humankind in the least».[69] Hence, the one who is 11.3
prepared for perfection manifests in a state of perfection; and the one who falls short of perfection becomes manifest with either average or below-average qualities of perfection. The one who is average stays such, and the one who is below average stays such: «there is no changing the words of God»;[70] «that is the ever-true religion».[71]

You must also examine outward appearances in order to recognize that He 11.4
is the truly Manifest, for the one who is superior is the one who is favored by the Real. Dear believer, you should therefore acknowledge His favor upon you in order to fall under its properties. For He is your Lord in the manner that He has favored you. If He favors you in one manner and you favor Him in another, then you are His lord in the manner He has favored you, and He is your lord in the manner that He has favored Himself. For lordship is not limited to a single level. It is a property that passes through all stages, and lordship manifests whenever one of its stages is actualized. The servant at the stage in which lordship manifests must therefore worship in a manner commensurate with the lordship it manifests. Not to do so is to be an unbeliever in the Lord in that presence; and unbelief in that presence is not helped by belief in the Lord in a different presence. For the servant is in blissfulness in the latter, and in chastisement in the former: in his case, both blissfulness and chastisement come together simultaneously. Do not ask, "How can opposites come together?" For we say, "They come together because of the tension between the two perspectives"—so make sure to understand that!

Know also, dear brother, that you are a wrongdoer each time you break the 11.5
balance and are punished by the measure of your wrongdoing with «a suitable recompense».[72] Therefore, if you are among those who have true witnessing in the first journey, you will perceive all things as beautiful. If you are among those who have true witnessing in the second journey, you will perceive beauty

عندك حسناً والقبح قبيحاً فاعرف مقامك وحقّق أحكامك وكن حيث تأكل فيه وتشرب فيه شرابك وطعامك لتكون من العدل على ﴿صِرَٰطٍ مُّسْتَقِيمٍ﴾ إمّا في عقوبة أو في تنعيم.

٦،١١ وحقيقة هذا الاسم تقتضي أن تعتبر التفضيل حيث كان يلزمك له التعظيم والتبجيل فإذا وجدت محلّ التعظيم فعظّمه وإن نهاك جاهل فعلّمه فإن أبى فحرّمه ومعنى التحريم عدم اجتماعك به فيما يوجب السكوت أو التكليم فإنّه من الذين حُرّموا قال الله تعالى ﴿حُرِّمَتْ عَلَيْكُمُ ٱلْمَيْتَةُ﴾ وهم الذين لا استعداد لهم لشهود الحقّ ﴿وَٱلدَّمُ﴾ وهم أهل الغضب فإنّ الغضب غليان دم القلب ﴿وَلَحْمُ ٱلْخِنزِيرِ﴾ وهم الذين لا غيرة لهم على أنفسهم وَمَا أُهِلَّ بِهِ لِغَيْرِ ٱللَّهِ وهم المُراؤون أهل الرِّياء ﴿وَٱلْمُنْخَنِقَةُ﴾ وهم الذين اختنقوا بتكلف ما لا يطاق وقِس على ذلك بقيّة الآية فإنّ ﴿ٱلْمُتَرَدِّيَةُ﴾ هم الذين وقعوا في شبهة منعتهم التوجّه إلى الله عزّ وجلّ ﴿وَٱلنَّطِيحَةُ﴾ وهم الذين أضلّهم غيرهم بوجه من الوجوه ﴿وَمَآ أَكَلَ ٱلسَّبُعُ﴾ وهم الذين تركوا شيخاً عارفاً بالتربية لمّا رأوا شيخاً عليه ظاهراً آثار العبادة وهو في نفسه جاهل فمالوا إلى تقليده دون العارف الأوّل وأمّا قوله ﴿إِلَّا مَا ذَكَّيْتُمْ﴾ فإنّ معناه إلّا ما حصّلتموه ممّا وقع فيه وعلى هذا التقدير فلا تنسب إلى ربّك تبارك وتعالى نقصاً بوجه من الوجوه وقم أنت في مقام أنْ تتلقّى عن ربّك تبارك وتعالى ما يتوجّه عليه فإنّه حضرة الذات لا حضرة الإله والمألوه في مقام الصفات.

٧،١١ قال الله تعالى ﴿وَلَوْ شَآءَ رَبُّكَ لَجَعَلَ ٱلنَّاسَ أُمَّةً وَٰحِدَةً وَلَا يَزَالُونَ مُخْتَلِفِينَ إِلَّا مَن رَّحِمَ رَبُّكَ وَلِذَٰلِكَ خَلَقَهُمْ﴾ فعلمنا من هذا أنّ من فضّله تعالى فإنّما فضّله باستحقاق ومن حقيقة قوله ﴿وَلِذَٰلِكَ خَلَقَهُمْ﴾ ولا ريب أنّ من إذا رأى من فضّله الحقّ تعالى عليه ولو في رتبة ناقصة فإنّه يجب له أن يفضّله على من دونه تفضيلاً مساوياً لاستحقاقه إن أمكن معرفة استحقاقه وإلّا فبقدر الإمكان

as beautiful, and ugliness as ugly. So know your station, realize your properties, and be present with God wherever He puts you so that you may walk with balance upon «the straight path»,[73] be it in punishment or in bliss.

The reality of this name dictates that you consider God's favor wherever veneration or honor is required. When you find a site of veneration, venerate it. Should an ignorant person reproach you, teach him; if he refuses, «forbid»[74] him. Forbidding here means not keeping his company, insofar as this obliges you to either remain silent or to speak out. He is therefore among those who are «forbidden»; God says: «Forbidden unto you are carrion»—namely, those who have no preparedness for witnessing the Real; «and blood»—namely, irascible people, since irascibility is the boiling of the blood of the heart; «and the flesh of swine»—namely, those who feel no protective jealousy for their own souls; «and what has been offered to other than God»—namely, those who make a show of things, or who have self-conceit; «and the animal that has been strangled»—namely, those who strangle themselves by burdening themselves with more religious obligations than they can bear. You can draw more analogies for the rest of the verse, since «the animal that has fallen to death» corresponds to those who fall into dubious practices that prevent them from orienting themselves to God; «the animal killed by the goring of horns» corresponds to those who were misguided by others in any way; and «the animal devoured by wild beasts» corresponds to those who abandon a master knowledgeable in the art of spiritual guidance when they see another master displaying more outward signs of piety but who himself is ignorant, and prefer to imitate him instead of the former recognizer. As for «save that which you have duly sacrificed», it means: except for what you have already done in the past. By the same measure, do not ascribe to your Lord deficiency in any respect. Stand at the station where you can receive from your Lord all that directs itself to Him, for that is the presence of the Essence, not the presence of lord and vassal at the station of the qualities. 11.6

God says: «Had your Lord willed, He would have made humankind one nation; but they continue in their differences, except those on whom your Lord has mercy; and for that end He did create them».[75] God teaches us here that when He favors people, He does so because of their worthiness, per the real meaning of the verse «and for that end He did create them». There is no doubt that whenever one sees a person who has been favored more than oneself, even if it be on a lower plane, it is necessary to favor such a person 11.7

وعبادة العارفين أكثرها من هذا الباب فإنّها عبادة بحسب ظهورات الحقّ كما قال الشاعر

مِنْ أَيِّ نَاحِيَةٍ تَجَلَّى ٱلْكَأْسُ قُمْتُ إِلَيْهِ وَاقِفْ

٨،١١ وقد ألّف الشيخ محيي الدين رضي الله عنه كتاباً سمّاه العبادلة وهو مختصّ بأهل المعرفة دون العبّاد وأهل الوقفة ومن فوقهم بل هو للعارفين فقط وذلك أنّه نسبهم إلى مراتب الأسماء الإلهيّة وسمّاهم بحسب تلك المراتب وإن لم تكن أسماؤهم التي سمّاهم بها أمّهاتهم وآباؤهم هي تلك الأسماء التي ذكرها الشيخ رضي الله عنه فإنّ العارف إنّما هو من عرف ربّه تبارك وتعالى من تعرّف اسم من اسمائه عزّ وجلّ أو من حيث صفة من صفاته ففني منه رسم ما يقابَل ذلك الاسم من العبوديّة وبقيّة رسومه باقية فهو باق من حيث ما بقي من الرسوم فانٍ من جهة ما فني منها فيكون ما بقي منه عبدا للمتجلّي سبحانه من مرتبة اسمه أو صفته الذين منهما أو منها حصل التجلّي فأمّا ما فني منه بالشهود في حضرة ذلك الاسم فإنّه التحق بالربوبيّة وصار هو المتجلّي بل ليس غيره لا أنّه هو أمّا من فنيت رسومه كلّها فهو في الوقفة وهو الذي قال فيه الشيخ محيي الدين رحمة الله عليه

ٱلرَّبُّ رَبٌّ وَٱلْعَبْدُ رَبٌّ يَا لَيْتَ شِعْرِي مَنِ ٱلْمُكَلَّفُ

٩،١١ وهي حضرة يعرفها أهلها ولا ينكرها أهل الإيمان بها أَوْ من ﴿أَلْقَى ٱلسَّمْعَ وَهُوَ شَهِيدٌ﴾ فالعارفون هم أهل عبادة المراتب الأسمائيّة ولكلّ واحد منهم عبادة تخصّه من حيث ما وقع له منها التجلّي ويكون عبداً لله تعالى من حيث ذلك الاسم ويسمّى بعبوديّته مرتبة فيكون من العبادلة وإن لم يكن في تسمية آبائه منهم وكلّ عابِد فمعبوده مفضّل عليه فالاسم المفضل تجري أحكامه في الحضرتين الربوبيّة والمربوبيّة.

over others in a manner corresponding to his worth, if determinable, and if not, then to the extent possible. The worship of the recognizers is mostly of this sort, for it is a worship in accordance with the manifestations of the Real. As one poet proclaimed:

> Wherever the cup is,
> there am I, standing before it.[76]

Shaykh Muḥyī l-Dīn ibn al-ʿArabī wrote a book entitled *The Servants of God*, which is specifically and exclusively for the recognizers, not the worshippers or those who have arrived at the station of halting and beyond. For he ascribes the servants of God to the levels of the divine names and gives each a name according to their specific level, even if those were not the names their parents gave them. The recognizer is the one who recognizes his Lord by recognizing one of His names or qualities, whereupon the trace of servanthood that stands as counterpart to that divine name passes away, while the rest of his traces remain.[77] The recognizer remains insofar as his traces remain, and he passes away insofar as his traces have passed away. What remains of him is a servant of the Self-Discloser at the level of the name or the quality from where the disclosure occurred. What passes away in the witnessing of the presence of that name joins the rank of lordship and becomes the Self-Discloser—in the sense that it is not other than He, not that it is He. As for the one whose traces have fully passed away, he has arrived at the station of halting, of which the shaykh[78] says in the verse: 11.8

> The Lord is a lord, and the servant is a lord;
> if only I knew who was burdened by the Law![79]

This is a presence that is recognized by those who abide in it. It is not denied by those who believe in it, nor by those who «give an ear while bearing witness».[80] For the recognizers are worshippers of the levels of the names, and each one has a unique worship that pertains to the disclosure that manifests for him therein. He is a servant of God in respect to that name, and he is named after his servanthood at that level and becomes one of the servants of God, though the name in question was not given to him by his parents. Every object of worship is given favor over its worshipper, and therefore the properties of the One Who Favors circulate in both the presence of lordship and of servanthood. 11.9

اسمه البصير تبارك وتعالى

ورد في البقرة في قوله تعالى ﴿وَٱللَّهُ بَصِيرٌۢ بِمَا يَعۡمَلُونَ﴾ وقد اتّفق على إيراده الأئمّة ١،١٢
الثلاثة رضوان الله عليهم والبصير هنا بمعنى المبصر كما ورد الأليم بمعنى المؤلِم و﴿بَدِيعُ ٱلسَّمَٰوَٰتِ﴾ بمعنى المبدع وأثبت أهل السنّة له تعالى البصر والسمع والكلام مع نفيهم التشبيه عنه وللظاهريّة والمجسّمة في أسماء الصفات أقاويل فأمّا أهل مقام التحقيق الذي هو فوق كلّ مقام فأثبتوا صحّة ما قالته كلّ طائفة من جميع الطوائف ولا لهم خلف مع موافق منهم ولا مخالف فقال الشيخ محيي الدين رضي الله عنه شعرًا

عَقَدَ ٱلخَلَائِقُ فِي ٱلإِلٰهِ عَقَائِدًا ‌ ‌ وَأَنَا ٱعۡتَقَدۡتُ جَمِيعَ مَا ٱعۡتَقَدُوهُ

وأمّا أنّهم كيف يوافقوا مع كلّ طائفة فذلك معلوم وهو أنّ كلّ طور من أطوار ٢،١٢
المخالفين فهو ظهور من ظهورات الحقّ تعالى عندهم فيثبتونه من حيث الظهور المشهود لهم لا من حيث إدراك تلك الطائفة فإنّ إدراكها إدراك محجوب وإلى الجهل وإن وافق العلم منسوب ولي في هذا المعنى شعر

مَنۡ كَانَ لَا يَدۡرِي ٱلصَّوَابَ ‌ ‌ فَذَاكَ أَخۡطَأَ إِذَا أَصَابَا
أَوۡ كَانَ لَا يَدۡرِي ٱلجَوَابَ ‌ ‌ فَمَا أَجَابَ وَإِنۡ أَجَابَا

لكن يصدق عند المحقّقين أن يقال إنهم أصابوا ويصدق أن يقال أخطؤوا أمّا الإصابة فلمصادفة ظهور الحقيقة من طورهم بمبلغهم فإنّها الظاهرة بكلّ مبلغ وأمّا الخطأ فلأنّهم لم يشهدوا جهة الإصابة ولأنّهم ما باشروا فيما قالوه برد اليقين ولا

Al-Baṣīr: The Seeing

This name is mentioned in the Surah of the Cow in the verse: «God sees what they do».[81] The three eminent scholars agree that it is a divine name. The Seeing here means the same as "the giver of sight," just as "painful" can mean the same as "causer of pain," and «Innovator of the heavens and earth»[82] means the same as "maker of innovations." The Sunnis affirm that God has sight, hearing, and speech while denying any comparability to Him. The literalist Ẓāhirīs and the Anthropomorphists,[83] for their part, hold many doctrines concerning the names of the divine qualities. Those who have attained the station of realization, which is above all stations, affirm the soundness of what each group says without disputing with those whose position agrees with or contradicts theirs. To this effect, Shaykh Muḥyī l-Dīn, God be pleased with him, said the following verse: 12.1

> God's creatures have devised many a belief about Him
> and I give credence to all that they believe.[84]

The manner in which they agree with every group is well known. For them, every one of the stages of the disputants is a manifestation of the Real. They affirm it with respect to the manifestation that is witnessed by them, not with respect to what that group perceives, for their perception is veiled and the result of ignorance, even when it happens to coincide with knowledge. On this point, I have composed the following verses: 12.2

> He who does not know what is right
> errs even if he hits the mark;
> He who does not know the answer
> has not answered, even if he answers.[85]

For those who know the reality of things, however, it would be true to say that they are right, and also that they are wrong. They are right in the sense that this reality happens to manifest at their stage of achievement; for reality is that which is manifest in every stage of achievement. They are wrong in the sense that they do not understand why they are right, nor do they experience the pleasure of certainty in what they say, nor has the joy of realization become

ظهرت عليهم بشاشة التحقيق و﴿إِنْ هُمْ إِلَّا يَظُنُّونَ﴾ ﴿إِنْ هُمْ إِلَّا يَخْرُصُونَ﴾ و﴿إِنَّ ٱلظَّنَّ لَا يُغْنِى مِنَ ٱلْحَقِّ شَيْـًٔا﴾.

٣،١٢ وأمّا طائفة أهل العرفان فمن كان منهم من أهل شهود الاسم السميع أو البصير أو المتكلّم وافقوا على ظاهر ما قاله أولئك المحجوبون ولم يتّخذوا المأخذ ولا ﴿تَشَٰبَهَتْ قُلُوبُهُمْ﴾ في المقصد ومن كان من أهل العرفان قد شهد من هذه الأسماء اسماً واحداً فقط أو اسمين فقط فإنّه يجهل ما لم يشهده فلا ينكر ولا يعترف إلّا بما شهد أمّا أنّه لا ينكر فلأنّ العارف مشغول بربّه عزّ وجلّ في طور ما شهد من أسمائه العلى غير متعرّض إلى ما خفي وبدا فإنّ طريقهم عدم التعرّض إلى السوى والتجنّب عن أهل الجدل والمراء وليست مداركهم من النطق وإن كان النطق معدوداً من الصدق بل من عين الحكم وهو العيان لا من الفكر ولا من الوهم ولا من الخيال اللواتي هي مادّة الأذهان.

٤،١٢ وإذا عُلم هذا فالاسم البصير عزّ وجلّ في كلّ مرتبة بحسبها فالبصر من قِبل الأعيان هو العلم وهو علم ذاتيّ لا تتعيّن فيه المعلومات صوراً علميّة متمايزة بل كعلم الماء بالتبريد ﴿وَٱللَّهُ بَصِيرٌۢ بِٱلْعِبَادِ﴾ من هذه الحضرة بكلّ اعتبارات الإطلاقات والتقاييد وأمّا في طور الظهور بالأعيان فبعدد ما ظهر من الكيان وتعدّد من الأكوان علوّاً وسفلاً وجزءاً وكلّاً فعلمه من طور العقل الأوّل علم بالكلّيّات وهو مقام الاسم الحيّ ومن هناك تتعيّن الحياة فإنّ قبل ذلك كان الموصوف منزّهاً عن ذكر الحياة وضدّها بل وعن الأسماء كلّها فإذاً تعيّن الحياة للحيّ تعالى إنّما هو من حيث ظهوره بالعقل الأوّل.

٥،١٢ وأمّا حضرة العلم فهي النفس ولذلك كانت النفوس هي الموصوفة بملكة العلم وأمّا مرتبة الإرادة فهي مقام الهيولى الكلّيّ وذلك أنّ الإرادة هي الميل إلى ظهور ما تظهره القدرة والهيولى هي حضرة الميل إلى ظهور عالَم الملكوت وهو الجسم الكلّيّ وقوم يسمّونه عالم الملك ولا تفاوت في التسمية وأمّا مرتبة القدرة فهي في مرتبة ظهور

manifest in them. «They are merely conjecturing»,[86] «they are merely surmising»,[87] «and conjecture avails naught against truth».[88]

Those recognizers who witness the Hearing, the Seeing, or the Speaking agree outwardly with what the veiled thinkers say. But they do not take their knowledge from the same source, nor are «their hearts similar»[89] with regard to their aim. Those recognizers who only witness one or two of these names have no knowledge of what they do not witness, and so they will only reject or affirm according to what they witness. Not rejecting is because the recognizer is preoccupied with his Lord at the stage of his witnessing of the exalted names. He is not distracted by what is hidden or by what is apparent. His way is to refrain from involvement in other-than-God, and to avoid those inclined to disputation and debate. He perceives things not on the basis of speech—although speech is counted as a type of truth—but on the basis of the property itself, and that is eyewitnessing. His perception is neither by way of reflective thought, nor delusion, nor imagination, all of which are products of the mind. 12.3

Given this, the Seeing is at every cosmic level and in keeping with it. As such, sight on the part of concrete entities is knowledge. It is essential knowledge in which the objects of knowledge are not determined as distinct cognitive forms, but rather as water knows how to cool things. «God sees the servants»[90] from this presence in respect to all their unqualifications and delimitations. The stage of the manifestation of concrete entities is per the number of beings that become manifest, and the number of existents that multiply above and below, both as particulars and as universals. His knowledge at the stage of the First Intellect is knowledge of universals, and that is the station of the Living, wherein Life becomes determined. For, prior to that, the Possessor of that quality of Life is hallowed not only beyond the mentioning of Life and its opposite, but also beyond all the names. Therefore, the distinct determination of Life for the Living is with respect to its manifestation through the First Intellect.[91] 12.4

The presence of knowledge is the Universal Soul. This is why souls are described as having an aptitude for knowledge. The level of Will is the station of the Universal Hyle.[92] For Will is the inclination to manifest whatever Power manifests, and the Hyle is the presence of the inclination to manifest the realm of Sovereignty, which is the Universal Body; some call it the realm of the Kingdom, but despite the nomenclature there is no disparity. The level of Power is at the level of the manifestation of the Universal Body, for it is the object that is brought into manifestation by Power. These four names, the Living, the 12.5

الجسم الكلّيّ فإنّه المقدور الذي أظهرته القدرة فهذه الأربعة أسماء هي في الأربعة المراتب الحياة في القلم الأعلى وهو العقل الأوّل والعلم في اللوح المحفوظ وهو النفس الكلّيّة والإرادة في الكتابة في النفس وهو الهيولى نفسها وأمّا القدرة فهي في المكتوب والمكتوب هو المراد الأوّل والعلّة الغائبة وظهوره يكون أخيرًا.

وتتداخل الأسماء كما قدّمنا فيكون الاسم البصير عزّ وجلّ بحسب هذه الأسماء ٦،١٢
الأربعة وبحسب كلّ منها فالبصر في العقل الأوّل حياةٌ وحقيقة الحياة الحسّ والحسّ في هذه المرتبة بحسبها فلا شكّ أنّ البصر حسّ لكنّه في هذه الحضرة حسّ إحساسه للكلّيّات إحساس ذاتيّ للعقل الأوّل فالحقّ تعالى من هذه الحضرة بصير بالكلّيّات لا على سبيل التمثيل كما يشير إليه أفلاطون من المُثُل الأفلاطونيّة بل مثلما إنّ الماء يحسّ إحساساً ذاتيّاً بما في ذاته من التبريد والسّيلان وذلك الإحساس بسيط فيكون جزؤه مساوياً لكلّه كما أنّ النقطة من الماء ماء هذا في المحسوسات الجسمانيّة فالمحسوسات العقليّة تكون بنسبة هذا لأنّ البساطة فيهما إمّا واحدة وإمّا في المعاني أبسط فهذا الإحساس هو البصر الذي يوصف به الحقّ تعالى في هذه الحضرة فيقال إنّه بصير أي بأطوار العقل فقد دخل البصير في الحيّ وإن شئت قلت الحيّ في البصير.

وأمّا ظهور الاسم البصير بالاسم العالم في حضرة النفس وظهوره بها مستصحباً ٧،١٢
للحياة المستفادة من مرتبة العقل من الاسم الحيّ فيكون البصير في طور العالم حيّاً وبما اكتسبه من طور النفس الكلّيّة يكون عالماً فيصير البصير في هذه المرتبة حيّاً عالماً بصيراً بصور الكتابة وهي العلم نفسه فالبصير تعالى في حضرة النفس عالم بالصور الروحانيّة ونسبتها إلى النفس الكلّيّة كنسبة التصوّرات الذهنيّة في أذهان الأناسي وكذلك هي كتابته في أذهان الأناسي أي في أنفسهم إذا كانت صحيحة فالبصير في النفس لا يغايره العالم فيكون البصر في هذه الحضرة يسمّى علماً باعتبار العالم ويسمّى بصراً باعتبار الاسم البصير وهذه الأمور اعتبارات ما ظهر الوجود إلّا بها ومَن تحقّقها زال عنه الجهل وخرج من عهدة التقليد.

Knowing, the Willing, the Powerful, are at the four cosmic levels: Life is in the Supreme Pen, which is the First Intellect; Knowledge is in the Preserved Tablet, which is the Universal Soul; Will is in the inscription upon the Soul, which is the Hyle itself; Power is in what is inscribed, and what is inscribed is God's first Will and the hidden cause, and its manifestation occurs last.

Moreover, the names interpenetrate, as we have said previously. The Seeing 12.6
therefore comes into being in keeping with these four names and in keeping with each name. Sight in the First Intellect is life, and the reality of life is sense perception. Sense perception, moreover, is in keeping with its level, and there is no doubt that sight is a sense perception. But in this presence, it is a sensation that senses the universals in an essential manner that pertains to the First Intellect. The Real in this presence sees the universals not by way of imaginalization as Plato alludes to in the Platonic Images, but rather in the same way as water is cognizant of its own natural properties of cooling and flowing. This sense perception is simple, such that its part equals its whole, just as a drop of water is water. All of this pertains to the corporeal sensory objects, because the intelligible sensory objects exist in relation to them. For simplicity in corporeal things is either a unity or, in the supersensory meanings, it is simpler still. This sense perception is the seeing that the Real is described by this presence, such that He can be called "Seeing." That is, He sees the stages of the First Intellect. Thus the Seeing is included within the Living; or you could say that the Living is included within the Seeing.

The manifestation of the Seeing through the Knowing is in the presence of 12.7
the Soul. Its manifestation thereby is accompanied by the life received from the level of the Intellect from the Living. As such, the Seeing at the stage of the Knowing is living, and through what it acquires from the Universal Soul it is also knowing. The Seeing in this level therefore lives, knows, and sees the forms of the Writing, which are Knowledge itself. The Seeing in the presence of the Universal Soul is therefore knowledge of the spiritual forms, whose relationship to the Soul is like the relationship of mental formations in the minds of people. So also is its writing in human minds; that is, in their souls when they are correct. For in the Soul, the knowing is no different from the seeing. Therefore, sight in the presence of the Soul is called knowledge from the perspective of the Knowing, and sight from the perspective of the Seeing. Moreover, it is only through these affairs, or perspectives, that existence manifests. Whoever realizes them rids himself of ignorance and emerges from the bondage of blind emulation.

٨،١٢ وأمّا ظهور الاسم البصير بمرتبة الكتابة وهي الهيولى الكلّي فذلك عالَم الإرادة والاسم البصير فيها ظاهر بالاسم المريد ويكون مستصحباً لحكم الحياة المستفادة من الحيّ ومستصحباً لمعنى العلم المستفاد من حضرة اللوح المحفوظ وهي النفس الكلّيّة وقائماً بالاسم المريد في حضرة الكتابة وهي معاني الهيولى التي ستصير صوراً جسمانيّة ولواحقها من المقدّمات والمتمّمات إلى أن ينقضي عالَم هذه الكرات والحقّ تعالى بصير في هذه الحضرة بما في القوّة القريبة من الفعل من حيث ما تهيّأت أن تظهر.

٩،١٢ وأمّا ظهور الاسم البصير بالاسم القادر فهو في حضرة ظهور المقدور وهو هنا الجسم الكلّي فيظهر البصير بالقادر مستصحباً للأسماء المذكورة قبل فيكون البصر المنسوب إلى الحقّ تعالى في هذه الحضرة هو نفس تقابل أجزاء الأجسام بعضها عند بعض فنفس ترائي الأشكال بعضها لبعض هو استجلاؤه ببصر القدرة جزئيّات المقدور استجلاءً حاليّاً يعرفه أهله ولا يسع العقل الروحانيّ جهله.

١٠،١٢ وأمّا عالم الأركان فإنّما تمايزت بما كان في الهيولى الكلّي من التمايز المعنويّ المناسب للحضرات التي قبلها وسأبيّن ذلك التمايز وهو أنّ الحياة لها في الهيولى حكم كان باطناً وظهر في النار الطبيعيّة وهي الحرارة لأنّ الحرارة حياة وبها يكون الحيّ حيّاً متحرّكاً لأنّ الحركة تتبع الحرارة كما تتبع الحرارة الحياة.

١١،١٢ التمايز الثاني هو أنّ للعلم في الهيولى نسبة وحكماً كان باطناً وظهر في الهواء الطبيعيّ وهي الرطوبة لأنّ الرطوبة علم إذ حقيقة العلم قبول صور المعلومات وقبول التشكّلات هو في الرطوبة فصار التصوّر يتبع الرطوبة وهي راجعة إلى حقيقة قبول النفس الكلّيّة للأشكال الكتابيّة التي هي العلم وصورتها في الحسّ الهواء.

١٢،١٢ التمايز الثالث وهو أنّ الإرادة من الاسم المريد لها حكم كان باطناً في الهيولى وظهر في الماء الطبيعيّ وذلك لأنّ حقيقة الماء الرطب البارد فهو بما فيه من الرطوبة هواء وبما في الهواء من الحرارة نار وبما في النار من الحياة حسّ أوّل وكما

The manifestation of the Seeing at the level of Writing, which is the Universal Hyle, is the realm of Will. The Seeing manifests therein through the Willing, and it is accompanied by the property of life that is taken from the Living. The Seeing is also accompanied by the pure meaning of knowledge that is taken from the presence of the Preserved Tablet, which is the Universal Soul, and it subsists through the Willing in the presence of Writing.[93] The latter consists of the pure meanings of the Hyle, which become corporeal forms, as well as the attendant prologues and epilogues of those forms,[94] until the realm of these spheres is completed. In this presence the Real sees by means of the potential proximate to actuality in the sense that it is ready to become manifest. 12.8

The manifestation of the Seeing through the Powerful is in the presence of the manifestation of the object of Power; namely, the Universal Body. The Seeing therefore becomes manifest through the Powerful, and is accompanied by the aforementioned names such that the sight that is ascribed to the Real in this presence is the opposition between certain parts of the bodies and others. Thus, the way in which shapes see one another is none other than His distinct manifestation of the particular objects of Power by the sight of Power, in an existential manner. This distinct manifestation is recognized by those who are qualified, and the intellect of the spirit cannot be ignorant of it. 12.9

The realm of the four elements becomes distinct through the intelligible differentiations that inhere in the Universal Hyle, which corresponds to the presences that precede it. Let me clarify this distinction: It is that life has a property in the Hyle that is nonmanifest, and is manifested in natural fire, which is heat. For heat is life, and through it the living comes to life and is put into motion, for motion follows heat just as heat follows life. 12.10

The second distinction is that knowledge has a relationship and property within the Hyle that is nonmanifest, and is manifested in natural air, which is wetness. For wetness is knowledge, since the true nature of knowledge is the reception of intelligible forms, and the reception of these configuring shapes occurs in wetness. The giving of forms therefore occurs after wetness, which derives from the reality of the Universal Soul's reception of the inscribed shapes that are knowledge, and whose form in the sensory realm is air. 12.11

The third distinction is that Will, from the Willing, has a property in the Hyle that is nonmanifest, and is manifested in natural water. For the true nature of water consists of cold wetness: it is air inasmuch as it contains wetness, and it is fire inasmuch as air contains heat, and it is primary sensation inasmuch as fire 12.12

أنّ البرودة تجمّد فهي كالميل الإراديّ إلى أن تثبت المرادات على أطوار ظهورها مقدورات على وفق ما سبق في القوّة والإمكان منها فالإرادة هي في الصور والأشكال عالم الماء.

١٣،١٢ وأمّا عالم الأرض وهو اليبس المحض فذلك عالم القدرة وكانت باطنة في الهيولى وظهرت باليبس الذي يجمّد السائل ليثبت في عالم الكثائف حتّى يتحقّق المقدور ظاهرًا ولولا ذلك لما ظهر في عالم القدرة والبصير هنا بحسب ما تدركه هذه الأركان بعضها من بعض حين تمازج ولولا البصر الإلٰهيّ لم يمتزج ما يولد المتولّدات فافهم وظهور المولّدات إنّما هو ببصر هو من الاسم البصير عزّ وجلّ.

١٤،١٢ واعلم أنّ الذي تقدّم ذكره إنّما هو ظهور في أطوار أربعة معانٍ هي الحياة والعلم والإرادة والقدرة وهي مرتّبة ترتيبًا طبيعيًّا للمعاني فإنّ للمعاني في ترتيبها طبيعة تخصّها غير محسوسة وحصل من هذه الأسماء الأربعة الحيّ والعالِم والمريد والقادر في أطوار هذه صفتها الحرارة والرطوبة والبرودة واليبوسة ثمّ تعيّنت من هذه التعيّنات تعيّنات هي مركّبات وبسائط تلك الأربعة المذكورة منها النار وهي من الحرارة والهواء وهو من الرطوبة والماء وهو من البرودة والأرض وهي من اليبس فمظهر الحياة والعلم والإرادة والقدرة الحرارة والرطوبة والبرودة واليبوسة ومظهر هذه هي النار والهواء والماء والتراب إذ هي مركّبة من تلك وفي شهود الشاهد لهذه الأربعة المركّبة يعلَم أنّ هذه ظهورات للاسم الحيّ والعالم والمريد والقادر في طور ثان فإنّه ما ظهر إلّا أحكام الأسماء وإن اختلفت التسمية عند المحجوبين والمتسمّي بها عند أهل الشهود واحد مشهود وهذه الأربعة الأركان تركّبت في المولّدات الأربع.

١٥،١٢ فأمّا عالم الإنسان منها في جسمه الأركان الأربعة والنار غالبة وما شاط أو شطّ[١] من عالم الإنسان فهو الشيطان والجانّ المخلوق ﴿مِن مَّارِجٍ مِّن نَّارٍ﴾ فعالم الإنسان

١ آ: شاطأ أو شطر؛ و: شاط أو شطن.

contains life. And just as cold can turn to freezing, its freezing is like the willful propensity of things to become fixed as determined objects, depending on their stage of manifestation and according to their preordained power and possibility. Therefore, within forms and shapes the divine Will is the realm of water.

The realm of earth, which is pure dryness, is the realm of Power, which is 12.13
nonmanifest in the Hyle, and is manifested through the dryness that freezes liquids. Liquids thereby become affixed in the realm of dense objects, such that the object of Power becomes realized in outward manifestation. Without the freezing, the object of Power would not manifest in the realm of Power.[95] The Seeing in this regard is in keeping with what these elements perceive of each other when they commingle. Were it not for divine seeing, the elements that mix to produce minerals, plants, and animals would not mix. Strive to understand this. The manifestation of the progeny is precisely through the sight that is from the Seeing.

You should know that what we have just mentioned is precisely a manifes- 12.14
tation at the stages of four suprasensory realities—namely, Life, Knowledge, Will, and Power. These are arranged according to their natural ranking; for in ranking them, each meaning possesses a specific non-sensory nature. These four names—the Living, the Knowing, the Willing, the Powerful—actualize the qualities of heat, wetness, cold, and dryness at their respective stages. From these determinations, other entities are determined, which are compounded and simple elements of the four elements: these include fire, which is from heat; air, which is from wetness; water, which is from cold; and earth, which is from dryness. The loci of manifestation of Life, Knowledge, Will, and Power are therefore heat, wetness, cold, and dryness, and their respective loci of manifestation are fire, air, water, and earth (as they are compounded from the former). Furthermore, through witnessing these four compounds, it is known that these are outward manifestations of the Living, the Knowing, the Willing, and the Powerful at a second cosmic stage. For nothing manifests other than the properties of the names, even if veiled intellects differ as to how they name them. The people of witnessing bear witness that the One who assumes those names is One. Moreover, these four elements are compounded in the four things generated from them: minerals, plants, animals, and humans.

In the human realm, man contains these four elements in his body. Fire is 12.15
dominant, and whatever is in excess (*shāṭa*) or goes to an extreme (*shaṭṭa*) is Satan (*Shayṭān*) and the jinn, created «from a smokeless fire».[96] In this realm,

هو الغالب على معنويّة نفسه وهي النار. وعالم الحيوان هو الغالب على معنويّة نفسه وهو الهواء فحياته بالحرارة والرطوبة ونفسه من النار إلّا أنّها مغلوبة وعالم النبات هو الماء ولذلك ضعف انتقاله كضعف انتقال الماء الناقص عن انتقال الهواء إلّا أنّ عالم الإنسان منصوب وعالم الحيوان مكبوب وعالم النبات مقلوب فرأس الإنسان إلى العلوّ ورأس الحيوان دونه معترض ورأس النبات في الأرض ورأس كلّ شيء ما منه يتغذّى.

١٦،١٢ أمّا الرابع وهو عالم المعادن فهو مغمور في الأرض لأنّ الأرض عالمه واليبس خاصّ بها فلهذا يتحرّك المعدن تحرّكاً يخرجه من الأرض مثل النبات إذ هو أقرب إلى النار التي هي النفس وقرب النبات حتّى شقّ الأرض ولبعده من النار بعداً هو أبعد من الهواء لم ينتقل النبات وانتقل الحيوان القريب من النار وهو عالم الهواء لكنّه لم يكن عالم النار نفسها فيكون منتصباً كالإنسان بل كان منحنياً ولم يكن منقلباً كالنبات لقربه وبعد النبات وكان الإنسان لأجل نفسه عالم النار والإنسان أكمل هذه الأربع لأنّ الإنسان فيه ما في الثلاثة ويختصّ بالنفس الناطقة مع أنّ فيه الحيوانيّة والنباتيّة والمعدنيّة والحيوان فيه النباتيّة والمعدنيّة وليس فيه الإنسانيّة والنبات فيه المعدنيّة وليس فيه الحيوانيّة ولا الإنسانيّة.

١٧،١٢ فالمولّدات على هذا هي أربعة وغلط من ظنّها ثلاثة فإنّه عدّ الإنسانَ من الحيوان ومعلوم أنّ النبات هو من المعدن والحيوان هو من النبات والإنسان هو من الحيوان لكنّه لا ينعكس فيها فيكون الحيوان من الإنسان والنبات من الحيوان والمعدن من النبات وهذا واضح بنفسه وظهور الاسم البصير في هذه الأطوار بمعنويّة ما يهتدي التركيب به فيها إلى الصواب وتكون الأسماء المذكورة منطوية فيه الحيّ والعالم والمريد والقادر ويدخل الظاهر في القادر فإنّ الظاهر بالقادر ظهر فيدخل الظاهر أيضاً في البصير بما به دخل القادر في البصير.

fire largely governs the self. In the animal realm, air largely governs the self. Thus, the animal's life is through heat and wetness, and its self is from fire, though it is dominated. The realm of plants, moreover, is water, which is why its motility is low, just as the motility of water is less than that of air. However, the human being is directed upward, while the animal is directed downward, and the plant is inverted. Thus, the head of a human being is uppermost, while the head of an animal stretches in front of it, and the head of the plant is in the earth. For the "head" of a thing is that by which it draws sustenance.

The fourth realm, the realm of minerals, is submerged in the earth: the 12.16
earth is its domain, and dryness is specific to it. This is why minerals, like plants, move in such a way that they come out of the earth, since dryness is closer to fire, which corresponds to the soul. Plants draw so close to the earth that they split it. They are more distant from fire than they are from air, which is why they do not move spatially, whereas animals, which are close to fire—the realm of air—move spatially. But since animals are not identical with the realm of fire, they cannot stand upright like a human being, but rather incline forward. Yet they are not entirely inverted like plants, for animals are close to fire, while plants are far from it. The human being corresponds to the realm of fire on account of his soul. He is therefore the most complete of these four worlds, for he contains what is in the other three and is distinguished by the rational soul while also containing the animal, vegetal, and mineral souls. The animal, for its part, contains the vegetal and the mineral realms, but not the human realm; and plants contain the mineral, but not the animal or human realms.

This being the case, the progenies are four, and those who think they are 12.17
three are mistaken. This is because they count the human being as an animal, it being well known that plants are from minerals, animals are from plants, and human beings are from animals. However, this succession is not reversible such that animals are from human beings, plants are from animals, and minerals are from plants. This much is self-evident. The manifestation of the Seeing at these stages accords with the pure meanings that ensure the process of compounding therein is appropriate. The Living, the Knowing, the Willing, and the Powerful are enfolded within these aforementioned names. The Manifest, moreover, is included within the Powerful, for the Manifest becomes manifest through the Powerful. Hence the Manifest is also included within the Seeing in the same manner as is the Powerful.

١٨،١٢ ولمّا كان الإنسان هو آخر الظهور والمتنوّر الذي أصله النور وظهر بما قبله من المراتب طالبته الأسماء السابقة على وجوده التي هي أصوله بأن تظهر أحكامها فيه مطالبة ذاتيّة فأجابها إجابته بالفعل فكان فيه الحيّ لأنّه حيّ وكان فيه العالم لأنّه عالم وكان فيه المريد لأنّه مريد وكان فيه القادر لأنّه قادر وكان فيه الظاهر لتعلّق الظاهر بالقادر في ظهوره فكان الإنسان ظاهرًا ولمّا كان السمع هو بصرما للأصوات فكان الإنسان سميعًا فكان بصيرًا بما سبق من الأطوار في وجوده لأنّا قد بيّنّا دخول هذه الأسماء في الاسم البصير فلمّا جمعها الإنسان وجب أن يكون بصيرًا فهو حيّ عليم قدير مريد ظاهر سميع بصير.

١٩،١٢ ولمّا كان العقل الأوّل الذي هو القلم الأعلى إنّما هو قلم لأنّه كاتب والكتابة نطق كان الإنسان هو القلم الأسفل فكان ناطقًا كنطق القلم إلّا أنّ القلم الأعلى كان نطقه معنويًا باطنًا وكان الإنسان في آخر السلسلة التي بين جسمه وبين القلم الأعلى فكان مقابلًا للقلم الأعلى فكان ناطقًا نطقًا مقابلًا لنطق المقابل له فكان نطق المقابل معنويًا فوجب أن يكون نطق الإنسان لفظيًا فنَطَق بالحرف والصوت وكان مجمع الحضرات الأسمائيّة بعد ترقّيه إلى الحضرة التي هي حضرة الحضرات وحينئذٍ يستحقّ أن يكون هو الحيّ العالم المريد القادر الظاهر السميع البصير المتكلّم. وظهر الحقّ سبحانه من طوره بهذه الأسماء ظهورًا بالفعل فإن شئت أن تجعل الحقيقة هي حياته وعلمه وإرادته وقدرته وظهوره وسمعه وبصره وإن شئت فاعكس فيه رؤيةَ وسمعَ الجزئيّات وكان ولا شيء معه حين فني في الذات.

Since the human being is the last in manifestation, and is the seeker of light whose origin is light, and is the one who manifests through the cosmic levels that precede him, the names that precede his existence and that are his roots seek him by their very essence in order to manifest their properties within him. He responds in actuality so that he has within him the Living because he is alive, the Knowing because he knows, the Willing because he wills, the Powerful because he has power, and the Manifest because the Manifest is attached to the Powerful when He manifests so that the human being is manifest. And since hearing is a kind of seeing of sounds, the human being hears. He also sees the cosmic levels that precede his existence, for we have explained how these names pertain to the Seeing, and he must necessarily be seeing since the human being brings together these names. He is thus living, knowing, powerful, willing, manifest, hearing, and seeing. **12.18**

Moreover, since the First Intellect, which is the Supreme Pen, is a pen precisely because it inscribes, and inscription is a form of rational speech, the human being is therefore the Lower Pen. He has rational speech just like the rational speech of the Pen, except that the rational speech of the Supreme Pen is nonmanifest and supersensory. The human being is at the end of the chain of being that extends between his body and the Supreme Pen. He is therefore the counterpart of the Supreme Pen, and he is endowed with rational speech in a manner that is a counterpart to the rational speech of the Pen. Since the rational speech of the Pen is supersensory, the human being's rational speech is necessarily verbal, such that he speaks in letters and sounds. He is, moreover, the gathering place of the presences of the names after his ascension to the Presence of Presences, whereupon he is worthy of being the living, the knowing, the willing, the able, the manifest, the hearing, the seeing, and the speaking. Moreover, the Real manifests at this stage through these names in an actual manner. You may thus consider His reality to be his life, knowledge, will, ability, manifestation, hearing, and seeing; or you may reverse it so that he is the sight and hearing of the particulars, and "he was and nothing was with him" when he passes away in the Essence. **12.19**

اسمه ذو الفضل

١،١٣ أوّل وروده في ترتيب سور الكتاب العزيز في البقرة في قوله تعالى ﴿وَٱللَّهُ ذُو ٱلْفَضْلِ ٱلْعَظِيمِ﴾ وانفرد بإيراده أبو بكر البيهقيّ رضي الله عنه وروي هذا الاسم عن محمّد بن إبراهيم عن أحمد بن محمّد بن غالب قال حدّثنا خالد بن محمد قال حدّثنا عبد العزيز بن حصين بن ثابت بن هشام بن حسّان عن محمّد بن سيرين عن أبي هريرة عن النبيّ صلّى الله عليه وسلّم وذكر الأسماء وقال في أوّلها الرحمٰن الرحيموقال في آخرها قبل ثلاثة أسماء وهي الخلّاق المولى النصير هذا الاسم الكريم وهو ذو الفضل ومعناه عند العلماء أنّه ذو فضل عظيم على عباده والفضل المزيد على تمام ما فيناسب أنّه العطاء لعباده عطاءً يفضل عن قدر حاجتهم لا عن قدر حاجته إذ لا حاجة له وهو الغنيّ بذاته فبقي أن يكون هو الزائد عن قدر حاجتهم.

٢،١٣ وهذا الاسم الكريم يتبع الاسم الخلّاق في إعطاء كلّ موجود خلقه ثمّ يتجاوزه في المزيد فيكون ذو الفضل خلّاقاً للمزيد فتدخل حقيقة الخلّاق في ذي الفضل في إعطاء المزيد فقط وإن شئت قلت إنّ ذا الفضل هو خصوص وصف في الخلّاق فإنّ الخلّاق تعالى خلق المزيد من مرتبة ذي الفضل والفاعل واحد وهو الله تعالى لكن من مراتب أسمائه العلى.

٣،١٣ وأوّل مراتب ظهور حكم هذا الاسم الكريم الذي هو ذو الفضل في سلسلة ترتيب عالمنا هذا لا في سلسلة أخرى من سلاسل لا تتناهى هو في مرتبة القلم الأعلى وذلك أنّ تعينه باعتبارين أحدهما أنّه صفة لموصوف أزليّ وهذا هو وجهه الذي لا يغايره الأزل فيه والثاني باعتبار أنّه موصوف بالإمكان فلذلك ظهر بعد فرض

Dhū l-Faḍl: The Bountiful

This name is first cited, according to the arrangement of the surahs of the Holy Book, in the verse: «God is magnificently bountiful».[97] Only al-Bayhaqī, may God be pleased with him, mentions this name as a name of God. It was reported in a prophetic tradition transmitted by Muḥammad ibn Ibrāhīm, from Aḥmad ibn Muḥammad ibn Ghālib, who cites Khālid ibn Muḥammad, who cites ʿAbd al-ʿAzīz ibn Ḥusayn ibn Thābit ibn Hishām ibn Ḥassān, from Muḥammad ibn Sīrīn, from Abū Hurayrah, from the blessed Prophet, who mentioned the names beginning with All-Merciful and Merciful, and ending with the noble name Bountiful, which is preceded by the names Ever-Creating, Patron, and Helper.[98] According to the scholars, the name the Bountiful denotes that He is magnificently bountiful toward His servants; and bounty here means an excess beyond the measure of fulfillment. It is thus appropriate to say that it is God's giving to His servants in a manner that bountifully surpasses the measure of their needs, not the measure of His need. For He has no need, since He is the Independent in His Essence. Therefore God's bounty is that which exceeds the measure of His servants' needs. 13.1

This noble name is subordinate to the Ever-Creating with regard to the bestowal of creation upon each existent. It then surpasses it in the excess of its giving, such that the Bountiful continuously creates in excess. The reality of the Ever-Creating is therefore included within the Bountiful only with regard to the excess of its giving. You may also say that the Possessor of Bounty refers to a specific quality in the Ever-Creating. For the Ever-Creating creates in excess from the level of the Bountiful. The agent is always the one God, though the actions proceed from the various levels of His supreme names. 13.2

The property of the noble name the Bountiful first becomes manifest at the level of the Supreme Pen. This, however, is with respect to the hierarchical chain of our world, not to any other of the infinite chains. For the Bountiful becomes actualized in two ways. On the one hand, bounty is the quality of an object that has no beginning—namely, the Pen. This is its aspect of beginninglessness that never undergoes change. On the other, the Bountiful assumes the quality of possibility. It therefore manifests in the wake of nonexistence—although, strictly speaking, nonexistence cannot be said to precede anything 13.3

سبق العدم له وإن لم يسبق العدم لشيء شيئاً إذ لا حقيقة للعدم وهذا هو وجه خلقيّة القلم الأعلى.

٤،١٣ فتتوجّه قوّة الاسم الخلّاق إليه حتّى يتعيّن تعيّناً مرتبياً فيكون مخلوقاً بالخلّاق تعالى ثمّ يظهر ذو الفضل في الخلّاق بعد تمام خلقيّة القلم الأعلى فيعطي الزيادة وهي ما في وجود القلم الأعلى بالقوّة من الموجودات التي بعده في السلسلة ولا شكّ أنّها فضل زائد على حقيقته فإذا تعيّن المزيد تعيّناً مرتبياً معنوياً تحقّق بذلك الترتّب حكم الاسم ذي الفضل تعالى.

٥،١٣ ثمّ يتسلّم الاسم الخلّاق ما هو بالقوّة في القلم الأعلى من تفاصيل الموجودات على ترتيب السلسلة التي هي عالم الخلق ويساوقها عالم الأمر مساوقة مساوية لتعيّناتها فلذلك يرى المشاهد سلسلة الترتيب التي هي عالم الخلق باعتبار ما أنّها عالم الأمر خصوصاً إذا غلب عليهم الفناء في التوحيد فإنّهم يعمون عن الخلق بالحقّ عمًى هو إبصار في التوحيد الصمديّ الذي لا نطول هنا بذكر شرحه فإذاً تلك المساوقة مستمرّة إلى عالم الإنسان الذي هو آخر المولّدات لكن تكون سلسلة الخلق أظهر حكماً عند المحجوبين بل لا يرون غير عالم الخلق كما لم ير الفانون في التوحيد الصمديّ شيئاً من عالم الخلق وإنّما الذين يرون الحالتين أعني السلسلة التي هي عالم الخلق والإطلاق الذي هو عالم الأمر المحقّقون وهم أهل نهاية السفر الثاني وربّما رأى ذلك أهل السفر الأوّل لكن يكونون مقهورين في غلبة رؤية عالم الخلق على عالم الأمر على قدر ما بقي فيهم من الغيريّة والمحقّقون ليس عليهم غلبة لمرتبة على مرتبة لأنّهم أهل العدل الإلٰهي.

٦،١٣ فنعود ونقول إنّ الاسم الخلّاق تعالى يتناول كلّ مرتبة من مراتب سلسلة عالم الخلق إذ هي مدرجته سلّماً يعطيها فيه خلقها ثمّ جميع ما يوجد فيها بالقوّة ممّا يتولّد عنها في المراتب التي بعدها في عالم الخلق هي مزيدات بالنسبة إلى خلقيّتها فيتولّاها

in anything, since it has no reality—and this is the created aspect of the Pen that undergoes change.

The potentiality of the Ever-Creating then approaches the Pen, which becomes determined in rank as a creation of the Ever-Creating. Once the Pen is created, the Bountiful manifests through the Ever-Creating by giving of its excess. This excess contains the subsequent existents along the chain that already exist in potentiality within the Pen, and which are undoubtedly a bounty that exceeds the reality of the Pen itself. Once this excess becomes determined as a supersensory rank, the property of the Bountiful is realized through that series of rankings. 13.4

The Ever-Creating then receives the potential particularities of existents in the Supreme Pen, arranged according to the hierarchy of the chain, which is the realm of creation. The realm of the command, moreover, transmits those particularities in a manner that corresponds to their determined entities in the realm of creation.[99] This is why the witnesser of the hierarchical chain—namely, the realm of creation—beholds it as though it were the realm of the command, especially if he is overcome by annihilation in divine oneness and is blinded by God from seeing created beings. This blindness is itself an insight into the oneness of divine self-sufficiency, which we shall not dwell on at length here. Thus, this correspondence between the two worlds persists down to the human realm: the human is the final progeny. However, the ruling properties of the chain of creation are more apparent to veiled intellects, who in fact behold only the realm of creation. Conversely, those who are annihilated in the oneness of divine self-sufficiency behold nothing whatsoever of the realm of creation. Those who behold both cases—the chain of the realm of creation, and non-delimitation, which is the realm of the command—are the ones who know the reality of things and who reach the end of the second journey. It may happen that those who are on the first journey also behold the realm of the command, but their beholding of the realm of creation overpowers that of the realm of the command to the degree that they retain a certain amount of alterity. By contrast, those who know the reality of things are not overpowered by one level over another, for they are the people of divine equilibrium. 13.5

To return to our initial point: We say that the Ever-Creating subsumes every level of the chain of the realm of creation. For these are arranged in degrees like a ladder, along the rungs of which the Ever-Creating creates them. Furthermore, all things that exist potentially in the chain are generated from it in the subsequent levels of the realm of creation. These are "excesses" in relation 13.6

الاسم ذو الفضل بما فيها من الفضل الزائد على وجودها وهكذا أبدًا كلّما أعطى الخلّاق الخلقيّة أعطى ذو الفضل المزيد في ترتيب أنّ كلّ شيء إنّما يكون من شيء فإنّ العدم لا يكون منه الشيء.

٧،١٣ فإذًا كلّ شيء من شيء إلى أن ينتهي الخلق إلى آخر السلسلة وهو طور الإنسان ونعني بالإنسان الإنسان الكامل ومن طور هذا الإنسان يرجع الاسم الخلّاق من خلقيّة صور الموجودات وأرزاقهم وأعمالهم وأزمنتهم وأمكنتهم وكيفيّاتهم وكمّيّاتهم وأوضاعهم وملكاتهم وأفعالهم وانفعالاتهم المعلومة في العقول إلى خلقيّات أخرى ترجع من الاسم الذي ظهر بالخلّاق أخيرًا وهو الاسم الآخِر باعتبار الخلقيّة إلى ما سنذكره وهو ما يرد على العارفين في سلوكهم ممّا يخلقه الاسم الخلّاق في بواطنهم من معاني المعرفة التي مدرجتها من الأذكار لا من الأفكار فتعيّن من هذه الخلقيّات أحوال في السلوكات بحسب كلّ سالك ما لا ينضبط تحت عبارة لكثرته وهي خلقيّات في أطوار سالكين إليه تعالى إلّا أنّ للاسم الخلّاق في هؤلاء مسلكين أحدهما ما ذكرناه والآخر ما يتعيّن بخلاقيّة الخلّاق في عقول المصيبين ظاهر الحقّ من أهل الأفكار وهم أقلّ من القليل.

٨،١٣ ويتعيّن من الخلّاق نسبة يمازجها الاسم المضلّ وهي ما يتعيّن في أذهان المحجوبين ممّا يظنّونه علمًا وليس به وما ليس به فقد يكون ظنًّا وقد يكون شكًّا وقد يكون وهمًا فهذه المخلوقات الذهنيّة أظهرها الاسم الخلّاق بممازجة اسم المضلّ ويتناول ذو الفضل في كلّ مرتبة ما يتعيّن أنّه يزيد على ما عيّنه الخلّاق من تلك الخلقيّات فيمضي فيه حكم ذي الفضل بمقدار ما يتعدّى مرتبة ذلك المخلوق وقبل تعيّن مرتبة ما سيُخلق منه فإذا أخذ الخلّاق في ظهور الطور الذي بعد المخلوق تقهقر ذو الفضل تقهقرًا مرتبيًا وخلّى بين الاسم الخلّاق تعالى وبين إنشاء ذلك المخلوق فإن كان ذلك المخلوق النفسانيّ تجلّيًا إلٰهيًا أو في مدرجة التعرّف الذي سوف يصير إلٰهيًا أو

to their createdness, and so the Bountiful presides over them inasmuch as they possess bounty that exceeds their existence. And so it is without end: each time the Ever-Creating bestows createdness, the Bountiful gives excess. This follows from the fact that all things that exist must proceed from something else, and nothing proceeds from nonexistence.

Therefore, all things proceed from other things until creation reaches the end of the chain. This is the stage of the human being; and by human being we mean the perfect human being. From the stage of this human being, the Ever-Creating begins its return from the state of createdness of the forms of existents and their provisions, deeds, times, places, modalities, quantities, situations, and habitudes, as well as the mental actions and reactions that occur in the intellects, in addition to other aspects of createdness. These return from the name the Last that finally manifests with respect to createdness from the Ever-Creating, unto what we shall now describe. These forms are what the recognizers experience in their wayfaring. They are pure meanings of recognition that are created by the Ever-Creating within them. Their provenance comes by way of invocations, not reflective thoughts. From these creations, the states of wayfaring become determined for each wayfarer, and they are too many to be captured in one sentence, for they are creations in the stages of the wayfarers to God.[100] However, the Ever-Creating follows two pathways for these wayfarers. The first is that of invocations, as we have just noted. The second is what becomes, through the creativity of the Ever-Creating, a determination in the intellects of those who, among those who reflect, attain the outward dimension of the truth—and they are the smallest minority. 13.7

There is also a relation that is determined by the mixing of the Ever-Creating with the Misguider. This is what becomes determined in the minds of veiled intellects, who mistake it for knowledge, though it is not; and if something is not knowledge, it can only be conjecture, doubt, or delusion. These mental constructs are manifested by the Ever-Creating when it mixes with the Misguider. The Bountiful, moreover, engages at every level with that which exceeds the created things that are determined by the Ever-Creating. The property of the Bountiful then subsumes that created thing according to the degree to which it surpasses that creature's level, stopping short of the determination of the level of that which is to be created from it. As such, when the Ever-Creating begins to manifest the successive stage of that created thing, the Bountiful withdraws progressively in rank, leaving a gap between the Ever-Creating and its configuration of that created thing. If the created thing happens to be 13.8

قد صار قائماً يشارك الخلّاق بالامتزاج الاسمُ الهادي لا الاسم المضلّ وإن كانت تلك المخلوقات الذهنيّة ليست في مدرجة التعريف الإلٰهيّ فإنّما يمازج الاسم الخلّاق فيها الاسم المضلّ.

٩،١٣ وفي هذه المعاني يحتاج السالكون إلى الشيخ الذي قد قطع السفر الثاني وهو في السفر الثالث ليخلّص السالكين ممّا يخلقه الاسم الخلّاق في أذهانهم وأنفسهم بالاسم المضلّ ممّا لا يتناسب السلوك الحقّ وذلك بأن ينهاهم الشيخ المذكور أن يتّبعوا ما خلقه الله تعالى في وجود أذهانهم ممّا رسمه الخلّاق بمدد الاسم المضلّ وينقلهم إلى ما رسمه الخلّاق في وجود أذهانهم وأنفسهم من أحكام الاسم الهادي فيحيي رقيقة حكم الاسم الهادي في وجود أنفسهم بالاسم المحيي عزّ وجلّ ويميت رقيقة حكم الاسم المضلّ في وجود أنفسهم بالاسم المميت إذ هو أعني الشيخ نائب حضرة الحضرات وحقيقة الحقائق ويسلك الشيخ بهم طريق استعداداتهم فلا يسلك بأحد في طريق استعداد غيره إلّا في أمور تشترك استعداداتهم فيها فتلك أمور يعطيهم القول فيها كلّيّاً وينفصل في وجود أنفسهم مفصّلاً لكنّه يكون متفاوتاً تفاوتاً لا يحسّونه هم ويحسّه الشيخ ويكون لفظ الشيخ كالاسم المشترك للمعاني التي تتعيّن لكلّ منهم بحسب استعداده فإنّ الاستعدادات أيضاً لا تتشابه ما تشابه منها من كلّ وجه ولا في كلّ معنًى واحد إذ لا تكرار في الوجود الحقّ ثمّ يبقى الخلّاق وذو الفضل تارة مع الاسم الهادي وتارة مع الاسم المضلّ إلى أن يصل أهل الاسم الهادي إلى مبالغ استعداداتهم فيقف كلّ واحد عند طوره الخاصّ به ويتعدّى الكُمّل إلى الحضرة الإلٰهيّة ويتفاوتون فيها إلى آخر الأسفار الأربعة.

١٠،١٣ وأمّا أتباع الاسم المضلّ فينقطعون في مبالغ جهلهم بحسب مراتب اسعداداتهم في ذلك الجهل أيضاً وينقسمون قسمين انقساماً مرتبياً يظهر حكمه في الحسّ قسم منهما يتخلّصون بالاسم السريع الحساب في موقف الآخرة فيلحقون بأولائك الذين هم أتباع الاسم الهادي وذلك لأنّ الاسم الهادي يتفقّدهم فيخلّص من النار من في قلبه حبّة

a divine self-disclosure within the soul, or if it ensues from a direct recognition that will become divine, or if it becomes a subsistent created form, then it shares in the Ever-Creating by mixing with the Guide, not the Misguider. But if the created things are mental and do not ensue from divine recognition, then it is the mixing of the Ever-Creating with the Misguider.

For these pure meanings, the wayfarers need a master who has traversed the second journey and is himself on the third. He can thereby free the wayfarers from what the Ever-Creating creates in their minds and souls through the Misguider, which is not proper to true wayfaring. The master will forbid them from following what God creates when the Ever-Creating inscribes in their mental existence with the ink of the Misguider. He directs them to what the Ever-Creating inscribes in their mental and psychological existence through the properties of the Guide, thereby giving life to the subtle properties of the Guide within their psychological existence through the Life-Giver, and terminating the subtle properties of the Misguider in their souls through the Death-Giver. For the master is the deputy of the Presence of Presences and the Reality of Realities. He will lead the wayfarers along the course of their own levels of preparedness, with the net effect that none is led along anyone else's path except with respect to what they share in terms of their levels of preparedness. The master will instruct them in these matters in general terms, but his instructions will be differentiated in particular details. This disparity is not sensed by them, though it is sensed by the master. For the speech of the master has many common meanings, and each word is understood differently by the disciples in accordance with their preparedness. The preparedness of one wayfarer is never identical to that of another in every respect, and not even in a single meaning, for there is no repetition in true existence. Therefore, the Ever-Creating and the Bountiful at times remain with the Guide, and at times with the Misguider, until those who follow the Guide reach their full potential, each arriving at his specific stage. The perfected wayfarers, moreover, go beyond to the divine presence, but there is also disparity among them until the end of the four journeys. 13.9

As for the followers of the Misguider, they vary in their measure of ignorance according to their levels of preparedness for ignorance. They are divided by rank into two groups in such a manner that their properties are manifest in the sensory realm. One group among them is saved by the Swift in Reckoning at the plane of the resurrection. They join the followers of the Guide, because the Guide seeks them out, saving from the Fire whoever has the slightest amount of good in his heart. The followers of the Misguider remain, and they are "the 13.10

من خردل من الخير ويبقى أتباع الاسم المضلّ وهم أهل النار الذين هم أهلها فإذا تجلّى الاسم الرحمٰن بأن تحوّل لهم في الصورة التي يعرفونه فيها كما ورد في الحديث سجدوا سجودًا على ظهورهم لأنّ التجلّي أتاهم من حيث لم يحتسبوا وهو الوراء المذكور فرأوا فيه عقائدهم من جهة وحدانيّة الاسم الأحد وهو أحديّة الجمع وحينئذ تغشاهم الرحمة فيتنعّمون بالنار وتكون ملائمة لهم بحيث يكون كملاءمة أهل الجنّة للجنّة فلا تشتهي طائفة من هاتين الطائفتين أن تنتقل إلى حيث الأخرى ويتولّى المزيدات من النعيم للطائفتين الاسم ذو الفضل تبارك وتعالى فسبحان من يتصرّف بوجوده في وجوده من مراتب أسمائه وصفاته على عدل من اسمه العادل عزّ وجـلّ.

اسمه الوليّ جلّ وعلا

آيتـه في البقرة و﴿مَا لَكُم مِّن دُونِهِۦ مِن وَلِيٍّ﴾ وهو ممّا اتّفق عليه الأئمّة الثلاثة ١،١٤
والولاية في لسان العلم لها مراتب فمنها ولايته تعالى للمؤمنين وهي بمعنى النصرة ولذلك نفى عن الكافرين النصرة والوليّ والنصير في هذه الرتبة بمعنًى واحد وقد يكون بمعنى المتولّي أمرهم ومنه وليّ الصبيّ والوليّ في عقدة النكاح ووليّ المال والولاية فوق هذا المقام وهو مقام الإحسان وهو مقام أن تعبد الله كأنّك تراه وهو أعلى من مقام فإنّه يراك وهذه الولاية بمعنى وليني أي ليس بيني وبينه حاجز كما تقول هذا يلي هذا لكنّ الولاية في هذا المقام هي على التشبيه بالولاية الحقيقيّة لا أنها هي إذ الولاية الحقيقيّة هي حضرة الاسم القيّوم وهو الذي قام به كلّ شيء.

people of the Fire who are its inhabitants."[101] When the All-Merciful discloses itself to them by becoming transformed into a form that they recognize, as mentioned in the well-known prophetic tradition, they prostrate themselves, but on their backs. For the self-disclosure reaches them from whence they do not expect, which is the "behind" mentioned in the prophetic tradition.[102] They see therein their beliefs in respect to the only-ness of the Only, which is the oneness of the all, and then mercy envelops them and they find bliss in the Fire. The Fire becomes agreeable to them just as the Garden is agreeable to the people of the Garden, such that no group has any desire to move to the other group's abode, and the Bountiful presides over the blissful excess for both groups.[103] So glory be to the One who governs His existence by His existence, from the levels of His names and qualities with justice, through His name the Just!

Al-Walī: The Guardian

This name, which occurs in the verse: «you have no Guardian other than He»,[104] is among the names that the three eminent scholars agree upon as being divine. In the language of scholarship, guardianship has several meanings. One of them is God's "assistance" for the believers, meaning His help. This is why He denies the unbelievers His help. In this level, the name Guardian is synonymous with Helper. Guardian can also mean a guardian over someone's affairs; whence the guardian of a child, the guardian of a marital contract,[105] and the guardian of a property. The guardianship above this level is the guardianship of spiritual excellence, which is the station of "to worship God as if you see Him,"[106] which is higher than the station of "He sees you."[107] This meaning of the word guardianship (*wilāyah*) derives from the verb "to follow" or "to lie next to" (*waliya*). In this sense, guardianship denotes that there is no barrier between me and him, just as one uses that verb to say "this adjoins that." But even the meaning of guardianship as used of this station is only a semblance of the true meaning of guardianship, and not identical with it, for true guardianship is the presence of the Self-Subsisting, the One by Whom all things subsist. 14.1

٢،١٤ ثمّ الولاية في المقام الذي فوق مقام الإحسان هي ولاية السكينة وحقيقتها أنّ العبد يحسّ بشهود الحقّ من وراء حجاب شفّاف فيسكن لما يرى من أنّه الفاعل رؤية شفّافة كالظلّ الذي هو على صورة الشخص وليس به إذ صاحب هذا المقام ثابت في برزخ بين الحجاب والكشف ولم يفن من رسمه بالتوحيد بعدُ شيء وأمّا ولاية ما فوق هذا المقام فإن كان أهله في مقام المحبّة وهي فوق مقام السكينة أيضاً بل هي من لواحقها فإنّ المحبّ يستجلي المحبوب في سرّه لا حقيقة بل تمثيلا كمقام السكينة فالسكينة كالباب للمحبّة أو المحبّة منتهى السكينة فإنّ السكن هو المحبوب في اللغة فإذا قال المحبّ يا سكني فإنّما قال يا حبيبي فإذاً مقام المحبّة متّصل بمقام السكينة والفرق بينهما أنّ صاحب مقام السكينة هو ساكن القلب إلى تجلّي المحبوب وأمّا المحبّ فطائر القلب متحرّك الجوانح مشتاق وصاحب مقام السكينة تعوزه هذه الحركة.

٣،١٤ واعلم أنّ بين كلّ مقامين مقام سكينة بنسبة تلك المقامات كان حقيقتها كسكون المصلّي بين الركعتين من الصلاة وكالاستراحة بين السجود والقيام وأمّا المحبّة فإنّها كالركن نفسه إلّا أنّ مقام المحبّة وإن كان فوق مقام السكينة فإنّ كلّاً منهما من مقامات المحجوبين ومن مراتب الطالبين لا المطلوبين.

٤،١٤ وإذا علمت هذا فاعلم أنّ الوليّ الحقّ تعالى لأهل هذين المقامين هو وليّ محادثة ومخاطبة تمثيليّة والخطاب بالحرف والصوت أكثره من هذا المقام فإن خوطب بها أهل الشهود الأسمائيّ فإنّما يخاطَبون بها بمقتضى ما بقي من رسومهم لا من حيث ما تجلّى لهم من التجلّيات الأسمائيّة وأكثر المدّعين للمشيخة هم من هذين المقامين وهم يظنّنون أنّه ليس فوق هذا شيء ولست أعني المشايخ الكاذبين نعوذ بالله من أولئك وإنّما المراد بالمشايخ الصادقون أهل الخطاب الواقفون على ما يظنّنون أنّه هو الباب

Then the guardianship in the station above the station of spiritual excellence is the guardianship of tranquility. Its true nature is that the servant witnesses the Real from behind a semitransparent veil, and is tranquil at the sight of Him as the agent. This vision is as translucent as a shadow that is in the form of a person, yet the shadow is not actually that person. For the one who is in this station is fixed in a liminal position between veiling and unveiling. Some of his traces have not yet passed away in divine oneness. As for the guardianship that is above this station, if the person is in the station of love—which is above the station of tranquility as well, and is in fact one of its ancillaries—then the lover uncovers the Beloved in his inmost heart; not in reality, but rather as an imaginal form that is like the translucent shadow in the station of tranquility, for tranquility is like a door to love, or love is the furthest boundary of tranquility. For, linguistically, tranquility refers to the beloved, as when a lover proclaims, "O my tranquility"; what he is actually saying is, "O my beloved." Therefore, the station of love is connected to the station of tranquility. The difference between the two is that the heart of the person in the station of tranquility finds tranquility in the disclosure of the Beloved, whereas the heart of the lover flies with the wings of yearning. But the person in the station of tranquility is incapable of such movement. 14.2

Between each station there is a station of tranquility that, in relation to them, is their reality. This is like the stillness of a person when he is between the two cycles of prayer, or like his position when he rests between prostration and standing. Love is like the pillar of prayer itself.[108] And although the station of love is above the station of tranquility, both are nonetheless stations of veiled intellects. They pertain to the ranks of those who are seekers, not those who are sought. 14.3

When you understand this, then you must understand that the true Guardian of those who stand in these two stations is the Guardian of imaginal discourse and speech. For most speech that occurs through sounds and letters arises from these stations. As such, when those who witness the names are addressed in this manner, they are addressed in this manner only insofar as some of their traces remain, not insofar as they have experienced the disclosures of the names.[109] Moreover, the majority of those who claim to be spiritual masters occupy one of these two stations, and they presume that nothing could be higher. Now, I do not mean the charlatan masters—we seek refuge in God from them—but rather the sincere masters who hear imaginal speech and who stand before what they consider to be the door. They stand there forever, 14.4

وأسرارهم أبدًا واقفة تنتظر أن يأتيها الفتّاح بعطايا الاسم الوهّاب فالاسم الوليّ هنا له ولاية لهم بمقدارهم وجارية في مضمارهم.

٥،١٤ وأمّا الولاية التي فوق هذا وهي ولاية أهل الشهود الجزئيّ الذي هو الأسمائيّ فهي ولاية الحقّ تعالى لعبده من حضرة ذلك الاسم الذي تجلّى له أو الأسماء التي تجلّى الحقّ تعالى لعبده من أطوارها وأهل هذا المقام هم العبادلة وقد ذكر الشيخ محيي الدين في معناهم كتابًا سمّاه كتاب العبادلة فإنّ من تجلّى له الاسم من حضرة المعطي فإنّما اسمه في هذه الحضرة عبد المعطي وكذلك سائر الأسماء فإنّ لكلّ اسم عبوديّة لعبد هو المختصّ بتلك الرتبة مع أنّ كلّ اسم فلله تعالى عباد من حيث ذلك الاسم متفاوتون في العبوديّة له في تلك الرتبة بحسب اختلاف مشاهدهم لذلك الاسم وتفاوت استعداداتهم في قبول تجلّيه والحقّ تعالى ليس له حسب من حيث ذاته وإنّما هي مراتب غيبيّة تظهر أحكامها في أهل مقامات التجلّي.

٦،١٤ وإذا حقّقت القول في هذا المقام الذي نحن في ذكره وجدت العبد باستعداده هو الذي أعطى الحقّ رتبة ربوبيّة له من ذلك الطور وحاصل هذا أنّ من وقف به الاستعداد عند طور عبوديّة قام في مقابلة وقوفه طور ربوبيّة له حتّى لو لم يقف الواقف ذلك الوقوف لم تكن للربوبيّة في ذلك المقام نسبة محقّقة وهذا الكلام ينكره القوم الذين لم يعرفوا معنى الحقيقة ويعترضهم الشكّ من جهة العقيدة فيقولون هل الحقّ هو الذي يسبق إلى إقامة الرتبة أو العبد فإن قلتم العبد كما قرّرتم كان للعبوديّة الرتبة العليا على الربوبيّة والأمر بالعكس.

٧،١٤ ولا يعلمون أنّ العبوديّة والربوبيّة اسمان من أسماء العزّة لا يفتخر السابق منهما على مسبوقه إذ ليس القائم في رتبة منهما غير القائم في الرتبة الأخرى باعتبار وحدانيّة الذات وإذا كانت الأحكام المتقابلة إنّما هي لواحد وفي واحد وبواحد

with their inmost secret waiting for the Opener to bring them gifts from the Bestower. Here, the Guardian has a guardianship over them commensurate with their measure, which floods their consciousness.

As for the guardianship that is above this, it is the guardianship of those who have partial witnessing, or the witnessing of the names. For this is the guardianship of the Real over His servant from the presence of the name that discloses itself to him, or the names that the Real discloses to His servant at different stages. Those who are in this station are the worshippers, about whom Shaykh Muḥyī l-Dīn ibn al-ʿArabī wrote his work *The Servants of God*. For when the name is disclosed to someone from the presence of the Giver, his name at that presence is none other than the Servant of the Giver. The same goes for all the other names. After all, every name possesses a type of servanthood specific to a servant singled out for that particular rank. And in fact, for each of His names, God has servants with respect to that name. There is a disparity in their servanthood at that rank, and this disparity is in respect to the differences in their witnessing of that name as well as their preparedness to receive the disclosure of that name. Yet the Real, in respect to His Essence, has no relationality; these are none other than unseen levels whose properties manifest within the disclosure stations of the wayfarers. 14.5

Now, if you truly understand the words we are saying in this station, you will discover that it is the servant's preparedness that bestows the rank of lordship upon the Real at any given stage. As a result, when the preparedness of the servant reaches a certain stage of servanthood, the corresponding stage of lordship stands counter to it. As such, if the servant were not to be in that standing place, the lordship appropriate to that station would not be actualized either. This discourse, however, is rejected by those who do not recognize the meaning of true reality and suffer from doubt in their creed. They say, "Is it the Real who first establishes the rank, or is it the servant? If you say it is the servant—as you claim—this would mean that servanthood possesses superiority over Lordhood, when in fact it is the opposite." 14.6

They do not know that servanthood and lordship are both names of exaltedness, and that neither is above the other. For, in view of the oneness of the Essence, the one who occupies one rank is precisely the one who occupies the other. And since opposing properties belong to, are in, and are through the One, how could some properties be more eminent than others? It is the words of the separative realm of all-comprehensive oneness that articulate relations between the two presences. These presences are exactly the same, whether one is the 14.7

فكيف يشرف فيها بعضها على بعض وإنّما ألسنة الفرق الجمعيّ الوحدانيّ تنطق بنسب ما بين كلّ حضرتين سواء كانت إحداهما حضرة ربوبيّة والأخرى حضرة عبوديّة أو كانت حضرتي ربّ أو حضرتي عبد أو كانت حضرة واحدة هي حضرة محو وسواء كان ذلك المحو حضرة جهل وغيبة كما في الأطفال والبله أو حضرة محو في التوحيد وتلك الألسنة الناطقة عن هذه المراتب هي المترجمة ولها لغة لا يعرفها إلّا الذاتيّون أعني أهل البقاء بعد الفناء من طور نهاية السفر الثاني وسيّد أهل هذا المقام هو القطب ووزراؤه هما الإمامان ومن هذه الطائفة الرسل في زمان الرسل والمسلّكون على سبيلهم من أتباعهم بعد زمان الرسل وهو الزمان الذي بعد زمان نبيّنا عليه السلام.

٨،١٤ فقد علمت مقام ولاية اسم الوليّ في أطوار العارفين وهم أهل التجلّيات الجزئيّة وليس للربوبيّة المختصّة بالولاية مقام فوق هذا المقام فإنّ المقام الذي فوق هذا لا يبقى فيه نسبة ربّ ومربوب فالولاية لا تكون في الفردانيّة بل في ثنويّة ما وأمّا الفردانيّة فمقام الوقفة إذ ليس فيها واقف وإلّا فلا وقفة والولاية لا تكون إلّا بين اثنين.

٩،١٤ وللاسم الوليّ حضرة مغايرة لهذه الحضرة التي سبق الكلام في تفصيلها ومنشأ حكم الاسم الوليّ في هذا الكلام المستأنف على العكس من منشأ حضرة الاسم الوليّ باعتبار الاسم الأوّل وذلك لأنّا اعتبرنا الابتداء هناك من مقام الإيمان ويكون الحقّ هو الوليّ تعالى لعبده وأمّا في هذا الاعتبار فيكون القطب تقدّس اسمه هو وليّ ربّه عزّ وجلّ ولاية يكون اشتقاقها من ولي الشيء إذا لم يكن بينه وبينه واسطة وذلك لأنّ القطب إذا أخذ في السفر الثالث وهو تنزّله إلى أطوار من دونه وهو لا يرى في الأطوار غيرًا فيقابل كلّ من يقابله مقابلة عبد يلي ربًّا يعرفه فينزل في الأطوار بأنواع الاعتبار فيجد في مقام المحجوبين ربّ العزّة ظهر بالذلّ والقادر ظهر بالعجز كما جاء في

presence of lordship and the other of servanthood, or whether both are presences of the lord, or whether both are presences of the servant, or whether it is one presence which is the presence of effacement and whether that effacement is the presence of ignorance and unawareness (as we find in children and simpletons), or the presence of effacement in divine oneness. These are the words that speak on behalf of those levels and are its spokespersons, and they possess a language that is recognized by none but those who are absorbed in the Essence—by which I mean those who subsist after annihilation in the stage of the second journey. The chief of those who occupy this station is the axial saint,[110] and his viziers are the two Leaders. Among this group are the Messengers in the age of Messengers, and their followers who travel the path in subsequent generations—that is, the generations that came after our blessed Prophet.

You now know the station of guardianship that comes from the Guardian and that pertains to the stages of the recognizers privy to partial self-disclosures. Moreover, the lordship of guardianship has no station above it, for in what is above this station there is no more Lord-vassal relationship. This is because guardianship does not pertain to nonduality but only to some form of duality. As for nonduality, it is to arrive at the station of halting where there is no one who halts.[111] And if there is no one who halts, then there is no halting. Guardianship, on the other hand, only occurs when there is both one who halts and halting. 14.8

The Guardian also has a presence that contrasts with what we have just explained in detail. The fountainhead of the property of the Guardian in the aforementioned discussion is the opposite of the fountainhead of the presence of the Guardian from the standpoint of the First. For in the former, we consider the starting point to be the station of belief, and the Real to be the Guardian over His servant. But from the perspective of the present discussion, it is the axial saint—blessed be his name—who is the guardian of his Lord. His guardianship derives from the verb "to lie next to a thing"—that is, there is no intermediary between him and Him. For when the axial saint sets out on the third journey, which is his descent to the stages of those beneath him, he sees no alterity in the stages and therefore encounters everything in the way a servant attached to a Lord would. He thus descends into the stages from various standpoints and discovers in the stations of veiled intellects the Mighty Lord manifesting Himself in lowliness, and the Powerful manifesting Himself in powerlessness. Thus, in the sacred tradition, God says, "I was hungry but you did not feed Me."[112] When the Mighty manifests Himself as the lowly, it is might; and when the Powerful manifests as the powerless, it is power. Moreover, the manifestation of each 14.9

حديث جعتُ فلم تطعمني وظهور العزيز بالذلّ عزّ كما أنّ ظهور القادر بالعجز قدرة وظهور كلّ حقيقة في طور مقابلها من الأسماء التي يجهلها المحجوبون ظهور ينزّهه القطب ويستمدّه الضدّ.

ومن لم ير الحقيقة في الظلم فما رآها في الأنوار وإنّما ينكر المتطوّر من أنكر الأطوار ١٠،١٤
وأنت تعلم من هذا أنّ القطب يلي كلّ حقّ متجلّ ولاية متحلّ غير متخلّ فيأنس الربّ في أطواره بعبده الجاري على مضماره ويقول له لسان الربّ من أطواره عبدي أنت الصاحب في السفر وأنت الخليفة في الأهل والمال والوطن وعلامة ما أقوله أنّ القطب علينا سلامه لا ينكره عقل ولا ذوق بل يجده كلّ صاحب مبلغ في مبلغه وتدّعيه كلّ طائفة إذا كاشفها في مبلغها وتراه عين مبلغها ولا شكّ أنّ الأطوار علوًّا وسفلًا ما عمرها إلّا الواحد فإن لحقه الاغتراب وبُعد كما بعدت بينه وبين الوحدانيّة الأنساب فوليّه العبد المتفرّق الذات على كلّ مراتب الحجاب فنفس وجدان حقيقة القطب في طور تجلّي الربّ هي الولاية منه لربّه التي يستأنس بها المتجلّي في أطوار حجبه وهو المنشد أعني الوليّ المذكور

وَمَا ٱسْتَلَمْتُ وَمَا قَبَّلْتُ مِنْ حَجَرٍ إِلَّا وَحَالُ سُلَيْمَى فِي مَكَامِنِهِ

اسمه النصير تبارك وتعالى

انفرد بذكره الغزاليّ رحمة الله عليه ومحلّه من سورة البقرة قوله تعالى ﴿وَلَا نَصِيرٍ أَمْ تُرِيدُونَ﴾ والنصير من النصرة فحيث وجدتها فثمّ النصير سبحانه وتعالى. ١،١٥

reality at the stage of a contrary name of which veiled intellects are ignorant is a manifestation through which the axial saint affirms divine transcendence and from which opposites derive.[113]

The one who does not see the truth in darkness will not see it in the light, and only those who deny the stages of wayfaring reject the one who is traversing them. From this you know that the axial saint is adjoined to every disclosed reality by way of adornment, not withdrawal. The Lord thus finds intimacy at each of His stages through His servant as he proceeds along his journey. About his stages, the Lord says, "My servant! You are the companion in My journey, the vicegerent over family, property, and homeland."[114] The proof of what I say is that the axial saint is not rejected by the intellect or by tasting, and whoever attains their furthest end finds him in his attainment, and each group claims him when he unveils himself to its members at the level of their attainment, and when they behold him with the eyes appropriate to their level of attainment. There is no doubt, moreover, that the stages above and below are occupied by none other than the One. And when the axial saint is overcome by separation, and grows distant just as the relations between him and divine oneness grow distant, then His guardian is the servant whose essence is dispersed across all the levels of the veil. Thus the experience of the reality of the axial saint at the level of the self-disclosure of the Lord is the very same as his guardianship of his Lord, through which the Discloser finds intimacy in the stages of His veils. He—this same Friend of God—sings: 14.10

Whenever I kiss or embrace the Black Stone,
I find my beloved Sulaymā hiding there.[115]

Al-Naṣīr: The Helper

Only al-Ghazālī mentions this name as a name of God. Its first place of occurrence is in the Surah of the Cow in the verse: «Apart from God, you have neither Guardian nor Helper».[116] Helper is from the word "help" or "assistance." The Helper is wherever you find help. 15.1

٢،١٥ واعلم أنّ الاسم النصير عامّ الحكم يدخل فيه الاسم الواسع فيسع كلّ طور فأمّا ظهوره أوّل ظهوراته المرتبيّة فهو أنّه نصر الغيب على الشهادة فأظهر الغائب على الشاهد فأقام الأزل في أطوار الحدوث إلى أن جلاّه بلسان الخاتم المبعوث هذا عند استعمال النصير للاسم الهادي وإقامته منه في مراتب البارئ وعند استعماله للمضلّ انتهى به من حضرة إبليس الأكبر إلى مرتبة الدجّال الذي سيظهر.

٣،١٥ واعلم أنّ كلّ مغالبة ظهر فيها أحد المتغالبين على الآخر فالاسم النصير بها عَلَم ولتصرّفه فيها حكم فإذا تقابلت الأسماء أو تمانعت الصفات ثمّ غلب غالب فبحكم للاسم النصير واعتبر ذلك في الحضرتين اللّتين انقسمت إليهما الأسماء وهما حضرة الله وحضرة الرحمٰن تجد بين الوجود وبين المراتب تباينًا وتغالبًا وذلك لأنّ المراتب عدميّة والرحمانيّة وجوديّة فالاسم النصير يتصرّف للمراتب فيجعل الوجود طوعها وذلك لأنّ المرتبة تنفعل فتوجد فعل الفاعل وتقسّم الوجود وتنقله من اسمه إلى اسم الموجود وتظهرا مرتبيّة.[1]

٤،١٥ ويقوم أيضاً بنصر الوجود فلا يبدو سواه ولا يخصّ[2] غيره فيكون مستعملاً في ذلك الاسم الظاهر. وللاسم النصير في مراتب العقول نصرة الحقّ على الباطل وفي مراتب الظنون نصرة الباطل على الباطل نصرة تشبه نصرة الحقّ على الباطل وليس بها وله في الخيال نصرة وفي المزاج نصرة فينصر أحد الممتزجات إمّا إلى تكوين وإمّا إلى إفساد فإنّ النصرة قد تكون للباطل قال عليه السلام لا تمنّوا لقاء العدوّ فإنّهم ينصَرون كما تنصَرون فللاسم النصير عناية بالكفّار كما له عناية بالمؤمنين الأبرار وإذا اعتبرت أحوال الاسم النصير تعالى لم تجد أكثر المراتب خالية عنه فإنّ الاسم النصير إذا نصر بلغ كلّ مبلغ فيما يؤلّف كنصرة الحقّ على الباطل والاعتدال على الانحراف وفيما ينكر بالعكس.

١ و: ويظهر أمرُ الله. ٢ آ: يخصّ؛ ب، ج: يحسن.

The property of the Helper is all-inclusive, and the All-Embracing is included within it so that it embraces every stage. Its very first manifestation of rank is that He gives help to the unseen over the visible, and makes the unseen manifest in the visible by placing that which is without beginning into the stages of temporality so that it is conveyed by the Seal of Messengers. However, this applies when the Helper employs the Guide, placing it in the levels of the Creator. When it employs the Misguider, it ultimately passes from the presence of the mightiest devil to the level of the Dajjāl who is yet to appear. 15.2

In every power struggle in which one side dominates another, the Helper, by virtue of exercising control over it, leaves its mark as well as its property. Thus, when the names clash, or when the qualities repel one another and then one name dominates the other, it is through the property of the Helper. Consider this with respect to the two presences into which the names divide—namely, the presence of Allāh and the presence of the All-Merciful—and You will discover that between existence and its levels there is a divergence and a mutual struggle. For the levels pertain to nonexistence, and all-mercifulness pertains to existence. The Helper therefore exercises control over the levels, rendering existence obedient to them. For the level is reactive, bringing the act of the agent into existence. It apportions existence, moving its name to the name of an existent, which together form the ranking of levels. 15.3

The Helper also helps existence, and thus nothing but it appears. Nor is it specified for anything other than existence, and in so doing it employs the Manifest. The Helper also helps truth overcome falsehood at the intellectual level. At the conjectural level, it helps falsehood to overcome falsehood in a manner that resembles how truth overcomes falsehood, although it is not the same. The Helper also helps the imagination and helps the bodily constitution by way of either generation or corruption. For help may take the side of falsehood, as the blessed Prophet said: "Do not seek to encounter the enemy in battle, for they are given help just as you are."[117] Thus the Helper has solicitude for unbelievers just as it has for believers. Moreover, if you consider the states of the Helper, you will discover that most levels are not devoid of it. For when the Helper gives help, all things are attained—such as truth overcoming falsehood and equilibrium overcoming disequilibrium, as well as the reverse. 15.4

٥،١٥ واعلم أنّ الانحراف إذا نُصر فظهر حكمه كان ظهوراً للحقّ بذلك الوصف وإذا غُلب فنصر عليه الاعتدال كان ظهوراً للحقّ بذلك والغالبيّة والمغلوبيّة هما متغالبان أيضاً تغالباً معنويّاً مرتبيّاً فالاسم النصير بإظهار الغالبيّة نصرها ونصر المغلوبيّة أيضاً في عين نصره للغالبيّة فتفطّن لهذا الاعتبار فإنّ النصرة للغالبيّة هي إظهار لحكم المغلوبيّة حتّى لو لم يكن هناك نصر للغالبيّة لم يكن للمغلوبيّة ظهور ولكانت معدومة وهذا الحكم سار في كلّ متضايفين لأنّ كلّ معنًى يطلب بالذات الاعتباريّ تعيّنه بالوجود الخاصّ به فكلّ ما أظهره فقد نصره النصير تعالى بترجيح وجوده على عدمه فيكون الاسم النصير في المغلوب كما هو في الغالب فتمّ[١] به الضدّان معاً فإنّ بنصر الغنيّ في الغنى ظهر حكم الفقر في الفقير فقد نصر الفقر بإظهار حكمه فما يخلو من الاسم النصير مكان ولا زمان وذلك لأنّ الوجود كلّه متحرّك في إظهار الصور الوجوديّات والعدميّات وكلّ ظهور فهو من نصر النصير تعالى وكلّ بطون فهو من نصره أيضاً ليظهر حكمه ويتسمّى فيقال باطن فيعطي ضرباً من الوجود يكون فيه منصوراً بالاسم النصير تعالى وللعبّاد من الاسم النصير نصرة إنشاط في العبادة على الكسل عنها ونصر خواطر الخير وظهور حكمها على حكم الاسم الهادي فتنصر على خواطر الشرّ فيخفي حكمها وللصوفيّ من الاسم النصير نصرة تبديل الأخلاق فيبدّل كلّ خلق دنيّ بكلّ خلق سنيّ فكلّ نصر فهو من اسمه النصير تبارك وتعالى ﴿وَمَا ٱلنَّصۡرُ إِلَّا مِنۡ عِندِ ٱللَّهِ﴾ .

---

١ آ، و: فتنعّم؛ ب: فتنقم.

You should also know that when disequilibrium is given help and its properties manifest, it is a manifestation of the Real through that quality. Moreover, when disequilibrium is overcome and dominated by equilibrium, it is a manifestation of the Real through that quality. Domination and defeat also rival each other at the supersensory level. The Helper helps domination by making it manifest, and it also helps defeat by helping domination itself. Ponder this point, for the help that is given to domination is a manifestation of the property of defeat; for if no help were given to domination, defeat would not be manifest and would remain nonexistent. This ruling property flows through all correlative pairs, for each pure meaning seeks through the perspectival Essence to become determined by the existence specific to it. Therefore, everything that the Essence manifests is given help through the Helper by giving preponderance to its existence over its nonexistence. The Helper is hence present in the vanquished as well as in the vanquisher such that both opposites subsist through this name. When the wealthy are assisted with their wealth, the property of poverty becomes manifest in the poor; and the Helper therefore helps poverty by manifesting its property. No place or time is devoid of the Helper. For all of existence is in motion, manifesting the forms of existence and nonexistence; and every manifestation is from the help of the Helper, just as every nonmanifest thing is also from the help of this name in order for its property to be manifest and to be named. It is called "nonmanifest" and then is given a type of existence that is given help by the Helper. Likewise, the worshippers receive help from the Helper in order to motivate them to worship instead of lapsing into laziness. It helps good thoughts manifest their properties according to the property of the Guide, thereby helping them to overcome thoughts that are evil and hiding their properties. The Sufi also receives help from the Helper in character transformation so that every base character trait is transformed into an exalted one. Thus, all help comes from the Helper, «and help is only from God».[118] 15.5

اسمه الواسع جلّ وعلا

اتّفق عليه الأئمّة الثلاثة ومحلّه من سورة البقرة قوله تعالى و﴿ ٱللَّهُ وَٰسِعٌ عَلِيمٌ ﴾ . ١،١٦
وهذا الاسم العظيم ألصق الأسماء بالرتبة الإنسانيّة الجامعة للغيب والشهادة وما ظهرت الذات المقدّسة بأكمل من ظهورها بهذا الاسم وحكمه الخاصّ به الانفعال فلا يكون فاعلاً إلّا في طور كون المنفعل علّة لفاعليّة الفاعل في مراتب غير متناهية وعدم التناهي مخصوص بالصفات الكونيّة معنويّة كانت أو روحانيّة أو حسّيّة وهذه السعة المنسوبة إلى الاسم الواسع لمّا كان اختصاصها بظهور أطوار الذات عمّ حكمها بجميع الصفات وليس للصفات جميع لأنّ ما لا يتناهى لا يقال له جميع ولمّا شهد أهل الشهود الذاتيّ هذا الاسم العظيم قال قائلهم في سعة ظهوراته

ٱلْعَرْشُ وَٱلْكُرْسِيُّ يَتْـلُوهُمَا   غَيْرُهُمَا مِنْ غَيْـرِ مَا عَـالَمِ
حُبَابَةٌ فِي بَحْـرِ إِطْـلَاقِهِ   مَا أَيْسَرَ ٱلْمَحْدُودَ فِي ٱلدَّائِمِ

ويعني بالدائم ما ليس بمحدود ولذلك قابل به المحدود ولولا ضرورته بحكم القافية لقال ما أيسر المحدود فيما ليس بمحدود.

٢،١٦ ومن ظنّ أنّ الأبعاد متناهية فإنّه اعتقد أن لا وجود لغير ما يحويه التاسع والتاسع عند الذاتيّين من المحقّقين بما فيه شخص واحد من أشخاص غير متناهية في النوع فكيف في الشخص ومن جعل الموجود معروضاً للوجود كان الوجود عنده عرضاً وليس عند أهل الحقيقة ذلك بل الموجود عرض في الوجود وإنّما ذكرتُ هذا لتعلم أنّ الواسع إنّما هو الوجود وأنّه يجوز فرض الأبعاد فيه غير متناهية وإلّا كان للعدم حقيقة محيطة

Al-Wāsiʿ: The All-Embracing

The three eminent scholars agree that it is a divine name. It occurs in the Surah of the Cow in the verse: «God is All-Embracing, Knowing».[119] This magnificent name adheres most closely to the human level that brings together the unseen and the visible. The Holy Essence does not manifest more completely than it does through this name. The property specific to it is passivity. It is not active except insofar as the recipient is a cause for the activity of the agent at endless levels. Moreover, infinitude is specific to engendered qualities, be they supersensory, spiritual, or sensory. Since the all-embracingness ascribed to the All-Embracing pertains specifically to the manifestation of the stages of the Essence, its property includes the totality of the qualities. Yet the qualities have no totality, for that which is endless cannot be called a totality. When those who witness the Essence witness this magnificent name, they describe the all-embracingness of its manifestations. To this effect, one of them said: 16.1

> The Throne and the Footstool are followed
> by many other worlds.
> A mere insect in the ocean of His non-delimitation;
> how puny is the delimited before the everlasting![120]

By "everlasting," the poet means the nondelimited, which is why he contrasts it with the delimited. If it were not for the constraints of the meter, he would have said: "how puny is the delimited before the nondelimited."

Those who suppose that spatial distances are finite believe there is no existence other than what is encompassed by the ninth sphere.[121] According to those who are absorbed in the Essence and who realize what is within it, the ninth sphere is merely an individual entity among an endless number of individual species, which is to say nothing of the individual entities themselves. The one who takes existents to be an accident for existence takes existence itself to be an accident. But such is not the case for those who know the reality of things, for an existent is indeed an accident of existence. I only mention this so that you can know that the All-Embracing is existence itself, and that it is possible to posit endless distances within it. Otherwise, nonexistence would possess an all-encompassing reality, in which case it would be an existent, not 16.2

وحينئذ يكون وجودًا لا عدمًا فعدم النهاية مساوق للاسم الواسع وأمّا عدم تناهي الصفات والأفعال فتابع لسعة الوجود.

٣،١٦ وليس في الوجود شيء ساكن إلّا سكونًا اعتباريًّا والمراد بحركة الوجود خروج موجوداته من الغيب إلى الشهادة في مراتب لا يتناهى عددها ولا أمدها وعود موجوداتها من الشهادة إلى الغيب عودًا غير متناهي العدد ولا الأمد والأزل فيه موصول بالأبد وليس في ذلك إلّا أحديّة الجمع وجمع الأحد وليس للعقول المحجوبة عثور على الإيمان بهذه الحضرة فكيف العيان لها فإنّ العقل من حيث فكره عقال وأضعف شيء في هذا المقام المقال وأعوز شيء في هذا المجال الرجال وليس للفحول أن تدركه فكيف للإناث أن تسلكه نعم للخنثى المشكل أن يملكه ولستُ أعني بالخنثى المشكل شخصًا حسّيًّا أو معنويًّا بل أعمّ من ذلك فهو حضرة الحضرات وحقيقة الحقائق والمطلق عن القيد والإطلاق ومنه تتعيّن أحكام الاسم الواسع ومن أحكام الاسم الواسع أحكام الأسماء والصفات والأفعال ويدخل فيه الاسمان العظيمان من وجه وهما الله والرحمٰن لاشتمال سعة الذات عليهما ويدخل الاسم الواسع في كلّ واحد منهما بطريق ظهوراته الجزئيّة.

اسمه البديع سبحانه

١،١٧ أوّل وروده في البقرة في قوله تعالى ﴿بَدِيعُ ٱلسَّمَٰوَٰتِ وَٱلْأَرْضِ﴾ وهو ممّا اتّفق عليه الأئمّة الثلاثة والبديع بمعنى المبدع وهو الذي أوجد ما لم يسبَق إلى مثله ويفهم منه

a nonexistent. Thus, infinity is coextensive with the All-Embracing. As for God's infinite qualities and acts, they are concomitants of the all-embracingness of existence.

In existence, things are only nominally still. What is meant by the motion of 16.3
existence is the emergence of existents from the unseen to the visible at levels that are infinite in their number and duration. The return of the levels' existents from the visible to the unseen is also a return that is infinite in number and duration. In existence, beginninglessness is joined to endlessness—here, there is only the unity of the all, and the all-ness of unity. Those who are obstructed by their intellects cannot attain this presence through faith, so how can they witness it directly? After all, the intellect is fettered by its act of reflection. The weakest thing in this station is speech, and the most deficient in this area are men. The strongest among them cannot perceive it, so how could females seek it? True, the androgyne that is simultaneously masculine and feminine may have ownership over it. But I do not mean by androgyne a sensory or supersensory individual; rather, I mean it in a more general sense. For it is the Presence of Presences and the Reality of Realities. It is that which is neither conditioned by delimitation nor non-delimitation, and from which the properties of the All-Embracing become determined.[122] And among the properties of the All-Embracing are the properties of the names, qualities, and acts. Moreover, the two magnificent names, Allāh and the All-Merciful, are included within it in a certain respect, for the all-embracingness of the Essence envelops them. The All-Embracing is also included within each by way of its partial self-manifestations.

Al-Badīʿ: The Innovative

It first occurs in the Surah of the Cow in the verse: «Innovator of the heavens 17.1
and the earth»,[123] and is among the names the three eminent scholars agree upon as being divine. The Innovative means the one who innovates; that is, the one who bestows existence upon that which has no precedent like it. However,

أهل العرفان أنّه في نفسه بديع أي وجوده لم يسبقه شيء فضلاً عن أن يسبقه ما يشبهه فقد أتى وجوده بما لم يُسبق إلى مثله.

٢،١٧ ولا شكّ أنّ العلماء قد قالوا أنّه أوجد الأشياء من عدم فإذاً أبدع ما في وجوده أن يوجِد من عدم وذلك لأنّ العدم لا يصلح أن يكون مادّة للموجود وقد أوجد الأشياء فأبدع من كلّ بديع أن يوجِد موجوداً ممّا لا يصلح أن يوجَد منه شيء فقد أتى بما لم يسبَق إلى مثله وهو الإيجاد ممّا لا يمكن أن يوجَد منه شيء.

٣،١٧ هذا إذا قلنا أنّ البديع بمعنى المبدع وإذا قلنا بما قاله أهل العرفان أنّه بديع في نفسه فإذاً ليس كنفسه شيء وهو بمعنى قوله ﴿لَيۡسَ كَمِثۡلِهِۦ شَيۡءٞ﴾ وهو إذا أردنا أن تكون الكاف زائدة وأمّا إن قلنا أنّها ليست زائدة فليس كالإنسان شيء فإنّ الإنسان مثله ولست أعني بالهاء التي هي الضمير الهويّة المطلقة بل الربوبيّة.

٤،١٧ وثمّ ليس كالإنسان شيء إذ كلّ الشيئيّات من الاسم الرحمٰن ونسبة الاسم الرحمٰن نسبة ربع الإنسان الغيبيّ المشتمل على الشهادة وهو إن كان غيبيّاً وشهاديّاً فنسبته إلى الغيب أولى لأنّه لمّا جمع الغيب والشهادة لم يعرفه أهل الغيب بما فيه من الشهادة ولم يعرفه أهل الشهادة بما فيه من الغيب فغاب عن الطائفتين فكانت نسبته إلى الغيب متعيّنة فإذاً ليس كالإنسان الغيبيّ ﴿شَيۡءٞۖ وَهُوَ ٱلسَّمِيعُ ٱلۡبَصِيرُ﴾ ونعني بالإنسان الإنسان الذي هو الإنسان وإذا قلنا إنّ الكاف زائدة فليس مثله شيء فهو البديع في نفسه سبحانه وتعالى.

٥،١٧ واعلم أنّ اسمه البديع عزّ وجلّ محيط بمراتب الوجود فإن كان بديعاً في نفسه فهو بديع في كلّ مرتبة من مراتب وجوده لأنّا لم نجد في موجوداته وهي كما علمت ظهوراته شيئاً مشبهاً من كلّ وجه لشيء آخر فإذاً كلّ موجود ليس مثله شيء فصحّ التلازم

those whose knowledge comes from direct recognition understand this name to mean that He is in terms of Himself Innovative. That is, His own existence was not preceded by anything at all, let alone anything similar to him; for His existence brought forth that which was not preceded by anything similar to it.

Scholars have certainly said that God brings things into existence from nonexistence. Accordingly, the greatest innovation is to bring into existence from nonexistence. This is because nonexistence cannot be a material substrate of existents; and yet God did bring things into existence. So the greatest innovator is He who brought things into existence out of something that was incapable of being their source. As such, He did something unprecedented—namely, to engender something from that out of which nothing could be engendered. 17.2

Now, this applies if we say that the Innovative means the one who innovates. But if we say what the recognizers say—namely, that He is in terms of Himself Innovative—then nothing is as His Self, in the sense of the verse: «nothing is as His like».[124] This is assuming that we read the particle "as" as pleonastic. However, if we say that it is not pleonastic, then it means that "nothing is like the human being" for the human being is God's like. And by the pronoun "His," I do not mean what denotes God's ultimate Identity; rather, by it I mean His lordship.[125] 17.3

Hence "nothing is like the human being" because all things are from the All-Merciful, and the All-Merciful is ascribed to the quarter of the unseen human being who encompasses the visible world. Moreover, although he belongs both to the invisible and the visible, his ascription to the invisible takes priority. After all, he brings together the invisible and the visible, and therefore those who experience the invisible do not recognize him on account of his visibility, and those who experience the visible do not recognize him on account of his invisibility. He is therefore invisible to both groups, and his ascription to the invisible is thereby determined. Thus nothing is as the invisible human being, and «he is the hearing, the seeing».[126] By "human being" we mean *the* human being.[127] However, if we read the particle "as" as pleonastic, then the verse in question means «nothing is as His like», as He in terms of Himself is Innovative. 17.4

Moreover, the Innovative encompasses the levels of existence. For if He is in terms of Himself Innovative, then He is Innovative at every level of His existence. For we do not find among His existents—which are His manifestations, as you know—anything that resembles some other thing in every regard. As such, nothing is like any other existent. The correlation is therefore established 17.5

فثبتت النتيجة وهي أنّه ليس مثله شيء فهو إذاً البديع الذي لم يسبَق إلى مثله وكيف يسبَق إلى مثله ولا مثل له تبارك وتعالى فهو البديع سبحانه.

٦،١٧ ثمّ إنّك قد علمت أنّ الإنسان المحجوب إذا محاه التجلّي خلعت عليه حضرة الربوبيّة أسماءها الحسنى وصفاتها العلى فيكون الإنسان الذي هو الإنسان أحقّ بهذه الرتبة فتكون له الأسماء الحسنى ومن جملتها البديع فيكون الإنسان هو البديع بهذا الاعتبار.

٧،١٧ وأمّا كيف يكون هو البديع فبيانه بأن نقول لا شكّ أنّه قد ثبت بما ذكرناه أنّه لَيْسَ مِثْلَهُ شَيْءٌ بنصّ قولنا ﴿لَيْسَ كَمِثْلِهِۦ شَيْءٌ﴾ ومثله هو الإنسان فإذاً ليس مثل الإنسان شيء أيّ الإنسان الذي هو الإنسان وإلّا فالأناسيّ كثير وإذا امتنع في الأناسيّ الكثيرين أن يشبه واحد منهم واحداً منهم من كلّ الوجوه فلأن يمتنع أن يشبه الكامل منهم أحداً من كلّ الوجوه من باب الأولى فإذاً ليس مثل الإنسان شيء فهو البديع سبحانه.

٨،١٧ وأمّا كيف يكون الإنسان الذي هو الإنسان بديعاً في كلّ مرتبة فهو ممّا يحتاج إلى البيان فنقول الإنسان الذي هو الإنسان إنّما نعني به الكامل الذي لا أكمل منه والذي لا أكمل منه فإمّا أن يكون معه من هو في درجته أو من هو دونه فأمّا من هو في درجته فالكلّ واحد قال

لَوْ أَنَّهُمْ أَلْفُ أَلْفٍ فِي عَدِيدِهِمُ   عَادُواْ إِلَى وَاحِدٍ فَرْدٍ بِلَا عَدَدِ

وذلك لأنّهم وإن خالفت بينهم الأزمنة والأمكنة والأسماء فإنّهم واحد أحديّ الجمع مجموع الأحديّة وذلك لأنّ كلّ شخص إنسانيّ فهو جسم وكلّ جسم فهو مادّة وصورة فالمادّة بين تلك الأشخاص كلّهم مشتركة والصور متشابهة في الاستعداد ولا يظهر عليهم إلّا ما هو بمقتضى استعداداتهم فيتشابهون في مذاهب قلوبهم وفي إدراك نفوسهم حتّى لو سئل أحدهم عن مسألة أجاب بجواب إذا سئل كلّ واحد منهم عن تلك المسألة أجاب بذلك الجواب ولا معنى لوحدانيّة ذواتهم إلّا هذا فصحّ قول الشاعر

and the conclusion is affirmed—namely, that «nothing is as His like». God is therefore the Innovative Who has no precedent like Him; and how could He be preceded by His like, if He has no like? Thus He is the Innovative.

You should also know that when God's self-disclosure effaces a veiled thinker, the presence of lordship confers upon him the garb of its beautiful names and exalted qualities. The human being who is *the* human being thus becomes worthy of this rank and the most beautiful names then become his. One of these is the Innovative, and from this perspective the human being thus becomes the innovative. 17.6

As for how the human being can be the innovative, we can say this much: It has been established beyond doubt that nothing is as God's like. This we plainly stated by citing the verse «nothing is as His like». Moreover, God's like is the human being. Therefore, nothing is like the human being; that is, the human being who is *the* human being. For there are many human beings, and since it is impossible for one of them to resemble another in every respect, the impossibility of the perfect human being resembling another in every respect is a fortiori even greater. Therefore, nothing is like the human being, for God is the Innovative. 17.7

How *the* human being can be innovative at every level calls for a clarification. We therefore say that the perfect human being, who in perfection is surpassed by none, has someone who is either at or below his level. As for the one who is at his level, they are all one. Someone said: 17.8

Even if they numbered a million,
they all go back to a single individual who has no number.[128]

For although they are separated by times, places, and names, they are nonetheless one; unified in their all-comprehensiveness, and comprehensive in their unity. For each human individual is a body, and each body is comprised of matter and form. Matter is shared by all these individuals, and their forms are exactly the same in preparedness, and nothing other than the dictates of their preparednesses manifests through them. As such, they resemble each other in the pathways of their hearts and the perceptions of their souls, so much so that if one of them were asked about a problem, he would give the same answer the other would have given. The singularity of their essences has no meaning other than this, and therefore the poet is correct in saying that:

لَوْ أَنَّهُمْ أَلْفُ أَلْفٍ فِي عَدِيدِهِمُ عَادُواْ إِلَى وَاحِدٍ فَرْدٍ بِلَا عَدَدِ

وأمّا الذي دون درجته فهو مغاير له قطعاً فإذاً ليس مثل الإنسان شيء وأمّا كيف يكون هو ﴿ٱلسَّمِيعُ ٱلْبَصِيرُ﴾ فهذا أمر محسوس لا يحتاج إلى بيان فإذاً ليس مثل الإنسان ﴿شَيْءٌ وَهُوَ ٱلسَّمِيعُ ٱلْبَصِيرُ﴾ وأيّ شيء أبدع ممّا ليس مثله شيء فهو إذاً البديع حقيقة.

٩،١٧ ولقائل أن يقول إذا كان هو ﴿لَيْسَ كَمِثْلِهِۦ شَيْءٌ﴾ والربّ سبحانه وتعالى ﴿لَيْسَ كَمِثْلِهِۦ شَيْءٌ﴾ فإذاً كلّ واحد منهما ﴿لَيْسَ كَمِثْلِهِۦ شَيْءٌ﴾ فتنتقض القاعدة بتشابههما إذ كلّ منهما مثل الآخر فلا يصحّ في حقّ كلّ واحد منهما أنّه ﴿لَيْسَ كَمِثْلِهِۦ شَيْءٌ﴾ أو ليس مثله شيء فقد بطل ما قرّرتموه بعين ما قرّرتموه.

١٠،١٧ وهذا هو التهافت بعينه فالجواب أنّ الحقّ تعالى من حضرة ربوبيّته له مثل وهو خليفته الذي أخبر عنه بقوله ﴿إِنِّي جَاعِلٌ فِي ٱلْأَرْضِ خَلِيفَةً﴾ والخليفة قطعاً من نوع المستخلف فإنّا ما رأينا إنساناً يستخلف بهيمة بل يستخلف مثله أو من هو فوقه ممّن يصلح للخلافة فهو إذاً مثله بصلاحه للاستخلاف فإذاً له مثل وللخليفة أيضاً مثل وهو المستخلَف لأنّ من ماثل شيئاً فكلّ واحد منهما مثل للآخر فصار للربّ مثل وللخليفة مثل.

١١،١٧ وأمّا الإنسان الذي هو الإنسان الغيبيّ فإنّه منزّه عن الخلافة ومحيط بحضرتي الربوبيّة والعبوديّة فهذا هو الذي لا مثل له لأنّ من درجتهم دون درجته فهم مغايرون له ولا مثل له فهو في نفسه البديع سبحانه وهو الذي صلّى له الربّ في قوله قف يا محمّد فإنّ ربّك يصلّي فأيّ بديع أبدع من هذا ويجب عليك أن تعلم أنّه لا تتناهى مراتبه ولا وجوده ولا ظهورات وجوده ولا وجود ظهوراته وإلّا لزمك أن تعتقد أنّه ليس ببديع لكنّه بديع فاعتقادك تناهي ما ذُكر باطل فهو البديع سبحانه.

١٢،١٧ واعلم أنّك أنت وأبناء نوعك مستعظمون هذه الكرات التسعة ومعتقدون أنّ الموجود محصور فيها ولو كان كذلك لكان الإنسان الذي هو الإنسان محصوراً فتشبهه

Even if they numbered a million,
they all go back to a single individual who has no number.

The one who is below this level certainly differs from the perfect human being. In this sense, nothing is like the human being. As for how he is the hearing and the seeing, this is an obvious sensory fact that does not need clarification. Thus, nothing is like the human being, «and he is the hearing, the seeing». And what could be more innovative than the one who is not like anything else? Thus, he is the truly innovative.

Someone may say: If nothing is like the perfect human being, and nothing 17.9
is like the Lord, then nothing is like either of them. If that is so, then it is a contradiction to say that they resemble each other. This means that it cannot be that nothing is as his like, or nothing is like him, and so the statement is self-refuting.

This statement is utter nonsense. The answer is that the Real, from the pres- 17.10
ence of His lordship, does have a like—namely, His representative, of whom He says: «I am placing a representative upon the earth».[129] A representative must definitely be of the same kind as the one who appoints him. For we never see a human being appointing a beast to represent him. Rather, he will appoint his like or someone above him who is suitable to represent him. The human being is therefore God's like by virtue of being suitable for appointment as His representative. The Lord therefore has a like, and the representative also has a like—namely, the One who appointed him. For whenever someone represents another, each of the two is like the other. Thus the Lord has a like, and the representative has a like.

The invisible human being is hallowed beyond the status of having a repre- 17.11
sentative, and he encompasses the presences of lordship and servanthood. This is the one who has no like, for those who are below his rank differ from him, which means he has no like. He himself is the innovative, and the one upon whom the Lord invokes blessings when He says: "Halt, O Muḥammad, for your Lord is praying."[130] What could be more innovative than this? You must also know that His levels and existence are infinite, just as the manifestations of His existence and the existence of His manifestations are infinite. Otherwise you would have to believe that He is not Innovative. But He is. Your belief that these things are finite would be false, and so He is the Innovative, blessed be He.

Now you and your ilk ascribe great importance to the nine spheres, holding 17.12
the belief that existents are confined therein. But if this were the case, then

كلّ ذرّة في الموجودات من جهة ما هي محصورة له مثله فلا يصحّ أن يقال أنّه ليس مثله شيء فإذًا لمّا ثبت أنّه ليس مثله شيء ثبت أنّ الموجود ليس بمحصور ومن هذه الجهة دخل الاسم البديع سبحانه في الاسم الواسع وظهر الاسم الواسع بوصف البديع سبحانه ورجعا معاً إلى الذات بوصف الأحديّة وما زالا في الأحديّة فإذًا ما انفصلا ولا اتّصلا فسبحان من جمع الأضداد وألّف بين الأنداد واتّصف بالأزواج والأفراد وجمع بالأحديّة فصمد النطق والسكوت في أحديّة الآزال والآباد وهذا السبحان لا بالنطق ولا بالحال بل يرجع ﴿إِلَيْكَ ٱلْبَصَرُ خَاسِئًا وَهُوَ حَسِيرٌ﴾ فافهم سرّ البديع ولا تكن بالمبدع.

اسمه المبتلي تبارك وتعالى

ورد في سورة البقرة في قوله تعالى ﴿وَإِذِ ٱبْتَلَىٰٓ إِبْرَٰهِـۧمَ رَبُّهُۥ بِكَلِمَٰتٍ﴾ وانفرد بذكره أبو الحكم بن برّجان الأندلسيّ رحمه الله واشتقاقه من الابتلاء وهو الامتحان والاختبار واختبار الحقّ تعالى لعبيده في لسان العلم هو لإقامة الحجّة عليهم وأمّا في لسان غيره فأمور أخرى يدقّ إدراكها على أهل العقول المحجوبة وتظهر ظهوراً واضحاً لأهل الأذواق والعقول المنوّرة فيرى أهل الأذواق تلك الأحكام حقائق ويراها أهل العقول المنوّرة مجازات وأمّا أهل العقول المحجوبة فيرون أنّها باطلة ممتنعة فلا يثبتون لإدراكها لالتباس الحقائق عليهم في امتيازها واشتراكها. ١٠١٨

the human being—that is, *the* human being—would be confined as well. Then every particle in existence would resemble him insofar as each is confined like him, and it would not be correct to say that nothing is like him. However, we have established that nothing is like him, and thereby we have established that existence is not confined by the nine spheres. It is also in this sense that the Innovative is included within the All-Embracing, and the All-Embracing manifests through the quality of the Innovative. Moreover, both names return to the Essence through the quality of unity, and they remain forever in unity. As such, they are neither differentiated from each other nor conjoined. Glory be to the One who brings together opposites, reconciles opponents, is conditioned by pairs and singles, and brings all things together through His unity so that speech and silence abide self-sufficiently in the unity of everything, without beginning and without end! This utterance of glory, moreover, is neither through speech nor state, but rather returns «your sight upon you dazzled and weary».[131] So understand the secret of the Innovative, and do not be a religious innovator!

Al-Mubtalī: The Tester

This name occurs in the Surah of the Cow in the verse: «when his Lord tested Abraham with some words».[132] Only Ibn Barrajān, may God have mercy on him, considers it to be a divine name. It derives from "testing," which is trial and examination. God's trial of His servants, according to exoteric discourse, is in order to establish the proof against them. According to a different discourse, there are other matters that are too subtle to be perceived by those whose intellects are veiled. These matters manifest in a clear manner for those who know through tasting and those whose intellects are illumined. Those who know through tasting see those properties as realities, while those whose intellects are illumined see them as metaphors. As for those whose intellects are veiled, they see them as unreal and impossible. They are unable to perceive such realities because they are confused by their distinctions and resemblances. 18.1

٢،١٨ ونحن إن كنّا إنّما نتكلّم بحسب أطوار العقول المحجوبة ضاعت المصلحة وتعيّنت المفسدة واعتقد الجاهل أنّ الفرق حقّ وأنّ الابتلاء إنّما هو الاختبار ولا شكّ أنّ الاختبار هو استخبار واستفهام وهو إنّما يكون عن جهل والحقّ تعالى منزّه عن الجهل فيكون ما ذهب إليه أهل العقول المحجوبة يلزمه أنّ الحقّ تعالى جاهل وهو باطل بالإجماع منّا ومنهم إلّا في اعتبار واحد تقصر أفهامهم عن إدراكه وهو أنّهم لا يعقلون أنّه تعالى لا يمتنع عليه أن يظهر حكم الجهل على فعل من أفعاله وذاته ليست مغايرة لذلك الفعل من طوره فيتّصف بالجهل من حيث كلّ جاهل ولا يضرّ كماله ذلك لاتّصافه بالعلم من حيث كلّ عالم أمّا لو كان في الوجود عالم غيره لا يكون له جهل لصحّ أن يقال إنّ ذلك العالم أكمل منه تعالى لأنّه يعلم ولا يجهل أمّا إذا كان لا علم إلّا له ولا جهل إلّا منه وبثبوت المرتبتين يكون الذي لا أكمل منه هو له تعالى وهل ظهور النقص من الكامل إلّا كمال.

٣،١٨ وإذا تحقّق هذا فالامتحان الذي هو الابتلاء في وحدانيّة العين إنّما معناها أن يكون الوجود إنّما أظهر ظهوراته ليتبيّن أيّ ظهور هو أكمل من أيّ ظهور آخر لا لأنّ الذات كانت جاهلة فعلمت ما ظهر بعد أن ظهر بل لأنّها هي بالفعل فلا يجوز أن يبقى في القوّة شيء لم يظهر فلمّا كانت الظهورات يتبيّن منها معاني ما في القوّة إذا ظهر بالفعل صحّ أن يقال إنّ الذات امتحنت نفسها لتظهر بالفعل صحّة كمالها فظهر ما ظهر وهو ناطق بلسان أنّ لتلك الذات القدرة على كلّ شيء فتحقّق اعتبار أنّ ممتحنًا لو امتحن أحكام هذه الذات في أنّها تقدر على كلّ شيء فلا شكّ أنّ ظهور القدرة على كلّ شيء هو جواب ذلك الممتحن وإن لم يكن هناك ممتحن فقامت حجّة الكمال في الكلام لأنّ هذا كلام الكمال لا كمال الكلام فحصل أنّ معنويّة الاسم المبتلي تحقّق

Now, if we were to speak only according to the levels of veiled intellects, then all that is advantageous would be lost and all that is disadvantageous would be gained. Moreover, the ignorant would believe that the realm of separation is real, and that God's trial is none other than a test. To be sure, a test is an interrogation and an inquiry, which are motivated by ignorance, yet the Real is hallowed beyond ignorance! Accordingly, the position of those whose intellects are veiled necessarily requires that the Real is ignorant, which is false by both our agreements, except for one consideration that is beyond their understanding, for they do not grasp that it is not impossible for Him to manifest the property of ignorance upon one of His acts, while His Essence is not opposed to that act on its own level such that He becomes characterized by ignorance in respect to every ignorant person. This does not diminish His perfection, because He is also conditioned by knowledge in respect to every knower. If there were another being in existence that possessed knowledge but not ignorance, then it would be correct to say that such a person was more perfect than God the exalted, for he would possess only knowledge and not ignorance. But since there is no knowledge except that it belongs to Him, and no ignorance except that it comes from Him, and since both levels are established, none is more perfect than Him. And is the manifestation of deficiency from one who is perfect anything but perfection? 18.2

If this is understood, then the testing, which is a trial in the view of divine oneness, means precisely that existence manifests whatever it manifests so that the most perfect manifestations may become clearly distinguishable from other manifestations. Now, this does not occur because the Essence was once ignorant and then came to know what manifested in the wake of its manifestation. Rather, it is because the Essence is actual, and it is not permissible for anything that has not manifested to forever remain in potentiality. Moreover, since the realities in potentiality become clearly distinguishable through the manifestations that manifest in actuality, it is correct to say that the Essence "tests" Its own Self in order to actually manifest Its genuine perfection, and that is why all that manifests becomes manifest. Manifestation, moreover, proclaims in its own language that the Essence possesses power over all things. The idea under consideration is thus confirmed: if someone were to test the properties of the Essence regarding its power over all things, the manifestation of power over all things would without doubt be the response to that test. And if there is no test, then the arguments for the perfection of the Essence are established in our discourse, because it is the discourse of perfection, not 18.3

في الحجاب وعند أهل الاغتراب بقوله ﴿وَلَنَبْلُوَنَّكُمْ حَتَّىٰ نَعْلَمَ ٱلْمُجَـٰهِدِينَ مِنكُمْ﴾ ويعكّر عليهم أنّه كان يعلم ويتحقّق بلسان المراتب التي بين أهل الحجاب وبين الذاتيّين الذي لا أكمل منهم.

٤،١٨ ولا يقال إنّ الاسم المبتلي إنّما ظهر بالاعتبار المحض لا بالوجود فإنّا نقول الاعتبارات في أطوارها هي الموجودات والوجود لها محقّق غاية ما في الباب أنّ هذا الاسم يرجع إلى الاسم الله من طريق الأوّلويّة ولا يدفَع عن اعتبار حكمه في الاسم الرحمٰن بحيث ينفي عن الوجود فإنّ الذي ينفي عن الوجود إنّما هو العدم وهو غير معقول فإن قال أحد إنّه يعقل العدم فيقال له إنّ الذي عقلته هو صورة ذهنيّة أحسست بما لها من الوجود الذهنيّ لأنّ العدم المحض لا يحَسّ به فإذاً الاسم المبتلي محقّق وحكمه سار في أطوار الظهورات الوجوديّة والمرتبيّة وظهوره بالاسم القادر من حيث يلحق بالقادر لحوقاً واجباً للاسم الظاهر.

٥،١٨ وأمّا تعلّق الاسم المبتلي بالاسم الباطن فضعيف إلّا باعتبارين أحدهما أنّ تعيّن الباطن هو ظهور ما ولو في صورة أنّه تعيّن فقط ولو لم يكن تعيّنه ظهوراً ما لكان معدوماً ولو كان معدوماً لم يلحقه الاسم فيقال الباطن فالباطن إذاً له ظهور ما وبقدر ذلك الظهور يتعيّن معه الاسم المبتلي والثاني أنّ البواطن إنّما هي بواطن باعتبار أنّها مقابلة للظواهر وأمّا في مقام بطونها فهي ظاهرة بعضها لبعض ظهوراً مرتبيّاً حتّى يقول المحقّق إنها في ذلك الطور هي الظواهر المحقّقة والظواهر التي هي ظواهر في مقابلتها هي بواطن بالنسبة إليها من حيث غيبتها عن حضرة البواطن والغيبة هي البطون فكانت الظواهر بواطن والبواطن ظواهر وقد كان العكس حقّاً وهذا أيضاً حقّ.

the perfection of discourse. What is gained from this is that the pure meaning of the Tester becomes realized in the veil. As for those who are seized by separation, it is realized in the verse: «verily We shall test you till We know those of you who strive hard»,[133] though they are confounded by the fact that God already knew this. This is realized by the language of cosmic levels that separates the veiled intellects from those who are absorbed in the Essence and who are unsurpassed in their perfection.

One should not say that the Tester only manifests purely theoretically and 18.4
not in actuality; for we say that all perspectival standpoints at their cosmic stages are existents, and their existence is realized. The main point here is that the Tester returns primarily to Allāh, yet its property in the All-Merciful should not be overlooked such that it is deprived of existence. After all, what is deprived of existence is none other than nonexistence, which is itself unintelligible. And if someone were to say that nonexistence is intelligible, then he should be told that what he has intelligibly conceived of is a mental form, and that he senses its mental existence. For absolute nonexistence cannot be sensed. Therefore, the Tester is realized, and its property flows through unfolding manifestations of existence and rank. Its manifestation, moreover, is through the Powerful insofar as the Powerful is necessarily joined to the Manifest.

However, the connection of the Tester to the Nonmanifest is weak, except 18.5
for two considerations. The first is that the determination of the Nonmanifest is a sort of manifestation, even if only in the form of being a determination. For if its determination were not a sort of manifestation, then it would be nonexistent, and if it were nonexistent, then it would not be joined to the name and hence be called "the Nonmanifest." Thus, the Nonmanifest possesses a sort of manifestation, and it is in the measure of this manifestation that the Tester becomes determined along with it. The second consideration is that nonmanifestations are nonmanifest precisely in view of the fact that they stand contrary to manifestations. Within their station of nonmanifestation, they are manifest to each other by rank. To this effect, the one who has verified the truth could say that at that stage, the nonmanifestations are the realized manifestations. The manifestations that stand contrary to them are themselves nonmanifestations relative to them, for they are absent from the presence of the nonmanifestations, and absence is nonmanifestation. As such, the manifestations are nonmanifestations, just as the nonmanifestations are manifestations. Just as the one is true, so is its opposite.

٦،١٨ فإذًا الاسم المبتلي يظهر حكمه في البواطن في الاعتبارات التي يقال فيها إنها ظواهر فيعمّ حكم الاسم المبتلي ولا يقال إنّ في التلاوة العزيزة قوله تعالى ﴿وَلَنَبْلُوَنَّكُمْ حَتَّىٰ نَعْلَمَ ٱلْمُجَٰهِدِينَ مِنكُمْ﴾ فعل الابتلاء لأجل العلم وأنت جعلت الابتلاء لأجل الظهور فإنّا نقول إنّ ظهوراته لا تغاير ذاته وعلمه لا يغاير ذاته فصار حاصل هذا ما معناه ﴿وَلَنَبْلُوَنَّكُمْ﴾ حتّى تظهر ذاتنا التي هي باعتبار صفاتنا وباعتبار ليست غيرنا فتحقّق بما قلناه حكم الابتلاء عامًّا وخاصًّا.

٧،١٨ ومن معاني قوله تعالى ﴿وَلَنَبْلُوَنَّكُمْ حَتَّىٰ نَعْلَمَ﴾ أي ولنظهرنّ لك العالم حتّى نظهر فيه إنسانًا فنعلم الجزئيّات بنفس علم الإنسان لعدم الغيريّة فانظر بعين الذات تتقدّس من الجهالات فتملك عنان الاسم الهادي في الخفايا والبوادي ﴿وَٱللَّهُ يَقُولُ ٱلْحَقَّ وَهُوَ يَهْدِى ٱلسَّبِيلَ﴾.

اسمه السميع تبارك وتعالى

١،١٩ هو من البقرة في قوله تعالى ﴿رَبَّنَا تَقَبَّلْ مِنَّآ إِنَّكَ أَنتَ ٱلسَّمِيعُ ٱلْعَلِيمُ﴾ وقد أورده الأئمّة الثلاثة والسميع بمعنى السامع كالقدير بمعنى القادر وقيل بمعنى المسمع كما قال عمرو بن مَعدي كرب

أَمِنْ رَيْحَانَةَ ٱلدَّاعِي ٱلسَّمِيعُ يُؤَرِّقُنِي وَأَصْحَابِي هُجُوعُ

Therefore, the property of the Tester becomes manifest in the nonmanifestations from the perspectives in which they can be called manifestations. The property of the Tester is therefore all-pervading. One must not say that the verse in the Holy Book reads: «verily We shall test you till We know those of you who strive hard», and that therefore He tests in order to gain knowledge. For in doing this, you make testing out to be for the sake of manifestation, whereas we say that His manifestations are not separate from His Essence, and that His knowledge is not separate from His Essence. What is gained from all this is that the verse «verily We shall test you» means in order for Our Essence to manifest, which from one consideration is Our qualities, and from another consideration is not separate from Us. This affirms the all-pervading and specific property of the divine testing. 18.6

Among the meanings of the verse «verily We shall test you till We know» is: We shall manifest the world for you till we manifest the human being therein. We will then know the particulars through the human being's own knowledge, because otherness does not exist. Look, then, with the eye of the Essence, and you will be exalted above ignorance. You will possess the reins of the Guide for all that is hidden, and all that is open. «And God speaks the truth, and He guides the way».[134] 18.7

Al-Samīʿ: The Hearing

This name occurs in the Surah of the Cow in the verse: «Our Lord, accept from us! Truly You are the Hearing, the Knowing».[135] All three eminent scholars cite it as a divine name. The Hearing can mean the one who hears, just as the Powerful can mean the one who has power. It is also said that it can mean "the one who causes hearing." To this effect, ʿAmr ibn Maʿdīkarib once said: 19.1

> Is it for Rayḥānah that he calls and shouts,
> keeping me awake while my companions sleep?[136]

أي الداعي المسمع وهو تعالى في لسان العلم سامع ومسمع والمسمع باعتبارين أحدهما خالق السمع في ذوات السامعين والثاني أنّه مسمع خطابه وكلامه لموسى الكليم ولمن قام في ذلك المقام من المخاطبين أهل التكليم.

٢،١٩ وأمّا في ألسنة الوجود وفي مراتب أهل الشهود فإن كان بلسان توحيد الفعل فلا سامع غيره إن جعلنا السمع فعلاً وإن جعلناه انفعالاً في السامع والفاعل وهو الأصوات فهو من باب توحيد الصفات وإن اعتبرنا أحديّة جمعه وجمع أحديّته فبلسان الذات.

٣،١٩ وقد تقدّم أنّ السمع يكون علماً في مقام والعلم يكون سمْعاً في مقام فتأخذ الأسماء أحكامها بعضها من بعض أخذاً ذاتياً في مراتب محفوظة النظام في الوجود فلا يقع منها شيء في غير موقعه لامتناع الظلم ولأنّ من أسمائه تعالى العادل وإن كانت الأسماء كلّها له فالظلم إنّما ينسَب إليه من أطوار الظالمين وهو من توحيد الفعل ومن أطوار المنحرفين ممّا لا يعقل وهي من توحيد الصفات ومن أطوار ذاتيّة وهي الكمالات فإنّ كمال الذات يقتضي ظهور اختلاف الصفات وكلّ ما أدّى إلى الكمال فهو كمال وذلك باعتبار وحدانيّة الوجود الذي من حضرته قيل ﴿مَا تَرَىٰ فِى خَلْقِ ٱلرَّحْمَٰنِ مِن تَفَٰوُتٍ فَٱرْجِعِ ٱلْبَصَرَ هَلْ تَرَىٰ مِن فُطُورٍ ثُمَّ ٱرْجِعِ ٱلْبَصَرَ كَرَّتَيْنِ يَنقَلِبْ إِلَيْكَ ٱلْبَصَرُ خَاسِئًا وَهُوَ حَسِيرٌ﴾ الآية.

٤،١٩ واعلم أنّ من سمعه تقدّس وعلا السمع الذي هو لمرتبة المراتب فإنّ الوجود الأزليّ له بالذات قول ﴿كُن﴾ ولهذا بالذات أن يسمع فهو السميع من حيث تتفصّل حقائقها في الظهور وهو الناطق بقول ﴿كُن﴾ ولذلك كانت أي ظهرت بالوجود وهو أيضاً سامع في نطقها فإنّ لها نطقاً ذاتياً بلفظة ﴿كُن﴾ أيضاً يسمعها من حيث قابليّته الذاتيّة بحسبها ومعنى قولها ﴿كُن﴾ أي تكثّر فسمعها بحقيقته وأجاب

"Calls and shouts" literally means "the person who calls and causes hearing." In the language of exoteric knowledge, God is both the Hearing and the One Who Causes Hearing. He causes hearing in two respects. The first is that He creates hearing within the hearers. The second is when He caused His address and speech to be heard by Moses, God's confidant,[137] and when He causes it to be heard by all those who stand in this station—namely, the addressees or those who converse with Him.

If the language of existence and the ranks of the people of witnessing is expressed in the language of the oneness of the divine acts, then there is no Hearing other than Him when we consider hearing as an act. But when we consider hearing as a reaction to sounds on the part of the hearer and the speaker, then it falls under the oneness of the divine attributes. But if we consider the unity of His all-ness and the all-ness of His unity, then this unitive all-ness is in the language of the Essence. 19.2

We have previously explained that hearing is knowledge at a certain station, and knowledge is hearing at a certain station. The names assume each other's properties in an essential manner at levels whose ordering is existentially exact. As such, nothing inexact ever occurs in them. For "wronging" is impossible,[138] and the Just is one of His exalted names. For although all the names belong to Him, wrongdoing is only ascribed to Him at the stages of the wrongdoers; and this pertains to the oneness of His acts. It can also be ascribed to Him at the stages of disequilibrium beyond the intellect; and this pertains to the oneness of the qualities. And it can be ascribed to Him at stages of the Essence, which are the perfections. For the perfection of the Essence entails the manifestation of diversity among the qualities; and whatever gives rise to perfection is itself perfection. This is from the perspective of the oneness of existence, from whose presence God says: «You will see no disparity in the All-Merciful's creation. Cast your sight again; do you see any flaw? Then cast your sight twice again and it will return to you humbled and wearied».[139] 19.3

One sort of hearing is His hearing at the Supreme Level. For the command «Be!»[140] belongs to the Essence in beginninglessness, and therefore it must be heard in the Essence. He is thus the Hearing insofar as the Essence's realities become differentiated in manifestation. He is the One who speaks the word «Be!» and thus the Essence's realities come into being; that is, they become manifest in existence. Moreover, He is the one who hears their speech, for the realities possess an intrinsic speech by virtue of the utterance «Be!», which He also hears inasmuch as He is intrinsically receptive to them. Moreover, the 19.4

بالسمع والطاعة فظهر بأحكامها فكان كثيراً وهو واحد ولم يكن لها أن تظهر بحكمه فتكون واحدة لأنّ حقيقتها تكثّر الواحد وحقيقة التكثّر لا يكون واحداً ﴿لَا تَبْدِيلَ لِكَلِمَٰتِ ٱللَّهِ﴾.

٥،١٩ فقد سمعت المراتبُ نطق الوجود كما سمع الوجود نطق المراتب وليس هناك غير الوجود والمرات والحقّ تعالى سميع من أطوارهما معاً فهو سميع من جميع الأطوار ومتكلّم من جميعها فلا سامع غيره ولا متكلّم سواه فإذا اعتبرت ذاته ناطقة لم تجد سامعاً وإلّا لكان معه غيره وإذا اعتبرت ذاته سامعة لم تجد ناطقاً وإلّا لكان معه غيره وقد ورد على بعض من ذاق هذا المقام خطاب بهذا المعنى وهو أنّه سمع نطقاً حاليّاً بلسان من الألسنة الناطقة عن حضرة الجمع يقول عبدي نطقت فلم أجد سامعاً وسمعت فلم أجد ناطقاً ومن حصّل شهود لغة الوجود وجده كلّه ناطقاً ووجده كلّه سامعاً وللشيخ محيي الدين في هذا شعر وهو

إِذَا نَطَقَ ٱلْوُجُودُ أَصَاخَ قَوْمٌ بِأَسْمَاعٍ إِلَى نُطْقِ ٱلْوُجُودِ

٦،١٩ واعلم أنّ نطق الوجود هو بألسنة الأحوال وليس له القول إلّا من حضرة جسم الإنسان وأمّا الخطاب الذي يسمَع بالحروف والأصوات لا من صورة الإنسان فصاحبه غالط في ظنّه أنّه بالحروف والأصوات بل هو معنى الكلام النفسيّ وللطافة إدراك المخاطب يتجسّد له في نفسه حتّى يصير كأنّه نطق بالصوت وذلك لأنّ لطيفته المدركة قويت حتّى صارت الخفايا عندها جلايا فغلب عليها قوّة الإدراك حتّى صار كلام النفس عندها حسّيّاً كأنّه كلام الجسم ولهذا إنّ من لطف مزاجه بالرياضة والخلوة أو غيرهما إذا سمع كلاماً يكاد ينزعج له فتشوّش عليه الأصوات الضعيفة فكيف

meaning of the Essence's command «Be!» is "multiply." He thus hears the Essence through His reality and responds by hearing and obeying. He manifests through the Essence's properties and multiplies even as He is One. The properties, for their part, do not manifest through His property by becoming one. For their reality is to multiply the One, and the reality of multiplication cannot become one: «There is no change in the words of God».[141]

Thus, the cosmic levels hear the speech of existence, and existence hears 19.5
the speech of the cosmic levels, for there is nothing but existence and cosmic levels. The Real, moreover, is the Hearing from both stages at once, for He is the Hearing from every stage, and He is the Speaking from every stage, and there is no Hearing or Speaking but He. Therefore, if you consider His Essence to be speaking, you will find no hearer, for the presence of a hearer would require that there is a partner alongside Him. And if you consider His Essence to be hearing, you will find no speaker, for the presence of a speaker would also entail that there is a partner alongside Him. One of those who tasted this station was once addressed in this regard: He heard an utterance in the language of the spirit, giving expression to the presence of all-comprehensiveness. It said, "O My servant, I spoke but found no hearer, and I heard but found no speaker." Whoever is made to witness the language of existence discovers that it all speaks and that it all hears. Shaykh Muḥyī l-Dīn ibn al-ʿArabī has a poem on this, in which he says:

> When existence speaks, one group
> lends its ear to the speech of existence.[142]

The speech of existence is expressed through the language of spiritual 19.6
states. It has no verbal expression except from the presence of the human body. The addressee is mistaken when he supposes that the address, heard through letters and sounds and not from a human form, is expressed through letters and sounds. For the address is the supersensory meaning of the speech of self, and by virtue of the addressee's subtle perception, it displays itself as a corporeal body within his soul until it resembles speech through sound. The reason for this is that the addressee's subtle perceptive faculty is strengthened to the point that hidden things become apparent for him. His power of perception becomes so predominant that the speech of self becomes part of the sensory domain as though it were the speech of the body. That is why the one whose temperament becomes benign through ascetic discipline, the spiritual retreat, or other practices is disturbed when he hears others speak. He finds the faintest

القويّة وذلك لأنسهم بالسكون والسكوت في الخلوة واستغنائهم بكلام النفس عن كلام الحسّ وصار ذلك إلفاً لهم وملكة عادية لهم فالنطق الحسّيّ عندهم يشوّش والنطق النفسيّ عندهم في الظهور مثل النطق الحسّيّ عند العامّة.

٧،١٩ فمن كان فيه منهم تمييز للحضرتين علم أنّ الخطاب نفسانيّ لا حسّيّ بالحرف والصوت فوعاه من مرتبة تعيُّنه ومن لم يكن له تمييز ذلك وغلب عليه اعتبار العادة الأولى صرفته العادة إلى أنّه حسّيّ بالحرف والصوت وهذا المعنى عند من جرّبه يعرفه معرفة جليّة وأمّا عند أهل الكثافة فيصعب إدراكه فإذاً الوجود كلّه ناطق بألسنة الأحوال والإنسان ناطق بألسنة الأحوال والأقوال ولعمري إنّ في بعض الحيوانات من ينطق بألسنة الأقوال بأصوات يفهمها بعضهم عن بعض وذلك لما فيهم من القرب إلى مرتبة ظهور جسم الإنسان وآخر كلّ شيء شبيه بأوّل الآخر.

٨،١٩ وإذا علمت أنّ الوجود ناطق فاعلم أنّ لكلّ نطق سمْعاً واعياً فالوجود سميع كلّه ولا كلّ له فالسميع سبحانه متصرّف فيما لا نهاية له واعلم أنّ كلّ فاعل في كلّ قابل فالفاعل ناطق والمنفعل سامع وكلّ منفعل أوجب فعل فاعل فيه فالمنفعل ناطق والفاعل سامع وذلك لأنّ المنفعل فاعل لفاعليّة الفاعل وفاعليّة الفاعل منفعلة عن فاعليّة انفعال المنفعل فتعاقبت حقائقها فعمّ حكم السميع فيهما وهذا مجال رحب لمن فُتح له بابه.

sounds distracting, let alone loud noises. He finds intimacy in stillness and in the silence of the spiritual retreat, for the speech of self obviates his need for speech of the sensory domain. As such, the speech of self becomes intimately familiar to him, and becomes a natural disposition. The speech of the sensory domain for him is distracting, while the speech of the self is as perceptible to him as the speech of the sensory domain is to common believers.

Those who can differentiate between these two presences know that the 19.7
address is from the self, not from the sensory domain of letters and sounds. They comprehend the address at the level of its own determination. Those who cannot differentiate between the two presences, whose predominant understanding is shaped by ordinary habit, are led by this habit to consider the address as pertaining to the sensory domain of sounds and letters. This reality is clear and obvious for those who have experienced it. For those who are dim-witted, it is very difficult for them to perceive it. Thus, all of existence speaks in the language of spiritual states, and the human being speaks both in the language of spiritual states and in verbal speech. By my life, there are even some animals that communicate among each other verbally in a manner that they understand. That is on account of how close they are to the level of manifestation of the human body, for the end of each thing resembles the beginning of the next.[143]

Now, if you understand that existence speaks, you must also understand 19.8
that every speech has a cognizant hearer. As such, the totality of existence hears, even though existence has no totality, and the Hearing exercises free control ad infinitum. Know too that every actor is contained within everything that is acted upon: the actor speaks, and the reactor hears. Furthermore, every reactor necessitates action from the one who acts upon him, and so in this sense the reactor speaks while the actor hears. The reactor activates the activity of the actor, and the activity of the actor reacts to the activity of the reactor's reactivity. As such, the realities of the actor and reactor succeed one another, and the property of the Hearing pervades both. This is a subject with much space to roam around in for those for whom it has been opened.

اسمه العزيز سبحانه

١،٢٠ ورد من البقرة في قوله تعالى ﴿وَيُزَكِّيهِمْ إِنَّكَ أَنتَ ٱلْعَزِيزُ﴾ واتّفق على إيراده الأئمّة الثلاثة واشتقاقه من العزّ الذي هو الامتناع وبهذا المعنى أورده النفّريّ في موقف العزّ لكنّه امتناع خاصّ وهو أنّ حضرة العزّة هي الوحدانيّة والامتناع فيها هو امتناع وجدان الغير معه فكأنّه امتنع عن الأغيار فيدخل في معناه الاسم الأحد سبحانه.

٢،٢٠ وإن أخذت العزّ الذي هو الغلبة كما قالت العرب من عزّ بزّ فيدخل فيه الاسم الغالب والقاهر وعلى كلا المعنيين فالاسم الأحد داخل في العزيز لأنّا إن اعتبرنا معنى الامتناع من وجدان الغير معه فالأحديّة ظاهرة.

٣،٢٠ وإن اعتبرنا معنى الغلبة فقد ذكرها النفّري في قوله وواقف بمعرفة أتعرّف إليه بالغلبة ومعنى الغلبة عنده ظهور حكم الفناء الماحي للأغيار ولا شكّ أنّ محو الأغيار هو ظهور معنى الأحديّة فالاسم العزيز يظهر بالمعنيين جميعاً في حقيقة معنى الاسم الأحد سبحانه.

٤،٢٠ وأمّا ظهورات الاسم العزيز فحيث وُجدت العزّة فإنّ الوجود للرحمٰن وحده فكلّ وجود وجد فهو للرحمٰن وحده فالعزّة إذا اتّصف بها وجود ما كان ذلك الوجود من ظهورات الاسم العزيز جلّ وعلا.

٥،٢٠ فإن استندت العزّة إلى الامتناع المرتبيّ اختصّ بها الاسم الله جلّت أسماؤه ويختلط بالاسم الرحمٰن في جمع الجمع حيث لا يعتبَر هناك اسم ولا مسمًّى وقولي هناك مجاز إذ ليس القصد المكان بل هو اعتبار قطع الاعتبارات وإنّما ألجأ إلى ذكر هذا ذكر

Al-ʿAzīz: The Mighty

This name is mentioned in the Surah of the Cow in the verse: «Truly You are the Mighty».[144] The three eminent scholars agree that it is a divine name. It derives from the word might, meaning impregnability. It is in the sense of impregnability that the Mighty is mentioned by al-Niffarī in his "halting at the station of might."[145] However, it is a particular kind of impregnability that is meant, for the presence of might is God's only-ness, an only-ness whose impregnability is the impossibility of anything existing alongside Him. As such, it is as though God makes Himself impregnable to all alterity. Thus, the Only is included within the meaning of this name. 20.1

However, if you take might to mean dominance in the sense used by the Arabs in the expression "whoever dominates, triumphs," then the Dominant and the Subjugator are included within it. Yet the Only is included within the Mighty in terms of both of these meanings, since if we consider the meaning of the impossibility of anything existing alongside Him, the attribute of uniqueness will obviously suggest itself. 20.2

And if we consider the meaning of dominance, to which al-Niffarī refers when he quotes God as saying: "One who attains Me with recognition, to whom I make Myself known through dominance"[146]—and by "dominance" he means the manifestation of the property of annihilation that obliterates all alterity—then there is no doubt that the obliteration of alterity is the manifestation of the meaning of God's uniqueness. Therefore, the Mighty manifests itself in both senses through the true meaning of the Unique. 20.3

As for the manifestations of the Mighty, wherever impregnability is found, its existence belongs solely to the All-Merciful; for every existent belongs solely to the All-Merciful. So when an existent becomes conditioned by the quality of impregnability, that being is one of the manifestations of the Mighty. 20.4

However, when exaltedness attributes itself to the impregnability of rank, then the majestic name Allāh lays special claim to it, and it mixes with the All-Merciful within the all-comprehensive totality, where neither the name nor the Named can be envisaged. This is metaphorical, because we are not really speaking of a place. Rather, it is a consideration that is severed from all other considerations, and I resort to mentioning it only in order to explain how the 20.5

عود العزيز باعتبار إلى الرحمٰن وباعتبار إلى الله فأردتُ أن أذكر المطلع الذي هو بين هذين الاسمين اللذين هما أصل الأسماء كلّها ولا شكّ أنّ المطلع هو حضرة جمعها وهو جمع الجمع فقد جاء الكلام بطريق ليس بالذات.

٦،٢٠ فنعود ونقول إنّ كلا المعنيين المقدّم ذكرهما قد تبيّن رجوعهما إلى الاسم الأحد وذلك لصدق الغلبة في الأحديّة والامتناع فيها فإذًا امتناعه تعالى عن الأبصار ظاهر فإنّه ﴿لَا تُدْرِكُهُ ٱلْأَبْصَـٰرُ﴾ فهو العزيز تعالى على مرتبة الأبصار والمعنى الذي به امتنع عن الأبصار هو بعينه يمتنع به عن إدراك الحواسّ كلّها وهو العزيز سبحانه بالنسبة إلى إدراك القوى الباطنة فإنّ ذاته مقدّسة عن أن يحضرها الخيال لأنّه لو أحضرها لحصرها وهي منزّهة عن الحصر وكذلك القوّة الوهميّة والذكريّة فإنّ القوّة الذاكرة لا تتعلّق بالذات بل إنّما تتعلّق بما يعيّنه الإيمان لا ما يتحقّق بالعيان والقوّة الحافظة إنّما تحفظ ما اتّصفت به المشاعر والمدارك.

٧،٢٠ ولقائل أن يقول إنّ العقل وحده هو المختصّ بهذا الشأن فنقول إنّ العقل في عقال عن رؤية الكنه وإنّما يتعلّق بالصفات وما علم الصفات أيضاً إلّا من الحسّ وإنّه لو لم ير الحيّ لم يعلم الحياة ولو لم يظهر له الموصوف بالعلم أو غيره لم تظهر له الصفة ولكان كالأكمه بالنسبة إلى إدراك عقله للألوان إذ لا يعرف منها إلّا أسماءها ومدركات الحسّ إذا قيست عليها معاني أسمائه تعالى لم ينهض قياس الغائب على هذا الشاهد لحصول معنى كنه الذات في العقل.

٨،٢٠ فالعزيز تعالى ظاهرة أحكامه في مراتب أطوار الإدراكات عقلاً وأمّا نقلاً فأمر إيمانيّ لا عيانيّ فهو العزيز تعالى عن إدراك أهل العقل وأهل النقل ومراتب العبّاد ومن فوقهم من الصوفيّة هي في ضمن المعقول والمنقول فليس لهاتين الطائفتين إلمام بكنه العزيز سبحانه وهاتان الطائفتان هما خواصّ العوامّ وأمّا الفلاسفة والمتكلّمون فهم

Mighty returns to the All-Merciful from one perspective and to Allāh from another. I therefore mention the horizon that lies between these two names, which are the root of all the names. Without doubt, the horizon is the presence that brings them together: the All-Comprehensive Totality. But this is not our chief concern here.

Let us then return to the matter at hand. We have shown how both these meanings of the Mighty revert to the Only, because it is correct to attribute both impregnability and dominance to His only-ness. That He is impregnable to eyesight is obvious, because «sight does not perceive Him»,[147] and so He is Mighty and beyond the level of eyesight. Moreover, the reality that makes it impossible to see Him is the same reality that makes it impossible to perceive Him through the other senses. He is, moreover, Mighty and beyond the perception of the inner faculties, since His Essence is hallowed beyond the presence of the imaginal realm. For if the imaginal realm were able to call the Essence into its presence, it would confine It, yet It is beyond confinement. The same goes for the faculties of imagination and memory, because the faculty of memory cannot attach itself to the Essence, but only to what is determined through belief, not what is realized through firsthand witnessing. The retentive faculty retains the qualities that are attributed to the organs of awareness and feelings. 20.6

Someone might say: only the intellect can lay claim to this matter. We say: the intellect is fettered and unable to get to the core; it only attaches itself to qualities, and knowledge of qualities only comes from sense perception. If the intellect did not see the living, it would not know life. If an object that possesses a quality, such as knowledge, were not manifest to the intellect, the quality would not be manifested to it either. Such an intellect would resemble a person blind from birth: he cannot perceive colors because he recognizes only their names. When one compares the objects that are perceived by the senses to the supersensory meanings of the divine names, the analogy between the invisible and the visible would not be enough for the pure meaning of the Essence to be attained by the intellect. 20.7

Therefore, the properties of the Mighty are manifest at the stages of sensory perception through reason. As for rote transmission of religious reports, that is a matter of belief, not direct witnessing, for He is Mighty beyond the perceptions of intellectuals and traditionalists alike. The levels of the worshippers and the Sufis who are above them lie within the realms of intelligible and transmitted reports. These two groups, despite being the elite among the ordinary believers, have no cognizance of the core of the Mighty. The philosophers 20.8

عوامّ فقط وأمّا أهل فروع الشريعة المطهّرَة فإن عملوا بما علموا منها فهم العبّاد وقد ذكر حالهم وإن لم يعملوا فهم في خطّة خسف لأنّ علمهم حجّة عليهم وإنّما لحقوا بالعبّاد إذا عملوا بما علموا لأنّ العبّاد لا يصلح لهم العمل بغير علم فالعمل بالشريعة هو مبدأ العبادة وهو من العمل الصالح إذا اتّصل به العمل بمقتضاه وإلّا فهو عمل قد حبط وهو أقرب إلى السيّئة لقيام الحجّة به على صاحبه فكان نجاة فصار هلكاً والعزيز بالنسبة إلى من ذُكر هو بمعنى الامتناع.

٩،٢٠ فإن قلت فمن هم الخاصّة إذا قرّرت أنّ من تقدّم ذكره هم طوائف العوامّ فالجواب أنّ الخاصّة هم أهل المعرفة ونعني بأهل المعرفة أهل التجلّيات والشهود الذين قد فنيت في التوحيد بعض رسومهم وبقي بعضها فهؤلاء هم الخاصّة وهم الذين يتعرّف الحقّ تعالى إليهم بالاسم العزيز لا بمعنى الامتناع المحض كما كان في حقّ من ذُكر قبل بل بمعنى الغلبة ويكون عزّ بمعنى غلب ومعنى الغلبة هنا كما قدّمنا هو استيلاء المحو على مراتب رسومهم بحسب طور التجلّي الحاصل لهم فهي غلبة لظهور الوحدانيّة على رسوم الكثرة فتقهرها كقهر النور للظلمة فإنّ الجهل ظلمة والتجلّي يرفع الظلمة ويبقى العزيز سبحانه في ذلك المقام وحده فإذاً معنى الغلبة ظاهر ومعنى الامتناع أيضاً ظاهر وذلك أنّ السالك يروم أن يرى الحقّ لغلبة شوقه عليه فإذا حصل له الشهود أفنى التجلّي اسم إرادة الرؤية من الرائي لأنّ المتجلّي يدكّ طور المتجلّى له و ﴿جَعَلَهُۥ دَكًّا وَخَرَّ مُوسَىٰ صَعِقًا﴾ وهذه غلبة وإن شئت قلت امتناع.

١٠،٢٠ وأمّا خاصّة الخاصّة فهم أهل الفناء الذي لا يبقى معه رسم ولا تعيّن فيه صفة ولا اسم وقولنا إنّهم خاصّة الخاصّة مجاز لأنّ مقامهم ليس ممّا فيه نسبة لخصوص أو عموم وأمّا من فوق هؤلاء وهم أهل البقاء بعد الفناء فلهم كلام غير هذا فإذاً الاسم العزيز تعالى ظاهر الحكم في أطوار الخاصّة أيضاً وهو أعظم ظهوراً في طور خاصّة

and theologians are just ordinary believers, and if the jurists who specialize in the sacred law act upon what they know, then they are ordinary worshippers whose state we have just mentioned. If, on the other hand, they do not act upon their knowledge, then they are in a state of abasement because their knowledge serves as evidence against them. The jurists only join the ranks of the worshippers when they act upon their knowledge, for the deeds of the worshippers are not acceptable without knowledge, and acting upon the revealed law is the cornerstone of worship. A deed is considered righteous if it is connected to its legal dictates. Otherwise it is one that "has come to naught"[148] and is closer to sin due to the evidence that stands against the one who performs the deed without knowledge. As such, what was deliverance becomes damnation. In relation to these types, the Mighty means the impregnable.

You may ask: who then are the spiritual elite, since you affirm that these 20.9
groups are ordinary believers? The answer is that the elite are those who know through recognition. By this we mean those who witness God's self-disclosures; those who are even partially annihilated in divine oneness. These are the elite. They are the ones to whom the Real makes Himself known through the Mighty; not in the sense of sheer impregnability, as is the case with the other groups, but in the sense of dominance. For them, to be mighty means to dominate, and the meaning of dominance, as we said, is their obliteration at each level and in keeping with the stage of self-disclosure being actualized in them. This is therefore a dominance due to the manifestation of oneness upon the traces of multiplicity. It subjugates multiplicity just as light subjugates darkness. For ignorance is darkness, and self-disclosure dispels the darkness so that the Mighty alone remains. So the meaning of dominance is evident, and the meaning of impregnability is also evident. The wayfarer strives to see the Real, since he is dominated by a yearning for God. Then, when witnessing occurs, the self-disclosure annihilates the desire to see from the person who sees, since the Self-Discloser causes the support upon which the recipient of disclosure stands to crumble to dust: «He made it crumble to dust, and Moses fell down in a swoon».[149] Such is divine dominance; or you could call it impregnability.

The elite of the elite are the annihilated ones of whom no trace remains. 20.10
No quality or name is determined in them. Calling them the "elite of the elite" is metaphorical because their station is beyond all relation to being elite or common. As for those who are above them still—the people of subsistence after annihilation—theirs is a different discussion altogether. As such, the Mighty is manifest in its properties at the stages of the spiritual elite as well,

الخاصّة لاصطلامه بالغلبة وأمّا أطوار أهل البقاء بعد الفناء فظهور الاسم العزيز هنالك كظهور سائر الأسماء لأنّها حضرة الذات في نفسها فتعيّن فيها أسماؤها لذاتها فلا أثر هنالك للأغـيار.

اسمه الكافي جلّ وعلا

١،٢١ شاهده في سورة البقرة قوله تعالى ﴿فَسَيَكْفِيكَهُمُ ٱللَّهُ﴾ ولم يذكره الغزاليّ والمراد الكافي خلقه أو الكافي من توكّل عليه فالاعتبار الأوّل هو قول الخلق بأسرهم علوّاً وسفلاً وجزءاً وكلاًّ وناطقاً وغير ناطق نطقياً حالياً ﴿حَسْبِيَ ٱللَّهُ﴾ ومعناه الكافي أمّا أنّه الكافي في إظهار الموجودات فلأنّه ما أظهرها غيره وهي قد ظهرت فلا شكّ أنّه الكافي في إظهارها وهي إمّا جواهر عقليّة أو نفسيّة أو روحانيّة أو جسمانيّة وإمّا أعراض على اختلافها والله تعالى في إيجادها هو الكافي وهذا من دخول الكافي في الاسم الخالق تعالى.

٢،٢١ ويدخل أيضاً في الاسم الرزّاق فيكون هو الكافي تعالى الكافل أرزاق العباد وأرزاق العباد مختلفة بحسب اختلاف أغذيتها فأمّا القلم الأعلى فرزقه التجلّي وهو مقتضى الاسم الرزّاق في حضرة الأزل والرزق هناك نور وحقيقته المدد الذي يتّصل بالقلم الأعلى فيصير كتابة عقليّة في صفحة اللوح المحفوظ والقلم في تلك الحضرة ليس له غذاء إلّا ذلك المدد فهو كاف تعالى في استمرار ذلك الرزق ويتفصّل ذلك الرزق في اللوح ويظهر فيما دونه إلى حضرة الأجسام فتغتذي

and it is even greater in manifestation at the stage of the elite of the elite where divine dominance is utterly overwhelming. As for the stages of those who subsist in God after annihilation, the manifestation of the Mighty at their stage is identical to the manifestation of all the other names because it is the presence of the Essence Itself. Therein, all the names become determined through the Essence, where there is no trace of alterity.

Al-Kāfī: The Sufficer

This name occurs in the Surah of the Cow in the verse: «God will suffice you against them»[150] and is not mentioned by al-Ghazālī as a divine name. It means either the One who suffices His creation, or the One who suffices those who trust in Him. In the first case, it is the entirety of creation—upper and lower, part and whole, rational and nonrational animals, expressing themselves through their states—that proclaims: «God suffices me»;[151] that is, He is the Sufficer. God is the Sufficer who makes existents manifest because only He brings them into manifestation; and since they are manifested, He is doubtless sufficient in making them manifest, either as substances of the intellect, the self, the spirit, or the body, or as accidents in all their diversity. So God is the Sufficer in existentiating these existents. In all of this, moreover, the Sufficer is included within the Creator. 21.1

It is also included within the Provider: He is the Sufficer in that He undertakes the provisions of His servants, and the provisions of His servants differ according to their different types of nourishment. The Supreme Pen provides self-disclosure, a dictate of the Provider in the presence of beginninglessness. There, provision is light, and its reality is the ink connected to the Supreme Pen, becoming an intellective inscription upon the surface of the Preserved Tablet. The Pen in that presence has no nourishment but for that ink. God suffices the continuation of the provision, which becomes differentiated in the Tablet and manifests beneath it in the presence of corporeal bodies. The corporeal bodies are nourished from it in diverse manners in accordance with 21.2

الأجسام منه أغذية مختلفة بحسب قوابلها فتتفصّل حقائق الاسم الكافي في أطوار الأرزاق إلى الأبد.

وإن أردت الاختصار في الاسم الكافي فلتقل إنّه كاف في ظهور مقتضيات الأسماء كلّها وهي لا تتناهى فيكون تفصيل الاسم الكافي لا يتناهى ولو أخذتُ في تفصيل أحكامه لاستنفذتُ عمر الدنيا ثمّ لا تكون نسبة ما ذكرتُه إلى ما لم أذكره إلّا كنسبة المتناهي إلى غير المتناهي إذ لا تحقّق بينهما نسبة محصّلة ثمّ إنّ كلّ شيء كفى شيئاً في شيءٍ أيّ شيء من الاعتبارات كان هو من تصرُف الاسم الكافي تعالى لأنّ المعاني لا يحملها إلّا الذات ولا ذات إلّا له وكلّ فعل أو صفة فله ذات ولا ذات إلّا له فيرجع الحكم إلى أن نقول لا هو إلّا هو ولنقف هنا فيكون هذا كافياً والكافي هو تعـالى. ٣،٢١

اسمه الرؤوف تعالى

وآيتـه من البقرة قوله تعالى ﴿إِنَّ ٱللَّهَ بِٱلنَّاسِ لَرَءُوفٌ رَّحِيمٌ﴾ وهذا الاسم الكريم ذكره الغزاليّ والبيهقيّ وأبو الحكم وفيه أربع لغات رَؤُوفٌ مضموم الهمزة مُشبعة ورَؤُفٌ مضموم الهمزة غير مُشبعة ورَأْف بإسكان الهمزة وحكى الكسائيّ والفرّاء رِئْف بكسر الراء وإسكان الهمزة. وقالوا في اشتقاقه من شدّة الرحمة رئف العراق لرأفته بأهله فمعنى الاسم شدّة الرحمة فيرجع إلى الاسم الرحيم بخصوص وصفه وأمّا بعموم وصفه فيرجع مع الأسماء الوجوديّة إلى الاسم الرحمٰن في حقيقة الاسم الرحيم وقد شُرحت فنستغني بها عن إعادتها هاهنـا. ١،٢٢

their receptivity. The realities of the Sufficer therefore differentiate endlessly throughout the stages of provision.

If you desire a summary of the Sufficer, you could say that God suffices in manifesting the dictates of all the names, which are infinite. As such, the differentiations of the Sufficer are infinite too. If I started to detail all the properties of the Sufficer, it would take the rest of time. Even then, the correspondence between what I did and did not mention would be like the correspondence between the finite and the infinite. For an actual correspondence between the two cannot be realized. Moreover, anything that suffices another thing, in any possible sense, comes from the controlling power of the Sufficer. Supersensory meanings are only borne by the Essence, and there is no essence but that it belongs to Him. And since every action or quality has an essence, there is no essence but that it belongs to Him. Thus, all we can say is that there is only He. Let us halt here, for this much suffices; and God is the Sufficer. 21.3

Al-Ra'ūf: The Kind

It occurs in the Surah of the Cow in the verse: «Truly God is Kind and Merciful toward people».[152] This noble name is mentioned by al-Ghazālī, al-Bayhaqī, and Ibn Barrajān as a divine name. The name *Ra'ūf* has four dialectical variants: *Ra'ūf* with a prolonged glottal stop and a long "ū" vowel; *Ra'uf* with a shortened glottal stop and a short "u" vowel; *Ra'f* with an unvoweled glottal stop; and, according to al-Kisā'ī and al-Farrā', *Ri'f* with the "r" taking an "i" vowel and followed by an unvoweled glottal stop. The latter variant is said to derive from the notion of intense mercy. The farmland of Iraq is known as *al-Ri'f* because of how kind it is to those who live off it. The name therefore denotes intense mercy, and it traces back to the Ever-Merciful through this specific quality. Its general quality is traced back along with the names of existence to the All-Merciful, through the reality of the Ever-Merciful. This has already been explained, so there is no need to repeat it here. 22.1

اسمه الإلٰه الواحد تعالى

وآيته من سورة البقرة ﴿وَإِلَٰهُكُمۡ إِلَٰهٞ وَٰحِدٞ﴾ وأجمع الثلاثة على ذكره وهو ١،٢٣
مشتقّ من الإلٰهة وهي العبادة ومعناه المستحق لعبادة خلقه دون من نسبوا إليه
الإلٰهة ولذلك أكّده بقوله ﴿إِلَٰهٞ وَٰحِدٞ﴾ أي المعبود حقيقة هو الإلٰه وحده تبارك
وتعالى والعبادة خضوع من العابد للمعبود ويظهر ذلك الخضوع بصور مشروعة
وتلك الصور مذكورة في العبادات من كتب الفقه وبصور أخرى في معنى الصور
المشروعة فهي كالمقيسة عليها فهي فروع إن صدق القياس وإلّا فشبيهة بالفروع
والمثمر من هذه الفروع هو ما صدق فيه القياس.

والثمرة بالنسبة إلى العبّاد حصول الوعد الجميل وبالنسبة إلى الصوفيّة تهيّؤ ٢،٢٣
النّفوس للعرفان بتزكيتها من الأخلاق المذمومة وفي ضمن ذلك محبّة الخلق لمن زكت نفسه وثمرتها بالنسبة إلى العارفين أهل السفر الأوّل أعلى من ثمرتها للمحبّين والمحبّون فوق رتبة الصوفيّة وتحت رتبة العارفين وثمرتها للمحبّين حلاوة المواجيد والأحوال ولذّتها دون مشاهدة فهم متنعّمون بعذاب الطلب الشديد وهم في الرتبة الأولى من مراتب أهل السماع وهم أحقّ به من الصوفيّة لا من العارفين ومن أنكر السماع على العارفين أو المحبّين فقد ظلم بوضع الإنكار في غير موضعه فيما ذكرنا بعض ثمرات العبادة والعبادة مختلفة بحسب مراتب العابدين وإن جمعتهم الصور المشروعة ظاهرًا فهم مختلفون في تناولها.

Al-Ilāh al-Wāḥid: The One God

It occurs in the Surah of the Cow in the verse: «Your God is One God».[153] All three eminent scholars agree that it is a divine name. It derives from "worship," and it means the One who deserves worship from His creatures, to the exclusion of all others to whom they may ascribe divinity. Thus He emphasizes it by saying: «One God»; that is, the only true Object of worship is the One blessed and exalted God. Worship, moreover, is the subordination of the worshipper to the Worshipped, and that subordination manifests through legally prescribed forms, which are mentioned in the discussions on ritual in the books of law. It also manifests through supersensory rituals that accord with the legally prescribed ones. These forms of worship are, as it were, analogously accordant with the legally prescribed forms. If the analogy is sound, then they are branches of the legally prescribed forms of worship; otherwise, they resemble them. Of these branches, those that accord with the legally prescribed forms are the ones that bear fruit. 23.1

The fruit for the worshippers is the fulfillment of the beautiful promise of the Garden. For the Sufis, it is the readiness of their souls for direct recognition by purifying them of blameworthy character traits; a further fruit resulting from this is that those whose hearts have been purified are loved by people. For the recognizers who are on the first journey, the fruit of worship is higher than the fruit of the lovers, and the lovers are higher in rank than the Sufis and lower than the recognizers. For the lovers, the fruit of worship is the sweetness of ecstasy and the delights of the spiritual states that they enjoy, but without witnessing the Real. They find enjoyment in the pain of their quest, and they occupy the first of the levels of those who participate in sessions of devotional music and poetry.[154] Moreover, they are more worthy than the Sufis, but less worthy than the recognizers. Those who disapprove of the recognizers and the lovers for participating in sessions of devotional music and poetry have done them wrong by censuring them inappropriately, per some of the fruits of worship that we have mentioned. For worship differs according to the ranks of the worshippers; they vary in how they partake of them even though they all outwardly share the same legally prescribed forms. 23.2

٣،٢٣ وأمّا في الفروع المقيسة عليها فليست الصور فيها إلّا بحسب أهل العبادة فلكلّ مقام منهم عبادة تصدر عنهم بل وبحسب كلّ استعداد بل وبحسب كلّ شخص بل وبحسب كلّ زمان ومكان بل وبحسب أمزجة العبّاد وما يلحق وجودهم من اللواحق والمقارنين وبحسب ما تصل قدرتهم إلى عمله أو إلى تركه فإنّ عبادتهم منها أفعال ومنها تروك هي في أثمارها كالأفعال في وقت أو حال أو مرتبة وفي وقت أو حال أو مرتبة هي أعلى وهذه الأفعال والتروك هي متنقّلة لا تستقرّ من أجل عدم استقرار أهل السلوك في مقام واحد وتلك التنقّلات تقتضي أنّ ما كان واجباً أن يُفعل فيصير واجباً أن يترَك وبالعكس ومنه قولهم حسنات الأبرار سيّئات المقرّبين وبالعكس ومن جملة التنقّل أنّ ما يكون بالأفعال البدنيّة يعتاض عنه بالتوجّهات القلبيّة والروحانيّة والمعنويّة العقليّة والذوقيّة والشهوديّة ومراتب فيما بين ذلك وفيما فوقه لا يعرفها ويرشد إلى سلوكه من غير غلط إلّا المكمّلون للسفر الثاني الآخذون في السفر الثالث.

٤،٢٣ وكلّ هذه مآخذ داخلة في العبادات التي يستحقّها الإله تعالى وله إلى كلّ عبادة نسبة تقتضي خصوصيّة بحسب الرتبة التي هي فيه ومن حصل له قطع أطوارها كلّها فقد حصلت له العبادة بحسبها كلّها وينال ثمرتها كلّها في نفَس واحد ويكون نومه ويقظته في حصول ذلك سواء وليس لصاحب مقام من هذه المقامات كلّها عليه اطّلاع وله الاطّلاع على كلّ عابد وعبادة ممّا تحت مقامه والغالب على من هذا حاله أن لا يعرَف ولا يعظَّم ولا يعترف به إلّا من قرب من مقامه ورمى في مرامي مرامه.

٥،٢٣ فقد ذكرتُ في هذا الكلام كلّيّات العبادة المختلفة الأحكام الخارج تفصيلها عن إدراك العوامّ وكلّها من مراتب تعلّقات الإله الواحد تعالى وللأسماء عبادة توجّهها إلى المسمّى والمسمّى واحد في المسمّيات وللصفات عبادة توجّهها إلى الموصوف بها كانت ما كانت في جميع أنواع الصفات وللذات توجّه بالعبادة باعتبار كلّ ما توجّه

The forms of the branches that are analogous to the legally prescribed acts of worship are in keeping with the particularities of the worshippers, for each of their stations has a form of worship that issues from it. In fact, the forms are in keeping with each worshipper's individual preparedness, with every time and place, with each worshipper's constitution and whatever is connected to their being, and with the worshipper's capacity to perform or not perform certain deeds. For their worship consists of actions and abstentions akin to actions in terms of their fruits, at specific times, states, or levels. At other times, states, or levels, the abstentions are higher still. These actions and abstentions, moreover, are in constant motion. They never settle, because the wayfarers never settle in one station. These constant motions require that what was once an obligatory action can become an obligatory abstention, and vice versa; whence the expression "The beautiful deeds of the pious are the ugly deeds of those brought near to God,"[155] and vice versa. An aspect of this constant motion is how that which takes place through bodily activity can be replaced by the turning of the heart and the spirit, and of supersensory intelligence, tasting, and witnessing. There are levels between and above these that are not known, and whose path is not discovered, except by those who have completed the second journey and are undertaking the third journey. 23.3

These variations all pertain to the forms of worship that God deserves. He in turn has a relation to every form of worship that is specifically in keeping with its level. The one who traverses all of its stages is able to actualize worship in keeping with every level, and in a single breath reaps all their fruits. These he attains during both sleep and wakefulness. Those who are only at one of these stations have no cognizance of him, yet he has cognizance of every worshipper and every form of worship beneath his station. Those who are in this state tend to be unrecognized, unacknowledged, and unacclaimed, except by those who are close to their station or who share the same hunting grounds. 23.4

I have mentioned in this discussion the universal forms of worship whose properties are diverse, and whose particularities are beyond the purview of the ordinary believers. These all pertain to levels of connection to the One God. Furthermore, the names themselves engage in worship by turning their face toward the Named, and the Named is One among the named things. The qualities also engage in worship by turning toward the object that they qualify, whatever that may be among the different kinds of qualities. Finally, the Essence Itself turns in worship with respect to all the names, acts, and qualities 23.5

إليها من الأسماء والأفعال والصفات بأنواع العبارات لقيامها في كلّ طور بوجوده وبمراتب وجوده وبرازخ ما بينهما كما قلتُ

فَمَا فِي تَصَارِيفِ مَعْنَى ٱلْوُجُودِ   مَجَـــالٌ لِشَيْئِيَّـــةِ غَـيْرِهِ
وَلَا فِيـهِ إِلَّا ٱلَّذِي مِنْـهُ فِي   تَنَوُّعِـــهِ فِي مَـدَى سَيْرِهِ
وَتِلْكَ شُؤُونٌ لَهُ مَـــا ٱلْوُجُو   دُ مِنْ خَيْرِهَا هِيَ مِنْ خَـيْرِهِ

اسمه الشديد العذاب جلّت قدرته

١،٢٤ آيتـه من سورة البقرة قوله تعالى ﴿وَأَنَّ ٱللَّهَ شَدِيدُ ٱلْعَذَابِ﴾ وانفرد بذكره أبو الحكم ابن برّجان وشدّة العذاب قوّته ومنه بلوغ الأشدّ أي كمال القوّة والعذاب ضدّ النعيم فالعذاب إدراك المنافر والنعيم إدراك الملائم إلّا أنّه لا يختصّ النّعيم والعذاب بأهل الإدراك وإن اشترك النّعيم والعذاب في الإدراك إلّا أنّ الإدراك في نظر أهل الأذواق أعمّ منه في اصطلاح العلماء وذلك لأنّ أهل الأذواق نظروا إلى حقيقة العذاب فوجدوه هو حقيقة النعيم لكنّ القوابل المختلفة أوجبت أن تكون الحقيقة الواحدة مختلفة وستجد مصداق ذلك في جميع مراتب الموجودات.

٢،٢٤ ألا ترى أنّ الأمزجة المختلفة كيف يختلف قبولها فيكون الإنسان الذي يغلب عليه البلغم يحبّ الحلو والصفراويّ يكرهه وتختلف الأمزجة في محبّة الطعوم وبغضها ويتنعّم إنسان بصحبة شخص من الأناسي وغيره يعدّ صحبته عذاباً ويتحابّ قوم ويتباغض

that turn toward It, in all their variety of expressions. For the Essence sustains their existence, their levels of existence, and the liminal positions between those levels. To this effect, I once wrote:

In the vicissitudes of the realm of existence
there is no room for the thing-ness of other-than-He.
All things therein come from Him,
as variegated as they are throughout the course of their journey;
Such are His workings, while existence
is choiceless, since it is as He chooses.[156]

Al-Shadīd al-ʿAdhāb: The Severe in Chastisement

It occurs in the Surah of the Cow in the verse: «God is severe in chastisement».[157] Only Ibn Barrajān mentions it as a divine name. The "severity" (*shiddah*) of chastisement denotes its full strength, as in the expression "to reach full maturity (*ashudd*)"; that is, full strength. Chastisement is the opposite of bliss; chastisement is to perceive that which is disagreeable, and bliss is to perceive that which is agreeable. However, bliss and chastisement are not specific to the perceivers, even though both are objects of perception. For perception, according to those who know through tasting, is more general in its meaning than it is in the conventional language of exoteric scholars. For those who know through tasting observe the reality of chastisement and see that it is the very reality of bliss, except that the diversity of receptacles necessitates diversity in the one reality. You will find the truth of this in all the levels of existents. 24.1

Do you not see that different bodily constitutions are diverse in their receptivity? Someone whose constitution is dominated by phlegm loves sweets, whereas someone who has a predominance of yellow bile hates them. Constitutions differ in love for and dislike of certain foods. Someone may find the company of a particular individual to be bliss, while another would consider his company to be torture. Some groups love each other, some hate each 24.2

آخرون ويتوسّط قوم الأمر ومراتب ما بين ذلك كثيرة منها ما تُحَسّ فيه المنافرة ومنها ما لا تُحسّ وكذلك الملاءمة ومتوسّطات كثيرة بين ذلك.

٣،٢٤ ويتجاوز أهل الأذواق هذا من الإنسان إلى الحيوانات فيرون ذلك في مآكلها ومشاربها ومسارحها في غذواتها ومراوحها في عشيّاتها ووحوش البرّ في اختلاف مطاعمها والطير من جوارحها وغير جوارحها وكيف بعضها يتنعّم بأكل اللحم وبعضها يتضرّر به أو لا يسيغه وتجاوزوا ذلك إلى النبات والمعدن فوجدوا ذلك كذلك وتجاوزوا ذلك إلى الأركان فوجدوه أيضاً كذلك فوجدوا أيضاً بين المعاني تناسباً وتنافرًا ورأوا النعيم عامّاً بكلّ شيء اتّصل به ملائمه ووجدوا العذاب عامّاً لكلّ شيء اتّصل به منافره وإن لم يكن له الإدراك المعروف حتّى إنّ النار إذا تمكّنت من الحطب تصوّت تنعّما لإدراك الملائم والحطب يصوّت لإدراك المنافر وبينهما نزاع وتغالب يستمرّ إلى أن يستحيل أحدهما إلى حقيقة صاحبه فيصير إيّاه وحينئذ يسكن التغالب وقد قال أهل الطبائع إنّ بعض الطبائع تفرح ببعض وبعضها تنفر من بعض وقد تحبّ الطبيعة طبيعة أخرى وتلك الطبيعة تبغضها وبالعكس في أطوار كثيرة.

٤،٢٤ وبالجملة فالعذاب حقيقة واحدة والنعيم ضدّها فالحقّ تعالى له من هاتين الحقيقتين اسمان المنعم والشديد العذاب إلّا أنّ أهل الشهود لمّا شهدوا وجدوا جيم الجنّة جيم جهنّم ووجدوا ما به يعذّب عين ما به ينعّم قاله النفّري فالمنعم هو الشديد العذاب ولو علم أهل الحجاب ما حقيقة العذاب لعلموا معنى المسألة التي حارت فيها أفكارهم وهي من المعضلات عندهم وذلك تحيّرهم في كون الحقّ تعالى حكم على قوم بالعذاب وحكم لقوم بالنعيم فقال هؤلاء إلى الجنّة ولا أبالي وهؤلاء إلى النار ولا

other, and still others find a middle way. There are many levels in between. In some cases, the disagreeability is perceived by the senses; in others, it is not. The same goes for agreeableness and its many intermediate levels.

Those who know through tasting take this further. They observe that one finds different tastes not only in humans, but also in animals. Animals differ in their food, drink, places of pasture, and evening resting places. The beasts of the wild differ in what they eat, as do predatory and non-predatory birds. Some eat flesh, while others are harmed by it or cannot swallow it. Those who know through tasting observe, moreover, that the same applies to plants and minerals, and even to the four elements. They also observe concordance and discordance in the supersensory meanings. They observe that bliss pervades everything that comes into contact with what it finds agreeable, and that chastisement pervades everything that comes into contact with what it finds disagreeable, even though these might not be perceived in the usual way. When fire takes hold of wood, it emits a sound of pleasure when it perceives what is agreeable to it; and wood also emits a sound when it perceives what it finds disagreeable. Contention and mutual struggle continue between them until one transforms into the reality of the other, and thereby becomes it, whereupon the conflict is resolved. Moreover, those who study the natural constituents say that certain natural constituents rejoice in one another, while others are repelled by one another. One natural constituent may love another, while the latter is repelled by it; and vice versa at many stages. 24.3

In sum, chastisement is a single reality, and blissfulness is its opposite. The Real has two names corresponding to these two realities: the Giver of Bliss and the Severe in Chastisement. However, to quote al-Niffarī, those who know through witnessing witness that "the *G* of the Garden is the *G* of Gehenna, and the source of chastisement is the source of blissfulness." The Giver of Bliss is therefore the Severe in Chastisement. If veiled intellects were to know the reality of chastisement, they would know the answer to the problem that perplexes their minds, one they consider to be an irresolvable dilemma—namely, the fact that God decrees chastisement for one group and bliss for another, thus proclaiming: "This group to the Garden, and I do not care! And this group to the Fire, and I do not care!"[158] Were the veiled intellect to realize the meaning of His proclamation "I do not care," they would know the answer to this problem. For our part, we intimate but cannot teach others, and we inspire but cannot feed others. The meaning of "I do not care" is an explicit statement 24.4

أبالي فلو حقّقوا معنى قوله لا أبالي لعلموا المسألة ونحن نلمع ولا نعلم ونطمع ولا نطعم وذلك أنّ معنى لا أبالي تصريح بالحلول في النعيم أمّا أهل الجنّة ففي الجنّة وأمّا أهل النار ففي النار.

٥،٢٤ وكيف لا تبالي الذات من استمرار منافرة الصفات وقد سبقت رحمتها غضبها وصحّتْ إذ حصحص حقّها بما أظهر إلى الرحمٰن نسبها لا نَسبها لكن لمّا انسبك ذهب الكيان بالشديد العذاب حُشر المتّقون منه إلى الرحمٰن فأهل الجنّة في الجنّة وأهل النار في النار والنعيم بعد العذاب شامل لهما في سائر الأطوار وأيّ عذاب أشدّ من عذاب يصيرّ المخالف مؤالفاً.

٦،٢٤ وقد علم أهل الطبيعة أنّ النار من شأنها أن تفرّق المختلفات وتجمع بين المؤتلفات وأجمع أهل الصنعة على أنّ مولودهم الفرّار يربىّ حتّى يصبر على النار وكيف لا يفترق الناس فرقتين أوَليس الهادي والمضلّ ضدّين فهما يختلفان لاختلاف الاسمين حتّى يذهب تخالف الرسمين فيتّفقا في الاسم الجامع فيتّفق في حقّهما الضارّ والنافع وهنالك يبطل حكم الشديد العذاب بدخوله في حقيقة الاسم الوهّاب.

اسمه الغفور تعالى

١،٢٥ أوّل وروده في البقرة في قوله تعالى ﴿فَلَآ إِثْمَ عَلَيْهِ إِنَّ ٱللَّهَ غَفُورٌ رَّحِيمٌ﴾ وقد اتّفق الثلاثة على إيراده واشتقاق الاسم الغفور من الغفر الذي هو السّتر ولذلك قيل المغفر والغفور والغفّار بمعنًى فقال العلماء المعنى الساتر للعقوبة عمّن عفا عنه وقيل

about dwelling in bliss: bliss for the People of the Garden in the Garden and bliss for the People of the Fire in the Fire.

And how could the Essence not care about qualities being mutually repellent, when Its mercy precedes Its wrath?[159] It can only not care when their truth is manifesting their primary relationship to, not their distant descent from, the All-Merciful.[160] However, when the gold of engendered things is separated from the dross by the Severe in Chastisement, "the God-fearing are assembled"—away from the Severe in Chastisement—"to the All-Merciful,"[161] and the People of the Garden are in the Garden, while the People of the Fire are in the Fire. Blissfulness, following chastisement, envelops both groups at every stage; and what chastisement could be more severe than a chastisement that renders the incompatible compatible? 24.5

Those who study nature know that fire's task is to separate incompatibles and bring together compatibles. All craftsmen agree that the alchemical element of quicksilver is mercurial, and that it is disciplined through exposure to fire. And how could it be that people do not separate into two groups? Are the names the Guide and the Misguider not opposites? The two groups differ on account of the difference between the two divine names so that there is no discordance between their traces and they can come together in the All-Comprehensive Name, where the Benefiter and the Harmer coincide. It is here that the property of the Severe in Chastisement is nullified by inclusion within the reality of the Bestower. 24.6

Al-Ghafūr: The Concealing

This name is first mentioned in the Surah of the Cow in the verse: «then no sin shall be upon him. Truly God is Concealing, Merciful».[162] The three eminent scholars agree that it is a divine name.[163] The etymological derivation of the name Concealing is from "to cover." Hence it is said that "the Coverer," "the Concealing," and "the Ever-Concealing" have the same meaning. The scholars say that it means "the one who covers the punishment to protect those whom 25.1

الساتر لذنوب من عفا عنه فيكون داخلاً في الاسم العفوّ بهذا المعنى ويدخل في الاسم الرحيم كما قال ﴿لَا تَقۡنَطُواْ مِن رَّحۡمَةِ ٱللَّهِ﴾ والمراد المغفرة بدليل قوله عقيب ذلك ﴿إِنَّ ٱللَّهَ يَغۡفِرُ ٱلذُّنُوبَ جَمِيعًا﴾ إشارة إلى الرحمة الخاصّة بالمغفرة وهي من الغفور سبحانه.

٢،٢٥ واعلم أنّ الاسم الغفور يستعمل معاني الأسماء كلّها ويظهر بأحكامها فيغفر الذنوب بصرافة الغفران ويغفر القبائح بنسبة الاسم الساتر أي يسترها وله مع الاسم الهادي نِسب مختلفة الصور فيغفر الشهوات أي يسترها عن قلوب الأولياء فلا تخطر لهم على بال ويستر الدنيا عن مطامح قلوبهم وهي مغفرة وهذه كلّها أحكام الاسم الهادي.

٣،٢٥ ويغفر الأخلاق المذمومة عن مقاصد الصوفيّة أي يسترها فلا تطمح إليها نفوسهم لأنّها قد صيّرت كرم الأخلاق ملكة فتنسى أضداده وذلك غفر وستر بنسبة الاسم الهادي ويغفر طلب الآخرة عن مطامح قلوب المحبّين فينسون ذكرها لشغلهم بالمحبوب وذلك غفران بنسبة الاسم الهادي ويغفر ذكر الحسنات عنهم فلا يرون لهم حسنة لأنّهم رأوها من الله لا من أنفسهم وذلك بنسبة الاسم الهادي ويغفر السوى أي يستره عن مطامح شهود أهل الوجود فلا يرون إلّا الواحد الحقّ وذلك بنسبة الاسم الهادي وإلى هنا ينتهي حكم الاسم الهادي.

٤،٢٥ وقد يبدو ساترًا بنسبة الاسم المضلّ فيغفر وجه المصلحة عن الضلّال فيعمون عنها وهو غفر منه ﴿بَاطِنُهُۥ فِيهِ ٱلرَّحۡمَةُ وَظَٰهِرُهُۥ مِن قِبَلِهِ ٱلۡعَذَابُ﴾ وهو الجهل وذلك بنسبة الاسم المضلّ ويغفر وجه الآخرة فلا تتعلّق به قلوبهم وهي نسبة الاسم المضلّ فإن ستر عنهم وجه حسن الدنيا أيضاً فؤلائك الآسفون[١] بنسبة الاسم المضلّ فلا يجدون حلاوة الدنيا ولا حلاوة طلب الآخرة ثمّ قد يستر عنهم وجه التوبة

١ آ، ب، ج: الاشقون.

He pardons." It is also said to mean "the coverer of the sins of those whom He pardons." Therefore, the Concealing is included within the Pardoner in this sense, just as it is included within the Ever-Merciful, for God says: «despair not of God's mercy», by which is meant concealment, as evidenced by what follows: «truly God conceals all sins».[164] This alludes to the mercy that is specific to concealment and is from the Concealing, may He be glorified.

The Concealing employs the pure meanings of all the names, and manifests itself through their properties. As such, He conceals sins through His pure concealment, and conceals ugly qualities through relation to the Coverer; that is, He covers them. Furthermore, this name relates in a variety of forms to the Guide so that He conceals (that is, covers) base desires from the hearts of His Friends so that these desires do not occur to them. He also covers the here below from the desires of their hearts, which is also a concealment. These are all properties of the Guide. 25.2

He also conceals blameworthy character traits from the aspirations of the Sufis; that is, He covers them so their souls do not aspire to them. For noble character traits become a disposition acquired by them while they forget the opposite traits, which is a kind of concealment and a covering pertaining to the Guide. He also conceals the pursuit of the hereafter from the hearts of the lovers so that they forget about it on account of their preoccupation with the Beloved. That is also a kind of concealment pertaining to the Guide. And He conceals the remembrance of beautiful deeds from them so that they do not see themselves as possessing any beautiful deeds, for they see them as coming from God, not from themselves. That also pertains to the Guide. He also conceals what is other than God; that is, He covers it from the witnessing of those who verify the reality of existence so that they see nothing but the Face of the Real. This also pertains to the Guide; and this is where the property of the Guide ends. 25.3

He also appears as the Coverer in relation to the Misguider in that He conceals what is in the interest of the misguided and blinds them to it. That is a concealment from Him, «the inside of which is mercy, and the outside of which is chastisement».[165] This entails ignorance, which pertains to the Misguider. He also conceals from them concern for the afterlife so that their hearts do not become attached to it, which also pertains to the Misguider. If He covers the beautiful aspect of this world from some, they are then unfortunate through the Misguider. For they do not experience the sweetness of this world, nor the sweetness of the pursuit of the next. He may also cover the 25.4

فلا يظهر الاسم التوّاب من مراتب وجودهم وقد يستر عن التائبين وجه حسن التقدّم إلى العمل الصالح فإنّ التوبة باب العمل فيقفون عنه وهم أهل الندامة على التفريط من غير استدراك الفائت وهي نسبة من الاسم المُضلّ وقد يستر عنهم وجوه الترقّيات فيقفون حيث انتهوا وهي دقائق الاسم المضلّ أيضاً إذ هو عيب كما قال

وَلَمْ أَرَ فِي عُيُوبِ ٱلنَّاسِ عَيْبًا كَنَقْصِ ٱلقَادِرِينَ عَلَى ٱلتَّمَامِ

٥،٢٥ وقد يبلغ الاسم الغفور بهم إلى أن لا يبقى في قلب أحدهم حبّة خردل من الخير وهم أهل النار الذين هم أهلها وأمّا من في قلبه حبّة خردل من الخير فهم آخِر من يخرج من النار كما ورد الحديث النبويّ وأمّا من خلا قلبه بالكلّيّة فهم أهل النار الذين هم أهلها وهم بعد العذاب أشدّ الناس نعيماً يوم تعمّ الرحمة فإنّ نسبة ﴿يُبَدِّلُ ٱللَّهُ سَيِّـَٔاتِهِمْ حَسَنَٰتٍ﴾ تلحقهم فتصير مراتب العذاب التي قطعوا أطوارها مظاهر للنعيم الذي لا يعرفه أهل الجنّة لكن أهل الجنّة لو عرض عليهم لكان عذاباً في حقّهم فلذلك اختصّ به هؤلاء.

٦،٢٥ وأصل هذه المسألة الذي يرجع إليه أنّ نعيم أتباع الاسم الهادي ضدّ لنعيم أتباع الاسم المضلّ وإن كان المنعم من حيث الذات واحداً والحقائق كلّها لا تتبدّل فلا جرم تتباين مداركهم في ملاقاة الملائم الذي هو النعيم حتّى يكون الذي ليس في قلبه حبّة خردل من الخير في نعيم مساو لنعيم الذي قد كمل الخير كلّه في قلبه.

٧،٢٥ وهي مرتبة طلبها السيّد المسيح أي تكملة أن يكون الخير كلّه في قلبه وشاهده قوله ليحيى عليه السلام عمّدني قال يحيى عليه السلام أنت أولى فقال له المسيح دعني فإنّي أريد أن أكمّل البرّ كلّه عندما أظهر التّلمذة لمن هو أولى أن يكون تلميذاً له منه.

face of repentance from them so that the Ever-Turning in Repentance does not manifest to them at their level of existence. To those who do repent, He may cover the beauty of carrying out righteous deeds—for repentance ought to be the door to action—so that they stop short of it. These are the remorseful ones who fall short without attempting to make up for what evaded them; and this also pertains to the Misguider. He may also cover from them the ways of ascension so that they halt at where they are; and these are also particularities of the Misguider, since it is blameworthy to halt. As al-Mutanabbī once said:

I have not seen a human flaw as bad
as falling short when you can attain perfection.[166]

The Concealing may even take them to the point where not even an iota of 25.5
good remains. Such are "the inhabitants of the Fire who are worthy of it."[167] Those whose hearts retain a slight amount of good shall be the last to be released from the Fire, as a prophetic report relates.[168] Those whose hearts are completely devoid of any good are "the people of the Fire who are worthy of it." After the chastisement, these are the ones who shall experience the most intense bliss on the day when God's mercy encompasses all things. For the verse «God will change their ugly deeds into beautiful deeds»[169] will finally overtake them, and the levels of chastisement they experienced will become loci for a manifestation of bliss unknown to the people of the Garden. Indeed, if the people of the Garden were exposed to it, it would be a chastisement, which is why it is specific to those people.

This matter is rooted in the fact that the bliss of the followers of the Guide 25.6
is the opposite of the bliss of the followers of the Misguider. For even though the Giver of Bliss is One with respect to the Essence, and even though the divine realities do not change, certainly their perceptions are dissimilar in their encounter with what is agreeable, which is bliss. As such, the one whose heart is devoid of even the slightest amount of good shall be in a bliss that is equivalent to the bliss of the one in whose heart goodness has reached its full measure.

That level—reaching the full measure of goodness in the heart—is what the 25.7
Messiah sought. This is attested in his saying to John the Baptist, "Baptize me." John replied, "You are more worthy of that." To this the Messiah responded, "Let it be so, for I wish to reach the full measure of righteousness."[170] Thus the Messiah displayed discipleship toward someone who was more worthy of being his own disciple.

فتكملة البرّ كلّه هو بتكملة الخير كلّه وهو مقام الجمال ويقابله مقام الجلال وهم ٨،٢٥
الذين كمّلوا البرّ كلّه فأخذتهم السطوة الإلٰهيّة حتّى بلغت إلى حدّ الاسم الشديد العذاب فكانت نهاية مطمح نظر الاسم المضلّ فتلقّاهم الاسم القيّوم عند المطلع الذي ﴿تَطَّلِعُ﴾ منه النّار ﴿عَلَى ٱلْأَفْـِٔدَةِ﴾ فناولهم إلى الاسم السلام فكانت النار إذ ذاك ﴿بَرْدًا وَسَلَٰمًا﴾.

ومن هناك ورد الوارد في قصّة إبراهيم خليل الرحمٰن فإنّ الرحمة تخلّلت منه ما ٩،٢٥
كان لولاها لتخلّلته النار فإذا تلقّاهم الاسم السلام أعطاهم الوصلة بالاسم المؤمن فأمنوا بعد الخوف وهيمن الاسم المهيمن بأن شملهم النعيم فتولّاهم الاسم العزيز فعزّوا بعد الذلّ وتناولهم الاسم الجبّار بمعنى الجبر فكبرت مراتب نعيمهم من حضرة الاسم المتكبّر لأنّ القوم إذ ذاك تنقّلوا في الحضرة من الحضرة بلا غيريّة فلذلك قال ﴿سُبْحَٰنَ ٱللَّهِ عَمَّا يُشْرِكُونَ﴾ فسبّح في هذه الحضرة عن الشرك وفي هذه الحضرة يكون الغفران والستر إنّما هو للسوى فيتستّر السوى عنهم بحقيقة الاسم الغفّار والغفور سبحانه.

فكلّ ستر في الوجود كان صنواً من حقائق الاسم الغفور ولذلك يرى أهل الكشف ١٠،٢٥
أنّ الحجب مجال للحقّ وحضرات لاستجلاء محاسن الحقيقة ولذلك لم يكن نسب الستر المكروه شرعاً وطبعاً وعقلاً ونقلاً خارجاً عن الاسم الغفور فتلك الأستار إنّما هي في الحقيقة أنوار وأين الظلم هايهات وهي العدم.

The full measure of righteousness is attained through perfecting all goodness, which is the station of beauty that stands in contrast to the station of majesty. These are the ones who fulfill all righteousness and are seized by the divine assault, which takes them to the boundary of the Severe in Chastisement, which lies at the furthest end of the gaze of the Misguider. Then they are received by the Self-Subsisting at the horizon of ascent where the Fire «ascends upon the hearts»,[171] and it takes them to the Giver of Safety, whereupon the Fire becomes «coolness and safety».[172] 25.8

The lesson from the story of Abraham, the Intimate Friend of the All-Merciful, unfolds from here. For mercy engulfed him; and were it not so, the fire would have engulfed him. When they are received by the Giver of Safety, He gives them access to the Giver of Security, and they feel secure after their fear. Then the Guardian guards over them by enveloping them in bliss, whereupon the Mighty presides over them and they are granted honor after abasement. Then they are subsumed by the Compeller—in the sense of compulsion—so that their levels of bliss become greater from the presence of the Proud. For in that station, they undergo a transition from and to the presence without alterity. Hence the verse «God be glorified above the partners they ascribe»,[173] for He glorifies Himself in this presence as transcending partners. In this presence, concealment and covering apply to everything other-than-God such that everything other-than-God is covered from them through the reality of the All-Concealing and the Concealing. 25.9

Hence, every covering in existence is an offshoot of the realities of the Concealing. This is why those who know through unveiling see the veils as loci of the Real and presences where reality discloses its splendors. This is also why the types of covering that are discouraged by law, nature, intelligence, and transmission do not fall outside the Concealing, for those coverings are in reality just lights. For where could there be darkness when it is sheer nonexistence? 25.10

اسمه القريب تبارك وتعالى

أوّل وروده في البقرة في قوله تعالى ﴿وَإِذَا سَأَلَكَ عِبَادِى عَنِّى فَإِنِّى قَرِيبٌ﴾ ١،٢٦
ولم يذكره الغزاليّ قال علماء الرسوم معنى قربه إحاطة علمه بكلّ شيء وأمّا القرب في اصطلاح هذه الطائفة فهو أنّه يصير سمع الشاهد وبصره وبالجملة جميع مشاعره ومداركه وفي الحقيقة أن يفنيه ويصير عينه قال الإمام زين العابدين لنا وقت يكوننا فيه الحقّ ولا نكونه وهو هذا المعنى وقال عليه السلام لي وقت لا يسعني فيه غير ربّي وهو هذا.

واعلم أنّ الحقّ لا يكون ذات الشاهد ما لم يفن وإليه أشار ابن الفارض في قوله ٢،٢٦

فَلَمْ تَهْوِنِي مَا لَمْ تَكُنْ فِيَّ فَانِيًا   وَلَمْ تَفْنَ مَا لَمْ تُجْتَلَى فِيكَ صُورَتِي

والمتصوّر عين هذه الصورة بلا حلول وإذا فني الشاهد في المشهود الحقّ كان الحقّ ولا شيء معه ولذلك قال النفّريّ الكبرياء هو العزّ والعزّ هو القرب والقرب فوت عن علم العالمين ومعنى الفوت عن علم العالمين أنّه لا يكون هناك معلوم إلّا فني فهذا هو الفوت عن علم العالمين.

فإذاً القرب هو أن يصير المشهود هو الشاهد وقد ذكر ذلك النفّري في قوله الشاهد ٣،٢٦
الذاكر إن لم يكن حقيقة ما شهد حجبه ما ذكر وفي رواية إن لم تكن حقيقته ما شهد حجبه ما ذكر ومن أهل الشهود من لا يصل إلى أن يرى أنّ الحقّ تعالى عين ذات الأشياء لكن يقرب من ذلك فقال النفّري في مثل حال هذا وقال لي أدنى علوم القرب أن ترى آثار نظري في كلّ شيء فيكون أغلب عليك من معرفتك به ومعناه أنّه ما رأى شيئاً إلّا ورأى الله تعالى عنده أظهر من ذلك الشيء فيغلب عليه أنّه الحقّ

Al-Qarīb: The Near

The first occurrence of this name is in the Surah of the Cow in the verse: «When My servants ask you about Me, truly I am near».[174] Al-Ghazālī does not mention it as a divine name. Exoteric scholars say that the meaning of God's nearness is that His knowledge encompasses all things. Nearness in the terminology of our camp means that God becomes the witnesser's hearing and seeing, and all his other faculties of awareness and perception. In reality, it means that He causes him to pass away entirely, until He becomes his identity. Imam Zayn al-ʿĀbidīn said: "We have moments when the Real becomes us, but we do not become Him."[175] Similarly, the blessed Prophet said: "I have moments when none but my Lord can embrace me."[176] 26.1

The Real does not become the essence of the witness so long as the latter has not passed away. Ibn al-Fāriḍ alludes to this in the following verse: 26.2

> As long as you have not passed away in Me, you do not long for Me;
> You will not pass away in Me as long as My form does not disclose itself within you.[177]

The one who assumes His form is the very form itself, without any indwelling. Moreover, when the witness passes away in the Witnessed Reality, then "The Real is, and nothing is beside Him."[178] That is why al-Niffarī says: "Self-Grandeur is exaltedness, and exaltedness is nearness, and nearness escapes the knowledge of the knowers." The meaning of "escapes the knowledge of the knowers" is that every object of knowledge passes away, and in this sense it "escapes the knowledge of the knowers."

Nearness, then, is that the Witnessed becomes the witness. To this effect, al-Niffarī says: "If the invoking witness does not become the reality he witnesses, then he is veiled by his invocation."[179] In another narration: "If his reality is not what he witnesses, then he is veiled by his invocation." Moreover, there are some among the witnesses who do not attain a vision of the Real as the very essence of all things, even though they come close to it. Describing their state, al-Niffarī says: "And God said to me: 'The lowest knowledge of nearness is to see the traces of My gaze in all things so that My gaze dominates your recognition of that thing.'"[180] This means that whenever the witness sees 26.3

أكثر ممّا يغلب عليه أنّه ذلك الشيء وهذا الشاهد فيه بقيّة هي التي أوجبت تردّده وإن كان رؤية الحقّ تعالى أغلب على نظره من رؤية الشيء فهو في ذلك قد نال أدنى علوم القرب.

٤،٢٦ وإذا عرفت هذا عرفت أنّ القرب عند هذه الطائفة معناه غير معناه عند المحجوبين ونحن إنّما نعتبر فيه معنى ما يقوله أهل الله تعالى لا غيرهم فنقول إنّه داخل في الاسم الأحد وفي الاسم الصمد في أحد معنييه.

٥،٢٦ واعلم أنّ باب القرب هو الفناء ولذلك قال وأنا العزيز الذي لا تستطاع مجاورته يعني أنّ مجاورته بالقرب تفني فكيف تستطاع مجاورة من مجاورته تفني ولي في هذا المعنى شعر

كَيْفَ يَرْجُو ٱلْحَيَاةَ وَهُوَ مَعَ ٱلْهَجْـ ـرِ قَتِيلٌ وَعِنْدَ رُؤْيَاكَ يَفْنَى

وإذا عرفت معنى القرب ظهر لك معنى القريب وإذا عرفت معنى القريب عرفت أنّ قربه تعالى هو بعده وليس قرب شيء هو بعده وأنّ قربه تعالى لا كقرب الشيء من الشيء وأنّ البعد هو عدم شهوده كما قيل في المواقف تراني ولا تراني ذلك هو البعد تراك وأنا أقرب إليك من رؤيتك ذلك هو البعد.

٦،٢٦ وأمّا قرب الحقّ تعالى بعلمه ففي حضرة الحجاب وقد ذكره العلماء وأمّا في حضرة الكشف فإنّ علم كلّ عالم هو علمه ولم يبق شيء إلّا علم فهو عالم بكلّ شيء فهو قريب من كلّ شيء قربًا هو عين واحدة.

something, God is more manifest to him than the thing is, so that he beholds it as the Real more than he beholds it as the thing itself. This witness retains a trace that causes him to waver, even though the vision of the Real overwhelms his vision of the thing and he thus attains the lowest knowledge of nearness.

If you know this, know also that nearness means something else to this camp than what it means to veiled intellects, and our only concern here is what it means to God's folk, not others. We therefore say that the Near is included within the Only, and within the Self-Sufficient in accordance with one of its two meanings. **26.4**

The door to nearness is annihilation, which is why al-Niffarī quotes God as saying: "I am the Exalted who cannot be taken as a neighbor";[181] that is, becoming God's neighbor by way of nearness causes annihilation. How then can someone become the neighbor of the One when being His neighbor causes annihilation? I once wrote a verse to this effect: **26.5**

> How can he aspire to live, when in avoidance
> he is dead, and upon seeing You he is annihilated?[182]

If you know the meaning of nearness, then the meaning of the Near will also be clear to you. And if you know the meaning of the Near, then you will know that His nearness is also His distance, even though the nearness of a thing is not its distance. You will also know that God's nearness is unlike the nearness of one thing to another, and that distance is to not witness Him. As stated in *The Book of Haltings*: "You see Me and you see Me not. That is distance. You see yourself, and I am nearer to you than your own sight. That is distance."[183]

God's nearness through His knowledge is within the presence of the veil, as scholars have discussed. In the presence of unveiling, His nearness through knowledge means that the knowledge of every knower is God's knowledge. And since all things are endowed with knowledge, He is the Knower through all things, and He is near to all things by a nearness that is a single entity. **26.6**

اسمه المجيب تبارك وتعالى

١،٢٧ أوّل وروده في البقرة وهو قوله تعالى ﴿أُجِيبُ دَعۡوَةَ ٱلدَّاعِ إِذَا دَعَانِ﴾ واتّفق عليه الأئمّة الثلاثة والمراد عند العلماء أنّه يجيب مسألة من سأله فيعطيه إمّا معجّلاً وإمّا مؤجّلاً وإمّا أن يكفّ عنه سوءاً يقوم له مقام ما سأله أو أعظم.

٢،٢٧ وأمّا أهل الله تعالى فيرون أنّه الداعي أيضاً ولذلك قرن قوله فقال ﴿وَإِذَا سَأَلَكَ عِبَادِى عَنِّى فَإِنِّى قَرِيبٌ﴾ ثمّ قال ﴿فَلۡيَسۡتَجِيبُواْ لِى﴾ فجعل الاستجابة لهم في مقابلة دعائه وإن كان معناه في التفسير غير هذا غير أنّ الكشف يرجّح هذا فيرجع المعنى عندهم إلى أنّه الداعي والمجيب.

٣،٢٧ وأمّا من امتحى عندهم رسم الأغيار فليس فيه عندهم داع ولا مجيب فهو الداعي وحده وهو المجيب نفسه والمحجوب يسمع الصدى ويعمى ويصمّ فلا يرى ولا يسمع الداعي الحقّ فمن كان في حضرة قولهم ما رأيت شيئاً إلّا رأيت الله قبله كان كما قال المتنبّي

فَدَعۡ كُلَّ شِعۡرٍ غَيۡرَ شِعۡرِي فَإِنَّنِي أَنَا ٱلنَّاطِقُ ٱلۡمَحۡكِيُّ وَٱلۡآخَرُ ٱلصَّدَى

ومن كان في حضرة قولهم ما رأيت شيئاً إلّا رأيت الله بعده والأمر عنده بالعكس من هذا ومن كان في حضرة قولهم ما رأيت شيئاً إلّا رأيت الله معه فهو كما قيل

رَقَّ ٱلزُّجَاجُ وَرَاقَتِ ٱلۡخَمۡرُ فَتَشَابَهَا فَتَشَاكَلَ ٱلۡأَمۡرُ

وموضع الإشكال قوله

فَكَأَنَّمَا خَمۡرٌ وَلَا قَدَحُ وَكَأَنَّمَا قَدَحٌ وَلَا خَمۡرُ

Al-Mujīb: The Responder

This name first occurs in the Surah of the Cow in the verse: «I respond to the call of the caller when he calls Me».[184] The three eminent scholars agree that it is a divine name. According to the scholars, what it means is that God responds to the request of the one who petitions Him by acceding to his request, sooner or later, or by withholding an evil from him in place of his request, which may be even greater than what was requested. 27.1

God's folk, for their part, see Him also as the Caller, and that is why after saying, «when My servants ask thee about Me, truly I am near», He follows with, «so let them respond to Me».[185] He thereby makes His response the counterpart of His call. And even though the normative interpretation of this verse differs from this reading, unveiling gives preponderance to it, which is where they derive the meaning that He is both Caller and Responder. 27.2

For those for whom the traces of otherness have been obliterated, there is no Caller and no Responder, for He alone is the Caller, and He Himself is the Responder. The veiled intellect hears mere echoes: it is blind and dumb, and cannot see nor hear the true Caller. In contrast, the one who is in the presence of the saying "I see nothing except that I see God before it" is as al-Mutanabbī puts it: 27.3

Cast aside all poetry except mine—
I am the celebrated wordsmith, others are my echo![186]

For the one who is in the presence of the saying "I see nothing except that I see God after it," the matter is the opposite. The one who is in the presence of the saying "I see nothing except that I see God with it"[187] is as the poet puts it:

Fine is the glass, and fine is the wine:
they resemble each other, and confusion ensues.[188]

The nature of this confusion is explained in the verse:

As though there were wine without a cup,
and a cup without wine![189]

وقد شهد أبو يزيد البسطاميّ هذه الثلاثة ونطق بها وأخبر عنها وقد نُقل قولهم ٤،٢٧
حُجبت فرأيت البيت فلم أر ربّ البيت ثمّ قال حجبت الثانية فرأيت البيت وربّ البيت
ثمّ قال حجبت الثلاثة فرأيت ربّ البيت ولم أر البيت ومعناه أنّه فني في نظره ما سوى
الحقّ تعالى فرأى صاحب البيت هو عين البيت فأثبت له العيان محو الكيان فكان في
نظره أنّ الله ولا شيء معه وهذا المقام فوق تلك المقامات الثلاث.

وأمّا كيف الإجابة في نظر المشاهد فتفصيل أحكامها لا تتناهى فمنه أنّ كلّ مجيب ٥،٢٧
فهي إجابة الحقّ تعالى فهذا باب من أبوابها.

واعلم أنّ الإجابة لأهل السلوك أشرف منها لغيرهم أعني في نظرهم وإلّا فهي ٦،٢٧
متساوية ومتفاوتة بحسب تفاوت مراتبها فمن إجابته لأهل السلوك ما قاله النفّري
وهو كلام هذا معناه إن عارضك السّوى فاصرخ إليّ فإن نصرتك فنم في نصري وإن
أقمتك في الصراخ فنم فيه وإقامتي لك في الصراخ هو من نصري لك فالحظ يا أخي
كيف يكون الصراخ معدوداً من النصر وذلك لأنّه إذا استمرّ في الصراخ كان خيراً
له من أن ينقطع باليأس من النصرة فإذاً ما أقيم إلّا في شيء هو خير فإذاً هو نصر من
الله تعالى وهي الإجابة للصارخ وهي من الاسم المجيب تعالى.

ومن جملة الاستجابة عند أهل الكشف إجابته ليونس عليه السلام في قوله ٧،٢٧
﴿فَنَادَىٰ فِى ٱلظُّلُمَـٰتِ أَن لَّآ إِلَـٰهَ إِلَّآ أَنتَ سُبْحَـٰنَكَ إِنِّى كُنتُ مِنَ ٱلظَّـٰلِمِينَ﴾ قال
الله تعالى ﴿فَٱسْتَجَبْنَا لَهُۥ﴾ ويعنون بهذه الظلمات ظلمات المحو وهي العدم الذي لا
أشدّ من ظلمته فلمّا فني في ظلمة العدم لاح له وجه الحقيقة فقال ﴿سُبْحَـٰنَكَ إِنِّى﴾
أنزهك عن أن يكون معك غيرك واعترف بما كان فيه قبل الشهود من اعتقاد أنّ
معه غيره فقال ﴿إِنِّى كُنتُ مِنَ ٱلظَّـٰلِمِينَ﴾ والظّلم هو وضع الشيء في غير موضعه في
لغة العرب فصرّح بأنّه كان ظالماً في اعتقاده وجود الأغيار والاستجابة له بالنسبة إلى

Abū Yazīd al-Basṭāmī witnessed three times and spoke of it. It is related that he said: "I was veiled, then I saw the House, but I did not see the Lord of the House." Then he said: "I was veiled a second time, and I saw the House and the Lord of the House." Then he said: "I was veiled a third time, and I saw the Lord of the House, but I did not see the House."[190] This means that everything but the Real passed from his sight, and he saw that the Owner of the House is the House itself, thereby affirming through vision the obliteration of engendered things. In his vision, he saw that there is God and none beside Him; and this station is above the other three stations. 27.4

The details of the response vis-à-vis the witness are infinite. One of them is that every responder is the response of the Real; this is one of the many topics that come under this heading. 27.5

The response for the wayfarers is more excellent than it is for others—from their view, I mean, for in fact they are equal or disparate in accordance with the disparity of their levels. One of His responses to the wayfarers is al-Niffarī's statement, which I paraphrase here: "If you are assaulted by other-than-God, then cry out to Me! If I come to your aid, then sleep in My aid. But if I leave you crying out, then sleep therein, for leaving you to cry out is My way of aiding you."[191] Take note, dear brother, how crying out to God is counted as divine aid. That is because to cry out persistently is better than to fall silent in despair of God's help. Thus, the caller is only made to abide in what is good, and so his crying out is an aid from God, just as His response to the one who cries out is a response from the Responder. 27.6

One of God's responses, according to those who know through unveiling, is His response to Jonah in the verse: «Then Jonah cried out in the darkness, "There is no god but You! Glory be to You! Truly I am one of the wrongdoers."» Then God says: «Then We responded to him».[192] Now, according to those who know through unveiling, «the darkness» refers to the darkness of obliteration, of nonexistence, than which there is no greater darkness. When Jonah passed away in the darkness of nonexistence, the face of Reality shone upon him and he cried out, «Glory be to You!» You are far above any alterity! He thus confessed how he had believed in alterity before witnessing the Real, and said, «Truly I am one of the wrongdoers». In Arabic, "wrongdoing" means to place a thing where it does not belong. Therefore, Jonah explicitly admitted that he had been a wrongdoer by believing in the existence of alterities. The response to Him in this presence was that God showed Jonah that 27.7

هذه الحضرة هي أنّه أراه أن ليس غيره فوجد بوجود الذات المقدّسة وهذا هو الذي يسمّونه البقاء بعد الفناء فإذاً هذه الإجابة هي من الاسم المجيب سبحانه واعتبارات هذا الاسم لا تنحصر ونحن الآن نقتصر.

اسمه السريع الحساب سبحانه

١،٢٨ أوّل وروده في البقرة ﴿سَرِيعُ ٱلۡحِسَابِ وَٱذۡكُرُواْ ٱللَّهَ فِيٓ أَيَّامٖ﴾ ولم يذكره الغزاليّ ومعناه أنّه عالم بأحوال عباده فيسرع حسابَه لهم عليها وهو عند هذه الطائفة أنّ حسابهم من أنفسهم وحقيقته أن يمتاز لكلّ أحد وجه الحقيقة فيظهر له هل هو من قسطها أو من قسط الباطل فمن كان من قسط الباطل احتاج إلى السّبك حتّى ينشأ نشأة أخرى ملائمة للحقيقة.

٢،٢٨ والحقيقة إمّا من قسط الاسم الهادي وإمّا من قسط الاسم المضلّ وكلا الحقيقتين تقتضي النعيم أمّا قسط المضلّ فيقتضي نعيمهم بعد سبكهم المعبّر عنه بالعذاب وأمّا قسط الاسم الهادي فمن أوّل الأمر إذ لا يحتاجون إلى السبك فإذاً ليس عذاب المعذّبين عند الاسم المضلّ إلّا رحمة وهو في نصيب الاسم الهادي يسمّى نقمة.

٣،٢٨ ولمّا كان الرسول عليه السلام رسالته من حضرة الاسم الهادي سمّي ذلك السبك عذاباً وهو حقّ فإنّ النطق إنّما هو عن ألسنة المراتب وكذلك كانت عبارات أهل الله تعالى عن الحقائق بمقتضى المراتب يشبه أنّها تجمع بين الأضداد وليس كذلك بل الحقائق لها عبارات مراتبيّة مختلفة بحسب اختلاف المراتب قد تكون متضادّة فينطق المحقّق في المسألة الواحدة بلسان مرتبة ما فيحسّن أمراً ربّما نطق عنه

there is none other than He. Jonah was then brought into existence through the existence of the Holy Essence, which is what they call "subsistence after annihilation." This response therefore came from the Responder. The considerations of this name cannot be exhausted, so we will keep it brief.

Al-Sarīʿ al-Ḥisāb: The Swift in Reckoning

This name first occurs in the Surah of the Cow in the verse: «God is Swift in Reckoning».[193] Al-Ghazālī does not mention it as a divine name. Its meaning is that He knows the states of His servants, and therefore His reckoning of those states' effect upon them is swift. According to our camp, however, this name means that the reckoning comes from the servants themselves. The reality of this name is that the true face of reality distinguishes itself to each person, and it becomes apparent to him whether he belongs to those who perceive reality or those trapped in falsehood. Whoever is trapped in falsehood has to be purified of dross in order to be configured "in another configuration"[194] that is conformable with reality. 28.1

Moreover, reality pertains either to the Guide or to the Misguider, and both realities ultimately entail bliss. The Misguider entails the bliss of its followers once they are purified of dross, which is conveyed by the word "chastisement." Blissfulness starts at the very outset for the followers of the Guide, for they do not need to be purified. Therefore, the chastisement of the chastised by the Misguider is mercy, even though with regard to the Guide it is called vengeance. 28.2

Since the message of the blessed Messenger comes from the presence of the Guide, the removal of the dross is called "chastisement." This is true, moreover, since speech can only use the languages of the cosmic levels. This is why the words of God's folk concerning the cosmic levels of reality appear to be self-contradictory. But they are not, for the realities are expressed at multiple levels in keeping with the differences between those levels. These levels may be opposites, such that the recognizer who verifies the truth speaks about one 28.3

بلسان مرتبة هي ضدّ تلك المرتبة فيقبّحه فيقول الجاهل المحجوب إنّه جاهل أو إنّه كاذب ولله درّ المتنبّي حيث يقول

وَكَمْ مِنْ عَائِبٍ قَوْلاً صَحِيحًا   وَآفَتُهُ مِنَ ٱلْفَهْمِ ٱلسَّقِيمِ

٤،٢٨ وإذا عرفتَ أنّ الحساب هو من نفس المحاسب اسم مفعول وكان كلّ أحد يشتغل بحساب نفسه فيكون مجموع محاسبات الأنفس هي حسابه لهم تعالى إذ ليست غيره فيسرع الحساب والصورة هذه ولو كان الحساب واحداً بعد واحد لما أسرع فإذاً هو سريع الحساب تعالى وتقدّس وقد ذكر لي سيّد من سادات العلماء كان قد وقف على كلامي على الفاتحة فقال إنّك قد أحسنت فيما ذكرته مثالاً في معنى سريع الحساب وكنتُ أنا قد أُنسيته فاعتمدت على قوله واختصرت هنا بنيّة الحوالة على ذلك الكلام فمن أراد البسط في هذا فليطالع ما ذكرته في شرح الفاتحة على ألسنة المراتب لا على ظاهر التفسير.

اسمه الحليم سبحانه

١،٢٩ هذا الاسم العظيم اتّفق على إيراده الأئمّة الثلاثة وآيته من البقرة قوله تعالى ﴿غَفُورٌ حَلِيمٌ﴾ حمل الحلم في لغة العرب مرّة على أنّه ضدّ الجهل ومرّة على أنّه ضدّ الانتقام من المذنب والحقّ عندي أنّه موافقة الصواب فلا تضع السيف في موضع النّدى ولا العكس.

٢،٢٩ وأمّا في حقّ الحقّ تعالى فهو العمل بمصلحة العبد فربّما رآه العبد من جهله أنّه انتقام ولو عرفه لعلم أنّه حلم وربّما رأى لطفاً فعلم أنّه حلم واعتقد أنّه كان يستحقّ العقاب

matter in the language of a specific level, declaring that matter to be beautiful; but when he speaks of it in the language of another level, he declares it to be ugly. The ignorant and veiled intellect will therefore accuse the recognizer of ignorance or deceit. How excellent is al-Mutanabbī's verse that reads:

> Many a people have criticized correct speech,
> yet they suffer from diseased minds.[195]

If you know that reckoning comes from the one who is reckoned, and that everyone is busy reckoning their own souls, then the totality of reckoned souls is God's reckoning. For there is no other reckoning, and hence the reckoning is swift when it is done this way. If the reckoning were to take place one by one, then He would not be swift. Therefore, He is Swift in Reckoning. In fact, one respected scholar once told me after reading my commentary on the Opening Surah: "Your example concerning the meaning of the Swift in Reckoning was well judged." At the time, I had forgotten what I had written, so I took his words to heart and summarize here the gist of my discussion. Whoever wishes a more elaborate discussion should consult what I wrote in my commentary on the Opening Surah in terms not of exoteric exegesis but of the registers of the cosmic levels. **28.4**

Al-Ḥalīm: The Forbearing

The three eminent scholars agree that this mighty name is a name of God. Its verse is in the Surah of the Cow: «Concealing, Forbearing».[196] "Forbearance" was sometimes taken by the early Arabs to mean the opposite of ignorance, and sometimes it is taken to mean the opposite of vengeance upon the one who has wronged you. For me, it really means coinciding with what is correct, such that one does not punish the one who deserves to be rewarded, or vice versa. **29.1**

With respect to the Real, forbearance is to act in the servant's best interest. In his ignorance, the servant may well see the treatment as vengeance, but if he were to know the Real then he would understand that it is forbearance. **29.2**

فعومل[1] باللطف وليس كذلك بل ما عامل أحداً إلّا بمستحقّه ولا يستحقّ أحد إلّا الإحسان ولكن يتلبّس الأمر على المحجوب فيعتقد أنّه سومح أو عوقب على غير ما يقتضيه مصلحة وهو جهل والحقّ تعالى لو صفح عمّن يستحقّ أن يظهر بالعقوبة لوضع الشيء في غير موضعه وهو الظلم ﴿وَمَا رَبُّكَ بِظَلَّٰمٍ لِّلۡعَبِيدِ﴾.

٣،٢٩ فإذاً عقوبته وصفحه كلاهما حلم لأنّ الحلم في الحقيقة هو موافقة الصواب وفعله لا يعدو الصوابَ فهو الحليم سبحانه بهذا التفسير لا بما يعتقده المخالف.

٤،٢٩ وإذا علمت هذا علمت أنّ تأثيرات الأسماء كلّها داخلة في معنى الاسم الحليم إذ هو موافقة الصواب في الفعل والترك وأحكام الأسماء كلّها صواب فهي كلّها داخلة في الاسم الحليم سبحانه فإن قلت إنّه إن فاته الحلم الذي هو الصفح عمّن يستحقّ العقوبة فاتته مَكرمة وكمال فالجواب إنّ كلّ من صفح عمّن يستحقّ العقوبة فهو صفحة لوحدانيّة الفاعل في الكلّ.

٥،٢٩ فإن قلت إنّك قد منعت من ظهوره بهذه الحقيقة تعويضاً عنها بمطاوعة الصواب والصفح عمّن يستحقّ العقوبة قد يكون ممّا لا يوافق الصواب فلا يكون الحقّ تعالى فاعلاً له فالجواب أنّ موافقة الصواب هي أعمّ ممّا أشرت إليه وهو أن يكون الصفح عن الجاني في نظر الأغيار صواباً مطلقاً ونحن لا نقول به ونقول إنّ الصواب في كلّ صورة صورة ممّا يقع هو الصواب الموافق للمصلحة ويكون قسط الحقّ تعالى في كلّ فعل موافقة الصواب وقسط الأغيار الفرق فيكون الصفح عن الجاني تارة صواباً وتارة خطأً وهما في نظر المكاشف سواء في أنّهما موافقان للصواب المحجوب عن نظر أهل الاغتراب فحصل من هذا أنّ فعل الحقيقة موافق للصواب مطلقاً وأفعال الأغيار ولا أغيار هناك

[1] آ، ب، ج: فقوبل.

A servant may also see gentleness and take it to be forbearance, believing that he deserves punishment but has been shown gentleness. But that is not the case, for God only treats His servants as they deserve, and no one deserves anything but beneficence. Yet the veiled intellect is duped by this and believes that he is forgiven or punished in a manner that is not in his best interest; and that is ignorance. For if God were to forgive the one who deserves to be punished, then He would put a thing somewhere it does not belong, which is the definition of wrongdoing; «And your Lord does not wrong His servants».[197]

Therefore, both His punishment and forgiveness are forbearance, because in reality forbearance is to coincide with what is correct, and God's act does not deviate from what is correct. He is therefore Forbearing according to this explanation, not according to what gainsayers believe. 29.3

If you understand this, then you will understand that all the traces of the names are included within the meaning of the Forbearing, because forbearance is to coincide with what is correct in both action and inaction, and all the properties of the names are correct, which means they are all included within the Forbearing. You might say: if God does not possess the attribute of forbearance in the sense of pardoning someone who deserves to be punished, this means that He is without a certain noble quality and perfection. The answer is: to pardon someone who deserves punishment is a pardon from God, because all acts are one. 29.4

You might then say: but you have discounted the possibility of His manifesting through this reality, and argued instead that He always conforms to what is right: forgiving someone who deserves punishment might not conform to what is right. How then can you say that it was the Real who enacted this forgiveness? The answer is: conformity to what is right is more comprehensive than what you allude to, for in the eyes of others it seems absolutely right to forgive the guilty. But that is not what we are saying. What we are saying is that what is right in each form is the form of what occurs that is right and advantageous: and in every act the Real shares in that which coincides with what is right, while that in which things other-than-God share is separation. Thus, to forgive the guilty is sometimes right and sometimes wrong. From the perspective of the unveiled thinker, both are exactly the same in that they coincide with the right that is veiled from the view of those in a state of separation. In sum, the action of the Real coincides absolutely with what is right, while the acts of other-than-God, which only exist from a certain 29.5

إلّا باعتبار أن يكون صواباً مرّة وخطأً مرّة أخرى وهذه المسألة غامضة تحتاج إلى ترقّ في النظر فهو الحليم بالمعنى الجامع سبحانـه.

اسمه الخبـير تبارك وتعالى

١،٣٠ أوّل وروده في البقرة في قوله تعالى ﴿وَٱتَّقُواْ ٱللَّهَ وَٱعْلَمُوٓاْ أَنَّ ٱللَّهَ بِمَا تَعْمَلُونَ خَبِيرٌ﴾ واتّفق عليه الأئمّة الثلاثة والخبرة خصوص وصف في العلم كما يقال الخبرة الباطنة والظاهرة ومستند العقل المحجوب في اعترافه له تعالى أنّه الخبير كونه خلق الخلق قال تعالى ﴿أَلَا يَعْلَمُ مَنْ خَلَقَ﴾ ثمّ أعقبها بقوله ﴿وَهُوَ ٱللَّطِيفُ ٱلْخَبِيرُ﴾ فإنّ اللطف في الإحاطة بالمعلومات أمكن ومجرى هذا اللطف هو القيّوميّة ومعناها قيام كلّ شيء به لطيفها وكثيفها ولمّا كانت الكثائف أهون إدراكاً من اللطائف نسب خبرته تعالى إلى اللّطف والعادة أن يقال إنّ فلاناً لطيف الإدراك أي غوّاص على المعاني الخفيّة والحقّ تعالى منزّه عن هذا غير أنّه خاطبنا على قدر العقول المحجوبة فعلى هذا يكون ذكر اللطف مناسباً لذكر الخبرة.

٢،٣٠ ولا شكّ أنّ وجوده سارياً بالقيّوميّة فيما لطف أو كثف فهو محيط ﴿بِكُلِّ شَىْءٍ عِلْمًا﴾ وعلمه ذاته فذاته محيطة ﴿بِكُلِّ شَىْءٍ﴾ وهي أعني الذات هي التي تشيّئ الشيئيّات وتمهّي الماهيات خلافاً لمن زعم أنّ الأعيان المعقولة غير مجعولات فهي كثيرة في عالم الحجاب واحدة الجوهر في وحدانيّة ذلك الجناب ولي في هذا المعنى بيت شعر وهو

perspective, are sometimes right and sometimes wrong. This is an obscure matter that requires a high level of reflection, and He is the Forbearing in an all-comprehensive sense.

Al-Khabīr: The Aware

This name first occurs in the Surah of the Cow in the verse: "So reverence God, and know that God is aware of what you do."[198] The three eminent scholars agree it is a divine name. Awareness is a specific quality of knowledge, just as one speaks of an "inner awareness" and an "outer awareness." That He created creation is used by veiled intellects as a basis for acknowledging that God is the Aware. God says: «Does the One Who created not know?», followed by «And He is the Subtle, the Aware».[199] For indeed, encompassing objects of knowledge in a subtle manner seems most plausible, and this subtlety flows through His quality of self-subsistence, which means that all things, both subtle and dense, are sustained by Him. Since dense things are more easily perceived than subtle things, He ascribes His awareness to subtlety. Furthermore, it is conventional to say "so-and-so has a subtle sense of perception"; that is, "he dives deep for hidden meanings." But the Real is hallowed beyond this, except in the sense that He addresses us according to the limitations of veiled intellects, which is why it is appropriate to mention subtleness along with awareness. 30.1

There is no doubt that His existence flows through His quality of self-subsistence in both subtle and dense things. For He encompasses «all things in knowledge»,[200] and His knowledge is His Essence. Therefore, His Essence encompasses «all things» and the Essence is what makes things things and quiddities quiddities. This is opposed to those who maintain that the intelligible entities are not made; for they are many in the realm of the veil, but one in substance with respect to their oneness. To this effect, I composed a verse of poetry that reads: 30.2

وَعَيْنِيَ مَا كَانَتْ وَلَكِنْ عُيُونُهَا   رَنَتْ فَانْتَشَتْ فِي طَيِّهِنَّ عُيُونِي

٣،٣٠ فسريان قيّوميّته تعالى في كلّ ذات وصفات وأفعال منها يقع العلم ﴿بِكُلِّ شَيْءٍ﴾ فهو يعلم الشيء من عين ذلك الشيء ومعلوم أنّ ذاته عين علمها وذاتها هي معلومها وعلمها وغيرهما ممّا لا ينحصر فهو الخبير سبحانه وتعالى وكيف لا تظهر الأشياء في وجوده ووجوده هو النور والنور أضاء في الظلمة وإنّما الظلمة لم تدركه وكيف تدركه الظلمة وهي إمّا عدم محض وإمّا سلوب عدميّة أو نسب إضافيّة وكلّ ذلك لا عين له في طور من الأطوار أمّا العدم الصرف فظاهر وأمّا السلوب والنسب فوجودها ذهنيّ والصور الذهنيّة من الوجود.

٤،٣٠ وإذا حُقّق الأمر وُجد ما في الذهن غير المعدوم الذي يتصوّره منه الذهن ثمّ إنّه من المستحيل أن يتصوّر الذهن أصلاً معدوماً خارجيّاً بل إنّما يقال إنّه تصوّر ما مصداقه خارجيّ هذا في تصوّر ما يتصوّره الذهن من الموجودات الخارجيّة فكيف النسب العدميّة فإذاً الظلمة لا تدرك النور والنور يدرك ذاته فيدرك في عين إدراكه كلّ شيء وأيّ خبرة أعظم من خبرة تكون في ضمن إدراك من أدرك ذاته وذلك لأنّ ذاته لا تغيب عنه فلا يغيب عنه شيء فهو الخبير سبحانه.

اسمه القابض جلّت قدرته

١،٣١ أوّل وروده في سورة البقرة في قوله تعالى ﴿وَٱللَّهُ يَقْبِضُ وَيَبْصُۜطُ﴾ واتّفق عليه الأئمّة الثلاثة وهو في رأي العلماء بمعنى المانع أي يمنع من يشاء وفيه معنى الإمساك

I myself have no existence, but as her existence unfolds,
mine grows within her fold.[201]

Therefore, His knowledge «of all things» occurs through His quality of self-subsistence that flows through every essence, quality, and act, such that He knows a thing through the very entity of that thing. It is well known, moreover, that His Essence is identical with His Essence's knowledge, and the essence of Its knowledge is Its objects of knowledge, Its knowledge, and other limitless things. He is thus the Aware; and how could things not manifest in His existence, when His existence is light? For light illumines darkness, and darkness does not perceive light, for how could darkness perceive light when it is either absolute nonexistence, privative forms of nonexistence, or relative nonexistents, none of which have a determined entity at any stage? Absolute nonexistence obviously does not perceive light, whereas privations and relativities exist in the mind, and mental forms are a part of existence. 30.3

Once this concept is realized, one discovers that what is in the mind is different from the nonexistence that is conceptualized by the mind. Moreover, it is categorically impossible for the mind to conceptualize an external nonexistent. The most that can be said is that the mind conceptualizes a thing that is evidenced externally. If this is the case for the mind's conceptualization of external existence, what then of relative nonexistents? Therefore, darkness does not perceive light, and light perceives its own essence, and so it perceives all things through its own self-perception. And what greater awareness is there than an awareness that is part of the perception of the One who perceives His Essence? For God's Essence is never hidden from Him, and therefore nothing is hidden from Him, and so He is the Aware. 30.4

Al-Qābiḍ: The Withholder

This name is first mentioned in the Surah of the Cow in the verse: «God withholds and lavishes».[202] All three eminent scholars agree it is a divine name. According to the opinion of exoteric scholars, the name means the Preventer; 31.1

قال الله تعالى ﴿وَيَقْبِضْنَ مَا يُمْسِكُهُنَّ إِلَّا ٱلرَّحْمَٰنُ﴾ والتحقيق فيه أنّ ما منع من المنع فهو من الاسم المانع ومرجعه إلى الاسم الله وما فيه من الإمساك فيرجع إلى الاسم الرحمٰن من حيث ما يدخل الاسم الرحمٰن في الاسم الله فإنّ الإمساك لا تكون فيه الرحمة بالذات بل بالعرض فإنّ الرحمة بسط والقبض ضدّ البسط فهو ضدّ حقيقة الرحمٰن.

٢،٣١ ولمّا نطقت التلاوة بقوله تعالى ﴿مَا يُمْسِكُهُنَّ إِلَّا ٱلرَّحْمَٰنُ﴾ علمنا أنّ المراد إمساك خاصّ تكون فيه الرحمة لكن بالعرض كما ذكرنا لأنّ الإمساك عند كمال مرتبة الظهور هو رحمة مثاله أنّ التكوين للولد في الأرحام لو استمرّ لزاد في الجنين أعضاءً أخرى غير ما جرت به العادة فتكون زائدة تؤدّي إلى عذاب فالإمساك عنها يكون رحمة وكذلك لو كانت الزيادة في طول الأعضاء أو عظمها خارجاً عمّا يُحتاج إليه لكانت عذاباً وكذلك لو كانت الزيادة أشكالاً أخرى غير أشكال أعضاء الإنسان لم تكن رحمة بل عذاباً وكذلك في كلّ موجود موجود لو زادت خلقته عن قدر الحكمة لم تكن رحمة وإن كانت الزيادات الوجوديّة كلّها منسوبة إلى الاسم الرحمٰن والرحيم بما فيها من الوجود الذي هو المادّة لكلّ موجود.

٣،٣١ وإذا علمت هذا علمت أنّ الإمساك عن تلك الزيادات المذكورة وأمثالها ممّا لا يتناهى هو رحمة فالإمساك إذاً بهذا التفسير يرجع إلى الاسم الرحمٰن لكنّ ذلك إذا استمدّه الاسم القادر فإنّ القدرة إنّما تظهر بالإمساك عند كمالات الموجودات إذ لو زادت عنها لانخرم وجود ذلك الموجود الذي تعلّقت به القدرة فالإمساكات هي تمام المقدورات فيكون القابض من موادّ الاسم القدير سبحانه لكن باعتبار الاسم الرحمٰن لا بحسب ذاته بل بحسب لواحقه فعلى هذا يكون الاسم القابض راجعاً للاسم الله بالذات وللاسم الرحمٰن بالعرض ويأخذ منه الاسم القدير قدر ما يتمّ به القدرة.

٤،٣١ وأمّا ما فيه من المنع فالقابض يكون في ذلك هو الاسم المانع وذلك لأنّ الاسم المعطي يبسط والاسم المانع يقبض فإذاً الاسم القابض إذا استعمله الاسم القادر كان فيه

that is, He who prevents whomever He wishes. It also comprises the meaning of holding back, for God says: «spreading out their wings; none holds them back except the All-Merciful».[203] The realization of the name is that all His acts of prevention are from the Preventer, and return to the name Allāh; and all His acts of holding back return to the All-Merciful, insofar as the All-Merciful is included within Allāh. For holding back does not involve mercy intrinsically, but only accidentally, since mercy is expansion, and withholding is its opposite: therefore, withholding is opposed to the reality of the All-Merciful.

Now, since revelation proclaims that «none holds them back except the All-Merciful», we learn that the meaning that is intended is a specific type of holding back that contains mercy, but only accidentally, as we said. For at the stage of full manifestation, holding back is a form of mercy. For instance, were the development of a child in the womb to continue beyond a certain point, the embryo would acquire an abnormal excess of limbs, and this would cause suffering. Therefore, it is a mercy to hold back excessive growth. Likewise, it would be a form of torment if there were to be an unnecessary increase in the length or size of our body parts. Also, it would not be an act of mercy but a torment if shapes alien to the shape of human body parts were to increase. The same holds for every single existent: if it were to grow beyond its wisely decreed measure, that would not be a mercy, even if all these existential growths are ascribed to the All-Merciful and the Ever-Merciful insofar as they comprise existence, the underlying material substrate for every existent. 31.2

If you know this, then you will know that it is a mercy to hold back such inordinate growths and countless other types of growth, and so according to this interpretation "holding back" goes back to the All-Merciful. However, if the holding back is supported by the Powerful, then power only manifests when the growth of complete existent things is held back. For if it were to continue growing, the existent dependent upon divine power would fall apart. Therefore, every act of withholding is a completion of an object of the divine power. Accordingly, the Withholder is one of the aspects of the Powerful, but only with respect to the All-Merciful, and with regard to its ancillary associations, not its essence. Thus, the Withholder returns to Allāh in an essential manner, and to the All-Merciful in an accidental manner; and the Powerful takes from it to the extent that power reaches its completion through it. 31.3

In the case of prevention, the Withholder becomes the Preventer, because the Giver expands, and the Preventer withholds. Therefore, if the Withholder 31.4

من الرحمٰن ممازجة بالعرض وإذا استعمله الاسم المانع لم يكن فيه من الاسم الرحمٰن إلّا مجرّد ما تقوم به حقيقة المنع وهي رحمة خاصّة تظهر بها حقيقة المنع فقط ولا يكون فيها للرحمٰن غير ذلك وبقيّة حقيقة الاسم المانع ترجع إلى الله لا إلى الرحمٰن وكلاهما أعني اسم الله والاسم الرحمٰن يرجعان إلى الذات لا بالحقيقة الاسميّة بل من حيث اعتبار أن تكون الذات ولا شيء معها.

اسمه الباسط تبارك وتعالى

١،٣٢ أوّل آية ذُكر فيها في ترتيب التلاوة في سورة البقرة في قوله تعالى ﴿وَٱللَّهُ يَقۡبِضُ وَيَبۡصُۜطُ﴾ واتّفق على إيراده الأئمّة الثلاثة وقد خصّه العلماء ببسط الرزق لقوله تعالى ﴿يَبۡسُطُ ٱلرِّزۡقَ لِمَن يَشَآءُ﴾ ويعنون بالرزق المقتات أو ما كان في معناه أو ما أدّى إليه ومعناه عند أهل الأذواق أعمّ وهي في مقابلة الاسم القابض فتكون معانيه معادلة لمعاني الاسم القابض في المقابلة ويُفهم من ذلك المراتب المذكورة في الاسم القابض فيطّلع منها على معاني الاسم الباسط وكذلك القول في العكس.

٢،٣٢ واعلم أنّ عالم الجمال هو داخل في الاسم الباسط وهو المقام الذي شُرّف بعيسى عليه السلام فكان لا ينظر إلّا الجمال ولا يتصرّف بشيء من أسماء الانتقام والمستولي عليه الاسم الرحمٰن فالاسم الباسط يستمدّه الاسم القادر في مبادئ الإيجادات وأوساطها فإذا أتت إلى نهاياتها تلقّاه الاسم القابض فوقّفها عند الغايات فيكون عطاء الاسم القابض المنع للقادر عن تعدّي ما لا يكون من تمامات الإيجاد فالاسم المعطي للباسط والاسم المانع للقابض.

is employed by the Powerful, it mixes with the All-Merciful in an accidental manner; but if it is employed by the Preventer, it merely partakes in the All-Merciful to the extent that the reality of withholding is sustained. That, moreover, is a specific mercy by which the reality of withholding alone manifests, and the All-Merciful has no other share in it. The remnant of the reality of the Preventer returns to Allāh, not the All-Merciful. And both—I mean Allāh and the All-Merciful—return to the Essence, not through the reality of the name but from the standpoint that the Essence is, and nothing is with It.

Al-Bāsiṭ: The Lavisher

The first verse in which this name is mentioned, according to the order in which the names occur in the Surah of the Cow, is: «God withholds and lavishes».[204] The three eminent scholars agree it is a divine name. Scholars limit the meaning of the name to the lavishing of provision, per the verse «God lavishes provision on whomsoever He will».[205] By "provision" they mean means of self-subsistence, or that which shares its meaning or leads to it. However, according to those who know through tasting, its meaning is more general than this. For it is a counterpart to the Withholder, and so its meanings are in precise contrast to those of the Withholder. The levels of the Withholder thus offer an overview of the meanings of the Lavisher, and vice versa. 32.1

The Lavisher includes the realm of beauty. This is the station that Jesus was honored by, for he saw nothing but beauty, and did not in the slightest conduct himself according to the names of vengeance. The All-Merciful presided over him. Thus the Lavisher is assisted by the Powerful at the early stages of existentiation, and also at the intermediate stages. When these existentiations reach their final stages, the Lavisher is met by the Withholder, which stops them when they reach their fullest extent. In this sense, the bestowal of the Withholder lies in how it prevents the Powerful from straying into anything detrimental to complete existentiation. The Bestower therefore pertains to the Lavisher, and the Depriver to the Withholder. 32.2

٣،٣٢ ولمّا كان الاسم الباسط هو الممدّ لعالم الجمال كان الاسم القابض هو الممدّ لعالم الجلال وهما حضرتان متقابلتان تجمعهما حضرة الكمال وحضرة الجلال هو المقام المتشرّف بموسى عليه السلام ولتقابل هاتين الحضرتين تقابل الفعل من موسى عليه السلام ومن عيسى عليه السلام فقتل موسى سبعين ألفاً في قوله ﴿ٱقۡتُلُوٓاْ أَنفُسَكُمۡ﴾ وقال عيسى عليه السلام إذا لطمك على خدّك فأدر له الخدّ الآخر.

٤،٣٢ فأسماء الانتقام للاسم الجليل من مقام الجلال وأسماء الإنعام للاسم الجميل من مقام الجمال والاسم المهيمن هو على الحضرتين من مقام الكمال وأهل غلبة الرجاء ينظرون بالاستعداد إلى حضرة الجمال وأهل الخوف ينظرون بالاستعداد إلى حضرة الجلال وهاتان الطائفتان هم العبّاد.

٥،٣٢ وأمّا الصوفيّة فليس الرجاء والخوف من أوصافهم وذلك لأنّ الرجاء طمع وهم يطالبون أنفسهم بمفارقة الطمع لأنّه من سفساف الأخلاق وأمّا الخوف فهو جبن وبخل إما بأنفسهم وإمّا بأموالهم وأيّ ما كان فهو من قسم سفساف الأخلاق.

٦،٣٢ ولم أقصد بالصوفيّة من سمّي بهذا الاسم بين الناس بل من تحقّق بمقام التصوّف وهو تبديل الأخلاق المذمومة بالأخلاق المحمودة إلّا أنّ بعض الناس يتوهّم أنّ الخلق الحسن هو أن لا يقابل السيّئة إلّا بالحسنة مطلقاً وليس كذلك لأنّ هذا يخصّ مقام الجمال والصوفيّ في تزكيته لنفسه إنّما يحاذي حضرة الكمال وهي الجامعة للجمال والجلال فيكون في الصوفيّ الإنعام والانتقام لكن لا ينتقم لنصرة نفسه ميلاً مع الهوى بل إن كان قد أقيم في مقام من يفوّض إليه إقامة الحدود فإنّه يقيمها ولا تأخذه فيها ﴿لَوۡمَةَ لَآئِمٍ﴾ كما قيل عن رسول الله صلّى الله عليه وسلّم إنّه ما انتقم قطّ لنفسه إلّا أن تنتهك حرمة هي لله فينتقم لله بها.

٧،٣٢ والفرق بين الصوفيّ والمحقّق وإن تساويا في الفعل أنّ المحقّق شهد حضرة الكمال وتحقّق بها والصوفيّ حُجب فيما لتلك الحضرة من الجلال وتحقّق بها فإذاً للصوفي قسط من الجمال والجلال والمحقّق فيهما المالك لذلك أو الواصل الذي به يهتدي كلّ سالك

Since the Lavisher replenishes the realm of beauty, the Withholder replenishes the realm of majesty, and these two opposite presences are brought together by the presence of perfection. The presence of majesty, moreover, is the station that honored Moses; and because of the contrariety between these two presences, the actions of Moses and Jesus stood in contrast to each other. Moses thus killed seventy thousand men by saying, «Kill yourselves»,[206] whereas Jesus said, "If he slaps you on the cheek, turn the other cheek."[207] 32.3

Therefore, the names of vengeance pertain to the Majestic in the station of majesty, and the names of bliss pertain to the Beautiful in the station of beauty, and the Overseer is in both presences in the station of perfection. The people who are dominated by hope look with preparedness to the presence of beauty, and those dominated by fear look with preparedness to the presence of majesty. These two groups constitute the worshippers. 32.4

As for the Sufis, hope and fear are not among their qualities, for hope is covetousness, and they seek to rid themselves of covetousness because it is a base character trait. Likewise, fear is cowardice and miserliness with regard to either the soul or wealth, both of which are base character traits. 32.5

By the term "Sufi," I do not mean all who are commonly designated thus. Rather, I mean the one who realizes the station of Sufism, which is the transformation of blameworthy character traits into praiseworthy ones. However, some people imagine that beauty of character means to always respond to an evil deed with a good deed. But that is not so, for this is specific to the station of beauty, and in purifying himself the Sufi is approximating the station of perfection, which combines beauty and majesty. As such, the Sufi contains both bliss and vengeance. Yet he does not exact vengeance in order to aid his own self by inclining toward his passions. Rather, if he is placed, for instance, in the position of someone responsible for upholding capital punishment, he applies the law and does not fear «the blame of any blamer».[208] To this effect, it is said that the blessed Messenger "never avenged himself, except if the inviolability of God were violated, whereupon he would avenge for the sake of God."[209] 32.6

The difference between the Sufi and the one who has verified the truth, though both may be equal in their actions, is that the one who has verified the truth witnesses and verifies the presence of perfection. The Sufi, for his part, is veiled by the majesty of the presence and verifies that. Therefore, the Sufi has a share of beauty and majesty, whereas the one who has verified the truth has mastery of both; he has arrived, and every wayfarer follows his guidance. In sum, all the properties of the aforementioned stations that pertain to the 32.7

فحصل ممّا ذكرناه أنّ ما كان في هذه المقامات المذكورة يخصّ جانب الإنعام فهو للاسم الباسط ومقابلات أحكامه هي للاسم القابض.

٨،٣٢ واعلم أنّ أوّل النهار للاسم الباسط إلى أن تزول الشمس ثمّ يتولّى بقيّة النهار الاسم القابض إلى أن تغرب ثمّ يتولّى الليل الاسم الباسط ليبسط البواطن من قوى الإنسان وذوات الحياة وقِوَى النبات وما تحته بسطاً طبيعياً فيحصل في الظواهر السبات وفي البواطن الحركات إلى مثل حدّ الزوال من النهار وذلك منتصف الليل ثمّ يتولّى الاسم القابض للبواطن فيكون الاسم الباسط ممدّاً للاسم الباطن في الليل وممدّاً للاسم الظاهر في النهار ويكون القابض على العكس من ذلك.

٩،٣٢ وكذلك أيضاً يقتسمان العام أعني الاسم الباسط والاسم القابض فتكون بينهما تلك النسبة بعينها هذا في الاقتسام التفصيلي وأمّا في الاقتسام الإجماليّ فيكون الشتاء والربيع للاسم الباسط فإنّ الشتاء والربيع حضرتان للإيجاد وهو بسط كما قال ابن عبّاس في قوله تعالى ﴿يَبْسُطُ ٱلرِّزْقَ لِمَن يَشَآءُ﴾ وفي قوله ﴿وَفِى ٱلسَّمَآءِ رِزْقُكُمْ وَمَا تُوعَدُونَ﴾ فقال هو المطر وهو عالم الشتاء الذي منه بسط الرزق وكذلك عالم الربيع فإنّ فيه يظهر حكم الإيجاد البسطيّ.

١٠،٣٢ وأمّا عالم الصيف والخريف فهما من عالم الاسم القابض لتمام إدراكات الثمار التي هي نهايات الإيجاد الشتويّ والربيعيّ كما قدّمنا من أنّ الاسم القابض له تعلّق بإتمام المقدورات وهو عالم الصيف والخريف فالاسم القابض له الصيف والخريف والاسم الباسط له الشتاء والربيع.

١١،٣٢ فإن قلت إنّا رأينا الحيوانات في الشتاء تنقبض وكلّ ما انقبض فهو للاسم القابض فالجواب أنّ ذلك بالعرض فإنّ كلّ عالم من عوالم الأسماء فيه كلّ عالم من عوالم الأسماء وإنّ كلّ شيء فيه كلّ شيء وإنّما الحكم للأغلب فينسب العالم إلى الاسم الذي هو أظهر حكماً في ذلك الزمان ويبقى من دونه منطوياً فيه.

١٢،٣٢ واعلم أنّ أعمار الحيوان ومن دونهم ومن فوقهم من الإنسان فإنّ فيها أسناناً مختلفة فسنّ النموّ للاسم الباسط إلى سنّ الوقوف ثمّ ينتقل الحكم إلى الاسم القابض

ambit of bliss belong to the Lavisher, whereas the opposite properties belong to the Withholder.

The first part of the day pertains to the Lavisher until the sun reaches its midpoint, and then the rest of the day until the sun sets is presided over by the Withholder. Then, until the counterpart to midday, which is midnight, the Lavisher presides over the night, lavishing in a natural manner the inner dimensions of the faculties of humans, living creatures, plants, and all that is below them, so they pass outwardly into torpor, while inwardly they move. Then the Withholder presides over their inner realities. As such, during the night the Lavisher replenishes the Nonmanifest, and during the day replenishes the Manifest, whereas the Withholder follows the opposite pattern. 32.8

Likewise, both the Lavisher and the Withholder divide the year into two, and share the exact same relation as far as particular divisions are concerned. As for general divisions, winter and spring pertain to the Lavisher, because winter and spring are presences of existentiation, which is a type of lavishing. To this effect, Ibn ʿAbbās said concerning the verses «He lavishes provision on whomsoever He wills»[210] and «In heaven is your provision and that which you were promised»[211] that "the provision is rain," which is the winter season from which provision is lavished. The same holds for the spring season, for in it the expansive property of existentiation becomes manifest. 32.9

Summer and autumn are from the realm of the Withholder because this is when fruits reach full maturity, which spells the end of the hibernal and vernal existentiation. For as we said previously, the Withholder pertains to the completion of the objects of power—namely, the realms of summer and autumn. Thus, summer and autumn belong to the Withholder, and winter and spring belong to the Lavisher. 32.10

If you were to say: We see animals seeking shelter during the winter, and everything that withdraws pertains to the Withholder, the answer is that this is accidental, for every name-world is contained within every other, and all things are contained within all things. The ruling property, however, is ascribed to the dominant one, and so the world is ascribed to the name whose property is most prominent at that time, while the other property remains enfolded within it. 32.11

The lifespans of animals and those beneath them, and of the humans above them, comprise different ages. For instance, the age of growth belongs to the Lavisher until the age of maturity, then from the age of maturity till the appointed time the property transfers to the Withholder. «For every 32.12

من سنّ الوقوف إلى أن يحلّ الأجل و﴿لِكُلِّ أَجَلٍ كِتَابٌ﴾ ولكلّ كتاب أجل والكتاب للاسم الباسط والأجل للاسم القابض فالقابض مانع والباسط معطٍ.

اسمه الحيّ تبارك وتعالى

١،٣٣ أوّل وروده في البقرة من قوله ﴿ٱللَّهُ لَآ إِلَٰهَ إِلَّا هُوَ ٱلْحَيُّ ٱلْقَيُّومُ﴾ واتّفق على إيراده الأئمّة الثلاثة وفسّره العلماء بأمرين أحدهما البقاء الذي لا فناء معه والآخر المعنى الذي به يكون حاله مخالفاً لحال الأموات ولا شكّ أنّه أمر غير نفس البقاء قال بعضهم إنّ معنى التحيّات لله أي الحياة لله والحياة له بذينك الاعتبارين المذكورين.

٢،٣٣ وأمّا أهل الأذواق فالحياة عندهم أخصّ أوصاف الوجود المطلق به وألصق الصفات له ومعنى الحياة هو وجوديّة الوجود وكونه لا عدم فيه باعتبار من الاعتبارات ويلزم من هذا أنّ كلّ من اتّصف بالوجوديّة فهو حيّ وإن كان الوجود له أقوى كانت حياته أقوى وأنّ كلّ حياة فهي حياة للوجود والوجود هو الموجود بوجه أشرف والموجود هو الوجود بوجه أكمل والكمال والشرف للحقيقة الوجوديّة فالحياة لها بما لا يتناهى من الاعتبارات.

٣،٣٣ ولمّا كانت الحياة إنّما هي للوجود الرحمٰن سبحانه وكان لو كانت حياته على نمط واحد نقص من أطوار حياته بمقدار ما فاته من ذلك لزم أن تختلف الحياة بالزيادات ولست أقول بالنُقصانات فإنّ النقص ليس في الوجود إلّا في طور هو شرط الكمال أو شرط لكمال ما هو أيضاً من شرط الكمال فلا نقص أصلاً فإذاً اختلاف الحياة هو

appointed time there is a Book»[212] and for every Book there is an appointed time. The Book pertains to the Lavisher, and the appointed time pertains to the Withholder. The Withholder deprives, and the Lavisher gives.[213]

Al-Ḥayy: The Living

This name is first mentioned in the Surah of the Cow in the verse: «Allāh, there is no god but He, the Living, the Self-Subsisting».[214] The three eminent scholars agree it is a divine name. The scholars interpret this name in two ways: the first is that it means subsistence that never passes away; the second is that it means the reality whose state is opposed to the state of the dead. But it is certainly not identical to subsistence. Some say that the meaning of "*taḥiyyāt* be to God"[215] is "life belongs to God." In any case, He possesses life in both abovementioned senses. 33.1

For those who know through tasting, life is the most specific quality of unconditioned existence, and the quality most closely attached to it. The pure meaning of life is the existential quality of existence and how it contains no nonexistence in any respect whatsoever. From this it follows that whatever is qualified by the quality of existentiality is living; and the stronger its existence, the stronger its life. It also follows that every individual life is a life of existence. Existence is the existent in a more excellent sense, and the existent is existence in a more perfect sense; and excellence and perfection pertain to the reality of existence. Therefore, there is no end to the considerations of life. 33.2

Life pertains precisely to the All-Merciful's existence; and if His life were of only one sort, its levels would be imperfect on account of its dearth of variety. Given this, there must necessarily be variety in life in the form of increase. I do not say decrease, for decreasing does not exist except at a stage that is a condition for perfection, or a condition for the perfection of something that itself is a condition for perfection; and so there is no imperfection to begin with. Therefore, the variety in all life belongs to the Living Subsisting One, and is one of the descriptions of the Living. All existents are living and speaking, but 33.3

للحيّ الباقي من نعوت الكمالات للاسم الحيّ فجميع الموجودات أحياء ناطقات لكن بنطق الوجود الذي يعرف ترجمته أهل الشهود

إِذَا نَطَقَ ٱلْوُجُودُ أَصَاخَ قَوْمٌ بِأَسْمَاعٍ إِلَى نُطْقِ ٱلْوُجُودِ

وكلّ ناطق حيّ والكلّ ناطق فالكلّ حيّ وهو الحيّ الذي لا إلٰه إلّا هو.

٤،٣٣ فإذا فسّرنا الحياة بمعنى البقاء فكلّ من بقي ولو في أن لا ينقسم فهو حيٌّ ما دام باقياً فإذا فارق الموجود صورته التي هو بها حيّ في طور من أطوار الوجود بقيت مادّته في صورة مادّيّته فكانت تلك المادّة لها الحياة مدّة بقائها في صورة المادّيّة فإذا لبست صورة أخرى إمّا على انفرادها وإمّا في اختلاطها بمادّة أخرى بقيت له حياة تناسب مرتبة تلك الصورة التي لبستها.

٥،٣٣ واعلم أنّ الموت إنّما يتحقّق بمفارقة الصور والصور عدميّة فالموت عدميّ مقترن بالعدميّات التي هي الصور وأمّا المتصوّر فهو الوجود الحقّ وله صفات سمّاها الحسّ المحجوب صوراً فالذي للصور من الوجود هو الحقّ الوجوديّ ونسبة العدم هي لذات الصورة وهي اعتباريّة فإدراكها على غير المشاهد عسر جدّاً وحقيقتها البرزخيّة هي الموجودات.

٦،٣٣ ولي في معنى البرزخيّة أبيات وهي هذه

لِلْبَرْزَخِيَّةِ مَعْنًى لَسْتُ أُبْدِيهِ إِلَّا لِمَنْ ظَهَرَتْ أَحْكَامُهَا فِيهِ
وَقَابَلَ ٱلْقَوْلَ بِٱسْتِعْدَادِهِ فَرَأَى نُقُوشَ أَشْكَالِ قَوْلِي فِي مَرَائِيهِ
أَمَّا ٱلَّذِي رَمِدَتْ عَيْنَا بَصِيرَتِهِ فَبَعْضُ أَنْوَارِ هٰذَا ٱلشَّيْءِ يُعْمِيهِ
فَإِنْ سَكِرْتَ بِهَا يَا صَاحِ فَٱصْحُ فَمَا إِسْكَارُهَا عَاشِقاً إِلَّا لِتُصْحِيهِ

they speak through the language of existence, whose meanings are only understood by those who witness:

> When existence speaks, one group
> lends its ear to the speech of existence.[216]

Every speaking entity is alive, and everything speaks, thus everything is alive; and He is the Living, there is no God but He.

Since we have explained that life means subsistence, everything that subsists—even by being indivisible—is alive so long as it subsists. But when at a certain stage of existence the existent is separated from the form through which it lives, its underlying material substrate subsists in the form of its materiality, and that substrate possesses life for the duration of its subsistence in its material form. When it takes on a different form—either by itself, or after mixing with another material—it retains life in keeping with the level of the form in which it clothed itself. 33.4

Moreover, death only becomes actualized through separation from form; and since forms pertain to nonexistence, death too must pertain to nonexistence. It is linked with nonexistents, which are forms. The one who assumes the form, however, is true existence whose qualities are named "forms" by veiled sensory faculties. Thus, the existence that the forms possess is existential reality, and the ascription of nonexistence pertains to the essence of the form, which is perspectival. Perceiving the perspectival relation between nonexistent forms and their real essence is very difficult for those who are not able to witness. Its liminal reality is the existents themselves. 33.5

I have composed the following verses concerning the meaning of liminality:[217] 33.6

> Liminality has a meaning that I will only disclose
> to the one in whom its properties are manifest;
> The one who, in his preparedness, is receptive of these words and sees
> the engraved shapes of my words in his field of vision.
> He whose eyes are inflamed, swollen by lack of insight,
> will be blinded by the slightest of these lights.
> So, if you are intoxicated by its light, dear friend, sober up! For
> they intoxicate the lover only to render him sober.

وَإِنَّهَا حَيْثُ تَنْفِي ٱلْعَقْلَ تُثْبِتُهُ بِهَا لَهَا لَا بِهِ كَمَا تُرَقِّيهِ
فَٱلْبَرْزَخِيَّةُ عَنْ بَحْرَيْنِ عَيْنُهُمَا إِلَى ٱلشَّهَادَةِ تَدْعُوهُ دَوَاعِيهِ
يَحُولُ بَيْنَهُمَا فَٱعْجَبْ لَهَا عَدَمًا سِرُّ ٱلْوُجُودَيْنِ فِيهَا وَهْيَ تُبْدِيهِ
وَمَا لَهَا فِيهِمَا أَيْنٌ يُقَيِّدُهَا إِذْنَ حَوَاهَا ٱلَّذِي بِٱلذَّاتِ تَحْوِيهِ
كَانَ ٱلْوُجُودُ بِلَا مَعْنًى لِوَحْدَتِهِ بَسَاطَةً وَهْيَ أَعْطَتْهُ مَعَانِيهِ
وَكَثْرَتَهُ وَلَوْلَا سِحْرُهَا لَغَدَا فَرْدًا بِلَا كَثْرَةٍ فِي عَيْنِ رَائِيهِ
فَإِنْ نَظَرْتَ إِلَيْهَا لَا بِأَعْيُنِهَا بَلْ عَيْنِهِ لَمْ تَجِدْ مِنْ كَثْرَةٍ فِيهِ

٧،٣٣ فحياة الأطوار كلّها هي للمتطوّر بها وحياة المتطوّر بها هي للاسم الحيّ والحياة وإن اتّحد معناها فلها ثلاثة اعتبارات إحداها حياة يقابلها الموت وحياة يزيدها قوّة ما يلحق الصور من الموت وحياة لا يزيد لها شيء ولا يقابلها شيء وهي الحياة السرمديّة التي بالحياة الأولى والأخرى لها بالعرض والذي لها من ذاتها إنّما هو البقاء السرمديّ الذي الأوّليّة والآخريّة به ومنه وله.

٨،٣٣ وله في هذه الثلاثة الاعتبارات الأولى منها تلحق الموجود من العرش إلى الفرش وما في ذلك وما بين ذلك والحياة والموت فيها باعتبارات مختلفات فموت الحيوان غير موت النبات وكذلك سائر الرتب الباقيات والفانيات الخلقيّات وأمّا الثانية فهي حياة الأسماء والصفات بمعان مختلفات وفيها الربوبيّة والعبوديّة وأمّا الثالثة فهي حياة لها جميع ما سبق ذكره من أنواع الحياة وفيها منها ما لا يقدر العقل أن يدركه إلّا بالتجلّيات الذاتيّات والاسم الحيّ مشتمل الحقيقة على كلّ ما ذُكر وما لم يذكَر ولو أخذنا نفسّر أنواع الحياة لاستغرق عمر الدنيا بشطره وما حُصر قليله فكيف كثيره.

For inasmuch as liminality negates intelligence, it also affirms it,
by and for it, not by the intellect itself, just as intoxication elevates it.
Now, liminality issues from two oceans; their fountainhead
calls its callers to bear witness;
It oscillates between the two, so wonder at its nonexistence!
The secret of the two existences lies within it, and reveals it,
Yet liminality has no "where" within the two oceans to delimit it,
so it is engulfed by the essence that engulfs it.
Existence had no meaning; its unity had
a simplicity, then liminality gave it its meanings
And its multiplicity; and but for its dawn, it would arise in the morning
as an indivisible entity without multiplicity in the eye of its observer.
So, when you behold liminality, not through its eyes,
but through His eye, you will not find any multiplicity therein.[218]

The life of all the stages therefore pertains to the one undergoing those stages, whose life pertains to the Living. And although the meaning of life is a single unity, it can be considered from three perspectives: life that is the counterpart of death, life that increases in power when forms conjoin with death, and life that neither increases nor stands counterpart to anything; this is the everlasting life, with respect to which the first and second types of life are accidents. What pertains to its essence is none other than the everlasting subsistence from which, by which, and for which there is firstness and lastness. 33.7

Regarding these three considerations: The first is connected to all existents, top to bottom, and all that they contain. There is life and death therein from various respects: the death of animals, for instance, differs from the death of plants; and the same holds for all the other subsistent levels and ephemeral existents. The second is the life of the names and qualities with all their diverse meanings, including lordship and servanthood. The third is life that possesses all these types of life, including life that the intellect can only grasp through disclosures of the Essence. The Living engulfs the reality of all that was mentioned and unmentioned. If we were to try to explain the types of life, it would take the entire lifespan of the world and half as much again to cover even a little of it, to say nothing of the majority of it! 33.8

اسمه القيّوم تبارك وتعالى

١،٣٤ شاهده من البقرة قوله تعالى ﴿ٱللَّهُ لَآ إِلَٰهَ إِلَّا هُوَ ٱلْحَيُّ ٱلْقَيُّومُ﴾ واتّفق عليه الأئمّة الثلاثة قال مجاهد القيّوم القائم بكلّ شيء وروي عن ابن عبّاس القيّوم الذي لا يزول وقال الضحّاك القائم الدائم وقال الربيع ابن أنس القيّوم ٱلْقَآئِمُ عَلَىٰ كُلِّ نَفْسٍ برزقه وحفظه قال أبو جعفر وتأويل مجاهد والربيع حسن مستقيم وصف الله عزّ وجلّ نفسه بأنّه القائم بأمر كلّ شيء في رزقه والدافع عنه وتقول العرب فلان القائم بأمر البلد ولا شكّ أنّ الموجودات كلّها بمنزلة البلدة وهو تعالى قائم بأمرها.

٢،٣٤ والقيام بأمر الموجودات هو قيام بما لا يتناهى فيكون القيام بأمره لا يتناهى خصوصاً إذا عُلم أنّ الذوات والصفات غير متناهية وليس قيام الحقّ تعالى بالموجودات في أرزاقها وحفظها فقط بل وفي ذواتها وصفاتها أمّا من علم أنّ العالم متجدّد أبداً كما قال تعالى ﴿بَلْ هُمْ فِى لَبْسٍ مِّنْ خَلْقٍ جَدِيدٍ﴾ فهو يعلم أنّ قيام الحقّ تعالى بكلّ تجدّد ومتجدّد هو قيام مستمرّ تجدّد به التعلّقات أو أنّه قام بنفسه فقام كلّ متجدّد به.

٣،٣٤ وإن قلنا أو قال قائل إنّه يستحيل عليه تجدّد التعلّق أو التجدّد مطلقاً فإنّ جوابه أن يقال لم يتجدّد له التجدّد فأين التجدّد وهذا المعنى من فهمه علم أنّ الحقّ تعالى لا يتجدّد له شيء وأنّ التجدّد ثابت وفهم هذا يحتاج إلى معرفة أصلين أحدهما وحدانيّة الذات والآخر تنوّع الصفات.

٤،٣٤ وأكثر ما يقع تعرّف الحقّ تعالى في بداية الأمر لأهل الترقّي هو من الاسم القيّوم وذلك لأنّ مبدأ تعرّف الاسم الظاهر هو من القيّوميّة في مبادئه فإن حصل التعرّف

Al-Qayyūm: The Self-Subsisting

This name occurs in the Surah of the Cow in the verse: «Allāh, there is no god but He, the Living, the Self-Subsisting».[219] The three eminent scholars agree that it is a divine name. Mujāhid says: "The Self-Subsisting (*al-qayyūm*) is the One who stands watch over all things (*al-qā'im*)." Ibn ʿAbbās is reported to have said: "The Self-Subsisting is the One who never ends." Al-Ḍaḥḥāk says: "The Self-Subsisting is the everlasting." Al-Rabīʿ ibn Anas says: "The Self-Subsisting is «He who watches over every soul»[220] by providing for it and protecting it." Abū Jaʿfar says: "The interpretations of Mujāhid and al-Rabīʿ are beautiful and clear." God describes Himself as standing watch over (*qā'im bi*) the affairs of all things by providing for them and repelling harm from them. Moreover, the Arabs say: "So-and-so is the one who attends to (*al-qā'im bi-*) the affairs of the land," and there is no doubt that the totality of existent things corresponds to the land, and that God attends to its affairs. 34.1

Attending to the affairs of existents is attendance to that which is infinite. Therefore, His attendance to His affairs is infinite, especially given that the essences and qualities of existents are infinite. Moreover, the Real's attendance to existents is not limited to their provision and preservation alone, but rather extends to their essences and qualities. Thus, the one who knows that the world is continuously being renewed—for God says: «Nay, but they are doubtful about a new creation»[221]—knows that the Real's attendance to every renewal and every thing that renews is a continuous attendance whose connections are constantly renewed. Alternatively, it is that He sustains Himself and thereby sustains everything that renews itself through Him. 34.2

If we or someone else were to say that it is impossible for God to renew connections, or that renewal is absolutely impossible for Him, the answer is that it is not on His side that the renewal takes place, for where is the renewal? Whoever grasps this meaning knows that for the Real nothing is renewed, yet the renewal is immutable. Grasping this requires direct recognition of two principles: the first is the oneness of the Essence, and the second is the multiplicity of the qualities. 34.3

Direct recognition of the Real mostly occurs at the incipient stages of those advancing on the Path from the Self-Subsisting. That is because the recognition 34.4

بقيّوميّته تعالى في الأفعال كان شهود المترقّي بأن يرى كلّ فعل هو من فعل الله تعالى فيظهر الاسم القيّوم من طور أفعال الموجودات فأوّل ما يغلب على الشاهد أن يرى الفعل للموجود لكن بقوّة الله تعالى فيجعل القوّة لله تعالى والفعل للعبد.

٥،٣٤ فإذا ظهر له في التجلّي مزيد في الشهود يرى أنّ الفعل لله تعالى لكن بواسطة العبد فإن تخلّص له الشهود الفعليّ بأن رآى أنّ الفعل لله وحده ويعزل العبد عن الفعل وحينئذ يرى أنّه حال العبادة لم يكن هو الفاعل فيسقط من قلبه اعتبار الأعمال الصالحة التي سلفت له وقد كان يعدّ أنّها ذخيرة له في الآخرة فينقطع أمله من المجازاة على تلك الأعمال إذ لم تكن صادرة عنه وهذا وإن كان ظاهره أنّه فاته ثمرات الأعمال فقد حصل له شهود الفاعل الحقّ فالذي حصل له أعلى ممّا فاته لكن شهود القيّوميّة إنّما يتعيّن في الأفعال حالة بقاء بعض الرسوم بحيث يرى أنّ الحقّ تعالى هو قوّى ذلك الفعل فأمّا إذا رأى أن لا فاعل إلّا الله فقد انتقل عن حضرة الاسم القيّوم إلى ما فوق مقامه.

٦،٣٤ فقد ظهر ممّا قلناه أنّ القيّوميّة من الاسم القيّوم وما هو فوقها وهو وحدانيّة الفعل وإفراد الفاعل الحقّ تعالى بالتصرّف لكن يبقى حكم القيّوميّة ثابتاً فيما بين الذات التي سُلب الفعل عنها وبين نفس الفعل ولو سُلبت القيّوميّة عنهما لم يكن للفعل نسبة إلى هذه الذات لا في العيان المحجوب ولا في العيان المكشوف لكنّ العيان يشهد باتّصال الفعل بهذه الذات حجاباً وكشفاً وسلبه عنها في الشهود الجزئيّ لا يقتضي سلبه عنها مطلقاً فتبقى بينهما إذاً رابطة وتلك الرابطة هي القيّوميّة وهي نصيب الاسم القيّوم في حال الفردانيّة المالكة للفعل.

of the Manifest starts with the beginning of divine self-subsistence. When recognition of His subsistence in the acts is attained, the spiritual traveler witnesses all acts as God's act. Thus, the Self-Subsisting manifests at the stage of the acts of existents, and the first thing that dominates the witness is the perception of how the existent has activity, but only through God's potential; so he assigns the potential to God, and the act to the servant.

Then, when his witnessing increases and manifests for him in the disclo- 34.5
sure, he sees that the act belongs to God but through the intermediacy of the servant. Then, when his witnessing of the acts is purified so that he sees that the act belongs to God alone, and he disassociates the servant from the act, at that moment he sees that in his state of worship he was not the actor. Thus, he eliminates from his heart any consideration of the righteous deeds that he had previously performed, and that he used to consider to be a repository for him in the hereafter. He no longer hopes for recompense for those deeds, since they did not issue from him. Even if in this state it may appear that the fruits of his deeds have escaped him, in fact he has experienced a witnessing of the true Actor, and thus what he has gained is greater than what he has lost. However, witnessing the quality of divine self-subsistence in the acts only occurs in a state where some traces still subsist, such that he sees that it is the Real who empowered the act. But once he sees that there is no actor other than God, he has passed from the presence of the Self-Subsisting to the station above it.

It is clear from what we have said that the quality of divine self-subsistence 34.6
derives from the Self-Subsisting, and what lies above it is the oneness of the act and ascribing agency to the Real Actor alone. However, the property of divine self-subsistence remains affixed between the individual from whom the act was stripped and the act itself. For were the quality of divine self-subsistence to be stripped of both, the act would have no relation to that individual, whether in the veiled or the unveiled visionary state. However, visionary experience testifies to the joining of the act and the individual in both the veiled and the unveiled state, and the stripping of the act from the individual during a partial visionary state does not entail that it is completely stripped away from the individual. Therefore, there remains a connection between them, and that connection is the quality of divine self-subsistence, which is the share of the Self-Subsisting in the state of exclusive singularity that takes possession of the act.

ثمّ إذا انتقل السالك في الترقّي إلى شهود وحدانيّة الصفة شرع نصيب الاسم ٧،٣٤
القيّوم ينفصل أوّلاً فأوّلاً حتّى تنسلب الصفة عن الذات بإفرادها عنه للحقّ تعالى
وهو مبدأ الفناء الذاتي فإنّ الفناء إذا ورد تدريجيّاً كان هكذا بأن تفنى الصفات
ثمّ تفنى بعد ذلك الذات أمّا إذا كان السالك مجذوباً وورد عليه الأمر بغتة بغير تدريج
كان الفناء دفعة واحدة كما قيل

ٱلْفَتَى مَنْ سَلَبَتْهُ جُمْلَةً   لَا ٱلَّذِي تَسْلُبُهُ شَيْئًا فَشَيْئًا

ونعود فنقول ما دام للرسم في الشاهد أثر فالقيّوميّة باقية وهو نصيب الاسم القيّوم ٨،٣٤
فأمّا إذا استغرق الفناء ارتفع حكم الاسم القيّوم وبقي الواحد الحقّ وتمامه أن يتّصل
به الصمد فيكون الأحد صمداً وهو قوله تعالى ﴿قُلْ هُوَ ٱللَّهُ أَحَدٌ ٱللَّهُ ٱلصَّمَدُ﴾
فالأحديّة تتبعها الصمديّة.

ونعود إلى الاسم القيّوم تعالى فنقول إنّ سلطانه على كلّ موجود يكون للحجاب فيه ٩،٣٤
حكم ما فهو رابطة بين الحقّ والخلق فهو كالسلك الذي يحمل فرائد العقد وجواهره
ولولاه لانفرط لكنّ انفراط القيوميّة بأن يفنى كلّ ما كان منظوماً لا بأن يتفرّق فحسب
بل أن يعدم فهذه مرتبة الاسم القيّوم في الوجود وهو شهود من قال ما رأيتُ شيئاً
إلّا ورأيتُ اللهَ معه وهو من المشاهد المشهودة التي يمرّ عليها أكثر السالكين في
السفر الأوّل.

When the wayfarer advances in his journey to witness the oneness of divine qualities, the portion of the Self-Subsisting begins to disengage progressively until the quality is stripped away from the individual and becomes exclusively ascribed to the Real, and that is the incipient stage of the individual's annihilation. For when annihilation occurs in degrees, it follows in this manner so that the qualities are annihilated, then the individual is annihilated. But if the wayfarer is divinely attracted and the matter occurs suddenly without a gradual progression, the annihilation occurs in a single swoop. As a poet once said: 34.7

Brave is he who is despoiled whole,
not the one who is despoiled bit by bit.[222]

Let us return to what we were saying. So long as a trace leaves its mark on the witness, the quality of divine self-subsistence continues to subsist, and that is the share of the Self-Subsisting. However, when annihilation becomes complete, the property of the Self-Subsisting is lifted and the One Real subsists. Its completion, moreover, occurs when it joins with the Self-Sufficient, whereupon the Only becomes Self-Sufficient. This is expressed in the verses: «Say, He, God, is the Only; God, the Self-Sufficient».[223] For self-sufficiency is subordinate to only-ness. 34.8

Let us return to the Self-Subsisting, and note that its realm of authority over every existent comprises a certain property of the veil, because this name is a connection between the Real and creation. Indeed, it is like the thread that ties together the pearls and gemstones of a necklace. Without the thread, it would fall apart. Yet the falling apart of the quality of divine self-subsistence means that everything that was tied together becomes annihilated. It does not merely scatter; it ceases to exist. This then is the level of the Self-Subsisting in existence, and this is what is witnessed by the one who proclaims, "I see nothing except that I see God with it." It is also one of the well-known contemplative stations through which most wayfarers pass during the first journey. 34.9

اسمه العليّ تعالى قدسه

شاهده في سورة البقرة وهو قوله تعالى ﴿وَلَا يَئُودُهُۥ حِفۡظُهُمَا وَهُوَ ٱلۡعَلِيُّ ٱلۡعَظِيمُ﴾ ١،٣٥
وهومّا اتّفق على إيراده الأئمّة الثلاثة وللعلماء في معناه مذهبان أحدهما أنّه العليّ عن أن يكون له شبيه في جميع صفاته العلا وأسمائه الحسنى ومنعوا في حقّه علوّ المكان المذهب الثاني من حمل الأمر على ظاهر قوله تعالى ﴿ٱلرَّحۡمَٰنُ عَلَى ٱلۡعَرۡشِ ٱسۡتَوَىٰ﴾ والعرش عالي المكان فقالوا إنّ الله تعالى هو العليّ على أمكنة عباده فالمذهب الأوّل يقولون إنّه تعالى لا يليق أن يخلو منه مكان وأمّا المذهب الثاني فبخلاف ذلك والرأي السديد عدم التعرّض لما ذكرت الطائفتان.

٢،٣٥ وترك التعرّض له مراتب أحدها مرتبة العبّاد فإنّهم مشتغلون بعبادة ربّهم تعالى عن الخوض في هذا إذ ليسوا مطالبين به المرتبة الثانية مرتبة الصوفيّة فإنّهم معرضون عن هذا لا شغلاً عنه بالعبادة بل لأنّهم أهل أدب لا يرضون أن يصفوا الله تعالى بما لم يروه عيانًا بل يقبلونه على مراد ربّهم ولا يتعرّضون إلى غير ذلك لأنّه يقدح في الصدق ويقتضي التهجّم والأدب لا يقتضي ذلك المرتبة الثالثة مرتبة أهل المحبّة وهم قوم مشغولون بالوجد وبالخوف من الفقد ولهم حالتان أحدهما أن يغلب عليهم إجلال المحبوب فتصغر أنفسهم عندهم أن ينظروا بعقولهم في صفاته لأنّهم يعلمون أنّه يراهم ويرى أسرارهم فلا يتهجّمون بأسرارهم على حضرة قدسه والحالة الأخرى حالة من يغلبهم العطش إلى مورد شهوده فيمثّله لهم الطمع فيكادون يجدونه في كلّ مرأى

Al-ʿAlī: The High

This name occurs in the Surah of the Cow in the verse: «Protecting them tires Him not, and He is the High, the Magnificent».[224] The three eminent scholars agree this is a divine name, and exoteric scholars typically take two approaches to its meanings. The first is that He is too High for anything to be like His exalted qualities and beautiful names. They also declare that it is impossible for highness in His case to be spatial. The second approach is to interpret this name according to the literal meaning of the verse: «The All-Merciful, upon the throne He sat».[225] Since a throne is a high place, they say that God is High above the locations of His servants. Thus, those who take the first approach maintain that it is inappropriate for any place to be devoid of Him, while the second approach takes the opposite position. The correct opinion, however, is to refrain from engaging with what either group says. 35.1

Refraining from engaging with these positions has many levels: The first level is that of the worshippers, for they are occupied with worshipping their Lord, rather than diving into this discussion, for they are not required to address it. The second level is that of the Sufis, who refrain from this debate, not out of preoccupation with worship, but out of courtesy to God. They do not approve of describing God in a manner that they have not seen with their own eyes. Thus, they accept the meaning of this name just as their Lord intended it, and they do not meddle any further because that would compromise their sincerity and constitute intrusive behavior, which is contrary to the dictates of etiquette when it comes to God. The third level is that of the lovers, who are preoccupied with finding mystical ecstasy and fear its loss. They have two states: The first is that of those who are overwhelmed in their declaration of the majesty of the Beloved, so that they deem themselves to be too small to reflect intellectually upon His qualities. They know that He sees them, and sees their innermost secrets, so they do not intrude upon His holy presence with their innermost secrets. The other state is that of those who are overcome with thirst for the spring of divine witnessing. Their burning desire causes the image of the spring to appear before them, and they well nigh find Him in every object of sight and every audible sound. For this group, intruding upon God takes priority over declaring His majesty, and is more in keeping with 35.2

ومستمع وعند هؤلاء أنّ التهجّم عليه هو أولى من إجلاله وأليق بالأدب فيكون الاسم العليّ عند طائفة الأولى بمعنى العظيم وعند الثانية بمعنى الودود.

ولي في حال الطائفة الأولى شعر وهو ٣٫٣٥

أَشْتَاقُهُمْ فَإِذَا لَاحَظْتُ عِزَّةَ مَنْ   أَشْتَاقُ أُطْرِقُ لِلتَّعْظِيمِ إِطْرَاقَا
وَإِنْ ذَكَرْتُ حَقَارَاتِي وَعِزَّهُمُ   خَجِلْتُ فِي ٱلْحُبِّ أَنْ أَبْكِي وَأَشْتَاقَا
عَزُّوا فَمَا ٱلسَّعْيُ بِٱلْمَوْصُوفِ عِنْدَهُمُ   هَلْ نَالَ نُجْحًا بِهِمْ أَوْ نَالَ إِخْفَاقَا
سِوَى أَمَانِيَّ إِنْ تَصْدُقْ فَفَضْلُهُمُ   أَعْطَى وَإِلَّا فَنُقْصِي دُونَهَا عَاقَا

ولي في حال الطائفة الثانية شعر وهو ٤٫٣٥

لَوْلَا ٱلْحَيَاءُ وَأَنْ يُقَالَ صَبَا   لَصَرَخْتُ مِلْءَ ٱلسَّمْعِ وَاطَرَبَا
حَضَرَ ٱلْحَبِيبُ وَغَابَ حَاسِدُنَا   مِنْ بَعْدِ طُولِ تَجَنُّبٍ وَخِبَا
فَٱلْيَوْمَ أَخْلَعُ يَا مَدَى أَمَلِي   فِيكَ ٱلْوَقَارَ وَأَطْرَحُ ٱلرُّتَبَا

فالاسم العليّ بمعنى العظيم عند أولئك وبمعنى الودود عن هؤلاء.

وأمّا من فوق المحبّين فهم العارفون وهم قوم ليس لهم من الأسماء الإلٰهيّة إلّا ما شهدوه فلا تعرّض لهم إلى اسم دون اسم حتّى يتجلّى لهم تعالى بما تعرّف به إليهم من أسمائه وصفاته وأفعاله فإن تجلّى لهم الاسم العليّ فهو عندهم بمعنى القريب لأنّ قربه يفنيهم فيتحقّق له العلوّ بالبقاء ولهم ضدّ العلوّ وهو الفناء وهذا العلوّ مرتبيّ ليس هو بمعنى شيء ممّا ذكره علماء الرسوم فالاسم العليّ بمعنى المميت وفي هذا المعنى قال من قال لن ترى الله حتّى تموت ولأهل الطريق في هذا ألفاظ مثل السّحق والمحق والمحو وأمثال ذلك. ٥٫٣٥

courtesy. As such, the High according to the first group means the Magnificent, and according to the second it means the Lover, the Kind.

I wrote the following verses about the first group: 35.3

I long for them, but when I see the exaltedness of those
I long for, I can only bow my head in awe;
And when I recall my lowliness and their exaltedness,
I feel ashamed to cry or yearn for love.
They are exalted, but what use could it be to beseech them?
Would it win them over, or merely lose their favor?
I have only wishes, which they might grant in their grace;
but if they do not, then the fault is mine alone.[226]

I wrote the following verses about the second group: 35.4

Were it not for shyness, and that I would be called infatuated,
I would shout at the top of my voice, "What joy!"
The Beloved is here, and he who envies us is absent
afte we have languished so long, veiled and sorrowful.
Today, O You in Whom is my every hope,
I abandon dignity and throw off formality.[227]

For the former, the High means the Magnificent, and for the latter, the Lover, the Kind.

Those above the lovers are the recognizers, who have none of the divine 35.5
names except for those they witness. They do not turn their attention to one name instead of another until God discloses Himself to them by His names, qualities, and acts, through which He makes Himself recognizable to them. Thus, when He discloses Himself to them as the High, for them it means the Near because His nearness annihilates them, and they come to realize His highness through subsisting in God after annihilation. This is the opposite of highness; that is, annihilation. This highness in rank has nothing to do with the meaning discussed by exoteric scholars. For the High means the Death-Giver, and it is because of this meaning that a recognizer once said: "You will not see God until you die."[228] Those who are on the spiritual path have various terms in reference to this, such as effacement, extermination, obliteration, and the like.

٦،٣٥ هذا وقد يلحظون في الاسم العليّ إذا تجلّى لهم الاسم الغالب بمعنى ﴿وَٱللَّهُ غَالِبٌ عَلَىٰٓ أَمۡرِهِۦ﴾ وكما قال في المواقف وواقف بمعرفة أتعرّف إليه بالغلبة والإشارة إلى المحو المذكور ومن لحظ معنى العليّ وجده في كلّ مستعل علوًّا مرتبيًّا كان أو جسمانيًّا وجده دائمًا لأنّ هذا الشاهد يلحظه في الاسم العليّ معنى الاسم المحيط لما علمت من أنّ كل اسم فيه كلّ اسم بل كلّ شيء فيه كلّ شيء.

اسمه العظيم جلّت قدرته

١،٣٦ أوّل وروده في البقرة وهو قوله تعالى ﴿وَلَا يَـُٔودُهُۥ حِفۡظُهُمَا وَهُوَ ٱلۡعَلِيُّ ٱلۡعَظِيمُ﴾ وقد اتّفق على إيراده الأئمّة الثلاثة والعظمة في حقّه تعالى التكبّر وهذا بالنظر إلى مدارك العقول.

٢،٣٦ وأمّا في نظر التوحيد فالتكبّر يقتضي أن يكون مع المتكبّر غيره فيتكبّر عليه وليس معه غيره وأمّا ما منه فيتكبّر باعتبار المراتب وأحكامها فيظهر بصفة العظمة التي معناها احتجابه عن العقول أن تدرك كنهه وهذه عظمة ظاهرة وتظهر بصفة العظمة التي معناها الغلبة فيكون بمعنى الاسم الغَالِبِ على الأَمْـر ويعظم في نفوس العبّاد حين يظهر لهم باسمه المعبود في اعتبار العبادة أو باسمه الربّ في اعتبار أنّهم عبيده ويقال إنّه عظيم في كلّ معاني الأسماء وهذا كلّه في لسان العلم.

٣،٣٦ وتظهر العظمة أيضاً في لسان المعرفة كمن شهد اسمه المحيط سبحانه فإنّه يشهد عظمة يكاد يتولّه من سطوة ظهورها وكذلك يظهر لمن شهد آياته في الآفاق فإنّه يرى

Furthermore, the recognizers may observe the High when the Dominant discloses itself to them in the sense of «God is dominant over His affair»,[229] or as stated in *The Book of Haltings*: "One who attains to Me with knowledge, to whom I make Myself known through dominance";[230] the allusion here is to obliteration. Those who witness the meaning of the High find it in every person of ascendancy, either in rank or in body, because the witness observes in the High the meaning of the Encompassing, for as you know, all names contain all the names, and in fact all things contain all things. 35.6

Al-ʿAẓīm: The Magnificent

The first occurrence of this name is in the Surah of the Cow in the verse: «Protecting them tires Him not, and He is the High, the Magnificent».[231] The three eminent scholars agree it is a divine name. For God, magnificence means pride, and that is from the viewpoint of what the intellect can perceive. 36.1

However, from the viewpoint of divine oneness, pride entails that there is another above whom the Proud proclaims His greatness—yet there is nothing other than Him. God's pride over what is from Him pertains to the cosmic levels and their properties. He thereby manifests through the quality of magnificence in the sense that He veils Himself from the intellects so that they cannot perceive His core, which is an obvious magnificence. Moreover, He manifests through the quality of magnificence in the sense of dominance, meaning "the one who dominates over the affair."[232] He also becomes magnificent in the souls of the worshippers when He manifests to them, with respect to their worship, as the Worshipped One, or with respect to them being His servants, as the Lord. It is also said that the concept of magnificence pervades all of His names. This entire discussion pertains to the language of exoteric knowledge. 36.2

The quality of magnificence also manifests in the language of direct recognition. For when someone, for instance, witnesses His name the Encompassing, he thereby witnesses a quality of magnificence so forceful in its manifestation that it almost causes the witness to become mad with ecstasy. Likewise, God 36.3

الأجسام والأجرام غير متناهية فإن شهد في تعظيم الآفاق وفي التعظيم الآفاقيّ اسمه الظاهر وهو تجلّي التدلّي من قوله ﴿ثُمَّ دَنَا فَتَدَلَّىٰ﴾ فضّل الأجسام على الأرواح ونطق لها بالحجّة وجعل الغيب خادماً للشهادة وجعل الباطن تبعاً للظاهر وكانت الغايات عنده عللاً للأوساط والبدايات وربّما رأى أنّ الأرواح مظاهرها أمزجة الأبدان وتكون نشأة الإنسان البدنيّة عنده عظيمة فيظهر الاسم العظيم بمعنويّتها فيكون الشاهد معظّماً لصور بني آدم على أيّ صفة كانت خصوصاً صورة ظهرت بالعلم فكيف إن ظهرت بالمعرفة فكيف إن غابت في الفناء في نظر صاحبها فكيف إن ثبتت بالبقاء في نظره.

٤،٣٦ ويعظّم أيضاً القضاة والولاة والأمراء والملوك والخلفاء تعظيماً إلٰهيّاً تعظيم كشف إلٰهيّ ولا يختصّ تعظيم هذه المراتب عنده بطائفة أو أهل مذهب دون أهل مذهب وتكون الملائكة عنده أفضل إلّا أنّ الأناسي يكون عنده أكمل وتظهر عنده الأفعال كلّها من الأغيار والأقوال أيضاً لطهارة مراتب الاسم الظاهر عنده من الأغيار ويكون بهذا النظر الشهوديّ في الغاية القصوى لا في مطلع الأضواء ويكون بين الناس محتجباً فلا ينشَر منشوره ولا يطوى فتعطيه حقيقة شهود الظاهر بطوناً عن إدراك الخلق له فيلحق آخر أطوار الظاهر بضدّه وهو الاسم الباطن في أوّل حدّه فيكون الاسم العظيم مشهوداً بالحواسّ الخمس موجوداً بتنويره الروح والنفس.

٥،٣٦ وقد يظهر الاسم العظيم بشهود ما وُجد في الأذهان من الأبعاد فيجد عدم التناهي لازماً لتعلّقها وإن لم يشهد لها عيناً في الوجود ولا أثراً في الجود فمعروضها خارجيّ لا هي والمحقّق من يعذر الغافل عنها واللاهي فيكون التعظيم في طورها اعتبارياً وقد

manifests Himself to the one who witnesses His signs on the horizons. Such a person sees bodies and corporeal entities in their infinitude. Upon witnessing the Manifest through the magnificent quality of the horizons, or through the horizons' magnification of God—which itself is a disclosure of divine descent, per the verse «then He drew nigh and descended»[233]—the witness deems corporeal bodies to be more excellent than spirits. He advances arguments in favor of corporeal bodies, and places the unseen in the service of the visible. He renders the nonmanifest subordinate to the manifest, and for him the ends become a means for the intermediaries and the beginnings. He may even behold that bodily constitutions are loci for the manifestation of spirits. For him, the bodily configuration of the human being has a quality of magnificence, and the Magnificent manifests in its pure meaning. Thereupon, the witness beholds the magnificent quality of human forms in whatever quality they assume, especially if it is a form that manifests as exoteric knowledge, to say nothing of when it manifests as direct recognition or of when it disappears in annihilation in the view of its possessor, or of when it is firm in subsistence in his view.

He also magnifies judges, patrons, emirs, kings, and caliphs with a divine 36.4
magnification rooted in divine unveiling. His magnification of these levels is not specific to one group, and it does not favor the followers of one school over another. For him, angels are more excellent, although human beings are more complete. Moreover, the actions that issue from things other-than-God, as well as their speech, become manifest to the witness by virtue of the purity of the levels of the Manifest from all things other-than-God; and through this witnessing gaze, the witness remains at the furthest limit, not at the starting point of the lights' ascent. He is veiled among the people, and what is sealed within him is neither announced nor concealed. The reality of witnessing the Manifest makes him hidden from the perceptions of others, and so he joins the final stages of the Manifest with its opposite, the Nonmanifest, at its first limit—such that the Magnificent is witnessed by the five senses, and exists by virtue of his illuminated spirit and soul.

The Magnificent can also manifest through witnessing the spatial distances 36.5
that exist within the mind. The witness therefore discovers that infinity is inseparable due to its attachment; and even if it has no entity in existence and no trace in the divine munificence, the subject of the accident of the mind is not itself but external to it. The one who knows the reality of things excuses the one who is heedless and unmindful of it. Thus, the magnification in this stage is conceptual. Moreover, magnificence may manifest in the infinity of numbers,

تظهر له العظمة في عدم تناهي العدد فيلحق به عدم تناهي المعدود وهذا الشهود عند أهل المعقول والمنقول مردود لا عند أهل الوجد بالوجود.

٦،٣٦ وأكثر ما يقع حكم الاسم العظيم لأهل الجلال وضدّه لأهل الجمال وتساويهما عند أهل الكمال والتعظيم الذي هو في عالم الحجاب يكون حرماناً للطلّاب لأنّه في الأفكار أعظم الأسباب وعند أهل الشهود يحسن القول بضدّه لأنّهم يرون التعظيم من بعد المحبوب وصدّه.

اسمه الغنيّ جلّ شأنه وتقدّس

١،٣٧ هـذا الاسم الشريف اتّفق عليه الغزاليّ والبيهقيّ وورد في سورة البقرة في قوله تعالى ﴿وَٱعۡلَمُوٓاْ أَنَّ ٱللَّهَ غَنِيٌّ حَمِيدٌ﴾ والغنيّ من له اليسار والغنيّ أيضاً من ليس له حاجة إلى أحد كما قال

كِلَانَا غَنِيٌّ عَنْ أَخِيهِ حَيَاتَهُ ... وَنَحْنُ إِذَا مُتْنَا أَشَدُّ تَغَانِيَا

وكلا المعنيين تصدق نسبته إلى الحقّ تعالى لكنّ الثاني أظهر لدلالة قوله تعالى في آية أخرى ﴿إِنَّ ٱللَّهَ غَنِيٌّ عَنِ ٱلۡعَٰلَمِينَ﴾ والاسم المعطي يشهد للمعنى الأوّل لأنّ العطاء إنّما يكون من يسار.

٢،٣٧ وإذا صحّ المعنيان فنقول على المعنى الأوّل إنّه المالك حقيقة الدنيا والآخرة وما فيهما والوحدانيّة تشهد أنّ ملك كلّ مالك إنّما هو مِلكه تعالى وليس معه غيره فلا يكون

so that it is joined to the infinity of the numbered objects. This manifestation is rejected by the experts of the intellectual and transmitted sciences, but not by the people who experience ecstasy in existence.

The property of the Magnificent most often occurs for the people of maj- 36.6
esty, while its opposite occurs for the people of beauty, and both occur equally for the people of perfection. The magnification that occurs in the realm of the veil is a deprivation for the seekers, because the most magnificent causes occur in reflective thought. For the witnesses, one could say the opposite, because they see that magnification is a result of distance and turning away from the Beloved.

Al-Ghanī: The Independent

This noble name is considered to be a divine name by al-Ghazālī and al-Bayhaqī. 37.1
It occurs in the Surah of the Cow in the verse: «know that God is Independent, Praiseworthy».[234] The independent is the one who possesses abundance. It is also the one who has no need for anyone. As someone once wrote:

> We each live our lives independently of each other,
> and when we die, we will be even more independent.[235]

Both meanings of abundance and freedom from need are applicable to God. However, the second meaning is more obvious because of the verse «Truly God is independent of the worlds».[236] The Giver, however, reinforces the first meaning of abundance, because giving is achieved from abundance.

Given that both meanings are correct, we say that, according to the first 37.2
meaning of abundance, He is the true Owner of the reality of this world and the next and everything that is within them. God's only-ness, moreover, bears witness to the fact that the ownership of every owner is God's possession, and that there is none alongside Him. Thus, the kingdom is none other than His. And if every gift is given by Him, it is also received by Him; He is at once the Giver, the Alms-Giver, and «the one who collects the alms».[237] Shaykh

الملك إلّا له فإذا كان كلّ عطاء فهو عطاؤه كان كلّ معطى هو له إلّا أنّه هو المعطي والمتصدّق وهو الذي ﴿ يَأْخُذُ ٱلصَّدَقَٰتِ ﴾ قال الشيخ محيي الدين رضي الله عنه من كانت هباته لا تتعدّى يديه فلا واهب ولا موهوب ومن كان عين الحجاب على نفسه فلا حاجب ولا محجوب فالواهب منه إليه وشاهد الحسّ يشهد للعلم فقط والمواجيد تشهد لما فوق العلم ولكلّ مقام مقال.

٣،٣٧ وعلى هذا التقدير يدخل اسمه مالك الملك في حقيقة الاسم الغنيّ إذ اليسار من جملة المُلك وكلّ مالك فيد الله يده ولست أقول يده يد الله فهو تعالى يملك كلّ مالك ومملوك ومُلك فإذا ظهر سلطان الوحدانيّة لم ير ممّا قلناه شيئاً وكان ولا شيء معه واليسار شيء فلا يكون معه يسار ولا غيره.

٤،٣٧ فيتعيّن بهذا الاعتبار اسمه الغنيّ بالمعنى الثاني الذي قلنا إنّ شاهده قوله تعالى وَٱللَّهُ ﴿ غَنِيٌّ عَنِ ٱلْعَٰلَمِينَ ﴾ فأمّا أهل السفر الأوّل فيقولون ﴿ إِنَّ ٱللَّهَ غَنِيٌّ عَنِ ٱلْعَٰلَمِينَ ﴾ قبل خلق خلقه وهو المقام الذي أخبر عنه بقوله كنتُ كنزاً لم أُعرف وأمّا أهل الوقفة فلا يرون له اسماً ولا غيره وأمّا أهل السفر الثاني فيقولون إنّه الآن على ما عليه كان أي إنّه غيب لم يدرَك وإن كانوا يرون الأغيار لكن في الاعتبار والعين الواحدة قائمة بذاتها والله تعالى عندهم ﴿ غَنِيٌّ عَنِ ٱلْعَٰلَمِينَ ﴾ أزلاً وأبداً.

٥،٣٧ وصلاة الاسم الغني سبوّح قدّوس والاسم الصمد هو المحيط به بأحد تفسيري الصمد وهو معنى أنّه الذي لا جوف له ونعني بالجوف الباطن فالاسم الغنيّ لا يناسبه في هذه المرتبة الباطن ولا الظاهر لأنّ غناه ﴿ عَنِ ٱلْعَٰلَمِينَ ﴾ ليس نسبة معقولة بينه وبين العالمين بل هو قطع النسبة واعلم أنّ لسان العلم يرجّح المعنى الأوّل ولسان التحقيق يرجّح الثاني.

Muḥyī l-Dīn ibn al-ʿArabī, God be pleased with him, said: "If your gifts do not extend beyond your hand, then there is neither giver nor gift. And if you are the veil over your own self, then there is neither veil nor veiled."[238] Thus, the bestowal is from Him and to Him. The person who only witnesses through the senses affirms only exoteric knowledge, while ecstatic experience bears witness to what lies beyond exoteric knowledge; and for every station there is a corresponding doctrine.

In this sense, the Owner of the Kingdom pertains to the reality of the Inde- 37.3
pendent, because abundance is an aspect of kingship. Moreover, for every owner, God's Hand is his hand—note that I do not say that his hand is God's Hand, for He owns every possessor, every thing possessed, and every possession. However, when the authority of God's oneness manifests itself, then none of the aforementioned remains, for "God was, and there is nothing with Him"; and since abundance is also a thing, neither abundance nor anything else remains beside God.

His name the Independent thereby becomes determined from this perspec- 37.4
tive by the second meaning, which is contained in the verse: «God is independent of the worlds». Those who are on the first journey say that He was «independent of the worlds» before He created creation, and this is the station described in the Holy Saying about the hidden treasure.[239] As for those who have arrived at the station of halting, they see no name or anything else beside Him. As for those who are on the second journey, they say that "He is now as He ever was." That is, He is unseen and has never been grasped. And even though they perceive the realm of other-than-God, they see it perspectivally, and the individual entity subsists through its Essence. For them, God is «independent of the worlds» for all eternity.

The prayer of the Independent is "All-Glorified, All-Holy!" Moreover, 37.5
the Self-Sufficient encompasses the Independent in respect to one of the two interpretations of the Self-Sufficient—namely, that He has no hollow interior, by which I mean a "nonmanifest dimension," for manifest and nonmanifest dimensions are inappropriate for the Independent in this level, since His «independence from the worlds» is not an intelligible relation between Him and the worlds, but rather a severing of relationality. Know that the language of exoteric knowledge gives preponderance to the first meaning of the Independent, while the language of realization gives preponderance to the second meaning.

اسمه الحميد تبارك وتعالى

أوّل وروده في الكتاب العزيز في سورة البقرة في قوله تعالى ﴿أَنَّ ٱللَّهَ غَنِىٌّ حَمِيدٌ﴾ ١،٣٨
ونعني بقولي أوّل وروده في ترتيب سور القرآن واتّفق على ذكره الأئمّة الثلاثة ومعناه مستحقّ الثناء سواء أحسن أو منع وأمّا الشكر فلا يكون إلّا عن إحسان وسيأتي ذكر ذلك في الاسم الشكور إن شاء الله تعالى وقد ذكرت في شرح الفاتحة معنى الحمد العائد إلى الله تعالى من كلّ موجود وبسطت فيه القول.

وبالجملة فالحمد يعود على الذات المقدّسة باعتبار كلّ صفة كمال لها والصفات لا ٢،٣٨
تتناهى فيكون الحمد العائد إليها لا يتناهى وعدم تناهيه مختلف فمنه عدم تناهي أنواعه فضلاً عن أشخاصه ثمّ يعود على كلّ حقيقة حقيقة من أثنى على الذات المقدّسة ثناءً مرتبياً ثناءً يشبه الشكر لها على ثنائها على الذات المقدّسة من حضرة الاسم الشكور وأنواع الشاكرين لا تتناهى فأنواع شكره لهم لا تتناهى إلّا أنّ ما يعود عليهم منه هو شكر وما يعود عليه منهم هو حمد وهنا دقيقة جليلة وهي أنّ الشكر مترتّب على الحمد فإنّ الشاكر إنّما يشكر من حمده أوّلاً ثمّ شكره على نعمة حصلت منه من حضرة الاسم المنعم فقد حمد ثمّ شكر.

والناطق بالحقيقة في هذا المجال له أن يقول إنّ الحميد الحقّ تعالى لم ير من حقائق ٣،٣٨
الموجودات شيئاً غير حامد حمداً بالذات وبلسان الحال لأنّ الموجود إنّما صار موجوداً بإخراجه من لا موجود إلى الموجود وذلك وصف كمال صار به موجوداً فإذاً له كمال ما فهو بذلك حامد وإلّا لم يكن له كمال فعين موجوديّته حامدة للموجد الحقّ حمد صفة لموصوفها إذ به قامت الصفة.

Al-Ḥamīd: The Praiseworthy

This name first occurs in the Holy Book in the Surah of the Cow in the verse: «God is Independent, Praiseworthy».[240] When we say that it first occurs, we mean according to the order of the surahs of the Qur'an. The three eminent scholars agree it is a divine name. It means "the one who is entitled to laudation, regardless of whether He deprives or acts magnanimously." Gratitude is only in response to magnanimity, as I will discuss under the Thankful, God willing. I also have an extensive discussion in my commentary on the Opening Surah on the meaning of the reflexive praise that returns to God from every existent. 38.1

In summary, praise goes back to the Holy Essence in view of each of Its qualities of perfection. The qualities are infinite, and the praise that goes back to It is therefore infinite. The infinitude of the qualities is varied, and includes the infinitude of species, not to mention the infinitude of individuals. Moreover, each time the Holy Essence is lauded, a laudation goes back to the reality of the lauder in accordance with its rank. This laudation is like a giving of thanks from the presence of the Thankful for having lauded the Holy Essence. Likewise, there are infinite types of thankers, and so the types of thanks are infinite, except that what returns to the thankful from Him is thankfulness, and what returns to Him from them is praise. This is a subtle and remarkable point—namely, that showing thanks is a consequence of giving praise, since the one who is thankful first gives thanks to the one who praises him, then gives thanks for a blessing that reached him from the presence of the Giver of Bliss; thus he praises, then gives thanks. 38.2

The person who speaks truth in this area should say that God, the truly Praiseworthy, sees none of the realities of these existents other than a praiser who praises through both the Essence and through the tongue of its spiritual state. For the existent only comes into existence when it emerges from the realm of nonexistence into existence, and that is a quality of perfection by which the existent comes to exist. Thus, the existent is endowed with a certain perfection and is a praiser through it. Otherwise, the existent would be devoid of perfection. Thus, the very fact of its existence praises the true Existentiator, in the same way as a quality praises the object that it qualifies, for it is through that object that the quality subsists. 38.3

لكن إذا اعتبرتَ وجدته الحامد من مرتبة ظهوراته وهو الشاكر لظهوراته فما عاد ٤،٣٨
عليه من حمدهم فصار حامداً شاكراً وتقول الحقيقة لذاتها إنّه حامد لذاته شاكر لها
من جهة أنّ الموصوف هو الصفة دون العكس.

وإذا فصّلت المراتب واعتبرت أنّه حامد لهم تعيّن للاسم الحميد معنًى ثالث وهو ٥،٣٨
أنّه حميد لعباده فيكون فعيل بمعنى فاعل أي حامد والمراد بعباده الذين هم عِباده أو عُبّاده فإنّ العبد أعمّ من العابد والفرق بين المعنيين أنّ الحميد بمعنى المحمود غير الحميد بمعنى الحامد وتفسير ﴿ٱلْحَمْدُ لِلَّهِ رَبِّ ٱلْعَٰلَمِينَ﴾ وافية بما لا يتناهى من حقائق الاسم الحميد بالاعتبارات كلّها وبكلّ واحد منها.

انتهت الأسماء الشريفة التي ذكرتُ ممّا تضمّنه سورة
البقرة وعدّتها أربعة وثلاثون اسمـاً.

However, upon reflection, you will find Him to be the Praiser at the levels of His manifestations, and the Thankful for His manifestations. As such, whenever their praise reaches Him, He is the true Praiser and the Thankful. Reality proclaims to the Essence that He praises His Essence and gives thanks to It, in the sense that the object of the quality is the quality, and not the reverse. 38.4

Furthermore, if you differentiate the levels and reflect on the fact that He praises them, a third meaning of the Praiseworthy is determined; namely, that He praises His servants. As such, the emphatic form (*faʿīl*) in praiseworthy (*ḥamīd*) takes on the meaning of the active form (*fāʿil*); that is, Praiser (*ḥāmid*). And by "His servants" I mean both servants as well as worshippers. For the servant (*al-ʿabd*) is more general than the worshipper (*al-ʿābid*), and the difference between the two meanings is that the Praiseworthy (*al-Ḥamīd*) in the sense of "the Praised One" (*al-maḥmūd*) is different from the Praiseworthy in the sense of the "Giver of Praise." The commentary on the verse «Praise be to God, Lord of the Worlds»[241] addresses the infinite realities of the Praiseworthy from each of its perspectives. 38.5

This is the end of my treatment of the eminent names contained in the Surah of the Cow, which contains thirty-four names in total.

سورة آل عمران

ولنذكر ما تضمّنه من الأسماء الإلٰهيّة إن شاء
الله تعالى وعدّتها اثنا عشر اسماً وأوّلها

اسمه المنتقم جلّت عظمته

أوّل ما استُخرج من سورة آل عمران وهو قوله تعالى ﴿وَٱللَّهُ عَزِيزٌ ذُو ٱنتِقَامٍ﴾ واتّفق على إيراده الأئمّة الثلاثة والانتقام هو المعاقبة وهذا الاسم من أسماء الجلال وهو بالذات من أقسام الاسم الله ويدخل في الاسم الرحمٰن لا بالذات فإنّ الرحمة تنافيه. ١،٣٩

وأمّا دخوله في الرحمٰن فمثل أن يعطي الاسم الرحمٰن لبعض الموجودات زيادة في القوّة رحمة لذلك الموجود فتدعوه تلك القوّة إلى لقاء الأقران ومعاندة أهل البطش أو أهل العدوان فتظهر فيه معاني الاسم المنتقم من مظاهر أهل البطش إمّا بإقامة حدود شرعيّة وإمّا سياسيّة وإمّا انتصاراً ومغالبة فيُقهر على يد أقوياء كلّهم مستمدّون من الاسم الرحمٰن القوّة والبطش فيكون ذلك الانتقام الصادر منهم سببه الرحمة الرحمانيّة الواصلة إليهم فيتعيّن الاسم المنتقم من الاسم الرحمٰن لا بالذات لأنّ القوّة الواصلة إلى الأقوياء الذين انتقموا إنّما وصلت إليهم بالذات من الاسم الرحمٰن. ٢،٣٩

The Surah of the House of ʿImrān

I shall mention the divine names that appear in this surah, God willing. They are twelve in number. The first of them is:

Al-Muntaqim: The Avenger

This is the first name derived from the Surah of the House of ʿImrān, where it occurs in the verse: «God is Exalted, Possessor of Vengeance».[242] The three eminent scholars agree it is a divine name. Vengeance is punishment. This name is one of the Names of Majesty, and is essentially one of the categories of names that pertain to Allāh; its inclusion within the All-Merciful is not essential, since mercy precludes it. 39.1

As for its inclusion within the All-Merciful, it applies, for example, when the All-Merciful gives someone an increase in power out of mercy for that person, and that power motivates him to meet opponents in battle and to stand up to violent and oppressive persons. The meanings of the Avenger therefore manifest in him, appearing as violent enforcement of legal punishments or political order, or as granting victory or assistance in a struggle. The enemy is thus subjugated at the hands of persons of power who all draw strength and violence from the All-Merciful. The vengeance they display is caused by the mercy of the All-Merciful that reaches them. As such, the Avenger is determined by the All-Merciful, but not essentially, because the power that reaches the persons of power who exact revenge reaches them essentially through none other than the All-Merciful. 39.2

٣،٣٩ وصيرورة البطش نقمة في حقّ ذلك الشخص هو لا بالذات وهو أنموذج يُفهم منه ما يقع بين العساكر من الوقائع والحروب كيف يحصل فيها انتقام من الاسم المنتقم وأصله من الاسم المنعم المنتسب إلى الرحمٰن بالذات وحصل منه الانتقام لا بالذات.

٤،٣٩ ويُفهم منه ما يقع من تصادم قوى الوجود في أطوار الموجود حتّى تلاطم الأمواج في البحار وعصف الرياح بالأشجار وأكل السباع من الوحش والطير لما يصيده في سائر الأقطار واغتذاء السمك بعضه ببعض حتّى ما يفرّق بين أجزاء الأرض من الزلازل في الأمصار وما يحصل من الألم في التخيّلات والأوهام والأفكار فإنّه تعالى لا يتحرّك ذرّة إلّا بإذنه فإن كانت ملائمة فمن إنعامه وإن كانت منافرة فمن انتقامه والمسبّب عند الأسباب وهو هي في رفع الحجاب.

٥،٣٩ وبالجملة فكلّ تألّم فمن انتقامه وكلّ تنعّم فمن إنعامه والانتقام للجلال والإنعام للجمال والتلذّذ بهما للكمال وكذلك من كان في السلوك متنعّماً بالآلام والأسقام كان استعداده للتجلّي المناسب للكمال وعلى قدر التفاوت في الزيادة والنقصان يكون الاستعداد الذي هو التهيّؤ لجود الاسم الجواد.

اسمه الوهّاب عمّت رحمته

١،٤٠ هو ثاني اسم ورد في سورة آل عمران في قوله تعالى ﴿إِنَّكَ أَنتَ ٱلْوَهَّابُ﴾ واتّفق على إيراده الأئمّة الثلاثة والوهّاب هو المعطي لا بسبب عوض بل منّاً وإحساناً والاسم المعطي أوسع دائرة منه وهو خصوص وصف في المعطي فإن اعتبرتَ أنّ كلّ ما وصل يقع إلى كلّ منتفع به فهو موهبة دخلت في ذلك الأمطار وما تبديه من ثمرات الأشجار وما ينتفع به ممّا يخرج من البحار وما اشتمل عليه الليل والنهار وما امتنّ

Moreover, the continued violence in the case of that individual does not pertain to its very essence. It is through this illustrative example that one understands how wars occur between armies, and how they mete out vengeance through the Avenger, whose root is from the Giver of Bliss, which in turn is ascribed to the All-Merciful in its very essence, and through which revenge is accomplished, rather than by way of its essence. 39.3

From this, one also understands the clashes of the powers of existence at the various stages of the existents: the crashing waves of the sea, the howling winds in the trees, the feasting of predatory animals, the birds of prey that hunt across the lands, the fish that devour each other, the earthquakes that cleave the land, and the pain that is experienced in the imagination, fantasies, and thoughts. For every particle moves by His permission. If it is agreeable, it is from His benefaction; if it is disagreeable, it is from His vengeance. The Causer of causes is with the causes, and is identical to them when the veil is lifted. 39.4

In summary, all pain comes from His vengeance, and all bliss comes from His benefaction. Vengeance pertains to majesty, while benefaction pertains to beauty, and the enjoyment of both pertains to perfection. Likewise, when a wayfarer finds enjoyment in pain and sickness, his preparedness for the disclosure is concordant with perfection. As such, the increase or decrease in that disparity determines his preparedness—that is, his readiness—for the munificence of the Munificent. 39.5

Al-Wahhāb: The Bestower

This is the second name that is mentioned in the Surah of the House of ʿImrān in the verse: «Truly You are the Bestower».[243] The three eminent scholars agree it is a divine name. The Bestower is the One who gives not in exchange for something, but out of gratuitous kindness and beneficence. The Giver is wider in scope, and this name is a specific quality of the Giver. For if you consider that when something reaches a beneficiary it is a bestowal, then bestowals include rains, the fruits that they yield on trees, the useful products of the 40.1

الله تعالى به على كلّ موجود ممّا يقيم وجوده في طور من الأطوار وكلّ ملاءمة تحصل حصل بها إشعار أو لم يحصل كمل بها العطاء أو لم يكمل فضل منها شيء عن قدر الحاجة أو لم يفضل.

٢،٤٠ وهذا الاسم من الاسم الرحمٰن بالذات وفيه من الاسم الله اعتبارات خصوصاً من الطور الذي يدخل منه كلّ اسم في معنى كلّ اسم حتّى يبلغ الإيجاد إلى دخول الأسماء ذوات التضادّ فإنّ الموهبة ربّما أدّت إلى طغيان فكان سبب منع الزيادة أو حصول النقصان فمن ذلك أن يوهَب شخص نعمة فتؤدّيه إلى منع استمرارها أو نقص ثمارها لطغيانه بها فيعرض معنى الاسم المانع لتلك المنافع.

٣،٤٠ وربّما كان الإيهاب من الاسم الوهّاب يقارنه شكر ويصحبه نشر فيستدعي المزيد ويتّصل في الدنيا والآخرة بالتأييد فيكون الرحمٰن غالباً على أمره وغيره وربّما كان اسمه الله غالباً على أمره والمجال في اعتبارات الأسماء أعلى من أن تنحصر وأسمى.

٤،٤٠ والاسم الشكور تعود أحكامه كثيرًا إلى هذا الاسم وتجري من شكر المواهب على رسم فإنّه ما شُكر مشكور في الوجود على وهب أو جود إلّا هو من معاني الاسم الشكور التي استدعاها الاسم الوهّاب وكان منه لها جميع الأسباب وهبات المسمّى بالوهّاب لا تتعدّى يديه ولا تعود منه إلّا عليه فلمّا كان عود هذا الاسم إلى الاسم الرحمٰن قيل في مسمّاه إنّ الخير كلّه بيديك والشرّ ليس إليك ويأتي ﴿كُلٌّ مِّنْ عِندِ ٱللَّهِ﴾ في اعتبار ليس هذا إيّاه.

oceans, everything that night and day comprise, anything that God gratuitously gives to any creature to enable its subsistence at any stage, and anything agreeable that becomes actualized, regardless of whether there is awareness of it or not, or whether the giving is complete or incomplete, or whether it surpasses the measure of what is needed or not.

This name pertains to the very essence of the All-Merciful. It also pertains to Allāh in several respects, especially at the stage where every name is included within the meaning of every other, until the bestowal of existence causes the oppositional names to interpenetrate. For bestowal may lead to an abuse, thereby causing increase to be withheld, or decrease to occur. For instance, a blessing may be bestowed upon an individual who then abuses it, thereby causing its continuous blessing to be withheld, or its fruits to decrease. Thereupon, the meaning of the Preventer covers those benefits. 40.2

Sometimes, the bestowal from the Bestower is met with gratitude and accompanied by growth, and that in turn invites an increase, which is connected to this world and the next by divine support. Therefore, the All-Merciful dominates over his affair and that of others. Sometimes, His name Allāh "dominates over His affair."[244] This area of discussion about the considerations of the names is too exalted and lofty to be restricted. 40.3

The properties of the Thankful often stem from this name. They flow from gratitude for bestowals upon traces of creation. For everything in existence that is thanked for a bestowal or an act of kindness is one of the meanings of the Thankful that are called upon by the Bestower. From it, all causes take place. And the bestowals of the so-called Bestower never extend beyond His Hands, nor do they return to anyone but Him. And since this name stems from the All-Merciful, the following is said about its Named Essence: "Verily all goodness lies within Your hands, and evil is not ascribed to You,"[245] whereas the verse «All is from God»[246] is to be understood from a different standpoint. 40.4

اسمه الجامع تبارك وتعالى

١،٤١ هـذا الاسم المحيط هو ثالث اسم في سورة آل عمران من جملة اثني عشر اسماً فيها وهو في قوله تعالى ﴿رَبَّنَآ إِنَّكَ جَامِعُ ٱلنَّاسِ لِيَوۡمٍ﴾ واتّفق الأئمّة الثلاثة على إيراده ومعناه عند العلماء ﴿جَامِعُ ٱلنَّاسِ لِيَوۡمٍ﴾ القيامة وهو اليوم الذي ﴿لَا رَيۡبَ فِيهِ﴾ ومثله ﴿يَوۡمَ يَجۡمَعُكُمۡ لِيَوۡمِ ٱلۡجَمۡعِ﴾.

٢،٤١ وفيه مجال رحب للكلام لأنّه تتعلّق به أوصاف ذلك اليوم وأسرار المعاد وذلك إذا انحرف مزاج العالم عند إرادة ذلك فيكون الاسم المميت قد توجّه إلى إماتة السبع السماوات والسبع الأرضين ويتوجّه الاسم المحيي إلى إحياء من مات من عالم الإنسان وعالم الملائكة وعالم الجنّ ومن شاء الله من ذوات النفس فإذا قاموا لم يجدوا ملجأً إلّا الله تعالى فإذا وقع الحساب كان حكم السريع الحساب تعالى وتقدّس وحقيقة الحساب معلومة ممّا نُقل عن الله تعالى وعن رسوله عليه السلام.

٣،٤١ ويصحب ذلك أنّ تجلّي الاسم الواحد يغشى أبصار أهل المحشر وبصائرهم وجميع مشاعرهم ومداركهم الظاهرة والباطنة فمن كان من أهل التوحيد في الدنيا لاءم الاسم الواحد فتعلّق بنوره فأولئك الذين يسرعون على الصراط كالبرق في السرعة أو دون ذلك أو أكثر منه.

٤،٤١ وأمّا أضداد أهل التوحيد فيقولون نعوذ بالله منك نحن هنا حتى يأتينا ربّنا ولسان الحال أفصح من لسان المقال فيكون أهل الاستجابة لتجلّي الواحد تعالى هم أهل التوحيد ويليهم في ذلك أهل الكفر الشديد ونعني بالكفر الشديد الذين لم تصلهم الدعوة الإلٰهيّة ويكونون عارين من العلم بالكلّيّة فيستجيبون لتجلّي الاسم الواحد ويسجدون لكن على ظهورهم كما ورد الحديث وهم يلون أهل التوحيد في إسراعهم

Al-Jāmiʿ: The Gatherer

This all-encompassing name is the third of the twelve divine names of the Surah of the House of ʿImrān. It occurs in the verse: «Our Lord, You are the Gatherer of humankind».[247] The three eminent scholars agree it is a divine name. Its meaning according to exoteric scholars is that He «is the Gatherer of humankind» for the Day of Arising, which is the Day about which «there is no doubt».[248] Similarly, this meaning is found in the verse: «the Day He gathers you for the Day of the Gathering».[249] 41.1

This is a broad subject of discussion because it is connected to the descriptions of that Day and the mysteries of the return. For when the constitution of the world enters a state of disequilibrium—when God wills this—the Death-Giver will turn in the direction of the seven heavens and the seven earths, in order to cause them to die, while the Life-Giver will turn toward those who have died from the realm of human beings, angels, and jinn and the animate creatures God wills to give life. Once they are resurrected, they will find no refuge except God.[250] Then, when the reckoning begins, the property of the Swift in Reckoning will take effect. The true nature of the reckoning is well known through the reports that have reached us from God and His blessed Messenger. 41.2

Together with this, the disclosure of the One will cover the sights, insights, and all the faculties of awareness and perception, both inward and outward, of the people of the Assembly. Those who adhered to the doctrine of divine oneness in this world will find the One agreeable and attach themselves to His light. It is they who will "rush across the bridge over the Fire at the speed of lightning, or slightly slower, or slightly faster."[251] 41.3

Their opposite numbers will cry out: "We seek refuge in God from you! We shall wait here until our Lord comes to us."[252] The spiritual state is more eloquent than speech.[253] The people who are responsive to the disclosure of the One will be those who proclaim divine oneness. These will be followed by the extreme unbelievers, by which we mean those whom the call to God never reached, so that they were entirely devoid of knowledge. They will respond to the disclosure of the One and prostrate themselves before God, but upon their backs, as mentioned in the Prophetic Tradition. They will follow the 41.4

إلى الاستجابة لأنّهم ليسوا أهل عقائد حتّى يتنظرون أن يأتيهم ربّهم في صورة اعتقادهم وكذلك ورد الخبر النبويّ فيتحوّل لهم في الصورة التي يعرفونه فيها فيقولون نعم أنت ربّنا أي يتحوّل لهم في صورة اعتقاداتهم وهذه الصورة التي تحوّل إليها هي تجلّي الاسم الجامع وفيه يقع الحساب مفصّلاً وفي أهل التوحيد وأهل الكفر يقع الحساب مجملاً.

٥،٤١ واعلم أنّ أهل التوحيد هم أهل شهود الوحدانيّة فقط وهم أهل مقام الوقفة التي هي نهاية السفر الأوّل سفر العارفين وإنّما ناسب الكفّار هؤلاء لأنّ أهل التوحيد كفروا العالم فما رأوا إلّا الحقّ تعالى وحده وهم كانوا أشعّة من نوره فرجعوا بالتجلّي من الاسم الواحد إلى حضرة عين الذات والطائفة الأخرى وهم أهل الكفر الذين كفروا الحقّ تعالى أي ستروه بسوء استعداداتهم ولم يتعلّقوا بغيره فكانوا سذّجاً فناسبتهم الوحدانيّة فأدركوها إدراكاً مقلوباً لجذبتهم من ورائهم إليها فيكون عذابهم الذي يسبكّون به حتّى يناسبوا الوحدانيّة بالمواجهة عذاباً بسيطاً ليس هو العذاب المعلوم ولا العذاب الموهوم.

٦،٤١ فإنّ هذين العذابين يختصّ بأهل الشرك من أهل العقائد والشرك مختلف بعضه خفيّ وبعضه جليّ فيلحق العذاب تفاصيل مشخّصات مسائل الشرك ودقائقه فيكون الشرك فيهم بمنزلة الزيت لشعلة الفتيلة تتبعه النار كما يتبع النار الحطب حتّى إذا استحال الشرك توحيداً طُهّروا فالعذاب تطهير وهو عند من عرفه مشتقّ من العذوبة لأنّ العذب هو الطيّب وقد وُجد هذا من هذه الطائفة الذي قال

proclaimers of divine oneness in their quick response because they have no creedal beliefs that would cause them to wait for their Lord to come to them in the form of their beliefs. It is related in the prophetic report that God will transform Himself into the form through which they recognize Him, and they will say, "Yes, You are our Lord." That is, He will transform according to the form of their beliefs. This form into which He will transform Himself, moreover, is the disclosure of the Gatherer. The detailed reckoning will take place therein, whereas the reckoning will take place in summary fashion for the proclaimers of divine oneness and the extreme unbelievers.

Moreover, the proclaimers of divine oneness are those who only witness 41.5
oneness. They are those who arrived at the station of halting, which is the end of the first journey, the journey of the recognizers. The unbelievers who cover the truth only correspond to them because the proclaimers of divine oneness disbelieved in the world, for they saw nothing other than the Real. They were rays of His light, and so they return through the disclosure of the One to the presence of the Essence Itself. The other group were the unbelievers who disbelieved in the Real, or covered Him with their ill-preparedness, but they also did not attach themselves to anything other than Him. They are primitives, and the Oneness is therefore congruent with them, though they perceive it in an inverse manner, which pulls them to it from behind. Therefore, the chastisement that removes their dross and enables them to find congruence in their face-to-face meeting with divine oneness is simple. It is neither the well-known chastisement nor an illusory chastisement.

Indeed, these forms of chastisement are specific to those believers in creeds 41.6
who associate partners with God. There are different types of associationism: some are hidden and others are apparent. As such, the chastisement is connected to the specific objects and details of the associationism. Associationism for them is like oil in relation to the flame of the wick. The fire follows it as surely as fire follows wood, until finally they become purified when associationism transmutes into divine oneness. Thus, chastisement is a purification; and according to those who recognize it, chastisement (*ʿadhāb*) is derived from fresh water (*ʿudhūbah*), because fresh water is pleasant to consume. Among our camp, some have attained an intimate awareness of this reality and have chanted:

أُحِبُّكَ لا أُحِبُّكَ لِلثَّوَابِ وَلٰكِنِّي أُحِبُّكَ لِلْعِقَابِ
فَكُلُّ مَآرِبِي قَدْ نِلْتُ مِنْهَا سِوَى مَلْذُوذِ وَجْدِي بِٱلْعَذَابِ

٧،٤١ والاسم الجامع هو المتولّي حساب أهل الموقف فإنّه جامعهم إلى الوحدانيّة إمّا بالمناسبة كما في مقام أهل الوحدة والوقفة ومن قرب من مقامهم وهم أهل المواجهة وبعدهم أهل الجهل المطلق المستجيبون استجابة مقلوبة وإمّا بالمنافرة وهم سائر الطوائف لكنّ أشدّهم عقوبة المشركون فإنّ المنافرة فيهم كثيرة وبعدهم المنافقون إذ لا يعذّبون إلّا ﴿فِى ٱلدَّرْكِ ٱلْأَسْفَلِ مِنَ ٱلنَّارِ﴾ لا في أعلاها الذي هو ظاهرها لأنّ ظاهرهم كان مسلماً مسلّماً والشرك متعلّق بباطنهم فكان عذابهم باطناً لذلك ثمّ يلي هؤلاء أهل الملل الحقّة على اختلاف طبقاتهم حتّى تنتهي العقوبة إلى حدّ التطهير وتقف.

٨،٤١ وأمّا أهل الملل الباطلة فيُخلّدون وهم أهل النار الذين هم أهلها فإن لحقتهم الرحمة فليس إلّا بأن يصيروا ناراً فتصير لهم ملائمة فيكونون فيها لا إلى نهاية لكنّهم لو سئلوا أن يخرجوا منها إذ ذاك لما أرادوا فإذا ظهر حكم الرحمة التي سبقت الغضبَ أو غلبت الغضبَ تخلّص أهل الملل الحقّة.

٩،٤١ واعلم أنّ نسبة أهل المعقولات الذين عدلوا عن اتّباع الأنبياء إلى المتّبعين للأنبياء نسبة المنافقين إلى المؤمنين فإنّ أهل العقول اعترفوا بالحقّ تعالى فوافقوا وخالفوا لعدم اتّباعهم الأنبياء فيعذّبون بجهة واحدة كما عوقب المنافقون بجهة واحدة وإذا شمل الحساب من السريع الحساب يشملهم باطن الاسم الجامع وهو الوحدانيّة فاجتمع الجميع في شهود التوحيد فيستوفي الاسم الجامع حقيقته تماماً.

I love You. I love you not for the recompense,
but rather I love You for the chastisement.
For all my needs I have attained from the recompense,
except my pleasure in the ecstasy of chastisement![254]

41.7 The Gathering presides over the reckoning of the people of the resurrection. It gathers them to oneness, either by way of affinity or by way of disagreeability. Affinity is the case of the station of those who know divine oneness and those who attain and whoever approximates their station—namely, those who experience the face-to-face encounter—and they are followed by the purely ignorant, who respond to God in an inverted manner. Disagreeability is the case for the remaining groups. However, among those who are repelled, the most severe in punishment are those who associate partners with God, for their disagreeability with oneness is manifold. These are followed by the hypocrites, for they are chastised in none other than «the lowest depths of the Fire»,[255] not in its higher level, which is the outward dimension of the Fire; for their outward dimension was that of a Muslim who surrenders to God, yet associationism was attached to their inner dimension, and so their chastisement is inward for that reason. These hypocrites are followed by those who hold true creeds, in all their variety, until the punishment reaches its purificatory end and stops.

41.8 Those who hold false creeds are eternalized. They are "the People of the Fire who are worthy of it."[256] When mercy reaches them, they become none other than Fire, such that the Fire becomes agreeable and they remain therein infinitely. If they were asked to leave the Fire at that moment, they would not want to do so. However, when the property of mercy becomes manifest—namely, the mercy that "precedes wrath" or "triumphs over wrath"[257]—then those who hold true creeds are delivered from their predicament.

41.9 Moreover, the relation between, on the one hand, those who follow their intellectual constructs and turn away from the Prophets, and on the other, the followers of the Prophets, is like the relationship between the hypocrites and the believers. For the intellectuals acknowledge the Real and conform, yet they oppose Him by refusing to follow the Prophets. They are therefore chastised in one aspect just as the hypocrites are punished in one aspect. Then, when the reckoning of the Swift in Reckoning encompasses them, they are encompassed by the nonmanifest dimension of the Gathering, which is divine oneness. Everyone is therefore gathered together in witnessing oneness, whereupon the Gathering fulfills its reality completely.

اسمه المقسط تبارك اسمه

١،٤٢ هو في آل عمران في قوله تعالى ﴿قَآئِمَۢا بِٱلۡقِسۡطِۚ لَآ إِلَٰهَ إِلَّا﴾ ولم يذكره أبو الحكم الأندلسيّ والقسط هو العدل قال تعالى و﴿ٱللَّهَ يُحِبُّ ٱلۡمُقۡسِطِينَ﴾ أي القائمين بالقسط وهذه المحبّة حصلت من تحقّق نسبتهم إلى الاسم المقسط لأنّه تعالى إنّما أحبّ وصفه وتلك المحبّة هي في ضمن محبّته لنفسه وسرت هذه الحقيقة في جميع مراتب موجوداته فما أحبّ أحد منها إلّا نفسه وهذه أيضاً من معاني قيامه تعالى ﴿بِٱلۡقِسۡطِ﴾.

٢،٤٢ ﴿وَأَمَّا ٱلۡقَٰسِطُونَ﴾ وهم الجائرون ﴿فَكَانُواْ لِجَهَنَّمَ حَطَبٗا﴾ والجور هو الخروج عن جادّة الطريق وجادّة الطريق هي العدل في الحقيقة وإنّما كان الجائرون حطباً لجهنّم لأنّ استعدادهم الذي اقتضى الجور هو انحراف ما والمنحرفات كلّها تُسبَك حتّى تعود إلى الاعتدال الذي هو العدل والمنحرفات من الموجودات هي محبوبة للحقّ تعالى من حضرة اسمه الجامع ومن حضرة اسمه المحيط وذلك لأنّ إحاطته تعالى توجب أنّ كلّ حركة من حركات الموجودات لا تكون إلّا إليه تعالى من أجل إحاطته فتوجّه المنحرفات إليه أيضاً في انحرافها فإنّ الانحرافات في نسبتها إليه هي اعتدالات بالنسبة إليه لأنّ وجوده تعالى لا ينافي شيئاً وكلّ شيء ينافي شيئاً آخر غيره بما به يغاير ذلك الشيء وفي هذا المعنى قال

فَمَا فِيَّ مِنْ شَيْءٍ لِشَيْءٍ مُوَافِقٌ   وَمَا مِنْكَ لِي شَيْءٌ لِشَيْءٍ مُخَالِفُ

٣،٤٢ ومن هذه الحقيقة احترق القاسطون وهم الجائرون المنحرفون لأنّ التجلّي الوحدانيّ إذا قالبته المنحرفات عنه قهرها بردّها إليه وذلك الردّ بالقهر هو العذاب وهو سبك لهم ليعودوا إلى الاعتدال قهراً لمحبّة الحقّ تعالى لهم لا من جهة الاسم المقسط فإنّ محبّته للموجودات من جهة اسمه المقسط هي محبّة لأهل الاعتدال وهم المقسطون.

Al-Muqsiṭ: The Equitable

This name occurs in the Surah of the House of ʿImrān in the verse: «Upholding equitability, there is no god but He».[258] Ibn Barrajān does not mention it as a divine name. Equitability means balance. God says: «God loves the equitable»[259]—that is, the upholders of balance—and they gain this love by realizing their relationship to the Equitable, for God loves none other than His own quality. This love is an aspect of God's love for Himself, and its reality flows through all the levels of His creation, none of which love anything but themselves. This too is one of the meanings of God's upholding of the balance. 42.1

As for «those who wreak iniquity»—the deviants—«they are kindling of the Fire».[260] Deviance is to stray from the middle of the road. The middle of the road is balance in reality, and the deviant are the kindling of the Fire precisely because their preparedness brings about deviance, which is a type of disequilibrium. All things that lack equilibrium must be cleared of their dross in order to be restored to a state of equilibrium, which is balance. Imbalanced existents are loved by the Real from the presence of the Gathering, and from the presence of the Encompassing. This is because His encompassment necessitates that all movements of existents are toward Him. Therefore, imbalanced existents also turn their attention to Him by their imbalance, for imbalances in relation to Him are balanced. This is because His existence is not incompatible with anything, whereas all things are incompatible with other things insofar as they are distinct from each other. This meaning is expressed in the following verse: 42.2

Nothing within me is compatible with anything,
and nothing within You is incompatible at all.[261]

It is through this reality that the wreakers of iniquity, who are imbalanced deviants, burn. For when the disclosure of oneness encounters those who deviate from oneness, it coerces them by returning them back onto itself. That return through coercion is the chastisement. It is a removal of their dross in order to restore them coercively back to equilibrium because God loves them, though not from the direction of the Equitable. For His love for existent things from the direction of the Equitable is a love for those who have equilibrium; that is, the equitable. 42.3

٤،٤٢ وأمّا محبّته للمنحرفين الذين هم القاسطون فإنّها محبّة من جهة اسمه المحيط فإنّ إحاطته تعالى ليست كإحاطة الشيء بالشيء على سبيل الظرفيّة بل إحاطته معنويّة ترجع إلى كون العين واحدة وإذا كانت حركات المنحرفين وحركات المعتدلين إنّما هي بمدد منه تعالى وهو غاية كلّ متحرّك في حركته منحرفة كانت الحركة أو معتدلة ف﴿إِلَيْهِ يُرْجَعُ ٱلْأَمْرُ كُلُّهُۥ﴾.

٥،٤٢ فإذًا هو تعالى يناسب بين حضرته وبين توجّهات موجوداته بحيطة وحدانيّته المنجذبة بسرّ أحديّته التي ثبتت بثبوت ذاته فمحبّته للمنحرفات هو من حضرة أعلى من حضرة محبّته للمعتدلات التي المقسطون منها ومحبّته للمقسطين هي من حضرة سفلى وإن كان المقسطون أعلى مرتبة لكن في الشرف وفي اعتبار آخر ليس لواحدة من الحضرتين شرف على الأخرى ولا علوّ وهذه الحضرة هي حضرة الاسم المحيط كما ذكرنا ﴿وَٱللَّهُ مِن وَرَآئِهِم مُّحِيطٌۢ﴾.

٦،٤٢ فالاسم المقسط يتوجّه به الوجود المحض في حركاته إلى التطوّر الذي هو تنوّع الوجود بأنواع هي موجوداته فإنّ الموجودات ليست هي غير تنوّعات الوجود والوجود هو أصل الجوهر وهو المادّة التي لا أبسط منها.

٧،٤٢ ولا يقال إنّ الوجود في الخارج بل الخارج في الوجود وليس الوجود عرضاً عندنا بل هو جوهر الجواهر وذات الذوات والموجودات كيفيّاته والكيفيّات منها غيبيّة ومنها شهاديّة ومنها معنويّة ومنها روحانيّة ومنها ذهنيّة فأحوال الوجود هي الموجودات هذا هو اصطلاح طائفة أهل الأذواق.

٨،٤٢ فحركة الوجود في هذه الأطوار المذكورة وفي ما لا يتناهى حركة ذاتيّة له تثبت له الحركة من حيث تثبت ذاته وثبوت ذاته له وجوبًا بها لا بغيرها فثبوت الحركة لها بها وجوبًا والنهايات مفقودة في الوجود وموجودة في كلّ موجود موجود وهذه الحركة يسري بها الوجود سريانًا ذاتيًا في طرق الاعتدال بحقيقة الاسم المقسط الذي هو العدل فإنّ العدل مأخوذ من الاعتدال فما دام السريان المذكور معتدلًا من كلّ وجه

His love for deviants, or wreakers of iniquity, is a love from the direction of the Encompassing. For His encompassment is not like the encompassment of one thing by another, in the manner of containment. Rather, it is supersensory, stemming from the fact that the entity is one. And since the movements of the balanced and the imbalanced alike only occur with His assistance, and since He is the ultimate end of every mover, whether that movement is imbalanced or balanced, then «to Him returns the entire affair».[262] 42.4

Thus, God effects a correspondence between His presence and the directions to which His existents turn. This He does by virtue of the scope of His oneness, which is drawn by the secret of His unity, which in turn remains fixed through the fixity of His Essence. As such, His love for imbalanced things is from a higher presence than His love for balanced things, which includes the equitable. His love for the equitable, for its part, is from a lower presence, even though the equitable enjoy a higher eminence. Yet, from a different perspective, neither of the presences is more eminent or higher than the other; and, as we said, that is the presence of the Encompassing: «God encompasses them».[263] 42.5

Thus, the movements of pure existence direct the attention of the Equitable to the unfolding of stages, which constitutes diversity in existence according to the diversity of existents. For existents are none other than diversities of existence, and existence is the original substance, which is the simplest underlying material substrate. 42.6

Furthermore, one must not say that existence is within the external realm. Rather, the external realm is within existence, because we do not hold existence to be an accident. Rather, existence is the substance of substances, and the essence of essences. Existents, for their part, are its modalities, and modalities are either invisible, visible, supersensory, spiritual, or mental. Existents represent the various states of existence. This is according to the terminology of those who experience direct tasting. 42.7

The motion of existence within these stages and within an infinity of others is, therefore, a motion that pertains to its essence. Motion is affixed to existence inasmuch as its essence is affixed to it, and the fixity of the essence to existence is necessary by its motion, not by anything else. Therefore, motion is affixed to existence in a necessary manner. Moreover, utmost ends are not found in existence, whereas they are found within every existing existent. Existence flows through this motion in a manner that pertains to its essence across the pathways of balanced equilibrium through the reality of the Equitable, 42.8

فهو من حقيقة الاسم المقسط وإذا لحقه الانحراف لحوقاً عرضيّاً فليس من الاسم المقسط وإن كان يرجع إلى الاسم المقسط بالقسط الثاني فإنّ الانحراف هو اعتدال في إقامة الذوات المنحرفة وهي ذوات ما فمن حيث أعطى تلك الذوات المنحرفة حقائقها كان اعتدالاً ما فيرجع بهذا الاعتبار إلى حقيقة الاسم المقسط ولأنّ كلّ اسم يدخل في حقيقة كلّ اسم ولأنّ مدخل الاسم المقسط في ذاته باعتبارين يرجع أحدهما إلى الآخر.

٩،٤٢ وأورد بعض المحجوبين على كلامي في هذا سؤالاً في قولي إنّ كلّ اسم يدخل في كلّ اسم فقال إنّ معاني الأسماء صفات والصفة لا تقوم بالصفة ولم يدر أنّ صفات الحقّ تعالى هي ذوات جوهرانيّة في الخارج وذلك لأنّ الحقّ تعالى عين صفاته وإن كانت صفاته ليست عينه وليس هذا مكان تحقيق هذا الكلام فإذا عرفتَ أنّ حركة الاسم المقسط تنتهي إلى إعطاء الموجودات ذواتها وصفاتها ومعانيها عرفت حقيقة الاسم المقسط والله أعلم.

اسمه مالك الملك جلّ سلطانه

١،٤٣ هذا الاسم الكريم أوّل وروده في سورة آل عمران في قوله تعالى ﴿قُلِ ٱللَّهُمَّ مَٰلِكَ ٱلْمُلْكِ﴾ ولم يذكره أبو الحكم وذكره الإمامان ومالك المُلك هو الملك بمزيد المُلك والمُلك هو حضرة الدنيا والآخرة فقد قال تعالى ﴿مَٰلِكِ يَوْمِ ٱلدِّينِ﴾ وهو يوم الآخرة وقال ﴿مَٰلِكِ يَوْمِ ٱلدِّينِ﴾ أيضاً ومالك المُلك هو مالك الدنيا والآخرة.

which is balance, because balance comes from equilibrium. Since this flow is characterized by equilibrium in every respect, it comes from the reality of the Equitable. But when it is qualified by disequilibrium in an accidental manner, then it does not come from the Equitable. Nonetheless, it too stems from the Equitable through the second type of equitability, for imbalance is a form of balance that upholds imbalanced essences, which, after all, are essences in a certain sense. Inasmuch as it gives these imbalanced essences their realities, it is a type of equilibrium. In this respect, it stems from the reality of the Equitable, since every name is included within the reality of every other name, and since the essential entry point of the Equitable goes back to two perspectives that stem from each other.

Some veiled intellects asked me a question about my claim that every name is included within every other. They held that the meanings of the names are qualities, and that one quality cannot abide within another. They did not grasp that the qualities of God are substantial essences in the external realm, because God is identical to His qualities even though His qualities are not identical to Him. But since this is not the place to pursue this discussion, if you recognize that the motion of the Equitable ultimately gives existents their essences, qualities, and meanings, then you will recognize the reality of the Equitable. And God knows best. 42.9

Mālik al-Mulk: The Owner of the Kingdom

This noble name is first mentioned in the Surah of the House of ʿImrān in the verse: «Say, "O God, Owner of the Kingdom."»[264] Ibn Barrajān does not mention it in his commentary, whereas the other two eminent scholars al-Ghazālī and al-Bayhaqī agree it is a divine name. The Owner of the Kingdom means the King of the ultimate kingdom, for His kingdom is the presence of this world and the next. For God says, «King of the Day of Judgment»,[265] which is the day of the next world, and He also says, «Owner of the Day of Judgment».[266] The Owner of the Kingdom is therefore the owner of this world and the next. 43.1

٢،٤٣ وحضرة هذا الاسم هي حضرة علميّة لتحقّق معاني الغيريّة فيها فإنّ المالك غير المملوك ولمّا كان المِلك لكلّ من له مِلك من دار أو غيره من الأعيان هو مِلك لله تعالى فالله تعالى هو مالك المُلك والملك فمملكة كلّ ملك هي مملكة لله تعالى فهو الملك في مراتب الممالك وهو المالك في مراتب المِلك فحقيقة مالك المُلك سارية في الممالك والمملوكات.

٣،٤٣ وإذا قال القائل هذا مِلكي سمعه المحجوب من لسان المخلوق وسمعه المكاشف من ناطق الحقيقة فينسب المكاشف المِلك لله تعالى في قوله مِلكي وينسبه المحجوب للمخلوق في قوله مِلكي والناطق في الحقيقة واحد.

٤،٤٣ قيل لبعض أهل الطريق كم نجب لله تعالى في كلّ أربعين شاة فقال عندنا أم عندكم أمّا عندنا فالكلّ فمن نسب قوله هذا إلى الإيثار قال إنّه باذل ملكه لله ومن نسبه إلى رفع الأغيار قال إنّما نطق بمعنى أنّ المِلك كلّه لله.

٥،٤٣ والفرق بين المِلك والمُلك مفهوم وبينهما مقاربة في المعنى فلذلك قيل مالك المُلك فجمع بين لفظة مالك التي تقتضي المِلك وبين لفظة المُلك.

٦،٤٣ واعلم أنّ من علم أنّ الحقّ تعالى هو مالك الملك حقيقة لا مجازًا لم يعترض على الملوك في ممالكهم بما تجري به أحكامهم فإنّ أحكامهم هي أحكام الله تعالى حقيقة ويد الله على قلب المَلِك وإن كان هذا لسان حجاب بل قلب الملك هو يد الله المتصرّفة يتصرّف أوّلًا في الخواطر ثمّ ينقلها إلى التعلّق بالظاهر فتجري أحكام الله تعالى فيها والناس ينسبون ذلك التصرّف إلى المخلوق والمشاهد ينسبه إلى الخالق تعالى ولذلك قيل مَن نظر إلى الناس بعين الحقيقة عذرهم ومن نظر إليهم بعين الشريعة مقتهم وسواء كانت الملوك من أهل ملّة الهدى أو من أهل ملّة الضلالة فإنّ الهادي هو الله تعالى والمضلّ هو الله تعالى والمتصرّف في الحضرتين هو الله تعالى ولو عزلنا تصرّفه تعالى عن حكم واحد من أحكام الحضرتين لم يكن مالك الملك.

The presence of this name is a presence of exoteric knowledge, because the meanings of otherness are realized through it: the owner is other than the owned. And since the ownership of anyone who owns anything, such as a house or any other kind of object, is God's ownership, God is the Owner of the Kingdom and the Owner of ownership. As such, the kingdom of every king is God's kingdom, because He is the King on the plane of kingdoms, and the Owner on the plane of ownership. The reality of the Owner of the Kingdom thus flows through all kingdoms and all ownerships. 43.2

Therefore, when someone says "this is mine," the veiled intellect hears that statement as an expression voiced by a creature, whereas those who know through unveiling hear it as an expression of truth. Those who know through unveiling ascribe ownership to God when someone says "this is mine," whereas the veiled intellect ascribes this to the creature. In reality, the speaker is one. 43.3

Someone on the spiritual path was once asked, "What alms tax must I pay for forty sheep?" He responded, "According to whom—us or you? According to us, you owe it all to God." The one who ascribes this statement to selfless altruism maintains that the Sufi freely gives up His possessions to God, whereas the one who ascribes it to the removal of other-than-God maintains that he said it in the sense that "all ownership belongs to God." 43.4

The difference between a possession (*milk*) and a kingdom (*mulk*) is understood, but they are proximate in meaning; hence the Owner of the Kingdom combines the word "owner," which implies possession, and the word "kingdom." 43.5

Whoever knows that God is the true, not the metaphorical, Owner of the Kingdom, does not protest against kings for what happens in their kingdoms through their rulings. For their rulings are really God's rulings, and the Hand of God rests upon the heart of the king. Nonetheless, this is an expression of the veil, because in fact the heart of the king is God's Hand, exercising dominant power. This He does first through the thoughts that occur to the king, which He transfers to an attachment in the external world, whereupon the divine rulings run their course. While people ascribe that dominating power to a creature, the witness ascribes it to the Creator. That is why it is said: "Excuse those who look at people with the eye of truth and abhor those who do so with the eye of the revealed Law." It makes no difference whether the kings hold sound belief or are misguided, because God is the Guide and the Misguider, and He exercises dominant power in both presences. If one were to sever God's dominant power from either of the two presences, then He would not be the Owner of the Kingdom. 43.6

٧،٤٣ وأمّا كون ظاهر الشريعة يخالف هذا فإنّما كان ذلك لتنزّل الخطاب الإلٰهيّ إلى أطوار عقول المحجوبين ليبيّن لهم وقد أُمر الأنبياء عليهم السلام أن يخاطبوا الناس على قدر عقولهم ويفقهم في طور منقولهم فمالك المُلك تعالى حكمه عامّ حقيقة في أطوار الممالك والأملاك ونور العرفان الشهوديّ شاهد بذلك وقد قال عليه السلام إنّ لصاحب الحقّ مقالاً فجعله صاحب الحقّ ولولا صحّة نسبة ذلك الحقّ إلى الله تعالى من مرتبة ذلك الشخص لما جعل له مقالاً فإنّ الأمر كلّه لله حقيقة لا مجازاً وإنّما كون الأمر لغيره في لسان الحجاب فذلك هو المجاز.

٨،٤٣ فتحقّق بحقيقة مالك الملك وانظر إلى دخول الاسم الجامع منه لكونه جمع له مراتب الممالك والأملاك ومراتب الملوك والملّاك وأراك حقيقة الحقّ فيها ظاهرة وأنوار وحدانيّته منها باهرة ومن شهد هذه الأنوار وجد أسرّة وجه الحضرة محرقة ما انتهى إليه بصرها من الخلق فإحراق الخلق ليس هو كإحراق النار بل شهود عدم الأغيار فالإحراق مجاز ونفي الأغيار حقيقة وبذلك تعلم حيطة اسمه مالك الملك تعالى ومن أقرّ بأنّ الله تعالى مالك الملك في الدنيا حقيقة لا مجازاً سهل عليه أن يعلم أنّه تعالى مالك الملك في الآخرة حقيقة لا مجازاً.

٩،٤٣ واعلم أنّ العبّاد والعلماء والصوفيّة هم أهل حضرة الملك وأمّا العارفون فيشهدون المالك وأمّا المحقّقون فيشهدون الملوك والملّاك في حضرة مالك الملك وأمّا الرسل فينطقون بنسب الأملاك إلى ملّاكها المخلوقين وبنسبة الممالك إلى ملوكها المخلوقين تنزّلاً إلى عقول المحجوبين ويعرضون بالقصد عن ذكر الحقيقة الجامعة ويعترفون بها باطناً ومن يأخذ علومه عن الرسل عليهم السلام فيجعل مالك الملك مجازاً لغلبة رؤية الملوك والملّاك المخلوقين عليه ظاهراً.

This is in opposition to the outward aspect of the revealed Law because, in order to clarify matters for people, God's address descends to the level wherein their intelligence is veiled. The Prophets, moreover, were commanded to address people at the level of their intelligence, and to restrict them to the level of transmitted reports. Therefore, the property of the Owner of the Kingdom in reality pervades the levels of kingdoms and ownership, and the light of recognition rooted in witnessing attests to this. To this effect, the blessed Prophet said: "A person who is owed a rightful due may speak."[267] The blessed Prophet thereby recognized the Bedouin as having rights, and were it not correct to ascribe that right to God at the level of that individual Bedouin, he would not have recognized his right to speak.[268] For the entire affair belongs to God in reality, and not metaphorically. The fact that it is ascribed to other than Him is an expression of the veil, which indeed is metaphor. 43.7

Realize, therefore, the reality of the Owner of the Kingdom, and observe how the Gathering is included within it inasmuch as it brings together the levels of kingdoms, ownership, kings, and owners. This name shows you the reality of the Real manifesting within it, and the lights of His oneness shine forth brilliantly from it. Whoever witnesses these lights discovers that the rays of the face of the Presence incinerate creation as far as his eye can reach. For this incineration of creation is unlike the burning of a fire: it is to witness the nonexistence of other-than-God. Burning is metaphorical, and the negation of other-than-God is real. Thus you know the encompassment of His name the Owner of the Kingdom; and whoever affirms that God is the Owner of the Kingdom in this life, in reality and not metaphorically, easily knows that He is the Owner of the Kingdom in the afterlife, in reality and not metaphorically. 43.8

Moreover, the worshippers, scholars, and Sufis are the people of the presence of the King, whereas the recognizers witness the Owner. The realized saints, for their part, witness the kings and ownerships within the presence of the Owner of the Kingdom. The Messengers speak to the relation between owned possessions and their created owners, as well as the relation between kingdoms and their kings. This they do in order to stoop to veiled intellects. Thus, even though they recognize it inwardly, the Messengers intentionally avoid speaking about the all-encompassing reality. As such, those who take their knowledge from the Messengers consider the Owner of the Kingdom to be a metaphor because they are dominated by the view of created kings and owners in the external realm. 43.9

وأمّا من ورد العين وجاوز المتى والأين فيرى تصرُّف الاسم الذي هو مالك الملك حقيقة في شهود المراتب وفي شهود الجمع ثمّ يرى أنّ الأسماء تدخل في حقيقة مالك الملك فإنّ الملك إذا تجبّر فقد دخلت حقيقة الاسم الجبّار في حقيقة مالك الملك وإذا قهر فقد دخلت حقيقة الاسم القهّار في حقيقة مالك الملك وإذا أعطى فقد دخلت حقيقة الاسم المعطي في حقيقة مالك الملك وكذلك كلّ معاني الأسماء الصفاتيّة والفعليّة تلحق بالاسم مالك الملك في تطوّرات تصوّراته وتصرّفاته ومعنويّاته وتعيين دخول كل اسم اسم في حقيقة مالك الملك سهل وإنّما تركناه اختصاراً وذكرنا منه أنموذجاً تذكاراً ومن كان من أهل الأنوار اكتفى بالإشارة فكيف من هو من أهل الأسرار ﴿وَٱللَّهُ يَقُولُ ٱلْحَقَّ﴾. ١٠،٤٣

اسمه المعزّ تعالى

ورد في آل عمران في قوله تعالى ﴿تُعِزُّ مَن تَشَآءُ﴾ وهو ممّا اتّفق عليه الأئمّة الثلاثة وحضرة الاسم المعزّ تحت حضرة الاسم العزيز فإنّ حقيقة الاسم المعزّ تثبت الأغيار في طور الاعتبار وحقيقة الاسم العزيز تنفي ذلك بالاستئثار والاسم المعزّ تعالى له طوران كلّيّان أحدهما في طور الحجاب ويظهر ذلك في كلّ قضيّة جزئيّة حصل فيها إعزاز عين ما من أعيان الموجودات. ١،٤٤

فإنّه تعالى أعزّ الملوك والخلفاء والأمراء وأهل المراتب الظاهرة وأعزّ الأنبياء والخلفاء والعلماء والعابدين بعزّ الطاعة وأعزّ العارفين برجوعهم عن غيره إليه تعالى وهذا عزّ باذخ وشرف شامخ وأعلى منه من رجع من حضرة الاسم المعزّ إلى حضرة الاسم ٢،٤٤

The one who arrives at the Source and passes beyond time and place truly sees the dominant power of the Owner of the Kingdom upon witnessing the levels and the all-comprehensive union.[269] Thereupon he sees how the names enter into the reality of the Owner of the Kingdom: When a king behaves tyrannically, it is the reality of the All-Dominating entering into the reality of the Owner of the Kingdom. When he subjugates someone, it is the reality of the All-Subjugating entering into the reality of the Owner of the Kingdom. When he gives gifts, it is the reality of the Giver entering into the reality of the Owner of the Kingdom. The same applies for all the meanings of the qualitative and actual names that connect to the Owner of the Kingdom at each respective stage of its form-giving, dominant power and transcendent meanings. Determining how each name enters into the reality of the Owner of the Kingdom is easy, but we have refrained from doing so here for the sake of brevity, and have mentioned just an example to serve as a reminder. The people of light[270] are content with an allusion, which is to say nothing of those who know the mysteries. And «God speaks the truth».[271] 43.10

Al-Muʿizz: The Exalter

This name is mentioned in the Surah of the House of ʿImrān in the verse: «You exalt whoever You will».[272] The three eminent scholars agree that it is a divine name. The presence of the Exalter pertains to the presence of the Mighty, for the reality of the Exalter affirms things other-than-God from the stage of perspectival considerations, whereas the reality of the Exalted negates things other-than-God by claiming exclusive possession. Furthermore, the Exalter comprises two universal stages. The first is the stage of the veil, which manifests in every particular situation wherein an existent entity becomes exalted. 44.1

For God exalts kings, caliphs, emirs, and persons of outward rank, just as He exalts prophets, scholars, and worshippers with the exaltedness of obedience. He exalts the recognizers by returning them from other-than-Him to Him, and that is a lofty exaltation and a magnificent honor. Higher still are 44.2

العزيز وذلك بفقدان الأنانيّة التي بها تثبت الإنيّة[١] الأصليّة وقد جاء في كتاب المواقف قوله يا عبدِ إذا لم أشهدك عزّي فيما أشهد فقد أقررتك على الذلّ فيه فإذًا من أشهده العزّ فإنّه ينقله إلى حضرة الاسم العزيز فيعزّ بعزّه عزّة هي عزّة أهل شهود حضرة الوقفة التي هي فوق العرفان.

٣،٤٤ فتصرّف الاسم المعزّ هو تحت حضرة الاسم العزيز وقد أعزّ الاسم المعزّ الأفلاك على السماوات وأعزّ السماوات على الأرضين وأعزّ المعادن على الجمادات فلم تقدر الجمادات أن تصل إلى عزّ المعادن وعزّها بنموّها وحركتها في أطوار مراتبها ثمّ أعزّ بعض هذه المعادن على بعض فإنّ النحاس لا يبلغ عزّة الذهب ويقاس على هذا بقيّتها ثمّ إنّه أعزّ النبات على المعادن وجعل النبات أشرف من المعادن في الرتبة لا في عرف العالم وما ذاك إلّا لأنّ المعدن مغمور في الأرض مستور بالغلبة والستر والنبات صحبته قوّة الاسم المعزّ فشقّ الأرض وعلا عليها إلى نحو الأفق والفوق وعزّته في تمكّن حركته فيما لا تقدر المعادن أن تحرّك فيه.

٤،٤٤ ومن جملة عزّة النبات أنّ جسمه تخلّص من الأرض ولم يبق منه فيها إلّا رأسه فإنّ رأسه هو الذي يكون منه الغذاء والاغتذاء وهو الذي هو في الأرض وبقيّة جسمه خالص ولمّا كان اغتذاء النبات إنّما هو من لطائف الأرض الممتزجة بالماء والأرض والماء كرة واحدة ثبت رأس النبات في الأرض لطلب الاغتذاء منها وتخلّص بقيّة جسم ما كان فيها فهذه عزّة ظهرت مِن الاسم المعزّ وتعلّق حكمها بالنبات كلّه ولا يلتفَت إلى عزّة الياقوت والذهب والفضّة وما عزّ من الأحجار عند الناس فإنّ تلك العزّةَ ليست عزّة إلٰهيّة بل عرفيّة بين الناس وإن كان العرف أيضاً راجعاً إلى الحضرة الإلٰهيّة.

٥،٤٤ وإذا أردت أن تعرف أنّ النبات أشرف من المعدن فانظر أيّهما أقرب إلى جسم الإنسان فإنّك تجد مرتبة النبات أقرب إذ هي تلي الحيوان الذي هو يلي الإنسان ولأنّ

١ التي بها تثبت الإنيّة: ساقطة من آ. الإنيّة: و: الأنانيّة.

those who return from the presence of the Exalter to the presence of the Exalted when they lose their I-ness through which the primordial is-ness is affirmed. As stated in *The Book of Haltings* of al-Niffarī, "O servant, if I do not make you witness My exaltedness in what I am witness to, then I have placed you in abasement within it."[273] Thus, the one who is made by Him to witness exaltedness is transported to the presence of the Exalted, whereby he becomes exalted through God's exaltedness. That exaltedness, moreover, pertains to those who witness the presence of the station of halting, which is beyond direct recognition.

Thus, the scope of the Exalter's activity lies below the presence of the 44.3
Exalted. For indeed, the Exalter exalts the celestial spheres above the skies, and the skies above the earths. The Exalter exalts minerals above other inanimate objects, and the inanimate objects are unable to attain the exaltedness of minerals. These He exalts by their growth and movements, each within the stage of its level. Then He exalts some of these minerals above others: brass does not attain the exaltedness of gold, and so on for the other minerals. Moreover, He exalts plants above minerals, and has made plants more eminent than minerals in rank, not in common custom, because minerals are buried beneath the earth, covered by the quality of divine dominance and hidden away. Plants, however, possess the strength of the Exalter, and thereby split the earth and rise above it, moving upward. The exaltedness of plants lies in their ability to move, whereas minerals are unable to move in the earth.

One aspect of the exaltedness of a plant is that its body frees itself from 44.4
the earth, so that all that remains is its head. For it is through the head of the plant that it nourishes itself. The head is what remains in the earth, while the rest of its body is free from it. Moreover, since the nourishment of plants is derived from the subtle properties of the earth that are mixed with water, and since earth and water form a single sphere, its head remains rooted within the earth in order to seek its nourishment therein, while the rest of its body frees itself from the earth. This, then, is an exaltedness that manifests through the Exalter, and its property is attached to all plants. And one should pay no regard to the exalted status of rubies, gold, silver, and precious stones among people, for that exaltedness is not from God, but from common custom; although common custom itself stems from the divine presence.

If you wish to understand how plants are more eminent than minerals, 44.5
then observe which of them is closer to the human body. You will find that the

النبات يكون غذاءً لجسم الإنسان ولا يكون المعدن كذلك ولأنّ المعدن مغصوب أي غصب الظهور وخصّ بالبطون فهو مغمور فذلّ.

٦،٤٤ وأمّا النبات فليس هو بمغصوب بل مقلوب أي رأسه إلى أسفل والمعدن كلّه أسفل ومن بعضه أسفل فهو أشرف ممّن كلّه أسفل لكنّ الحيوان قد حصل له من الاسم المعزّ نصيب هو أكمل من نصيب النبات ومن نصيب المعادن فإنّه قد ظهر من الأرض ولم يبق رأسه فيها كما بقي رأس النبات وانتقل ولم ينتقل النبات إلّا أنّه مكبوب لكنّ المكبوب أشرف من المقلوب فقد فضل على النبات واغتذى منه فإنّ كلّ جسم يغتذي ممّا تحته فإنّ الذي تحته هو ممّا يحكم عليه ولا يلتفت إلى كون بعض النبات أطول من الحيوان فإنّ المطاولة إنّما هي بالرؤوس ورؤوس الحيوان فوق ورؤوس النبات أسفل.

٧،٤٤ فإذاً حكم الاسم المعزّ في الحيوان أظهر منه في النبات ولكلّ منهما نصيب منه إلّا أنّ الحيوان أقرب إلى الإنسان فكان أشرف لكنّه وإن شرف على النبات فإنّ شرف الإنسان على الحيوان ظاهر فكان نصيبه من الاسم المعزّ أقوى وبيان شرفه لا يخفى وذلك بالنطق في المعاني وبالصورة في الأجسام فإنّ الحيوان مكبوب والنبات مقلوب والمعدن مغصوب وأمّا الإنسان فمنصوب وذلك لأنّ قامته منتصبة ورأسه إلى جانب العلوّ ورأسه أعلى من بدنه بخلاف النبات ورأس الحيوان مساو لبدنه في حقيقة المكبوبيّة.

٨،٤٤ واعلم أنّ حقّ المعدن أن يغتذي من الأرض إذ هي تحته وحقّ النبات أن يغتذي من الماء إذ هي تحته لكن تداخَل الماء والأرض فاغتذى النبات منهما وحقّ الحيوان أن يغتذي من النبات إذ هو تحته وحقّ الإنسان أن يغتذي من الحيوان إذ هو تحته وليس شيء فوق الإنسان فيكون الإنسان غذاءً له هذا هو الترتيب الأصليّ ثمّ انحرفت بعض موجودات هذه المراتب فاغتذى سائح[1] الطير والوحش من الحيوان

[1] و: سباع.

rank of plants is closer, for it follows that of animals, which follows the human being. Plants are also a nourishment for the human body, but minerals are not. Moreover, since minerals are constrained—that is, constrained from manifesting themselves and thus confined to nonmanifestation—they are submerged and therefore lowly.

Plants, for their part, are not constrained but inverted. That is, their heads 44.6
are turned upside down, in contrast to minerals, which are entirely underground. Something that is partially submerged is more eminent than something that is entirely submerged. However, the animal attains a share of the Exalter that is more complete than that of the plant and the mineral. It comes from the earth, but its head does not remain in the earth like that of a plant. Moreover, an animal moves about, in contrast to a plant, even though its head is stretched in front of it. Yet an animal whose head is stretched in front of it is more noble than a plant whose roots are in the ground. As such, it is more eminent than the plant, and takes its nourishment from it. For every body takes its nourishment from what is beneath it, since what is beneath it is what it rules over. One should pay no regard to the fact that some plants are taller than animals, because the measurement of tallness is based on the position of the head, and the heads of animals are higher than the heads of plants.

Thus, the property of the Exalter in the animal is more manifest than it is 44.7
in the plant, though each has its share of this name. However, the animal is closer to the human being than the plant, and thus is nobler. And although it is nobler than a plant, the nobility of the human being in relation to the animal is obvious, and hence the human's share of the Exalter is stronger. An explanation of human nobility, moreover, is not ambiguous: it lies in his articulation of meanings, and his bodily form. For the animal has a head that stretches to the front, the plant is inverted, and the mineral is deep underground, whereas the human being is upright. His posture is upright, and his head is raised high atop his body. This is unlike the plant or the head of the animal, which is parallel to its body because it is stretched in front of it.

The mineral has a right to take nourishment from the earth, because the 44.8
earth lies beneath it. Likewise, the plant has a right to take nourishment from water, for water is beneath it. But water and earth interpenetrate, and therefore the plant takes its nourishment from both. Moreover, the animal has a right to be nourished from the plant, for the plant lies beneath it. Nothing, however, is above the human, for which he may serve as nourishment. This, then, is the

وهو على غير القاعدة ووُجد هذا في المراتب كلّها لكنّه يقلّ في الإنسان وأمّا أنّ الإنسان يغتذي بالنبات فلأنّ الأعلى له أن يتصرّف في الأدنى وأنّ اللحم هو أنسب لجسم الإنسان.

٩،٤٤ وقد عرفت تصرّف الاسم المعزّ في هذه المراتب وسيأتي ذكر الاسم المذلّ فيكون ما أعزّه الاسم المعزّ على غيره فقد أذلّ الاسم المذلّ ذلك المفضول فكأنّ الاسم المذلّ يأخذ ما أبقاه الاسم المعزّ فيقتسمان والله أعلم.

اسمه المذلّ تبارك اسمه

١،٤٥ ورد في آل عمران في قوله تعالى ﴿تُعِزُّ مَن تَشَآءُ وَتُذِلُّ مَن تَشَآءُ﴾ وقد اتّفق على إيراده الأئمّة الثلاثة ومحلّ تصرّفه في كلّ الموجودات التي تثبت لغيرها عليها مزيّة فإنّ حقيقة هذا الاسم ليست مقصودة بالقصد الوجوديّ بل بالقصد المرتبيّ فإنّه لمّا عزّ غيره عليه ذلّ فكان القصد بالذات عزّة ما أُعزّ فحصل بالعرض ذُلّ ما ذلّ إلّا أنّه لمّا كان ما ذلّ ليس خارجاً عن القصد الذاتيّ الجامع المحيط لم يكن هذا خارجاً لكن بالقصد الثاني وقد عرفت تناسب العزّة في ترقّيها ممّا ذُكر في الاسم المعزّ فيقابلها من الاسم المذلّ ما يقابل تلك الأحكام المذكورة ﴿جَزَآءً وِفَاقًا﴾.

٢،٤٥ واعلم أنّ بين الأناسي أيضاً أحكاماً في معنى الذلّ الذي حصل من الاسم المذلّ أمّا ذلّ الرعيّة للملوك فمن الاسم المذلّ وذلّ الفقراء للأغنياء فمن الاسم المذلّ وذلّ الضعفاء للأقوياء فمن الاسم المذلّ وبالجملة فكلّ ذلّ حصل على اعتبارات اختلافاته

fundamental hierarchy, although some creatures deviate from these ranks. For instance, birds and beasts of prey take nourishment from other animals, and that is an exception to the rule. This deviation occurs at all levels, but it is rare among human beings. The human being will take nourishment from plants, because what is higher exercises control over what is lower, but eating flesh is more appropriate for the human body.

You now know how the Exalter exercises control at the cosmic levels. We shall now turn to the Abaser, for whenever the Exalter exalts one thing over another, the Abaser abases the latter. In a sense, the Abaser takes what the Exalter leaves, so they work as a pair. And God knows best. 44.9

Al-Mudhill: The Abaser

This name is mentioned in the Surah of the House of ʿImrān in the verse: «You exalt whoever You will and abase whoever You will».[274] The three eminent scholars agree it is a divine name. The Abaser exercises its control over existent things that are inferior in relation to others. For in reality, the purpose of this name is not existence but rank. As such, whenever one entity is exalted above another, then the latter is abased in relation to it, and the essential purpose is to exalt the one that is exalted. As such, the abasement of the one that is abased occurs accidentally. But since the one that is abased does not lie beyond the all-comprehensive and all-encompassing purpose of the Essence, it is not outside of it. Rather, its purpose is secondary. You know how exaltedness, which was discussed in our commentary on the Exalter, corresponds in its ascension to the contrasting properties of the Abaser in «a suitable recompense».[275] 45.1

Moreover, there are also properties of abasement among human beings that occur through the Abaser. For instance, the abasement of subjects before their king is from the Abaser, and the abasement of the poor before the rich is from the Abaser, and the abasement of the weak before the strong is from the Abaser. In short, every abasement that occurs in a variety of respects is from the Abaser. For there is nothing in existence other than the properties of the 45.2

فمن الاسم المذلّ فإنّه ما في الوجود إلّا أحكام الأسماء ومن الذلّ أن لا تدرك بعض الموجودات علم مسألة ما ويدركها غيره فيعزّ المدرك ويذلّ الجاهل وإن لم يحسّ الجاهل بالذلّ لكنّ الذلّ لازم له.

٣،٤٥ واعلم أنّ عدم الإدراك في الحقيقة ليس يخصّ من جهل ما صنّفه العلماء من العلوم فقط بل هو فيما أُدرك من العلم بالله ولم يدركه غيرهم أقوى أعني أنّ ذلّ من لم يدرك الحقيقة هو الذلّ المحقّق فيكون العلماء أذلّة بالنسبة إلى العارفين والعارفون أذلّة بالنسبة إلى الواقفين والواقفون أذلّة بالنسبة إلى المحقّقين والرسل من المحقّقين أعزّ من المحقّقين وعود الرسل بجمع الأحديّة هو ما يجعلهم أعزّ من الأنبياء فقط وأمّا أهل العمل فمن حصل له الإخلاص هو أعزّ ممّن هو خالط عمله الرياء وأهل التصوّف من العبّاد أعزّ من أهل العبادة فقط والمحبّون أعزّ من الصوفيّة والعارفون أعزّ من المحبّين وتتّصل السلسلة المذكورة آنفاً.

٤،٤٥ واعلم أنّ حقيقة الاسم المذلّ لمّا أحسّ بها المحبّون من وراء حجاب رقيق وجدوا في أذواقهم نسبتها إلى اسم محبوبهم فتمسّكوا بالذلّ لعزّ محبوبهم والذلّ في نفسه حقيقة واحدة لكنّها للمحبّين شرف لأنّها إنّما كانت منهم لتسليمهم العزّة للمحبوب الحقّ فصبغها المحبوب الحقّ بشرفه فشُكرت تلك الذلّة شرعاً ورآها المحبّون أصلاً وإن كانت فرعاً.

٥،٤٥ وأمّا العارفون فإنّهم شهدوا الاسم المذلّ من حضرة المسمّى الحقّ فذلّوا إذ لا يرونه عزّاً وهم فيه على قدر مراتبهم فمن بقيت فيه بقيّة من حضرة المحبّة كان ذلّه من تلك الحيثيّة ذلّ المحبّين ومن كانت ذلّته إنّما هي ذلّة لعزّة الربوبيّة بالشهود كان ذلّه ذلّ العارفين.

٦،٤٥ ومن كان الشطح غالباً عليه في البوح بوارداته كانت ذلّته ذلّة المغلوبين ومن كانت ذلّته ذلّة تنزّل إلى عقول المحجوبين كان ذلّه اختيارياً وتقيّة من المنكرين وقد قال الجنيد

names. Moreover, when some creatures comprehend a subject and others do not, that is a type of abasement, for the one who comprehends it is exalted and the one who is ignorant is abased. And even if the ignorant do not sense their abasement, it is nonetheless inseparable from them.

A lack of comprehension is not specific to those who are ignorant of what exoteric scholars have written. It also pertains to the knowledge of God that is comprehended by some and not others. And this—I mean the abasement of those who do not comprehend the truth—is stronger. It is the true abasement. As such, exoteric scholars are abased in relation to the recognizers, and the recognizers are abased in relation to those who have arrived at the station of halting, and those who have arrived at the latter are abased in relation to the truth-verifiers, and the Messengers among the truth-verifiers are more exalted than the rest. The Messengers, moreover, are more exalted than the Prophets because of how they are made to return to God's All-Comprehensive Oneness. Among people given to religious deeds, those who attain sincerity are more exalted than those whose deeds are tainted by conceit. Moreover, the Sufis among the worshippers are more exalted than simple worshippers, just as the lovers are more exalted than the Sufis, and the recognizers are more exalted than the lovers, and so on, as was just described. 45.3

Moreover, the lovers sense the reality of the Abaser from behind a thin veil, and they directly experience its relation to the name of their Beloved. Thereupon they cling to their abasement on account of the exaltedness of their Beloved. Now, abasement in itself is one reality, but for the lovers it is eminence, because their abasement lies in how they concede exaltedness to none other than the true Beloved, and therefore the truly Beloved colors their abasement with His eminence. Thus, abasement is praised by the revealed Law, and the lovers consider it to be a foundational root, even though it is a secondary branch of the Law. 45.4

The recognizers, for their part, witness the Abaser from the presence of the true Bearer of the Names. Thereupon, they enter into abasement, for they do not see it as exaltedness. In this, moreover, they differ according to their levels. Those in whom there is a remnant of the presence of love are abased in the manner of lovers, while those who are abased purely through the exaltedness of lordship by direct witnessing are abased in the manner of recognizers. 45.5

Furthermore, those who are so dominated that they proclaim ecstatic utterances and divulge their inrushes are abased in the manner of the dominated. The abasement of those who are abased such that they descend to the level 45.6

رضي الله عنه عطّل ذلّي ذلّ اليهود وقال نحن قوم كنس الله بأرواحنا المزابل وأمثال هذه الأحكام وكلّها من حقائق الاسم المذلّ.

٧،٤٥ وَٱلْأَرْضُ ذَلُولٌ وكلّ المعادن والنبات والحيوان ذلولات للإنسان ذلًّا مرتبيًا وإن سطا به بعض هذه الموجودات فبجسمه لا بنفسه والإنسان إنّما هو النفس وإلّا فالأنبياء والرسل دخل على أجسامهم الضرر ممّن هو دون مراتبهم ولم يقدح ذلك في العزّة الإلٰهيّة الثابتة لنفوسهم ولمّا لحق الحضرة الإلٰهيّة الغيرة على مرتبة الاسم المذلّ في توجّهه إلى حظّ محلّ تصرّفاته أُعطيت حقيقته بدلًا في بعض المراتب فكان الذل من تلك الجهة سببًا للعزّ فقيل شعر

وَكَمْ عِزَّةٍ قَدْ نَالَهَا ٱلْمَرْءُ بِٱلذُّلِّ

٨،٤٥ واعلم أنّ ذلّ العبوديّة ممّا هو منسوب إلى عزّ الربوبيّة ولو لم يكن إلّا بالمضايفة فإنّ المضايفة قرب ما إذ المضايف أقرب من غير المضايف إلى من ضايفه ومن عزّة العبوديّة أنّها كالثمن للربوبيّة فإنّ السالكين إذا تحقّقوا بمعنى العبوديّة تمامًا عُوّضوا عنها بعزّ الربوبيّة ومن هذه الحضرة شطح الحلّاج وأضاف اسم الربوبيّة إلى ذاته ومن هذه الحضرة قال أبو يزيد سبحاني إلى غير ذلك وقال في المواقف أعطني اسمك حتّى ألقاك به وقال لا تتسمّ ولا تتكنَّ والمراد بذلك خروجه عن اسمه ومسمّاه حتّى تحقّق العبوديّة المحضة وهو العدم حتّى لا يكون ﴿شَيْـًٔا مَّذْكُورًا﴾ وعند ذلك تتبدّل أسماؤه.

٩،٤٥ ولي في ذلك شعر

أَرَى رَسْمَهَا عِنْدِي يُعَوِّضُ عَنْ رَسْمِي فَمَا بَالُهُمْ فِي ٱلْحَيِّ يَدْعُونَنِي بِٱسْمِي
وَلَكِنْ إِذَا أَفْنَتْكَ عَنْكَ عَلَى عِلْمِ إِذَا مَا دَعَى ٱلدَّاعِي بِعَلْوَةَ فَٱسْتَجِبْ

of veiled intelligence is voluntary and a cautious dissimulation in the face of deniers. Al-Junayd said: “My abasement nullifies the abasement of the Jews.”[276] He also said: “We are a people whose spirits God uses to clean out dunghills,”[277] and other such sayings, which all come from the realities of the Abaser.

Moreover, «the earth is abased»,[278] and all minerals, plants, and animals are abased in rank relative to the human. When a creature attacks a human, it attacks with its body, not its soul; and the human is none other than the soul. Even Prophets and Messengers have suffered bodily harm from those who are beneath their rank, yet that does not detract from the divine exaltedness firmly rooted in their souls. Now, since the divine presence is seized by a jealous pride toward the level of the Abaser as it turns its attention to a locus that partakes in its free activity, the reality of abasement is inverted at some levels, whereby abasement becomes a cause of exaltedness. To this effect, a poet once said: 45.7

> Many an exaltation has been earned through abasement![279]

Among the states ascribed to the exaltedness of lordship is the abasement of servanthood, even though it is only by way of relative correlation. For relative correlations are also a type of proximity, and that which has a relative correlation to its counterpart is closer than that which has no relative correlation. Moreover, servanthood is qualified by exaltedness because it is the price, as it were, for lordship. For when the wayfarers realize the pure meaning of servanthood completely, they are compensated for it with the exaltedness of lordship. It was from this presence that al-Ḥallāj made his ecstatic utterance and ascribed the designation of lordship to himself. It was also from this presence that Abū Yazīd al-Basṭāmī said: “Glorified am I!” and so forth. Al-Niffarī quotes God in *The Book of Haltings* as saying: “Give Me your name so that I may meet you therein,” and “Do not adopt a name or a moniker,”[280] by which He refers to setting aside one’s own name in order to realize absolute servanthood (which is nonexistence) so that one can become «a thing unremembered»,[281] at which point one’s names are supplanted. 45.8

On this topic I have the following verses: 45.9

> I see Her traces replace mine within me—
> why then do they call me by my name in the neighborhood?
> When someone calls out, “ʿAlwa!”[282] then answer,
> but only if She has caused you to pass away from yourself
> knowingly . . .[283]

فقوله ﴿وَلَكِنْ إِذَا أَفْنَتْكَ عَنْكَ عَلَى عِلْمٍ﴾ إشارة إلى التحقّق بالعبوديّة وحينئذ تتبدّل الأسماء فيتبدّل الذليل بالعزيز فيكون في هذه الحضرة قد وصل تنزّل الاسم المذلّ فوجد في مقابلة وجهه الاسم المعزّ فصار التحت فوقاً والصعب طوقاً والله أعلم.

اسمه الحَكَم تبارك وتعالى

١،٤٦ موضعه من آل عمران قوله تعالى ﴿فَأَحْكُمُ بَيْنَكُمْ فِيمَا كُنتُمْ فِيهِ تَخْتَلِفُونَ﴾ وقد اتّفق على إيراده الأئمّة الثلاثة ولهذا الاسم أحكام في الدنيا والآخرة فيحكم بين عباده يوم القيامة وأمّا في الدنيا ففي شمول قوله تعالى ﴿إِنِ ٱلْحُكْمُ إِلَّا لِلَّهِ﴾ ﴿ذَٰلِكُمْ حُكْمُ ٱللَّهِ يَحْكُمُ بَيْنَكُمْ﴾ فإذا ظهرت حقيقة اسمه الحكيم تبارك وتعالى في مظاهر الوجود الظاهر شهده أهل الكشف في حقائق القضاة والولاة وأرباب المراتب ممّن يتولّى أمور الناس ويشهدونه أيضاً في أطوار غير الأناسيّ فيحكم المالك للدوابّ بين دوابّه بالعدل فلا يمكّن شيئاً منها من التعدّي على شيء ويحكم الجنّان والبستانيّ بين النبات فلا يترك بعضها يتعدّى على بعض ولذلك ينزع الغريبة من بين الأشجار والضارّة بها وكلّ هذه وأمثالها ممّا لا يتناهى هي مظاهر للاسم الحكيم تعالى فإنّ الحكم حقيقة إنّما هو لله تعالى.

٢،٤٦ واعلم أنّ العارفين لمّا تحقّقوا باسمه الحكم تبارك وتعالى لم يغلّطوا حكم حاكم باجتهاده فعندهم كلّ مجتهد مصيب وحكمه تعالى بين عباده فيما ﴿هُمْ فِيهِ يَخْتَلِفُونَ﴾ يعرفه أهل الله فيشهدون ﴿مَا هُمْ فِيهِ يَخْتَلِفُونَ﴾ فيرون الحكم العدل تعالى قد أثبت لكلّ

The hemistich "but only if She has caused you to pass away from yourself knowingly" is an allusion to the realization of servanthood, when the names are replaced, such that the abased is replaced with the exalted. In this presence, the servant arrives at the descent of the Abaser, and he finds himself facing the Exalter. Low becomes high, and the intractable comes within reach. And God knows best.

Al-Ḥakam: The Ruler

This name is found in the Surah of the House of ʿImrān in the verse: «I shall rule between you as to that wherein you used to differ».[284] The three eminent scholars agree it is a divine name. This name has properties in both this world and the hereafter. For He will judge between His servants on Resurrection Day, and He judges in this world by virtue of the all-inclusive verses «the rule only belongs to God»[285] and «that is God's judgment; He rules between you».[286] Therefore, when the reality of the Ruler manifests in the loci of external existence, those who know through unveiling witness it through the realities of judges, governors, and persons of rank who preside over the affairs of people. Those who know through unveiling also witness this reality at the stages of nonhumans: an owner of animals rules over his animals justly, ensuring that no animal assaults another. The cultivator and the gardener also rule over plants and prevent some from aggressing against others by removing harmful weeds from between trees. All of these examples and countless others are loci of the Ruler because true rulership belongs to God alone. 46.1

Since the recognizers verify the Ruler, they do not find fault with a ruler for ruling according to his independent judgment because, for the recognizers, "every independent judgment is correct."[287] Furthermore, His rule over His servants «in that wherein they differ»[288] is recognized by God's folk[289] who, upon witnessing «that wherein they differ», see the Just Ruler at each level of difference, establishing a ruling that contains truth. Therefore, God speaks through their witness on the tongue of the Ḥanafī jurist through the truth of 46.2

مرتبة من المختلف فيه حكماً هو فيه الحقّ فينطق الحقّ في شهودهم من لسان الحنفيّ بالحقّ الحنفيّ وفي لسان كلّ مخالف له بالحقّ المنسوب إلى ذلك الطور ويشهدون أحوال العباد مختلفة فيجدون الأحكام تختلف بحسب اختلافها أمّا في المسألة الواحدة فلأنّ حكم المسافر في الصوم غير حكم المقيم وحكم الحائض غير حكم الطاهر وحكم الجنب غير حكم المتطهّر وأحكام العبادات مختلفات على عدد اختلافها من صلاة وصوم وجهاد وحجّ وزكاة وتتطوّر في مراتب السنّة والنافلة والمستحبّ والمباح والمحرّم والمكروه وغير ذلك والعبادات القلبيّة والعبادات البدنيّة فإنّ الحقّ تعالى يحكم بين هذه الأحكام أيضاً فلا يدع حكماً منها يتعدّى طوره ولا تدخل حقيقة في حقيقة أخرى إلّا من وجه يجوز لمثلها أن تدخل وهذا كلّه حكومة معنويّة يتصرّف فيها الاسم الحَكَم العدل تبارك وتعالى.

٣،٤٦ واعلم أنّ المظالم لا تختصّ بالأفعال بل حتّى في المعتقدات فإنّ الظلم وضع الشيء في غير موضعه والحَكَم الحقّ يحكم بين المراتب فكلّ نفس اعتقدت عقيدة إمّا حقّة وإمّا باطلة فإنّ الحقّ تعالى يحكم في ذات كلّ واحد ممّن تلبّس بتلك العقيدة فيجازيه على عقيدته إن صالحة فصالحاً وإن فاسدة ففاسداً قال تعالى ﴿سَيَجْزِيهِمْ وَصْفَهُمْ﴾ ومعنى فاسداً هو كقوله تعالى ﴿وَجَزَٰٓؤُاْ سَيِّئَةٍ سَيِّئَةٌ مِّثْلُهَا﴾.

٤،٤٦ واعلم أنّ المظاهر الذي لا يحكم بالعدل إنّما يرجع إلى حكم الحَكَم تبارك وتعالى من طور ظهور الاسم المضلّ في الاسم الحكم فإنّ الجائر في حكمه حَكَم بحكم الله تعالى من حضرة اسمه الحَكَم في تآمره في ظهور حقائق الاسم المضلّ فإنّ ظهورات محالّ تصرّفات الاسم المضلّ إنّما تحقّق في كلّ الأطوار ومن جملة الأطوار الحكم بالجور فيجب أن يكون الحكم بالجور حكماً لله تعالى من حضرة الاسم المضلّ لا بأمره فإنّه تعالى هو الذي ﴿يُضِلُّ مَن يَشَآءُ﴾.

٥،٤٦ كما أنّ الحكم بالعدل في مراتب ظهورات الحكّام بالعدل على اختلافهم إنّما هي ظهورات أحكام الاسم الهادي من طور الحَكَم تبارك وتعالى فظهر أنّ الأحكام من

the Ḥanafī jurist, and on the tongue of those who differ by the truth that is related to that stage. Likewise, they witness the varying states of the servants, and discover that their rulings differ according to their differences. A single legal issue features different rulings because the ruling regarding fasting for the traveler is different from the ruling for the non-traveler, and the ruling for the menstruating woman is different from that for the woman in a state of ritual purity, and the ruling for the one in a state of ritual impurity is different from that for the one in a state of ritual purity. There is a similarly broad variance in the rulings of worship for such matters as prayer, fasting, jihad, pilgrimage, and charity, and these change according to various levels; namely, that of the prophetic practice of the legal categories of the voluntary, the encouraged, the permitted, the prohibited, the discouraged, and so on.[290] The same applies to acts of worship of the heart and those of the body. For the Real decrees these rulings as well, and He does not allow for one ruling to transgress its stage, nor for one reality to encroach upon another except from a certain angle where it is permissible for it to do so. All of this is a supersensory domain of rulership where the Just Ruler exercises free control.

Moreover, wrongdoings are not just specific to deeds, but also to beliefs; for 46.3
to wrong means to place a thing where it does not belong. The true Ruler rules over all levels, and therefore the Real rules over each soul that holds a belief, whether it be one that is true or false. When an individual espouses a belief, He recompenses them for their belief with righteousness if it is a sound belief, and with corruption if it is a corrupt belief. God says: «He will recompense them for that which they ascribe».[291] The meaning of corruption, moreover, is in following verse: «The recompense of an ugly deed is an ugly deed like it».[292]

When a possessor of dominion does not rule in a just manner, this stems 46.4
from the rulership of the Ruler from the stage of manifestation of the Misguider through the Ruler. For the oppressive ruler in fact rules by God's rulership through the presence of the Ruler when he sets himself up as a lord, manifesting the realities of the Misguider. For the manifestations of authority of the Misguider are realized at all stages, and one of them is oppressive rule. Thus, oppressive rule must necessarily be a rulership that belongs to God through the presence of the Misguider, but not from His prescriptive command, for it is He who «misguides whoever He wills».[293]

Likewise, when just rulership manifests at the levels of just rulers in all their 46.5
variety, those are none other than manifestations of the Guide through the

الحاكمين أناسيّ كانوا أو غير أناسيّ فإنّها أحكام الله تعالى فإن اقتضت تلك الأحكام رجوعات رجعت في الحقيقة إلى الاسم الرحمٰن وإن كانت عدميّات مرتبيّات رجعت في الحقيقة إلى الاسم الله ويرجعان معاً إلى الاسم الهو وهي الهويّة وترجع الهويّة إلى نفسها بقطع الإشارة والعبارة.

٦،٤٦ وهذه الرجوعات المذكورة يتصرّف فيها الحَكَم تبارك وتعالى فلا يترك مرتبة تدخل في قسيمتها ولا يترك راجعة منها ترجع عن حكم رجعتها وتعطي الطبيعة نيابته تعالى فتكون الطبيعة حكيمة فتحكم بين الكيفيّات وتغاير بين الكمّيّات وتقابل بين الإضافات وتحفظ نسبة المتمكّنات إلى الأمكنة في الإضافات وتحفظ مراتب الأزمنة في الدهر فلا تترك الحاضر من الآتي ولا الماضي من الحاضر والآت وتعدل في العدل بالعدل وتعدل في الجور بالجور وترجعهما معاً إلى عدل الذات وتحكم بين المختلفات بالمختلفات وبين المؤتلفات بالمؤتلفات فإنّ الاختلاف في مراتبه عدل والائتلاف في مراتبه عدل والخلط بينهما عدول وجور يرجع إلى الاسم الجامع وهو عدل.

٧،٤٦ فإنّ مراتب الاختلاط تثبت فيما بين المحيط والمحاط حتّى لا يخرج شيء عن الوجود أبداً ولا يقع شيء من الاختلاف في الاختلاف والائتلاف سرمداً ولا تقع حكومة صغرت أو كبرت إلّا وتجد لها من الحَكَم الحقّ مدداً ويستمرّ ذلك على حكم ذلك أمداً ومدداً ويشتمل هذا الحكم من الحَكَم تبارك وتعالى دنياً وأخرى وسرّاً وجهراً وحدانيّة وتوحيداً وإيماناً وكفراً فأحكام الاسم الحَكَم مكتوبة في ذوات الوجودات والمراتب سطراً سطراً فمن صبغ نظره النور الكشفيّ فإنّه لتلك السطور يقرأ ومن عمي عنها فإنّ استعداده قد أوسعه عذراً وإن كان له عذراً والله أعلم.

stage of the Ruler. Thus, it is clear that the rulings of rulers, whether they are human or nonhuman, are rulings of God. Moreover, if those rulings entail a return, they return in reality to the All-Merciful. And if they are nonexistential ranks, they return in reality to Allāh, while both return to the name "He," which is God's Identity, which returns to Itself by removing from Itself all allusions and expressions.

Moreover, the Ruler exercises control over these returns, for He does not let 46.6
any level partake in their portions, nor does He allow any one of these returns to defy the predetermined property of its return. He also gives nature His deputyship so that nature possesses wise rulership. It thus rules over modalities, differentiates between quantities, counters correlations, preserves the relation between emplaced things and places in correlations, and preserves the levels of time within the aeon so that it does not abandon the present for the future, or the past for the present and the future; and it upholds a balance of justice, strikes a just balance in things that are in disequilibrium, and brings them both to the just balance of the Essence; and it rules over incongruities by incongruity and over the compatible by compatibility. For incongruities at their own levels are an equilibrium, and compatibility at its level is an equilibrium, whereas mixing the two is a disequilibrium and deviation that harks back to the All-Comprehensive, which itself is a just equilibrium.

For the levels of mixing are affirmed between the Encompassing and that 46.7
which is encompassed such that nothing ever goes out of existence. Nor are there ever any incongruities within incongruity or within compatibility, nor is an ordinance set forth, however major or minor, except that it is perpetually sustained by the true Ruler. Thus it continues to be sustained to the end, and that ruling from the Ruler includes both this world and the next, secretly and openly, in only-ness and oneness, belief and disbelief. For the properties of the Ruler are inscribed upon the essences of existents and the levels, line by line. Whoever adorns his sight with the light of unveiling is able to read those lines; and whoever is blind to them, then his preparedness is a sufficient excuse for him, though he may have other excuses on top of that. And God knows best.

اسمه الناصر تبارك وتعالى

١،٤٧ ورد في آل عمران في قوله تعالى ﴿ٱللَّهُ مَوْلَىٰكُمْ وَهُوَ خَيْرُ ٱلنَّٰصِرِينَ﴾ انفرد بإيراده البيهقيّ رحمه الله معنى النصرة ظاهر في المعنى[١] على من تغالبه والاسم الناصر تعالى له اعتباران كلّيّان أحدهما وجوديّ يرجع إلى الاسم الرحمٰن والثاني مرتبيّ يرجع إلى الاسم الله فالنصر الوجوديّ مثل نصر الخصب بالمطر على الجدب ونصر السمن بالاغتذاء على العجف في الكسب ويظهر حكمه في تغيّر الأحوال بغلبة النموّ على الاضمحلال والزيادة على النقصان في الزرع والميزان والمكيال وفي دفع السقم بالشفاء والغدر بالوفاء والكدر بالصفاء والفراق باللقاء والسقوط بالارتقاء والعدم بالوجود والمنع بالعطاء والجود كلّ ذلك ممّا ذاته في الخارج ممّا يرتقي في الوجوديّة في مدارج ومعارج.

٢،٤٧ وأمّا المرتبيّ فعكس ما ذُكر فإنّ نصر الجدب نفي الخصب وهو مرتبيّ عدميّ ونصر العجف عدم السمن ونصر الاضمحلال هو عدم النموّ ونصر النقصان هو عدم الزيادة ويقاس ما بقي على ما ذُكر وهذا النصر المرتبيّ يرجع إلى الاسم الله وكلاهما يرجع إلى الهو وهو حضرة الثبوت التي هي أعمّ من الوجود والعدم في اصطلاح أمّة من الأمم والاسم الناصر تبارك وتعالى يتولّى أحكام هذه المراتب في الطورين ويعمّ مقاماتها بالأمرين فهو يعطي الشيء وضدّه ويجعل المتقابلين أعوانه وجنده.

٣،٤٧ وأحسن مواقعه في النصر السلوكيّ فإنّ السالك إذا عاقته العوائق ورام أن يكون السابق فأعوزه حتّى أن يكون اللاحق فصرخ إلى الله من جور السوى وممانعة الهوى فسقط عن أفق التقدّم وهوى فإن وافاه حكم الاسم الناصر اجتمع من التفرقة عن

١ و: المُعِين.

Al-Nāṣir: The Assister

This name occurs in the Surah of the House of ʿImrān in the verse: «God is your Patron, and He is the best of assisters».[294] Only al-Bayhaqī mentions it as a divine name. The meaning of divine assistance is evident to those who experience God's assistance. The Assister has two universal considerations. The first pertains to existence and stems from the All-Merciful. The second pertains to rank and stems from Allāh. Existential assistance is like when dry land is assisted with abundant rains, or when an emaciated body is assisted with fatty foods. This name's property also manifests in changes of state whereupon growth dominates over recession, and increase dominates over decrease in crops, weights, and measurements; and in the removal of disease through antidotes; or when loyalty replaces treason; purity replaces turbidity; union replaces separation; ascent replaces descent; existence replaces nonexistence; or charity and generosity replace deprivation. The same holds for any entity in the external realm that existentially climbs in ascending pathways and degrees. 47.1

God's assistance in rank is the opposite of the above. For assisting aridity means the negation of fruitfulness, which is a nonexistential rank; and assisting emaciation means the nonexistence of plumpness; and assisting diminishment means the nonexistence of growth; and so on for the rest. This assistance in rank stems from Allāh, and both stem from the divine pronoun He. This, moreover, is the presence of fixity, which, according to the terminology of a certain group, is more inclusive than existence and nonexistence. Furthermore, the Assister presides over the properties of these levels at both stages, and it subsumes their stations in both cases. Thus it gives a thing as well as its opposite, and it turns contrary objects into its allies and its troops. 47.2

This name's most beautiful mode of descent is when it assists the wayfarer. For when the one who attempts to advance is obstructed by an impediment that renders him incapable of moving forward, he cries out for God to assist him in overcoming the tyranny of the realm of other-than-God and the opposition of his caprice. He loses sight of the horizon toward which he is advancing and falls down. But when the property of the Assister comes to his aid, he overcomes his separation and finds union with his Lord. The remembrance of his Beloved blinds him to his good deeds and sins. Flashes of lightning assist 47.3

ربّه وعمي بذكر محبوبه عن رؤية حسنته وذنبه ولاحت له بوارق تنصره على السوى إن كان هو مغالبه أو على ما عداه من أحكامه التي تطالبه فيكون اجتماعه نصراً حين ﴿تَنفَعَهُ ٱلذِّكۡرَىٰٓ﴾ وإن لم يرد عليه ما يجمعه ولا يتّفق له حضيض السقوط ما يرفعه فإن أقام في الصراخ فذلك نصر له وإن انقطع باليأس فاستعداده بالحرمان قتله فالصراخ نصر والرجاء إذا ركب مركبه حمله بحر.

٤،٤٧ وأمّا النصر المعروف الذي هو بين الناس مألوف فهو أيضاً من الاسم الناصر جلّت قدرته ولا يلتفَت هل انتصر فيه حزب الإيمان أم حزب الكفر فإنّهم ينصَرون كما تنصَرون والناصر واحد وهو الحقّ ومن كان مع الحقّ تعالى من حيث حضرة اسمه الناصر تعالى فإنّه يرى النصر ﴿مِنۡ عِندِ ٱللَّهِ﴾ كما قال تعالى ﴿وَمَا ٱلنَّصۡرُ إِلَّا مِنۡ عِندِ ٱللَّهِ﴾.

٥،٤٧ وقد حكي عن أبي مدين رحمه الله أنّ إنساناً دخل إليه فقال إنّ الفرنج نُصروا على المسلمين فقال الحمد لله ولم يتأثّر فعجب الحاضرون من عدم تأثّر الشيخ رضي الله عنه فمدّ الشيخ إصبعيه وأشار إلى أحدهما فقال هذا الهادي وأشار إلى الآخر وقال هذا المضلّ ثمّ وضع إصبعه على موضع اجتماعهما من ظاهر الكفّ وقال قلبي هاهنا فعرف العارفون إشارته ومعناها أنّ من كان قلبه مع الله تعالى لم تختلف عليه معاني الأسماء ولولا اعتبار الشيخ حقيقة الاسم الناصر لم يتساو عنده الأمران فإذاً حقيقة الاسم الناصر شاملة وحقيقته في الناقصات ناقصة وفي الكاملات كاملة والنقص والكمال في طيّ الأكمليّات.

٦،٤٧ واعلم أنّ العابد المحجوب إذا آنس من همّته فتوراً وعن إطالة أوراده قصوراً دافع الفترة وطلب من الله النصرة فإن وجد عقيب طلبه نشاطاً وبعد انقباضه انبساطاً فهو من نصر الله مِن حضرة اسمه الهادي لكن على نسبة الملك فإنّ ما يجدونه من الخير فمن لمّة الملك وما يجدونه من الشرّ فمن لمّة الشيطان فقد أدركه الاسم الناصر.

him in overcoming the realm of other-than-God if he was struggling against it, or in overcoming the enmity of parts of his own self holding him back. His attainment of union is thus a display of divine assistance when «the remembrance benefits him».[295] But if the assistance of union does not reach him and nothing lifts him from the lowliness of his fall, and if he continues crying out to God, then that itself is an assistance given to him. But if he lets himself fall into despair, then his preparedness for divine deprivation shall be his ruin. For to cry to God is a divine assistance, and to embark upon the ship of hope is to be carried upon an ocean.

Military assistance, widely recognized, is also from the Assister, regardless 47.4
of whether it is the army of belief or unbelief that is victorious. For "the unbelievers are assisted just as you are assisted,"[296] and the Assister is One, the Real. He who is with the Real with respect to the presence of the Assister sees that all assistance comes «from God» just as God says: «assistance is from none other than God».[297]

It is said that Abū Madyan was once visited by a man who told him that "the 47.5
Franks were victorious over the Muslims," whereupon he responded, "Praise be to God!" and did not overreact. Those in Abū Madyan's company expressed surprise that the shaykh did not overreact. Thereupon he extended two of his fingers and, pointing to one, said, "This is the Guide." Then he pointed to the other and said, "This is the Misguider." He then pointed to the place where the two fingers meet on the back of his hand and said, "My heart is here."[298] The recognizers recognized his allusion. What it means is that those whose hearts are with God are not confounded by the realities of the names. And were it not for the shaykh's consideration of the reality of the Assister, the two outcomes would not be equivalent for him. Thus, the reality of the Assister is all-inclusive. Its reality among imperfect things is imperfect, and among perfect things is perfect. Imperfection and perfection, moreover, are aspects of ultimate perfection.

When the veiled worshipper feels a lack of spiritual resolve and falls short 47.6
in his long litanies,[299] he fights against his lack of spiritual resolve and asks for God's assistance. If he finds enthusiasm in the wake of his request, and expansion in the wake of his contraction, then that is God's assistance through the presence of the Guide. However, the assistance reaches him through an angel, for "whatever good he encounters is from the prompting of an angel, and whatever evil he encounters is from the prompting of Satan,"[300] for Satan too is overtaken by the Assister.

٧،٤٧ وأمّا من كان من طور التصوّف من العبّاد وقد حاول تبديل خلق دنيّ بخلق سنيّ واستعصت عليه نفسه أو دعا إلى إظهار المحاسن جسمه فغلبت عليه نفسه فلجأ إلى الله نصره في شدّة ما دعاه ودعا الله لمّا عصاه حاله حين دعاه فإن وجد النفس قد أصبحت بعد الشماس وأعطته فيها الرجاء بعد اليأس فهو من الاسم الناصر تعالى في حضرة برزخ بين الملك والاسم الهادي لكن في حقيقة الاسم الهادي.

٨،٤٧ وأمّا من كان في طور العرفان ولجأ إلى الله تعالى في طلب النصرة على الفقد طالباً للوجدان فإن صرفت عنه ظلم تراكم الأغيار وحدانية هي الأنوار فأشرق أفقه وأقلع غسقه فهو نصر من الاسم الناصر وذلك أيضاً من حضرة الاسم الهادي إلّا أنّ الاسم الهادي والحالة هذه يتولّاه تولّياً ذاتياً لأنّ الاسم في هذه الحضرة هو بالمسمّى فالنصر من هذه الحضرة أشرف من غيره وأسمى.

اسمه المحيي دام مدد جوده

١،٤٨ موضعه من آل عمران قوله تعالى ﴿وَٱللَّهُ يُحۡيِۦ وَيُمِيتُ﴾ وهو ممّا اتّفق عليه الأئمّة الثلاثة والإحياء منه تعالى لا تتناهى مراتبه فأوّل إحيائه إعطاؤه الوجود تعينّه فإنّ بساطة الوجود سابقة في الرتبة على تعينّه فأوّل حياة حصلت تعيّن المتعيّن الذي يظنّ أنّه أوّل متعيّن ومن ظنّ أنّ للمتعيّنات أوّلاً فقد حصر ما لا ينحصر لكنّ كلّ متعيّن فله الأوّل أمّا أنّ التعيّن له أوّل فهذا يقتضي أن يكون للوجود المحض بداية ولست أقول لكلّ موجود فإنّ لكلّ موجود بداية وليس للوجود بداية وذلك

When a worshipper engaged in inner purification tries to change a base character trait into an exalted one, his soul may become defiant or he may be tempted to display his physical beauty, and then he is overcome by his lower self and seeks refuge in God. God thus assists him through his intense supplication, and he calls out to God after being defied by his spiritual state. If he then finds that his soul becomes radiant after its obstinacy, and it gives him hope after his despair, then that is from the Assister in a liminal presence between the angel and the Guide, but through the reality of the Guide. 47.7

For the one at the stage of direct recognition seeking refuge in God's assistance in order to recover lost ecstasy, if the accumulated darkness of things other-than-God are dispelled by the oneness of the lights, whereby his horizon brightens and his darkness is dispelled, then that is an assistance through the Assister. It is, moreover, through the presence of the Guide, except that the Guide and this spiritual state preside over him directly, because the name in this presence is within the named. The assistance in this level is therefore loftier than the others. 47.8

Al-Muḥyī: The Life-Giver

It occurs in the Surah of the House of ʿImrān in the verse: «God gives life and causes death».[301] The three scholars agree it is a divine name. His gift of life occurs at infinite levels. He first gives life by giving distinct determination to existence; for the uncompounded simplicity of existence precedes the level of its distinct determination. Therefore, life is first actualized when the so-called first determined entity is determined. However, those who presume that determined entities have a "first" have limited that which cannot be limited. For although every determined entity does have a first, if determination as such were to have a first, then it would imply that absolute existence had a beginning. I am not saying that existents do not have a beginning, for each existent does have a beginning. Existence as such, however, does not have a beginning, because existence is necessity according to the established 48.1

لأنّ الوجود هو الواجب على اصطلاح الذوق والموجود هو الممكن فيه منه به على ما يقتضيه الذوق أيضاً.

٢،٤٨ فأوّل حياة هي تعيّن المتعيّن في أزليّة السبق وسبق الأزليّة ثمّ تنفصل الحياة بتنوّع غير متناهي الحقائق فضلاً عن العدد فكلّ تمايز يحصل في العين الواحدة ففيه حياة التعيّن وحياة المتعيّن وحياة الاشتراك مع غيره في العين الواحدة وحياة ما به الامتياز عن غيره فيها فإن تسلسل تعيّن المتعيّنات في الأسباب والمسبّبات كانت هناك حياة أخرى وهي حياة الارتباط بين تلك الذوات على ما نسب تسلسلها في التقدّم والتأخّر وتوسّط ولست أعني بالتسلسل توقّف شيء على شيء لا إلى نهاية بل النهاية مفروضة.

٣،٤٨ والاسم المحيي تعالى متولّي ذلك كلّه ثمّ بعد ذلك تُعتبر حياة ما بعد التعيّن فحياة نفس الحياة هي من الحقائق التي بعد التعيّن ومعنى الحياة كون العين الواحدة وجوداً لا حظّ للعدم فيه ثمّ حضرة حياة العلم وهو كون المتعيّن يقبل أن تتشكّل فيه صور ما تشكّلاً في قوّة تلك العين الواحدة وذلك هو حياة العلم فإنّ العلم هو تعيّن الصور في حضرة انفعال النفس عنها ولمّا كانت الحياة تنشأ كما ينشأ ما يحيي بها كانت النفس إذا حييت في ذاتها حييت حياة النفس الخاصّة بها لأنّ الحياة المختصّة بالنفس المذكورة لم تكن سابقة للنفس بل نشأت معها وذلك لأنّ التهيّؤ الذي هو التسوية يلزم منه النفخ ويلحقه لحوقاً واجباً من ذات المتهيّئ لا من غيره فكما أنّ النفخ يوجِد حياة المتهيّئ والمتهيّئ وجد حياته وحياة حياته بتهيّئه فالاسم المحيي يتولى إحياء الشيء وإحياء حياته في كلّ مرتبة مرتبة ثمّ إنّ ميل النفس إلى أن تتعيّن فيها مادّة تقبل شكل الجسم من ذاتها هو الإرادة ولها حياة تخصّها وحياة حياة أيضاً كما ذكرنا والاسم المحيي معطي ذلك.

٤،٤٨ والكلام في مرتبة الإرادة كالكلام الذي كان في مرتبة العلم سواء ثمّ يكون الكلام في مرتبة القدرة كذلك أيضاً سواء فإنّ القدرة التي أظهرت المقدور للحسّ هي شكل

terminology of those who know through tasting, whereas the existent is possible within, from, and through existence according to direct tasting.

Thus, the determination of the determined entity in the beginninglessness of pre-eternity and in the pre-eternity of beginninglessness is the first life. Life then differentiates into an infinite variety of types. Each distinction that occurs within a single entity comprises the life of the determination, as well as the life of the determined entity, the life of its association with other entities within a single entity, and the life of its distinction from other entities. Moreover, it is another life if a successive regression of determined entities occurs within the realm of secondary causes and effects. This is the life of the interconnection prior to, after, and in between the regressing essences of the entities. By regression I do not mean the infinite dependence of one thing upon another, for an end is assumed for the regression. 48.2

The Life-Giver presides over all of this. After that, consider the life that follows the entity's determination. For the life of the Soul is one of the realities that follow the entity's determination. Life, moreover, means that an entity exists in a state wherein nonexistence has no share. Then follows the presence of the life of Knowledge, which means that the determined entity is receptive to taking on forms in accordance with the potential of that single entity. That is the life of Knowledge, because Knowledge is the determination of forms within the Soul's reception of activity. Given that Life is configured just as that which it enlivens is configured, when the essence of the Soul is enlivened, the life of the Soul specific to it is also enlivened. For the life specific to this Soul does not precede the Soul; rather, it is configured along with it. This is because the predisposition, which is its proportioning, entails the inblowing of the spirit, and the latter necessarily accompanies the predisposed essence. Thus, just as the inblowing of the spirit gives existence to the life of the predisposed essence, and the predisposed essence finds its life, and the life of its life is through its predisposition, the Life-Giver presides over life-giving to the thing, and over giving life to its life at every single level. Moreover, the Soul's inclining toward the determination of a material substratum within it that is essentially receptive to the shape of the body is Will, which also has a life that is specific to it, and a life of its life as well, as we said, and the Life-Giver bestows that too. 48.3

Furthermore, Speech at the level of Will is no different from Speech at the level of Knowledge. Following that, Speech at the level of Power is no different from Speech at the level of Will, for the Power that makes its objects of power manifest in the sensory domain is the shape of the material issuing from the 48.4

المادّة الصادرة عن النفس وذلك هو من النفس فإنّ الحقيقة الإيجاديّة ليست تأتي من غير الموجود بها وذلك لإيجاد العين في نفسها.

٥،٤٨ وأمّا ما بعد الجسم الكلّي فإنّ تصرّف الاسم المحيي فيه ظاهر للعيان أو مثل ظاهر للعيان فإنّ تصرّف الطبيعة فيما تحتها قد تكلّم فيه أهله وإنّما نتكلّم نحن في كون المتعيّن منها تكون له حياة تخصّه فإنّ الأجسام لها حياة تخصّها وبتلك الحياة بقاؤها والأركان كذلك والمولّدات أشدّ ظهوراً في ذلك وفي الحيوان والإنسان فهو باتّفاق وأمّا النبات وما قبله فهو خفيّ عند أهل الحجاب وأمّا أهل الكشف فيرون ذلك عياناً جليّاً فالاسم المحيي متصرّف فيما ذكرناه تصرّفاً ظاهراً.

٦،٤٨ وهذا الكلام الذي ذكرناه محصور فيما يخصّ كرة دنيانا بما أحاط بها من الأفلاك وأمّا الواقع في نفس الأمر فليس الاسم المحيي مختصّاً بإحياء ما ذكرناه بل هو يتصرّف في مقتضيات الوجود وهي لا تتناهى وأمّا الموجود المخصوص فقد ذكرنا أحكامه فإذاً الاسم المحيي غير متناهي التصرّف إذا ذكرنا أحكام الوجود المطلق.

٧،٤٨ واعلم أنّ النفخ الذي يساوق التسوية هو تصرّف الاسم المحيي وهو الإحياء نفسه فالتهيّؤ والإحياء متلازمان أزلاً وأبداً وتفاصيل جزئيّات ذلك لا تحتاج إلى ذكر أنموذج منها في بعض محالّها فإحياء الأرض بعد موتها إحياء واهتزازها بنباتها إحياء ونموّها حتّى تبلغ إلى غاياتها إحياء وظهور زهرها وثمرتها إحياء واغتذاء الحيوان بما يأكله منها إحياء واغتذاء الحيوان بالحيوان إحياء واغتذاء الإنسان بالحيوان والنبات إحياء ونموّ الحيوان والإنسان والتولّد إحياء وحركاتها في مراتبها بما هو من شأنها إحياء وتغذّي النفوس بتعلّم علوم الحسّ إحياء وتدرّجها ممّا علمت منه إلى ما لم تعلم إحياء بشرط أن تكون ممّا تقتضيه الفطرة.

٨،٤٨ وأمّا الأوهام الكاذبة فهو إحياء للأوهام وإماتة للحقائق ففيها نصيب للاسم المميت وأمّا الترقّي في السلوك إلى الله تعالى على المدرجة الصحيحة فهو إحياء وتوصّل

Soul. That, moreover, comes from the Soul, for the existentiating reality does not come about without the thing that it existentiates, for the entity is existentiated within itself.

The control the Life-Giver exercises over what comes after the Universal Body[302] is manifest—or virtually manifest—to the eye. Nature's control over its domain has been discussed by the experts in that subject. What we speak of, however, is how what is determined by nature has a life specific to it. For bodies have a life specific to them, and their subsistence is through that life. The same is true for the elements. The three kingdoms, moreover, are more intensely manifest in this regard. In animals and humans, it is by consensus. The life of plants and what is below them is hidden from veiled intellects. Those who know through unveiling, for their part, witness their life clearly with the eye, for in a manifest manner the Life-Giver exercises control in everything we have said. 48.5

Everything we have said is specifically restricted to the sphere of our lower world and the surrounding spheres. As for what actually occurs, the Life-Giver is not limited to giving life just to what we have mentioned. Rather, it exercises control over the dictates of existence, which are infinite. We have mentioned the properties of the specific existent. Thus, the activity of the Life-Giver is infinite when we speak of the properties of unconditioned existence. 48.6

Moreover, the inblowing of the spirit,[303] which coextends with the proportioning of the body, is the activity of the Life-Giver, and is identical with the giving of life. For predisposing to and giving life are inseparable for all eternity. Specific details of such loci by way of illustrative examples are hardly necessary. For reviving the earth after its death is a giving of life; and its stirring forth with plants is a giving of life; and their growth until they reach their fullest extent is a giving of life; and the appearance of flowers and fruits is a giving of life; and their eating by animals is a giving of life; and the eating of some animals by other animals is a giving of life; and the nourishment of humans from animals and plants is a giving of life; and the growth and procreation of animals and humans is a giving of life; and their movements through their levels according to what pertains to their status is a giving of life; and the nourishment of souls by learning physical sciences is a giving of life; and their gradual ascent from what they know to what they did not know is a giving of life, on the condition that the knowledge to which they ascend is innate to the human disposition. 48.7

False illusions, for their part, are an enlivening of illusion and a death of realities, and thus the latter have a share in the Death-Giver. As for advancing 48.8

السالكين بالعلم النافع والعمل الصالح إحياء وتدرّج السالك بالعمل إلى ثمرته ثمّ ذوقه ثمّ إلى شهود وجوده ثمّ الترقي بالاعتدال إحياء تمام والله أعـلم.

اسمه المميت عمّ حكمه

١،٤٩ محلّه من آل عمران قوله تعالى ﴿وَٱللَّهُ يُحۡيِۦ وَيُمِيتُۗ﴾ وهومما اتّفق عليه الأئمّة الثلاثة وهذا الاسم يساوق الاسم المحيي ويأخذ ما ترك فكلّ مرتبة ذكر فيها الاسم المحيي اسم فله في حلّ ما أبرمه حكم ونسبة عدميّة بخلاف الاسم المحيي ومرجعه إلى الاسم الله تعالى لأنّه مرتبيّ لا وجوديّ وذلك لأنّ التهيّؤ للبقاء من الحيّ ما دام قابلاً للمدد الوجوديّ الإلهيّ فالاسم المحيي متصرّف فإذا وقف تهيّؤ القبول المذكور وقف حكم التسوية فبطل النفخ واتّصل به حكم الاسم المميت.

٢،٤٩ فهو أعني الاسم المميت يتبع النقصان والاضمحلال والفساد وتحلّل الكيفيّات والكمّيّات والإضافيّات وانقضاء الأزمان والحركات وتبدّل الحالات كالفقر بعد الغنى والعدم بعد الملكة أو الحال والانتقال من صورة وجوديّة إلى عدمها لا إلى صورة أخرى فإنّ الصورة الأخرى نصيب الاسم المحيي فإنّ الاستحالات التي تلحق الكيفيّات قد يكون فساد ما فسد منها سبباً لوجود شيء آخر فنفس فسادها للاسم المميت ونفس وجود ما كان الفساد المذكور سببه هو للاسم المحيي.

in one's journey to God on the right path of ascent, that is a giving of life. The wayfarers' attainment through beneficial knowledge and righteous deeds is also a giving of life; and the wayfarer's gradual climb from spiritual practice to its fruit, then to tasting, then to witnessing his existence, then ascending to a state of equilibrium, is a complete giving of life; and God knows best.

Al-Mumīt: The Death-Giver

It occurs in the House of 'Imrān in the verse: «God gives life and causes death».[304] It is one of the names the three eminent scholars agree is a divine name. The Death-Giver is coextensive with the Life-Giver; it claims whatever the latter leaves behind. At every level in which the Life-Giver is mentioned, the Death-Giver leaves its opposing property and nonexistential ascription by untying what was tied by the Life-Giver. The Death-Giver, moreover, returns to Allāh, for it is a name of rank, not of existence. After all, the predisposition of subsistence pertains to the Living so long as it continues to be receptive to the replenishment of divine existence. The Life-Giver thus exercises control, and when it ceases to be predisposed to existential sustenance, then the property of proportioning ceases too, and the inblowing is nullified, whereupon it joins to the property of the Death-Giver. 49.1

The Death-Giver pertains to deficiency, dwindling, corruption, and the decomposition of modalities, quantities, and correlations. It pertains to the termination of times and motions, and to the alteration of states such as poverty after wealth or lack after possession, and to the transition from an existential form to a nonexistential one (but not to an alternative form). For transitioning into an alternative form would belong to the share of the Life-Giver. After all, when a transformation is associated with a modality, then the corruption it undergoes may cause the existence of another thing. In that case, its corruption pertains to the Death-Giver, whereas the existence that was caused by that corruption pertains to the Life-Giver. 49.2

٣،٤٩ فانتشاء السحاب للاسم المحيي وتحلّله للاسم المميت ونزول القطر للاسم المحيي وذهاب صورة مائيّته بأن تشربه الأرض فتذهب كيفيّته هو للاسم المميت واغتذاء النبات به هو للاسم المحيي وتحويل البذرة نباتاً فالتحوّل نفسه للاسم المميت ونموّ النبات للاسم المحيي والآفات التي تعرض للنبات للاسم المميت وانتقال النبات إلى أن يكون غذاءً للحيوان هو للاسم المحيي والجهل من الجهّال هو للاسم المميت وانصرام الدنيا وما فيها هو للاسم المميت وقيام الآخرة وما فيها هو للاسم المحيي وعالم البقاء وعالم الجنّة للاسم المحيي وإدراك المنافر في جهنّم وغيرها من عدميّاته للاسم المميت ووجوديّاته للاسم المحيي فتلهّب النار في ذاتها هو للاسم المحيي إذ تلهّبها حياتها وتفريق أجزاء ما لابسها من المحترقات هو للاسم المميت ونعيم الآخرة كلّه هو للاسم المحيي وبعض عذاب الآخرة فقط هو للاسم المميت.

٤،٤٩ وقبول النفس لتصوّر المتصوّرات الذهنيّة والتصديقات الذهنيّة والتنبّهات الذهنيّة هو للاسم المحيي ونسيان ذلك أو عدم قبول النفس لذلك هو للاسم المميت والمنع والبخل هو للاسم المميت والعطاء والجود هما للاسم المحيي وعالم الظهور للاسم المحيي وعالم البطون أيضاً إذا قصدته الموجودات فهو للاسم المحيي وأمّا إذا لم تقصده فهو للاسم المميت.

٥،٤٩ وحركة الإطلاق الذاتيّة هي لحركة المحيي ومقابلها من السكون هو للاسم المحيي وعدمها للاسم المميت وتوجّهات الصفات والأسماء والأفعال هي للاسم المحيي وعدمها للاسم المميت وبدايات الأشياء وتوسّطها للاسم المحيي ونهايات ذلك للاسم المميت والكلام والأقوال للاسم المحيي والسكوت وعدم الفهم للاسم المميت والإصغاء للقول وفهم معانيه للاسم المحيي وكلال الذهن وملاله وتبلّده وسهوه للاسم المميت.

Thus, the formation of clouds pertains to the Life-Giver, and their dissipation pertains to the Death-Giver. Precipitation pertains to the Life-Giver, and the disappearance of the form of water when it is absorbed by the earth and loses its modality pertains to the Death-Giver. The nurturing of plants by underground water pertains to the Life-Giver. The process of the transformation of seed into plant pertains to the Death-Giver, whereas the growth of the plant pertains to the Life-Giver. The blights that befall plants are from the Death-Giver, and the process by which plants turn into nourishment for animals pertains to the Life-Giver. The ignorance of ignorant persons pertains to the Death-Giver. The passing of this world and everything upon it pertains to the Death-Giver. The coming of the next world pertains to the Life-Giver, and the realm of subsistence and the realm of the Garden pertain to the Life-Giver. The perception of what is disagreeable in the Fire and other nonexistential things pertains to the Death-Giver, while existential things are from the Life-Giver. Thus, the blazing of the Fire within itself pertains to the Life-Giver, for its blazing is its life, whereas the disintegration of its flammable parts pertains to the Death-Giver. Bliss in the next world pertains entirely to the Life-Giver, and only part of the torment of the next world pertains to the Death-Giver. 49.3

The soul's receptivity to conceptualizing mental concepts, affirmations, or remarks pertains to the Life-Giver, whereas forgetting them, or the soul's unreceptivity for them, pertains to the Death-Giver. Stinginess and greed are from the Death-Giver, whereas gift-giving and generosity are from the Life-Giver. The realm of manifestation pertains to the Life-Giver, and the realm of nonmanifestation also pertains to the Life-Giver, but with respect to those existents that are made for it. The existents that are not made for manifestation pertain to the Death-Giver. 49.4

Moreover, the Essence's unrestricted motion pertains to the motion of the Life-Giver; and its counterpart, rest, also pertains to the Life-Giver, while its absence pertains to the Death-Giver. The orientations of the qualities, names, and acts pertain to the Life-Giver, while their nonexistence pertains to the Death-Giver. The beginning and intermediary stages of things pertain to the Life-Giver, and their end stages pertain to the Death-Giver. Discourse and speech pertain to the Life-Giver; silence and non-apprehension pertain to the Life-Giver. Listening to someone's words and understanding their meanings pertains to the Life-Giver; mental fatigue, weariness, stupidity, and negligence pertain to the Death-Giver. 49.5

وانفعال الأجسام الإنسانيّة لفعل الاختلاط[1] للاسم المميت وفعل الاختلاط[2] ٦،٤٩
في قابليّاتها للاسم المحيي وتقهقر الأخلاط لبنية[3] قوى طبيعة الجسم الإنسانيّ ودفعها للأخلاط للاسم المحيي ودبيب البرء في السقم للاسم المحيي ودبيب السقم في الصحّة للاسم المميت وعالم الجمال للاسم المحيي وعالم الجلال أكثره للاسم المميت والدم والصفراء للاسم المحيي والبلغم والسوداء للاسم المميت إلّا إذا كان بالبلغم وبالسوداء اعتدال ما خاصّ بالنسبة إلى مزاج خاصّ فهو وهما للاسم المحيي والشجاعة للاسم المحيي والجبن للاسم المميت والهمّة والرأي واليقظة للاسم المحيي والفشل والكسل والحياء والتراخي للاسم المميت والهرب للاسم المميت والطلب للاسم المحيي والهمّ والغمّ والحزن للاسم المميت والسرور والطرب والنشوة للاسم المحيي والفصاحة والبيان للاسم المحيي والعيّ واللكنة للاسم المميت وحركات الضلال موت متتابع وسكونها حياة وهميّة فالأوّل للاسم المحيي والثاني للاسم المميت والبرازخ التي بين الأشعّة والضلال للاسم المميت ونفس الأشعّة ونفس الضلال للاسم المحيي وتحلّل الأعراض من جواهرها كلّه للاسم المميت وخلقها كلّه للاسم المحيي.

واعلم أنّ العدم المطلق ليس له حقيقة فهو ما كان قطّ وما سيكون أبدًا فللاسم ٧،٤٩
المميت به تعلّق ما وهميّ لا حقيقيّ وأمّا الأعدام الإضافيّة فهي في الأذهان للاسم المحيي وفي الأعيان للاسم المميت وكلّ ما قد كان ومضى فهو للاسم المميت وكلّ ما سيأتي فهو للاسم المحيي والممكنات كلّها المتساوية الطرفين جانب الوجود منها للاسم المحيي وجانب العدم منها للاسم المميت وحضرة الاسم الله تعالى ممّا تختصّ مراتبه دون ثبوتها الذهنيّة هو للاسم المميت وحضرة الاسم الرحمٰن لما يختصّ مرتباته الوجوديّة هو للاسم المحيي والله أعلم.

---

[1] و: الأخلاط. [2] و: الأخلاط. [3] آ، و: لتنبه.

The reaction of human bodies to the commingling of the humors pertains to the Life-Giver, and the act of commingling within the parts that are receptive to it also pertains to it. The backward movement of the humors into the structures of the natural faculties of the human body and how these faculties repel the humors pertain to the Life-Giver. The penetration of a cure into an illness pertains to this name, but the penetration of illness into health pertains to the Death-Giver. The realm of beauty pertains to the Life-Giver. The realm of majesty mostly pertains to the Death-Giver. Blood and yellow bile pertain to the Life-Giver. Phlegm and black bile pertain to the Death-Giver, except when phlegm and black bile establish an equilibrium specific to a particular constitution, when the equilibrium as well as the phlegm and black bile are from the Life-Giver. Courage pertains to the Life-Giver, and cowardice pertains to the Death-Giver. Saintly aspirations, dreams, and states of wakefulness pertain to the Life-Giver. Weakness, indolence, bashfulness, and laxity pertain to the Death-Giver. Flight pertains to the Death-Giver, and seeking pertains to the Life-Giver. Concern, sorrow, and sadness pertain to the Death-Giver. Joy, delight, and rapture pertain to the Life-Giver. Eloquence and clear speech pertain to the Life-Giver. Ineloquence and stammering pertain to the Death-Giver. The movements of the misguided are successive deaths, and their rest is an illusory life. The latter therefore pertains to the Life-Giver, and the former pertains to the Death-Giver.[305] The thresholds between radiance and darkness pertain to the Death-Giver, while the rays and the darkness themselves pertain to the Life-Giver. The dissolution of accidental qualities from their substances always pertains to the Death-Giver; and their creation pertains entirely to the Life-Giver. 49.6

Absolute nonexistence has no reality, for it never was and never will be. The Death-Giver thus has a type of illusory association with it, not a real one. Relative nonexistents pertain to the Life-Giver within the mind, and to the Death-Giver within the entities themselves. Moreover, everything that was and has passed pertains to the Death-Giver, and everything that will come to be pertains to the Life-Giver. Possibles that are equal at both ends pertain to the Life-Giver in terms of existence, and to the Death-Giver in terms of nonexistence. That which is specific to the levels of Allāh's presence, not its mental immutability, pertains to the Death-Giver. That which is specific to the existential levels of the All-Merciful pertains to the Life-Giver. And God knows best. 49.7

اسمه الوكيل تبارك وتعالى

١،٥٠ هو آخر اسم خرّجه الأئمّة الثلاثة من سورة آل عمران فهو كمال الاثني عشر اسمًا فيها وموضعه منها في قوله تعالى ﴿قَالُواْ حَسۡبُنَا ٱللَّهُ وَنِعۡمَ ٱلۡوَكِيلُ﴾.

٢،٥٠ ومن اتّخذ الحقّ تعالى وكيلًا في مقام الأمر وهو قوله تعالى ﴿فَٱتَّخِذۡهُ وَكِيلًا﴾ فهم أهل التوكّل على الله عزّ وجلّ من العبّاد ولولا الإذن في اتّخاذ الحقّ تعالى وكيلًا لكان الأدب تركه.

٣،٥٠ وأمّا من اتّخذه تعالى وكيلًا حسن ظنّ به أنّه يجود عليه تعالى بما لو كان له وكيل غيره قادر لم يتجاوزه فهذا هو من مقام التصوّف وهو فوق مقام العابدين فإنّ حسن الظنّ خلق جميل وهو من أوصاف الصوفيّة ولو لم يرد الإذن به لم يكن اعتماده سوء أدب كما لو فُرض ذلك في مقام العبّاد.

٤،٥٠ وأمّا ما فوق التصوّف من مقام المحبّة فالمحبّ إذا اتّخذه وكيلًا فقد باين أحوال المحبّين وهو في سوء أدب أشدّ من أحوال أهل مقام العبادة إن لو لم يؤذن لهم في اتّخاذه وكيلًا وذلك لأنّ المحبّ لا تبقى فيه فضلة عن محبوبه يتوجّه بها إلى ما يوكّله فيه فلا تتوجّه له نسبة إلى الاسم الوكيل من مقام من صحّت محبّته.

٥،٥٠ وأمّا فوق مقام المحبّة وهو مقام العرفان فالعارف في هذا المقام يشهد الحقّ تعالى شهودًا بحسب مقامه فيراه يقوم عنه بما هو يقوم به الوكيل فيكل الأمر إليه تعالى تكلانًا يراه ضروريًا لا مندوحة عنه فالاسم الوكيل في هذا المقام أشدّ ظهورًا وأخفى حقيقة أمّا شدّة ظهوره فلأنّ العارف يرى الحقّ تعالى قائمًا عنه مقام الوكيل رؤية أظهر من الحسّ وأمّا أنّها أخفى حقيقة فلأنّ الوكالة إنّما تكون بموكِّل والموكَّل هنا قد

Al-Wakīl: The Trustee

This is the last of twelve names from the Surah of the House of ʿImrān cited by the three scholars. It occurs in this verse: «They say: "God is sufficient for us, and an excellent Trustee is He"».[306] 50.1

Those who take the Real as their trustee in response to the command of the verse «so take Him as your Trustee»[307] are those worshippers who trust in God. Were it not for the permission to take the Real as one's Trustee, the proper courtesy would be to refrain from doing so. 50.2

Then there is the one who takes Him as his Trustee out of a belief rooted in the good opinion that He is munificent toward him so that this individual would look no further were there an able trustee other than God. This is the station of Sufism, which is above the station of the worshippers. For it is a beautiful character trait to hold a good opinion, and it is one of the qualities of the Sufis. Moreover, even if permission were not given to take God as a Trustee, the Sufi's reliance upon God would not count as a lack of courtesy as this form of trusteeship is only appropriate for worshippers. 50.3

As for what lies beyond Sufism—namely, the station of love—if the lover takes Him as his Trustee he thereby forsakes the state of lover, and exhibits discourtesy more grave than it would be for those in the station of worship, had they not been permitted to take Him as their Trustee. The lover has no remnant left to entrust to His Beloved. As such, for those whose love is genuine in this station there is no relation to the Trustee. 50.4

As for recognition, which lies above the station of love—the recognizer in this station witnesses the Real in respect to where he stands. He sees God attending on his behalf in the same way as the Trustee does. Thus he entrusts his affairs to Him, putting Him in charge out of unavoidable necessity. The Trustee in this station is therefore more intensely manifest, just as its reality is more hidden. It is intensely manifest because the recognizer sees, with more clarity than in the sensory realm, that the Real attends to him in the station of the Trustee. It is hidden in its reality because entrusting can only come from someone who entrusts, and in this case the entruster has passed away from some of the traces of his lower human nature, and thus, to the extent that his 50.5

في بعض رسمه فذهب من إنائه الموكّل بمقدار ما انمحى من رسمه فبقي التوكّل ناقصاً يشبه المجاز.

٦،٥٠ فإذا فني رسم العارف كلّه لم يبق هناك وكالة فينتقل حكم الوكيل إلى حكم الموكّل فيصير الفرع أصلاً كما لم يزل ويصير الأصل فرعاً يرجع إلى الصفة وإذا كان الوكالة ساقطة في حقّ العارف فلأنْ تكون ساقطة في حقّ الواقف من باب الأولى فكيف من فوق الواقف.

٧،٥٠ واعلم أنّ الأسماء كلّها نافعة لأهل الذكر من المتوجّهين إلى الحقّ سبحانه لكنّ لكلّ اسم خاصّيّة في النفع أو خواصّ والخواصّ المذكورة ينتفع بها من يحتاج إليها وبعض خواصّها ما لا يليق بكلّ مقام بل كلّ من له مقام في السلوك وطلب منها الاسم الذي من خواصّه أن ينتفع به ذلك السالك حتّى لو تعاطى ذكر اسم يكون خاصّيّته مضادّة للاسم النافع له لا نضرّ بذكره فيما يرومه لا مطلقاً وفي هذا المعنى يحتاج إلى الشيخ المربّي ليعطيه من الأذكار ما يناسب استعداده.

٨،٥٠ وكنت عند كتابة هذا الاسم وما قبله معرضاً عن ذكر خواصّ الأسماء في حقّ السالكين إلى الله تعالى فنبّهني لذكر ذلك أخي في الله تعالى وفي الخرقة الشريفة خادم شيخنا الشيخ الوارث قطب الحقيقة صدر الدين محمّد بن إسحاق رضي الله عنه وهو السيّد العارف ضياء الدين محمّد بن محمود متّع الله بطول حياته فشعرت من هذا الاسم أن أذكر الخواصّ وألحق فيما سلف من الأسماء حواشي في معاني الخواصّ أيضاً لنكون قد ذكرنا خواصّ الأسماء كلّها في معنى السالكين لا غير وإلّا فلها خواصّ أخرى لم نتعرّض لذكرها.

٩،٥٠ فنقول إنّ الاسم الوكيل تقدّس ذكره إنّما ينتفع به من السالكين من غلب عليه تعاطي الأسباب وأراد شيخه أن ينقله عنها إلى التجريد لعلمه بمنفعة ذلك عنده فهو ينقله إلى ذكر الاسم الوكيل من غير أن يعلم مقصوده في ذلك فإنّ السالك إذا داوم

traces are obliterated, entrusting has disappeared from his vessel. The trust remains deficient, appearing to be, as it were, metaphorical.

No entrusting remains when the trace of the recognizer passes away entirely. Thereupon, the property of the Trustee passes onto the property of the entruster. The branch then becomes the root, as it always was, and the root becomes the branch that stems from the divine attribute. Moreover, if entrusting is absent in the case of the recognizer, it is even less applicable in the case of the halter who has completed the journey to God, which is to say nothing of the one above the halter.[308] 50.6

Moreover, all the names are beneficial for those who invoke and turn their attentiveness toward the Real. However, each name has one or more beneficial effects. These effects are beneficial for those who are in need of them, but certain effects are not appropriate for every station. In fact, for whoever has a station in wayfaring and seeks to benefit from a name whose properties are beneficial to him, if he takes up the invocation of a name whose specific benefit is contrary to the name that benefits him, then he would be harmed by his invocation in that specific sense, but not in a general manner. But in this situation he would be in need of a master to give him the invocations appropriate to his level of preparedness. 50.7

When writing on this and the previous names, I refrained from mentioning the specific characteristics of the names for the wayfarers to God. Then I was approached by my spiritual brother, the servant of our master the inheritor shaykh and axial saint Ṣadr al-Dīn Muḥammad ibn Isḥāq (God be pleased with him)—namely, the esteemed recognizer Ḍiyāʾ al-Dīn Muḥammad ibn Maḥmūd (God give us the joy of prolonging his life). So I decided from the point of this name onward to mention these specific characteristics, and to add a gloss about the meanings of the specific characteristics of the other names as well, so that we will have mentioned the specific characteristics of all the names in the case of the wayfarers alone. For the names do have specific characteristics that we will not mention. 50.8

Thus we say: The Trustee, may its invocation be hallowed, is especially beneficial to those wayfarers who are given to the pursuit of worldly ends and whose shaykh wants them to transition from the world of means[309] to full withdrawal from the world, knowing that it will be beneficial. Thus he ensures he transitions to invoking the Trustee, even though the wayfarer does not know his shaykh's aim. For when the wayfarer persists in invoking this name, he himself 50.9

ذكر هذا الاسم طلب الانتقال إلى التجريد من نفسه وعزفت نفسه عن الأسباب فتركها من قلبه حتّى لو أمر الشيخ بتركها قبل تعاطيه ذكر هذا الاسم شقّ عليه ذلك وربّما امتنع وانقطع.

١٠،٥٠ فإن لازم هذا الذكر ترقّى به هذا الذكر إلى سقوط الوكالة إمّا بالعرفان وإمّا بالوقفة وعلامة التجريد بصحّة التوكّل على الله الوكيل سبحانه ألّا يضطرب السالك عند الفاقة ولا يختلف حاله عند المصيبة ولا يتّهم الوكيل سبحانه فيما يجد من شدّة تعرض أو واقعة تُفرض بل يرى أنّ الوكيل سبحانه عوّضه عن الفانيات خيرًا منها ووقاه بالحادثات ما هو أتعب منها حتّى يذهل عنها ما دام في مقام دون العرفان فأمّا إن أُلحق بالعارف فهو يرى الوكيل سبحانه قائمًا بالاسم المقسط تعالى في حقّه وفي إعطاء مستحقّه فيثبت بالله لا بنفسه وكان مع الله تعالى لا مع حسّه ورقّاه الحقّ تعالى به إلى مراتب قدسه حتّى يكون ولا شيء معه كما كان الحقّ تعالى في شهوده ولا شيء معه والحقّ يقول الحقّ.

asks to withdraw from the world. His soul turns away from the world of means and his heart abandons them. It would cause him hardship if the shaykh were to command him to abandon the world of means before practicing the invocation of this name, and the wayfarer might refuse and cut himself off.

Continued practice of this invocation advances him to the point where he eliminates his entrusting either through direct recognition or through reaching the station of halting. Moreover, the sign of genuine withdrawal from the world with sound trust in God, the Trustee, is that the wayfarer does not become agitated by poverty, nor does his state change because of an affliction, nor does he have doubts in the Trustee when a hardship befalls him or when an unfortunate incident imposes itself upon him. Rather, he sees that the Trustee has replaced transient things with more permanent ones, and so has shielded him from other events that would have caused him greater suffering. Thus he overlooks his afflictions as he continues to advance in stations short of the station of recognition. But if he is brought to the station of the recognizer, he sees that for him the Trustee subsists through the Just, bestowing that which is rightfully deserved. He thereby stands firm through God, not through himself, and remains with God, not with his sensory faculties. The Real then advances him through the levels of His holiness to the point that "God was, and there was nothing with Him," just as in his witnessing the Real was, and there was nothing with Him; and the Real says what is real.[310] 50.10

سورة النساء

وفيها ثمانية أسماء

ذكر ما ورد في سورة النساء من الأسماء الإلٰهيّة

اسمه الرقيب تبارك وتعالى

الآية التي هو فيها قوله تعالى ﴿إِنَّ ٱللَّهَ كَانَ عَلَيْكُمْ رَقِيبًا﴾ واتّفق على إيراده ١،٥١
الأئمّة الثلاثة وللاسم الرقيب تبارك وتعالى نسب إلى العبّاد تختلف بحسب اختلاف مراتبهم فبعضها في عالم الحجاب وبعضها في عالم الكشف فأمّا مراتب الحجاب فمثل ما يؤمن به أهل الإيمان من اطّلاع الباري تعالى على ظواهرهم وبواطنهم وأنّه تعالى ﴿يَعْلَمُ ٱلسِّرَّ وَأَخْفَى﴾ والإيمان بقوله تعالى ﴿مَا يَكُونُ مِن نَّجْوَىٰ ثَلَٰثَةٍ إِلَّا هُوَ رَابِعُهُمْ وَلَا خَمْسَةٍ إِلَّا هُوَ سَادِسُهُمْ وَلَآ أَدْنَىٰ مِن ذَٰلِكَ وَلَآ أَكْثَرَ إِلَّا هُوَ مَعَهُمْ﴾ الآية فالرقيب متولّي هذه المراتب الأسمائيّة[١] لأنّه تابع للاسم العليم والاسم العليم ﴿لَا يَعْزُبُ عَنْهُ مِثْقَالُ ذَرَّةٍ﴾ الآية.

٢،٥١ وأمّا في مرتبة الإحسان فهو أظهر لأنّ مقام الإحسان هو أن تعبد الله كأنّك تراه فإن لم تكن تراه فإنّه يراك فإن كنت كأنّك تراه فأنت الرقيب به له وإلّا فهو الرقيب بك لك وهو الرقيب تعالى من المقامين.

٣،٥١ وأمّا من مقام السكينة فمعناها أن تسكن إلى أحكام مقام الإحسان التي شرحناها

١ آ، و: الإيمانيّة.

The Surah of Women

Discussion of the eight names mentioned in the Surah of Women.

Al-Raqīb: The Watchful

The verse in which this name occurs is: «Truly God is watchful over you».[311] 51.1
The three eminent scholars agree it is a divine name. The Watchful has different relations to the worshippers according to their different levels. Some are in the realm of the veil, others in the realm of unveiling. For those in the levels of the veil, it is similar to the belief that believers have that God is cognizant of their outer and inner dimensions, and that «He knows the secret and what is more hidden».[312] It is the belief in the verse: «Three people do not secretly converse together but that He is the fourth of them; nor do five people but that He is the sixth of them; nor do fewer than these or more, but that He is with them wherever they are».[313] Because it is subordinate to the Knowing, the Watchful thus presides over these levels of the names, and «not so much as the weight of an atom escapes»[314] the Knowing.

This is all the more evident at the level of spiritual excellence because the 51.2
station of spiritual excellence is "to worship God as if you see Him, for if you do not see Him, He nonetheless sees you."[315] If you are in the state of "as if you see Him," then you are watchful of Him through Him. Otherwise, He is Watchful of you through you, for He is the Watchful from both stations.

In the station of tranquility, which means finding rest in the properties of 51.3
the station of spiritual excellence that we have previously explained, tranquility is a specific quality of the station of spiritual excellence, and the Watchful

فالسكينة خصوص وصف في مقام الإحسان وللاسم الرقيب في مراتب العبّاد أحكام تختلف بحسب اختلاف العبادات.

٤،٥١ وأمّا نسبة الصوفيّة إلى الاسم الرقيب فهو أنّ حكم الصوفيّ في تبديله الصفات الذميمة بالصفات المحمودة أن يراقب الحقّ تعالى بحيث يكون فعل ذلك إنّما هو لله تعالى مخلصاً لا لأن يقال إنّ الله تعالى فضّله على الناس بهذه الأخلاق ولا لأن يكون له عند الناس جاه بحسن الخلق فملاحظة الصوفيّ أنّ الله تعالى مطّلع عليه عند تعاطيه إصلاح أخلاقه هو نسبة للاسم الرقيب تعالى.

٥،٥١ وأمّا مقام المحبّة فظهور أحكام الاسم الرقيب فيها أقوى لأنّ المحبّ لا يغيب قلبه عن محبوبه وإذا كان محبوبه هو الحقّ تعالى علم أنّ محبوبه مراقب له في حركاته الظاهرة والباطنة وفي سكون الظاهر والباطن هذه بعض أحكام الاسم الرقيب في مراتب الحجاب.

٦،٥١ وأمّا مراتب أهل الكشف فالعارفون يرونه رقيباً عليهم من نفس مراقبتهم لأنفسهم من حيث يرونه هو الرقيب في رقبة كلّ رقيب بل لا يرون رقيباً غيره فهم لا يوافقون المحبّين على ذمّ الرقيب لأنّ الرقيب عندهم ليس إلّا الحقّ تعالى في كلّ طور وفي كلّ آن وفور ويرون مراتبهم هم لمراتب شهوده عزّ وجلّ هو أيضاً له فيكون هو الشاهد والمشهود فهو الرقيب من كونه شاهداً ثمّ إنّ العارف يراه رقيباً في كلّ منظور من إنسان وحيوان ونبات ومعدن وأصول هذه وفي قواها فهو لا يرى شيئاً إلّا ويرى الله به رقيباً إذ لا يمكنه أن يرى شيئاً إلّا ويرى الله قبله.

٧،٥١ قال النفريّ وقال لي أدنى علوم القرب أن ترى آثار نظري في كلّ شيء فيكون أغلب عليك من رؤيتك إيّاه فتجد معنى الاسم الرقيب محيطاً فيدخل في حقيقة الاسم المحيط وفي حقيقة الاسم المهيمن ويظهر ظهوراً واضحاً فيدخل في حقيقة الاسم الظاهر.

٨،٥١ وإنّما يدخل في حقيقة الاسم الباطن باعتبار أهل الإيمان بالغيب فيكون الرقيب عندهم بمقتضى العقيدة لا أنّه مشهود وهؤلاء هم العوامّ وأهل الغفلة من المؤمنين ويدخل فيهم أهل الكتاب فإنّهم يؤمنون به على مقتضى عقائدهم المخالفة للإسلام

at the levels of the worshippers has properties that differ according to the different forms of worship.

The Sufis' relationship to this name involves the transformation of their blameworthy character traits into praiseworthy ones; therefore, they are watchful of the Real in order to ensure that this transformation is done for the sake of God alone, not so that people will say that God has favored them above others with these traits, nor so that they can enjoy some kind of rank by virtue of their beautiful character. Therefore, the Sufis' relation to the Watchful pertains to their regard for God's gaze upon them as they transform their character. 51.4

The manifestation of the properties of the Watchful is even stronger in the station of love. For a beloved is never absent from the heart of its lover. Since the Real is the Beloved, the lover knows that his Beloved is watchful of both his outward and inward motions and his moments of stillness. These then are some of the properties of the Watchful at different levels of the veil. 51.5

As for the levels of those who know through unveiling, the recognizers see Him watching over their own self-surveillance inasmuch as they see Him as Watchful through every watch. In fact, they see no other watcher but Him. For they disagree with the lovers who blame the watchful. They consider the Watchful to be none other than the Real at every stage, in every instant, and at every moment. They also see their own levels as levels of His witness such that He is witnesser and witnessed. He is the Watchful by virtue of being the Witness. Moreover, the recognizer sees that through the sight of every human, animal, plant, mineral, or element, or through their other faculties, He is Watchful. No matter what the recognizer sees, he sees that God is watchful through it since he cannot see anything without seeing God before it. 51.6

Al-Niffarī says: "God said to me: 'The lowest knowledge of nearness is to see the traces of My gaze in all things so that My gaze overwhelms your recognition of that thing.'"[316] Here you can discover that the meaning of the Watchful is encompassing, and thus is included within the reality of the Encompassing, as well as the reality of the Overseer. And since the meaning of the Watchful is plainly manifest, it is also included within the reality of the Manifest. 51.7

This name is only to be included within the reality of the Nonmanifest in the view of those who believe in the unseen so that the Watchful for them is a matter of creed—it is not witnessed. These then are the commoners and the heedless believers. The People of the Book are included in this category as well, for they believe in Him according to their own articles of belief contrary 51.8

فيعترفون بأنّه رقيب عليهم وإن لم يشهدوا ذلك فيكون الاسم الرقيب عند هؤلاء داخلاً في الاسم الباطن.

وأمّا ما ذكره المُحاسِبيّ رضي الله عنه في كتاب الرعاية من تدقيقه في محاسبة النفس فالاسم الرقيب ظاهر الحكم من حيث تلك المراتب التي ذكرها وحاسب نفسه فيها فإنّ من استعمل ما ذكره ولم يكن يعلم أنّ الحقّ تعالى رقيباً عليه فما هو الذي ذكره المحاسبيّ. ٩،٥١

وكان بعض المشايخ يلقّن تلاميذه ما صورته الله معي الله ناظر إليّ إنّ الله يراني ويأمرهم بتكرار ذكر ذلك بألسنتهم وقلوبهم دائماً ومراده في ذلك أن يداوي مرض قلوبهم من داء الغفلة فينبّههم بالذكر على معنى الاسم الرقيب تبارك وتعالى فيحصل لهم الحضور مع الله تعالى بالأدب وهو حال أهل العبادة القلبيّة وأكملهم في ذلك رجال الأنفاس وهم الذين لا يجتذبون نفَساً إلّا وهم حاضروا القلوب مع الله تعالى ولا يطلقون نفَساً إلّا وهم حاضرون معه عزّ وجلّ وهو مقام صعب على أهل الحجاب جدّاً فشقّ عليهم إذ لا يبقى مع مراعاته حظّ من حظوظ العادات البشريّة إلّا وتعطّل. ١٠،٥١

وهذا الاسم إذا استعمل ذكره أهل الغفلة استيقظوا من سنتها وإن استعمله أهل اليقظة داموا فيها ووفّوا فإن استعمله أهل العبادة خلصوا من الرياء وكذلك أهل التصوّف وأمّا العارفون فلا يحتاجون إلى ذكر وليس فيه نسبة للواقفين لأنّهم قطعوا الأسماء. ١١،٥١

to Islam. They acknowledge Him as being Watchful over them even though they do not witness it, and therefore the Watchful in their case is included within the Nonmanifest.

In *Observing the Rights of God*, al-Muḥāsibī writes about taking the soul carefully into account[317] and notes that the properties of the Watchful are evident with respect to the levels he mentions and wherein we are supposed to take account of our souls. To practice this method without knowing that the Real is Watchful over us is not to practice what al-Muḥāsibī discusses. 51.9

Some shaykhs used to instruct their disciples the repeat the formula: "God is with me. God is looking at me. Verily God sees me."[318] They would order them to constantly repeat this invocation verbally and internally. Their goal was to cure their disciples' hearts of the disease of heedlessness and through the invocation to draw their attention to the meaning of the Watchful so that they would obtain presence with God through courtesy.[319] That is the state of those who worship with their hearts. The most perfect in this regard are the "people of the breaths": those who do not inhale without their hearts being present with God, and who do not exhale without being present with Him. This is an extremely difficult station for veiled intellects. It creates hardship because no trace of human habit remains in observing it. 51.10

When the invocation of this name is practiced by heedless people, they awaken from their stupor. When awakened people practice it, they abide therein and fulfill their responsibilities.[320] When worshippers practice it, they are cleansed of pretension, as is the case with the Sufis. The recognizers have no need for remembrance. This name, moreover, has no relation to those who have arrived at the station of halting,[321] because they have gone beyond the names. 51.11

اسمه الحسيب تبارك وتعالى

١،٥٢ هـذا الاسم الكريم هو ثاني اسم خرج من سورة النساء وجملة ما في النساء ثمانية أسماء وقد اتّفق على إيراده الأئمّة الثلاثة وشاهده من سورة النساء قوله تعالى ﴿وَكَفَىٰ بِٱللَّهِ حَسِيباً﴾ والحسيب قد يكون بمعنى المحسب مثل البصير بمعنى المبصر والأليم بمعنى المؤلم ويكون حينئذ بمعنى الكافي وقد يكون الحسيب بمعنى المحاسب كما يقال حسيبك أي محاسبك مثاله الأكيل بمعنى المؤاكل وقد يكون بمعنى القادر قال الله تعالى و﴿كَانَ عَلَىٰ كُلِّ شَيْءٍ حَسِيباً﴾.

٢،٥٢ فإن كان بمعنى المحسب فهو الكافي في إعطاء الخلق فيكون داخلاً في الخالق وقد يكون في إعطاء الخُلق فيدخل في الاسم الوهّاب سواء كان الخُلق محموداً أو غيره فإنّ إيجاده ذا خلقٍ هبة خير من عدمه وقد يكون الكافي في الرزق فيدخل في الاسم الرازق وفي إعطاء أمد الأجل فيدخل في الاسم الـمميت وتفاصيل هذه لا تتناهى.

٣،٥٢ وإن كان بمعنى المحاسب فيأتي شرحه في سريع الحساب وقد ذُكر وإن كان بمعنى القادر فيأتي فيه والمحسب بمعنى الكافي ظاهر فيه وكونه تعالى كافياً لأنّه عند الطائفة ليس معه غيره فإن لم يكن هو الكافي لم يوجَد كاف أصلاً فكلّ موجود وجد كفاية في طور من الأطوار فهو تعالى موجدها فهو الحسيب سبحانه وتتعلّق به معان من الاسم الوكيل سبحانه إذا اتّخذته وكيلاً لأنّ الكفاءة في الوكيل مطلوبة ولذلك قرن به ﴿كَفَىٰ﴾ في قوله ﴿وَكَفَىٰ بِٱللَّهِ حَسِيباً﴾ أي كفايته كافية أي كاملة شاملة.

Al-Ḥasīb: The Reckoner

This noble name is the second drawn from the Surah of Women, which includes a total of eight names. The three eminent scholars agree it is a divine name. It occurs in the verse: «God suffices as a reckoner».[322] The Reckoner can mean provider of sufficiency, *muḥsib*, just as endowed with sight, *baṣīr*, can mean provider of sight, *mubṣir*, and hurting, *alīm*, can mean giver of pain, *mu'lim*. Thus, the Reckoner can mean the Sufficer. Furthermore, *ḥasīb* can mean *al-Muḥāsib*, the One Who Reckons, just as you can say the one who takes your accounts, *ḥasībuka*, to mean your reckoner, *muḥāsibuka*; or *akīl*, a person who eats, can mean a person who joins you in eating, *mu'ākil*. Moreover, it can mean the Powerful. God says: «God is powerful over all things».[323] 52.1

If this name means provider of sufficiency, then it means that He suffices in what He bestows upon the external aspects of creation. In that case, it is included within the Creator. It may also refer to the bestowal of an inward character trait, whereupon it is included within the Bestower, regardless of whether that trait is praiseworthy or not. For giving existence to it in someone who possesses a character trait is a bestowal that is better than its nonexistence. Moreover, He may be the Sufficer in provision, in which case it is included within the Provider; or in giving an appointed term its duration, in which case it is included within the Death-Giver, and so on. 52.2

If this name is taken to mean the One Who Reckons, then its explanation pertains to the Swift in Reckoning, which was discussed earlier. If it is taken to mean the Powerful, this will be discussed later. Moreover, the Provider of Sufficiency, in the sense of the Sufficer, is self-evident. His sufficiency, according to the perspective of our school, lies in how there is none other with Him. Moreover, there would be no sufficiency in the first place if He were not the Sufficer. Thus, whenever an existent finds its sufficiency in any of its stages, it is He who gives it existence. He is the Reckoner, and meanings from the Trustee are associated with it when you take Him as your Trustee, because the ability to suffice is required from a trustee. It is for this reason that He connects the verb "to suffice" with a reckoner in the verse: «God suffices as a reckoner».[324] That is, His sufficiency is sufficient, which is to say that it is complete and all-inclusive. 52.3

أمّا إذا اعتبرتَ الأكوان وكونها تجري على نظام متقن من دوران الأفلاك وبـ﴿ تَقۡدِيرُ ٱلۡعَزِيزِ ٱلۡعَلِيمِ ﴾ وإشراق كواكبها والدراري الجواري بأمره والمدد الذي يتّصل بالمولّدات واغتذاء بعضها ببعض بحيث ينقام الملك بغير نقص إلّا النقص الذي هو من شرط الكمال فإنّه لو لم يكن في الموجودات نقص لم تعلم حقيقة الكمال فهو حسيب في ترتيب موجوداته على ما هو مشهود منها ولن تموت نفس حتّى تستوفي رزقها فهو الحسيب الكافي في إيصال الأرزاق. ٤،٥٢

وأنت تجد معنى الكافي في الأسماء كلّها أمّا في الاسم الله فما ولّه خلقه فيه غيره فهو كاف في ذلك وفي الإصلاح وهو حقيقة الربّ في بعض معانيه وفي الرحمة وهو من الرحمٰن الرحيم فهو كاف فيها وهو كاف في المملكة من اسمه الملك وفي الإحاطة من اسمه المحيط وفي القدرة من اسمه القدير وفي العلم من اسمه العليم. ٥،٥٢

وبالجملة إنّ اسمه الحسيب بمعنى الكافي يرد معناه في معاني الأسماء كلّها فيدخل بالإحاطة في الاسم المحيط ويستدعي بحقيقته حقيقة الاسم الوكيل من حيث أنّه إذا كان حسيباً أي كافياً دعا ذلك أن يتّخذ وكيلاً فإنّه يتّخذ وكيلاً من كان كافياً وقد شرحنا لمعة من معنى الاسم الوكيل. ٦،٥٢

وإذا كان بمعنى المحاسب دخل فيه الاسم الرقيب فإنّه إنّما تكون المحاسبة على ما يُعلم وما يُعلم لا يكون دون مراقبة المعلوم وقد مضى شرح معنى الرقيب ومن حاسب نفسه فبمعنى الحسيب حاسبها وكذلك من حاسب غيره فإنّ المعاني إنّما هي له تعالى سواء كانت علويّة أو سفليّة لأنّ الوجود له تعالى حقيقة فإن فُرض وجودُ غيرِه فمجاز فما حاسب أحدٌ أحداً إلّا والإشارة عند الموحّد إلى أنّه تعالى الذي حاسب نفسه حقيقة وإن لم يدرك ذلك أهل العقول المحجوبة. ٧،٥٢

When you consider the cosmos and how it is patterned according to a precise arrangement of cyclical spheres by «the determination of the Exalted, the Knowing»,[325] its resplendent planets running their course by His command, and the beneficial replenishment that reaches minerals, plants, and animals, and how each takes nourishment from the other such that God's kingdom subsists without any imperfection—except for the imperfection that is a condition of perfection, for if there were no imperfection in existents, then the meaning of perfection would be unknown—then He is sufficient in arranging all existents that one witnesses, and no soul shall die before it is given the provision that is rightfully due to it. He is thus the Sufficient Reckoner in how He ensures that their provisions reach them. 52.4

One also discovers the meaning of the Sufficer in all the names. In Allāh, for instance, none other than Allāh enthralls His creatures, and in that sense He is sufficient. He is also sufficient in the sense of restoring good order, and that is the reality of certain meanings of the Lord. In mercy, which is from the All- and Ever-Merciful, He is also sufficient. He is sufficient too in the kingdom through the King, and in encompassing all things through the Encompassing, and in power through the Powerful, and in knowledge through the Knowing. 52.5

In short, the meaning of the Reckoner in the sense of the Sufficer overlaps with the meanings of all the names, and in being thus encompassed it is included within the Encompassing. Moreover, its reality entails the reality of the Trustee in view of the fact that since He is Sufficient then that entails that He is taken as a Trustee, for only one who suffices is taken as a trustee. We have already spoken briefly about the meaning of the Trustee. 52.6

Now, if this name it is taken to mean the One Who Reckons, then it pertains to the Watchful. For reckoning is only applied to something that is known, and what is known is only known if it is watched over. We have already explained the meaning of the Watchful. Moreover, the one who takes his soul to account reckons it in accordance with the meaning of the Reckoner. Likewise, when someone takes others into account, the meanings pertain to none other than Him, be they high or low, for existence is really His. If one were to suppose an existence other than His, it could only be metaphorical. As such, whenever someone takes account of anyone else, the spiritual allusion for the monotheist is that it is He who takes Himself into account, even if this is not perceived by the one whose intelligence is veiled. 52.7

وهذا الشهود هو ممّا أجمع عليه أهل السفر الثاني لأنّهم أهل تفصيل التوحيد ٨،٥٢
فيثبتون الأغيار في عين الوحدانيّة والكمّل في السفر المذكور الذي هو الثاني هم الأقطاب وهم القوم الذين فارقتهم الأحوال والهمم وتنزّهوا عن الجهل من كلّ وجه حتّى جهل العارفين والواقفين وهو الجهل الصعب فإنّ العارف تغلبه الأحوال فيظنّ في الحقيقة أموراً لا تمكن منها أنّهم يرون أنّ الكامل يجب في حقّه ظهور خرق العادات ولا يعلم أنّ ذلك للرسل عليهم السلام لإقامة الحجّة.

وسمعتُ ابن هود يقول إنّه إن لم تدخل يدي في النار فلا أتألّم لم تثبت لي ولاية وهو ٩،٥٢
في ذلك ذو عقيدة وورد فيما نقله القشيريّ أنّه قال إذا برقت بارقة من التحقيق لم يبق حال ولا همّة وأمّا المحجوبون من أهل السنّة فكلّهم يعتقدون ذلك.

واعلم أنّ الاسم الحسيب يظهر حكمه في مراتب هؤلاء المذكورين وذلك لأنّ من ١٠،٥٢
جهل شيئاً فعاداه فالله حسيبه بمعنى محاسبه على جهله فلا يعطيه ما يعطي من لم يجهل ذلك الجهل فيكون حسيباً في المجازات بمعنى كاف في المحاسبة.

ومن ثمرات من يلازم ذكر هذا الاسم الكريم أنّه إن كان مشغوفاً بالأسباب خرج ١١،٥٢
عنها إلى التجريد اكتفاءً بالحسيب تعالى أي الكافي وإن لحظ فيه معنى القادر علق بقلبه أن لا قدرة لغيره عزّ وجلّ.

والقاعدة أنّ من ذكر ذكراً وكان لذلك الذكر معنى معقول تعلّق أثر ذلك المعنى بقلبه ١٢،٥٢
وتبعته لواحق ذلك المعنى حتّى يتّصف الذاكر بتلك المعاني إلّا إذا كانت الأسماء من أسماء الانتقام لم يكن كذلك بل تعلّق بقلب الذاكر الخوف فإن حصل له تجلّ كان من عالم الجلال والله أعلم.

This contemplative station is agreed upon by those who are on the second journey, because they are the folk of the differentiation of unity. They affirm the domain of separative entities within unity itself. The perfect ones of this second journey, moreover, are the axial saints. It is they who are divorced from states and aspirations and are free of ignorance from every angle, including the ignorance of the recognizers and those who have arrived at the station of halting, which is the most intractable ignorance. For the recognizer is overcome by states and thus has conviction in things that are otherwise impossible. Among these is that they hold that the perfect ones must display miracles, not knowing that it is for the Messengers to establish proofs.[326] 52.8

To this effect, I heard Ibn Hūd say, "If my hand goes into the fire and I feel pain, then I am not a Friend of God."[327] This was a matter of conviction for him. Moreover, it is related that al-Qushayrī said, "After a flash of realization, no state or saintly aspiration remains."[328] All veiled thinkers among the Sunnis hold this belief. 52.9

The property of the Reckoner manifests in these aforementioned levels. When someone is ignorant of a thing and opposes it, then God is His Reckoner, which is to say that He takes him into account for his ignorance and does not bestow upon him that which He bestows upon the ignorant. As such, He is the Reckoner in compensating, in the sense that He is sufficient in reckoning. 52.10

Among the fruits for those who persist in invoking this noble name is that those who are obsessed with secondary causes abandon them and withdraw from the world. They suffice themselves with the Sufficer. Moreover, if they behold the meaning of the Powerful in it, their hearts become attached to the fact that none but He has power. 52.11

The principle is that when someone practices an invocation that carries an intelligible meaning, its imprint takes hold of his heart, and its consequences become attached to him until he assumes the qualities of those meanings. However, that does not occur if the names he invokes are among the names of vengeance. Rather, fear takes hold of his heart, and when he experiences a disclosure, it is from the realm of majesty. And God knows best. 52.12

اسمه الشهيد تبارك وتعالى

١،٥٣ هو ثالث اسم خرج من سورة النساء في قوله تعالى ﴿إِنَّ ٱللَّهَ كَانَ عَلَىٰ كُلِّ شَيْءٍ شَهِيدًا﴾ وهو ممّا اتّفق عليه الأئمّة الثلاثة وهو بمعنى الشاهد قال الله تعالى ﴿شَهِدَ ٱللَّهُ أَنَّهُۥ لَآ إِلَٰهَ إِلَّا هُوَ﴾ وأمّا عطف ﴿ٱلْمَلَٰٓئِكَةُ وَأُوْلُواْ ٱلْعِلْمِ﴾ عليه تعالى فهو من باب مخاطبته على قدر العقول فالمعطوف مجاز والمعطوف عليه هو الحقيقة هذا إذا اعتبرتَ الحال من مقام العرفان وأمّا من مقام الأقطاب فالكلّ حقيقة فإنّ المراتب كلّها مغمورة به فيه منه فلا ميزة إلّا في الحجاب فالاسم الشهيد تعالى قد غمر الأطوار.

٢،٥٣ ومن طرائف ما يحكى أنّ الملك الكامل محمّد بن أيّوب رحمه الله حضر عنده بعض أمراء الأكراد على السماط فأكرمه السلطان بتقديم حجلة مشويّة إليه فضحك الأمير الكرديّ فقال له الملك الكامل ما الذي يضحكك قال إنّي كنت في زمن الصبا في بلادي فلقيت رجلاً فقطعت عليه الطريق وأخذت ما معه ورميته إلى الأرض لأذبحه فقال لي لا تفعل لئلّا يأخذك السلطان بدمي فقلت له ومن يشهد عليّ وما هنا أحد فقال ذلك الطائر وأشار إلى حجلة هناك فضحكت من اعتقاده أنّ الحجلة تشهد وذبحته فقال له السلطان ذبحته قال نعم فقال له قد شهدت الحجلة وقبلت الشهادة وأمر بصلبه فصُلب.

٣،٥٣ فهذه شهادة لو لم تكن متّصلة بالاسم الشهيد سبحانه لم تؤثّر فإنّ التأثير هو بقوّة و﴿ٱلْقُوَّةَ لِلَّهِ جَمِيعًا﴾ قال عليه السلام أنتم شهداء الله في الأرض والمراد ظهورات شهادة الشهيد سبحانه ويدخل معناه في معنى الرقيب وقد ذُكر شرحه في الاسم العليم.

٤،٥٣ وبالجملة كلّ الأسماء تدخل في معنى كلّ الأسماء وأشرف مظاهر الاسم الشهيد وأكملها هو قطب الأقطاب وذلك لتمركزه في دوائر الموجودات من الأناسيّ وغيرهم

Al-Shahīd: The Witness

This is the third name drawn from the Surah of Women in the verse: «Truly God is witness over all things».[329] It is among the names that the three scholars agree upon as divine. It means "the one who bears witness." God says: «God bears witness that there is no god but He».[330] The conjunctive phrase «and the angels and the possessors of knowledge»,[331] moreover, is an example of God addressing the level of the intellect. For the conjunction is metaphorical, and that to which it is conjoined is what is real. This, moreover, is in view of the station of direct recognition. From the station of the axial saints, however, everything is real, for all the levels are inundated by Him, in Him, and from Him, and there are no distinctions except in the veil. Thus, the Witness inundates all the stages. 53.1

A curious story is told about Sultan al-Kāmil Muḥammad ibn Ayyūb, may God have mercy on him. Some Kurdish emirs were present during a meal and the sultan honored them by serving roasted partridge. A Kurdish emir laughed at the sight of this. The sultan asked, "What's so funny?" He replied, "In my homeland, when I was young, I robbed a man, stealing his possessions, and when I threw him to the ground to kill him, he screamed, 'Don't kill me! If you do, the sultan will deal with you!' I said to him, 'And who will bear witness against me when there's no one here?' He replied, 'That bird!' And he pointed to one of those partridges over there. I laughed at the fact that he believed a partridge could testify against someone. Then I killed him." "You killed him?" the sultan asked, and the emir replied in the affirmative. The sultan then said, "The partridge has indeed testified against you, and I accept its testimony!" He ordered that the emir be crucified, which he was. 53.2

If the testimonial were not connected to the Witness, it would have had no effect because effects occur through power, and «power altogether belongs to God».[332] The blessed Prophet says: "You are God's witnesses on earth,"[333] by which he meant manifestations of the testimony of the Witness. Moreover, its meaning is included within the meaning of the Watchful, which was commented upon under the Knowing. 53.3

In short, all the names are included within the meanings of all the names, and the most eminent and perfect locus of manifestation of the Witness is the 53.4

فيشهد أحوالهم المختلفات بحسبها فيكون مع كلّ شيء ولا يقدر أن يكون معه شيء لأنّ له المطلع على كلّ مطّلع فيكون الاسم الشهيد ظاهرًا في مرتبته فيحيط بكلّ شيء ولا يحيط به شيء.

٥،٥٣ واعلم أنّ القطب قد يخفى عنه بعض الكشف الصوريّ ولا يصحّ أن يقال أنّه جاهل بها لأنّه يعلمها علماً كليّاً ولولا تقيّده بصورة جسميّة لم يخف عنه منها شيء فهو مظهر الاسم الشهيد.

اسمه المرسل جلّت هدايته

١،٥٤ هذا الاسم الكريم رابع اسم خرج من سورة النساء وشاهده منها قوله تعالى ﴿وَمَآ أَرۡسَلۡنَا مِن رَّسُولٍ إِلَّا لِيُطَاعَ﴾ وانفرد بإيراده أبو الحكم بن برّجان الأندلسيّ ولمّا كانت الرسالة إنّما هي من الله تعالى بحقيقة اسمه الهادي لم يكن للرسل عليهم السلام توجّه إلّا إلى مراتب ظهورات الاسم المضلّ وذلك لأنّ بين حقيقتي الاسم الهادي والاسم المضلّ حربًا معنويًّا من جهة تقابل معنييهما ولا بدّ من ظهور أحكام كلّ منهما في مراتبها.

٢،٥٤ فالرسل عليهم السلام جاؤوا من حضرة الاسم الهادي إلى حضرة الاسم المضلّ وهي الحضرة التي أضلّ الله منها من شاء قال تعالى ﴿يُضِلُّ مَن يَشَآءُ﴾ فكانت الحروب بين الحضرتين في أيّام الرسل عليهم السلام قائمة والمراسلات بينهما متردّدة والحرب بينهما سجال ولم يزل ذلك كذلك ولولا ذلك أعني لولا أنّ حضرة الضالّين

supreme axial saint,[334] for he is at the center of the circles of being, human and otherwise. He thus bears witness to all their different states in accordance with each one, and he is with all things, whereas nothing can be with him. For he has an overview over every horizon, and the Witness is therefore manifest at his level, and he encompasses all things, although he is encompassed by nothing.

The unveiling of certain forms may be hidden from the axial saint, but it is not correct to say that he is ignorant of them, for he knows them in a universal sense. But for his delimitation in bodily form, no form would remain hidden from him, for he is the locus of manifestation of the Witness. 53.5

Al-Mursil: The Sender

This is the fourth noble name drawn from the Surah of Women, and it occurs in this verse: «We sent no Messenger except that he should be obeyed».[335] Only Ibn Barrajān cites it as a divine name. Now, since the message comes only from God through the reality of the Guide, the Messengers—peace be upon them—turn their attentiveness solely to the levels in which the Misguider manifests. This is because a supersensory war is waged between the realities of the Guide and the Misguider, inasmuch as their meanings are mutually contrary and inasmuch as each of their properties must become manifest in their respective levels.[336] 54.1

God's Messengers—peace be upon them—thus come from the presence of the Guide to the presence of the Misguider, which is the presence from which God misguides whoever He wills, as He says: «He misguides whoever He wills».[337] Thus, throughout the eras of the Messengers wars were waged between both presences: messages were exchanged back and forth between them, and the guided and misguided fought each other with varying degrees of success. Indeed, this war never ended; for were it not so—that is, if the presence of the misguided were not drawing from His name the Misguider—then the misguided would never be helped in the first place. Yet the blessed Prophet 54.2

مستندة إلى اسمه المضلّ سبحانه لم ينصر الضالّون أصلاً لكنّه عليه السلام قال لا تمنّوا لقاء العدوّ فإنّهم ينصَرون كما تُنصرون.

٣،٥٤ وهذه العداوة أصلها من تقابل الاسم الهادي والمضلّ ﴿وَلَوْ شَآءَ رَبُّكَ لَجَعَلَ ٱلنَّاسَ أُمَّةً وَٰحِدَةً﴾ من حضرة قوله ﴿وَٱللَّهُ غَالِبٌ عَلَىٰٓ أَمْرِهِۦ﴾ ﴿وَلَا يَزَالُونَ مُخْتَلِفِينَ﴾ لإحياء مراتب ظهورات أسمائه تعالى ﴿إِلَّا مَن رَّحِمَ رَبُّكَ﴾ أي لحقه تجلّي الرحمة إمّا من حضرة حجاب فهو بأن يرجع إلى الهداية فيتبع الرسل أو من حضرة شهود عرفانيّ فيتبع تجلّيات الحقّ بلا واسطة أو من حضرة القطبيّة فتكون الأسماء تحت مقامه فيكون في غيب الذات وشهادتها هو هو وهو نهاية السفر الثاني.

٤،٥٤ فإن تنزّل بحقيقة السفر الثالث إلى أن يدعو ﴿إِلَى ٱللَّهِ عَلَىٰ بَصِيرَةٍ﴾ يعني إلى الاسم الهادي فإن كان في زمان الرسل لم يدع إلّا إلى الاسم الهادي وإن كان في غيره وصل به كلّ أحد إلى مقام خلاصه كان في ظاهر الحال ممّن ظهر بأحكام الاسم الهادي أو لم يظهر بل كان ظاهراً بحقائق الاسم المضلّ ﴿أَلَآ إِلَى ٱللَّهِ تَصِيرُ ٱلْأُمُورُ﴾.

٥،٥٤ قال الشيخ والمستقيم منها ما شُرع ومصير الجميع إلى الله ذكر ذلك في كتاب العبادلة فالاسم المرسل داخل في الاسم الهادي والرسالة دون النبوّة والنبوّة دون الولاية أمّا الرسول فجامع الثلاث مراتب فهو وليّ نبيّ رسول قال الشيخ

مَقَامُ ٱلنُّبُوَّةِ فِي بَرْزَخٍ دُوَيْنَ ٱلْوَلِيِّ وَفَوْقَ ٱلرَّسُولِ

says: "Do not seek to encounter the enemy in battle, for they are given help just as you are."[338]

Furthermore, this opposition originates in the confrontation of the Guide and the Misguider: «Had your Lord willed, He would have made humankind one nation»—from the presence of the verse «and God presides over His affair»—«but they continue in their differences»[339] in order to give life to the levels of manifestation of His names, «except for those on whom your Lord has mercy»;[340] that is, those who receive the disclosure of mercy. This disclosure may come from the presence of the veil, whereupon he will return to guidance and follow the Messengers. Alternatively, it may come from the recognizer's presence of witnessing, whereupon he will follow the disclosures of the Real with no intermediary. Or it may come from the axial presence, whereupon the names will be beneath his station, for he will be traveling in the unseen realm of the Essence, and their witnessing will be he himself. That is the end of the second journey. 54.3

Thereafter, he may descend back through the reality of the third journey and call «to God based on insight»;[341] that is, call to the Guide. If he lives during the era of the Messengers, then he calls unto none but the Guide. If he lives during a different period, everyone reaches their station of deliverance through him, regardless of whether his state outwardly manifests the properties of the Guide or not, and even if he manifests by the realities of the Misguider, «Surely all matters go back to God».[342] 54.4

The shaykh says: "Upright things include those that are set down as Shariah, and all things go back to God."[343] He mentions this in his book, *The Servants of God*. Thus, the Sender pertains to the Guide. Messengerhood is above prophethood, and prophethood is above friendship. The Messenger brings together these three levels and is thus a Friend-Prophet-Messenger. The shaykh says: 54.5

> The station of prophethood is located in an isthmus
> between the Friend and the Messenger.[344]

اسمه المقيت تبارك وتعالى

١،٥٥ هو خامس اسم خرج من سورة النساء شاهده قوله تعالى ﴿وَكَانَ ٱللَّهُ عَلَىٰ كُلِّ شَيْءٍ مُّقِيتًا﴾ وانفرد بإيراده أبو الحكم والمقيت في اللغة المقتدر أي القادر على أن يعطي القوت كلّ محتاج إليه وقد جاء بمعنى الحفيظ والأوّل أظهر.

٢،٥٥ واعلم أنّ مراتب ظهورات الاسم المقيت عامّة فلا تقتصر على الأجسام التي تلقّب بالمغتذّي فإنّه من شهد الوجود وجد موجوداته كلّها تطلب القوت وذلك راجع إلى حقيقة المدد الإلٰهيّ فإنّ القلم الأعلى قوته من الغيب الإلٰهيّ واللوح قوته من القلم واللوح المحفوظ إنّما قوته العلم والبسائط الجسمانيّة قوتها من اللوح والأجسام قوتها بعضها من بعض فالماء والتراب يستحيل بعضها إلى بعض فيقتات ما استُحيل إليه ممّا استحال وكذلك الهواء يقتات لطيفه من كثيفه والمعادن تقتات من الأرض والنبات منها ومن الماء والحيوان من النبات وبعضه من بعض.

٣،٥٥ والإنسان تقتات نفوس الكمّل منهم من الحقائق ونفوس العارفين من المعارف ونفوس المحجوبين من العلوم العقليّة والنقليّة والجهّال تقتات نفوسهم من التخيّلات والتوهّمات إذ يتوهّمون أنّها علوم وأمّا أجسام الأناسيّ كلّهم محقّقهم وعارفهم ومحجوبهم فغذاؤه معلوم فالاسم المقيت معط في هذه المراتب كلّها حقيقة القوت وألذّ أقوات الأجسام ما لاءم الحسّ وجانس الجسم وأمدّ القوى إمدادًا معتدلًا وألذّ أغذية الأنفس ما ناسبها وتغذّي النفوس بالواردات والأحوال والتجلّيات هي ألذّ أغذيتها ولذلك يكون أهل البداية ألذّ عيشًا من الكمّل لمكان قبولهم للتجلّيات وواردات الأحوال.

Al-Muqīt: The Nourisher

This is the fifth name drawn from the Surah of Women, and it occurs in the verse: «God nourishes all things».[345] Only Ibn Barrajān cites it as a divine name. Linguistically, the Nourisher means the Powerful; that is, the one who has the power to provide nourishment to anyone in need. It can also mean the Preserver, but the first definition is more apparent. 55.1

Levels of manifestation of the Nourisher are all-pervasive. They are not restricted to what are classified as bodies that feed. For the one who witnesses existence discovers that all of its existents seek nourishment, and this derives from the reality of divine replenishment. For the nourishment of the Supreme Pen is from God's unseen realm. The nourishment of the Tablet, for its part, is from the Pen. The Preserved Tablet's nourishment is none other than divine knowledge, and the nourishment of the simple elements is from the Tablet.[346] The nourishment of bodies is from each other: water and earth transmute into one another, such that the transmuted element is nourished by that which transmutes into it. Similarly, subtle winds are nourished by dense winds, minerals are nourished by the earth, plants are nourished by the earth and by water, and animals are nourished by plants and by one another. 55.2

Among humans, the perfected souls are nourished by esoteric realities. The souls of the recognizers are nourished by direct recognition. The souls of the veiled intellects are nourished by the intellectual and transmitted sciences. The souls of the ignorant are nourished by mental images and fantasies, which they imagine to be science. Without exception, the nourishment of human bodies—including the bodies of those who have verified the truth, the recognizers, and the veiled intellects—is well known. The Nourisher provides nourishment at all these levels. Moreover, the most pleasurable nourishment for the body is what is agreeable to the senses, congenial to the body, and replenishing to the faculties in a balanced manner. The most pleasurable nourishment for souls is that with which they have affinity. Souls are nourished by inrushes, spiritual states, and disclosures, which are the most pleasurable of their nourishments. That is why beginners experience more pleasure than the perfected, for they are receptive to disclosures, inrushes, and spiritual states. 55.3

٤،٥٥ قال الجنيد رحمه الله واشوقاه لأيّام البداية وذلك لما رأى فيها من التلذّذ بتلقّي التجلّيات وأمّا الكمّل فلمّا انقطع عنهم الواردات والتجلّيات بطلت لذّاتهم ورجعوا إلى الحسّ بالكلّيّة فأشبهت ظهواهرهم ظواهر العوامّ فجُهلوا بِخلاف أهل الترقّي فإنّ نفوس العوامّ تنفعل لهم ويعتقدون أنّهم أكمل وهو غلط منهم.

٥،٥٥ وذكر اسم المقيت يفيد التجريد عن الأسباب ويعطي التوكّل والله أعلم.

اسمه الصادق عزّ وجلّ

١،٥٦ هذا الاسم الكريم لم يذكره الإمام أبو حامد الغزاليّ وذكره الإمامان البيهقيّ وأبو الحكم وشاهده من سورة النساء قوله تعالى ﴿وَمَنْ أَصْدَقُ مِنَ ٱللَّهِ حَدِيثًا﴾.

٢،٥٦ واعلم أنّ الاسم الصادق عامّ الحكم شامل الحقائق لا تخلو منه رتبة من رتب الوجود أمّا صدقه على ألسنة الرسل فشاهده المعجزات وأمّا صدقه على ألسنة الناطقين فشاهده الحسّ والعقل.

٣،٥٦ والكلّ صدق الاسم الصادق وأمّا صدقه في كلّ المراتب فلأنّ الكاذب صادق باعتبار أنّه إنّما أخبر عن وجود موجود أو موجودات لكنّ ذلك الموجود أو تلك الموجودات في الذهن فإنّه صوّر في ذهنه بحقيقة الاسم المصوّر ما[1] أخبر عنه والاسم المصوّر هو الذي صوّر الإخبار أيضاً فوقع الإخبار عن موجود محقّق.

٤،٥٦ وإن كان السامع يظنّه أخبر عن الموجود في الخارج فالخطأ من السامع فإن قلت إنّ الصدق إنّما هو ما كان الإخبار به عن موجود في الخارج فالجواب أنّا نقول إنّه

١ آ، ب، ج: وما.

Al-Junayd, may God have mercy on him, said: "How I yearn for the early days!"[347] because of the pleasure he took from the disclosures he experienced then. Inrushes and disclosures are cut off from the perfected, and therefore their pleasures are nullified and they return fully to their sensory faculties. Outwardly they thus resemble ordinary believers, and they pass unnoticed, in contrast to those who are still on the path of ascent, to whom the souls of the ordinary believers are receptive and whom they hold to be more perfected, which is a mistake on their part. 55.4

Invoking the Nourisher is helpful in withdrawing from the realm of secondary causes, and gives trust in God. And God knows best. 55.5

Al-Ṣādiq: The Truthful

This noble name is not mentioned by al-Ghazālī, but it is mentioned as a divine name by al-Bayhaqī and Ibn Barrajān. It occurs in the Surah of Women in the verse: «who is more truthful in speech than God?»[348] 56.1

The property of the Truthful is all-pervasive, its realities all-inclusive, and no level of existence is devoid of it. His truthfulness on the tongues of the Messengers is attested by miracles. His truthfulness on the tongues of speakers is attested by sense perception and intelligence. 56.2

Everyone, moreover, affirms the truthfulness of the Truthful. His truthfulness obtains at all levels, because the liar is also truthful in view of the fact that he merely reports on the existence of one or several existents. That existent, however, is in his mind, for through the reality of the Form-Giver he forms the thing he reports in his mind. The Form-Giver also gives form to his report-giving. As such, he reports about an actual existent. 56.3

Furthermore, the error is from the listener if the listener assumes that the liar is reporting on a thing that exists externally. For if one were to contend that truthfulness is essentially reporting on something external, we would say that to report on something external is to report on what is in the mind, except that 56.4

إن[١] أخبر أحد عمّا في الخارج إنّما يخبر عمّا في الذهن في الحالين لكن اتّفق أن صادف موافقة الداخل للخارج ولهذه الحقيقة من لم يتصوّر ما يخبر عنه لم يخبر عنه إذ لا شعور له به فتفطّن لهذا الأمر.

واعلم أنّ الباطل حقّ باعتبار أنّه وجود والوجود هو الحقّ وكلّ نطق لوجود فهو نطق ٥،٥٦
الوجود قال الشيخ رضي الله عنه

إِذَا نَطَقَ ٱلْوُجُودُ أَصَاخَ قَوْمٌ   بِأَسْمَاعٍ إِلَى نُطْقِ ٱلْوُجُودِ

ونطق الحقّ حقّ كما قلتُ في اسمه العليم تبارك وتعالى

لَا تُنْكِرِ ٱلْبَاطِلَ فِي طَوْرِهِ   فَإِنَّهُ بَعْضُ ظُهُورَاتِهِ
وَأَعْطِهِ مِنْكَ بِمِقْدَارِهِ   حَتَّى تُوَفِّي حَقَّ إِثْبَاتِهِ
أَظْهِرْهُ فِي ذَاتِكَ مُسْتَكْمِلاً   خَشْيَةَ أَنْ تَظْهَرَ فِي ذَاتِهِ

فالاسم الصادق هو لسان الوجود والناطق هو لسان حقيقة الحقائق وهي مرتبة القطب فالاسم الصادق مساوق للاسم المحيط في مظاهر الوجود كلّه.

وذكر هذا الاسم يعطي للمحجوب صدق اللسان وللصوفيّ صدق القلب وللعارف ٦،٥٦
التحقيق والله أعلم.

---

١ و: ما.

the internal and the external thing happen to be identical. Therefore, not to conceptualize what one is reporting on is not to report on it at all, because it is to be unaware of it. So ponder this matter!

Falsehood is truth inasmuch as it is an existent, and existence is real, and the uttering of every existent is a speech of existence. To this effect, the shaykh, may God be pleased with him, says: 56.5

When existence speaks, one group
lends its ear to the speech of existence.[349]

Furthermore, the speech of the Real is true, as I said concerning the Knowing:

Do not deny falsehood within its stage
for it is a part of His self-manifestation.
Give it its measure of yourself,
thereby fulfilling its due by affirming it.
Manifest it in your being, seeking perfection,
lest it be you that manifest in its being.[350]

The Truthful is therefore the mouthpiece of existence, and the speaker is the voice of the Reality of Realities, which is the level of the axial saint. The Truthful is thus coextensive with the Encompassing in all manifestations of existence.

The invocation of this name gives a truthful tongue to the veiled thinker, 56.6
a truthful heart to the Sufi, and realization to the recognizer. And God knows best.

اسمه الشاكر جلّ جلاله

١،٥٧ انفرد بإيراده البيهقيّ وشاهده من سورة النساء قوله تعالى ﴿وَكَانَ ٱللَّهُ شَاكِرًا عَلِيمًا﴾ ومعناه عند العلماء أنّه يشكر للعبد الصالح عملَه أي يثيبه عليه.

٢،٥٧ ومعنى الاسم الشاكر عامّ الحكم في كلّ قابل للأثر متأثّر من الفعل ينجح فيه قصد الفاعل ويظهر فيه مقصود المؤثّر فيجمع بين شكر الإحسان المعلوم وشكر إظهار المنّة وهو قبول الأثر كشكر الأرض للمطر بظهور النبات وشكر الأغصان للأصول بإظهار الثمرات فقبول القلم الأعلى مدد الغيب شكر وقبول اللوح المحفوظ منه شكر وانقياد الأفلاك بطبعها لحركة دوريّة شكر وتمازج طبائع ما تحتها بسرّ المدد الإلٰهيّ شكر وظهور المولّدات عنها شكر وقبول الإناث تأثيرات ذكورها شكر وانفعال الفاعل بالمفعول بتملّقه له شكر ونطق الناطقات شكر وصمت الصامتات شكر لأنّه مطلوب منها أن تصمت وذلك لانقطاع المدد عنها لأنّ الأعدام لا تكون بتأثير مؤثّر بل بضدّه والحركة الذاتيّة شكر للوجود المطلق وهو الشكر العامّ الذي كلّ شكر من تفصيله.

٣،٥٧ والاسم الشاكر في هذه المراتب كلّها ناطق بالشكر الراجع إلى الذات المقدّسة وليس في الموجودات موجود لا شكر له حتّى جحود الجاحد فإنّه شكر لأنّه مطلوب منه بالتأثير أن يكون جاحداً فقد تأثّر وأظهر المراد منه فكان شاكرًا لأنّه لو لم يكن متأثّرًا لناسب العدم.

Al-Shākir: The Grateful

Only al-Bayhaqī considers it to be a divine name. It occurs in the Surah of Women in the verse: «God is Grateful, Knowing».[351] According to the scholars, it means that God shows gratitude toward the righteous servant for his deeds; that is, He rewards him for them.[352] 57.1

The property of the Grateful, moreover, pervades everything that is receptive of influence and is influenced by an act, through which the aim of an agent is carried out, and in which the intended goal of an exerter of influence becomes manifest. Thus, the Grateful brings together common gratitude in response to a beautiful action, and the gratitude of displaying the blessings that one has received; that is, being receptive to the agent's influence. Examples of this include the growth of plants as the gratitude of the earth for rain, and the production of fruit as the gratitude of branches to their roots. Thus, the following constitute gratitude: the receptivity of the Supreme Pen to replenishment from the unseen; the receptivity of the Preserved Tablet to the Pen; the natural submission of the spheres to circular motion; the mixing of the natural constituents below the spheres through the secret of divine replenishment; the manifestation of minerals, plants, and animals thereby; the receptivity of females to the influence of males; and the passivity of the object to the subject by ingratiating itself to it. Moreover, the speech of rational speakers is gratitude, just as the silence of silent things is also gratitude, for they are expected to stay silent because the divine replenishment has been cut off. After all, nonexistents do not come about as effects of something that produces effects, but rather by its opposite. Moreover, the motion of the Essence is gratitude to unconditioned existence, and the latter is the all-pervading gratitude from which all forms of gratitude receive their differences. 57.2

At all these levels, the Grateful expresses the gratitude that stems from the Holy Essence, and there is no existent devoid of gratitude. This includes the ingratitude of the ingrate, for it too is gratitude since he is expected to display the behavior of ingratitude. Given that he displays effects and manifests what is intended for him, the ingrate is actually being grateful; for if he were not to display the effect of ingratitude, then he would correspond to nonexistence. 57.3

٤،٥٧ واعلم أنّ خاصّيّة الوجود المطلق هو التأثّر لا التأثير فالانفعال أسبق من الفعل وسرّ هذا لا يقال إلّا مشافهة فتطوّرات الوجود كلّها ألسنة ناطقة تشكر الحقّ جلّ جلاله فهو شاكر لنفسه إذ لا يستحقّ الشكر غيره ولا يستحقّ أن يكون شاكرًا سواه.

٥،٥٧ والشكر والذمّ كلاهما شكر واقع على القطب لأنّه الذي صدرت عنه الأحكام من حيث مرتبة لا من حيث صورة جسميّة والأسماء كلّها إليه ترجع الحسنى وغير الحسنى فليس الشاكر وحده راجعاً إليه وهذا واضح عندهم فلا تراه خفيّاً.

٦،٥٧ والاسم الشاكر يعطي أهل الذكر له مقام المحبّة إن كانوا صوفيّة ومقام الوقفة إن كانوا عارفين ومقام القطبيّة إن كانوا واقفين وهو حضرة قدس محفوفة بالأنس ونفع هذا الاسم في الخلوة بالغ والله أعلم.

اسمه العفوّ سبحانه

١،٥٨ هذا الاسم الكريم اتّفق على إيراده الأئمّة الثلاثة وشاهده من سورة النساء قوله تعالى ﴿إِنَّ ٱللَّهَ كَانَ عَفُوًّا قَدِيرًا﴾ وهو آخر ما خرج من سورة النساء ومعنى العفوّ الساتر ذنوب العاصين بالمسامحة لهم وصيغته فعول للمبالغة بمعنى كثرة العفو منه تعالى.

٢،٥٨ واعلم أنّ العفو منه تعالى له اعتباران أحدهما يخصّ مرتبة العلم والآخر يخصّ مرتبة المعرفة فالذي يخصّ مرتبة العلم هو أنّ الحقّ تبارك وتعالى يسامح عبده بأن لا يعاقبه على ذنبه وأصعب الذنوب كلّها الشرك قال الله تعالى ﴿إِنَّ ٱللَّهَ لَا يَغْفِرُ أَن يُشْرَكَ بِهِۦ﴾ وإنّما توجب العقوبة على العبد بدعواه نسبة الفعل إلى

Moreover, the characteristic of unconditioned existence is the reception, not the display, of effects; for reaction precedes action. But this secret can only be shared orally, since all stages of existence express gratitude to the Real. After all, He is grateful to Himself, since none is worthy of gratitude but He, and none is worthy of showing gratitude but He. 57.4

Furthermore, gratitude and blame are both cases of gratitude actualized by the axial saint, because in respect to his cosmic level, not in respect to his bodily form, all properties come forth from him. Moreover, all the names, both the most beautiful ones and the others, return to him. As such, it is not only the Grateful that stems from him; this is clear for the axial saints, seeing it as they do without any ambiguity. 57.5

The Grateful gives those who invoke it the station of love if they are Sufis, the station of halting if they are recognizers, and the station of axial sainthood if they have arrived at the station of halting. It is a presence of holiness that is wrapped in intimacy. The benefit of this name for the spiritual retreat[353] is far-reaching. And God knows best. 57.6

Al-ʿAfū: The Forgiver

This noble name is mentioned by the three eminent scholars as a divine name. It occurs in the Surah of Women in the verse: «God is indeed forgiving, powerful».[354] It is the penultimate name in this surah. The meaning of the Forgiver is He who conceals the sins of the disobedient by pardoning them. Its form (*faʿūl*) denotes emphasis, meaning that forgiveness from Him is abundant. 58.1

Forgiveness from Him has two considerations. The first pertains specifically to the level of knowledge, and the second pertains specifically to the level of direct recognition. The first consideration is that the Real pardons His servant by not punishing him for his sins. The most terrible of all sins, moreover, is to associate partners with God. God says: «God indeed does not forgive that a partner be associated with Him».[355] In such cases, a person's punishment is necessary because he ascribes the act to himself, and is thereby guilty of 58.2

نفسه فأشرك بدعواه أنّ مع الحقّ تعالى فاعلاً غيره فلمّا فعل العبد ما خالف الشرع استحقّ العقوبة.

٣،٥٨ وأصل العفو عن الذنوب معنى التوحيد والتوحيد أصل الحسنات بسرّ قوله لا حول ولا قوّة إلّا بالله فالراجع إلى الحقّ تعالى بالاستغفار يشبه من رجع إليه بالتوحيد لأنّ المستغفر يبرأ إلى الله تعالى من ذلك الفعل المعبَّر عنه بالذنب والبراءة من الفعل يشبه من نسب الفعل إلى الله تعالى فناسب التوحيد فاستحقّ العفو ونهاية توحيد أهل الحجاب أن يتحقّقوا بمعنى لا حول ولا قوّة إلّا بالله لأنّهم لا يقدرون على نسبة الفعل كلّه لله فهذا موضع تصرّف الاسم العفوّ في مراتب المحجوبين.

٤،٥٨ وأمّا في اعتبار مراتب أهل الكشف فيشهدون أنّ الأمر كلّه لله شهودًا لا يجدون فيه شكًّا فلا جرم أنّ الحساب ساقط عنهم لخالهم حال المعفوّ عنهم فالاسم العفوّ يلحقهم في مبادئ شهودهم فإذا انكشف أن لا فعل إلّا لله عزّ وجلّ فلا تعلّق لهم بغير ما شهدوه واستغفار هؤلاء إنّما هو من أنفسهم كما ورد عن بعضهم أنّه خوطب بما صورته حوِّل الرداء إذا استسقيتني أسقك واستغفرني منك أرسل سماء تعرّفي عليك مدرارًا فجعل الاستغفار لا من الذنب بل من رؤيته لنفسه.

٥،٥٨ وهذا الاسم يليق بأذكار العوامّ لأنّه يصلحهم وليس من شأن السالكين إلى الله ذكره لأنّ فيه ذكر الذنب وذكر القوم لا يكون فيه ذكر الذنب بل ولا ذكر الحسنة قال الواقف وقال لي يا عبد اجعل ذنبك تحت رجليك واجعل حسنَتك تحت ذنبك فإذا ذكرته العامّة حسن حالهم والله أعلم.

associationism by claiming that there is an actor other than God. Given that the servant has violated the revealed Law, he merits punishment.

The root of forgiveness from sin is the meaning of divine oneness. Divine oneness, moreover, is the root of beautiful deeds through the secret of the saying: "There is no strength and no power but through God." Turning to God by asking for forgiveness is like turning to Him by declaring His oneness. This is because the seeker of forgiveness acquits himself before God of the act that is referred to as a sin, and this acquittal is akin to ascribing the act to God. It thus concords with declaring God's oneness, and is worthy of forgiveness. Moreover, the highest declaration of divine oneness by veiled intellects is to realize the meaning of "There is neither strength nor power but through God," for they are unable to ascribe all acts to God. This then is where the Forgiver exercises control at the levels of the veiled intellects. 58.3

From the perspective of their levels, those who know through unveiling witness that the entire affair belongs to God and have no doubt in their witness. The reckoning therefore does not apply to them, for theirs is the state of those who are forgiven. Thus, the Forgiver seizes them at the first stages of their witnessing, but when it is revealed to them that there is no act but God's, they have attachment only to what they witness. These types seek forgiveness from none other than themselves. To this effect, one of them heard a voice saying something like this: "Turn the mantle inside out when you ask Me for rain, and I will send rain down on you; seek My forgiveness from yourself and I will unburden the sky of My true knowledge upon you in torrents."[356] He thus asked forgiveness not from sin, but from seeing himself. 58.4

The invocation of this name is appropriate for the ordinary believers because it rectifies them. However, it is not appropriate for the wayfarers to God to invoke it because it involves the mention of sin, and the invocation of the Folk should not involve any mention of sin, or even any mention of beautiful deeds. The one who arrives at the station of halting quotes God as saying: "He said to me: O servant, place your sins under your feet, and place your beautiful deeds under your sins."[357] Thus, when ordinary believers invoke this name, their state improves; and God knows best. 58.5

سورة الأنعام

وفيها ستّة أسماء

اسمه الفاطر جلّ اسمه

١،٥٩ ذكره أبو الحكم دونهما وشاهده قوله تعالى ﴿فَاطِرِ ٱلسَّمَٰوَٰتِ وَٱلْأَرْضِ﴾ والفاطر معناه الخالق وقد يكون من فطر الشيء إذا شقّه قال الله تعالى ﴿أَنَّ ٱلسَّمَٰوَٰتِ وَٱلْأَرْضَ كَانَتَا رَتْقًا فَفَتَقْنَٰهُمَا﴾ وهو بمعنى شققناهما ليوافق قوله تعالى ﴿فَاطِرِ ٱلسَّمَٰوَٰتِ وَٱلْأَرْضِ﴾ أي شقّها ومعنى فطرها أي فتح في مادّتها صورتها الخاصّة بها فهو راجع أيضاً إلى الخالق فإنّ الخالق هو الذي أوجد الصورة.

٢،٥٩ واعلم أنّ نصيب العلم النقليّ أنّ الله تعالى أوجد الأشياء من عدم والظاهر أنّ تقديره عن عدم فمن بمعنى عن والفرق بينهما أنّ عن بمعنى أنّ الأشياء لم تكن فوُجدت بعد عدم وأمّا مِن على أن تُجعل مادّة الوجود عدماً فهو عسر الفهم.

٣،٥٩ وأمّا نصيب الشهود فقال الشيخ إنّه تعالى اقتطع قطعة من نوره ففتح فيها صورة العالم فيكون إذاً مادّة العالم ذلك النور فالخلق يتعلّق بالصور لا بالنور فإنّ نوره منه متّصل بصور العالم ولهذه الحقيقة حصل فيهم معنى قوله تعالى ﴿ٱللَّهُ نُورُ ٱلسَّمَٰوَٰتِ وَٱلْأَرْضِ﴾ على حذف المضاف تقديره ﴿ٱللَّهُ﴾ مفيض ﴿نُورِ ٱلسَّمَٰوَٰتِ وَٱلْأَرْضِ﴾

The Surah of the Cattle

The Surah of the Cattle has six divine names.

Al-Fāṭir: The Cleaver

It is mentioned by Ibn Barrajān alone. It occurs in the verse: «Cleaver of the heavens and the earth».[358] The meaning of the name is the Creator. It can also denote to cleave something, or to split it. God says: «The heavens and the earth were a stitched mass, then We cleaved them apart»,[359] meaning We split them apart. It thus concords with the verse «Cleaver of the heavens and the earth»; that is, the one who split them apart. Moreover, the meaning of "He cleaved them" is that He opened their specific form within their material substratum. Thus it stems also from the Creator, for it is the Creator who brings the form into existence. 59.1

According to transmitted knowledge, God brought things into existence "from" nonexistence. The plain sense of this is that it means "of" nonexistence. For "from" can mean "of," and the difference between them is that "of" means that things were naught, and they were brought into existence after nonexistence. "From" would imply that the substratum of existence is nonexistence, and that is difficult to understand. 59.2

According to direct witness, the shaykh says: "God took a piece of His light, and then opened within it the form of the cosmos."[360] Light is therefore the material substrate of the cosmos, and creation takes forms as its object, rather than light, because His light is from Him and connected to the forms of the cosmos. It is through this reality, then, that they interpret the verse «God is the light of the heavens and the earth»[361] as omitting the genitive apposition, 59.3

والمراد ذلك النور الذي فتح فيه صور العالم وربّما لم يعتبر بعض أهل الشهود حذف هذا المضاف وحملوا الأمر على ظاهره وهو حقّ فالاسم الفاطر يتعلّق بإيجاد الصور في حضرة الحجاب.

٤،٥٩ وأمّا نصيب الكشف فإنّ الاسم الفاطر معناه الظاهر ويرون الظاهرات تجلّيات من غيب إلى شهادة ومن باطن إلى ظاهر ليس هو غيره حتّى يصحّ اعتبار أنّه ﴿ٱلْأَوَّلُ وَٱلْـَٔاخِرُ وَٱلظَّٰهِرُ وَٱلْبَاطِنُ﴾ والتجلّيات ترى بعينه وأهل الحجاب لا يعلمون قال الشيخ

إِذَا تَجَلَّى حَبِيبِي بِأَيِّ عَيْنٍ أَرَاهُ
بِعَيْنِهِ لَا بِعَيْنِي فَمَا رَآهُ سِوَاهُ

فعلى هذا الاسم الفاطر معناه الظاهر.

٥،٥٩ واعلم أنّ الاسم الفاطر بمعنى الظاهر لا يختصّ بالظاهر للحسّ بل ظهورات المعنويّات فطور وتخيّلات عالم الخيال فطور وبدوّ الباديات من مكاشفات القلوب فطور وفناء الصور في الذات الواحدة فطور للوجود الواحد فإنّ قيام الوحدانيّة من الكثرة فطور لها وأوسع دوائر الفطور تفصيل الوحدانيّة في السفر الثانيّ لاشتمالها على العوالم التي لا تتناهى ولا تخرج عنها شيء.

٦،٥٩ وأمّا ثمرة هذا الاسم إذا ذُكر في الخلوة فيعطي شهود الاسم الخالق ويفرّق عن التوحيد فلا يناسب طالب الواحدانيّة والله أعلم.

so that it is taken to mean «God is» the effuser of «the light of the heavens and the earth». And what is intended is the light wherein He opens the forms of the cosmos. Some witnesses may not take this omission of the genitive apposition into consideration, and they interpret the verse according to its surface meaning, which is true too, for the Cleaver is connected to the bestowal of existence upon the forms in the presence of the veil.

According to unveiled thinkers, the Cleaver means the Manifest. They see manifest things as being disclosures from the unseen to the visible, or from the nonmanifest to the manifest, and as none other than Him. They therefore genuinely consider Him to be «the First and the Last, the Manifest and the Nonmanifest».[362] Disclosures, moreover, are seen through His eye, but the veiled intellects do not know that. The shaykh says: 59.4

When my Beloved discloses Himself,
through what eye do I see Him?
Through His eye, not mine,
for none sees Him but He.[363]

Accordingly, the Cleaver means the Manifest.

The Cleaver in the sense of the Manifest is not specific to what is manifest to the senses. Rather, the manifestations of supersensory meanings are a cleaving manifestation; imaginalizations of the Imaginal world are a manifestation; the very initial stages of the unveilings of the heart are a manifestation; the annihilation of forms in the Unique Essence is a manifestation of the one existence, for the subsistence of oneness through many-ness is its manifestation. Moreover, because it comprises all the infinite worlds, and nothing is excluded from it, the differentiation of oneness during the second journey is the broadest circle of manifestation. 59.5

As for the fruit of this name, when it is invoked in a retreat it allows one to witness the Creator, but it cuts one off from divine oneness and is therefore inappropriate for the seeker of oneness. And God knows best. 59.6

اسمه القاهر جلّت قدرته

١،٦٠ هو من سورة الأنعام في قوله تعالى ﴿وَهُوَ ٱلْقَاهِرُ فَوْقَ عِبَادِهِۦ﴾ واتّفق على إيراده أبو الحكم والبيهقيّ ومعناه الغالب والمتكبّر بقدرته والغلبة هنا لها اعتبارات.

٢،٦٠ منها أن تكون غلبة الرحمة للغضب كما حكى الرسول عنه تعالى أنّه يقول غلبت رحمتي غضبي ومعناه ظهور أحكام الرحمة فيمنع أحكام الغضب التي هي صورة الانتقام فيكون هذا حال رحمته لعباده ولذلك نسبهم إليه في قوله تعالى ﴿وَهُوَ ٱلْقَاهِرُ فَوْقَ عِبَادِهِۦ﴾ أي فوق مرتبة المؤاخذة لهم بذنوبهم.

٣،٦٠ ومنها أنّ الغلبة لله تعالى على من يحاربه عزّ وجلّ من معنى قوله ﴿فَأْذَنُواْ بِحَرْبٍ مِّنَ ٱللَّهِ﴾ والحرب هنا مجاز فيكون معنى الغلبة المعاقبة لهم بذنوبهم ومنها أن يكون القاهر بمعنى أن يقهرهم على يد رسوله والمؤمنين بأن ينصر أولياءه على أعدائه فهو الغالب تعالى من حقيقة ألا ﴿إِنَّ حِزْبَ ٱللَّهِ هُمُ ٱلْغَٰلِبُونَ﴾.

٤،٦٠ ومنها أن تكون الغلبة له تعالى في مراتب العبّاد بأن ينصرهم على الشياطين بملائكته فإنّه عليه السلام قال قلب العبد بين لمّتين لمّة الملك ولمّة الشيطان فما تجدونه من الخير فمن لمّة الملَك وما تجدونه من الشرّ فمن لمّة الشيطان فإذا قوي لمّة الملك غلب وقهر لمّة الشيطان فهو القاهر سبحانه.

٥،٦٠ ومنها أن ينصر عباده الصوفيّة بأن يقوّيهم على تبديل أخلاقهم المذمومة بما هو محمود من الأخلاق ومنها ما يخصّ المحبّين بأن ينصر الغرام بجلاله تعالى على التشاغل عنه بعواذل الأكوان أو بالغرام بمحاسن الصور فيشغلهم بصور المحاسن القدسيّة.

Al-Qāhir: The Triumphant

60.1 This is from the Surah of the Cattle in the verse: «He is the triumphant over His servants».[364] Both Ibn Barrajān and al-Bayhaqī agree it is a divine name. It means He who predominates and is Proud through His power. In this context, predominance has many meanings.

60.2 Among them is the predominance of mercy over wrath. To this effect, the blessed Messenger quotes God as saying: "My mercy triumphs over My wrath,"[365] which means that the manifestation of the properties of mercy withhold the properties of wrath, or the form of vengeance. This then is the state of His mercy toward His servants, and that is why He ascribes them to Him in the verse: «He is the Triumphant over His servants»; that is, He is above the level of making them account for their sins.

60.3 Also among them is God's predominance over those who wage war on Him, according to the meaning of the verse «Be aware that God will war with you».[366] War here is metaphorical, and predominance here is taken to mean punishment for their sins. Among these meanings, moreover, is that He predominates over them through the hand of His Messenger and the believers by assisting His friends over His enemies, for He is the Triumphant through the reality of «Indeed the party of God are the triumphant».[367]

60.4 Another example: Predominance belongs to Him at the levels of the worshippers, in that He gives them victory over the devils through His angels, for the Messenger says: "The heart of the servant is caught between two promptings: the prompting of an angel and the prompting of Satan. Thus, whatever good you encounter is from the prompting of an angel, and whatever evil you encounter is from the prompting of Satan."[368] When the prompting of the angel is strengthened, it predominates and triumphs over Satan, and so God is the Triumphant.

60.5 Another example: He assists His servants among the Sufis by giving them the strength to transform their base character traits into praiseworthy ones. Another: He assists the lovers' passion against distraction by the reproach of others, or helps them to overcome their attraction to forms by busying them with the splendors of holiness.

٦،٦٠ ومنها نصر العارفين بتجلّيه لهم بما يفنيهم عن ذواتهم ظاهرها وباطنها حتّى يلحقون بمقام الوقفة إمّا دفعة وإمّا بالتدريج فتكون الغلبة قهر العرفان للنكران وغلبة الأنوار للأغيار.

٧،٦٠ ومنها غلبة التفصيل للوحدانيّة المطبقة والمغالبة هنا من مراتب إلٰهيّة معنويّة يتَمَعّنَاها المسافر في السفر الثاني فيكون باطنه ميدان هذه المحاربة إلى أن يتغلّب مقام الوقفة بنصرة الحقّ تعالى لمقام القطبيّة وثَمّ اعتبارات أخرى كثيرة يطول ذكرها.

٨،٦٠ وأمّا ثمرة هذا الذكر بهذا الاسم فإنّها تظهر بحسب هذه المراتب التي ذُكرت فمن كان من أهل مقام منها وذكر هذا الاسم في خلوته حصلت له غلبة مراده على ضدّه والله أعلم.

اسمه القادر جلّت قدرته

١،٦١ هو من سورة الأنعام في قوله تعالى ﴿قُلْ هُوَ ٱلْقَادِرُ عَلَىٰٓ أَن يَبْعَثَ عَلَيْكُمْ﴾ وانفرد بإيراده أبو الحكم ومعنى القدرة التمكّن ممّا أراده فهو قادر على الفعل والترك الوجوديّين لأنّ العدم لا يقبل الفعل ولا الترك وهو قسم المستحيل والتمكّن هو في حضرة الإمكان لأنّه تعالى هو الذي صيّره ممكنًا بقدرته كما يصيّر المستحيل على تلك الحالة.

٢،٦١ واعلم أنّ القدرة خصوص وصف في الإرادة لأنّها ظهور المراد على وفق العلم الذاتيّ الناشئ عن الحياة الذاتيّة وقولي الذاتيّ ليخرج العلم المتشكّل في الأذهان الذي يفسده

Another example: The assistance He gives to the recognizers by disclosing Himself to them such that He causes them to pass from their own selves, both outwardly and inwardly, until they arrive at the station of halting either all at once, or gradually in degrees. This predominance is the triumph of direct recognition over obliviousness, and the predominance of light over separative entities. 60.6

Another: The predominance of differentiation over multilayered oneness. The predominance here is from the divine supersensory levels, whose meanings are assumed by the journeyer during the second journey. Thus his inner dimension is the site of this contest until the station of halting is predominated by God's assistance of the station of axial sainthood. And there are many more considerations too long to mention. 60.7

The fruits of invoking this name manifest according to the aforementioned levels. The person who belongs to one of these stations and invokes this name in his retreat will achieve a predominance of his intended goal over its opposite. And God knows best. 60.8

Al-Qādir: The Able

This name is from the verse of the Surah of the Cattle: «Say: He is able to send upon you».[369] Only Ibn Barrajān mentions it as a divine name. The meaning of "ability" is to possess the power to achieve what one desires. He thus has the ability for both activity and inactivity. For nonexistence, which has no receptivity for activity or passivity, pertains to the category of impossibility. Ability, however, pertains to possibility because it is God who renders it possible through His ability, just as He renders the impossible impossible. 61.1

Power is a specific quality of Will, because it is the manifestation of what is desired in accordance with the essential Knowledge that issues from essential Life. I say "essential Knowledge" in order to distinguish it from knowledge constructed in the mind that can be corrupted by forgetfulness. For God is exalted above such knowledge. However, the latter kind of knowledge may be 61.2

النسيان جلّ الله تعالى عن ذلك وإن كان ثابتاً له في مراتب القائمين به على معنى نفي الأغيار وبذلك الاعتبار.

٣،٦١ وأصل القدرة للرحمٰن تبارك وتعالى إذ هو الوجود المحض إذ لا حظّ للعدم فيه فلا يقف تصرّفه عند غاية ولا نهاية وبذلك ﴿هُوَ عَلَىٰ كُلِّ شَيْءٍ قَدِيرٌ﴾ والقدرة كلّها لله تعالى فلا يكون مقدور بين قادرين فالفعل كلّه فعله ولذلك من رآى الأشياء كلّها منه تعالى فقد برئ من الشرك وسلم من الحساب وأمّا من ادّعى أنّ الفعل له فالحساب متوجّه في حقّه ومن نوقش الحساب عُذّب.

٤،٦١ وإثبات أنّ القدرة لله تعالى ظاهر حتّى للأطفال فإنّ احتياج المقدور إلى قادر هو في بداية العقول والموجودات مصنوعة في العقول واحتياج المصنوع إلى الصانع ضروريّ وهذه المسألة يعسر على السالكين الخلاص فيها إلّا بعد مشقّات في المجاهدة وترقّيات في السلوك حتّى يحصل الفناء فيكون النظر نظر الحقّ تعالى فيرى نفسه فيجد الحقّ وينتفي المقدور بالجملة والمصنوع وهذا هو رفع الحدث والوضاءة الإلٰهيّة في قول من صحّت نيّته في قوله نويتُ بوضوئي هذا رفع الحدث.

٥،٦١ فالقادر في مراتب الحجاب هو الحاكم على عقول أهل الاغتراب وتعلّق القدرة بقوله ﴿كُن فَيَكُونُ﴾ هو تعلّق الشيء بنفسه باعتبارين مختلفين فإنّ قوله فعله وقد ورد في الحديث النبويّ إنّ الله تعالى خلق الجبال وقال بها على الأرض هكذا وأشار بيده فعبّر عن القول بالفعل وعن الفعل بالقول.

٦،٦١ وثمرة هذا الذكر تنفع أهل استبعاد خرق العوائد فإذا ذكره في خلوته انغمر باطنه بصحّة ذلك بوجه ما والله أعلم.

affirmed in Him with respect to the levels of those who, in subsisting through Him, negate the realm of separative entities.

The root of power pertains to the All-Merciful, because the latter is pure existence and nonexistence has no share therein. His dominating power thus has no limit and no end, and it is in this way that «He has power over all things».[370] All power belongs to God, and all objects of power are controlled by His ability alone. For all activity is His activity. Therefore, to see that all things are from Him is to be exonerated from the sin of associationism and to be safe from the reckoning. The reckoning is aimed at those who claim to act: "And whoever is interrogated during the reckoning will be chastised."[371] 61.3

Affirming that power belongs to God is even obvious to children, for the dependence of an object of power on an able subject is ingrained from childhood. Moreover, existents are constructed by the intellect, and the dependence of the construct upon a constructer is self-evident. This issue, however, is difficult for wayfarers to overcome without hardship in spiritual struggle and ascension to the point of attaining annihilation. With this, their gaze becomes the gaze of the Real, and they find the Real each time they see themselves, when, along with the constructs, the objects of power are entirely negated. This is the "removal of impurities" and the divine ablutions of the person with sound intention when he says: "Through performing the ritual ablution I intend to remove impurities of temporality."[372] 61.4

Thus, at the levels of the veils, the Able rules over the intellects of those who experience separation from God. The attachment of power to an object in the verse: «"Be!" And it is»[373] is the attachment of a thing to itself in two different respects. For His speech is His act, and it is related that the blessed Prophet said, "God created the mountains, and He said, 'Let them be upon the earth like so,'" making a gesture with his hand.[374] Thus he expressed speech by reference to act, and act by reference to speech. 61.5

The fruits of this invocation are beneficial for those who doubt the likeliness of supernatural events. When invoked during a retreat, in a certain sense their inner being is inundated by its truth. And God knows best. 61.6

اسمه القاضي عزّ وجلّ

١،٦٢ هو في سورة الأنعام في قوله تعالى ﴿وَٱللَّهُ يَقۡضِي بِٱلۡحَقِّ﴾ وفي سورة النحل ﴿يَقۡضِي بَيۡنَهُمۡ﴾ واتّفق على إيراده البيهقيّ وأبو الحكم دون الغزاليّ ومعناه أنّه الذي يرجَع إلى حكمه بالطاعة وقضاة الحقّ مستندون إلى هذا الاسم وهم القضاة الذين هم في الجنّة قال عليه السلام القضاة ثلاثة قاض في الجنّة وقاضيان في النار.

٢،٦٢ والاسم القاضي يرجع إلى الاسم العالم والاسم القاهر فهو تعالى يقضي بين عباده أمّا في الدنيا فعامّ فيها حتّى بين طبائع الموجودات فيحكم بينهما حكمًا إيجاديًا حتّى بين أمزجة المعادن والنبات والحيوان والإنسان فيعطي كلّ مرتبة حقّها في تفاصيل حقائق ذواتها الظاهرة والباطنة وفي أخلاق موجوداته الظاهرة والباطنة فيجزي كلّ موجود وصفه كما قال تعالى ﴿سَيَجۡزِيهِمۡ وَصۡفَهُمۡ﴾ أي يجري أحكام أوصافهم عليهم فهو قضاء منه تعالى بينهم بالحقّ.

٣،٦٢ وهو تعالى القاضي بين الأناسيّ في مظاهر ذواتهم فيقضي على ألسنة الخلفاء والسلاطين والأمراء والقضاة وفروع هؤلاء بالحقّ الذي هو وصف المقضيّ عليهم فأمّا من حكم منهم بالحقّ فظاهر أنّه حكم الله تعالى وأمّا من حَكَم بالباطل فموجّه بوجه وصف المقضيّ عليهم كما تكونوا يولّى عليكم يد الله على قلب المِلك فالحقّ تعالى هو القاضي في الأقضية كلّها وسواء كان الملوك مسلمين أو غيرهم فمن شهد أنّ الله هو القاضي لم يمقت أحدًا منهم بحكم حكم به.

٤،٦٢ وأمّا أقضيته في الآخرة فهو الحساب وقد ذُكر في اسم غير هذا وأقضيته تعالى إنّما هي تجلّيات وفي القيامة يظهر ذلك ظهورًا تامًّا ويرى الناس العدل الإلهيّ ﴿فَلَا تُظۡلَمُ نَفۡسٞ شَيۡـٔٗاۖ وَإِن كَانَ مِثۡقَالَ حَبَّةٖ مِّنۡ خَرۡدَلٍ أَتَيۡنَا بِهَا﴾ ومحاكمة كلّ

Al-Qāḍī: The Judge

This is from the verse in the Surah of the Cattle: «God judges according to the truth»,[375] and in the Surah of the Bee: «He judges between them».[376] Both al-Bayhaqī and Ibn Barrajān agree it is a divine name, but al-Ghazālī does not. It means the one whose decree is met with obedience. Truthful judges draw support from this name, and they are described as the judges of the Garden. The blessed Messenger says: "There are three types of judges: one in the Garden, and two in the Fire."[377] 62.1

Moreover, the Judge stems from the Knowing and the Triumphant, for He judges between His servants. In this world, His judgment pervades all things, including the natural constituents of existents, which He judges through His existentiating decree. It also includes the constitutions of minerals, plants, animals, and humans, for He gives each level its rightful due by inwardly and outwardly differentiating the realities of their essences. And it includes the outer and inner character traits of His creatures, for He recompenses each according to their qualities, as He says: «He shall recompense them for their qualities»;[378] that is, He recompenses them according to the properties of their qualities. This therefore is a judgment according to the truth among them. 62.2

Furthermore, He judges between humans according to the outward appearances of their souls. He issues His judgments through the tongues of caliphs, sultans, emirs, judges, and their subordinates according to the truth, and the truth is the quality of those who are judged. It is obvious that the judgment of those who judge according to the truth is God's judgment. Those who judge according to falsehood are directed by the quality of those upon whom the judgment is carried out. "As you are, so shall you be presided over";[379] "The Hand of God is upon the king's heart."[380] In all cases, the Real is the Judge, regardless of whether the kings are Muslim or not. Therefore, whoever witnesses that God is the Judge will not be hostile to any judge because of the judgment that they decree. 62.3

His decree in the next world is the Reckoning, which has been discussed under another name. His decrees, moreover, are actually self-disclosures. At the Resurrection, this will be completely manifest and people will see the divine justice. «No soul will be wronged in the least; even if a deed is the 62.4

أحد يوم ذلك هو من نفس وجوده وليست المحاسبة على تعاقب لكلّ أحد بمفرده بل يحاسَبون جميعهم دفعة واحدة حتّى يعتقد كلّ أحد أنّ المحاسبة معه وحده وذلك لإحاطة الحقّ تعالى بالظواهر والبواطن فهو يحاسب كلّ موجود من نفسه وفي الحقيقة إنّما يحاسب نفسه ومن هنا كانت محاسبة الإنسان نفسه أنفع من محاسبة غيره له قال صلّى الله عليه وسلّم استفت قلبك وإن أفتاك المفتون.

٥،٦٢ وينتفع من ذكر هذا الاسم في الخلوة خصوصاً لمن يتردّد في الأمور جهلاً فيقضي الله تعالى له في باطنه بشهود الحقّ تعالى والله أعلم.

اسمه الفالق دام جوده

١،٦٣ هو من سورة الأنعام في قوله تعالى ﴿فَالِقُ ٱلْحَبِّ وَٱلنَّوَىٰ﴾ انفرد بإيراده أبو الحكم وله معان كثيرة كـ﴿فَالِقُ ٱلْإِصْبَاحِ﴾ لأنّ الفلق هو الصباح والمراد بـ﴿فَالِقُ ٱلْحَبِّ وَٱلنَّوَىٰ﴾ أنّه تعالى الذي يفلق الحبّة بالنبات منها وكذلك النواة والحبّة هي حبّة الحنطة والشعير وسائر الحبوب والنواة من التمر معروفة.

٢،٦٣ وفي الآية أعقب تعالى قوله ﴿فَالِقُ ٱلْحَبِّ وَٱلنَّوَىٰ﴾ بقوله ﴿يُخْرِجُ ٱلْحَيَّ مِنَ ٱلْمَيِّتِ وَمُخْرِجُ ٱلْمَيِّتِ مِنَ ٱلْحَيِّ﴾ وفي هذا مفهومان أحدهما إخراج ﴿ٱلْحَيَّ مِنَ ٱلْمَيِّتِ﴾ عموماً فيدخل هذا الاسم في الاسم المحيي وكذلك القول في إخراج ﴿ٱلْمَيِّتِ مِنَ ٱلْحَيِّ﴾ فيدخل في الاسم المميت أيضاً والثاني أن يريد بإخراج

weight of a mustard seed, We shall bring it forth».[381] The judgment of each individual on that day will be in terms of their own existence. The process of reckoning will not take place sequentially, individual by individual. Rather, they will all be called to account simultaneously, such that each will believe that he alone is being called because the Real encompasses them inwardly and outwardly. Thus, through His very Self He calls each existent to account, for in reality He is calling into account none but Himself. It is in this sense that it is more beneficial for a human being to call himself to account than for another to do so. The blessed Messenger says: "Consult your heart, regardless of what counsel others may offer you."[382]

Invoking this name in the retreat is beneficial, especially for the person indecisive in his affairs due to his ignorance. By granting him inward witness of the Real, God will judge for him. And God knows best. 62.5

Al-Fāliq: The Splitter

It is from the verse of the Surah of the Cattle: «He who splits the grain and the date pit».[383] Only Ibn Barrajān considers it to be a divine name. It has many meanings, such as «He who splits the sky into dawn»[384] because the "split" is the morning. Moreover, what is meant by «He who splits the grain and the date pit» is that He splits the seed as well as the date pit by the plant inside. A seed, moreover, can be a seed of wheat, barley, or any kind of grain, whereas a date pit is well known. 63.1

In this verse, God follows «He who splits the grain and the date pit» with «He brings forth the living from the dead, and He brings forth the dead from the living».[385] Two points can be understood from this. The first is that He brings forth the living from the dead in general. As such, this name is included within the Life-Giver. The same holds for His bringing forth the «dead from the living», whereby this name is included within the Death-Giver as well. The second point is that bringing forth the «living» refers to plants, since their growth heralds their life. Moreover, bringing forth the «dead from the 63.2

﴿ٱلْحَىِّ﴾ يعني النبات لنموّه المؤذن بحياته وإخراج ﴿ٱلْمَيِّتِ مِنَ ٱلْحَىِّ﴾ أي يميّز ما مات من الحبّة والنواة حال الإنبات عمّا نمى منها فكان نباتاً وهذا المفهوم خاصّ فأمّا عموم المفهوم فسيأتي وقد ذُكر في الاسم المحيي والاسم المميت.

٣،٦٣ وأمّا المفهوم الخاصّ بالحبّ والنّوى فهو اعتبار دخول الاسم الفالق في الاسم الرازق قال ابن عبّاس في تفسير قوله تعالى ﴿وَفِى ٱلسَّمَآءِ رِزْقُكُمْ وَمَا تُوعَدُونَ﴾ أنّه المطر والمقصود نبات الزرع والرزق من الرازق تعالى في مضمون قوله تعالى و﴿رِزْقُكُمْ﴾ في السماء ﴿وَمَا تُوعَدُونَ﴾ نبات الزرع ففيه معنى فالق الحبّ.

٤،٦٣ وإذا فُرّع على[١] قاعدة المفهوم العامّ كان كلّ نكاح منتج في معنى ﴿فَالِقُ ٱلْحَبِّ وَٱلنَّوَىٰ﴾ وقد وقع في نفوس الناس أن يفرّقوا بين فالق الحبّة بقولهم بارئ النّسمة فيقولون في القسم وغيره فالق الحبّة وبارئ النّسمة مجمعون في المعنى الواحد بين فالق الحبّة وبارئ النّسمة فقد جعلوا النكاح من المعنى بعينه فكلّ نتاج داخل في معنى هذا الاسم.

٥،٦٣ ومن تحقّق سرّ الله تعالى في طبائع الموجودات جعل تولّد المعادن أيضاً من هذا المعنى فإنّ السرّ الإلهيّ واحد في الجميع والمدد متّصل فيه من غيب الذات المقدّسة إلى عالم شهادتها متّصلاً غير منفصل وهذه أحكام الاسم الخلّاق يجري بها الاسم الفالق في طرق الإيجاد.

٦،٦٣ وهذا الاسم ينفع أرباب الخلوات في ذكرهم إيّاه نفعاً بالغاً ويسرع بالفتح عليهم إذا كان معه الاسم القيّوم أو الحيّ ويبطئ إذا ذُكر مع لا إله إلّا الله والله أعلم.

---

١ آ: معنى. ساقطة من: ب، ج.

living» means that He sets apart that which during the plant's growth died within the grain and the date pit from that which grew out of it to become a plant. This is the specific understanding of the verse. The general understanding will come later, and it has also been discussed under the Life-Giver and the Death-Giver.

The specific understanding of «the grain and the date pit» is to consider how the Splitter pertains to the Provider. In his comment on the verse «In the sky is your provision and what you were promised»,[386] Ibn ʿAbbās says that it means rain and refers to the sowing of plants. Moreover, the provision from the Provider is implied in the verse «in the sky is your provision» and the sowing of plants «you were promised». This is how it encompasses the meaning of «He who splits the grain». 63.3

When this general principle is applied to specifics, then every act of procreation that produces offspring pertains to the meaning of «He who splits the grain and the date pit». In fact, it occurs to people to make a further distinction in «He who splits the grain» by using the expression "The Creator of living creatures" so that in taking an oath, for instance, they say, "He who splits the grain and creates living creatures," bringing together both He who splits the grain and He who creates living creatures under one meaning. Thus they identify the act of procreation with its basic meaning, wherefore the production of any offspring pertains to the meaning of this name. 63.4

Whoever attains realization of God's secret within the natural constituents of existents takes the generation of minerals as pertaining to this meaning as well. For the divine secret is one within all things, and His replenishment extends from the unseen realm of the Holy Essence to its visible realm of the all. His replenishment is continuous, not disconnected, and it consists of the properties of the Ever-Creating. The Splitter runs its course by these properties through the pathways of existentiation. 63.5

The invocation of this name has a far-reaching benefit for those in spiritual retreat. If accompanied by the Self-Subsisting or the Living, it hastens their spiritual opening and delays it if invoked with "no god but God." And God knows best. 63.6

اسمه اللطيف تبارك اسمه

١،٦٤ هو من سورة الأنعام في قوله تعالى ﴿وَهُوَ يُدْرِكُ ٱلْأَبْصَـٰرَ وَهُوَ ٱللَّطِيفُ﴾ واتّفق على إيراده الأئمّة الثلاثة.

٢،٦٤ واعلم أنّ الاسم اللطيف يلحق الاسم الخالق والاسم المصوّر والاسم الهادي. فأمّا لحاقه للاسم الخالق فللطف مدارجه الخلّاقيّة في التوصيل إلى إعطاء وجود المتكوّنات من المعادن والنبات وسائر أنواع الحيوانات في ظلمات الأرض في المعدن وفي أصول الأشجار والنبات وفي بطون البحار فيما يتكوّن من السابحات وفي ظهور الآباء وأرحام الأمّهات كلّ ذلك من الاسم اللطيف سبحانه فإنّ مدارج التكوين لطيفة لصغر أجزاء ما يتصرّف فيه منها فكأنّها تصغر لطفاً عن الحواسّ المحسّات وتدقّ للطفها عن مواقع المعاينات.

٣،٦٤ وأمّا لحاقه للاسم المصوّر فإنّ نصيب الخلّاق تخليق المادّة أي تقديرها فمعنى خلق قدّر وبعد الخلق يكون التصوير وهو نصيب الاسم المصوّر ومعنويّة الاسم اللطيف في التصوير العصمة اللازمة من الغلط في التصوير فإنّ اللطف أيضاً التأنّي والرفق وبهما تقع العصمة في التصوير فلا يتصوّر من مادّة إلّا ما يخصّ نوعاً هو المطلوب منها.

٤،٦٤ وأمّا لحاقه بالاسم الهادي فإنّ الهادي إنّما يهدي بحقيقة اللطف فإنّ مدارج الهداية لطيفة وإذا اعتبرت أنّ اللطف ملاقاة كلّ موجود بما يستحسنه منك فاشهد معنى الاسم اللطيف في كلّ ما تستلطفه من استنشاق النسيم إذا هبّ وارتشاف الماء العذب وإدراك الملائم من الأغذية والفواكه والمحسوسات ممّا تشاكل عنها وتشابه واستخراج ما في الضمائر من السرّ المصون من مواقع ملاحظات العيون وانفعال الأسماع من لطف ما يلائم من السماع وتنعّم الأرواح من الرياحين وغيرها وطيب الأرواح ولذاذة اللمس والذوق وسريان نشوة المحبّة والشوق وما وُعد به من النعيم المقيم من مواهب الجواد الرحيم كلّ ذلك من الاسم اللطيف الذي هو بمعاني الرحمة مطيف.

Al-Laṭīf: The Subtle

This is from the verse of the Surah of the Cattle: «but He perceives the faculty of sight, and He is the Subtle».[387] The three scholars agree it is a divine name. 64.1

The Subtle joins to the Creator, the Form-Giver, and the Guide. Its association with the Creator is due to the subtlety of its creative pathways in bestowing existence upon engendered phenomena among minerals, vegetation, and every kind of living thing within the depths of the earth, such as metals and the roots of trees and plants, and in the deep seas where aquatic creatures are engendered, and in the loins of fathers and the wombs of mothers. All of that is from the glorious name the Subtle. Its engendering pathways are subtle due to the smallness of the parts it exercises control over. They are too small for the sensory faculties, and too minute to be seen. 64.2

It is associated with the Form-Giver: the function of the Ever-Creating is to create the material substratum; that is, to measure it out, since "to create" means "to measure out." After creation comes form-giving, and this is the function of the Form-Giver. At the supersensory level, the Subtle protects the process of form-giving from error. For subtlety is also gentle deliberation, and this is how form-giving is protected from error. Thus, a material substratum only takes on a form applicable to its specific species. 64.3

It is associated with the Guide: The Guide only guides through the reality of subtle gentleness, for the pathways of guidance are subtle. When you consider that subtle gentleness is the joining of every existent with what it finds pleasing, then you witness the meaning of subtle gentleness in everything you deem to be subtly gentle, including inhaling a fragrant scent; sipping fresh water; enjoying agreeable foods, fruits, or similar sensorial objects; extracting the inmost secret from a soul through the glance of an eye; listeners reacting to the soothing gentleness of devotional music and poetry; the joy that one's spirit finds in fragrant herbs, pleasant scents, touch, and taste; the intoxicating flow of love and yearning; and His promise of enduring bliss as a gift from the Munificent Merciful One. All of that is from the Subtle, which circumambulates around the transcendent meanings of divine mercy. 64.4

وذكر هذا الاسم ينفع في الخلوة كثيف الطبع فيلطف وأهل المشاهدة يقوى به ٥،٦٤
شهود من منهم يضعف والله أعـلم.

Invoking this name in a retreat will benefit someone with a dense natural constitution, because it will render him subtler. It will strengthen a witness's witnessing if it has weakened. And God knows best. 64.5

سورة الأعراف

وفيها ثلاثة أسماء

اسمه البادئ سبحانه

١،٦٥ هذا الاسم الكريم أوّل الثلاثة الأسماء التي في سورة الأعراف وموضعه فيها قوله تعالى ﴿ كَمَا بَدَأَكُمْ تَعُودُونَ فَرِيقًا هَدَىٰ ﴾ انفرد بتخريجه البيهقيّ دونهما ومعناه أنّه فعل الخلق ابتداءً فلم يسبَق ففيه معنى البديع سبحانه.

٢،٦٥ واعلم أنّ البداءة والابتداء لاحقة لموجود موجود بما لا يتناهى والناس ﴿ فِي لَبْسٍ مِّنْ خَلْقٍ جَدِيدٍ ﴾ إلّا أنّ الابتداء لا ابتداء له فإنّه خلّاق بالفعل لا من بداءة وإنّما أشار بقوله ﴿ بَدَأَكُمْ ﴾ يعني عالمنا هذا وهو محدث كان الله ولا شيء معه ثمّ خلق الخلق وبسط الرزق والعوالم التي لا بداية للابتداء فيها لم يخاطب بها لأنّ الأنبياء عليهم السلام إنّما خاطبوا الناس على قدر عقولهم وعقولهم لم تدرك ما لا بداءة له ولا نهاية له ثمّ إنّ كلّ عالم عالم محدث لكن ليس للعوالم كلّ وهذه المسألة عسرة الفهم على العقول المحجوبة لأنّهم لا يعقلون عدم تناهي ما دخل في الوجود.

٣،٦٥ وإذا علمتَ أنّ معقول الابتداء المطلق لم نخاطَب به وأنّ الذي خوطبنا به هو ابتداء مضاف إلى هذا العالم فمعنى الاسم البادئ متعلّق بهذا العالم بحسب الخطاب لنا

The Surah of the Heights

The Surah of the Heights contains three names.

Al-Bādiʾ: The One Who Originates

This noble name is the first of the three in the Surah of the Heights, in the verse: «As He originated You, so will you return».[388] Al-Bayhāqī alone cites it as a divine name. It means that He actualizes creation from the beginning and has no precedent. Therefore, it contains the meaning of the Innovator. 65.1

Beginning-ness and origination are associated with every single existent, which are infinite in number, although people «are in uncertainty as to a new creation».[389] Origination, however, has no origination of its own, for He is Ever-Creating in actuality, not just in the beginning. When He says «He originated you», He alludes to our world, originated in time: "God was, and there was nothing with Him, then He created creation and lavished provision."[390] God does not speak directly about the universe, whose origination has no beginning, because the blessed Prophets only address people according to their intellectual capacities, and their intellects are incapable of grasping that which has no beginning and no end. Furthermore, each universe is a universe originated in time, although there is no totality to the universes. However, this issue is difficult to understand for the intellect that is veiled because it cannot conceive of an infinity of things entering into existence. 65.2

If you understand that God does not address us concerning unconditioned origination inasmuch as it is intelligible, and that He only addresses us concerning the origination of this universe, then the meaning of the One Who Originates is associated with this universe in respect to His address to us. But it is 65.3

وهو متعلّق بكلّ عالم عالم ممّا لم نخاطَب به لا إلى نهاية ولا من بداية وهذا هو اللائق بسعة الحقّ تعالى ولا يلزم ممّا قلناه قِدَم العالم بل قدم الخالق تعالى.

٤،٦٥ ومن شهد هذا الاسم رآى أثر الحقّ تعالى في كلّ مبتدأ وإنّما ابتداُه الحقّ تعالى أي أوجده ابتداءً ليقع عنه إخبار ما فكلّ مبتدأ له خبر وهي أحكام أحواله وأقواله وأفعاله في دنياه وأخراه من جليل أمره وحقيره وليس من شرط الإخبار أن يخبر عنها يخبر بل نفس تهيّئ الموجود لأن يخبر عن وجوده أو ذاته أو أحواله وأقواله وأفعاله هو إخبار بلسان الحال فالحقّ تعالى بدأها وبدأ إخبارها وهو محيط بالخبر والمخبَر به وعنه.

٥،٦٥ والذاكر لهذا الاسم ينتفع بالبدايات في أوّل بدءها ويشهد البدأ للاسم البادئ والله أعلم.

اسمه الهادي عمّت رحمته

١،٦٦ هو ثاني أسماء سورة الأعراف وشاهده قوله تعالى ﴿مَن يَهْدِ ٱللَّهُ فَهُوَ ٱلْمُهْتَدِى﴾ وهو ممّا اتّفق عليه الأئمّة الثلاثة ومعاني الاسم الهادي ذكرنا فيها وحدها ستّة كراريس في شرح الفاتحة في قوله تعالى ﴿ٱهْدِنَا ٱلصِّرَٰطَ ٱلْمُسْتَقِيمَ﴾.

٢،٦٦ وقد تقدّم في شرح الاسم المرسل أنّ الرسالة هي من الله تعالى بحقيقة اسمه الهادي عزّ وجلّ فتُعتبر معاني الهداية في كلّ مرتبة مرتبة من مراتب الأمّة مثل الإسلام والإيمان والإحسان والسكينة وهي معنى قوله تعالى ﴿فَٱسْتَقِمْ كَمَآ أُمِرْتَ﴾

also associated with every single universe that we are not addressed about, and these universes are infinite in number and without beginning. This, moreover, befits the all-embracingness of the Real. But what we have said does not necessarily imply that the universe is eternal, only that the Creator is eternal.

To witness this name is to see the trace of the Real in every beginning. For it 65.4
is the Real who begins it; that is, He brings it into existence at the beginning, in order for a report to be given about it. For each subject with a beginning has a predicated report, which are its properties, states, sayings, and acts in this life and in the next, whether great or small.[391] Moreover, report-giving is not contingent upon a report being provided by a report-giver. Rather, the predisposition of the existent itself to report about its existence, essence, states, sayings, and acts is a report expressed through the language of its state. For the Real begins it, and He begins its report-giving, and He encompasses the report, the report-giver, and the subject of the report.

To invoke this name is to benefit from the beginning of things when they 65.5
begin, and to witness that this beginning pertains to the One Who Originates. And God knows best.

Al-Hādī: The Guide

This is the second name in the Surah of the Heights, in the verse: «Whomso- 66.1
ever God guides, he is rightly guided».[392] It is one of the divine names agreed upon by all three eminent scholars. Our discussion of this name alone fills six booklets in our *Commentary on the Opening Surah* under the verse: «Guide us upon the straight path».[393]

We previously said in our commentary on the Sender that the Message 66.2
comes from God through the reality of the Guide. The realities of guidance can thus be observed from the standpoint of each level within the Muslim community, including submission, belief, spiritual excellence, and tranquility. The latter, moreover, corresponds to the meaning of the verse «So be upright as you have been commanded»;[394] that is, having uprightness, finding

أعني الاستقامة مع الطمأنينة بها وعدم منازعة النفس لمخالفتها فتشتمل على أداء الفرائض وزيادة النوافل الذين هما سبب حصول محبّة الحقّ تعالى لعبده من مضمون قوله عليه السلام ما تقرّب إليّ المتقرّبون بأفضل من أداء ما افترضته عليهم ولا يزال عبدي يتقرّب إليّ بالنوافل حتّى أحبّه ومن جملة النوافل مقام التصوّف وهو التخلّق بالأسماء الحسنى فإذا أحببته كنتُ سمعه الذي يسمع به وبصره الذي يبصر به معناه أريته ذلك وإلّا فكلّ أحد به يسمع وبه يبصر وإنّما الاختصاص أن يريه ذلك عياناً فهو الاصطفاء فهذه هي مدرجة الاسم الهادي في حقيقة الاسم المرسل.

وللاسم الهادي هداية أخرى هي في حقّ من لم تبلغه الدعوة مثل قسّ بن ساعدة ٣،٦٦
فإنّه هداه الله تعالى لا بواسطة رسول فلذلك كان أمّة وحده أو أمّة واحدة كما ورد الحديث وهذا هو ظاهر الاسم الهادي.

وثَمّ هداية أخرى شاملة يهتدي بها كلّ موجود إلى مصلحته دنيا وآخرة فإنّ ٤،٦٦
الطرق كلّها إليه تعالى تصل ومن هذه الحقيقة يدخل ظاهر الاسم المضلّ في حقيقة باطن الاسم الهادي ويتعيّن من باطن الاسم المضلّ مراتب تباين معنى باطن الاسم الهادي فإنّ ظاهر الاسم المضلّ إنّما باين ظاهر الاسم الهادي لا باطنه والذي باين باطن الاسم الهادي إنّما هو باطن الاسم المضلّ فبين كلّ مرتبتين في مقام واحد حدّ وفوقه مطلع يجمع بينهما فيه ثمّ يتعيّن في عين ذلك المطلع تباين آخر في مقام واحد غير ذلك المقام فتقع بينهما المباينة ثمّ يكون في ذلك المقام الآخر حدّ بين الاسمين المذكورين وفوقه مطلع كما ذُكر قبل حتّى ينتهي إلى الوحدانيّة المطبقة[١] والنهاية في تعداد المراتب متعذّرة لعدم تناهي ما يقع فيه التباين من موجودات لا نهاية لها وإنّما المراد

١ آ، ب، ج: المنطقة.

rest therein, and not struggling against opposition from the lower self. It thus includes the performance of the obligatory works, in addition to supererogatory devotions, which are a means to attaining God's love for His servant, as stated in His Holy Saying: "Those who seek My proximity do not draw near to Me through anything greater than what I made obligatory upon them. And My servant continues to draw near to Me through supererogatory devotions until I love him." The station of Sufism, which is the assumption of the traits of the most beautiful names of God, is one of these supererogatory devotions. The hadith continues: "And when I love him, I am the hearing with which he hears, and the seeing through which he sees."[395] That is, I show him that I am his hearing and seeing, for in fact everyone hears through Him and sees through Him. But to be elected is to be allowed to witness it with one's own eyes; it is to be chosen. This then is the route of ascension of the Guide through the reality of the Sender.

The Guide includes another type of guidance for those whom a Prophet's 66.3
call has never reached, such as Quss ibn Sāʿidah, whom God guided without the intermediacy of a Messenger. That is why he was "a nation unto himself" or "a single nation" as is narrated in the Prophetic Tradition;[396] and this is the outward dimension of the Guide.

There is another type of guidance that is all-inclusive. Through it, every 66.4
existent is guided to its worldly and otherworldly well-being. For every path leads to Him, and it is by virtue of this reality that the outer aspect of the Misguider is included within the inner reality of the Guide. Moreover, several levels are designated within the inner aspect of the Misguider, and these levels stand in contrast to the inner meaning of the Guide. For the outer aspect of the Misguider only stands in contrast to the outer aspect of the Guide, not to its inner aspect. Moreover, what stands in contrast to the inner aspect of the Guide is none other than the inner aspect of the Misguider. Therefore, there is a border between every two levels of a single station. Above that station lies a place of ascent that brings the two levels together, and within that place of ascent another contrast is designated by a station that is not that station, such that a further contrast occurs between them. In the following station, there is also a border between the two aforementioned names, with a place of ascent above it as previously mentioned, until it finally reaches multilayered unity. The end of this plurality of levels cannot be perceived because of the infinity of places where contrast occurs between an infinity of existents. So, what is

بوصول الأمر إلى الوحدانيّة المطبقة[١] لا أنها غاية بل أنّ الأسماء كلّها تفصيلها وشرح ما قُلتُه يذكَر مشافهة.

٥،٦٦ وذكر الاسم الهادي نافع جدًّا في الخلوة في كلّ مرتبة والله أعلم.

اسمه المضلّ

نعوذ به منه كما قال نعوذ بك منك

١،٦٧ هو ثالث اسم خرج من سورة الأعراف وهو كمال ما خرج منها وشاهده منها قوله تعالى ﴿وَمَن يُضۡلِلۡ فَأُوْلَٰٓئِكَ هُمُ ٱلۡخَٰسِرُونَ﴾ وانفرد بتخريجه البيهقيّ دونهما.

٢،٦٧ وقد ذكرنا بعض معانيه في شرح الاسم الهادي ومعاني الضلال كثيرة والمراد منها هنا ما قابل الرشاد وباينه وأصله أن يضيع عن القصد فلا يعرفه وأصله عند أهل الأذواق انحراف ويحصل في سلسلة عالم الخلق فيقع في عالم الأمر لأنّ عالم الخلق بالقصد الأوّل الذاتيّ يكون وعالم الأمر كاللازم اللاحق لحوقًا واجبًا لعالم الخلق وهما لله تعالى من حضرة الاسم الرحمٰن قال الله تعالى ﴿أَلَا لَهُ ٱلۡخَلۡقُ وَٱلۡأَمۡرُ﴾ ﴿تَبَارَكَ ٱللَّهُ أَحۡسَنُ ٱلۡخَٰلِقِينَ﴾ فنسب الحسن للخلق ولم ينسبه للأمر في قوله ﴿أَحۡسَنُ ٱلۡخَٰلِقِينَ﴾ وذلك لأنّ الانحراف عن مدرجة عالم الخلق يقع في عالم الأمر والانحراف لا ينسَب إليه الحسن إلّا من حضرة المطلع الجامع بين المتقابلين كما ذكرنا في الاسم الهادي.

---

١ آ، ب، ج: المنطقة.

meant by the attainment of multilayered unity is not that it is a furthest limit, but that the entirety of the names is its differentiation. However, what I have just said can only be explained orally.

During the retreat, invoking the Guide is very beneficial at every level. And God knows best. 66.5

Al-Muḍill: The Misguider

We seek refuge from Him, for as the blessed Prophet said, "With You, we seek refuge from You."[397]

This is the third and last name taken from the Surah of the Heights, from the verse: «Whoever He misguides, they are the losers».[398] Only al-Bayhaqī includes it as a divine name. 67.1

In our commentary on the Guide, we have mentioned some of its meanings, and the meanings of misguidance are many. Here, what is meant by them is what stands counter and in contrast to right conduct. The root of misguidance is to lose sight of, and to not recognize, one's intended goal. According to those who know through tasting, it is at root a deviation that is attained in the chain of the realm of creation, and then occurs in the realm of command. For the realm of creation comes into existence by the primary intent of the Essence, whereas the realm of command is like a concomitant joined by necessity to the realm of creation. Both, moreover, come from God through the presence of the All-Merciful. God says: «Surely to Him belongs the creation and the command»; «Exalted is God, the most beautiful of creators».[399] Thus He ascribes excellence to creation and not to command when He says: «the most beautiful of creators». This is because deviation from the path of ascension of the realm of creation occurs in the realm of command, and excellence is not ascribed to deviation except from the horizon that brings together the two contrasts, as we mentioned under the Guide. 67.2

٣،٦٧ وفي المطلعات يلوح للسالك وجه الحقيقة وتُجمع له معاني الأضداد ويأتلف في المختلف كما يتألّف في المؤتلف ولي في المؤتلف والمختلف بيتان وهما

عِنْدِي بِكَ عِلْمٌ عَنْهُ تُطْوَى ٱلصُّحُفُ … فِيهِ أَبَدًا يَأْتَلِفُ ٱلْمُخْتَلِفُ
ٱللَّامُ خِلَافُهُ إِذَا مَا ٱنْفَرَدَتْ … لَكِنْ هِيَ هُوَ إِنْ عَانَقَتْهَا ٱلْأَلِفُ

٤،٦٧ فالاسم المضلّ يقابل الاسم الهادي في كلّ مرتبة مرتبة ممّا يظهر فيها حكمه أو ممّا يمكن أن يظهر فيها حكمه ولا يزال ذلك كذلك أبدًا أمّا في عالمنا فينتهي إلى الخلود في الجنان ويقف وإنّما يتعلّق التأبيد بالعوالم التي لا تتناهى فإنّ الاسم الهادي والاسم المضلّ يجريان في الأطوار إلى غير نهاية فيما لا نهاية له والإحاطة بما لا يتناهى هي أن يكون الواحد عين ما لا يتناهى لا إحاطة الشيء بالشيء غيره.

٥،٦٧ ولمراتب الاسم المضلّ وحدانيّات جزئيّة تنظم شمله في تعدادها حتّى ينغمس أهل تلك المراتب في الضلال وهم يرونه هدًى انغماسًا يعمون فيه عن رؤية ضدّه ولذلك إنّ كلّ ملّة ﴿بِمَا لَدَيْهِمْ فَرِحُونَ﴾ لأنّهم حزب وكلّ أمّة تخالف غيرها فإنّها تقاتل وتناضل عمّا يخصّ مقامها فينعكف كلّ على حاله ولي شعر يشبه هذا المعنى وهو

وَعَاكِفِينَ عَلَى ٱلصَّهْبَاءِ قَدْ جُمِعَتْ … شَتَاتُ شَمْلِهِمْ فِيهَا وَهُمْ فِرَقُ
طَوَتْهُمُ أَعْيُنُ ٱلسَّاقِي وَأَكْؤُسُهُ … حَتَّى كَأَنَّهُمُ فِي كَفِّهِ وَرَقُ
لَا يَعْرِفُونَ طَرِيقَ ٱلصَّحْوِ مُذْ سَكِرُوا … وَلَا ٱلظَّمَا بَعْدَمَا مِنْ رَاحَتَيْهِ سُقُوا

فهذه الغمرة هي وحدانيّة ما يرجع إلى الله تعالى من حضرة الاسم الجامع.

٦،٦٧ ولا يذكر هذا الاسم في الخلوة إلّا من لاح له وجه الحقّ منه والله أعلم.

The face of the Truth shines forth for the wayfarer from all horizons. Therein, the opposites come together. He finds compatibility in opposition, just as he finds compatibility in compatibility. Concerning opposition and compatibility, I wrote the following two verses: 67.3

Through You, I gain a knowledge that folds away the scrolls;
in that knowledge, oppositions are rendered forever compatible.
When it stands alone, the *lām* of the definite article (*alif-lām*) is opposed to it,
but becomes identical to it when embraced by the *alif*.[400]

Thus the Misguider stands face-to-face with the Guide at every level where the latter's properties either become or can become manifest. So it continues forever. In our universe, it ends at the eternal Garden. However, endlessness is associated with the infinite number of cosmoses, for the Guide and the Misguider flow infinitely through the infinite stages. Moreover, in order to encompass something that has no end, the One must be identical to the infinite and not such that one thing is encompassed by another thing. 67.4

Moreover, the levels of the Misguider comprise individual parts that bring together its numerical unity so those who pertain to levels of misguidance may plunge themselves into misguidance—even while they see it as guidance—in a manner that blinds them from seeing its opposite. That is why every community «rejoices in what they have»,[401] for they are different parties, and every nation disputes with other nations. Each fights and struggles for the station specific to it, and thus each one clings to its state. To this effect, I wrote the following verses: 67.5

Clinging to the wine that brought them together,
scattered as they were, separated into groups.
They are folded within the eyes of the wine pourer and his cups,
so they are like paper in his palm.
After intoxication, they have known neither the path of sobriety,
nor, after being sated through His hands, of thirst.[402]

This inundation is a oneness that harks back to God through the presence of the Gatherer.

This name is only invoked in the retreat by those upon whom the face of Reality shines through it. God knows best. 67.6

سورة الأنفال

وفيها اسم واحد يذكّر وهو

اسمه المغيث شمل جوده ورحمته

١،٦٨ هـذا الاسم الكريم خرج وحده من سورة الأنفال وشاهده قوله تعالى ﴿إِذْ تَسْتَغِيثُونَ رَبَّكُمْ فَٱسْتَجَابَ لَكُمْ﴾ وإنّما يستجيب للمستغيث الاسم المغيث وانفرد بتخريجه البيهقيّ رحمه الله وهو في معنى الناصر ﴿وَمَا ٱلنَّصْرُ إِلَّا مِنْ عِندِ ٱللَّهِ﴾ ويدخل في الاسم المجيب فلذلك حسن قوله تعالى ﴿فَٱسْتَجَابَ لَكُمْ﴾.

٢،٦٨ والاستغاثة طلب من المغيث على وجه الدعاء في حقّ الله تعالى وهو إنّما يعقل عند نازلة أو شدّة من الأمر ومراتب النوازل لا تنحصر في معاني الدنيا والآخرة وللمستغيث أن يقول واغوثاه فإن قالها ويريد ربّه تعالى فإنّما يريد يا مغيث وإن أراد بعض مخلوقاته فالإرادة مخطئة[١] بالنسبة إلى قصده وغير مخطئة[٢] في نفس الحقيقة إذ لا غوث إلّا بالله وأيضاً فما ثَمّ غيره وإن لم يعلم المستغيث.

٣،٦٨ فإن استغاث من نازلة الجوع فإنّما يطلب من الاسم المغيث بما فيه من معنى الاسم الرزّاق وإن استغاث من نازلة الفقر فإنّما يدع[٣] المغيث بما فيه من معنى الاسم المغني والغنى يتنوّع بما لا يحصر أنواعه وإن استغاث من نازلة الذلّ فإنّما يدعوا

١ و: محيطة. ٢ و: محيطة. ٣ و: يسأل.

The Surah of the Spoils

The Surah of the Spoils contains one name.

Al-Mughīth: The Deliverer

This noble name envelops His existence and mercy. It appears in the Surah of the Spoils in the verse: «When you called upon your Lord to deliver you and He responded to you».[403] It is only through the Deliverer that the petition of the caller for God's deliverance is granted. Of the three eminent scholars, only al-Bayhaqī affirms that this is a name of God. The Deliverer is synonymous with the Helper—«help is only from God»[404]—yet it also pertains to the Responsive, which is why He said: «and He responded to you». 68.1

Calling for deliverance is an appeal to the Deliverer by way of a supplication to God. It is invoked only during a crisis or a state of hardship—and the cosmic levels of such states are not limited to the meanings in this world and the next. The petitioner may say, "O my deliverance!" If he means to address his Lord, then he actually means "O Deliverer!" However, if he means to address some creature, then what he means is mistaken with respect to his intent, although in actuality it is also correct since there is no deliverance except God's. Besides, there is none but He, regardless of whether the petitioner for deliverance knows this or not. 68.2

When the petitioner calls for deliverance from a crisis of hunger, then he is appealing to the Deliverer insofar as it shares in the meaning of the Provider. When he calls for deliverance from a crisis of poverty, then he is beseeching the Deliverer insofar as it shares in the meaning of the Enricher—and the variation in types of enrichment is unlimited. When he calls for deliverance from a 68.3

الاسم المغيث بما فيه من الاسم المعزّ وبالجملة فالأسماء تتداخل ومعانيها تتفصّل بحسب القوابل والفواعل.

٤،٦٨ وحضرة الاسم المغيث تلاقي كلّ أحد بما سأل حاله فإنّ لسان الحال لا يخطئ ولسان المقال قد يخطئ وإن استغاث من نازلة دينيّة فقد استغاث بالاسم المغيث من حضرة الاسم الهادي ثمّ يصيبه من إغاثة المغيث بحسب ما يقتضيه حاله من طور هدايته الخاصّة بحاله ثمّ نوازل الدين كلّها من الاسم المضلّ في أطوار العبادة والتصوّف والعرفان والوقفة والتفصيل وليس في القطبيّة ضلال إذا صحّت أعني نهاية السفر الثاني وكذلك السفرين الأخيرين ليس فيهما ضلال.

٥،٦٨ ولا يمكن أنّ أحداً يستغيث إلّا ويغاث إمّا ظاهراً وإمّا باطناً وأمّا في مراتب نوازل الدنيا إذا فاته الغوث عُوّض عنه في مراتب الآخرة وأقلّ درجاته أنّ انفعال باطنه لطلب الغوث هي صفة كمال استيقظت فيها النفس لطلب منفعتها من سنة الغفلة التي اقتضاها رجاء الحال وعافية الجسم والدين والنفس المغمورة في ظلم لا تستبين ثمّ إنّ من استغاث الله عزّ وجلّ فلم ير ظاهر صورة الغوث فليعلم أنّ استمراره في الإغاثة هي من إغاثة البارئ عزّ وجلّ فإنّ حال المستغيث منه قربة.

٦،٦٨ وذكر هذا الاسم ينفع في الخلوة ينفع في وجود التفرقة والقساوة فيرفعهما والله أعلم.

crisis of abasement, then he is calling upon the Deliverer insofar as it partakes in the Exalter. In sum, the names interpenetrate and their meanings differ with respect to the passive recipients and the active agents involved.

The presence of the Deliverer also reciprocates the demands of each person's state. For direct, spiritual speech does not err, whereas non-direct, ordinary speech may err. When the petitioner calls for deliverance from a crisis of religion, then he is imploring the Deliverer from the presence of the Guide. He receives deliverance from the Deliverer in accordance with the dictates of his state at its specific stage of guidance. Moreover, all moments of religious crisis ensue from the presence of the Misguider in the stages of worship, Sufism, recognition, halting beyond all stations, and separation; but there is no misguidance at the level of the axial saint when it is truly attained—that is, the end of the second journey. Likewise, there is no misguidance in the two final journeys. 68.4

It is impossible for someone to call for deliverance without being delivered either outwardly or inwardly. However, if he does not receive deliverance from the levels of worldly crises, then he is compensated in the levels of the hereafter. The least of his degrees of deliverance is his own inward impulse to call upon deliverance, which is a quality of perfection that awakens in the soul. The soul thereby seeks to avail itself from the slumber of heedlessness caused by hankering after spiritual states and bodily and financial well-being, and by a soul that is submerged in desolate darkness. Moreover, whoever calls upon God for deliverance but fails to recognize its outward form should know that persistence in petitioning is an aspect of the deliverance of the Maker. For the state of petitioning is itself a cause of nearness to God. 68.5

Invoking this name during the spiritual retreat benefits the one who is in a state of dispersion and hardness of heart, for it removes these states. And God knows best. 68.6

سورة يونس عليه سلام

وفيها اسمان

اسمه الضارّ

نعوذ بالله منه اتباعًا للرسول عليه السلام

١،٦٩ هـذا الاسم الكريم ممّا اتّفق عليه الأئمّة الثلاثة وشاهده في سورة يونس قوله تعالى ﴿وَإِن يَمْسَسْكَ ٱللَّهُ بِضُرٍّ﴾ وهو في مقابلة الاسم النافع وسيأتي الكلام على الاسم النافع.

٢،٦٩ والضرر قد ينسَب إلى الله من حيث المراتب وقد ينسَب إلى الاسم الرحمٰن من حيث الإفراط في الرحمة وأمّا صور المراتب فمثل من هو في رتبة لا يقبل ما يريده من النفع ويحتاج إليه فيقع له الضرر لا بوجه وجوديّ بل بوجه عدميّ فيكون الاسم الضارّ في حقّه من لواحق الاسم الله.

٣،٦٩ وأمّا من يتعيّن في حقّه الضرر من مراتب الاسم الرحمٰن في ظهوراته الوجوديّة فمثل ما يزيد الاغتذاء عن قدر حاجة الجسم فينضرّ من وجه كان منفعة فزادت وكانت وجوديّة فأدّت إلى العدم ومثل من يصيبه المطر فيموت أو يتضرّر به وهو رحمة صارت في حقّه نقمة فنُسبت إلى الاسم الضارّ من حيث رجوعه إلى الاسم الرحمٰن بوجوديّته إذ معنى الرحمة هو الوجود وهو النافع بالقصد الأوّل ويلحقه من حيث أطواره أن يتعيّن به الاسم الضارّ وتفاصيل المعنيين المذكورين لا تتناهى

The Surah of Jonah

The Surah of Jonah has two divine names.

Al-Ḍārr: The Harmer

We seek refuge in God from Him, as the Prophet did.

This is one of the names all three scholars agree upon as divine. It occurs in the Surah of Jonah in the verse: «If God should touch you with harm, none can remove it».[405] It stands opposite to the Benefiter, which we will discuss below. 69.1

Harm can be ascribed to Allāh with respect to the levels, and it can be ascribed to the All-Merciful with respect to an excess of mercy. In terms of the forms of the levels, it is like the one who is at a level where he is not receptive to the benefit he desires and needs, and therefore experiences harm not in an existential, but in a privative sense. For him, the Harmer is therefore associated with the name Allāh. 69.2

He who experiences harm at the levels of existential manifestation of the All-Merciful is like someone who ingests more food than the body needs. He is thereby harmed by something beneficial that became excessive, or by something necessary for existence that led to privation. Another example is when rain causes death or inflicts harm. Rain is a mercy, but in this case it turns into a punishment ascribed to the Harmer inasmuch as it traces back to the All-Merciful existentially. For mercy means existence, and in its primary intent it is a cause of benefit. However, with respect to its stages, it joins with determinations of the Harmer. The details of these meanings are endless, and anyone who is graced with light should be able to distinguish between the 69.3

وكلّ أحد ممّن له نور يدرك أن يفصل هاتين المرتبتين على معانيه الجزئيّة ويردّ كلّ حقيقة من حقائق الاسم الضارّ إلى أصلها.

٤،٦٩ والاسم الضارّ كالاسم المضلّ في أنّه من عالم الأمر لا من عالم الخلق فإنّه ليس بالقصد الخلقيّ يكون الضرر ولا في صورة واحدة من صور المرتبتين المذكورتين لكن يلحق لحوقاً واجباً للوجود الرحمانيّ والرتب الإلٰهيّة ووقوعُ ذلك في مراتب غير متناهية.

٥،٦٩ وقد يدعو المضرور بمقابله أو بلسان حاله الاسم الواقي أو الدافع أو المغيث أو النافع فتقع الإجابة إمّا ظاهرة وإمّا باطنة ولو في كونه صار داعياً فإنّه لابس صورة عبادة نافعة فقد أجابه الاسم النافع ووقاه الواقي والدافع بذلك القدر من النفع وقد يستجاب له بعين مراده وبأبلغ ممّا كان في اعتقاده فيلحقه غوث الاسم الجواد بما فوق ٱلْحُسْنَىٰ وَٱلزِّيَادَةَ على العادة وبما هو خارق للعادة وذو الفضل يؤتي فضله من يشاء والرازق ﴿يَرْزُقُ﴾ عبده ﴿بِغَيْرِ حِسَابٍ﴾.

٦،٦٩ والضرر الواقع في حقّ المحجوب عن المطلوب في السلوك إلى وحدانيّة علّام الغيوب كلّها من النسب العدميّة من حضرة الاسم الله والذي يقع منها بالنسبة إلى الاسم الرحمٰن فهو قليل ومثاله من غلب عليه حرارة دم القلب فيغلي قلبه غضباً فيُحجب عن الانقياد إلى شيخه فيفوته المطلوب وسببه زيادة ما كان نفعاً لولا زيادته وكذلك السمن والشبع والجاه والمال والشباب اللواتي يحجبن.

٧،٦٩ وهذا الاسم لا ينفع في الخلوة إلّا لمن له مثل مقام أبي يزيد في قوله رضي الله عنه

أُحِبُّكَ لَا أُحِبُّكَ لِلثَّوَابِ   وَلٰكِنِّي أُحِبُّكَ لِلْعِقَابِ

فلو أجيب لا ينفع بحصول مطلوبه والله أعلم.

two levels according to their particularities, and to trace back to its root each reality of the Harmer.

Furthermore, the Harmer resembles the Misguider. It too is from the realm of command, not from the realm of creation. For harm does not come by way of creative design, nor does it appear in only one form from among the forms of these two levels. Rather, it necessarily joins to the existence of all-mercifulness and the levels of divinity, and it occurs at infinite levels. 69.4

The person who is afflicted by harm may call out to its opposing name, or he may call out in spiritual, nonverbal language to the Protector, or the Repeller, or the Deliverer, or the Benefiter. Thereupon, the response occurs either outwardly or inwardly. It may even occur by the fact that he has become someone who supplicates God, for he has clothed himself in a beneficial form of worship. In this sense, the Benefiter will have responded to him, the Protector will have protected him, and the Repeller will have brought him benefit. This person may also receive the exact response that he asked for, or even more than he had expected. He is therefore joined to the assistance of the Munificent in a manner that surpasses "that which is most beautiful and even more,"[406] either with or without a supernatural event. For the Bountiful bestows His bounty upon whomever He desires, and the Provider «provides» to His servant «without reckoning».[407] 69.5

The harm that afflicts the person who is veiled from progressing to the oneness of the Knower of the unseen comes from the nonexistential relations of the presence of Allāh. It is only rarely that harm comes from them in a way that pertains to the All-Merciful. An example of this is when a person is overcome by the heat of the blood in his heart so that he starts to boil in anger, and his anger veils him from surrendering to his spiritual master, and thus the object of his quest escapes him. The cause here is an excess in something that would have been beneficial were it not excessive. The same goes for being overweight, eating to the point of satiety, wealth, and youth, which can all veil him when in excess. 69.6

This name does not benefit in the retreat except for the one who has the station of the likes of al-Basṭāmī, may God be pleased with him, who said: 69.7

I love You, not for Your recompense,
    but rather for Your chastisement.[408]

Were he to receive a response, he would not benefit from the Object of his quest. And God knows best.

اسمه النافع عمّ خيره

١،٧٠ هـذا الاسم الثاني من سورة يونس وهو آخر ما خرج منها في قوله تعالى ﴿وَإِن يُرِدْكَ بِخَيْرٍ فَلَا رَآدَّ لِفَضْلِهِۦ﴾ وهو ممّا اتّفق عليه الأئمّة الثلاثة.

٢،٧٠ واعلم أن الاسم النافع عامّ في مراتب الاسمين الذين هما أصل الأسماء كلّها وهما الاسم الله والاسم الرحمٰن وذلك لأنّ النفع يوجد في مراتبه ولا إشكال في أنّه غير متناه لعدم تناهي مراتبه ويوجَد في المراتب المقابلة لمراتبه من الاسم الضارّ فيما لا يتناهى أيضاً وذلك لأنّ كلّ ضرر فهو نفع لظهور مراتب الضرر في الإيجاد حتّى الضرر في مصيبة الموت فإنّ الجسد ينتفع به الهوامّ ويزيد في كمّيّة الأرض وتتأهّل به الأرض إلى حصول كيفيّة لم تكن عليها ويكون بذلك الموت حياة اصطلاحيّة وغير اصطلاحيّة.

٣،٧٠ فلا وجود للضرر من كلّ وجه أصلاً فالنفع متعيّن في كلّ طور ولا كلّ للأطوار لعدم تناهي أنواعها فضلاً عن أشخاصها فيكون معنى الاسم النافع مساوقاً للاسم الخالق والمحيي والمميت بل ولأسماء لا تتناهى فإنّ أسماء الحقّ تعالى غير متناهية.

٤،٧٠ وسأضرب لك مثلاً في ذلك أمّا إن علمت أنّ عوالم الله لا تتناهى فسهل عليك أن تعترف بما نذكره وإن لم تعترف فسوف تعلم أن تنعّمات أهل الجنّة لا نهاية لها وللحقّ تعالى في طور كلّ موجود أو طور كلّ تنعّم معنًى يخصّ ذلك الموجود أو ذلك التنعّم فيستحقّ ذلك المعنى اسماً يمتاز به عن غيره في نفس الأمر وإن لم تعرفه أنت وأيضاً فإنّ اسم كلّ موجود وغير موجود ممّا لا يتناهى فإسميّته الخاصّة به لله تعالى لها نسبة إليه خاصّة تستحقّ اسماً إلٰهيّاً يميّزها عن غيره.

Al-Nāfiʿ: The Benefiter

This is the second and the last name taken from the Surah of Jonah, in the following verse: «should He desire any good for you, none can stand in the way of His bounty».[409] It is one of the names the three eminent scholars agree are divine. 70.1

The Benefiter pervades all levels of the two names that are the roots of all the names; namely, Allāh and the All-Merciful. For there is benefit in the levels of both root names. Moreover, the Benefiter's properties are without doubt infinite, since the levels of the root names are themselves infinite. Benefit is also found within the opposing levels of the Harmer, which are infinite too. Indeed, every harm is itself a benefit, including the harm of the affliction of death, since it is the manifestation of the levels of harm in existentiation, for by fertilizing the earth corpses provide benefit, and through them the earth is able to actualize a mode it did not previously have. In this way, in both the conventional and unconventional senses of the term, death becomes life. 70.2

Fundamentally, therefore, harm has no existence because benefit is actualized in every stage of existence, although the term "all" is not applied to these stages since their species are infinite, let alone their individuals. Thus, the supersensory meaning of the Benefiter is co-extensive with the Creator, the Life-Giver, the Death-Giver, and in fact with an infinite number of names, since the names of the Real are infinite. 70.3

I will give you an example. If you know that God's realms are infinite, then it will be easy for you to acknowledge what we are saying. But if you do not acknowledge this, then you will know that the pleasures of the people of the Garden are infinite, and that at the stage of every existent, or at the stage of every enjoyment, the Real has a supersensory meaning that is specific to that existent or that enjoyment such that the supersensory meaning is entitled to a name that distinguishes it from other similar things, regardless of whether you are aware of it or not. Furthermore, the name of each of the infinite existents and nonexistents has a name-ness that is specific to it, which in turn has a specific relation to God that entitles it to a divine name and distinguishes it from others. 70.4

٥،٧٠ فأمّا إن علمت أنّ ما في الوجود إلّا وجوده تعالى فالأمر أظهر ومن رأى وجه الحقيقة شهد هذا المشهد العزيز ومن آمن بهذا فهو وليّ ومن أنكره فإنكاره ظهور من ظهورات عالم الأمر الانحرافيّ الذي يُشهد من حضرة الاسم الجامع فيوجَد المنكر والإنكار كلاهما بالذات يعترفان بمعنى ﴿وَإِلَيْهِ يُرْجَعُ ٱلْأَمْرُ كُلُّهُۥ فَٱعْبُدْهُ﴾ ومن عبده من حيث رجوع الأمر كلّه إليه كان مع كلّ طائفة بما هي هي فيجده عندها وهو لا يجدها عنده فيسبق كلّ أحد إلى مبلغه ولا مبلغ له يقف عنده هو ولا غيره.

٦،٧٠ فإذا علمت هذا وعلمت أنّ النفع حاصل في كلّ طور ممّا يسمّى نفعاً وممّا يسمّى ضرراً علمت أنّ الاسم النافع عامّ الحكم دنياً وآخرة وظاهراً وباطناً وغيباً وشهادة خصوصاً في مقام المحبّة فإنّ المحبّ لا يرى ضرراً إلّا وجده من محبوبه نفعاً فهو نفع لتنعّم المحبّ به وتلذّذه بمواقع تصرّفه فيه كما قيل

وَيَقْبُحُ مِنْ سِوَاكَ ٱلْفِعْلُ عِنْدِي وَتَفْعَلُهُ فَيَحْسُنُ مِنْكَ ذَاكَا

٧،٧٠ وذكر هذا الاسم النافع نافع في الخلوة والجلوة والله أعلم.

If you know that there is nothing in existence except His existence, then the matter becomes more evident. The one who sees the face of truth witnesses this exalted contemplative station. The one who believes in this is a friend of God; and the one who denies it, his denial is one of the manifestations of the realm of the aberrant command that is witnessed from within the ambit of the All-Comprehensive. Therein one finds that the person who denies as well as the act of denying are both essentially an acknowledgment of the meaning of «to Him returns the entire affair, so worship Him».[410] Thus, the one who worships Him with respect to the return of the entire affair to Him is with each group as it is in itself. He finds Him in the group, but not the group in Him. He therefore overtakes the point each group has reached, yet for his part he has no limit at which he or anyone else would halt. 70.5

If you know this, and if you know that benefit occurs at every stage—both those called beneficial and those called harmful—then you know that the properties of the Benefiter pervade this world and the next, the manifest and the nonmanifest, the unseen and the visible. This is particularly true in the station of love since the lover experiences harm from his beloved as benefaction. It is a benefaction since the lover finds bliss in it and takes pleasure in his beloved's domination. To this effect, it has been said: 70.6

An act from anyone other than You is ugly to me,
but when it comes from You, it is utterly beautiful.[411]

Invoking the Benefiter is beneficial both in seclusion and in public, and God knows best. 70.7

سورة هود عليه السلام

وفيها ستّة أسماء

اسمه القويّ جلّت قدرته

١.٧١ هـذا الاسم الكريم شاهده من سورة هود قوله عزّ وجلّ ﴿إِنَّ رَبَّكَ هُوَ ٱلْقَوِيُّ﴾ متّفق عليه بين الأئمّة الثلاثة والضعف ضدّ للقوّة والقوّة خصوص وصف في القدرة كأنّها كمال القدرة فتدخل في معنى الاسم القدير سبحانه.

٢.٧١ وأسماء الله تعالى وصفاته كلّها ذوات جوهرانيّة فلا يقال كيف يدخل بعضها في بعض أو يتّصف بعضها ببعض وهي أعراض والعرض لا يقوم بالعرض فإنّ ذلك القول خطأ وهي من جهة انتسابها للاسم الرحمٰن جواهر كلّها أشرف من جواهر الأجسام ولها معان هي اعتباريّة أيضاً.

٣.٧١ واعلم أنّ القوّة الإلٰهيّة هي التي جعلت الممكنات ممكنة فإنّ الممكن لولا الترجيح لم يوجَد فذلك الترجيح هو من معنى الاسم القويّ وكثيراً ما يغلط قوم في صفة الإمكان فيعتقدون أنّها قائمة بالممكن وهي في الحقيقة صفة للقوّة الإلٰهيّة أي في قوّته أن يفعل ما أراد فإنّ قولك أمكنه أن يفعل كذا بمعنى تمكّن أن يفعله وأمّا الممكن قبل وجوده فإنّه معدوم الذات والصفات لا يقوم به شيء ولا يقوم بشيء.

The Surah of Hūd

The Surah of Hūd has six names.

Al-Qawī: The Strong

71.1 This noble name occurs in the Surah of Hūd in the verse: «Indeed your Lord is the Strong».[412] The three eminent scholars agree it is a divine name. Weakness is the opposite of strength, and strength is a specific quality of power. It is, as it were, the perfection of power. As such, it pertains to the meaning of the Powerful.

71.2 All of God's names and qualities are substantial essences. Therefore, one must not ask: "How could some be included within others, or be conditioned by others, if they are accidents, given that an accident does not subsist through another accident?" For such a question is unsound. With regard to their ascription to the All-Merciful, the names are substances more noble than the substances of bodies, and they have supersensory meanings that are perspectival as well.

71.3 Moreover, divine strength is what makes possible things possible. For were it not for the preponderance of a possible thing, it would not exist; and this preponderance stems from the reality of the Strong. Many err with respect to the quality of possibility, and they believe it subsists in the possible. But in reality, possibility is an attribute of divine strength. That is, it is within His strength to do whatever He desires. For when you say, "It is possible for him to do such and such," it means he is able to do it. However, prior to its existence, possibility is nonexistent in its essence and qualities, nothing is sustained by it, and it sustains nothing.

والذي يتخيّـل منه في الذهن هو من قبيل المفروضات فيفرض كما يفرَض المحال ٤،٧١
وأولى ثمّ يحكَم على ذلك المفروض أنّه قابل للوجود في نفسه والممكن في نفسه غير ذلك المفروض وصحّ هذا لأجل الضرورة ولأنّ المفروض وجوديّ أي موجود في الذهن وهو غير المعدوم المذكور وقولهم إنّه لا يقبل الوجود صحيح مجازًا وأمّا قولهم يقبل العدم أيضاً فهو باطل فإنّ المعدوم لا يقبل العدم لأنّه تحصيل الحاصل والقوّة غير متناهية التعلّق فليس في الإمكان أبدع من العوالم التي هي غير متناهية بالنوع وليس كما قال الغزاليّ رحمه الله أنّه ليس في الإمكان أبدع من هذا العالم ويعني من محدث[1] التاسع إلى نقطة مركز الأرض فإنّ هذا أقلّ من أنْ ينسَب إلى أنّه مبلغ مقدور الله تعالى.

وهذا الاسم يتصرّف في الأسماء كلّها فإنّ معاني الأسماء كلّها موصوفة بالقوّة من ٥،٧١
حقيقة الاسم القويّ وكذلك صفاته وأفعاله وكلّ قوّة فهي قوّة الله تعالى من كلّ قويّ فإنْ قلت كيف تقوم القوّة الواحدة بأقوياء غير متناهية فاعلم أنّه ليس مع الله غيره في الوجود.

واعلم أنّ الاسم القويّ ينفع ذكره لمن مرض في الخلوة أو آنس ضعفاً من الذكر أو ٦،٧١
تفرّق فإنّه يجتمع والله أعلم.

اسمه الحفيظ تبارك وتعالى

متّفق على تخريجه بين الأئمّة الثلاثة وشاهده من سورة هود قوله تعالى ﴿إِنَّ رَبِّى عَلَىٰ ١،٧٢
كُلِّ شَىْءٍ حَفِيظٌ﴾ والحفيظ والحافظ بمعنى أي يحفظ عباده ويحرسهم وفيه معنى

١ ب، و: محدَّب؛ ج: محذب.

What the mind imagines is a supposition: It is a supposition just as the impossible a priori is a supposition. This supposition is deemed to be receptive to existence in itself. But the possible in itself is different from that supposition, and this is true both by necessity and because the supposition is existential; that is, it exists in the mind, which is different from nonexistence. It is metaphorically correct to say that it is not receptive to existence; but it is false to say it is receptive to nonexistence as well, for it is tautological to call a nonexistent "receptive to nonexistence." The objects of strength, moreover, are infinite. Wherefore, nothing in possibility is more perfected than the worlds whose species are infinite. It is not as al-Ghazālī—may God have mercy upon him—said: "Nothing in the realm of possibility is more wondrous than this world,"[413] by which he meant our temporally originated universe. For surely our universe is too little to be described as the extent of what comes under God's power. 71.4

This name, moreover, exercises control over all the names. For the meanings of all the names are qualified by strength through the reality of the Strong. The same holds for His qualities and acts. Moreover, all strength belongs to God's strength through everyone who possesses strength. Thus, if you say, "How can a single strength be sustained through infinite possessors of strength?," the answer is that there is nothing in existence but God. 71.5

The invocation of the Strong is beneficial for those who fall ill in the spiritual retreat, or discern weakness or a lack of focus in his invocation, for it will pull him together. And God knows best. 71.6

Al-Ḥafīẓ: The Preserving

The three eminent scholars agree it is a divine name. It occurs in the Surah of Hūd in the verse: «Indeed my Lord is preserver over all things».[414] The Preserving and the Preserver have the same meaning; namely, that He preserves His servants and guards over them. It also contains the meaning of the Watchful, because preservation is watchfulness with an aim to the good. The Real 72.1

الاسم الرقيب فإنّ المحافظة هي المراقبة بقصد الخير فالحقّ تعالى يحرسهم بالحفظة الذين هم الملائكة وهم دقائق[1] اسمه الحفيظ وفروع تجلّيه أومّا الملك الذي هوكاتب السيّئات وهوكاتب الشمال فراجع إلى اسمه الرقيب وهو من مادّة قوله تعالى على لسان رسوله صلّى الله عليه وسلّم ﴿وَمَآ أَنَا۠ عَلَيۡكُم بِحَفِيظٖ﴾ .

٢،٧٢ واعلم أنّ منّ وجوده يعمّ جميع خلقه فمن نفس معرفتهم لنفوسهم ومراقبتهم لها تكون مراقبة الحقّ تعالى لهم فهو أقرب إلى كلّ شيء منه لنفسه وحفظه تعالى لموجوداته ظاهر فإنّ القوّة المستمسكة هي من قوّة حفظه وبقيّة القوى كالدافعة والجاذبة وغيرهما يقع بها الحفظ واعتدال الهواء يقع به الحفظ وإنبات الحبوب والفواكه والأدوية يقع بها الحفظ ووجود الأنعام وتولّدها يقع به الحفظ للإنسان ويقع لها الحفظ بالإحسان والجميع من الاسم الحفيظ.

٣،٧٢ والأبنية يقع بها حفظ الحفيظ سبحانه وما يتّخذ من الأوبار والأشعار وما يقوم مقامها كلّه من حفظ الحفيظ عمّ وجوده ورحمته ونظام الشرائع وسياسة الملوك للرعايا هو من الاسم الحفيظ ووجود المياه والكلأ والنار والكواكب ذوات الأنوار يقع بها الحفظ ووجود السماء لتظلّ الأرض والأرض لتقلّ وأعلامها ليُستدلّ لوجود الحفظ من الحفيظ تعالى والقوى النفسانيّة من ذكر وفكر وتخيّل وتوهّم وحسّ كلّه فيه حفظ الحفيظ سبحانه.

٤،٧٢ وأصل حفظه لنا هو حفظه لنفسه وأصل حفظه لنفسه وجوب بقائه الذاتيّ له الذي يثبت له من حيث تثبت ذاته وهو جهة وجوب الوجود بذاته ولوجوب بقائه لذاته وجب بقاء النفس الإنسانيّة أبداً وسرمداً لأنّها على صورته التي هي الحياة والعلم والإرادة والقدرة والسمع والبصر والكلام وما تفرّع من هذه الأصول الكرام وهل الجسم للنفس إلّا بمنزلة البيضة للفرخ يتكوّن فيها ويبقى بعد فسادها وإنّما استحقّت النفس البقاء لتشابه الخليفة المستخلف.

---

١ و: رقائق.

guards over them through the guardian angels, who are subtle realities and branches of disclosure of His name the Preserver. The angel who keeps the record of ugly deeds on the left side stems from the Watchful, and is from the substance of God's utterance on the tongue of His blessed Messenger: «I am not a guardian over you».[415]

The gratuitous favor of His existence pervades all of His creation. For the Real's watchfulness over them is identical with their own self-knowledge and watchfulness over themselves. For He is more proximate to each thing than it is to itself. Moreover, His preservation of existents is obvious. For the force of cohesion derives from the force of His preservation, whereas other forces, such as repulsion and attraction, are forces through which preservation happens. Thus, preservation happens through the balance of air, and through the growth of grains, fruits, and medicinal plants. The preservation of humans occurs through the existence and reproduction of livestock. The preservation of livestock occurs through their fair treatment. And all of the above is due to the Preserver. 72.2

Moreover, the preservation of the Preserver happens through artifacts. The use of furs, pelts, and everything that serves that purpose is due to the preservation of the Preserver, may His existence and mercy pervade! The order of revealed Laws and the rule of kings over their subjects occur through the Preserver. Preservation occurs through the existence of water, pasturage, fire, the luminous planets, and the sky that shades the earth, the earth that carries us, and its guiding landmarks; all of this is through the existence of the Preserver's preservation. What is more, all the faculties of the soul, including those of memory, thought, estimation, imagination, and sensation, are due to the preservation of the Preserver. 72.3

His self-preservation is the root of His preservation of us, and the root of His self-preservation is the necessity of His own essential subsistence, which is immutable since His Essence is immutable, which is what necessitates existence itself.[416] Moreover, it is on account of His Essence's existential necessity that the human soul necessarily subsists eternally and forever, for it is created upon His form, which is Life, Knowledge, Will, Power, Hearing, Seeing, and Speech, and all that is derived from these noble foundations. After all, is not the body to the soul as the egg is to the chick? It comes into being within the egg, and subsists after its decay. The soul, moreover, is only worthy of subsistence on account of the resemblance between the representative and He who appoints the representative. 72.4

وهذا الاسم الكريم ينتفع بذكره من يخشى على أحواله أن تحول فينحفظ بالذكر حاله والله أعلم. ٥،٧٢

اسمه المجيد سبحانه

١،٧٣ اتّفق على إيراده الأئمّة الثلاثة وشاهده من سورة هود قوله تعالى ﴿إِنَّهُۥ حَمِيدٌ مَّجِيدٌ﴾ والمجيد في اللغة هو الكريم بآبائه قديماً والحقّ تعالى مجيد بآلائه أزلاً ومجد كلّ ماجد هو به تعالى فإنّه معطي المجد.

٢،٧٣ وأكثر ما يعتبَر حكم الاسم المجيد سبحانه في مراتب ظهوراته فحيث ثبت مجد ما لمن نسب إليه المجد فإنّما نُسب إلى الحقّ تعالى من حقيقة اسمه المجيد ومن شهد أن لا ظهور إلّا له تعالى علم أنّ الظهور ظهوراته إذ لا غير يشاركه في الوجود ويتحقّق هذا عند الشاهد بكون صفاء الشهود خصوصاً إذا ظهر المجد بمظهر أشرف موجود وهو محمّد صلّى الله عليه وسلّم فإنّه المجيد بآبائه المورث المجد لأبنائه.

٣،٧٣
قَدْ وَرِثَ ٱلْمَجْدَ بِآبَائِهِ   وَوَرَّثَ ٱلْمَجْدَ لِأَبْنَائِهِ
وَقَامَ قُطْباً لِمُحِيطِ ٱلْعُلَى   وَٱلْمَجْدُ قَدْ حَفَّ بِأَرْجَائِهِ
وَطُهِرَتْ أَجْزَاؤُهُ فَٱغْتَذَى   يُطَهِّرُ ٱلْكُلَّ بِأَجْزَائِهِ
وَكَانَ ظِلاًّ فَمَحَاهُ ٱلسَّنَا   وَمُثْبِتاً فَانٍ بِأَفْنَائِهِ
فَكَانَ فِي غَيْبَةِ أَكْوَانِهِ   يَقْطُرُ مَاءُ ٱلْمَجْدِ مِنْ مَائِهِ

Invoking this noble name benefits those who fear that their spiritual state will change, whereupon this state shall be preserved. And God knows best. 72.5

Al-Majīd: The Glorious

The three eminent scholars agree it is a divine name. It occurs in the Surah of Hūd in the verse: «Truly He is Praiseworthy, Glorious».[417] Linguistically, glorious means someone who is noble by virtue of an ancient ancestry. The Real, for His part, is glorious by His blessings from pre-eternity, and the glory of every glorious person is through Him, for He is the giver of glory. 73.1

The properties of the Glorious are mostly considered at the levels of His manifestations. For whenever some type of glory is affirmed in someone to whom glory is ascribed, then it is ascribed to none other than the Real through the reality of the Glorious. Moreover, to witness that there is no manifestation but His is to know that all manifestation is His, for He partners with no other in existence. This is realized, moreover, by the witness through the purification of his witnessing, especially when glory manifests in the locus of manifestation of the noblest being, blessed Muḥammad, who is glorious by his ancestry and bequeaths glory to his progeny. 73.2

He inherited glory from his ancestors, 73.3
and bequeathed glory to his progeny.
He established himself as the axis of the upper sphere,
and glory surrounded him from all sides.
His parts were purified, so he went forth
to purify the whole with his parts.
He was a shadow, then radiance effaced him;
Immutable, yet annihilated among his surroundings.[418]
From his invisible existential states,
the water of glory poured forth from his water.[419]

٤،٧٣ فهو عليه السلام مجد الله الظّاهر وواسطة عقد الأوّل والآخر وقوله حالة فنائه وظهور بارئه هٰذه يد ٱلله وشهادته فيه ﴿إِنَّ ٱلَّذِينَ يُبَايِعُونَكَ إِنَّمَا يُبَايِعُونَ ٱللَّهَ﴾ و ﴿مَن يُطِعِ ٱلرَّسُولَ فَقَدْ أَطَاعَ ٱللَّهَ﴾.

شعر

هٰذَا هُوَ ٱلْمَجْدُ ٱلَّذِي قَدْ غَدَا لَا يُوصِلُ ٱلْكُلُّ إِلَى بَعْضِهِ
سَمَاؤُهُ فِي أَرْضِهِ وَهِيَ لَمْ تَكُنْ لِتَعْلُو بِسِوَى أَرْضِهِ
فَكُلُّ مَنْ قَامَ بِهِ حُبُّهُ قَامَ بِفَرْضِ ٱللهِ فِي فَرْضِهِ
عَيْنُ رِضَى ٱللهِ رِضَاهُ فَمَنْ أَرَادَ يُرْضِي ٱللهَ فَلْيُرْضِهِ

٥،٧٣ وهذا الاسم الكريم لا يستعمله في الخلوة أهل البداية وأمّا أهل التوسّط فيجب أن يذكروه في وقت تجلّي الحقّ تعالى لهم بالتدلّي إلى حضرات التقييد فإنّ ذكر المجيد يرفع الإشكال والله أعلم.

اسمه الودود شملت رحمته

١،٧٤ هذا الاسم الكريم متّفق عليه بين الأئمّة الثلاثة وشاهده من سورة هود قوله تعالى ﴿إِنَّ رَبِّى رَحِيمٌ وَدُودٌ﴾ قال بعضهم إنّه بمعنى مودود أي محبوب مثل هبوب بمعنى مهبوبٍ وقال قوم فعول بمعنى فاعل مثلَ غفور بمعنى غافر أي وادّ لعباده الصالحين وهذا الأخير هو الذي يقتضيه الذوق بالأصالة والأوّل يقتضيه الذوق أيضاً لكن بالقصد الثاني.

For the blessed Prophet is God's manifest glory, and the intermediary link between beginning and end. During his state of annihilation and the manifestation of his Creator, he said: "This is the hand of God,"[420] and God bears witness to that in the verse: «Truly those who pledge allegiance unto thee pledge allegiance only unto God»[421] and «whosoever obeys the Messenger has obeyed God».[422] Poem: 73.4

His is the surpassing glory
  that no one can attain even partially.
His heaven lies over his earth, and his heaven would not
  be raised above anything but his earth.
Thus, those in whom his love subsists
  have performed God's command through his command.
God's own approval is his approval, so let anyone who
  wishes to please God please him.[423]

This noble name is not to be used by beginners in the spiritual retreat. Intermediates ought to invoke it at the moment of the Real's disclosure to them through His descent into delimited presences, for invoking the Glorious removes confusion; and God knows best. 73.5

Al-Wadūd: The Loving

The three eminent scholars agree it is a divine name. It occurs in the Surah of Hūd in the verse: «Indeed my Lord is Merciful, Loving».[424] Some say that it means the Beloved (*mawdūd*) or the Loved One (*maḥbūb*) just as the rising (*habūb*) means the risen one (*maḥbūb*). Another group says that the active form *fa'ūl* denotes *fā'il*, or the agent, just as the Concealing (*ghafūr*) means the One Who Conceals (*ghāfir*). Thus, the Loving (*wadūd*) means the One Who Loves (*wādd*); that He loves His righteous servants. The latter is what experiential knowledge primarily entails; it entails the former too, but only by secondary intent. 74.1

٢،٧٤ قال الله تعالى ﴿ يُحِبُّهُمْ وَيُحِبُّونَهُۥٓ ﴾ وإنّما كان الثاني هو الأصل لأنّ محبّة الله تعالى سابقة وهو قوله كنتُ كنزًا لم أعرَف فأحببت أن أعرَف فخلقت خلقاً وتعرّفت إليهم فبي عرفوني فمحبّته اقتضت وجود أفعاله الذين هم مخلوقاته فإن أحبّوه بطريق التبع فبحبّه لنفسه أحبّوه.

٣،٧٤ ثمّ إنّه من هذه الحقيقة يُشهد أنّه ما أحبّ المحبّون إلّا أنفسهم فهو تعالى الودود في ودّ العبيد له وفي ودّه للعبيد فتفطّن لسرّ التوحيد وفي ضمن هذا التوحيد تفاصيل يترتّب بعضها على بعض في أطوار العلم فإنّ من لم يعلم أنّ الحقّ تعالى ما أحبّ في محبّته للموجودات إلّا نفسه فإنّه ما يمكنه أن ينكر أنّ الله تعالى قال ﴿ يُحِبُّهُمْ وَيُحِبُّونَهُۥٓ ﴾ ولعلّه يفسّر محبّته لهم إنّما هي بطريق الرحمة ويجعل الاسم الودود راجعاً إلى الاسم الرحمٰن والأمر كذلك ويرى تنزيه الحقّ تعالى عن حقيقة المحبّة التي توجب افتقار المحبّ إلى المحبوب وينسى أنّ الرحمة شجنة من الرحمٰن باستلزام أنّ الرحمة مشتقّة من الرحم والرحيم شجنة من الرحمٰن فيلزم أن تكون الرحمة شجنة من الرحمٰن أيضاً وإذا كانت الرحمة قرابة ورحماً فنطق الاشتقاق بالتوحيد ظاهر.

٤،٧٤ فالودود سبحانه قد ودّ نفسه فودّ بودّه نفسه جميع الموجودات فإن ظننتَ أنّ ودّه تعالى يجب أن يودّ به المتّقين فقط أو المسلمين دون غيرهم فاعلم أن ذلك صحيح في مرتبة رجوع الاسم الودود إلى الاسم الهادي وذلك هو بعض أحكام الاسم الودود لا كلّها فإنّ مراتب أحكام الاسم الودود لا يتناهى تفصيلها ولا ينحصر اعتبارها وتأويلها فهو ودود لكلّ مخلوقاته ولا كلّ لها إذ لا نهاية لعدد أنواعها فضلاً عن أشخاصها وإنّما عالمنا نحن متناه والعوالم غير عالمنا غير متناهية فلا يلتفَت إلى قول من يقول إنّ كلّ ما دخل في الوجود فهو متناه فإنّ ذلك قول من يظنّ أنّ الوجود عرض.

٥،٧٤ وهذا الاسم الكريم إذا ذكره أرباب الخلوة حصل لهم الأنس والمحبّة والله أعلم.

God says: «He loves them, and they love Him».[425] The second clause is primary, because God's love precedes theirs, per the saying: "I was a hidden treasure who was not known; and I loved to be known, so I created humankind so that I may make myself known to them, and so that they may come to know Me through Me."[426] Thus, His love dictates the existence of His acts, which are His creatures, and when they love Him reciprocally, it is through His love for Himself that they love Him. 74.2

Furthermore, through this reality one witnesses that those who love love none other than themselves. He is the Loving through the love servants have for Him, and through the love He has for His servants. Be astute, therefore, concerning the secret of divine oneness, for within this divine oneness are the particulars that derive mutually from each other in the stages of knowledge. For the one who does not know that by loving His creatures, the Real loves none other than Himself, still cannot deny that God says: "He loves them, and they love Him." He might explain God's love for them as occurring through mercy specifically. He thus states that the Loving stems from the All-Merciful—which is the case—and deems the Real to be far above the reality of love, because love entails the lover's need for the beloved. Yet he forgets that mercy (*raḥmah*) is a derivative from the All-Merciful (*al-Raḥmān*), by virtue of the fact that mercy is derived from womb (*raḥim*) and therefore the Ever-Merciful (*al-Raḥīm*) must be a derivative from the All-Merciful as well. Furthermore, explaining how it derives from divine oneness is evident since mercy is a maternal relation and a connection through the womb. 74.3

Thus, the Loving loves Himself, and through His love for Himself He loves all creatures. Moreover, if you suppose that with regard to His intense love, He must only have love for the pious or for Muslims and no one else, then you should know that this is correct at the level in which the Loving stems from the Guide. But that is only one, not all, of the properties of the Loving. For the levels of the properties of the Loving are infinite in their detail, and their considerations and interpretations cannot be confined. He is Loving toward all His creatures—though His creatures have no "all" because their species are infinite, let alone their individuals. It is precisely our world that is finite, whereas worlds other than ours are infinite. One should pay no regard to those who say that everything that enters into existence is finite, for that is the doctrine of those who opine that existence is an accident. 74.4

If this noble name is invoked by those who are in spiritual retreat, they attain intimacy and love. And God knows best. 74.5

اسمه الأليم الأخذ نعوذ به منه

١،٧٥ هذا الاسم الكريم انفرد بإيراده أبو الحكم بن برّجان وشاهده من سورة هود قوله تعالى ﴿إِنَّ أَخْذَهُۥٓ أَلِيمٌ شَدِيدٌ﴾ والأليم بمعنى المؤلم مثل السميع بمعنى المسمع قال

أَمِنْ رَيْحَانَةَ ٱلدَّاعِي ٱلسَّمِيعِ

أي المسمع والألم هو الوجع والمؤلم الموجع والأخذ من المؤاخذة على الذنب ويكون من الأسر الذي هو ضدّ الإطلاق فإنّ الأخيذ هو الأسير وورد في الحديث إنّ الله يمهّل الظالم فإذا أخذه لم يفلته والمراد أنّه الأليم الأخذ أي شديد العقاب.

٢،٧٥ واعلم أنّ اسمه الأليم الأخذ إنّما يتعيّن تصرّفه في مراتب الاسم الله بطريق الأصالة وإنّما يلحق الاسم الرحمٰن من طريق كونه محيطاً فقط فإذاً اسمه الأليم الأخذ هو من أحكام المراتب الإلٰهيّة وكذلك الشديد العقاب وطريق فهم هذا أنّ الحقّ تعالى في حقيقة اسمه الموجِد أعطى كلّ موجود قدراً به يمتاز عن غيره وقدراً يشارك به الموجودات والقدر المشترك الذي هو المادّة إنّما هو الوجود وهو اصطلاح أهل شهود الوحدانيّة.

٣،٧٥ فإذا علمت هذا فاعلم أنّ التجلّي من حضرة الاسم القهّار إذا ورد فإن صادف من موجود ما ملائمة له من أنّه شهده بالقدر المشترك تنعّم به وكانت النسبة للاسم الرحمٰن وإن صادف من الموجود القدر الذي به يمتاز نافره التجلّي القهّاريّ فعجز عن

Al-Alīm al-Akhdh: The Painful in Retribution

This noble name is only considered divine by Ibn Barrajān. It occurs in the Surah of Hūd: «Surely His retribution is painful, severe»[427]—"painful" (*alīm*) in the sense "He causes pain" (*mu'lim*), just as "hearing" (*samīʿ*) can mean "the one who enables hearing" (*musmiʿ*). A poet said: 75.1

> Is it for Rayḥānah that he calls and shouts?[428]

Here the word *samīʿ*, which usually means "hearing," is used to mean "aloud"—that is, one who causes hearing (*musmiʿ*). Furthermore, pain is suffering, and so the painful is the one who causes suffering. Retribution (*akhdh*) comes from taking to task for sins, and also from captivity (*asr*), which is the opposite of manumission. For the one who is taken for ransom (*akhīdh*) is a captive (*asīr*). To this effect, there is a prophetic tradition that states: "God gives respite to the wrongdoer, but when he seizes him, he does not get away."[429] What is intended by the Painful in Retribution is the Severe in Punishment.

Moreover, His name the Painful in Retribution exercises control primarily at the levels of Allāh. However, it joins to the All-Merciful only in the sense that the latter is all-encompassing. Thus, the Painful in Retribution is one of the properties of the levels of Allāh, and the same holds for the Severe in Punishment. Now, the way to understand this is that the Real, through the reality of His name the Existentiator, gives each existent a measure that distinguishes it from others and a measure that it shares with other existent things. The measure the existents have in common, or their material substratum, is existence according the terminology of those who witness divine oneness. 75.2

If you know this, then you should know that when the disclosure from the presence of the All-Subjugating occurs, it may encounter something concordant within an existent. For the existent witnesses the disclosure through the measure shared with other existents, whereupon there is enjoyment, and that relationship is ascribed to the All-Merciful. However, the disclosure may also encounter the measure that distinguishes the existent, whereupon the subjugating disclosure is disagreeable and is incapable of being repelled by the Protector. In this case, the disclosure overwhelms through disagreeability; and the definition of pain is experiencing the disagreeable. Therefore, to experience 75.3

دفعه بالاسم الواقي فاستولى عليه التجلّي بنسبة المنافرة وإدراك المنافرة هو الألم فإذًا من كانت منافرته للأسماء الإلٰهيّة حاصلة تعذّب وعوقب على قدر المباينة.

٤،٧٥ وهذا الكلام عند أهل الأذواق واضح بخلاف ما هو عليه عند المحجوبين وتنتهي مراتب أهل المباينة والمنافرة إلى حدّ يكون فيه ذلك المباين أشدّ أهل النار عقوبة فإذا عمّت الرحمة صار أقوى أهل النار نعيمًا بالنار وإدراك المنافرة يكون دنيًا وآخرة فما يعذَّب أحد إلّا والله تعالى هو الذي عذّبه بمباينة ما وشرح هذا طويل لا يسعه هذا الكتاب وينتهي أهل الملاءمة إلى أن يتنعّموا بجميع ما يُتنعّم به وبجميع ما يكون به العذاب.

٥،٧٥ ومن هذه الحضرة أنشدهم قائلهم

أُحِبُّكَ لا أُحِبُّكَ لِلثَّوَابِ   وَلٰكِنِّي أُحِبُّكَ لِلْعِقَابِ
فَكُلُّ مَآرِبِي قَدْ نِلْتُ مِنْهَا   سِوَى مَلْذُوذِ وَجْدِي بِٱلْعَذَابِ

فأسماء النقمة في حقّ هذا رحمة.

٦،٧٥ ولا يذكر هذا الاسم في الخلوة إلّا طالب العقوبة مثل صاحب هاتين البيتين المذكورين والله أعلم.

اسمه الفعّال تبارك وتعالى

١،٧٦ انفرد به البيهقيّ وشاهده من سورة هود ﴿إِنَّ رَبَّكَ فَعَّالٌ لِّمَا يُرِيدُ﴾ واعلم أنّ الاسم الفعّال يتعيّن من الاسم المريد والإرادة هي الميل المعنويّ إلى حقيقة ظهور المراد ومظهرها قابليّةٌ هي انفعال مادّة المراد انفعالًا مناسبًا للمراد منه وذلك

disagreeability vis-à-vis the divine names is to be tormented and punished to the degree of incompatibility.

This discussion is evident to those who know through tasting, in contrast to those who are veiled. Moreover, the utmost level of those who experience incompatibility and disagreeability is the person whose incompatibility is so intense that he is the most severely punished inhabitant of the Fire. But once divine mercy prevails, he becomes the inhabitant of the Fire who experiences the most intense enjoyment in the Fire. Moreover, the experience of disagreeability occurs in this world and in the next, and all chastisement is God's chastisement through some sort of incompatibility. Explaining this, however, would take too long for this book. In the end, those who experience compatibility end up finding enjoyment in all things that cause enjoyment and in all things that cause chastisement. 75.4

It is from this presence that someone proclaimed: 75.5

> I love You. I love You not for the recompense,
> but rather I love You for the chastisement.
> For all my needs I have attained from the recompense,
> except my pleasure in the ecstasy of chastisement![430]

Thus, the names of vengeance in his case are a mercy.

This name is only invoked in the spiritual retreat by those who seek punishment, such as the person who composed these two verses. And God knows best. 75.6

Al-Faʿʿāl: The Fully Active

This name is only mentioned by al-Bayhaqī. It occurs in the Surah of Hūd in the verse: «Truly your Lord acts fully on what He desires».[431] Moreover, the Fully Active becomes determined through the Willing. Will is the supersensory inclination toward the actual manifestation of what is willed. Its locus of manifestation is receptivity, which is the reactivity of the willed object's 76.1

هو المقتضى فإذا صحب ذلك انتفاء المانع وجب الفعل وبالفعل يكون المفعول في المادّة فالاسم الفعّال من لواحق الاسم المريد والقادر يدخل في الاسم الفاعل كالصفة له وهذه الأحكام كلّها تنبعث من النور الذي هو الوجود.

٢،٧٦ واعلم أن ما ذكرناه هو من أحكام الاسم الفعّال إذا لحق الاسم الرحمٰن في نهاية ترقّيه إليه فإن أخذت معناه في أوسع من دائرة الاسم الرحمٰن قبل أحكاماً أخرى باعتبارين أحدهما أن ينسَب إلى المراتب فيكون للاسم الله فيكون فعّالاً أفعالاً مرتبيّة مثاله أنّ النقيضين لا يجتمعان ولا يرتفعان والفاعل الذي فعل هذا الحكم وهو كونهما لا يجتمعان ولا يرتفعان هو الفعّال تعالى لا من جهة وجوديّة بل من جهة أخرى مرتبيّة وهذا أولى من أن يقال إنّها غير مجعولة ولا مفعولة وكذلك اجتماع الضدّين لشيء واحد في آن واحد لا ينقسم فإنّ هذه أفعال[1] مفعولة للفعّال باعتبار الرتب فقط ونسبتها إلى الاسم الله لا إلى الاسم الرحمٰن إلّا من حيث دخول الاسم الرحمٰن في الاسم الله بإحاطة الاسم الله وكذلك الحكم في الاسم الرحمٰن عندما يدخل تحته الاسم الله.

٣،٧٦ والاعتبار الثاني المفعول الفعّال منسوب[2] إلى الذات في معنًى أعلى من الوجود والمراتب ولسان ذلك ما فوق الصمت والفعّال إذ ذاك قوّة الذات في ذاتها والمنفعل عنها ذاتها إلّا أنّ هذه الحضرة الانفعال فيها سابق لفعل الفعّال في الانفعال من حيث أنّ الانفعال فاعل في الفاعل أن يصير فاعلاً فهو بهذا الاعتبار فعّال بالانفعال في الفاعل حتّى يكون كونه فاعلاً هو عين انفعاله فتتعاكس الحقائق في ثاني النظر وبادئه ولم تتعاكس في حقيقة الأمر أصلاً.

٤،٧٦ وهذه الحضرة هي حضرة الحضرات ومرتبتها هي مرتبة المراتب وحقيقة الحقائق ومنها تنبعث الأصول ونطقها الصمت وهو ناطق بكلّ نطق وبكلّ صمت وإليه ترجع الأصول والفروع وفيه يفنى الرجوع وفيه تقوم الحقيقة في أعيان القطبيّة بذاتها لذاتها

---

١ و: أحكام. ٢ آ، ب، و: منسوبًا.

material substratum in a manner that corresponds to what is desired of it, for that is its dictate. When this is accompanied by the self-negation of the impediment, then the act becomes necessary. It is through the act, moreover, that what is acted upon takes place within the material substratum. The Fully Active is thus a subsequence of the Willing, and the Able is included within the Active as a quality of it. These properties, moreover, all arise from light, which is existence.

Our discussion pertains to the properties of the Fully Active when associated with the All-Merciful at the end of its ascent thereto. But if you apply its meaning beyond the scope of the All-Merciful, then from two perspectives it assumes further properties: The first is that it is ascribed to the ranks, wherefore it pertains to Allāh, and its acts are fully active at the ranks. For example: contraries neither join together nor detach from each other, and the actor who enacts this property—the property of them neither joining together nor detaching from each other—is the Fully Active, though not from the perspective of existence but of rank. This is more apt than describing it as neither done nor enacted. The same goes for the joining all at once of opposites into a single indivisible thing. For these acts are enacted by the Fully Active in view of the levels alone, and its relationship is to Allāh, not to the All-Merciful except inasmuch as the All-Merciful is included within Allāh by virtue of the encompassment of Allāh. The same goes for the property of the All-Merciful when Allāh is included within it. 76.2

The second consideration is that what is at once enacted and fully active is ascribed to the Essence through a meaning higher than existence and its levels, whose language goes beyond silence. The Fully Active therein is the force of the Essence in Itself, and what reacts to It is Its Essence, except that in this presence, that reactivity precedes the act of the Fully Active in its reactivity, such that the reactivity activates the agent to become an agent. He is, from this standpoint, fully active by the reactivity in the agent, such that His activity is His own reactivity. The realities are thus reversed at first and at second glance, though they are not reversed in reality whatsoever. 76.3

This presence is the Presence of Presences. Its level is the Level of Levels, and the Reality of Realities. From it, the roots grow. Its speech is silence, yet it speaks through every speech and through every silence. To it return all roots and branches, and in it the return is obliterated. In it, reality is sustained in the entities of the axial saint, by their Essence and for their Essence, without the 76.4

من غير غيبة شيء من أفعالها ولا أسمائها ولا صفاتها فتكون هي فقط وقولنا هي تنقيص لها إذ لا قول.

وهذا الاسم الكريم ينفع ذكره لمن يريد التأثيرات والكرامات والله أعـلم. ٥،٧٦

absence of any of its acts or names or qualities. Thus, only It is; though even to say “It” is an injustice, for in It there is no speech.

The invocation of this noble name benefits those who desire to produce effects and miracles. And God knows best. 76.5

سورة يوسف عليه السلام

وفيها اسمان

اسمه الحافظ تبارك اسمه

١،٧٧ انفرد به البيهقيّ وشاهده من سورة يوسف قوله تعالى ﴿فَٱللَّهُ خَيْرٌ حَٰفِظًا﴾ وقرئ حَافِظًا وقد تقدّم ذكر الحفيظ سبحانه وبين الحفيظ والحافظ سبحانه ما بين فعيل وفاعل من المبالغة وتركها.

٢،٧٧ فمن حفظ الحافظ سبحانه ما يخصّ النور الذي فيه صُوَر العالم وهو الوجود لأنّه عندنا هو المادّة التي تُعرض لها منها الصور لا من غيرها ومثال حفظها أنّه متى انحلّ نظام موجود بمفارقة صورته الخاصّة به خلفتها في تلك المادّة صورة أخرى إمّا خير من الأُولى وإمّا مثلها وإمّا دونها فلا تتعطّل المادّة أصلاً بأن تنعدم من الخارج بل المادّة باقية في صور غير باقية فالاسم الحافظ متولّي حفظ المادّة بلحاق تصرّف الاسم المصوّر لها بإيجاد صورة أخرى.

٣،٧٧ وانظر إلى المادّة التي يسمّيها قوم بالعناصر تجد ما يحلّ من الأرض إذا فارقته صورة الأرضيّة صار ماءً بتصوير الاسم المصوّر فيها صورة المائيّة وكذلك ما يحلّ

The Surah of Joseph

The Surah of Joseph has two names.

Al-Ḥāfiẓ: The Preserver

Only al-Bayhaqī mentions it as a divine name. It occurs in the Surah of Joseph in the verse: «God is the best for preservation»,[432] where preservation can also be read as Preserver. We have already spoken about the Preserving. The difference between the Preserving and the Preserver is like the difference between the emphatic and non-emphatic forms of the active participle, *faʿīl*, ever-active, and *fāʿil*, active. 77.1

One aspect of the Preserver's preservation pertains to the light in which the universe—that is, existence—was formed. For, according to our school, it is actually the underlying material substrate in which, and from which, the forms display accidents. One example of its preservation is that each time the structure of an existent decomposes and is separated from its specific form, another form takes place within its material substratum. The latter is either superior, similar, or inferior to the first. In the external realm the material substrate, therefore, is never destroyed or reduced to nonexistence. Rather, it subsists within perishing forms. The Preserver presides over the preservation of the material substratum by bringing the activity of the Form-Giver to bear upon the existentiation of a new form. 77.2

When you consider the material substrate that one school calls the "elements," you notice that when something loosens from the earth and loses its terrestrial form, it becomes water because the Form-Giver gives it an aquatic form. Likewise, when the element of water expands, it assumes the accidents 77.3

من عنصر الماء وينبسط فإنّه يعرض له بتصوير الاسم المصوّر صورة الهواء وكذلك نسبة الهواء إذا انحلّ ولطف عرضت له صورة النار فكان من النار فالجوهر الذي هو المادّة محفوظة بالاسم الحافظ سبحانه.

٤،٧٧ وكذلك القول فيما يتكاثف من جرم النار بصورة الاسم المصوّر هواءً فتنحفظ المادّة بالاسم الحافظ وكذلك يتكاثف الهواء فيكون ماءً والماء فيكون أرضاً وكذلك ما يستحيل من الأرض والماء إلى المعدن تحت الأرض وإلى النبات فوقها وتحتها وإلى الحيوان فوقها كلّها تتعاقب فيه الصور بالخلع والتلبّس من نفس المادّة بتصوير الاسم المصوّر تعالى فيوجب ذلك بقاء المادّة فيتعيّن بينهما حكم الاسم الحافظ تعالى.

٥،٧٧ واعلم أنّ الصور كلّها أعراض للمادّة منها فلا يلتفَت إلى قول المخالفين الذين يقولون إنّ الصورة المقوّمة هي جوهر في الجوهر والصورة المتمّمة قد تكون عرضاً بل الجميع أعراض وكلّ صورة فهي مقوّمة بجميع ما عرضت له فإنّه إنّما تكوّن هو بجميع متمِماته حتّى بالغواشي الغريبة كالثوب فإنّه إنّما هو مجموعه وهيئاته إنّما هو بأن يعتبَر معه ثوبه ذلك فإذا أزاله كان مجموع آخر هذا في الغواشي الغريبة فكيف فيما هو من الموجود نفسه.

٦،٧٧ واعلم أنّ خاصّة هذا الذكر حفظ الحال فيذكره من يخاف المكر.

of the form of air through the form-giving of the Form-Giver. Likewise, when a part of air becomes subtler, it is exposed to and becomes a part of the form of fire. The substance, which is the underlying material substrate, is preserved through the Preserver.

The same can be said for the body of fire that assumes density and becomes air through the Form-Giver. Wherefore, the material substrate preserves itself through the Preserver. Likewise, air assumes density and turns into water, and water into earth, just as things made of earth and water transform into minerals inside the earth, into plants that grow above and below the earth, and into animals that live above the earth. In each case, the forms succeed one another by casting off or assuming forms of the same underlying material substrate through the form-giving of the Form-Giver. This necessitates the subsistence of the material substrate, and thus the property of the Preserver becomes determined between the two forms. 77.4

Moreover, all forms are accidents of their underlying material substrate. Therefore, we pay no regard to the doctrine of our opponents who say that the constituting form is a substance within a substance, while the completing form could be an accident.[433] Rather, both are accidents, for every form is a constituent of all the accidents it is exposed to, and the thing is what it is precisely because of the totality of the elements that complete it. These include all coverings, including clothing; for the thing is its totality, and its configurations are taken into account, including its clothes. Thus, if it is stripped of its clothes, then it is a new totality. This is true for all coverings, to say nothing of what pertains to the existent itself. 77.5

The characteristic of this invocation is that it preserves one's spiritual state. It should therefore be invoked by the one who fears deception. 77.6

اسمه الرافع تبارك وتعالى

١،٧٨ اتّفق على إيرادِه الأئمّة الثلاثة رضوان الله عليهم وشاهده من سورة يوسف عليه السلام قوله تعالى ﴿نَرْفَعُ دَرَجَٰتٍ مَّن نَّشَآءُ﴾ واعلم أنّ من جملة أحكام هذا الاسم العظيم أن يعتبَر فيه ثلاث اعتبارات أحدهما عامّ والآخر خاصّ والآخر أخصّ.

٢،٧٨ فالعامّ رفعه تعالى لموجوداته في أحكام دنياهم فيرفع فيها درجات من يشاء من الخلفاء والملوك والأمراء والحكّام وأرباب المراتب على اختلافها فإنّ ذلك لا يكون إلّا برفعه تعالى لهم ويكون ذلك في سائر اعتبارات ما يرفع فيه الموجود حتّى في المآكل فبعضها أرفع من بعض وفي المشارب وفي المساكن وفي الملابس وفي المراكيب ولمّا سُبقت ناقة النبيّ صلّى الله عليه وسلّم وأُخبر بذلك قال إنّ حقًّا على الله تعالى ألّا يرفع شيئًا من الدنيا إلّا وضعه فسمّى سبقها لغيرها رفعًا وسمّى كونها سُبقت وضعًا ويتعدّى[١] هذا الحكم إلى النبات والمعادن وأُصولها.

٣،٧٨ وأمّا الخاصّ فهو رفعه تعالى للعلماء على الجهّال ورفعه للعابدين على العلماء غير العابدين إذا عمل العابدون العمل الصالح بالعلم النافع ورفعه للصوفيّة العابدين على العابدين فقط وإن كانوا علماء ورفع المحبّين مطلقًا على الصوفيّة ورفع العارفين على المحبّين ورفع الواقفين على العارفين والوقفة هي نهاية الخواصّ فهذه أحكام كلّها تكون من الاسم الرافع جلّ عطاؤه لأهل السفَر الأوّل ومن قبلهم.

٤،٧٨ وأمّا الاعتبار الأخصّ فهو مراتب ترقّي الواقفين في السفر الثاني وهم أهل البقاء بعد الفناء وأهل التلوين في التمكين وأهل تفصيل العين ونقش الواحد بالإثنين وهؤلاء هم أهل الترقّي الذاتيّ ومنتهاهم إلى حقيقة القطبيّة فيمرّون على مراتب ما قبل النقباء ثمّ على النقباء ومن بعدهم من الأوتاد والإمامين فإذا تعيّن لأحدهم القيام بحقيقة القطبيّة كانت مرتبة القطبيّة به لا له وكانت القطابة حكمًا من أحكامه فيكون في

١ و: وتقدير.

Al-Rāfiʿ: The One Who Elevates

The three eminent scholars, God be pleased with them, agree it is a divine name. It occurs in the Surah of Joseph in the verse: «We elevate the ranks of whomever We wish».[434] Know that the properties of this supreme name involve at least three considerations. The first property is general, the second specific, and the third more specific still. 78.1

The general consideration is the elevating of His creatures in their worldly properties. He elevates the ranks of those He wills, be they caliphs, kings, emirs, rulers, or notables of various types. Indeed, this elevation only occurs because He elevates their rank. Moreover, this occurs in all other considerations in which He elevates an existent, including foodstuffs (for some are loftier than others), drinks, dwellings, clothes, and riding animals. Once, when the blessed Prophet was informed of the defeat of his she-camel in a race, he said, "Indeed, God's right is that whenever He elevates something in this world, He lowers it."[435] The blessed Prophet called her victory an elevation, and her defeat a lowering. This principle, moreover, extends to the vegetal and mineral realms, as well as their fundamental constituents. 78.2

The specific consideration is that He elevates scholars above the ignorant, and elevates pious scholars above impious scholars, provided that beneficial knowledge informs the performance of righteous deeds by the pious. Furthermore, He elevates pious Sufis above pious non-Sufis even if they are scholars, He elevates the lovers categorically above the Sufis, the recognizers above the lovers, and those who arrive at the station of halting above the recognizers. The station of halting, moreover, is the end of the spiritual elite, and thus these properties all occur through the Uplifter, both for those who are on the first journey and for those in their wake. 78.3

The most specific consideration is the levels of ascent of those who have arrived at the station of halting and are on the second journey. These are the people of subsistence after annihilation; the people of variegation in stability; the people of differentiation of identity and the imprinting of the one by the two. They are those who ascend to the Essence, whose extreme limit is the reality of the axial saint. Thus they pass through the levels preceding the Chiefs, then the Chiefs, then the Pegs and the two Leaders.[436] When one 78.4

الوقت الواحد آلاف كلّهم أقطاب وحكم الجميع حكم الواحد فيسمّون واحدًا بالمقام وإن كانوا أعدادًا بالأشخاص ومن هؤلاء يكون الرسل والكلّ من المشايخ أهل التربية وهم رسل للخواصّ فافهم.

٥،٧٨ وأمّا هذا الذكر فإنّه نافع لمن غلب عليه التواضع في التصوّف فيذكره في خلوته فينصلح.

is appointed to reside through the reality of the axial saint, the level of the axial saint is engendered by him, rather than for him, and axiality becomes one of his properties, so that at any given moment he is thousandfold, each of whom is an axial saint, and the property of all is the property of the one. Whereupon, these are called "one" by virtue of station, even though they are multiple in terms of individuals. The Messengers come, as well as the perfected shaykhs of spiritual training, who are Messengers for the elite, from their number. So understand!

This invocation is beneficial for those given to excessive humility in their Sufi demeanor. It may be invoked in the spiritual retreat in order to be rectified. 78.5

سورة الرعد

وفيها ستّة أسماء

اسمه المدبّر تبارك وتعالى

انفرد به البيهقيّ وشاهده من سورة الرعد قوله تعالى ﴿يُدَبِّرُ ٱلْأَمْرَ يُفَصِّلُ ٱلْآيَٰتِ﴾ ١،٧٩
ومعنى ﴿يُدَبِّرُ ٱلْأَمْرَ﴾ يحكمه و﴿ٱلْآيَٰت﴾ العلامات والمراد علامات وحدانيّة الحقّ سبحانه فعلامات وحدانيّته قد فصّلها تدبيره الأمر وليس المراد بالتدبير التفكّر فإنّ ذلك شنيع أن ينسَب إلى الحقّ تعالى لأنّه عالِم من غير تفكّر لكنّ صدور موجوداته تعالى محكَمة هو المراد بالتدبير وهو خطاب لنا بما نألف.

٢،٧٩ ولا نشكّ في إتقان هذا العالم وكون الخلق والأمر فيه متساوقين على نظام يقتضي أن يكون العالم علامة على الحقّ ولذلك قرن قوله تعالى ﴿يُدَبِّرُ ٱلْأَمْرَ﴾ بقوله ﴿يُفَصِّلُ ٱلْآيَٰتِ﴾ والتفصيل في محلّ عالم الخلق و﴿يُدَبِّرُ ٱلْأَمْرَ﴾ هو في عالم الأمر قال الله تعالى ﴿أَلَا لَهُ ٱلْخَلْقُ وَٱلْأَمْرُ تَبَارَكَ ٱللَّهُ﴾ فأمّا عالم الخلق فظاهره تعلّق المسبّبات بأسبابها ظاهرًا وأمّا عالم الأمر فوجود الحقّ ظاهرًا وباطنًا بأسمائها وصفاتها وأفعالها من حيث ما هو موجود منه ذواتها فالمحجوبون يشهدون عالم الخلق وأهل الكشف

The Surah of the Thunder

The Surah of the Thunder has six names.

Al-Mudabbir: The Governing

Only al-Bayhaqī mentions this as a divine name, from the verse: «He governs the command and differentiates the signs».[437] The meaning of «He governs the command» is He presides over it. Moreover, these «signs» are marks; that is, marks of the unity of the Real, and they are differentiated by His governance of the command. Rational deliberation is not what is meant here by governance. For it is absurd to ascribe such a thing to the Real, because He knows without rational deliberation. Instead, what is meant by governance is the emergence of existents in a well-designed fashion; it is a way of addressing us in a manner we are familiar with. 79.1

Furthermore, we do not doubt the meticulous perfection of this world, or the fact that in it the creation and the command concur according to an orderly arrangement that entails this world is a mark of the Real. For this reason, He links the assertion «He governs the command» with «He differentiates the signs». The "differentiation" occurs in the realm of creation, whereas «He governs the command» occurs in the realm of command. God says: «Verily the creation and the command belong to Him; blessed is God».[438] The manifest effects of the realm of creation are connected to their causes outwardly. The realm of command[439] is the Real's existence, both outwardly and inwardly, through its names, qualities, and acts inasmuch as their essences exist through Him. As such, veiled intellects witness the realm of creation, whereas those who are unveiled witness the realm of command. For their part, those who are 79.2

يشهدون عالم الأمر والذاتيّون يشهدونهما في غيبة منهما في إحاطة قدس الذات فلهم شهود الخلق والأمر لأنّهم في حضرة ﴿تَبَارَكَ ٱللَّهُ﴾ من حيث هو هو وفي ضمن ذلك ثبوت حضرة كونه ﴿رَبِّ ٱلْعَٰلَمِينَ﴾ .

٣،٧٩ ولمّا ذكر الشيخ محيي الدين بن العربيّ قدّسه الله ترقّي السالك بتقليد الشارع وترقّي الفيلسوف بفكره جعل مبيت المتشرّع في السماء الدنيا عند آدم عليه السلام ومبيت الفيلسوف عند القمر ثمّ ذكر القصّة كلّها وأنّ المتشرّع ينزل في كلّ سماء عند نبيّ والفيلسوف عند كوكب حتّى بلغا إلى العقل الأوّل فوقف الفيلسوف عنده لأنّه به سلك وتعدّاه المتشرّع إلى حضرة ربّه عزّ وجلّ لأنّه به سلك فكان الفيلسوف أبدًا في عالم الخلق والمتشرّع في عالم الأمر وهما متجاوران ظاهرًا ومتباينان حقيقة وباطنًا.

٤،٧٩ واعلم أنّ كلّ ظهور ففيه علامة على وحدانيّة الحقّ من حيث يعرج ذلك الظهور بقوله أنا والقائل أنا عند قول كلّ قائل هو الواحد تعالى إذ لا يستحقّ الأنانيّة غيره فالتدبير بين عالم الأمر والخلق ظاهر ومنه تعيّن الاسم المدبّر تعالى ويدخل الاسم الحكيم في حقيقة الاسم المدبّر ويظهر حكم الهادي في تفصيل الآيات.

٥،٧٩ ويصلح للسالك ذكر هذا الاسم إلّا أن يخاف عليه الشيخ من غلبة الوجد[١] والله أعلم.

١ آ، ب، ج: التوحيد.

absorbed in the Essence witness both, in their absence from them and within the all-encompassing holy Essence. They witness the creation and the command because they are in the presence of «Blessed is God» insofar as He is He; and within «Blessed is God» is the immutability of the presence of Him as «Lord of the worlds».[440]

When Shaykh Muḥyī l-Dīn ibn al-ʿArabī, may God sanctify him, mentions how the wayfarer ascends by following the Lawgiver, and the philosopher ascends by following rational thought, he designates the dwelling of the Shariah-bound wayfarer in the lowest heaven with Adam, and the dwelling of the philosopher in the moon. He goes on to detail this in its entirety, including the fact that the Shariah-bound wayfarer pauses in every heaven at a Prophet, while the philosopher pauses at a celestial object, until both attain the First Intellect. The philosopher halts there because his wayfaring was through it, whereas the Shariah-bound wayfarer goes beyond it to the presence of his Lord, for his wayfaring was through Him. Thus, the philosopher always remains in the realm of creation, while the Shariah-bound wayfarer is in the realm of command. Both are outwardly parallel, but are distinct inwardly and in truth.[441] 79.3

Moreover, each manifestation contains the mark of unity of the Real, insofar as that manifestation ascends by the word "I," and the one who says "I" within each speaker is the One, for none other is worthy of selfhood but He.[442] Thus, governance between the realm of command and the realm of creation is evident, and it is through the latter that the Governing becomes determined. Furthermore, the Wise is included within the reality of the Governing, and the property of the Guide manifests through the differentiation of the signs. 79.4

Invoking this name is suitable for the wayfarer, unless the shaykh fears that he will be overwhelmed by ecstasy. And God knows best. 79.5

اسمه القهّار جلّت قدرته

١،٨٠ اتّفق عليه البيهقيّ والغزاليّ ولم يذكره أبو الحكم وشاهده من سورة الرعد قوله تعالى ﴿وَهُوَ ٱلْوَٰحِدُ ٱلْقَهَّـٰرُ﴾ والقهر الغلبة ومراتب قهره لا تحصى فإنّ من غُلب فإنّ الحقّ تعالى هو الغالب القاهر له.

٢،٨٠ وليس في الوجود الذي لا تتناهى أنواعه نوع إلّا وهو مقهور قهرًا يجده ولا يجد منه بدًّا ولو في انحصاره فإنّ الوجود نفسه غير منحصر والموجود كيف كان فهو منحصر منقهر فرجوع الموجودات بالموت والفناء إليه تعالى قهر وافتقارهم إليه مع اجتهادهم أن يستغنوا قهر وتوقّف المسبَّبات على أسبابها هو من قهره لها إذ لا تقدر أن تكون واجبة الوجود من غير شرط وانقياد العوالم إليه تعالى طوعًا هو قهر لأنّه هو الذي جعلها طائعة وظهور ما خالف منها بالمخالفة هو من قهره تعالى لهم حتّى خالفوا من جهة أنّه ﴿لِذَٰلِكَ خَلَقَهُمْ﴾ وشهوات النفوس والأجسام وغيرها هو من قهره تعالى لها حيث غلبها على أن توجَد كذلك فإنّه ليس لشيء من نفسه أن يظهر بما أراد بل بما يراد منه ﴿وَهُوَ ٱلْقَاهِرُ فَوْقَ عِبَادِهِۦ﴾ والفوقيّة علوّ معنويّ لا حسّيّ وكلّ قاهر في الوجود هو مقهور حتّى في كونه قاهرًا لم يكن قاهرًا من تلقاء نفسه بل قُهر على أن يصير قاهرًا فالقهر الإلٰهيّ شامل.

٣،٨٠ وبالجملة فمن علم أنّ الموجود منقهر الوجود فقد عرف المقصود والوجود هو الذي هو في الخارج والداخل والمحيط الذي لا يحاط به وقوّته هي القاهرة لِما ظهر بها من وجودها وهذه القوّة القهّارة هي منقهرة أيضًا له تعالى من جهة انفعاليّة وجوده لتظهر فيها أحكام القهّاريّة فصار المنفعل مقهورًا لكن لذاته وهو قهر يصيّر المنفعل

Al-Qahhār: The All-Subjugating

Al-Bayhaqī and al-Ghazālī agree it is a divine name, while Ibn Barrajān does not mention it in his commentary. It occurs in the Surah of the Thunder in the verse: «He is the One, the All-Subjugating».[443] Subjugation is dominance, and the levels of His dominance are innumerable, for when anyone is dominated, it is God who dominates and subjugates him. 80.1

All the infinite species in existence find themselves subjugated. There is no escape from their subjugation; even by the mere fact they are circumscribed. For existence itself is not circumscribed, yet existents of all types are circumscribed and subjugated. Thus, the return of existents to Him through death and annihilation is subjugation. Despite their efforts to be independent, their dependence on Him is subjugation. The confinement of effects to their causes is from His subjugation, for they cannot be existentially necessary in an unconditional manner. The willful submission of the worlds to Him is subjugation because He made them obedient. The presence of those who are disobedient is from His subjugation over them, in that they are disobedient, for «this is why He created them».[444] The appetites of the souls, the bodies, and others are from His subjugation inasmuch as He compels them to exist in that way. For nothing manifests itself in the way that it wills, but rather in the way that is willed for it. «He is the subjugator above His servants».[445] "Above" here is meant in a supersensory, not spatial, sense. Furthermore, every subjugator in existence is subjugated even by the fact that he is a subjugator. For he is not a subjugator of his own accord, but rather is compelled to be one. Thus, divine subjugation is all-encompassing. 80.2

In short, whoever knows that all existent things are in a state of existential subjugation understands what is meant. Existence, moreover, is what is both in the external and the internal realm. It is the circumference that cannot be circumscribed. Its power subjugates all things that become manifest through its existence. This all-subjugating power, moreover, is itself subjugated by God with regard to its receptivity of His being in order for the properties of subjugation to become manifest within it. Thus, that which is being acted upon becomes subjugated, but through its own essence, and that is a subordination that turns the passive subject into an active agent which acts upon another 80.3

بمعنويّته فاعلاً في الفاعل في أن يصير فاعلاً فالقهر عامّ فرعاً وأصلاً وجزءاً وكلاًّ وغيباً وشهادة فالقهر يدخل في الاسم المحيط.

٤،٨٠ واعلم أنّ رجوع الاسم القهّار بالذات للاسم الله من جهة أنّه مرتبيّ وأمّا باعتبار بعض الظهورات الوجوديّة كما يفرط النافع فيصير ضارّاً لا بالذات بل بالعرض فالقهّار في تلك الرتبة راجع إلى الاسم الرحمٰن ويتداخل الاسمان في الإحاطة فيصير القهّار محيطاً بهما من حيث الذات ومن القهّاريّة الإلٰهيّة قهر التوحيد للشرك في أطوار شهود أهل المعارف وأهل المواقف.

٥،٨٠ وخاصّيّة هذا الذكر يرجع إلى سلوك الملوك والجبابرة فإنّهم إذا ذكروه جمعهم على الحقّ والله أعلم.

اسمه الكبير تبارك وتعالى

١،٨١ هذا الاسم الكريم متّفق عليه بين الأئمّة الثلاثة وشاهده من سورة الرعد قوله تعالى ﴿عَٰلِمُ ٱلْغَيْبِ وَٱلشَّهَٰدَةِ ٱلْكَبِيرُ﴾ واعلم أنّ الكبير هنا بمعنى العظيم ومنه يُشتقّ الكبرياء وهو له تعالى لا لغيره وذلك لأنّ كلّ عظمة نُسبت إلى عظيم استحقّها تعالى لأنّ وجوده عين وجودها وتنزّه عن أن يكون وجودها عين وجوده.

٢،٨١ ثمّ إنّ له تعالى الكبرياء مطلقاً أمّا إن اعتبرت الذات فانفرادها بوجوب وجودها بها لا بغيرها عظمة وكبرياء لا يشارَك فيه وكذلك إن اعتبرت صفتها فإنّ اعتبارات الصفات إمّا مرتبيّة وإمّا وجوديّة فالمرتبيّة لها من قبل الاسم الله وأمّا الوجوديّة فمن قبل الاسم الرحمٰن.

active agent, making it active. Subordination is thus universal, and it includes the branch and the root, the part and the whole, the visible and the invisible. Subjugation thus pertains to the Encompassing.

Because it pertains to the ranks, the All-Subjugating returns to the Essence through Allāh. However, with regard to certain manifestations of existence—such as when an excess of benefit becomes harmful in an accidental, not essential, manner—then at that level the All-Subjugating derives from the All-Merciful, and the two names interpenetrate in their universal encompassment. Thereupon, the All-Subjugating encompasses both names with respect to the Essence. One aspect of divine subjugation is the subjugation of monotheism over polytheism at the stages of witness by the people of the sciences of direct recognition and those who have arrived at the station of halting. 80.4

The special characteristic of this invocation relates to the spiritual wayfaring of kings and tyrants. For, when they invoke this name, it brings them back to the Real. And God knows best. 80.5

Al-Kabīr: The Great

The three eminent scholars agree it is a divine name. It occurs in the Surah of the Thunder in the verse: «Knower of the unseen and the seen, the Great».[446] Moreover, the Great here means the Magnificent. Self-grandeur (*kibriyā'*) is derived from the Great (*al-Kabīr*) and it belongs only to Him. After all, the magnificence that is ascribed to anything magnificent belongs rightfully to God, since His existence is identical with its existence, though its existence is not identical with His transcendent existence. 81.1

Furthermore, to Him belongs unconditional greatness. If you consider the Essence, then the singularity of Its necessary existence within Itself, and not through anything other than Itself, is a quality of magnificence and greatness that is not shared by anyone. Likewise, if you consider Its qualities, they either pertain to rank or to existence. The qualities of rank are from Allāh, whereas the qualities of existence are from the All-Merciful. 81.2

٣،٨١ وله تعالى الكبرياء في معاني صفاته الحسنى فله العظمة في الاسم الله من جهة أنّ العقول مولّهة فيه وله العظمة من قبل الاسم الرحمٰن من جهة وجود كلّ عظيم وعظمة الوجود أيضاً ولكلّ صفةٍ عظمة يعتبَر فيها الاسم الكبير تعالى. وله الكبرياء من جهة أسمائه من جهة أنّه لا يقع اسم إلّا عليه لغلبته على الوجود واستئثاره به.

٤،٨١ والأسماء والصفات والأفعال إذا نُسبت إليه من الوجه الذي يشهده أهل الله كانت كلّها كبرياء وعظمة وهذا المشهد صعب سماعه على العقول المحجوبة أمّا العقول التي كانت عين معقولها فإنّها لا ترى غيره وتعرف وجه الكبرياء فيه ولذلك لا يصغر عند العارفين شيء بل يرون الموجودات بعين التعظيم لظهور العظيم بها فإن ضعفت عن سماع هذا فبظهورها بالعظيم تعالى فهو الكبير جلّ جلاله وتقدّس عمّا يتوهّم المحجوب من لوازم هذا الكلام في ذهنه الناقص عن الكمال.

٥،٨١ فمن كان من أهل المشهد عظّم كلّ شيء ورأى الاسم الكبير جلّ جلاله وإن لم يكن من أهل هذا المشهد فأقلّ أقسام أن يلاحظ كبرياء الكبير عند رؤية كلّ كبير فإنّه تعالى هو معطي ذلك الكبير ما به سمّي كبيراً ومعطي العظمة أعظم من المعطى فالله تعالى هو الكبير عند كلّ كبير وقبله وبعده وفي الشهود هو وحده.

٦،٨١ ولقد عجز من ظنّ أنّ العالم كبير وهو صغير إذ هو يعني أنّ العالم هو هذه الأفلاك وما اشتملت عليه ولو كان كذلك لما كانت كبرياء الله تعالى العائدة إليه من العالم إلّا بقدر هذا العالم المحصور كلّا بل عظمة الكبير سبحانه غير متناهية في كلّ آن.

٧،٨١ واعلم أنّ هذا الاسم يأمر الشيخ تلميذه أن يذكره إذا غلب عليه تجلّي القرب وخاف عليه الوله منه والله أعـلم.

He also possesses greatness within the pure meanings of His beautiful qualities. Thus, He possesses magnificence within Allāh in regard of the fact that intellects are utterly confounded in Him. He possesses greatness, moreover, in view of the All-Merciful through the existence of all magnificent things, as well as the magnificence of existence. Each quality possesses a quality of magnificence in which the Great can be taken into account. He possesses greatness in His names too, in that all names are affected by it, for it dominates existence, and because existence displays its traces.[447] 81.3

When the names, qualities, and acts are ascribed to Him in terms of what God's folk witness, then they are entirely great and magnificent. This contemplative station is difficult for the puny-minded. Intellects that are identical with their intelligible objects see only Him, and they recognize the greatness therein. For this reason, the recognizers consider nothing to be low in rank. Rather they view everything as magnificent because the Magnificent becomes manifest therein. When they are too weak to hear this, it is because of their manifestation through the Magnificent. Thus He is the Great, and He is hallowed beyond the putative implications of this discussion within limited veiled minds. 81.4

The people of this contemplative station proclaim the magnificence of all things and see the Great. For those who are not the people of this contemplative station, the lowest category is beholding the grandeur of the Great upon seeing anything great. For it is He who bestows greatness on that thing, and the bestower of magnificence is more magnificent than its recipient. Thus, He is the Great along with, before, and after all the great ones. In witnessing, however, He is alone. 81.5

Weak is he who supposes the cosmos is great and he is small. For he supposes that the cosmos consists of the spheres and all that they contain. But if that were the case, then the divine greatness attributable to God from the cosmos would be restricted to the limited measure of this cosmos. Far from it! The magnificence of the Great—glory be!—is infinite in every sense. 81.6

The shaykh instructs his disciple to invoke this name when overwhelmed by a disclosure of His proximity, fearing that the disciple may lose his mental stability. And God knows best. 81.7

اسمه المتعال جلّ وعلا

١،٨٢ اتّفق عليه الغزاليّ والبيهقيّ ولم يذكره أبو الحكم وشاهده من سورة الرعد قوله ﴿عَٰلِمُ ٱلْغَيْبِ وَٱلشَّهَٰدَةِ ٱلْكَبِيرُ ٱلْمُتَعَالِ﴾.

٢،٨٢ وعلوّه تعالى في ذاته معنويّ وفي بعض أطوار متجلّياته حسّيّ والحسّيّ هو من لواحق اسمه الظاهر وبهذا الاعتبار هو تعالى يُرى لكن بعينه لا بعين الرائي ﴿لَّا تُدْرِكُهُ ٱلْأَبْصَٰرُ﴾ وهي أبصارنا فإذا كان سمعنا وبصرنا رأيناه به رؤية بصر هو بصره لأنّه البصير سبحانه.

٣،٨٢ وفي هذا المعنى نظم ومنه قولي

وَلَوْ لَمْ يَكُنْ مَعْنَاكَ فِي ٱلْكَوْنِ مُطْلَقًا   يَـدُلُّ عَلَيْـهِ مِـنْكَ حُسْنٌ مُـقَيَّدُ
لَمَا أَبْصَـرَتْ عَيْنٌ جَـمَالَكَ جَهْـرَةً   وَمَنْ لَمْ تُشَاهِدْ عَيْنُهُ كَيْفَ يَشْهَدُ

٤،٨٢ فالمتعالي سبحانه له العلوّ بالاعتبارات التي لا تتناهى وفي الاسم المتعالي معنى الاسم المتكبّر ومعنى الاسم القدّوس ومعنى الاسم العزيز بمعنى الامتناع وفيه معنى ﴿سُبْحَٰنَ ٱللَّهِ عَمَّا يُشْرِكُونَ﴾ فيدخل فيه الاسم الواحد.

٥،٨٢ ويدخل فيه الاسم الكبير سبحانه من حقيقة قوله الله أكبر خصوصاً في تكبيرة الإحرام فإنّها تصحب ظهور وصف العبوديّة للحسّ من المصلّي فيتعالى سبحانه عن وصف العبيد إلّا في تنزّله عندما يصلّي فيقوم بوصف عبده وجوداً ويظهر حينئذ الاسم المتعالي للعيان في وصف الكيان ويكون العلوّ في هذه المرتبة عن استئثاره بوصف كلّ ذي وصف حتّى لا يكون غيره الموصوف فهو تعاليه سبحانه عن أن يشارَك في حقيقة الوحدانيّة ولذلك تحقّق عندنا قوله ﴿سُبْحَٰنَ ٱللَّهِ عَمَّا يُشْرِكُونَ﴾.

Al-Muta'ālī: The Transcendent

This name is agreed upon as divine by al-Ghazālī and al-Bayhaqī but is not mentioned by Ibn Barrajān. It occurs in the Surah of the Thunder in the verse: «Knower of the unseen and the visible, the Great, the Transcendent».[448] 82.1

His transcendence within His Essence is supersensory; at certain stages of His disclosure it is sensory. The sensory aspect pertains to the Manifest, for from this perspective God is visible, but through His own eyes, not through the eyes of the seer. «Sight does not perceive Him»[449]—that is, our sight—but when He is our hearing and our seeing, then we see Him with a vision that is His, because He is the Seeing. 82.2

To this effect, I wrote the following verses: 82.3

If Your absolute reality
could not be indicated by delimited beauty
No eye would ever see Your beauty,
for how can a blind eye ever see?[450]

Thus, the Transcendent possesses transcendence from an infinity of perspectives. Moreover, the Transcendent comprises the meaning of the Proud, and the meaning of the Holy, and the meaning of the Mighty in the sense of impregnability. It also comprises the meaning of the verse: «God be glorified above what they associate»,[451] and therefore the One is included within it. 82.4

Furthermore, the Great is included within it with respect to the reality of the expression "God is Greater" (*Allāhu akbar*). This is especially so when the phrase is pronounced upon entering into the ritual prayer, for it goes hand in hand with the tangible manifestation of the quality of servanthood upon the person who is praying. God then transcends the quality of His servants, except with respect to His descent when they pray. He then assumes the description attributed to Him by His servant existentially, and at that moment the Transcendent manifests to the eye through the quality of his being. God's transcendence in this level lies in His sole claim to the qualities that are attributed to every qualified thing, such that He alone is qualified by a quality. Such is His transcendence beyond sharing in the reality of His oneness. In this way, we realize His words: «God be glorified above what they associate». 82.5

٦،٨٢ فالمتعالي عن الشرك هو أن يظهر بالأوصاف وكيف لا يظهر بوجود الصفات من استأثر بظهور وجود الذوات حتّى يكون هو المتعيّن ومخلوقاته هي التعيّنات وهي عدميّات في أنفسها وفي اعتبار قيامها في الذهن هي وجوديّات.

فَمَا فِي تَصَارِيفِ مَعْنَى ٱلْوُجُودِ   مَجَالٌ لِشَيْئِيَّةٍ غَيْرِهِ
وَلَا فِيهِ إِلَّا ٱلَّذِي مِنْهُ فِي   تَعَيُّنِهِ فِي مَدَى سَيْرِهِ

٧،٨٢ وهذا الاسم مثل الكبير في كونه ينفع من غلبه القرب وكاد يولّهه فإذا ذكره عاد إلى الحسّ والله أعلم.

اسمه الواقي به العصمةُ ومنه الرحمة

١،٨٣ انفرد به البيهقيّ وشاهده من سورة الرعد قوله تعالى ﴿وَمَا لَهُم مِّنَ ٱللَّهِ مِن وَاقٍ﴾ مع أنّ هذه الآية لا تشهد بأنّ هذا الاسم من أسمائه تعالى فتأمّلها تجد ذلك غير أنّه من أسمائه تعالى في قوله ﴿فَوَقَٰهُمُ ٱللَّهُ شَرَّ ذَٰلِكَ ٱلْيَوْمِ﴾ وهو بمعنى الحفيظ والحافظ وقد تقدّم ذكرهما.

٢،٨٣ وكيفيّة الوقاية تختلف اعتباراتها فمنها أنّ قوله تعالى ﴿سَرَٰبِيلَ تَقِيكُمُ ٱلْحَرَّ وَسَرَٰبِيلَ تَقِيكُم بَأْسَكُمْ﴾ فإنّما يريد أنّني الواقي لكم بها أمّا أوّلاً فلأنّها من وجوده وَجُوده وأمّا ثانياً فإنّ قوّتها من قوّته ﴿أَنَّ ٱلْقُوَّةَ لِلَّهِ جَمِيعًا﴾ وأمّا بعد فإنّ ظهورها من اسمه الظاهر وقهرها لما وقت منه من اسمه القاهر.

Thus, His transcendence beyond partnership is to be made manifest through the qualities. And how could He not become manifest through the existence of qualities, when He is the One who has sole claim to the manifestation of the existence of essences? For He is the One who determines, while His creatures are but determinations, and are nonexistent in themselves, and only seem to exist because of their conception in the mind. 82.6

In the vicissitudes of the realm of existence
there is no room for the thing-ness of other-than-He.
All things therein come from Him,
as variegated as they are throughout the course of their journey.[452]

This name is similar to the Great in that it benefits those who are overwhelmed by divine proximity to the point that they nearly lose their balance. When they invoke it, they return to their senses. And God knows best. 82.7

Al-Wāqī: The Protector

Only al-Bayhaqī cites it as a divine name. It occurs in the Surah of the Thunder in the verse: «they have no protector from God»,[453] and although this verse does not attest that it is one of His names—contemplate the verse and you will discover as much—it is one of His names in the verse: «so God protected them from the evil of that day».[454] As we discussed earlier, this name can mean the Preserver and the All-Preserving. 83.1

The modality of God's protection involves various considerations. For example, the verse «He has made coats for you that protect you from the heat, and coats that protect you from your own might»[455] actually means "I am your Protector through them." This is because these things are, first, from His existence and His munificence, and, second, their power is from His power, since «power belongs altogether to God».[456] Finally, it is because their manifestation is through the Manifest, and they control whatever the coats protect against through the All-Subjugating. 83.2

٣،٨٣ وهو الواقي تعالى بالطعام من ألم الجوع بحقيقة اسمه الرزّاق وبالصّون باسمه المعزّ من الذلّ والخضوع وهو الواقي تعالى باسمه الشافي من المرض وباسمه الكافي ممّا لولاه لَعرض ومن أين للحصون تمنّع لولا اسمه المانع ومن أين للبّاس والنجدة أن تدفع لولا اسمه الدافع فهو الواقي سبحانه بمعاني الأسماء ما ينزل إلى الأرض من آفات السماء وهو الواقي سبحانه باسمه المؤمن لهب النار والمطفئ باسمه العفوّ غضب اسمه الجبّار وكيف لا يكون واقياً من الشرور وهي كلّها ظلم وهو النور والشرّ غضب والرحمة منه سبقت الغضب فهو الواقي بالسبق والسابق بالوقاية.

٤،٨٣ والشرّ ينتهي إلى الخير والخير بلا نهاية فما اندفع عن شيء من الأشياء سوء إلّا والواقي هو الذي حفظه ومن هذه الحقيقة قوله عليه السلام اللّٰهمّ إنّي أدرء بك في نحورهم وأشار أيضاً إلى ظهوره في طوري الخير والشرّ بقوله أعوذ بك منك فهو الواقي سبحانه في كلّ ما يتعوّذ به منه ويفزع إليه عنه.

٥،٨٣ ولقد جرت لي في السفر من الديار المصريّة إلى زيارة قبر الخليل عليه السلام مع بعض المشايخ يقال له جمال الدين بن النويريّ واقعة في طريق الرمل وذلك أنّا جلسنا على الرمل فسعى إلينا الدلم وهو دويبة تؤلم بقرصها وتؤذي المكان الذي تقرصه من الجسم فجعلت أنا أصرفه عنّي مشاهداً لاسمه الواقي تعالى وصبر هو على ألمه وضرّه واعتذر بأنّه لا يريد أن يظهر عليه أحكام البشريّة فقلت له ما أنا الواقي بل شهدت الواقي الحقّ فعرف غلطه وجلس على يدي في الخلوة في حرم الخليل بعدما صرف أصحابه عنه وتجرّد.

٦،٨٣ واعلم أنّ الاسم الواقي لا يذكر في الخلوة لأنّ شرطها بذل النفس والله أعلم.

Furthermore, He protects them with food from the pain of hunger through the reality of the Provider; and with safety from abasement and meekness through the Exalter. Through the Healer, He is the Protector from illness; and through the Sufficer from what would otherwise become susceptible. For how could fortresses protect anything were it not for the Preventer; or how could clothing and reinforcements repel anything were it not for the Repeller? Through the pure meanings of the names, therefore, He is the Protector from the tribulations that descend to earth from heaven. Through the Giver of Safety, He is the Protector from the blaze of the Fire, and through the Forgiving, He is the extinguisher of the wrath of the All-Dominating. For how could He not be a Protector from evil things, all of which are darkness, when He is the Light? Evil is wrath, and mercy from Him precedes His wrath. Thus, He is the Protector by precedence, and He it is who takes precedence in protecting. 83.3

Furthermore, evil ultimately reaches the good, and the good is infinite. Thus, no ugliness is ever removed from a thing except that it is the Protector who preserves it. It is from this reality that the blessed Prophet said: "O God, I fend them off through You!"[457] He also alluded to His manifestation at both stages of evil and good when he said: "I seek refuge in You from You."[458] For He is the Protector from all things from which refuge is sought in Him, and from which flight is made to Him. 83.4

Once I was on a trip from Egypt to visit the tomb of God's Intimate Friend Abraham, peace be upon him. I was with a shaykh called Jamāl al-Dīn ibn al-Nuwayrī,[459] and we conversed as we made our way across the sands. When we sat on the sand, insects started to crawl over us—the little insects that inflict painful bites—so I began to shoo them away from me as I invoked the Protector. The shaykh, for his part, endured the pain and explained to me that he did not wish to exhibit natural human traits during the ordeal. I said to him, "I am not the protector, but rather I invoked the true Protector." He thus recognized his mistake. After dismissing his disciples and withdrawing from the world, the shaykh entered into the spiritual retreat under my supervision at the tomb of the Intimate Friend. 83.5

The Protector should not be invoked in the spiritual retreat because it is conditional upon freely giving up one's soul. And God knows best. 83.6

سورة إبراهيم عليه السلام

وفيها اسم واحد

اسمه المنّان شمل منّه ورحمته

١،٨٤ انفرد به أبو الحكم بن برّجان وشاهده من سورة إبراهيم قوله تعالى ﴿وَلَٰكِنَّ ٱللَّهَ يَمُنُّ عَلَىٰ مَن يَشَآءُ مِنْ عِبَادِهِۦ﴾ والمنّ الإنعام وهو أبلغ من الاسم المنعم لما في الصيغة من المبالغة.

٢،٨٤ والمنّ من كلّ مانّ إنّما هو من الاسم المنّان تعالى واليد العليا في الصدقة أشرف من السفلى عند رؤية الفرق لأنّ المنّان هو المنعم بها فإن لم يحصل الفرق وحصل النظر بعين الجمع فالصدقة تقع في يد الحقّ قبل أن تقع في يد السائل وحقيقة ﴿مَن ذَا ٱلَّذِى يُقْرِضُ ٱللَّهَ﴾ تنفي السائل وحقيقة اليد العليا أشرف تنفي المسؤول والحقّ تعالى في الطرفين يبلّغ السؤل يقول شيخنا محيي الدين بن العربيّ رضي الله عنه وأرضاه من كانت هباته لا تَتَعَدَّى يديه فلا واهب ولا موهوب ومن كان عين الحجاب على نفسه فلا حاجب ولا محجوب.

٣،٨٤ فالمنّ الإلٰهيّ عامّ فإعطاؤه صور الإيجاد منّ وإبقاؤه لمن أوجد ولما أوجد منّ وتعليق المسبّبات بالأسباب منّ والمدد الدائم منه منّ وإعطاؤه قوّة الاستمداد منّ وإخلاف

The Surah of Abraham

The Surah of Abraham has one name.

Al-Mannān: The Gracious

Only Ibn Barrajān cites it as a divine name. It occurs in the Surah of Abraham in the verse: «but God is gracious toward whomever He wills among His servants».[460] Grace, or voluntary kindness (*mann*), means to give a blessing (*inʿām*). But this name reaches further than the Giver of Blessings (*al-Munʿim*) because of the emphasis expressed in the form of the word (*faʿʿāl*). 84.1

Any act of voluntary kindness from a gracious person is from the Gracious. Furthermore, when the realm of separation is beheld, the hand that gives is nobler than the hand that receives, because the Gracious is the one who gives the blessing. However, when the realm of separation is not experienced, and when one experiences through the eye of union, then the charity is received by the hand of the Real before it is received by the hand of the beggar. The reality of «who shall lend God a loan?»[461] negates the beggar, whereas the reality of "the higher hand is nobler" negates the donor; and the Real delivers the request on both sides. Our shaykh Muḥyī l-Dīn ibn al-ʿArabī, may God be pleased with him and may He please him, said: "If your gifts do not extend beyond your hand, then there is neither giver nor gift. And if you are the very veil over your own self, then there is neither veil nor veiled."[462] 84.2

God's grace is therefore all-inclusive. His giving of the forms of existentiation is grace. His assuring the subsistence of what He existentiates is grace. The connection that links cause and effect is grace. The perpetual replenishment that comes from Him is grace. His giving of the ability to be receptive to this 84.3

ما يفنى من الفانيات منّ وإعطاؤه ﴿كُلَّ شَيْءٍ خَلْقَهُۥ﴾ منّ وكونه هداه حتّى استوفى حقّه منّ.

٤،٨٤ فالاسم المنّان تعالى عامّ الحكم في طوري المعرفة والعلم وأمّا في المقام الأسمى المتجاوز طوري الصفات والأسماء فلا نطق ولا صمت وأمّا في حضرة الأسماء فأهل شهود الاسم المنّان لا يأخذون إلّا منه ولا يعطون إلّا ويرون أنّه المعطي ومقام هؤلاء لا يناسبه الورع والجهّال في إعراضهم نفع ويتوهّمون فيهم عدم الدّين وهيهات هم أهل اليقين وسكّان حضرة الأنوار النافية ظلمات الأغيار ولا يضرّهم إنكار المنكر لأنّهم يرونه من لواحق الاسم المتكبّر ويرون أنّ الله الكبير وإليه المصير.

٥،٨٤ ولمّا علم المشايخ ذلك رأوا أنّ أجلّ[١] ما يكتسَب إذ كان لا معطي إلّا الله أنّهم يرتّبون لهم خدّاماً يسألون الكسرة من الناس بمقدار ما تحصل به البلغة وذلك لأنّ الكسرة أو قيمتها لا تضرّ المعطي ولا تنقص ممّا في يده ولا يقلّد الفقير بإعطائه إيّاها منه والفقير أيضاً يأخذها من يد المنّان سبحانه فلا يتكلّف فيها شكر غيره تعالى.

٦،٨٤ وذكر هذا الاسم الكريم في الخلوة نافع جدّاً لمن فارق حظوظ النفس ويضرّ لمن حاجات نفسه باقية والله أعلم.

---

١ و: أحلّ.

replenishment is grace. His replacement of everything that perishes is grace. His «giving of everything its creation»[463] is grace, and His «guiding it»[464] to fulfill its rightful due is grace.

Thus, the property of the Gracious is all-inclusive at the stages of direct recognition and discursive knowledge. At the loftiest station, which surpasses the stages of the qualities and the names, however, there is neither speech nor silence. Moreover, in the presence of the names, the people who witness the Gracious receive only from Him, and they do not give except that they see Him as the Giver. Their station is not compatible with abstinence. In the turning away of the ignorant from them, there is a benefit. The latter presume them to be lacking in religion. Far from it! They are the people of certainty. They inhabit the presence of lights that negate the darkness of separative entities. They are not harmed by the censure of those who censure them, because they see them as generated by the Proud. They see that God is the Great, and that to Him is the return. 84.4

Since the Sufi shaykhs know this, they consider that the best way to earn a living—for there is no Giver apart from God—is to hire servants to solicit enough pieces of bread to meet their needs. After all, a piece of bread or its equivalent neither puts stress on the donor nor reduces what he possesses. Moreover, in asking for pieces of bread, the servant does not imitate the poor person, because he gives the poor person a part of that piece of bread. The poor person, for his part, receives it from the hand of the Gracious as well. Therefore, he need not burden himself with stilted expressions of gratitude apart from toward God. 84.5

Invoking this name is very beneficial during the spiritual retreat for those who have renounced selfish interest. But it harms those who still are tainted by selfish interest. And God knows best. 84.6

سورة النحل

وفيها اسم واحد

اسمه الكفيل تبارك وتعالى

١،٨٥ اتّفق عليه البيهقيّ وأبو الحكم دون الغزاليّ وشاهده من سورة النحل قوله تعالى ﴿وَقَدْ جَعَلْتُمُ ٱللَّهَ عَلَيْكُمْ كَفِيلًا﴾ فأمّا أنّه كفيل بأرزاق العباد فمن اسمه الرازق وبإيجادهم فمن اسمه الخالق وبما يرجونه من البرّ فمن اسمه البرّ وبدفع ما يخشونه من الضرّ فمن اسمه الواقي والدافع والكفيل الضمين فهو يعطي المكفول ﴿كِفْلَيْنِ مِن رَّحْمَتِهِۦ﴾ والكِفل الضِعف فهو ﴿يُضَٰعِفُ لِمَن يَشَآءُ﴾.

٢،٨٥ وعلى وجوده ضمان كلّ شيء لكن يعيده بإعادة المثل لا العين فإنّه لا تكرار في الوجود ولا ضيق في سعة الجود فهو كافل للّيل أن يعود وللنهار أن يرجع إذا أدبر ولليقظة أن تعود بعد النوم وللنوم بعد اليقظة بين الليلة واليوم وهو الكفيل بقوى الحركات أن تعاقب السكون وتترادف اللحظات على العيون والكفيل بعود ما سلف أن تذكره القوّة الذاكرة من أمر الدنيا والآخرة فإنّه الفعّال للأفعال ومعطي الحسّ والخيال لكونه كفيلًا بما يحتاج إليه العباد وضامن للمريد حصول المراد ولولا الوثوق بكفالته

The Surah of the Bee

The Surah of the Bee has one name.

Al-Kafīl: The Guarantor

Both al-Bayhaqī and Ibn Barrajān agree it is a divine name, but not al-Ghazālī. It occurs in the Surah of the Bee in the verse: «you have made God a Guarantor over you».[465] God guarantees His servants' provisions through the Provider. His bringing them into existence, moreover, is through the Creator. The loving-kindness that they hope from Him is through the Kind Lover. His repelling of harms that they fear is through the Protector and the Repeller. Furthermore, guarantor (*kafīl*) means sponsor, and He gives His sponsored subject «a twofold portion, (*kiflayn*) of His mercy».[466] *Kifl* means "double," and hence He «doubles for whoever He wills».[467] 85.1

The guarantee of all things rests upon His existence. However, He returns the thing by returning its equivalent, not the thing in itself, because there is no repetition in existence, and there is no constraint on the breadth of divine munificence. Therefore, He guarantees the return of the night, and the regress of the day after night departs, the wakefulness that returns after sleep, and the sleep that returns at night after wakefulness. He is the Guarantor of the faculties of motion that come after rest, and of the glances that are successively bestowed upon the eyes. He guarantees the return of what has passed such that the faculty of memory recalls its affairs in this world and the next. He is the agent behind all acts, and the Bestower of sense perception and imagination in that He guarantees the needs of His servants for those faculties. He guarantees that the seeker shall attain what he seeks. No soul would entertain any hope 85.2

للمهل لما طمعت نفس في بلوغ الأمل فكفالته تبسط النفس ولولاها لأزال توهّم وحشة العدم وجود الأنس وإلّا فمن أين لمن له العدم من نفسه بقاء إلى غده أو ثبوتٌ بعد فناء أمسه.

ولكنّ الاسم الكفيل تجده النفوس فتركن إليه وتعوّل فيما تأمّله عليه وذلك من حيث لا يَشعر المحجوب فأمّا الشاهد فيراه عياناً والمؤمن يثبته إيماناً وأنت تأكل الطعام وتأمل أن تشبع ولولا كفالته لم تطمع ولولا رؤية ضمانه ما كنت بقدر الكفاية تقنع لأنّك كنت لولاه تشره ولا تأمن فتظنّ وقوع ما تكره لكنّ إحساس النفوس بالاسم الكفيل يوجد فيها رجاء الجميل ومن كان وثوقه بالاسم الكفيل أكثر كان سكونه تحت مجاري الأقدار أوفر وإنّما يكون الوثوق بحسب كمال النفس وبحسبه يكون استعدادها وإلى حكمه في الوثوق بالاسم الكفيل يكون استنادها وكلّ كفالة وقعتْ فوثقت بها النفس فهي فرع لكفالته عزّ وجلّ. ٣،٨٥

٤،٨٥ وهذا الذكر لمن أراد أن يحصّل مقام التوكّل نافع جدّاً والله أعلم.

of attainment were it not for the confidence in His guarantee of moments of respite. His guarantee expands the soul, but for which the terror of nonexistence would eradicate all intimacy. Otherwise how could we in whom nonexistence is intrinsic continue to exist until tomorrow, or how could we even remain steadfast after yesterday?

Nonetheless, souls find within themselves the Guarantor and they depend 85.3
on it, placing their hopes in it. This occurs in such a way that the veiled intellect is unaware. The witness sees it with his own eyes, just as the believer affirms it through belief. You eat food and expect to become full; but for His guarantee, you would have no hope. For if you did not behold His guarantee, you would not be content with your fill, and would become covetous. You would never feel secure and would always expect the worst. However, souls sense the Guarantor, and that inspires them to hope for the best. The more one places confidence in the Guarantor, the more one finds serenity in the flow of destiny. This confidence, moreover, is precisely commensurate with the perfection of the soul, and the soul's preparedness is in accordance with it. The soul finds support through the property of the Guarantor. Every guarantee that takes place in which a soul finds confidence is a branch of His guarantee.

This invocation is very beneficial for those who wish to attain the station of 85.4
trust in God. And God knows best.

سورة سبحان

وفيها اسم واحد

اسمه المكرّم تعالى

١،٨٦ انفرد به البيهقيّ وشاهده ﴿وَلَقَدۡ كَرَّمۡنَا بَنِيٓ ءَادَمَ﴾ أي جعلناهم كراماً وليس المراد بالكرم ما يقابل البخل بل هو صفة كمال خُصّ به بنو آدم وهو كونهم على الصورة وإن كان إنّما يكون على الصورة من بلغ حدّ مقام القطبيّة لكن لمّا كان الكمال المشار إليه لا يوجَد إلّا في الإنسان عمّ ذكره بني آدم وإن كان إنّما يُطلق لفظُ ابن آدم حقيقة على من ورث مقام آدم عليه السلام وهو الكمال الذي به استحقّ أن يكون خليفة في الأرض.

٢،٨٦ والمراد بالأرض الحرف ونعني الموجود لأنّ الحروف كلّها موجودات والهمزة منها فأمّا الألف التي تنشأ عن امتداد النفَس مع الفتح فتلك هي مادّة الحروف بمنزلة الوجود والحروف بمنزلة الموجود والخلافة في الأرض هي الخلافة في الحروف أي خلافة على الموجودات كلّها.

٣،٨٦ وكرامة ابن آدم بالعقل وهي الكرامة العامّة وأمّا الكرامة الخاصّة فهي فوق طور العقل المحجوب من حيث ما هو مفكّر لا من حيث ما هو قابل لخلافة المحجوب على المحجوبين

The Surah of the Night Journey

The Surah of the Night Journey has one name.

Al-Mukarrim: The Ennobler

Only al-Bayhaqī mentions it as a divine name. It occurs in the verse: «We have indeed ennobled (*karramnā*) the children of Adam».[468] That is, We have made them noble. Now, the term *karam* here is not being used in the sense of "generosity," but rather in the sense of "nobility," which is a quality of perfection specific to the children of Adam; namely, their being created in the image of God. However, the individual who is actually in the image of God is the one who reaches the degree of the axial saint. Nonetheless, since this perfection is only encountered in a human being, all the children of Adam are mentioned in the verse, even though in reality, the term "child of Adam" only applies to the individual who has inherited the station of Adam, peace be upon him, and that is the perfection by virtue of which he is worthy of being God's representative on earth.[469] 86.1

The meaning of "earth" is the letter, by which we mean the existent, because all letters are existents. The *hamzah* is one of them. The *alif*, created by drawing out the breath with an open vowel, is the underlying material substrate of the letters that corresponds to existence, whereas the letters correspond to existents. Moreover, vicegerency on earth is vicegerency among the letters. It is, in other words, a vicegerency over all existents. 86.2

The child of Adam is noble by virtue of his intellect, and that is universal nobility. Particular nobility is beyond the stage of the veiled intellect inasmuch as it is a reflective faculty, but not inasmuch as it is a receptive one. Thus, the 86.3

وخلافة الأقطاب على الواقفين ويعمّ ما تحتهم بهم من العارفين ويُطلَق على ترتيب أمور المحجوبين بالحكمة لا بالحكيم وب﴿ تَقْدِيرُ ٱلْعَزِيزِ ٱلْعَلِيمِ ﴾.

٤،٨٦ ومن جملة تكريم المكرّم أنّه جعل الرسول يشرع ما يريد وحكّمه في أن يقول ما يرشد إلى التوحيد من شرك التقاييد فإنّ الرسالة مطلقة وهو يعيّن أحكامها بحسب الوقت والحال وقابليّات المكلّفين بالأعمال ومن هذه الحقيقة وقع نسخ الشرائع ورفع أحكام بعضها ببعض لما فيه من المنافع فغلط اليهود في تسميته بالبداء وصمّوا حين ناداهم بنسخ التوراة إلى مصلحتهم فما سمعوا النّداء وأيّ كريم أعظم كرامة ممّن يجعل أمر التشريع إليه جعلها إلى رسوله وأطلق تصرّفه في تحريم الشيء وتحليله ويكون في ذلك ﴿مَا يَنطِقُ عَنِ ٱلْهَوَىٰٓ إِنْ هُوَ إِلَّا وَحْيٌ يُوحَىٰ﴾ والوحي منه إليه وعوده عنه عليه ومن لم يحكّم رسوله ﴿فِيمَا شَجَرَ﴾ ولا يجد في نفسه ﴿حَرَجًا﴾ ولا ضجر ويُسَلِّمَ تَسْلِيمًا فما آمن بل كفر وهذا تكريم لعبده وتشريف له من عنده.

٥،٨٦ وهذا الاسم الكريم يأمر الشيخ به المريد إذا حقر نفسه وعدم بالاستصغار أنسه والله أعلم.

vicegerency of the veiled intellect is over veiled individuals; and the vicegerency of the axial saint is over those who have arrived at the station of halting and includes the recognizers beneath them. Furthermore, vicegerency is ascribed to the sequential arrangement of the affairs of veiled intellects through wisdom, not through the Wise, and «through the measuring of the Mighty, the Knowing».[470]

One of the honors given by the Ennobler is that He appoints the Messenger to legislate as he sees fit. He endows him with a firm ability to give instructions that lead toward divine oneness and away from polytheistic delimitations. For the Message is unconditioned, and a Messenger determines its rulings according to the time, context, and receptivity of those upon whom the Law is imposed. Moreover, it is through this reality that the supersession of revealed religions takes place, as well as the abolishment of certain rulings by other rulings when this is beneficial. It was thus a mistake for the Jews to call abrogation "alteration," and they turned a deaf ear when blessed Muḥammad called them to what is in their best interest by abrogating the Torah; and thus they did not hear the call.[471] And who is greater in nobility than He who sets forth the task of Law-giving, then assigns it to His Messenger, granting him unrestricted authority to proscribe and prescribe rulings, in all of which «he does not speak out of caprice; it is naught but a revelation revealed»?[472] The revelation is from Him to Him, and its return is from Him to Him. And «whoever does not make» His Messenger «the judge in his disputes, and finds resistance» or discontent «in his soul» and does not «surrender with full submission»[473] does not believe, but rather is an unbeliever. This therefore is an honor for His servant, and an act of ennobling from Him. 86.4

The shaykh may instruct his disciple to invoke this noble name when the disciple holds himself in disdain and loses his spiritual intimacy through his self-belittlement. And God knows best. 86.5

سورة الكهف

اسمه المقتدر

١،٨٧ اتّفق عليه البيهقيّ والغزاليّ دون أبي الحكم وشاهده قوله تعالى ﴿وَكَانَ ٱللَّهُ عَلَىٰ كُلِّ شَيْءٍ مُّقْتَدِرًا﴾ ومعناه القادر.

٢،٨٧ وسمّى المعدومات التي تظهر بالقدرة كلّ منها شيئاً مجازاً لأنّ الشيئيّة لاحقة للتعيّن والمجاز لا بدّ فيه من علاقة بها يصحّ الإطلاق وهي هنا أمور منها أنّ الموضوع الذي تتعيّن فيه صور الموجود بالإيجاد هو النور الذي فيه تُفتح صور العالم وهو المادّة فقد وُجد بعض الموجود الذي يسمّى شيئاً فساغ أن يسمّى شيئاً ولو اعتبرنا الصورة وجدناها ﴿لَمْ يَكُن شَيْـًٔا مَّذْكُورًا﴾ وكذلك قوله ﴿خَلَقْنَـٰهُ مِن قَبْلُ وَلَمْ يَكُ شَيْـًٔا﴾.

٣،٨٧ الثاني وهو أقرب من الأوّل وجود انفعال المادّة وتهيّئها لقبول الصورة مثل وقوع النطفة في الرحم والحبّة في الأرض المبلولة أو تعفين يلحقُ الأرض فينشئ المقتدر تعالى فيها صوراً إيجاداً منه في كلّ طور ما يناسبه لعلمه باستحقاق الموادّ ما يبديه فيها منها وطاعة المادّة له تعالى هي القدرة لأنّه يأخذها منها بها فيكون الخلق طبيعيّاً لها وهو معنى قوله تعالى ﴿قَالَتَآ أَتَيْنَا طَآئِعِينَ فَقَضَىٰهُنَّ سَبْعَ سَمَـٰوَاتٍ﴾ وقوله ﴿فِى يَوْمَيْنِ﴾ أي خلق اليومين معها فالمظروف مع الظرف لا يسبق أحدهما الآخر في الإيجاد

The Surah of the Cave

Al-Muqtadir: The Potent

Al-Bayhaqī and al-Ghazālī agree that is a divine name, but not Ibn Barrajān. 87.1
It occurs in the verse: «God is potent over all things».[474] It means able.

He calls all nonexistents that manifest through divine power "things" metaphorically, because thing-ness is joined to determination. To be deployed properly, a metaphor must possess a relationship of some sort. In this case, there are several matters to consider: First, the subject in which the forms of existents, through the bestowal of existence, become determined is the light wherein the forms of the cosmos are opened. That is the underlying material substrate. For a part of the existent, the so-called "thing," was brought into existence, and thus it may be called a "thing." However, if we consider the form, we find that «it is a thing unmentioned»[475] and: «We created him before, when he was not a thing».[476] 87.2

Second—and this is more apposite than the first point—is the underlying material substrate's receptivity to activity, and its predisposition to receive the form. This, for instance, is when a drop of sperm is ejaculated into the womb, or when a seed is planted in moist soil, or when soil is fertilized, and the Potent configures forms, bringing them into existence at every stage in a manner appropriate to each, and according to His knowledge of what configurations are suitable to the material substrate. The material substrate's compliance with God is divine power, because He derives the material substrate from itself and by itself, such that creation is imprinted upon its very nature. This is the meaning of the verse «then He turned to heaven while it was smoke and said to it and the earth, "Come willingly or unwillingly!" They said, "We come willingly." Then He decreed that they be seven heavens», to which He adds: «in two days»,[477] which is to say that He created the two days with them. Thus, that which is contained is with the container, and neither precedes the other in 87.3

ويشبه هذا المعنى دوران الأفلاك فإنّها طبيعيّة وكون دورها طبيعيًا هو معنى طاعتها لمدبّرها الحقّ.

٤،٨٧ فنعود ونقول إنّ وجه الشبه بين دورانها وبين خلق اليومين مع مظروفهما معًا أنّ دورانها وإن كان طبيعيًا هو عند كلّ نقطة تتعيّن من حركته في مكانه يتهيّأ الفلك بها بحركته لموازاة نقطة أخرى ومن هنا ينحلّ الشكّ الذي يتخيّله الفيلسوف من أنّه لو كان دورها طبيعيًا لما كان دورًا للزوم أنّ الطبيعة التي تقصد به جهة يمتنع عليها أن تقصد ضدّها ولم يدر أنّ استعداد الفلك في دورانه متجدّد في كلّ موازاة نقطة من مكانه ويتعيّن بدورانه آنات زمانيّة والقدرة هي الفاعلة لكلّ جزء ولكلّ حال وتعيّن معنويّ أو غيره فالمقتدر هو المتصرّف تعالى.

٥،٨٧ وهذا الاسم يذكره من يريد منه الشيخ ظهور الكرامات دون التوحيد والله أعلم.

existence. This concept resembles the rotation of the spheres, which is natural; and the fact that its rotation is natural is the meaning of its willing compliance to its true Governor.

Returning to our discussion: The resemblance between spherical rotation and the creation of the two days together with their contents is that by rotating—albeit naturally—at each point, its motion in space determines the predisposition of the sphere to be equivalent to the next point. This is where the doubt imagined by the philosophers vanishes—namely, that if its rotation were natural, it would not be a rotation at all, because it is impossible that nature could drive the sphere both toward a certain location and toward the opposite location. They are unaware that the predisposition of the sphere to rotate renews itself with every equivalent point in space, that units of time are determined by its rotation, and that divine power acts upon every part, every state, and every determination—supersensory or otherwise—and thus the Able is exercising control. 87.4

This name should be invoked by a disciple whose master wants him to perform miracles, instead of focusing on divine oneness. And God knows best. 87.5

سورة مريم

اسمه الحنّان تبارك وتعالى

١٫٨٨ انفرد به البيهقيّ دونهما وشاهده قوله تعالى ﴿وَحَنَانًا مِّن لَّدُنَّا وَزَكَوٰةً﴾ ولدن وإن كانت بمعنى عند لا يلزم منها أن يعود بها وصف عليه تعالى لكنّ ذوق التوحيد يقتضي أنّ العنديّات كلّها تعود بالوصف عليه لِما تشهد من فناء ما سواه في وجوده ونحن إنّما نتكلّم بلسان الوحدانيّة الناطقة لا الصامتة خصوصاً.

٢٫٨٨ والحنان هو الرحمة فهو الراحم سبحانه وأطوار الحنان لا نهاية لها وقد ورد إنّه تعالى خلق الرحمة مائة جزء وادّخر منها للآخرة تسعة وتسعين وجعل منها جزءاً واحداً في الدنيا فيها تراحم الموجودات بعضها على بعض فجعل رحمة الموجودات بعضها على بعض من إيجاده وهي رحمة حقيقة لأنّ الرحم شجنة من الرحمٰن أي قرابة.

٣٫٨٨ وأصل الحنان الرحمٰن تعالى وأصل الحنين الذي هو الشوق الحنان لأنّ المشتاق يرحم غربة نفسه فيتوق إلى اتّصالها إلى وطن طلبها ولمّا كانت الوحدانيّة أصل كلّ كثرة عذر المشتاقون إلى رؤية جهة الوحدانيّة برؤية وجه الحقيقة وهي مادّة ذواتهم فاشتاقوا الذات الجامعة وهي حضرة الجمع وأمّا ضعفاء الاستعداد فلمّا عموا عن الشعور بذلك الوطن حنّوا إلى الأوطان البدنيّة ومراتع لهو الصبى وملاعب أترابه.

٤٫٨٨ ووصف الحنان جميل من كلّ ظاهر به لثبوت جماله منسوباً إلى جناب الرحمة وقد ورد في الحديث النبويّ قوله عليه السلام ألا أخبركم بأقربكم مِنّي مجالس يوم القيامة

The Surah of Mary

Al-Ḥannān: The Tender

Only al-Bayhaqī mentions it as a divine name. It occurs in the verse: «We gave John judgment as a child, and a God-given tenderness, and purity».[478] Although "God-given" can mean "from Us," this does not necessarily entail that the quality goes back to God. However, the direct tasting of divine unity entails that all "froms" are qualities that go back to Him, since they witness the annihilation of other-than-Him in His existence. Moreover, we speak here in the language of God's spoken oneness, not specifically His silent oneness. 88.1

Tenderness is mercy, so the Tender denotes the Merciful. The stages of His tenderness are infinite, and we know of a report that "God created one hundred parts of mercy, and He reserved ninety-nine of them for the hereafter, and assigned one part for the here below. Through it, existent things show mercy to each other."[479] Thus, the mercy that existents show each other are from His existentiation. This is real mercy, because "the womb is intimately connected to the All-Merciful,"[480] meaning that it is in a maternal relationship. 88.2

The root of tenderness is the All-Merciful, just as the root of longing—that is, yearning—is tenderness; for the person who longs has mercy toward his soul in exile, and thus aspires to unite it with the homeland it seeks. Since unity, moreover, is the root of all multiplicity, those who experience longing are excused for seeing oneness wherever they see the face of reality, which is the underlying material substrate of their essences. Thus, they long for the all-comprehensive Essence, which is the presence of union. Those whose preparedness is weak are blind to awareness of the spiritual homeland, and instead incline toward the bodily homeland, the pastures of diversion, and the places where they would relax with companions. 88.3

The quality of tenderness beautifies all who display it, because its beauty is firmly ascribed to the side of divine mercy. To this effect, we know of a report 88.4

ثمّ قال أحاسنكم أخلاقًا الموطّؤون أكنافًا الذين يألفون ويؤلفون والألفة من الحنان الذي أصله الحنّان عزّ وجلّ.

٥،٨٨ ومن حقيقة الحنان وجود المحبّة التي هي أشرف مقامات العوامّ فهي فوق العبادة وفوق التصوّف فإنّ الحنان والحنين يقارنها أبدًا وبذلك تكون الأشواق ومحبّة العبد لربّه عزّ وجلّ فرع عن محبّة الربّ لعبده ﴿جَزَآءً وِفَاقًا﴾ فتصاريف الاسم الحنّان في كلّ ملاءمة وقعت في الوجود أو تقع فيه بطريق الكرم والجود.

٦،٨٨ ويذكر الاسم الحنّان في الخلوات فيقوّي الأنس إلى أن يبلغ بصاحبه إلى المحبّة والله أعلم.

اسمه الوارث إليه المصير

١،٨٩ انفرد به الغزاليّ رحمه الله وشاهده من سورة مريم قوله تعالى ﴿إِنَّا نَحْنُ نَرِثُ ٱلْأَرْضَ وَمَنْ عَلَيْهَا وَإِلَيْنَا يُرْجَعُونَ﴾ فأمّا العلماء فيقولون إنّه تعالى يرث الأرض بعد موت أهلها ويرثهم بعودهم إلينا أي إليه تعالى وهذا هو المفهوم الذي يتبادر إلى الأفهام وله معنيان غير هذا سيأتي ذكرهما إن شاء الله.

٢،٨٩ فنعود ونقول إنّ الميراث هنا مجاز إذ المُلك أوّلًا وآخرًا هو له تعالى وقد جعلنا ﴿مُّسْتَخْلَفِينَ فِيهِ﴾ والاستخلاف لا ينقل المُلك إلى الخليفة عن مستخلفه فهو باق حقيقة وأمّا بطريق المجاز فيصحّ.

that the blessed Prophet said: "Shall I not inform you about those who will be assembled closest to me on the Day of Resurrection? It is those with the most beautiful character, who are easygoing, friendly, and bring people together."[481] Friendliness is from tenderness, whose root is the Tender.

The true nature of tenderness gives rise to love, which is the noblest station of the ordinary believers, since it is above worship and above Sufism. For tenderness and longing are always linked to love, and therefore the servant's yearning and love for his Lord is an offshoot of the Lord's love for His servant as «a fitting recompense».[482] The activities of the Tender occur within everything in existence that is agreeable, or that happens therein through generosity and munificence. 88.5

When the Tender is invoked during the spiritual retreat, it strengthens one's intimacy until the invoker attains divine love. And God knows best. 88.6

Al-Wārith: The Inheritor

Only al-Ghazālī, may God have mercy on him, considers this a divine name. 89.1
It occurs in the Surah of Mary in the verse: «surely We shall inherit the earth and whatsoever is on it, and to Us they shall return».[483] The scholars say that God inherits the earth after the death of its inhabitants, just as He inherits them by their return to «Us»; namely, to God. This is the most intuitively obvious meaning of the verse, but there are two other meanings that we shall mention shortly, God willing.

To return to our discussion: Inheritance here is metaphorical, for the 89.2
kingdom is His in the beginning and in the end, and He has appointed us «as representatives over it».[484] However, the appointment of a representative does not transfer the kingdom to the representative from the One who is represented. For it is God who subsists in reality, and so the transfer is only metaphorical.

ثمّ إنّ ﴿ٱلْأَرْضَ وَمَنْ عَلَيْهَا﴾ معروفان لكنّ الأرض التي يشهدها أهل الله تعالى هي غير متناهية العدد وهذه واحدة منها فيكون ميراثه للأرضين متجدّداً أبداً ويعرف هذه المسألة من عرف الوجود وهو لا يعرَف إلّا به تعالى. ٣،٨٩

ثمّ إنّ الموجود أيضاً غير متناهي العدد لأنّ عنصره ومادّته هو الوجود وهو متطوّر أبداً لأنّ حقيقته لا تقتضي إلّا الإيجاد في مادّة غير متناهية الأبعاد ولا يقال إنّ الأبعاد لا تكون إلّا في الجسم فإنّ الوجود هو قابل للجسم أي يكون جسماً والجسم قابل للأبعاد وقابل القابل قابل فهو قبول بالتقدير لكنّه تقدير واجب فقبول الأبعاد إذاً واجب. ٤،٨٩

وأمّا المعنيان الآخران فأحدهما أن يكون الاسم الوارث بمعنى أنّه يرث الصور التي كانت مقدّرة في المتصوّرات وهي تعيّنات فتنحلّ إلى بسيطها فتذهب التعيّنات في بسيطها لأنّ لها ضرباً من الوجود وإليه ترجع إذ لا تنحلّ إلى العدم المحض إذ لا حقيقة له فهو ميراث للاسم الوارث تعالى وهذا الاعتبار هو فناء الصور في المتصوّر بها وهو واجب وجودها الذي هي ممكناته فيكون الميراث للمراتب فقط فهو رجوع إلى الاسم الوارث من جهة ما هو في الاسم الله. ٥،٨٩

والثاني أن يكون الميراث للاسم الوارث مع بقاء الصور ولا تحتاج في تحقيق الميراث إلى انعدامها ولهذا نظير وهو قول الصوفيّة مخبرين عن قائله كان الله ولا شيء معه وهو الآن ما عليه كان وهذا الفناء الذي يعنونه العارفون والواقفون وحاصله أنّ ما ثَمّ صور ولا متصوَّر غيره تعالى فمن شهد هذا علم أنّه وارث مع بقاء كلّ شيء بحاله والميراث هنا أن يكون عين الأشياء لا أنّ الأشياء عينه وهذا هو الفرق بين هذا المعنى وبين ما قدّمناه أوّلاً من أنّ الأشياء باقية على ملكه تعالى فإنّ هناك قد ٦،٨٩

Furthermore, «the earth and whatsoever is on it» are both well known. However, the earths witnessed by God's folk are infinite in number, and our earth is but one of them. Wherefore, His inheritance of the earths is constantly renewed. This matter is known by those who know existence, and existence is known only through Him. 89.3

Existents are also infinite in number, because existence is their elemental component and material substrate. Existence, moreover, unfolds eternally from stage to stage, because its true nature entails precisely the giving of existence to a material substrate whose spatial distance is infinite. One must not say that spatial distance only exists in corporeal bodies, for existence is receptive of corporeal bodies, which is to say that it can become a body. A body, moreover, is receptive to spatial distance; and that which is receptive to a receptacle is itself a receptacle. Its receptivity is therefore supposed, which is necessary; therefore, the body's receptivity to spatial distances is necessary. 89.4

One of the two other meanings is that the Inheritor can mean that He inherits the forms that were assumed by the formations, which are the determinations. These determined forms disintegrate into their simple element because they possess a type of existence. Moreover, they return to Him, and do not vanish into absolute nonexistence, because the latter has no reality. This then is an inheritance of the Inheritor. This consideration, moreover, is the annihilation of forms into the underlying material substrate that receives those forms. The underlying material substrate is the necessary aspect of their existence, and they are its possibilities. The inheritance is thus only for the levels, and that is a return to the Inheritor inasmuch as it pertains to Allāh. 89.5

The second consideration is that the inheritance pertains to the Inheritor while the forms subsist. The inheritance is not contingent upon the nonexistence of the forms. This is like when the Sufis respond to the divine dictum "God was, and there was nothing with Him" by saying "and He is now as He ever was."[485] This is what the recognizers and those who have arrived at the station of halting mean by annihilation, and what comes from it is that there are neither forms nor receptacles of forms apart from Him. Whoever witnesses this knows that He is the Inheritor even while things continue to subsist in their state. The inheritance here means that He is identical with the things themselves, not that the things themselves are identical with Him. Herein, moreover, lies the difference between the second and the first meaning in which things continue to exist within His kingdom. For in the latter, we affirm 89.6

أثبتنا مالكًا ومملوكًا بلسان العلم الحجابيّ والعلم أبدًا في الحجاب وأمّا بالكشف فهذا الأخير هو المعنيّ.

وهذا الاسم يصلح للعارفين فيكون جاذبًا لهم إلى الفناء المطلق وهو مقام الوقفة ٧،٨٩
والله أعلم.

both the Owner and the possession in the language of veiled knowledge; and knowledge is forever behind the veil. Through unveiling, however, it is the former meaning that we have in mind.

This name is suitable for the recognizers, for it draws them toward uncon- 89.7
ditioned annihilation, which is the station of halting. And God knows best.

سورة طه

ثلاثة أسماء

اسمه الباقي عزّت فردانيّته

١،٩٠ هـذا الاسم العظيم متّفق عليه بين الأئمّة الثلاثة وشاهده من سورة طه قوله تعالى ﴿وَٱللَّهُ خَيۡرٞ وَأَبۡقَىٰٓ﴾ وبقاؤه تعالى هو لا من بداية ولا إلى نهاية.

٢،٩٠ واعلم أنّ هذا البقاء هو المعبّر عنه بالدهر في قوله عليه السلام لا تسبّوا الدهر فإنّ الله هو الدهر ففيه حذف مضاف وإقامة المضاف إليه مقامه وهو مجاز معروف وأمّا الزمان فإنّه مفروض في الدهر بعدد دوّرات الأفلاك ما دامت دائرة أو بمقادير لو أديرت الأفلاك لكانت مساوية لأزمنتها فإنّه ليس واجباً أن تبقى هذه الأفلاك لأنّ الذي يدوم إنّما هو الوجود المحض وهو للحقّ تعالى وأمّا الموجود فكلّ متناه وإن طال أمده فإنّه يحلّ لا محالة.

٣،٩٠ والفلاسفة وأهل علم الهيئة ينكرون هذا القول ﴿وَٱللَّهُ يَعۡلَمُ إِنَّهُمۡ لَكَٰذِبُونَ﴾ فإنّ اسمه الوارث تعالى لا يبقي غيره وليس هو ممّا يتسمّى إذ ذاك موجوداً بل وجوداً وبين هاتين اللفظتين ومعنييهما ما بين الواجب والممكن ونعني به الممكن العامّ المسلوب ضرورة العدم فقط وأمّا الممكن الخاصّ وهو المسلوب الضرورتين فهو في نفس

The Surah of Ṭā Hā

The Surah of Ṭā Hā has three names.

Al-Bāqī: The Everlasting

90.1 The three eminent scholars agree that this august name is divine. It appears in the Surah of Ṭā Hā in the verse: «God is better, and everlasting».[486] His everlastingness is without beginning and without end.

90.2 Moreover, this everlastingness is described as the aeon in the prophetic tradition: "Do not curse the aeon! For God is the aeon."[487] Here, the first noun of the genitive construction is dropped and replaced by the second noun, which is a well-known metaphorical construct.[488] Time is supposed within the aeon according to the number of spherical rotations, so long as they continue to rotate, or according to a measure temporally equivalent to the rotations of the spheres. For it is not necessary for these spheres to subsist, because what lasts forever is pure existence, and that belongs to the Real. As for existents, anything that is finite—no matter how long its duration—will inevitably disintegrate.

90.3 The philosophers and astronomers reject this doctrine, «and God knows that they are liars».[489] For His name the Inheritor assures the subsistence of none beside Him. Hence, He is not called an "existent" but rather "existence." What lies between these two terms and their meanings is what lies between the necessary and the possible. Moreover, by possible we mean universal possibility alone, which is stripped of the necessity of nonexistence. Particular possibility—which is stripped of necessary existence and nonexistence—is unreal in itself, and its nature is impossible in itself. Such possibility is only

الأمر باطل وطبيعته في نفس الأمر ممتنعة وإنّما يثبت في جهل الجاهل حيث لا يعلم أنّه يكون أو لا يكون وليس الواقع في نفس الأمر إلّا أحدهما فأهل الله المحقّقون لا يتكلّمون إلّا في الواقع في نفس الأمر وليس إلّا الواجب والممتنع.

٤،٩٠ قالوا أيضاً والممتنع هو الذي ما كان قطّ ولا يكون أبدًا وهذا الطور عندهم ممّا يقبح الكلام فيه عندهم لأنّهم أهل الوجود والممتنع عدم صرف وقولنا عدم صرف هو اسم على غير مسمّى والمقصود به التفهيم فهو يفرض لينفى لا ليثبَت.

٥،٩٠ ونعود فنقول إنّ الأفلاك فانية علم ذلك من علم وجهله من جهله والذي علينا هو نطق بالأذواق وليس علينا أن نفهم أهل الشّقاق ولا نسمع ﴿مَن فِي ٱلْقُبُورِ﴾ وهم في قبور الحجاب وأمّا الذي يسمعه أهل القبور فهو نطق الوجود قال شيخنا محيي الدين ابن العربيّ رحمة الله عليه

إِذَا نَطَقَ ٱلْوُجُودُ أَصَاخَ قَوْمٌ بِأَسْمَاعٍ إِلَى نُطْقِ ٱلْوُجُودِ

٦،٩٠ فاسمه الباقي يستأثر بالبقاء ويدخل في معناه الاسم الوارث والبقاء له تعالى هو بذاته التي هي الوجود إذ كان الوجود لا يقبل العدم كما يقبله الموجود وقد جهل علماء الرسوم فجعلوا الوجود عرضاً وكأنّهم يعنون بالوجود الوجدان فإنّ الوجدان يتجدّد وهو عرض يقع بالتضايف.

٧،٩٠ وهذا الاسم الكريم ينفع ذكره لمن عجز عن بذل نفسه لربّه تعالى فإذا ذكره دواماً خرج عن نفسه والله أعلم.

affirmed by an ignoramus insofar as he does not know whether it is being or nonbeing, though in itself it can only be one of the two. Thus, the People of God who are realized speak solely about what is actually the case, which is only the necessary and the impossible.

Those who are realized also say that the impossible is that which never was and will never be. Furthermore, this stage is an unappealing subject of discussion for them, because they are the People of Existence, and impossibility is pure nonexistence. "Pure nonexistence" is a phrase that has no corresponding reality. Its purpose is to aid the understanding, for it is posited in order to be negated, not affirmed. 90.4

Returning to our discussion: The spheres are evanescent, regardless of whether this is known by those who have knowledge, or unknown to the ignorant. It is our responsibility to speak through direct tasting, not to persuade those who stir up discord. We cannot cause «those who are in the graves to hear»,[490] for they are in the graves of the veil. What the people of the graves hear[491] is the language of existence. Our shaykh Muḥyī l-Dīn ibn al-ʿArabī, may God have mercy on him, writes: 90.5

> When existence speaks, one group
> lends its ear to the speech of existence.[492]

Thus, the effects of everlastingness are displayed upon the Everlasting, and the Inheritor is included within its meaning. Everlastingness thus belongs to Him through His Essence, which is existence. For existence rejects nonexistence, in contrast to existent things. The exoteric scholars, moreover, are ignorant when they make existence an accident, as though existence meant consciousness, for consciousness is ever-renewing, and is an accident that occurs correlatively. 90.6

This eminent name benefits the person who is incapable of giving himself up freely to God. When he invokes it consistently, he transcends his lower self. And God knows best. 90.7

اسمه المعطي جلّ ثناؤه

١،٩١ هـذا الاسم الكريم انفرد به أبو الحكم دون الإمامين وشاهده من سورة طه قوله تعالى ﴿أَعۡطَىٰ كُلَّ شَيۡءٍ خَلۡقَهُۥ ثُمَّ هَدَىٰ﴾ .

٢،٩١ وأوّل عطاء قبله قابل منه تعالى القابليّة ثمّ أعطى القابل ما قبل فأعطى الإيجاد وهو من جملة ما قبله القابل ثمّ تسمّى القابل بأنّه أوجده الفاعل من جهة أنّ القبول عطاء أيضاً ثمّ إن كان الإعطاء مستمرًّا وهو بمعنى الإيجاد إلى أن وصل إلى مراتب الحجاب فكان الإعطاء يتقبّل[١] وهو إعطاء التلبّس بالملك أو ما هو شبيه الملك.

٣،٩١ والعطاء عامّ فكلّ ما لاقاك فقد أعطاك الموازاة وإن أدركته ببعض محسّاتك فقد أعطاك الإدراك والمرآة تعطيك صورتك وأنت تعطيها الموازاة والقوى تعطي المنافع بحسبها والنيران تعطي الأضواء والأضواء تعطي الأبصار والسماء تعطي الأرض المطر والأرض تعطي السماء ظهور عطاياها في النبات والنبات يعطي البهائم أغذيتها ويعطي المحسّات ما يدركه منها والحيوان يعطي الإنسان أغذيته وحدّته وملكه ولين مفاصل الحيوان يعطيه أوضاعه التي تستريح بها فإنّ كلّ حيوان كانت أوضاعه أكثر كانت استراحته أكثر والإنسان يعطي الأشياء أسماءها في نطقه وكتابته ويعطيها إظهار منافعها ومضارّها وهو الناطق عنها فألسنتها هي لسانه الناطق وهو كتابها المبين الذي يظهر مضمرها.

٤،٩١ والإنسان يعطي حضرة الحقّ تعالى أسماءها النطقيّة ويعطيه بارئه منها البقيّة فيقيم مجد ربّه تعالى فإنّ المرزوق هو معطي اسمه الرازق والمخلوق هو معطيه اسمه الخالق وكذلك المقول في كلّ مطابقة[٢] وقعت بين العبد وربّه وهو أيضاً أعطى الحقّ الصمد إن صار عبداً وأنزله في مراتب تدلّيه فاتّصف بكلّ جزئيّة وأسدل الحجاب على النقائض فنسبها لنفسه والقيّوميّة تأبى ذلك والفردانيّة تعدمه والمضايفات

[١] و: تنقيلاً. [٢] و: مضايفة.

Al-Muʿṭī: The Giver

91.1 This noble name is cited by Ibn Barrajān, but not by the other two eminent scholars. It occurs in the Surah of Ṭā Hā in the verse: «He gives everything its creation, then guides it».[493]

91.2 Receptivity is the first gift from Him to any individual. He then gives him the things to which he is receptive, whereupon He bestows existence, which is one such thing. It is then that a person can be called a person by virtue of having been brought into existence by an agent because receptivity is also a gift. Moreover, if bestowal is continuous—in the sense of existentiation—it reaches the levels of the veil, and the bestowal is met with receptivity, for it is a bestowal clothed in ownership, or something that resembles ownership.

91.3 Furthermore, bestowal is all-pervasive, and everything that you encounter gives you an equivalent bestowal. When you perceive bestowal through your senses, it is He who gives you that perception. A mirror shows you your form, and you give it the equivalent bestowal. The faculties give benefits according to what they are; fire gives light, and light gives vision; the sky gives the earth rain, and through its plants the earth gives the sky the sign of its gift; and the plants give the beasts their nourishment. Plants also give creatures endowed with sense perception whatever they perceive therefrom. Animals give humans their nourishment, energy, and the fact of their ownership. The joints of animals give them the positions they rest in, and the more bodily positions an animal can assume, the more it will find rest. Through speech and writing, the human being gives things their names. He gives them the displays of their benefits and harms, and he speaks on their behalf, for their tongues speak through his, and he is their Clear Book that displays their content.[494]

91.4 The human being provides the Presence of the Real with its names that are spoken, and their Author gives the human being the remainder. Thus, man affirms the glory of his Lord, because the one who receives provision gives Him the name the Provider, and the one who is created gives Him the name the Creator. The same can be said of every correspondence between the servant and his Lord. By becoming a servant, the servant also gives to the Self-Sufficient. The servant brought the Lord down to the levels of His descent, so that He assumes all particular qualities, and He drapes the veil

وإن أعطت فهي اعتباريّة مرتبيّة لكنّ مقامها شريف وبينها وبين الوجود ما يشبه ما بين الاسم الله والاسم الرحمٰن فأنت إذا أسفر لك وجه المعطي تبارك وتعالى لم تر حركة في وجوده إلّا وهي عطاء.

٥،٩١ وبالجملة لا فعل إلّا وهو عطاء ولو لصورة حركته في نفسه فإنّها عطاء ولا قابل إلّا وهو آخذ من المعطي تعالى وذلك الأخذ هو من المعطي تعالى عطاء لإيجاد حقيقة الأخذ فهو من هذه الجهة عطاء والمحوطات أعطت المحيطات إحاطتها والمحيطات أعطت المحوطات محوطيّاتها والكلّ للاسم المُعطي تعالى.

٦،٩١ وهذا الاسم تعالى أقرب الأسماء المذكورة في الخلوة إلى الفتح لكنّه فتح ضعيف في الغالب والله أعلم.

اسمه الغفّار تبارك عفوه

١،٩٢ انفرد به الغزاليّ رحمه الله وشاهده من سورة طه قوله تعالى ﴿وَإِنِّي لَغَفَّارٌ لِّمَن تَابَ﴾ الغفّار والغفور وغافر الذنب كلّه من الستر للعبد من العقوبة أو لستر الذنب لأنّ الغفر هو الستر وهذا القدر هو نصيب العلم والعلماء.

٢،٩٢ وثَمّ اعتبارات أخرى بحسب بعض المراتب فمنها أنّه غفّار لمن تاب أي رجع فإن كان رجوعه إلى نفسه في حضرة الحجاب فالغفر ستر الغفّار له عن ملاحظة الخوف

over opposites and ascribes them to Himself, even while the quality of self-subsistence rejects this, and the quality of exclusive singularity nullifies it, and correspondences—although they do give—are still suppositions of rank, even though their station is sublime. Moreover, the disparity between these suppositional correspondences and existence resembles the difference between Allāh and the All-Merciful. Thus, when the blessed face of the Giver shows itself to you, you will not notice any movement in His existence but that it appears as a gift.

In summary, every act is a gift. Even the form of its movement within 91.5
itself is a gift. Moreover, every receptacle receives from the Giver, and that receiving is one of the gifts of the Giver because He existentiates the reality of receiving. In this regard, it is therefore a gift. Furthermore, things that can be encompassed give the encompassments to those who encompass them. The latter, for their part, give the encompassments their encompassed-ness. All that belongs to the Giver.

When invoked during the retreat, this name is the most effective at bring- 91.6
ing about a spiritual opening; usually, however, it is an incomplete opening. And God knows best.

Al-Ghaffār: The All-Concealing

Only al-Ghazālī, may God have mercy on him, mentions it as a divine name. 92.1
It occurs in the Surah of Ṭā Hā in the verse: «Surely I conceal the one who turns in repentance».[495] The names the All-Concealing (*al-Ghaffār*), the Concealing (*al-Ghafūr*), and the Concealer of Sin (*Ghāfir al-Dhanb*) all relate to shielding the servant from punishment or covering his sin, because a concealment is a type of covering (*satr*). This much exoteric scholars understand.

Beyond this, there are other considerations in accordance with some of the 92.2
levels of manifestation. One of them is that He is the All-Concealing for the one who repents; that is, who turns. If he turns toward himself in the presence of the veil, then the All-Concealing covers him from experiencing fear

من الاسم الشديد العذاب فهو لا يتقي ولا يعرف التقوى لأنّ التقوى إنّما يكون ممّن ينكشف له ما يخافه ويحذره والاسم الغفّار في هذه المرتبة ساتر عليه وجه التقوى وحاجب له عنها من حضرة كونه تعالى ﴿أَهْلُ ٱلْمَغْفِرَةِ﴾ وذلك حقيقة الاسم المضلّ فيدخل الغفّار هنا في حقيقة الاسم المضلّ ويكون معنى أنّه ﴿أَهْلُ ٱلْمَغْفِرَةِ﴾ في خصوص هذه الرتبة أنّه المضلّ.

٣،٩٢ وفي غير هذا الاعتبار ممّا يقابله وهو أن يكون قد أحاطت به حقيقة ﴿أَهْلُ ٱلتَّقْوَىٰ﴾ فإن كان غَفَّاراً لِّمَن تَابَ أي رجع إليه تعالى عن حضرة المعصية إلى حضور الطاعة فالحقّ تعالى في حقّه ﴿هُوَ أَهْلُ ٱلتَّقْوَىٰ﴾ فهو غفّار له بستر أحكام الاسم المضلّ وإظهار أحكام الاسم الهادي فينبّه للتقوى لأنّه مستور عن أحكام الاسم المضلّ وهذا غفر لوجوه الشهوات المحرّمة وأحوال أهل الضلالة فهو الغفّار تعالى وهذا الحكم هو المشهود[1] عند أهل العلم.

٤،٩٢ واعتبار آخر أن يكون معنى الغفر هو ستر الغفّار تعالى له عن ملاحظة أنّه الفاعل برؤية أنّ الفاعل هو الحقّ تعالى فلا يرى لنفسه حسنة وينسب الخير كلّه لربّه عزّ وجلّ وهذا هو توحيد الفعل وهو من مقامات العارفين في مبادئ المعرفة.

٥،٩٢ وثَمّ اعتبار فوق هذا وهو أن يستره الغفّار تعالى عن رؤية ذاته بالقيّوميّة الإلهيّة فيشهد الاسم القيّوم فيذهل بشهوده عن رؤية ما قام به وهو ستر لذاته كما قيل

تَسَتَّرْتُ عَنْ دَهْرِي بِظِلِّ جَنَاحِهِ فَعَيْنِي تَرَى دَهْرِي وَلَيْسَ يَرَانِي
فَلَوْ تَسْأَلِ ٱلْأَيَّامَ مَا ٱسْمِي لَمَا دَرَتْ وَأَيْنَ مَكَانِي مَا عَرَفْنَ مَكَانِي

[1] آ، ب، ج: المشهور.

from the Severe in Chastisement. Such a person has no reverential fear, and does not know what reverential fear means, because reverential fear is only for those who perceive an object worthy of fear and caution. In this level, the All-Concealing covers the person with respect to reverential fear. It veils him from it inasmuch as God is «most worthy of concealing»;[496] and this is the reality of the Misguider. In this case, the All-Concealing is included within the reality of the Misguider, and God is «most worthy of concealing» in this specific level in the sense that He is the Misguider.

Another consideration, in contrast to the former, is that the reality of God who is «most worthy of reverential fear»[497] encompasses the one who turns in repentance. Given that God «conceals the one who turns in repentance»[498] or who turns to Him from a state of disobedience to a state of obedience, then God in his case is «most worthy of reverential fear». Thus He is All-Concealing to the repenter by covering the properties of the Misguider and manifesting the properties of the Guide. Thereupon, his reverential fear is awakened, because he is concealed from the properties of the Misguider. This is a concealment of the various unlawful appetites and the states of the people of misguidance. He is therefore the All-Concealing, and this is the property witnessed by the exoteric scholars. 92.3

A further consideration of the meaning of concealment is that the All-Concealing covers a person from observing his own agency by beholding that God is the true Agent. Thereupon, he does not regard himself as the possessor of a beautiful deed, and ascribes all good to his Lord. This is the oneness of divine acts, and it is among the stations of the recognizers at the early stages of direct recognition. 92.4

There is yet another consideration beyond this one—namely, that through the divine quality of self-subsistence, the All-Concealing covers the person's self-perception, so that he witnesses the Self-Subsisting. Through that act of witnessing, he becomes oblivious to the deeds he has performed, and that is a covering of his essence. To this effect, a poet said: 92.5

I shield myself from my fate in the shade of His wing
  so that I see my fate, but it does not see me.
So, if you were to ask time my name, it would not know;
  and it would not know my whereabouts either.[499]

٦،٩٢ وهذا مقام توحيد الصفات لأنّ الذوات المتكثّرة كلّها صفات في الحقيقة ولذلك لا تقوم بأنفسها بل إنّما تقوم بالقيّوم سبحانه وأمّا كيف ذلك فأهل الشهود يعرفونه فهو الغفّار سبحانه في هذا المقام هذا النوع من الغفر.

٧،٩٢ وثمّ اعتبار آخر وإن كانت الاعتبارات لا تنحصر وهو عود الأشياء إليه تعالى فلا يبقى غيرُه وهو دخول الغفّار في حقيقة الاسم الباقي.

٨،٩٢ وخاصّيّة هذا الذكر تنفع أهل الخوف من العقوبة ويحصّل الأنس والله أعلم.

This is the station of the oneness of the qualities, for the multiple essences are in reality qualities, which is why they do not sustain themselves, but rather are sustained through the Self-Subsisting. How they are sustained is recognized by the witnesses. Thus, He is the All-Concealing in this station in this manner. 92.6

There is yet a further consideration—though considerations are inexhaustible—which is the return of things to God such that nothing subsists apart from Him. Here, the All-Concealing is included within the reality of the Everlasting. 92.7

The special property of this invocation benefits those who are afraid of divine punishment. It generates intimacy with God. And God knows best. 92.8

سورة الأنبيـاء

وفيها اسمان

اسمه الراتق تعالى

انفـرد به أبو الحكم الأندلسيّ وشاهده من سورة الأنبياء قوله تعالى ﴿ كَانَتَا رَتْقًا ﴾ ١،٩٣
أي كان الحقّ راتقها فهي رتق بذلك وحقيقة الرتق بساطة النور فإذا انفتحت فيه صوره التي هي صورة الموجودات فقد انفتق واعلم أنّ الرتق هو الأصل لأنّ الوحدانيّة هي السابقة لكن بالمرتبة فإنّ خلاّقيّة الخالق تعالى أزليّة لم تزل ولا تزال بالفعل.

وقوله عليه السلام كان الله ولا شيء معه ثمّ خلق الخلق وبسـط الرزق يحتمل ٢،٩٣
ثلاثة معان أحدها أنّه تعالى الآن على ما عليه كان أعني ولا شيء معه فإنّه الموجود تعالى وصفاته وأفعاله والموجودات هي أفعاله والفعل يرجع إلى الصفة على ما حقّقه أهل الشهود.

والمعنى الثاني أن يكون معنى ولا شيء معه يعني هذا الموجود الذي هو عالمـنا ٣،٩٣
الخاصّ بنا وهو من محيط التاسع إلى نقطة مركز الأرض وهذا لا شكّ أنّه موجود بعد أن لم يكن فهو المراد بقوله ثمّ خلق الخلق وبسط الرزق.

The Surah of the Prophets

The Surah of the Prophets has two names.

Al-Rātiq: The Stitcher

Only Ibn Barrajān mentions it as a divine name. It occurs in the Surah of the Prophets in the verse: «The heavens and the earth were stitched together».[500] That is, God stitched them, so thereby they were stitched together. The true nature of the stitched mass is the unrefracted purity of white light. When the forms of existents open up within it, then the light is unstitched; that is, refracted into the various colors. Moreover, the stitched mass is the origin, because oneness comes first. However, this is in view of rank. For the divine quality of ever-creating in actuality has no beginning and no end. 93.1

As for the prophetic tradition: "God was, and there was nothing with Him, then He brought forth creation and spread out the provision,"[501] it carries three possible meanings. The first is that "He is now as He ever was";[502] that is, when "there was nothing with Him." For He exists, and the qualities, acts, and existents are His acts, and acts return to qualities according to truth verified by the witnesses. 93.2

The second possible meaning is that "and nothing was beside Him" refers to the realm of existence that is our specific world, and that extends from the ninth sphere to the center point of the earth. There is no doubt that this exists after it did not. This is therefore what is meant by his saying: "then He created creation and spread out the provision." 93.3

الثالث أن يكون معنى قوله كان الله ولا شيء معه إشارةٌ إلى سبق المرتبة كسبق العلّة للمعلول وإن لم يكن يفارقها فإذا تعيّن الاسم الراتق هو باعتبار كان الله ولا شيء معه والاسم الفاتق هو باعتبار قوله ثمّ خلق الخلق وبسط الرزق. ٤،٩٣

وأحكام الاسم الراتق تعالى متجدّدة مع الآنات فإنّه ما تخلو دقيقة من دقائق الزمان من[1] عدم صورة من صور العالم فذلك الانعدام هو رتق لفتق الوجود ويكون الاسم المميت تبعاً لهذا الاسم في هذا المعنى فإنّ الموت يختصّ بصور الحيوان الناطق وانعدام الصور أعمّ فلاسم المميت هو بخصوص وصف في الاسم الراتق تعالى. ٥،٩٣

فسكون البحار بعد تموّجها رتق وانحلال السحب بعد تراكمها رتق وسكون الحيوان أو بعضه بالنوم رتق ورجوع الأفق إلى الظلمة بغيبوبة الشمس رتق وعود النهار بطلوعها هو لليلِ رتق وللنهار فتق وانحلال النبات من صورة إلى صورة فوقها هو رتق باعتبار الصور السابقة وفتق باعتبار الصور اللاحقة وكذلك صور الحيوان والمعدن ورجوع الأمور إلى الله تعالى بشهود التوحيد رتق ورجوعها إليه تعالى بأن يصعق ﴿مَن فِى ٱلسَّمَٰوَٰتِ وَمَن فِى ٱلْأَرْضِ إِلَّا مَن شَآءَ ٱللَّهُ﴾ رتق وبالنفخة الثانية فتق. ٦،٩٣

وهذا الاسم الكريم يأمر الشيخ بذكره من يُخاف عليه منه نكوص الاستعداد فيُحجب عنه التجلّي والله أعلم. ٧،٩٣

[1] و: مع.

The third possible meaning is that "God was, and there was nothing with Him" is an allusion to precedence of rank, just as a cause precedes its effect, even though the two are not separate. Thus, when the Stitcher becomes determined, it is in respect to "God was, and there was nothing with Him," whereas the Unstitcher is in respect to his saying: "then He brought forth creation and spread out the provision." 93.4

Furthermore, the properties of the Stitcher are renewed at every instant. No single unit of time passes without one of the forms of the world ceasing to exist. The disappearance of the form is the stitching together of the unstitching of existence. The Death-Giver, moreover, is subordinate to the Stitcher in this sense. For death is specific to the forms of the rational animal, whereas the existential disappearance of the forms is more general. Thus, the Death-Giver is a specific quality of the Stitcher. 93.5

Thus, the stillness of the oceans in the wake of a storm is a stitching together. The scattering of clouds after their amassing is a stitching together. The resting of animals, or of some animals, when they sleep is a stitching together. The return of darkness to the horizon after sunset is a stitching together. The return of day at sunrise is a stitching for the night, and an unstitching for the day. The decomposition of plants from one form to the next is a stitching in respect to the previous forms and an unstitching in respect to the subsequent forms. The same goes for the forms of animals and minerals. The return of all matters to God through witnessing divine oneness is a stitching together, just as their return to Him «when the trumpet will be blown, whereupon whoever is in the heavens and on the earth will swoon, except those whom God wills»[503] is a stitching together; and when the trumpet is blown a second time, it is an unstitching. 93.6

A shaykh may prescribe the invocation of this name to someone who fears he may be insufficiently prepared, and so it veils the self-disclosure from him. And God knows best. 93.7

اسمه الفاتق تبارك تعالى

١،٩٤ انفرد به أبو الحكم وشاهده من سورة الأنبياء قوله تعالى ﴿فَفَتَقْنَٰهُمَا[١] وَجَعَلْنَا مِنَ ٱلْمَآءِ كُلَّ شَىْءٍ حَىٍّ﴾ فقرن الفتق بالإحياء لأنّه بمعناه.

٢،٩٤ فالاسم الفاتق أعمّ من الاسم المحيي تصرّفًا والاسم الفاتق يساوق الاسم الراتق بمعنى أنّه لا تنفتق صورة إيجاد موجود إلّا عن عدم صورة مادّته السابقة فإنّه لا تكون صورة في غير مادّة وسواء كانت الصور عقليّة ومادّتها النور أو نفسانيّة ومادّتها العقل أو تخيليّة ومادّتها ما في بطون المقدّم من الدماغ في الإنسان أو أصل مادّة الجسم وهو اللوح المحفوظ أو صور الأركان ومادّتها ما إليه يستحيل أو ما بعد ذلك فالاسم الفاتق يعدم بإيجاد الصورة اللاحقة ما قبلها من الصور السابقة فتتعيّن أحكام الاسم الراتق بتعيّن أحكام الاسم الفاتق فالاسم الفاتق والاسم الراتق متعاقبان في أحكامهما حتّى يصحّ أن ينسَب فعل كلّ واحد منهما إلى الآخر فإنّ فتق الصورة هو رتق الأخرى السابقة ورتق السابقة هو بعينه فتق الأخرى اللاحقة ففعل كلّ واحد من هذين الاسمين الكريمين هو فتق وهو رتق ويمتاز كلّ واحد منهما عن الآخر باعتبار فإقامة الصورة للفاتق وإعدام ما قبلها للراتق وذلك الرتق فتق كما ذلك الفتق رتق.

٣،٩٤ واعلم أنّ الوجود لمّا كان لا يمكن السكون منه ولا في دقيقة من الزمان وإن لم يشعر بذلك أهل النقصان فإنّ الصور[١] فيه أعني في الوجود لا تزال في فتق ورتق أبد الآباد دنيا وآخرة فتنعّمات أهل السعادة صور فتقٍ ورتق وعذاب أهل الشقاء صور فتق ورتق وحركات الأفلاك صور فتق ورتق للهيئات والقرانات وما يلحق ذلك من الأحكام والتأثيرات ومطاردة الفصول الأربعة بعضها لبعض من[٢] التعاقب صور

١ ب، ج: الأمر. ٢ و: في.

Al-Fātiq: The Unstitcher

Only Ibn Barrajān mentions it as a divine name. It occurs in the Surah of the Prophets in the verse: «The heavens and the earth were stitched together, then We unstitched them, and we made every living thing from water».[504] God associates unstitching with life-giving because they have the same meaning. 94.1

Thus, the control that the Unstitcher exercises is broader than that of the Life-Giver. Moreover, the Unstitcher is coextensive with the Stitcher in the sense that the form of an existent is not unstitched existentially until the preceding form of its material substrate has disappeared. For forms only exist in material substrates. The Unstitcher causes one form to disappear by bringing the subsequent form into existence from the previous, regardless of whether those forms are intellectual (their material substrate is light), or pertain to the soul (their material substrate is the intellect), or to the imaginary (their material substrate is the frontal lobe), or to the origin of the material substrate of the body (the Preserved Tablet), or to the forms of the four elements (their material substrate is whatever substance they transmute into). Thus, the properties of the Unstitcher become determined in tandem with the determination of the properties of the Stitcher. The properties of these two names therefore follow successively, such that it is correct to ascribe the act of each to the other. For the unstitching of one form is the stitching of the previous one, just as the stitching of one is itself an unstitching of the other. Thus, the activity of each of these noble names is at once a stitching and an unstitching, while each one is distinguished from the other in a certain respect. Establishing the form belongs to the Unstitcher, and eliminating the previous form belongs to the Stitcher. The stitching is an unstitching, just as the unstitching is a stitching. 94.2

Since nothing in existence can be still, not even for a single moment in time—even though deficient intellects are unaware of this—then the forms in existence are continuously unstitching and stitching, forever and ever, in this world and in the next. Therefore, the joys of the joyful are forms of unstitching and stitching, as is the punishment of the wretched. The movements of the spheres are forms of unstitching and stitching of the heavenly constellations and astronomical conjunctions, as are the properties and effects joined to them. The successive transformations of the four seasons are forms of 94.3

فتق ورتق وتوابع تلك الفصول من تكوين ما يتكوّن في كلّ فصل ممّا يخصّه صور فتق ورتق وحركات الأفكار والتخيّلات والتوهّمات والظنون والشكوك وما يلحق ذلك من تخالفها واتّفاقها واتّصالها وافتراقها كلّه صور فتق ورتق وأحلام النائمين ومرائيهم الصادقة والكاذبة والممزوجة صور فتق ورتق من الاسم الراتق تعالى.

وهذا الاسم الكريم لا يذكره أهل البداية لأنّ مقصودهم الرتق ويذكره العارفون. ٤،٩٤

unstitching and stitching. The effects of the seasons, including the generation of season-specific things, are forms of unstitching and stitching. The movement of thoughts, imaginings, suppositions, fantasies, doubts, and their effects, as well as the incompatibility and compatibility, union and separation that are joined to them, are all forms of unstitching and stitching. The dreams of sleepers, along with their true, false, and mixed visions, are forms of unstitching and stitching from the Unstitcher.

This noble name is not invoked by the beginners because their goal is stitching. The recognizers may invoke it. 94.4

سورة الحجّ

فيها ثلاثة أسماء

اسمه الباعث تعالى

انفرد به الغزاليّ رحمه الله وشاهده من سورة الحجّ قوله تعالى ﴿يَبۡعَثُ مَن فِى ٱلۡقُبُورِ﴾ وخصّ بعث القبور لأنّه مثال[١] على القدرة التي لا يقدر عليها إلّا هو وإن كان لا قدرة لغيره عند أهل الشهود فيكون البعث أعمّ من بعث القبور وهو نشر الموتى وإنشاره تعالى لهم وهو الباعث تعالى في كلّ اعتبارات البعث فإذا توفّى الله تعالى الأنفس في منامها ثمّ استيقظت فهو بعثها وإرسالها وبعثها بمعنًى. ١،٩٥

وقوله عليه السلام ينزل ربّنا تبارك وتعالى إلى سماء الدنيا حين يبقى ثلث الليل الآخر فيقول من يدعوني فأستجيب له ومن يسألني فأعطيه ومن يستغفرني فأغفر له هو لأنّه تعالى يبعث الناس من آخر الليل لأسفارهم وللعبادة للعابدين منهم ولعزائم أهل العزم منهم في الأمور الدنيويّة والأخرويّة والإلٰهيّة فهو يبعثهم له تعالى بحقيقة اسمه الباعث. ٢،٩٥

واعلم أنّ بعثه تعالى للموجودات هو بعث طبيعيّ وما سوى الطبيعيّ فهو لاحق للطبيعيّ إلّا فيما فوق الطبيعة فإذا كان في أواخر الليل كانت الشمس متوجّهة إلى حيّز ٣،٩٥

---

١ ب، ج: دالّ؛ آ: ذاك.

The Surah of the Pilgrimage

The Surah of the Pilgrimage has three names.

Al-Bāʿith: The Resurrector

95.1 Only al-Ghazālī, may God have mercy on him, mentions it as a divine name. It occurs in the Surah of the Pilgrimage in the verse: «He resurrects whoever is in the graves».[505] He singles out the resurrection from the grave because it is an example of His unmatched power, even though no one else has any power according to the witnesses. Thus, the resurrection is more encompassing than the resurrection from the graves, which means the quickening and raising of the dead. He is the Resurrector in every sense of the term. Thus, He resurrects souls when He takes them in sleep and they wake up. Moreover, "to send forth" and "to resurrect" are synonyms.

95.2 The blessed Prophet said: "Our Lord descends to the lowest heaven during the last third of the night, and He says, 'Who is calling out to Me, that I may respond to him? Who is asking of Me, that I may give him? Who is asking for My forgiveness, that I may forgive him?'"[506] God resurrects people at the end of the night to pursue their journeys,[507] and worshippers to conduct their worship, as well as people of resolve for worldly, otherworldly, or divine matters. He thus resurrects them to Himself through the reality of the Resurrector.

95.3 His resurrection of existents is a resurrection that is joined to the realm of nature. Unless it is above it, whatever is not within the realm of nature is still connected to nature. Hence, toward the end of the night, when the sun nears the line of the horizon, it is sensed by the natural constituents of existents. These begin to move because the heat produced in them is concordant with

الطلوع فتحسّ طبائع الموجودات بذلك فتتحرّك بالحرارة التي تنشأ فيها بمناسبة أنّها حرارة هذا العالم السفليّ والحرارة ترجع إلى الحياة وهي من الاسم المحيي المستند إلى الاسم الحيّ تعالى فإذا أحسّت بذلك تحرّكت بالطبع فيتلقّاها البارئ تعالى بمعاني قوله مَن يدعوني فأستجيب له ومن يسألني فأعطيه ومن يستغفرني فأغفر له وهذا القول منه هو بلسان الحال.

٤،٩٥ وكذلك نزوله تعالى هو نزول أحكام الإجابة للسائل والداعي والمستغفر ولسنا ننكر النزول لكن على الوجه الذي هو عليه عرفناه أو لم نعرفه فأمّا أهل الله تعالى فيعرفون ذلك على حقيقته أعني الذاتيّين فالحقّ الباعث تعالى يبعث اليقظة إلى النيام فيستيقظون ثمّ إنّ يقظاتهم تستدعي المدد من الاسم الباعث في توجّهات مقاصدهم استدعاءً ذاتيًّا فيجيبهم الاسم الباعث بالمدد فهو الباعث في المطلوب والطلب والمسبّب والسبب.

٥،٩٥ وهذا الاسم لا يذكره أهل طلب الفناء ويذكره أهل الغفلة والله أعلم.

اسمه الحقّ تبارك وتعالى

١،٩٦ متّفق عليه بين الأئمّة الثلاثة وشاهده من سورة الحجّ قوله تعالى ﴿ذَٰلِكَ بِأَنَّ ٱللَّهَ هُوَ ٱلۡحَقُّ﴾ فسّره بعض العلماء بأنّه بمعنى صاحب الحقّ والحقّ خلاف الباطل والكشف يقتضي أنّه الحقّ وما سواه باطل ومنه قول النبيّ صلّى الله عليه وسلّم أصدق كلمة قالها شاعر قول لبيد ألا كلّ شيء ما خلا الله باطل ومعنى الباطل العدم كأنّه قال ألا كلّ شيء ما خلا الله عدم وذلك لأنّ الوجود له تعالى ف﴿هُوَ ٱلۡأَوَّلُ وَٱلۡـَٔاخِرُ

the heat of this lower world. Heat, moreover, derives from life, and life derives from the Life-Giver, which in turn draws from the Living. Thus, when they apprehend it, they naturally start to move, and the Maker welcomes them through the meanings of His words: "Who is calling out to Me, that I may respond to him? Who is asking of Me, that I may give him? Who is asking for My forgiveness, that I may forgive him?" He expresses these words through the spiritual tongue.

Likewise, His descent is a descent of the properties of responsiveness to the petitioner, the supplicant, and the seeker of forgiveness. We do not deny His descent, but affirm that it is as it is, whether we recognize it or not. God's folk—by which I mean those who are absorbed in the Essence—recognize His descent as it really is. For the Resurrector, the Real, sends wakefulness to sleepers, and they awaken. With an essential attraction, their wakefulness attracts replenishment from the Resurrector through the direction of their intentions, whereupon the Resurrector responds to them with replenishment. He is therefore the Resurrector for the object sought and the quest, as well as the effect and the cause. 95.4

This name should not be invoked by those in pursuit of annihilation. It should be invoked by the heedless. And God knows best. 95.5

Al-Ḥaqq: The Real

The three eminent scholars agree it is divine. It occurs in the Surah of the Pilgrimage in the verse: «that is because God is the Real».[508] Some scholars interpret this name to mean the possessor of truth; truth being the opposite of falsehood. However, unveiling yields the conclusion that He is the Real, and that all but He is falsehood. To this effect, the blessed Prophet said: "The truest thing ever said by a poet was said by Labīd: 'Indeed, all but God is unreal.'"[509] Here, unreality means nonexistence. It is as if Labīd had said: "Indeed, all but God is nonexistent." For existence belongs to Him, since «He is the First and the Last, the Manifest and the Nonmanifest, and the Knower of all things»;[510] 96.1

﴿وَٱلظَّٰهِرُ وَٱلۡبَاطِنُۖ وَهُوَ بِكُلِّ شَيۡءٍ عَلِيمٌ﴾ أي محيط فقد استحقّ بهذه الأسماء ألّا يكون معه غيره.

٢،٩٦ والحقيقة مشتقّة من الحقّ فإذاً حقيقة الشيء هي الحقّ فلا يستحقّ الشيئيّة غيره والشيئيّة هي الوجود والموجود عرض فيه منه ولك أن تقول إنّ الشيئيّة هي اسم للموجود وأمّا الوجود فهو مشيّئ الشيئيّات وممهّي الماهيات لا بمعنى قال لها كوني فكانت فقط بل لأنّ المادّة نوره ونوره هو الوجود والوجود هو حقيقة الشيء في نفس الأمر فإذا عرضت له الصور صارت أشياء فعلى هذا يكون الشيء هو جنس الأجناس.

٣،٩٦ وأمّا من اقتصر على أنّ أجناس الأجناس عشرة فهو والله إمّا غالط وإمّا متغالط وذلك لأنّ الأجناس هي كلّيات والكلّيات ليست في الخارج فإذاً هي اعتبارات ذهنيّة فيا ليت شعري كيف جاز أن يجعل الأجناس بمجرّد الذهن فيما دون الموجود وحرّمه على الموجود وهل المراد بالجنس إلّا الاعتبار الذهنيّ الجامع لحقائقِ ما تحته على وجه أن يكون ضابطاً ذهنياً فقط لا أنّه في الخارج فلِمَ لا يكون الموجود ضابطاً للأجناس العشرة فإنّ الجوهر والأعراض التسعة محتاجة إلى ضابط واحد كما احتاجت كلّ كثرة إلى ضابط واحد في الذهن يسمّى جنساً للحقائق التي تحته.

٤،٩٦ وإنّما أرسطو ومن ناسبه كرهوا قول برمانيدس ومالسس وهو أنّ الموجود واحد فاختاروا ألّا يجعلوا جنساً هو الموجود لئلّا يقال إنّ الموجود واحد بالجنس فيصير واحداً في الجملة وهم لا يختارون أن يسلّموا أنّه واحد لما التزموه من المراء والجدل المخرج عن الحقّ المحوج إلى التزام الباطل ونحن فنعتصم بالحقّ عن اعتماد الباطل.

٥،٩٦ وأمّا قولهم إنّ الكلّيّ الطبيعيّ في الخارج فقد كذبوا ليس في الخارج كلّيّ إنّما في الخارج حصص الكلّيّ الذهنيّ والحصص بمنزلة الجزئيّات لأنّها متحصّصة في الخارج فهي أشخاص فلا رضي الله عمّن يترك الحقّ ويعتمد الباطل مقلّداً كان أو عالماً فإذاً

that is, He encompasses all things. Through these names, therefore, He rightfully establishes that there is none but He.

Furthermore, "reality" derives from "real," and the reality of a thing is the real. Thus, only He can rightfully lay claim to being a thing. Thingness, moreover, is existence, and an existent is an accident within and from existence. Or you could say that thingness is another name for the existent, whereas existence is the thingifier of things, and the quiddifier of quiddities, not only in the sense that God says to the thing, "Be!" and it is, but in the sense that the material substrate is His light. His light, moreover, is existence, and existence is the reality of the thing in itself. The forms become things when exposed to it. Accordingly, the thing is the genus of the genera. 96.2

To limit the genera to ten, is, by God, to be either mistaken or a sophist. For the genera are universals, and there are no universals in the external realm since they are only mental constructs. By my life! How can Aristotle consider it permissible to say that the genera are purely mental for everything beneath the level of the existent, and still deny it for the existent? Is not the sole purpose of a genus to serve as a mental construct that comprises the realities beneath it, given that it is only a mental universal, not one in the external realm? Why then is the existent not a universal for the ten categories? For the substance and the nine accidents require a single universal, just as all multiplicities require a single universal in the mind, which we call a genus, with subdivisions beneath it. 96.3

However, Aristotle and his followers detested the doctrine of Parmenides and Melissus, who held that there is one existent. They chose not to designate the existent as a genus so that it not be said that the existent is one as a genus, and thus become one as a whole. They refused to acknowledge that it is one because they are set in their obstinacy and disputatious ways, which leads away from the truth and obliges one to follow falsehood. For our part, we take protection in the Real so as not to rely on what is false. 96.4

Their doctrine that the natural universal is extramental is false: there is no universal in the external realm.[511] Rather, in the external realm there are only subdivisions of the mental universal. The subdivisions correspond to the particulars because they are subdivided in the external realm. They are thus individuals. God is not pleased with those who forsake the truth and rely upon falsehood, be they scholars or uncritical followers of authority! Thus, the existent is a genus, and the nonexistent is a genus, and they are two species: one is 96.5

الموجود جنس واللاموجود جنس وهما نوعان أحدهما يسمّى الشيء والآخر أن لا شيء وهما نوعان للمفهوم فهو جنس الأجناس والشيء جنس أجناس الموجودات.

وذكر هذا الاسم الذي هو الحقّ أنفع الأذكار لمن أراد التوحيد والله أعلم. ٦،٩٦

اسمه المولى تبارك وتعالى

هو ممّا انفرد به أبو الحكم وشاهده قوله تعالى و﴿ٱعۡلَمُوٓاْ أَنَّ ٱللَّهَ مَوۡلَىٰكُمۡۚ نِعۡمَ ٱلۡمَوۡلَىٰ﴾ ١،٩٧ ومعناه هنا الناصر والجار والسيّد وهذه المعاني كلّها مجاز لنزاهة الحقّ تعالى عن مضايفة إذ هو وحده فقط لكنّ هذه المجازات حسنة فإنّ من صرخ إلى الله تعالى فأغاثه فهو مولىً له أي ناصر وهو تعالى قد جعل من جاور بيته الحرام جاراً فهو جاره أيضاً وأمّا السيّد فإنّ الحقّ لمّا كان يملك الوجود والموجود فهو سيّده لكنّ ملكه للشيء باستيلاء معنويّ لا ثنويّة فيه بخلاف مِلكنا بعضنا لبعض فهو السيّد بالمعنى اللائق به والسيّد منّا هو سيّد بما هو معروف عندنا من السيادة.

فالاسم المولى على ما قرّرناه وقد يعتبر في المولى الولاء الذي هو القرب ف﴿وَٱللَّهُ ٢،٩٧ وَلِيُّ ٱلۡمُتَّقِينَ﴾ ومولاهم وكونه تعالى مستأثراً بالوجود يقتضي أنّ كلّ من نُسب إليه اسم المولى فالله تعالى أولى منه بذلك الاسم لأنّه فيه حقيقة وفي غيره مجازاً وهذا نظر شهوديّ فهو جار في مرتبة كلّ جار وسيّد في مرتبة كلّ سيّد وناصر في مرتبة كلّ ناصر.

فأحكام سيادته في مراتب العبّاد أنّهم أشباه العبيد لا عبيد فما يستحقّون من ٣،٩٧ سيادته لهم إلّا شبه السيادة وأمّا من هم في مراتب التصوّف فيستحقّون السيادة

called a thing, and the other a non-thing. Conceptually speaking, they are two species. Species is the genus of genera, and the thing is the genus of the genera of existent things.

Invoking this name, the Real, is the most beneficial invocation for those seeking divine unity. And God knows best. 96.6

Al-Mawlā: The Patron

This is one of the names mentioned by Ibn Barrajān alone. It occurs in the verse: «Know that God is your Patron; an excellent Patron He is!»[512] Here it means the Helper, the Neighbor, and the Master. These meanings are all metaphorical, because the Real is free from all comparisons; only He alone is. Nonetheless, these metaphors are beautiful, because when someone calls upon God and is delivered by Him from distress, then He is his Patron; that is, his Helper. God, moreover, designates as His neighbors those who take up residence near His sacred house. He is therefore their Neighbor. Since the Real possesses existence and existents, He is their Master. However, His ownership is supersensory and without duality, in contrast to our quotidian ownership. He is thus the Master in a sense appropriate to Him, while human masters possess mastership in the common sense of the term. 97.1

The Patron is thus what we have affirmed. But one may also think of divine friendship and proximity (*walā'*) in the Patron (*al-Mawlā*). Wherefore «God is the Friend (*walī*) of the God-fearing».[513] He is their Patron. Because He alone claims existence, He is worthier of that name than anyone referred to by the name of patron. For God is the Patron in actuality; all others can be patrons only metaphorically. This viewpoint, moreover, pertains to witnessing. For He is the Neighbor at the level of every neighbor, the Master at the level of every master, and the Helper at the level of every helper. 97.2

As such, the properties of His mastership display themselves at the levels of the worshippers in that they resemble worshipful servants, but are not really, and so are only worthy of a semblance of His mastership. Those at the level of 97.3

عليهم بمعنى أنّهم عبيد لأنّهم لا يرون أخذ العوض ولو كانوا كذلك لتوهّموا الحرّيّة وهي رعونة والصوفيّة قد صفوا من أكدار الطمع ومن كلّ وصف ذميم فهم عبيد حقيقة فيستحقّون أن يكون الحقّ تعالى لهم مولًى بمعنى سيّد حقيقة وأمّا معنى الناصر فلا يمكن أن يكون معناه في حقّ الصوفيّة فإنّهم لا ينتصرون لأنفسهم ولا يطلبون منه النصرة فضلاً عن أن يطلبوها من غيره فالحقّ تعالى لا يقال إنّه مولًى لهم بمعنى الناصر فهو مولًى لهم بمعنى السيّد فقط وأمّا معنى الجار فهم جيران له لقطعهم العلائق من غيره فهي مجاورة معنويّة.

٤،٩٧ وأمّا العارفون فهو مولًى لهم بمعنى الجار ما دام شيء من رسمهم باقياً فإذا فنيت رسومهم وأدركهم الفناء في التوحيد فقد ذهب عنهم اسم أنّه مولى لهم بمعنى الجار وثبت لهم العتق والحرّيّة المطلقة لأنّ العارفين لا يسمّون عارفين إلّا ولهم رسم باق والمكاتب عبد ما بقي عليه درهم واحد.

٥،٩٧ وأمّا من فوق الواقفين فهم القائمون بالأطوار فتكون أجسامهم عبيداً وقلوبهم فوق السيادة والعبوديّة وإليهم يعود أمر الترتيب.

٦،٩٧ وهذا الاسم لا يذكره إلّا العبّاد لاختصاصهم به فإن ذكره من فوقهم فبمعنى اسم آخر والله أعلم.

Sufism are worthy of His mastership in the sense that they are servants. For they do not think they deserve any compensation. If they did, then they would have the illusion of freedom, which is a frivolity of the lower self. But the Sufis have purified themselves from the turbidity of cravings and from all blameworthy traits. They are true servants and are worthy of having the Real as their Patron, in the sense that He is their true Master. The meaning of the Helper is impossible in the case of the Sufis. For they do not seek help for themselves, and they do not ask for assistance from Him, let alone from others. Thus, one should not say that He is their Patron in the sense that He is their Helper, for He is their Patron only in the sense that He is their Master. As for the meaning of the Neighbor, they are His neighbors because they have cut off attachments from everything apart from Him. It is a supersensory neighborliness.

He is the Patron of the recognizers in the sense that He is their Neighbor so 97.4
long as a trace of them remains. When their traces pass away and they are overcome by annihilation in divine unity, then the Patron, in the sense of Neighbor, leaves them. They become emancipated and unconditionally free. For the recognizers are only called recognizers if they continue to retain a trace of themselves, in the same way as a ransomed slave remains enslaved so long as he owes a single dirham.

Those who attend to the stages are above the ones who have arrived at the 97.5
station of halting. Their bodies are servants, whereas their hearts are above mastership and servanthood. To them returns the task of ordering the hierarchy.

This name is invoked only by the worshippers, because they are singled out 97.6
by it. If those who are above them invoke it, it is according to the meaning of a different name. And God knows best.

سورة النور

وفيها أربعة أسماء

اسمه المزكّي تبارك وتعالى

انفرد به أبو الحكم وهو في نسخة له الزكيّ والأوّل هو الموافق لشاهد الآية وهي قوله ١،٩٨
تعالى ﴿وَلَٰكِنَّ ٱللَّهَ يُزَكِّى مَن يَشَآءُ﴾ والثاني أشهر والزكيّ الممدوح ومنه قولهم زكى
نفسه أي مدحها قال تعالى ﴿فَلَا تُزَكُّوٓاْ أَنفُسَكُمْ هُوَ أَعْلَمُ بِمَنِ ٱتَّقَىٰٓ﴾ والمدح
له تعالى والثناء والحمد.

وإذا اعتبرت الزكاة بمعنى الزيادة فهو لوجوه[١] الخلّاق إذ خلّاقيّته تتزيّد أبدًا فلا ٢،٩٨
تقف سرمدًا فيكون الزكيّ من معاني الخلّاق تعالى وإن كان بمعنى الممدوح فكلّ ثناء
وحمد وُجد في العوالم التي لا نهاية لها هو راجع إليه تعالى حقيقة وفي غيره مجازًا
في حضرة الحجاب.

١ آ، و: لوجوده.

The Surah of Light

The Surah of Light has four names.

Al-Muzakkī: The Purifier

98.1 Only Ibn Barrajān mentions it as divine, and in one manuscript copy it reads *al-Zakī*. The first (*al-Muzakkī*) accords with the Qur'anic citation «but God purifies whomsoever He wills»,[514] whereas *al-Zakī* is more famous and means "praised," whence the expression "to praise oneself" (*zakā nafsahu*). God says: «Do not praise yourselves; He knows best the God-fearing».[515] All honor, laudation, and praise belong to Him.

98.2 If you consider *zakāh* in the sense of increase, then it pertains to different aspects of the Ever-Creating. For the divine quality of continuous creation increases forever and never stops. Accordingly, the Ever-Increasing (*al-Zakī*) is one of the meanings of the Ever-Creating. However, if it means the extolled one, then every laudation and praise that is found in any of the infinite worlds is in reality attributable to Him, and in the presence of the veil attributable to other-than-He metaphorically.

اسمه الوفيّ تعالى

١،٩٩ انفرد به البيهقيّ وشاهده من سورة النور قوله تعالى ﴿ يَوْمَئِذٍ يُوَفِّيهِمُ ٱللَّهُ دِينَهُمُ ٱلْحَقَّ ﴾ وهو الوفيّ سبحانه للممكنات بما يظهرها في وجوده باسمه الموجد وتفصيل الإيجاد إذا شُرح لا يتناهى فتفصيل معاني الاسم الوفيّ لا يتناهى.

٢،٩٩ قال تعالى ﴿ فَوَفَّىٰهُ حِسَابَهُۥ وَٱللَّهُ سَرِيعُ ٱلْحِسَابِ ﴾ وقال تعالى ﴿ فَيُوَفِّيهِمْ أُجُورَهُمْ ﴾ وهو الوفيّ تعالى منهم أيضاً فإنّهم وفّوه ما أراده منهم بمقتضى الاسم المريد وتوفيتهم إيّاه هو من توفيته إيّاهم فيما قبلوه من حضرة الإمكان إذ من جملة ما قبلوه من اسمه الموجد أن أوجد فيهم أن يوفّوه فتوفيتهم إيّاه من عين توفيته إيّاهم فهو الوفيّ تعالى في الاعتبارين.

٣،٩٩ وذكر هذا الاسم في الخلوة يعطي نهاية ما في الاستعداد من القبول وهو ذكر المتوسّطين.

اسمه النور تبارك وتعالى

١،١٠٠ انفرد به أبو الحكم وشاهده من سورة النور قوله تعالى ﴿ ٱللَّهُ نُورُ ٱلسَّمَٰوَٰتِ وَٱلْأَرْضِ ﴾ قال العلماء النور بمعنى المنوّر فكأنّهم قالوا ليس هو النور بل هو المنوّر وهذه الطائفة لا يمنعون أن يكون هو النور ثمّ إنّ النور منوّر.

٢،١٠٠ وهذا الاسم هو له تعالى من قِبل اسمه الموجد فإنّ الإيجاد يظهر كما أنّ النور يظهر والنور الإيجاديّ هو أصل النور الكونيّ والأنوار لا تتناهى ومنها نور البصيرة

Al-Wafī: The Fulfiller

Only al-Bayhaqī mentions it as a divine name. It occurs in the Surah of Light in the verse: «On the Day God will fulfill them their rightful due».[516] He fulfills the possibilities by making them manifest in His existence through the Existentiator. If we were to explain the details of existentiation, we would never stop, and thus the detailed meanings of the Fulfiller are without end. 99.1

God says: «He then fulfilled him his reckoning; and God is swift in reckoning».[517] He also says: «He will fulfill them their rewards».[518] He is also the Fulfiller through them, for they fulfilled what He willed for them through the dictates of the Willing, and their fulfilment to Him is from His fulfillment to them inasmuch as they are receptive to the presence of possibility. For one of the things they received from His name the Existentiator is that He gave existence to their fulfillment, and thus their fulfillment is from His own fulfillment to them. God is thus the Fulfiller in both respects. 99.2

Invoking this name in the spiritual retreat provides the most preparedness that one can receive. It is an invocation for those who are at the intermediate stages. 99.3

Al-Nūr: The Light

Only Ibn Barrajān mentions this name. It occurs in the Surah of Light in the verse: «God is the light of the heavens and the earth».[519] The scholars say that the Light means the Illuminator, as if to say that He is the Illuminator, not the Light itself. Our group of scholars, however, does not deny that He is the Light; and in any case, light is what provides illumination. 100.1

This name belongs to God in respect to the Existentiator, because existentiation makes manifest just as light makes manifest. The existentiating light is the root of the engendered light, and the lights are infinite. The light of inward 100.2

بالفطرة وأقوى منه نور الكشف والشهود والأنوار معروفة في الوجود وبالجملة فكلّ ما أظهر فهو نور حتّى الظلم في إظهار الأشياء للخفّاش وما ناسب الخفّاش في البصر هي أيضاً أنوار في تلك الأطوار.

٣،١٠٠ واعلم أنّ من جملة الأنوار الكاشفة الظنون والأوهام والشكوك فإنّها تظهر حقائق المظنونات والموهومات والمشكوكات ولولاها لخلا الوجود من هذه المعاني الثلاثة فهو نور إضافيّ ولا يضرّكون هذه ناقصة عن الحقّ الحقيقيّ فإنّ المعقولات إذا أدركت الحقائقَ على ما هي عليه لكن من طور أفكارها فهي أيضاً ناقصة فإنّ الكاملة ليس إلّا إدراك العقول من حيث هي قابلة للفناء في المتجلّي الذي هو النور الحقيقيّ حتّى لا يكون المدرك حقيقة إلّا النور الحقيقيّ أدرك ذاته وأسماءه وصفاته وأفعاله فما رأى غيره ففنيت الرؤية لاقتضائها الثنويّة وبقي الباقي كما لم يزل.

٤،١٠٠ وهذا الاسم يسرع على أهل الخلوات الفتح لكنّه يأتي بالتدريج ولا يعطي الفتح الكلّيّ إلّا نادراً والله أعلم.

اسمه المبين جلّ جلاله

١،١٠١ انفرد به أبو الحكم وشاهده من سورة النور قوله تعالى ﴿وَيَعْلَمُونَ أَنَّ ٱللَّهَ هُوَ ٱلْحَقُّ ٱلْمُبِينُ﴾.

٢،١٠١ واعلم أنّ الاسم المبين له اعتباران أصليّان كلّيّان ينفصل من كلّ منهما حقائق لا تتناهى أحدهما وهو يتعلّق بالاسم الموجد والاسم النور في إبانتهما ما كان لا يبين قبل الإيجاد والظهور فحيث أبان الاسم الموجد ما أبان بالإيجاد فالحقّ تعالى هو المبين من هذه الحقيقة.

vision through the innate human disposition is one of these lights. A stronger light is the light of unveiling and witnessing. The lights, moreover, are well known in existence. In sum, anything that makes something manifest is a light. Even darkness, which makes things manifest for bats—or whatever has a faculty of sight similar to that of a bat—is also a light at those levels.

In addition, you should know that conjectures, illusions, and doubts are types of lights. For they make manifest conjectured, illusory, and doubtful realities, of which existence would be devoid were it not for them. They are thus relative lights. There is no harm in the fact that they fall short of what is truly real; for when the intellects perceive realities as they are in themselves—but at the level of their thoughts—they too are deficient. Perfect vision is none other than the perception of an intellect inasmuch as it has receptivity for annihilation in the Self-Discloser which is the true light, so that the only true perceiver is the true Light that perceives its Essence, names, qualities, and acts. Thus He sees none other than Himself, and because it implies a duality, vision vanishes, whereas the Everlasting continues to subsist forever. 100.3

This name hastens the spiritual opening of those who practice the spiritual retreat. But the opening comes in degrees, and it rarely bestows it in full. And God knows best. 100.4

Al-Mubīn: The Clarifier

Only Ibn Barrajān mentions this name. It occurs in the Surah of Light in the verse: «They will know that God is the clarifying truth».[520] 101.1

The Clarifier has two original and universal considerations, from which infinite realities differentiate. The first is associated with the Existentiator and the Light, in that they make clear what was unclear before the bestowal of existence and outward manifestation. For inasmuch as the Existentiator clarifies by bestowing existence, it is the Real who through this reality is the Clarifier. 101.2

٣،١٠١ والثاني وهو أمر ذوقيّ يشير إلى أنّ الإبانة الحاصلة من الإنسان حيث كان يبين المعاني بلفظه وخطّه وإشارته ونحو ذلك فهو مبين وإبانته من عين إبانة ربّه عزّ وجلّ إذ كان الوجود له تعالى فالحقّ تعالى هو المبين في طوره الخاصّ المسمّى إنسانًا.

٤،١٠١ وهذا الاسم الكريم ينفع ذكره أهل الاستعدادات المختلطة فإذا عرف الشيخ اضطراب استعداد المريد لقّنه هذا الاسم.

The second consideration, which is a matter of direct tasting, alludes to how the human being who clarifies meanings verbally, in writing, by gesture, and so on, is a clarifier. His clarity comes from the very same clarity of his Lord, since existence belongs to Him. The Real is therefore the Clarifier in this specific level called "human." 101.3

The invocation of this eminent name benefits those whose preparedness is mixed. When the shaykh recognizes an agitation in the disciple's preparedness, he prescribes this name to him. 101.4

سورة الفرقان

فيها اسم واحد

اسمه المقدّر جلّ جلاله

انفرد به أبو الحكم وشاهده من سورة الفرقان قوله تعالى ﴿فَقَدَّرَهُۥ تَقۡدِيرٗا﴾ والاسم ١،١٠٢
المقدّر يمازج الاسم الحكيم وخصوص وصف يلحقه من الاسم المريد وهو بين يدي
تصرّف الاسم الخالق لأنّ التقدير في عالم الخلق وأمّا عالم الأمر فقائم من غير تقدير
لإضافته إلى الاسم الواحد والأحد.

فظهور حكمه في المهندسين وأرباب المهن والحرف والصناعات وجميع تصرّفات ٢،١٠٢
من ذُكر ومن لم يذكر هي من تصرّفات الاسم المقدّر بين يدي تصرّف الاسم الخالق
وكلّ ما لم يلحقه تصرّف الاسم المقدّر وظهر مخالفاً فالاسم الخالق تصرّف به بحكم
الاسم المضلّ ويسمّى في الأكوان غلطاً وفي حضرة المكوّن إضلالاً فإنّ الطبيعة
حكيمة ما دامت في تصرّف الاسم المقدّر تعالى ولا تغلط وهي في تصرّفه أصلاً
فإن اتّخذتها أحكام أسماء أخرى خرجت عن الحكمة بقدر مفارقتها للاسم المقدّر
تعالى وأغاليط الأطبّاء في مداواة أجسام الناس هو من اعتوار أحكام الأسماء

The Surah of the Criterion

The Surah of the Criterion has one name.

Al-Muqaddir: The Determiner

Only Ibn Barrajān mentions this name. It occurs in the Surah of the Criterion in the verse: «He determined it precisely».[521] The Determiner commingles with the Wise, and it is associated with a specific quality that joins to it from the Willing. Furthermore, it comes under the control of the Creator, because determination occurs in the realm of creation, whereas the realm of divine command exists independently of any determination since it is related to the One and the Unique. 102.1

Thus, the manifestation of its properties among geometers and experts of disciplines, professions, and crafts, as well as its activity among those we have mentioned and those we have not mentioned, are all part of the authority of the Determiner through the authority of the Creator. In addition, if anything is not joined to the authority of the Determiner and manifests in opposition to it, then the Creator continues to exercise control over it through the property of the Misguider. In the realm of engendered things, this is called a mistake. In the presence of the One Who Engenders, it is called misguidance. For nature is wise as long as it is under the control of the Determiner. As long as it is under its control, it does not commit a mistake. However, when seized by the properties of other names, nature deviates from wisdom inasmuch as it is separated from the Determiner. Thus, the mistakes of doctors in their medical treatment of human bodies are caused by the miscellaneous properties of the various names. After all, the potency of remedies, medicines, and treatments 102.2

المختلفة فإنّ قِوى العقاقير والأدوية والمعالجات لا تكون إلّا عن تصرّفات الحقّ تعالى بمقتضى أسمائه.

٣،١٠٢ واعلم أنّ تقدير الاسم المقدّر غير حقيقة القدَر فإنّ حقيقة التقدير المنسوب إلى الاسم المقدِّر يكون بمقتضى الاسم الحكيم والأقدار الإلٰهيّة قد تخالف الحكمة وتوافق الإرادة إذ تعلّق الاسم المريد أوسع دائرة من تعلّق الاسم الحكيم وتعلّق ما يلحقه لكنّ الإرادة لا توافق إلّا الذات الجامعة وفي موافقتها للذات الجامعة قد تخرم أحكام الاسم المقدّر بمخالفة ترتيبه خرماً يزيل مخالفة الذات المقدّسة لأنّ رجوع الأشياء كلّها إلى أحكام الذات ﴿وَٱللَّهُ غَالِبٌ عَلَىٰٓ أَمْرِهِۦ﴾ وعالمُ الخلق والأمر مغلوب له غلباً هو مقتضى الذات.

٤،١٠٢ وهذا الاسم يلقّنه الشيخ لأهل الإعراض عن حكمة الحكيم فيجمعهم إليه.

come from none other than the control of the Real in accordance with the dictates of His names.

Moreover, the apportionment of the Determiner differs in reality from the apportionment of destiny. For the reality of apportionment ascribed to the Determiner accords with the dictates of the Wise. In contrast, the apportionment of destiny may contradict His wisdom but conform to His will. For what pertains to the Willing has a broader scope than what pertains to the Wise and the concomitants joined to it. Divine will, moreover, only conforms to the all-comprehensive Essence, and by conforming to the all-comprehensive Essence, it may obliterate the properties of the Determiner by opposing its arrangement in a manner that causes its opposition to the Holy Essence to disappear. For all things derive from the properties of the Essence, and «God is dominant over His affair».[522] Likewise, the worlds of creation and command are dominated in a manner required by the Essence. 102.3

This name is given by the shaykh to those who oppose the wisdom of the Wise, and it brings them back to Him. 102.4

سورة الشعراء

وفيها اسم واحد

اسمه الشافي عمّت بركتُه

١.١٠٣ انفرد به البيهقيّ وشاهده من سورة الشعراء قوله تعالى ﴿وَإِذَا مَرِضْتُ فَهُوَ يَشْفِينِ﴾ والشافي خلاف الممرض والشفاء والمرض متقابلان والمشهور أنّهما في أبدان الإنسان وبالعموم الحيوان والحقّ أنّ المرض والشفاء أعمّ فإنّ المرض هو خروج البدن عن الاعتدال وعن عرضه الذي تتردّد فيه صحّة كلّ بدن بحسبه.

٢.١٠٣ هذا في الخصوص وفي العموم هو خروج كلّ موجود عن الاعتدال الخاصّ به وعن عرضه الذي يتردّد فيه فيكون الشفاء رجوع البدن أو الموجود إلى ما خرج بالمرض عنه فيدخل الأمراض في الموجودات بأسرها ما كان منها يعمّ الجسم الكلّيّ وما كان منها يعمّ الطبيعة أو الطبائع وما كان منها يعمّ الموادّ وصورها وما كان منها يعمّ النفوس والعقول ولواحقها من الإدراكات والآراء.

٣.١٠٣ وممّا يعمّ الجسم الكلّيّ حركات الأفلاك فإنّ لها خروجاً ما يقتضيه تناهي أجرامها وقواها وكونها محدثة بعد أن لم تكن خلافاً لزاعمي أزليّتها ولعلّ خروجها المذكور هو الذي اقتضى اختلال ما وجدوه قد انخرم من مقتضيات الإرصاد في المدد الطوال وهو من الأمراض.

The Surah of the Poets

The Surah of the Poets has one name.

Al-Shāfī: The Healer

Only al-Bayhaqī mentions it as a divine name. It occurs in the Surah of the Poets in the verse: «When I fall ill, it is He who heals me».[523] The Healer contrasts with the one who causes illness, just as health and illness are opposites. It is well known that these conditions occur in humans and in animals in general. But the truth is that health and illness are general, since illness is the body's loss of equilibrium and of the normal condition wherein each body maintains its health in keeping with itself. 103.1

This pertains to the specific. The general is the existent's loss of the equilibrium specific to it and of the condition it normally inhabits. Healing, therefore, is the return of the body or the existent to what it lost on account of the illness. These two matters pertain to all existents: those that pervade the Universal Body; those that pervade nature or the natural constituents; those that pervade the material substrates and their forms; and those that pervade souls, intellects, and the perceptions and views they produce. 103.2

The movements of the spheres are among the things that pervade the Universal Body. For they too experience a loss that entails the finitude of their bodies and their strength. In addition, they are temporally originated after being nonexistent, contrary to those who claim that they are eternal. Their loss, moreover, may be what causes the disintegration that can be observed in the stars over long periods of time; and that is a type of illness. 103.3

وإذا عرفت عموم المرض فاعرف في مقابلته مواقع تصرّف الاسم الشافي في عود ٤،١٠٣
ما خرج عن الاعتدال إلى الاعتدال والله تعالى هو الشافي في ذلك جميعِه.

If you recognize the pervasiveness of illness, then you recognize by contrast the places where the Healer exercises control by bringing back things from disequilibrium to equilibrium, and God is the Healer in every single instance. 103.4

سورة النمل

وفيها اسم واحد

اسمه الكريم جلّ وعلا

١٠١٠٤ متّفق عليه بين الأئمّة الثلاثة وشاهده في سورة النمل قوله تعالى ﴿إِنَّ رَبِّى غَنِىٌّ كَرِيمٌ﴾ والكريم هنا بمعنى المكرم مثل السميع بمعنى المسمع وهو أولى من جعل الكريم هنا أنّه المقابل للّئيم فإنّ الحقّ تعالى تنزّه عن هذه المقابلة إذ لا يُتوهّم فيه قبول وصف اللؤم فيُرفع ذلك التوهّم بوضع اسمه الكريم عليه تعالى فإذا قلنا إنّه بمعنى المكرم فيكون من جملة كرمه إعطاء الكرماء وصفاً هو الكرم المقابل للّؤم.

٢٠١٠٤ واعلم أنّ الوصفين له تعالى إذ كان معطيهما أعني الكرم بمعنى المكرم والكرم المقابل للّؤم لكونه يوجدهما وليس المكرم غيره عزّ وجلّ ﴿وَمَن يُهِنِ ٱللَّهُ فَمَا لَهُۥ مِن مُّكْرِمٍ إِنَّ ٱللَّهَ يَفْعَلُ مَا يَشَآءُ﴾ كما أنّه من يكرم فما له من مهين.

٣٠١٠٤ وأوّل إكرامه عزّ وجلّ لخلقه بأن خلقهم ثمّ بأنْ أمدّهم بالبقاء مدّة واستأثر بدوامه وحده وأكرم من أكرم بتمام ما هو أكمل من غيره وكرّم بني آدم ورزقهم مِنَ ٱلطَّيِّبَاتِ ثمّ أكرم بعضهم بالإيمان ورفع بعضهم فوق بعض درجات في السلوك إلى العرفان

The Surah of the Ants

The Surah of the Ants has one name.

Al-Karīm: The Noble

The three eminent scholars agree that it is a divine name. It occurs in the Surah of the Ants in the verse: «Indeed my Lord is Independent, Noble».[524] Here, the Noble (*al-Karīm*) means the Ennobler (*al-Mukrim*), just as the Hearing (*al-Samīʿ*) can mean the one who makes it possible to hear (*al-Musmiʿ*). This is more fitting than to put the noble in opposition to the ignoble, for the Real is hallowed beyond this opposition. Indeed, one cannot imagine Him as receptive of the quality of ignobility, such that the Noble would remove that imagined supposition. Therefore, if we say that the Noble means the Ennobler, then part of His nobility is that He confers the quality of nobility—which is the opposite of ignobility—upon the noble. 104.1

The two qualities belong to Him, for He confers both; that is, nobility in the sense of the Ennobler, and the nobility that is the opposite of ignobility. This is because He bestows existence upon them, and there is no Ennobler other than He. «Whoever God disgraces, none can ennoble. Truly God does whatever He wills».[525] Similarly, whoever God ennobles, none can disgrace. 104.2

God first confers nobility upon His creatures by creating them, then by extending the duration of their subsistence, reserving the quality of permanence for Himself. He ennobles whoever He ennobles by completing their perfection over others. He ennobles the children of Adam, and «provides them with pleasant things»,[526] then ennobles some with faith, and raises some in degrees as they journey toward direct recognition. He singles out the 104.3

واختصّ الخواص وخواصّ الخواص إلى القطبيّة فيقف العمل وينقطع الأمل لا باليأس بل ببلوغ ما لا يأخذه الحصر والقياس قال بعضهم

أَصْبَحْتُ لَا أَمَلًا وَلَا أُمْنِيَّةً   أَرْجُو وَلَا مَوْعُودَةً أَتَـرَقَّـبُ

elite, and the elite of the elite, for axial sainthood, at which point the performance of deeds ceases and hope is cut off, not because of despair but because they have attained that which cannot be measured or described by analogy.[527] It was said:

> I no longer have any expectation or desire
> to hope for, nor do I anticipate a reward.[528]

سورة القصص

وفيها اسم واحد

اسمه المحسن تبارك وتعالى

١،١٠٥ انفرد به أبو الحكم وشاهده من سورة القصص قوله تعالى ﴿وَأَحْسِن كَمَآ أَحْسَنَ ٱللَّهُ إِلَيْكَ﴾ وإحسان الحقّ تعالى لا ينحصر أمّا أوّلاً فلأنّ كلّ إحسان صدر عن محسن فهو خلقه وإيجاده فهو المحسن به وأمّا ثانياً فلأنّ كلّ ما يتوهّم أنّه إساءة فله فيه لطف فمن ذلك اللطف ما يدرَك ومنه ما لا يدرَك ومنه ما يعجّل ومنه ما يؤجّل.

٢،١٠٥ ومن عرف أنّ مراد الحقّ تعالى بكلّ موجود إنّما هو بمصلحته عرف صحّة هذا حتّى إنّ أهل النار لهم في دخولها مصلحة لا يعرفها الناس ولولا ذلك لما كانوا إذا عمّت الرحمة لو خُيّروا في الانتقال إلى الجنّة لرجّحوا نعيم النار على نعيم الجنّة فلم يختاروا الانتقال وذلك حين غلبت الرحمة على الغضب لمضمون قوله غلبت رحمتي غضبي فالإحسان عامّ لا يتناهى ولا يمكن حصره.

٣،١٠٥ وذكر هذا الاسم الشريف يوجب الأنس ويسرع بالفتح ويداوى به المريد من رُعب عالم الجلال ويصلح للعوامّ إذا أريد منهم تحصيل مقام التوكّل.

The Surah of the Story

The Surah of the Story has one name.

Al-Muḥsin: The Benevolent

Only Ibn Barrajān mentions it as divine. It occurs in the Surah of the Story in the verse: «be benevolent, just as God is benevolent to you».[529] The benevolence of the Real is unlimited because, first, every act of benevolence that stems from the Benevolent is His creation and existentiation, and He shows benevolence through it. Second, every supposed harm contains gentle grace, some of which is perceived, and some is not perceived; some of it is immediate, and some is yet to come. 105.1

Whoever recognizes that God's intent for every existent is what is in their best interest will recognize the truth of this. Even the inhabitants of the Fire have an advantage in entering it that people do not recognize. Were this not so, they would not freely choose the bliss of the Fire over the bliss of the Garden when divine mercy pervades. Wherefore, they will not choose to be transferred from the Fire when mercy finally triumphs over wrath, as implied by God's statement: "My mercy triumphs over My wrath."[530] Benevolence is thus all-inclusive and infinite, and it is impossible to limit it. 105.2

The invocation of this eminent name brings about intimacy with God, hastens the spiritual opening, and is used to heal the disciple from the shock of the realm of majesty. It is also suitable in assisting the ordinary believer to attain the station of trust. 105.3

سورة الروم

وفيها اسمان

اسمه المبدئ تبارك وتعالى

١،١٠٦ متّفق عليه بين الأئمّة الثلاثة وشاهده من سورة الروم قوله تعالى مجده ﴿وَهُوَ ٱلَّذِى يَبۡدَؤُاْ ٱلۡخَلۡقَ﴾ ويُبْدِئُ ويَبْدَأُ بمعنى واحد يفعل وأمّا يُبْدِيهِ إذا أظهره فهو غير مهموز فالمبدئ هنا بمعنى الخالق وهو خطاب فيه تنزّل إلى أفهام أهل الحجاب إذ هو الظاهر عند أهل الشهود.

٢،١٠٦ ومدارك العقول من حيث ما هي مفكّرة لا تعقل إلّا الصانع والمصنوع وبذلك وقع الخطاب الإلٰهيّ وسائر الطوائف تحت قهر حجابيّة احتياج المصنوع إلى الصانع حتّى يقولون إنّ هذه المسألة ضروريّة بديهيّة وعند احتياج أهل الاستعداد الكامل إلى التجريد في طلب التفريد والعمل بالعزم الشديد على تحصيل الأذواق والمواجيد يقاسون في الخلاص من هذه المسألة تمزّق القلوب وتفتّت الكبود فيصقلون بالرياضة مرائي العقول فتحكم العقائد على عقولهم الصقيلة فيتجلّى عليهم افتقار المصنوع إلى الصانع فيضيع ما تاجروا فيه من تلك البضائع ويحجب عنهم الاسم المعطي ويظهر لهم جلال القهر من الاسم المانع فلا يرون إلّا ﴿ظُلُمَٰتُۢ بَعۡضُهَا فَوۡقَ بَعۡضٍ﴾.

The Surah of the Byzantines

The Surah of the Byzantines has two names.

Al-Mubdiʾ: The Originator

The three eminent scholars agree that it is divine. It occurs in the Surah of the Byzantines in the glorious verse: «He it is Who originates (*yabdaʾ*) creation».[531] Both verbs *yubdiʾ* and *yabdaʾ*, with the letter *hamzah*, mean "to do." As for *yubdī*, without the *hamzah*, it means to make manifest. Thus, the Originator (*al-Mubdiʾ*) here means the Creator. This address features a descent to the level of understanding of veiled intellects, for He is the Manifest according to the witnesses. 106.1

Insofar as intellects are cogitative, they perceive only the Artisan and His artisanry, and the divine address was sent down accordingly. All schools of thought, moreover, are veiled and beholden to the idea that creation needs a Creator. They go so far as to say that this matter is necessary by self-evidence. However, those who are fully prepared to withdraw from the world and to seek God's exclusive singularity, and who strive with intense resolve to attain tasting and ecstatic states, suffer heartbreaks and severe afflictions in their attempts to emancipate themselves from this idea. Thus, with ascetic discipline they burnish the mirrors of their intellects, yet still these knots of belief take hold of their burnished intellects, and the artisanry's need for the Artisan discloses itself to them, whereupon they lose the prize they labored after. The Giver becomes veiled from them, and the majesty of His overwhelming power manifests itself to them through the Withholder, and they see nothing but levels of «darkness, one above the other».[532] 106.2

وكلّما طلبوا أسماء الخلاص نكص بهم العقل المحجوب إلى الانتقاص فتمرّ الأزمان الطوال وهم لا يظفرون بطيف الخيال وكلّما توغّلوا في العبادة والورع ولزوم الجوامع والجمع علق بهم حبّ الأعمال وافتخروا وهم علماء عاملون افتخار الجهّال وكيف لهم بالبقاء[1] وهم متوجّهون إلى الفناء وكيف يحمدون السُرى ونفوسهم تسمع وترى هيهات لا يعلق القلب بالحقّ وفي وجوده بقيّة شعور بعالم الخلق وسبب حرمانهم وتضييع زمانهم أنّهم أهل أغراض في طلب نعيم الجنان وطلب الخلاص من النيران والطمع طبع وكيف يظفر بالحقّ صاحب غرض في العرض. ٣،١٠٦

اسمه المعيد تبارك وتعالى

١،١٠٧ اتّفق عليه الأئمّة الثلاثة وشاهده من سورة الروم قوله تعالى ﴿وَهُوَ ٱلَّذِى يَبْدَؤُا۟ ٱلْخَلْقَ ثُمَّ يُعِيدُهُۥ﴾ ومعنى يعيده إلى الحال التي كان عليها وهو أنّه تعالى أبدأهم منه وفيه يعيدهم خلق السماوات والأرض ﴿جَمِيعًا مِّنْهُ﴾ و﴿كَمَا بَدَأَكُمْ تَعُودُونَ﴾ وفي شهود الوقفة ما صدروا حتّى يرجعون هم أفعاله وأفعاله من صفاته وصفاته من ذاته.

٢،١٠٧ وهذا الاسم يلقّنه الشيخ لمن يريد أن يحجبه إذا خاف عليه من الكشف أن يتولّه.

١ آ، و: بالفناء.

Each time they seek the names of deliverance, their veiled intellects pull them back to a state of deficiency. Long periods of time pass, and they never catch even a fleeting shadow. The more these pious scholars immerse themselves in scrupulous piety and worship, frequently visiting mosques, and performing the Friday prayers, the more attached they become to the love of pious deeds, boasting like ignoramuses. How can they attain subsistence in God when they devote their attention toward annihilated things? How could they praise the Almighty if their souls hear and see? But oh! No heart is attached to the Real as long as it keeps within it a trace of awareness of the created order. The reason these veiled thinkers waste their time and are deprived is that they have a personal desire to seek the bliss of the Gardens and deliverance from the Fires. Greed is imprinted by nature, and how can the Real be attained by a seeker who has a personal desire for impermanent goods? 106.3

Al-Muʿīd: The Restorer

The three eminent scholars agree that it is a divine name. It occurs in the Surah of the Byzantines in the verse: «He it is Who originates creation, then brings it back».[533] "Brings it back" means that He restores it to its original state. For it is He who originated them from Him, and then He brings them back to Him. He created the heavens and the earth «altogether from Him»,[534] and «Just as He originated you, so shall you return».[535] From the perspective of witnessing the station of halting, however, they never emerged in the first place such that they could return. They are His acts, and His acts derive from His qualities, and His qualities derive from His Essence. 107.1

The shaykh gives this name to the one he wants to veil if he fears that unveiling will confound him. 107.2

سورة الأحزاب

وفيها اسم واحد

اسمه الطاهر جلّ جلاله

انفرد به أبو الحكم وشاهده من سورة الأحزاب قوله تعالى ﴿وَيُطَهِّرَكُمْ تَطْهِيرًا﴾ ١،١٠٨
والطاهر في ذاته المقدّسة هو المطهّر سبحانه والطهارة والتقديس واحد فالطاهر بمعنى القدّوس تعالى وطهارته هو أن ليس معه غيره.

وهذا الاسم يلقّنه الشيخ لمن غلبت عليه العقيدة وانفتح له الطاهر فيردّه إلى التنزيه. ٢،١٠٨

The Surah of the Parties

The Surah of the Parties has one name.

Al-Ṭāhir: The Pure

Only Ibn Barrajān mentions it as a divine name. It occurs in the Surah of the Parties in the verse: «He purifies you completely».[536] The Pure in His holy Essence is the Purifier, and purity and holiness are the same. Thus, the Pure can mean the Holy, and His purity is that there is none beside Him. 108.1

This name is given by the shaykh to those who are obsessed with creedal belief. The Pure opens itself to him, and restores them to the profession of divine transcendence. 108.2

سورة سبأ

وفيها اسمان

اسمه الفتّاح تعالى

١،١٠٩ اتّفق عليه الإمام الغزاليّ والإمام أبو بكر البيهقيّ وشاهده من سورة سبأ قوله تعالى ﴿وَهُوَ ٱلْفَتَّاحُ ٱلْعَلِيمُ﴾ والاسم الفتّاح بمعنى الفاتق وقد تقدّم الكلام عليه وهو أنّه يفتح صور العالم في جوهر النور فيكون مستولياً على كلّ مراتب الظهور.

٢،١٠٩ وذكر هذا الاسم يسرع الفتح.

اسمه العلّام تبارك وتعالى

١،١١٠ انفرد به البيهقيّ وشاهده من سورة سبأ قوله تعالى ﴿يَقْذِفُ بِٱلْحَقِّ عَلَّٰمُ ٱلْغُيُوبِ﴾ والعلّام بمعنى العليم وهو بمعنى العلم وعلمه ذاته وعلم كلّ عالم هو علمه في مراتب ظهوراته وكلّ موجود هو عالم علماً ما بالذات وأمّا الجهل فأحكامه من أحكام النسب والإضافات.

The Surah of Sheba

The Surah of Sheba has two names.

Al-Fattāḥ: The Opener

The two eminent scholars al-Ghazālī and al-Bayhaqī agree that it is divine. It occurs in the Surah of Sheba in the verse: «He is the Opener, the Knowing».[537] The Opener can mean the Unstitcher, which we have previously discussed, in the sense that He opens the forms of the world within the substance of the light, and thus He masters all the levels of manifestation. 109.1

Invoking this name hastens the spiritual opening. 109.2

Al-ʿAllām: The Ever-Knowing

Only al-Bayhaqī mentions it as a divine name. It occurs in the Surah of Sheba in the verse: «My Lord casts the truth; He is the Ever-Knowing of things unseen».[538] The Ever-Knowing means the Knowing, in the sense of divine knowledge. His knowledge, moreover, is His Essence; and the knowledge of every knower is His knowledge at their levels of manifestation. Every existent, moreover, possesses an essential knowledge. The properties of ignorance pertain to relations and relativities. 110.1

٢،١١٠ ومن علوم الأشياء خواصّها التي في ذواتها والطبيعيّون والأطبّاء يرون طبائع المعادن والنبات والحيوان فمنافع الأشياء ومضارّها هو سلوك منها في التأثير على طريقة علمها الذاتيّ وهي تنطق عنه بلسان الحال والإنسان يعبّر عن نطقها بالمقال فعلم كلّ شيء هو علم العلّام.

٣،١١٠ وذكر هذا الاسم ينبّه من الغفلة ويحضر القلب مع الربّ ويعلّم الأدب في المراقبة فيتأكّد الأنس عند أهل الجمال ويتجدّد الخوف والهيبة عند أهل عالم الجلال.

Among the kinds of knowledge possessed by things are the unique properties within their essences. The naturalists[539] and physicians observe the natural constituents of minerals, plants, and animals. The beneficial or harmful effects they possess are simply ways of displaying their essential knowledge, and they articulate these through the language of their state, just as humans express them through the spoken word. Thus, the knowledge of all things is the knowledge of the Ever-Knowing. 110.2

Invoking this name rouses one from heedlessness. It makes the heart present with the Lord, and teaches one to observe courtesy during self-examination. It thus strengthens the intimacy of the people who inhabit the realm of beauty, and renews the fear and awe of the people who inhabit the realm of majesty. 110.3

سورة فاطر

وفيها اسم واحد

اسمه الشكور تعالى

اتّفق عليه الأئمّة الثلاثة وشاهده من سورة فاطر قوله تعالى ﴿إِنَّهُۥ غَفُورٌ شَكُورٌ﴾ ١،١١١
والشكور بمعنى المشكور كما ورد الحلوبة بمعنى المحلوبة ويجوز أن يشكر نفسه عن عبده بمعنى أنّه يثيبه ثواب الشاكرين إذا علم عجزه عن الشكر فهو شكور وفي تجلّيات أهل المعارف يرونه قائماً بالشكر في شكر كلّ شاكر حتّى في شكر العبيد بعضهم لبعض ذلك من توحيد الفعل فلا شكور عندهم غيره تعالى.

وهذا الذكر من الأذكار المختصّة بالخاصّة أهل الوصول. ٢،١١١

The Surah of the Cleaver

The Surah of the Cleaver has one name.

Al-Shakūr: The Thankful

The three eminent scholars agree it is a divine name. It occurs in the Surah of the Cleaver in the verse: «Truly He is Concealing, Thankful».[540] The Thankful (*al-Shakūr*) can mean the one who is thanked (*al-Mashkūr*) just as a she-camel that gives milk (*ḥalūbah*) can mean a she-camel that is milked (*maḥlūbah*). Furthermore, it is possible for Him to thank Himself on behalf of His servant in the sense that He rewards him just as He would reward those who are thankful when they recognize their inability to show thankfulness. Thus, He is the Thankful. The recognizers, moreover, see Him in their disclosures as attending to thankfulness whenever a thankful person is thankful, and this includes the thankfulness of His servants toward each other. That, moreover, is part of the oneness of divine acts; and according to the recognizers, none is thankful apart from Him. 111.1

This is one of the invocations that pertains specifically to the elite who have attained annihilation in God. 111.2

سورة غافر

وفيها أربعة أسماء

اسمه الغافر جلّ جلاله

١،١١٢ خرّجه البيهقيّ وهو بمعنى الغفور وشاهده من سورة غافر قوله تعالى ﴿غَافِرِ ٱلذَّنۢبِ﴾ والغفر الستر وقد مرّ الكلام على الاسم الغفور وأحسن مواقع الغفران أن يستر الحقّ تعالى عن لطيفة عبده المدركة رؤية غيره تعالى.

٢،١١٢ واعلم أنّ المشايخ لا يلقّنون هذا الذكر إلّا لعوامّ التلاميذ وهم الخائفون من عقوبة الذنوب وأمّا من يصلح للحضرة فذكرمغفرة الذنب تورث عندهم الوحشة وكذلك ذكر الحسنة توجب رعونة تجدّد للنفس تشبه المنّة على الله تعالى بخدمته في الطاعة وضرر ذكر الحسنة أكثر من ضرر ذكر السيّئة والله أعلم.

The Surah of the Concealer

The Surah of the Concealer has four names.

Al-Ghāfir: The Concealer

112.1 Al-Bayhaqī mentions it. It means the concealing. It occurs in the Surah of the Concealer in the verse: «The Concealer of sin».[541] *Ghafr* is a cover, and we have previously discussed the Concealing. The most beautiful instance of concealment is when the Real covers His servant's faculty of perception from seeing other than Him.[542]

112.2 The shaykhs prescribe this invocation only to the ordinary believers among their pupils; namely, those who fear being punished for their sins. The recollection of sin makes those who are suitable for the presence feel estranged. Similarly, remembering beautiful deeds necessarily generates a frivolity of the lower self that is tantamount to reminding God of one's favor to Him by serving Him obediently. The harm of remembering a beautiful deed is greater than the harm of remembering an ugly deed, and God knows best.

اسمه ذو الطول جلّ جلاله

انفرد به أبو الحكم وشاهده من سورة غافر قوله تعالى ﴿شَدِيدِ ٱلْعِقَابِ ذِى ٱلطَّوْلِ﴾ ١،١١٣
والطول الفضل و﴿فَضْلُ ٱللَّهِ يُؤْتِيهِ مَن يَشَآءُ﴾ ومن فضل الله علينا الإسلام ثمّ الإيمان ثمّ الإحسان ثمّ السكينة ثمّ الاستقامة ثمّ التصوّف ثمّ العرفان ثمّ الوقفة ثمّ التحقّق بالمراتب ثمّ الخلافة.

وهذا الذكر فيه إسراع بالفتح. ٢،١١٣

اسمه الرفيع تعالى

انفرد به أبو الحكم وشاهده من سورة غافر قوله تعالى ﴿رَفِيعُ ٱلدَّرَجَٰتِ﴾ يجوز أن ١،١١٤
يكون الرفيع بمعنى الرافع مثل القدير بمعنى القادر ويجوز أن يراد بالارتفاع الذي هو العلوّ القهر كما قال تعالى ﴿وَهُوَ ٱلْقَاهِرُ فَوْقَ عِبَادِهِۦ﴾ ومعنى الرفعة هي معنويّة الرتبة المختصّة بالربوبيّة وتقابلها مرتبة العبوديّة وجميع الحضرات فيها ربوبيّة في مقابلة عبوديّة.

فالإشارة بالارتفاع إلى خصوصيّة الربوبيّة وظهوره تعالى بصفات عبيده في ٢،١١٤
أسمائه الحسنى فيه تأنيس لأهل العرفان برؤيته في حضرات تنزّله وتدلّيه وقيامه بالظهورات الجزئيّة في حيث رأوه منها فعرفوه فإنّه ما ظهر سواه.

وهذا الاسم الكريم يلقّنه الشيخ لمن غلب عليه القرب حتّى كاد أن يتولّه. ٣،١١٤

Dhū l-Ṭawl: The Abundant

Only Ibn Barrajān mentions it as a divine name. It occurs in the Surah of the Concealer in the verse: «The Severe in Punishment, the Abundant».[543] Abundance means bounty: «God's abundance, He bestows it upon whomsoever He will».[544] God's abundance to us includes submission, belief, then spiritual excellence, tranquility, rectitude, Sufism, recognition, halting, realizing the levels of being, and vicegerency. 113.1

This invocation hastens the spiritual opening. 113.2

Al-Rafīʿ: The Uplifter

Only Ibn Barrajān mentions it as a divine name. It occurs in the Surah of the Concealer in the verse: «the Uplifter of Ranks».[545] It is permissible to say that the Uplifter (*al-Rafīʿ*) means the One Who Elevates (*al-Rāfiʿ*) just as the Powerful (*al-Qadīr*) means the One Who Is Able (*al-Qādir*). Moreover, ascension or elevation can also mean dominance. To this effect, God says: «He is dominant over His servants».[546] The meaning of elevation is the supersensory level specific to lordship, and it stands counter to the level of servanthood. Each presence contains lordship, which is in contrast to servanthood. 114.1

The allusion to His ascension as a specific characteristic of lordship, and to His manifestation through the qualities of His servants within His beautiful names, gives intimacy to the recognizers. For they see Him in His presences of descent,[547] and in His attending to the partial manifestation wherein they see Him and through which they recognize Him. For indeed, nothing manifests other than Him. 114.2

The shaykh may prescribe this noble name for one who is so overcome by divine proximity that he almost becomes mad with ecstasy. 114.3

اسمه ذو العرش

انفـرد به أبو الحكم وشاهده من سورة غافر قوله تعالى ﴿ذُو ٱلۡعَرۡشِ يُلۡقِي ٱلرُّوحَ﴾ ١،١١٥
العرش سرير الملك وهو هنا العزّ لأنّ العرب تقول ثُلّ عرشه أي ذهب عزّه فهو بمعنى العزيز ذي العزّ الذي لا يضام.

٢،١١٥ واعلم أنّ العرشَ إذا اعتُبر بمعنى العزيز كان من تجلّيات الاسم الظاهر وبمعنى ما ناسبه من الاسم القاهر وفيه شهود يسهّل على أهل الكشف تجبُّرَ المتجبّرين وعلوّ عروش الملوك من المخالفين والموافقين للزوم التجلّي في نظرهم وانغمار المراتب كلّها بالحقّ تعالى عندهم.

٣،١١٥ وهذا الاسم الكريم يلقّنه الشيخ لمن غلب عليه التنزيه فيعتدل به نظره ويأنس بالتجلّيات الظاهـرة.

Dhū l-ʿArsh: The Possessor of the Throne

Only Ibn Barrajān mentions it as a divine name. It occurs in the Surah of the Concealer in the verse: «Possessor of the Throne, He casts the Spirit».[548] The throne is the seat of a king, and here it means might, because the Arabs say "his throne is weakened" when they mean that his might has gone. Thus, it means the mighty One whose might does not diminish. 115.1

If the throne is considered to mean the Mighty, then it is among the disclosures of the Manifest, and it corresponds in a certain sense to the Overpowering. Moreover, to those who know through unveiling it provides a witnessing that eases the tyranny of tyrants and allows them to bow down before the exalted thrones of kings, whether just or unjust. For the divine self-disclosure is ever-present in their vision, and they witness the Real through all the levels. 115.2

The shaykh may instruct the one who is overcome by divine transcendence to invoke this name in order to restore the equilibrium of his vision and grant him intimacy in outward disclosures. 115.3

سورة الحجرات

وفيها اسم واحد

اسمه الممتحن جلّ جلاله

١،١١٦ انفـرد به أبو الحكم وشاهده من سورة الحجرات قوله تعالى ﴿ٱمْتَحَنَ ٱللَّهُ قُلُوبَهُمْ لِلتَّقْوَىٰ﴾ والامتحان الاختبار ويعبّر عنه بالمنتقم إذا أريد بالمحنة المصيبة.

٢،١١٦ وهذا الاسم الكريم من خواصّه أنْ يستعمل معناه المشايخُ أهل التربية تلاميذهم بما يختبرون به استعداداتهم ليعرفوا أيّ طريق يسلكون بهم فيه إلى الله عزّ وجلّ ولا يلقّنونه في الخلوة إلّا لِمن أصابته بلوى فهو يذكّره بربّه عزّ وجلّ.

The Surah of the Private Chambers

The Surah of the Private Chambers has one name.

Al-Mumtaḥin: The Setter of Trials

Only Ibn Barrajān mentions it as divine. It occurs in the Surah of the Private Chambers in the verse: «God has tested their hearts for reverence».[549] To put to a trial is to examine. When "trial" is used in the sense of misfortune, it pertains to His name the Avenger. **116.1**

One of the unique characteristics of this noble name is that its meaning is used by the shaykhs, who use it in training their disciples, to test their preparedness in order to know which path to guide them along toward God. They do not instruct them to invoke it in the spiritual retreat unless they are afflicted with a tribulation, for it reminds them of their Lord. **116.2**

سورة الذاريات

وفيها اسمان

اسمه الرزّاق شمل جوده

١،١١٧ اتّفق عليه الغزاليّ والبيهقيّ وشاهده من سورة الذاريات ﴿إِنَّ ٱللَّهَ هُوَ ٱلرَّزَّاقُ﴾ وصيغة فعّال فيه للمبالغة وتحقّقه في الخارج بوجود المرزوق وهو من أتباع الاسم الرحمٰن ومن توابع الرزّاق الاسم المعطي والجواد والمحسن من أتباع الاسم المعطي لأنّهما أخصّ منه وليس الأعمّ تابعاً للأخصّ في الوجود في ذوق أهل الله تعالى خلافاً لِمن عكس الأمر.

٢،١١٧ والرزق فرزق العقول الشهود ورزق النفوس العلوم ورزق قابل الجسم الصور ورزق الأجسام الغذاء والغذاء في الأفلاك الحركة وفي الأركان الاستحالة بعضها إلى بعض وفي المولّدات لطائف الأرض بمشاركة من لطائفها وهي الثلاثة الأركان ويتنوّع الغذاء الجسمانيّ بحسب قابليّة المغتذي.

٣،١١٧ وذكر هذا الاسم الكريم في الخلوة يصلح لكلّ الطوائف وأرباب المراتب والله أعلم.

The Surah of the Scatterers

The Surah of the Scatterers has two names.

Al-Razzāq: The All-Provider

Al-Ghazālī and al-Bayhaqī agree that it is a divine name. It occurs in the Surah of the Scatterers: «Indeed, God is the All-Provider».[550] Its verbal form (*faʿʿāl*) is for emphasis. The All-Provider is realized in the external realm through the existence of someone to receive provision. This is one of the names that are subordinate to the All-Merciful, while the names that are subordinate to the All-Provider include the Giver. The Munificent and the Benevolent, for their part, are subordinate to the Giver because they are more specific than it. The more general names are not subordinate to the more specific ones in existence according to the direct tasting of God's folk, in contrast to those who invert this. 117.1

The provision of intellects is witnessing; the provision of souls are the sciences; the provision of that which is receptive of bodies are the forms; the provision of bodies is nourishment; the nourishment of the spheres is movement; and in the four elements it is the transmutation of certain parts into others; and in minerals, plants, and animals it is their own subtle elements—the four bases of material life—in association with the subtle elements of the earth; and the nourishment of the body is varied according to the receptivity of the one taking nourishment. 117.2

Invoking this noble name in the retreat is suitable for all groups and for those who have mastered the levels of wayfaring. And God knows best. 117.3

اسمه المتين

١٬١١٨ اتّفق عليه الأئمّة الثلاثة وشاهده من سورة الذاريات قوله تعالى ﴿ذُو ٱلْقُوَّةِ ٱلْمَتِينُ﴾ اعلم أنّ المتين هو الصلب وهو هنا مجاز يعبّر به عن القوّة الشديدة والحقّ تعالى متين أي صلب لكنّ الصلابة منه تعالى ألّا ينقهر لشيء أصلاً غيره لأنّه ﴿ٱلْقَاهِرُ فَوْقَ عِبَادِهِۦ﴾ وله ﴿ٱلْحُجَّةُ ٱلْبَٰلِغَةُ﴾ والكلمة الواجبة.

٢٬١١٨ وقهر كلّ قاهر له تعالى لأنّه الظاهر بالقهّاريّة وحده عزّ وجلّ حتّى من كونه منفعلاً انفعالاً يفعل في الفاعل فهو يستأثر بالأحكام وتكون من غيره قبيحة فتحسن إذا أضيفت إليه تعالى لأنّ القبح عارض والشرّ ليس في الأصل والقبح من الشرّ ومن هذا قول القائل

يُكَمِّلُ نُقْصَانَ ٱلْقَبِيحِ جَمَالُهُ   فَمَا ثَمَّ نُقْصَانٌ وَلَا ثَمَّ بَاشِعُ

٣٬١١٨ فكلّ من رأيت فيه متانة[١] أو كلّ ما رأيت فيه متانة فهو من المتين الحقّ جلّ جلاله والمتانة مبالغة في القوّة ومنه قوله عليه السلام إنّ هذا الدين متينٌ فأوغلوا فيه برفق فإنّ المنبتّ لا ظهراً أبقى ولا أرضاً قطع ومتانة الدين مِن متانة الديّان تعالى.

٤٬١١٨ وهذا الذكر يضرّ أرباب الخلوة وينفع أهل الاستهزاء بالدين ويردّهم بطول ذكره إلى الخشوع والخضوع والأسماء كلّها لها خواصّ والمسلّكون من الشيوخ يعرفون ذلك والله أعلم.

---

١ آ: مكانه.

Al-Matīn: The Firm

The three eminent scholars agree that it is a divine name. It occurs in the Surah of the Scatterers in the verse: «the Possessor of Strength, the Firm».[551] Know that firm means solid, and here it is a metaphor that expresses intense strength. The Real is firm, or solid, except that His firmness means that He is never overpowered by anyone other than Himself, for He is the «triumphant over His servants»,[552] and to Him belongs «the conclusive argument»[553] and the necessary word. 118.1

Moreover, the subjugation of any subjugator belongs to God. For He alone manifests through the quality of subjugation, even in being receptive in a manner that acts upon an agent. Thus He lays sole claim to the properties; and while this is unsightly in others, it is beautiful when ascribed to Him. For unsightliness is an accidental quality, and there is no evil in principle. Unsightliness, moreover, is from evil. To this effect, someone wrote: 118.2

His beauty perfects the defect of unsightliness.
Thus, there is no defect, and there is nothing repulsive.[554]

Thus, whenever you see firmness in someone or in something, then it is from the One who is truly Firm. Firmness, moreover, is extreme strength, hence the blessed Prophet's saying: "Verily, this religion is firm, so delve deeply into it with gentleness, for the fervent traveler whose riding animal breaks down does not cover any distance and does not preserve his riding animal."[555] The firmness of religion is from the firmness of the Requiter. 118.3

This invocation harms those who frequent the retreat, though it benefits those who mock religion and, by invocation over long periods, brings them back to fear and humility. All the names, moreover, have specific properties, and the shaykhs who guide along the path know them. And God knows best. 118.4

سورة والطور

وفيها اسم واحد

اسمه البرّ تبارك وتعالى

١،١١٩ متّفق عليه بين الأئمّة الثلاثة وشاهده من سورة والطور قوله تعالى ﴿إِنَّهُۥ هُوَ ٱلْبَرُّ ٱلرَّحِيمُ﴾ والبرّ هنا هو الذي أولى البرّ رحمة منه فالبرّ من خواصّ الاسم الرحيم[1] الراجع إلى الرحمٰن تبارك وتعالى.

٢،١١٩ وذكر هذا الاسم يعطي الأنس ويسرع بالفتح الجزئيّ لا التوحيد والله أعلم.

١ آ: الرفيع.

The Surah of the Mount

The Surah of the Mount has one name.

Al-Barr: The Clement

The three eminent scholars agree that it is a divine name. It occurs in the Surah of the Mount in the verse: «Truly He is the Clement, the Ever-Merciful».[556] The Clement here is the one who shows kindness out of His mercy. The Clement is therefore one of the unique qualities of the Ever-Merciful, deriving from the All-Merciful. 119.1

Invoking this name gives intimacy and hastens the partial spiritual opening, not divine oneness. And God knows best. 119.2

سورة النجم

وفيها اسم واحد

اسمه المغني تعالى

اتّفق عليه الغزاليّ والبيهقيّ وشاهده من سورة النجم قوله تعالى ﴿وَأَنَّهُۥ هُوَ أَغْنَىٰ وَأَقْنَىٰ﴾ ١،١٢٠
ويرجع إلى الاسم الوهّاب والاسم الرحمٰن المستولي على مراتبه ويستلزم الاسم الغنيّ
لأنّ إنّما يغني من هو الغنيّ.

وذكر هذا الاسم نافع لمن طلب التجريد فلم يقدر عليه والله أعلم. ٢،١٢٠

The Surah of the Star

The Surah of the Star has one name.

Al-Mughnī: The Enricher

120.1 Al-Ghazālī and al-Bayhaqī agree that it is a divine name. It occurs in the Surah of the Star in the verse: «It is He who enriches and satisfies».[557] It derives from the Bestower and the All-Merciful, the latter of which presides over its levels. It is inseparable from the Independent, because only the Independent can free one from dependence.

120.2 Invoking this name is beneficial for those who wish to withdraw from the world but are unable to do so. And God knows best.

سورة الرحمٰن

وفيها اسمان

اسمه ذو الجلال تعالى

١،١٢١ متّفق عليه بين الأئمّة الثلاثة وشاهده من سورة الرحمٰن قوله تعالى ﴿وَيَبۡقَىٰ وَجۡهُ
رَبِّكَ ذُو ٱلۡجَلَٰلِ وَٱلۡإِكۡرَامِ﴾ ومعناه ذو العظمة بطريق الهيبة والقهر أيضاً وهو
يعدل ثلث معاني الأسماء فإنّ عالم الجلال يقابل عالم الجمال ويليهما عالم الكمال.
٢،١٢١ ويصلح في الخلوة لأهل غلبة الغفلة والله أعلم.

اسمه ذو الإكرام تعالى

١،١٢٢ متّفق عليه أيضاً وشاهده من سورة الرحمٰن قوله تعالى ﴿وَيَبۡقَىٰ وَجۡهُ رَبِّكَ ذُو
ٱلۡجَلَٰلِ وَٱلۡإِكۡرَامِ﴾ ومعنى الإكرام معطي الكرم الذي به يقال إنّ فلاناً كريم والكرم

The Surah of the All-Merciful

The Surah of the All-Merciful has two names.

Dhū l-Jalāl: The Possessor of Majesty

The three eminent scholars agree that it is a divine name. It occurs in the Surah of the All-Merciful in the verse: «There remains nothing but the face of your Lord, the Possessor of Majesty and Honoring».[558] It means magnificent by virtue of His augustness and overwhelming power. This name equals one-third of the meanings of the names, because the realm of majesty stands in contrast to the realm of beauty, and these are followed by the realm of perfection.[559] 121.1

This name is suitable in the retreat for those overcome by heedlessness. And God knows best. 121.2

Dhū l-Ikrām: The Honorer

It is also agreed upon as being a divine name. It occurs in the Surah of the All-Merciful in the verse: «There remains nothing but the face of your Lord, the Possessor of Majesty and Honoring».[560] The meaning of honoring is the bestowing of honor, just as one says, "So-and-so has honor." Honoring is 122.1

أعمّ من الجود فإن اعتبرت معنى أنّ الكرم هو الحسب والشرف فهو للاسم الخالق وإلّا كان للرزّاق.

وذكره في الخلوة يعطي الأنس ويبطئ بالفتح والله أعلم. ٢،١٢٢

broader than generosity. If you consider that the meaning of honor is dignity and nobility, then it belongs to the Creator; otherwise it belongs to the Provider.

Invoking this name in the retreat bestows intimacy, and slows down the spiritual opening. And God knows best. 122.2

سورة الحديد

وفيها أربعة أسماء

اسمه الأوّل جلّ ثناؤه

١،١٢٣ متّفق عليه بين الثلاثة وشاهده من سورة الحديد قوله تعالى ﴿هُوَ ٱلْأَوَّلُ﴾ قال العلماء هو الذي لا سابق له في وجوده والحقّ أنّ الأوّليّة اعتبار أنّه عند صدور الموجودات فهو السابق لها فإن اعتُبر هذا العالم الذي نحن فيه فقد كان ولا شيء معه ثمّ خلق الخلق.

٢،١٢٣ وذكره في الخلوة يعطي الزهد فيما سواه تعالى والله أعلم.

اسمه الآخر تعالى

١،١٢٤ متّفق عليه وشاهده قوله ﴿هُوَ ٱلْأَوَّلُ وَٱلْـَٔاخِرُ﴾ والمراد أنّ بقاءه إلى لا نهاية فيه وفيه معنى الوارث والباقي وبمضايفة الآخريّة للأوّليّة بثبوت لام العهد فلا شيء

The Surah of Iron

The Surah of Iron has four names.

Al-Awwal: The First

The three eminent scholars agree that it is a divine name. It occurs in the Surah of Iron in the verse: «He is the First».[561] The scholars say it means He who has no precedent in His existence. But the truth is that firstness is in respect to His preceding the emergence of existents. If one takes this world of ours into consideration, then He was and there was nothing with Him, and then He created creation. 123.1

Invoking this name in the retreat allows for renunciation of everything apart from Him. And God knows best. 123.2

Al-Ākhir: The Last

It is agreed upon as a divine name. It occurs in the verse: «He is the First and the Last».[562] What this means is that He subsists infinitely. It also contains the meaning of the Inheritor, and the Everlasting. Moreover, the correspondence between lastness and firstness is affirmed by the definite article of specificity, implying that there is nothing with Him, to say nothing of the affirmation of 124.1

معه فكيف بثبوت لام الجنس ويدلّ عليه مطابقتهما للاسمين الظاهر والباطن فلا شيء غيره.

٢،١٢٤ وذكره في الخلوة يعطي الزهد فيما سواه تعالى.

اسمه الظاهر تقدّس وعلا

١،١٢٥ متّفق عليه بينهم وشاهده من سورة الحديد قوله تعالى ﴿هُوَ ٱلْأَوَّلُ وَٱلْـَٔاخِرُ وَٱلظَّٰهِرُ﴾ ومن شهد هذا الاسم علم أنّ ما ظهر غيره في أطوار غير متناهية بطريق استغراق الظهور ولا يدركه إلّا من عينه هي حقيقة النور ف﴿لَا تُدْرِكُهُ ٱلْأَبْصَٰرُ﴾ وهي إبصارك فاتركها له تره.

٢،١٢٥ وذكر هذا الاسم ينفع في السفر الثاني جدّاً والله أعلم.

اسمه الباطن شمل جوده

١،١٢٦ متّفق عليه بينهم وشاهده من سورة الحديد قوله تعالى ﴿هُوَ ٱلْأَوَّلُ وَٱلْـَٔاخِرُ وَٱلظَّٰهِرُ وَٱلْبَاطِنُ﴾ ومن شهد هذا الاسم علم أنّه باطن الأشياء كلّها بسرّ القيّوميّة فإنّ الظاهر مطابقه وليس بينهما فاصل في الخارج بل مرتبة ذهنيّة فهو واحد تعالى.

٢،١٢٦ ويذكر هذا الاسم من غلب عليه تجلّي الظاهر وخيف عليه الوله والله أعلم.

the definite article of genus. This is evidenced by their correspondence to the Manifest and the Nonmanifest; thus, there is nothing other than Him.

Invoking this name in the retreat allows for renunciation of everything apart from Him. And God knows best. 124.2

Al-Ẓāhir: The Manifest

It is agreed upon by them as being a divine name. It occurs in the Surah of Iron in the verse: «He is the First and the Last, the Manifest».[563] The one who witnesses this name knows that nothing other than Him manifests within the infinite levels, through total immersion in manifestation. But this is only perceived by him whose eye is identical to the reality of the light, for «sight does not perceive Him»;[564] that is, your sight does not perceive Him. So abandon it for Him and you will see Him! 125.1

Invoking this name is very beneficial during the second journey. And God knows best. 125.2

Al-Bāṭin: The Nonmanifest

It is agreed as being a divine name. It occurs in the Surah of Iron in the verse: «He is the First and the Last, the Manifest and the Nonmanifest».[565] Whoever witnesses this name knows that He is the nonmanifest aspect of all things through the secret of divine self-subsisting. For this name coincides with the Manifest, and in the external realm there is no line of demarcation between the two. It is simply a mental division, for He is One. 126.1

The one who is overwhelmed by the disclosure of the Manifest and risks becoming mad with ecstasy should invoke this name. And God knows best. 126.2

سورة الحشر

وفيها تسعة أسماء

اسمه القدّوس عزّ قدسُه

اتّفق على إيراده الأئمّة الثلاثة ومنه يُشتقّ التقديس الذي هو التطهير والقدس الطّهر ١،١٢٧
وهو في حقّه تعالى تنزيه عن الشريك في الذات والوصف والقول والفعل.

وفي ضمن هذه النزاهة معنى أنّه ليس معه غيره من حضرة وقفة الوقفة وفي حضرة ٢،١٢٧
المعارف فالتقديس التطهيرُ لأهل الشهود الجزئيّ بالتجلّيات التي تمحوا منهم ما انتهى التجلّي إليه من رسومهم وذلك هو تطهيرهم وتتكامل لهم الطهارة في آخر السفر الأوّل وهو مقام الوقفة فالحقّ تعالى في الحضرة مقدّس لهم وفي مقام الوقفة يتعيّن أنّه التنزيه الرافع للأغيار وأمّا في حضرة العلم وهو مقام الحجاب فالتنزيه يكون بالإيمان لا بالعيان وطوره النقل والعقل وما قالته العلماء في كتبهم يكفي فإنّ مقام العلم قد أكثر فيه العلماء بِقَدر مبلغهم من العلم.

وهذا الاسم الكريم يأمر المشايخ بذكره لمن يكون دخل الخلوة واعترضته شبه أهل ٣،١٢٧
التجسيم والتشبيه ولمن كانت عقيدته تناسب ذلك فينتفع بذكر هذا الاسم انتفاعاً كثيراً ولا يأمر المشايخ رضوان الله عليهم غير هؤلاء بذكره وخصوصاً من كانت عقيدته أشعريّة فإنّه يبعد عليهم الفتح ويعوّضهم المشايخ عن ذكر الاسم القدّوس بذكر الاسم

The Surah of the Gathering

The Surah of the Gathering contains nine names.

Al-Quddūs: The Holy

The three eminent scholars agree that it is a divine name.[566] From it derives "to hallow," which means "to purify," for holiness is purity. In His case it means transcendent freedom from partnership in Essence, quality, speech, and act. 127.1

The meaning that there is nothing along with Him is included in this transcendence. This is from the presence of the station of halting. Hallowing, in terms of the mystical sciences, is the purification of those who are given partial witnessing. This occurs through the disclosures that obliterate what is left of the recognizers' traces. This is their purification, which becomes complete at the station of halting, the end of the first journey. Thus, in this presence it is the Real who makes them holy, whereas at the station of halting it becomes determined as a transcendence that removes all otherness. In the presence of knowledge—the station of the veil—the profession of transcendence is through belief, not eyewitnessing. Its domain is that of tradition and intellect, and what the scholars have said about it in their works is sufficient, for the station of knowledge has been discussed extensively by the scholars in accordance with the extent of their knowledge. 127.2

The shaykh prescribes this noble name to those who enter the retreat and are impeded by the obfuscations of the corporealists and anthropomorphists, as well as those who have similar beliefs. They benefit enormously from invoking this name. The shaykhs—may God be pleased with them—do not prescribe this invocation to anyone else, especially to the followers of the Ashʿarite 127.3

القريب والرقيب والودود وشبه هذه الأسماء فإنّ ذكرهذه الأسماء الحسنى هي أدوية لِمراض القلوب ولا يستعمَل الدواء إلّا في الأمراض التي يكون ذلك الاسم نافعاً فيها وحيث يكون مثلاً الاسم المعطي نافعاً لمرض قلب مخصوص فالاسم المانع ليس بمطلوب فيه وقِسْ على هذا المعنى.

اسمه السلام تبارك وتعالى

١٠١٢٨ هذا الاسم الكريم اتّفق على إيراده الأئمّة الثلاثة أيضاً وشاهده من سورة الحشر قوله تعالى ﴿ٱلْمَلِكُ ٱلْقُدُّوسُ ٱلسَّلَٰمُ﴾ وفي التسمية إشعار بتكثير السلام منه تعالى على أهل الخصوص من عباده ومن حصل له السلام منه تعالى فقد سلم من كلّ محذور وإذا قال المؤمن لأخيه السلام عليك فإنّما معناه سلام الله عليك فالسلام كلّه من الله تعالى فهو السلام ومنه السلام وإليه يعود السلام بحقيقة الوحدانيّة.

٢٠١٢٨ ومن خواصّه لأهل السلوك أن يفيدهم الأنس به تعالى إذا داوموا ذكره.

اسمه المؤمن تعالى

١٠١٢٩ هوممّا اتّفق عليه الأئمّة الثلاثة وشاهده في سورة الحشر قوله تعالى ﴿ٱلسَّلَٰمُ ٱلْمُؤْمِنُ﴾ وهو الذي يؤمّن عباده من المخاوف يوم القيامة قال تعالى ﴿يَٰعِبَادِ لَا خَوْفٌ عَلَيْكُمُ

creed, because it distances the spiritual opening from them. Instead of invoking this name, the shaykh has them invoke the Near, the Watchful, the Lover, and suchlike. For the invocation of these beautiful names is an antidote to the diseases of the heart, and antidotes must only be used to treat the diseases that they are effective against. Thus, the Withholder is uncalled for where the Bestower is effective against a particular disease of the heart. This principle may be applied to the other names.

Al-Salām: The Peace

The three eminent scholars agree that it is a divine name. It occurs in the Surah of the Gathering in the verse: «The King, the Holy, the Peace».[567] This appellation denotes an abundance of peace from Him upon His chosen servants. Moreover, all those who obtain peace from Him are safe from misfortune. When a believer says to his brother, "Peace be upon you," it actually means: God's peace be upon you. All peace is from God, for He is Peace, and from Him is peace, and to Him returns peace through the reality of divine unity. 128.1

One of the unique characteristics of this name for the wayfarers is that it gives intimacy with Him when they persevere in invoking it. 128.2

Al-Mu'min: The Faithful

The three eminent scholars agree that it is a divine name. It occurs in the Surah of the Gathering in the verse: «The Peace, the Faithful».[568] It means He who makes His servants secure from the fears of the Day of Arising. God says: «O My servants, no fear shall be upon you today, nor shall you grieve».[569] 129.1

﴿ٱلۡيَوۡمَ وَلَآ أَنتُمۡ تَحۡزَنُونَ﴾ ويجوز أن يُلحظ فيه معنى التصديق لعباده الذين ﴿صَدَقُواْ مَا عَٰهَدُواْ ٱللَّهَ عَلَيۡهِۖ﴾ .

٢،١٢٩ ففي الاعتبار الأوّل يدخل فيه الحليم والرحيم والواقي وما يناسب ذلك ممّا يؤمّن الخائفَ وكلّ من أمّن غيره من مخوف فإنّه من فعل المؤمن تعالى لأنّ أفعال العبيد هي تفاصيل فعله تعالى من اسمه الله إذ لا فاعل للخير غيره تعالى من جهة الاسم الرحمٰن ولا فاعل لمقابله غيره تعالى من جهة اسمه الله.

٣،١٢٩ وأمّا الاعتبار الثاني ومعناه المصدّق فكلّ تصديق من قول أو معناه هو منه تعالى وهو الصادق والمصدّق فإنّه تعالى عند لسان كلّ قائل لا بمقاربة بل عنديّة تختصّ بجلاله يرجع معناها إلى أنّه وحده لا معه غيره.

٤،١٢٩ وذكر هذا الاسم يصلح في الخلوة لمن استولى عليه مخاوف الخيال ومن حكم عليه رعب الحالـــ.

اسمه المهيمن تعالى

١،١٣٠ اتّفق على إيراده الأئمّة الثلاثة وأصله آمن فهو مؤيمن ثمّ قُلبت الهمزة هاءً وشاهده في سورة الحشر قوله تعالى ﴿ٱلۡمُؤۡمِنُ ٱلۡمُهَيۡمِنُ﴾ وفيه معنى ما قبله ومعنى الاسم المحيط فيدخل في الأسماء كلّها وتدخل فيه الأسماء كلّها بالاعتبارات المرتبيّة اللائقة بجلاله تعالى وهو معنى الاسم الواحد والأحد فإنّ الأحديّة هي مجرى الإحاطة في الوجود الحقّ إذا نسب هذا الاسم للاسم الرحمٰن عزّ وجلّ وإذا نُسب الاسم إلى الله كانت

It is also permissible to note in this name the meaning of "faithfulness" to His servants who «were faithful to their covenant with God».[570]

In the first consideration, the Forbearing, the Ever-Merciful, the Protector, and others that involve giving security to the fearful, pertain to the name's meaning of Security-Giver. Whenever security from a source of fear is provided, it is the act of the Security-Giver. For the acts of servants are differentiations of God's act by way of His name Allāh. Indeed, there is no agent of good other than He, and that is in respect to the All-Merciful. Nor is there an agent for His counterpart other than He, and that is in respect to His name Allāh. 129.2

Concerning the second consideration, which means the Faithful, every assent to the truthfulness of a speech or its meaning comes from Him. After all, He is the Truthful and the Assenter to Truthfulness. For He is on the tongue of every speaker, not in spatial proximity, but in a type of togetherness that is particular to His majesty and whose meaning derives from the fact that He alone is, while there is nothing else with Him. 129.3

Invoking this name is beneficial in the retreat for those who are overcome by fearsome thoughts and those whose condition is dominated by dread. 129.4

Al-Muhaymin: The Overseer

The three eminent scholars agree that it is a divine name. Its root is from *āmana*, to give security. Thus He is the Security-Giver (*al-mu'aymin*), but the *hamzah* was turned into a *hā'*, and it is read *al-Muhaymin*. It occurs in the Surah of the Gathering in the verse: «The Faithful, the Overseer».[571] It contains the meaning of the preceding name, as well as the meaning of the Encompassing. Thus, it is included within all the names, and all the names are included within it, in view of the ranks appropriate to His majesty. This is the meaning of the One, and the Only. For only-ness is the scope of His all-encompassing quality in real existence when this name is ascribed to the All-Merciful. However, when it is ascribed to Allāh, then the overseeing is with 130.1

الهيمنة من جهة مرتبة المراتب وحقيقة الحقائق وهي الإنسانيّة العليّة الغيبيّة التي لا يتناهى ظهور أحكامها في وجود الذات.

اسمه الجبّار تبارك وتعالى

١٫١٣١ اتّفق على إيراده الأئمّة الثلاثة وشاهده في سورة الحشر قوله تعالى ﴿ٱلْعَزِيزُ ٱلْجَبَّارُ﴾ فإن حُمل معناه على الجبر الذي يُفهم منه مقابل الكسر كان من أسماء الرحمة وإن اعتُبر فيه معنى الجبروت وهو القهر كان من أسماء النقمة.

٢٫١٣١ وهذا الاسم الكريم يصلح أن يلقّنه الشيخ في الخلوة لِمن غلب عليه شهود الجمال وخيف عليه من البسط الذي يجده أهل الطريق من تجلّي الاسم الباسط وهو من رقائق جمال الحضرة الإلٰهيّة.

٣٫١٣١ ومقام المسيح عليه السلام هو جامع معاني الجمال فيقابَل بذكر ما يناسب مقام موسى عليه سلام وهو جامع من معاني الاسم الجبّار فإنّ موسى عليه السلام هو علَم على مقام الجلال والجبروت منه فإذا ذكر من حاله البسط هذا الاسم عرض له القبض فيعتدل في سلوكه فإنّ الأسماء الإلٰهيّة أدوية علل السالكين إلى الحضرة الإلٰهيّة.

respect to the Level of Levels, and the Reality of Realities, which is the lofty human nature of the absent realm whose properties manifest infinitely in the existence of the Essence.

Al-Jabbār: The All-Dominating

The three eminent scholars agree that it is a divine name. It occurs in the Surah of the Gathering in the verse: «The Mighty, the All-Dominating».[572] If it is interpreted to mean *jabr* in the sense of "mending"—in contrast to "breaking"—then it is one of the names of mercy. But if understood in the sense of domination—which is coercion—then it is one of the names of vengeance. 131.1

It is appropriate for the shaykh to assign this noble name in the retreat to those who are overcome by their witnessing of beauty, and there is reason to be afraid for them because of the overwhelming expansion from the self-disclosure of the Expander experienced by the travelers on the path. This is one of the intangible realities of the divine presence of beauty. 131.2

The station of the Messiah,[573] peace be upon him, brings together the meanings of beauty. It is counterbalanced by invoking what corresponds to the station of Moses, who brings together the meanings of the All-Dominating. After all, Moses is a signpost of the station of divine majesty and compulsion. Therefore, when a person who is in a state of expansion invokes this name, he experiences a constriction that restores his equilibrium in wayfaring. For the divine names are antidotes to the diseases of those en route to the divine presence. 131.3

اسمه المتكبّر جلّ جلاله

ذكره البيهقيّ والغزاليّ ولم يذكره أبو الحكم وشاهده من سورة الحشر معروف وهو مناسب للاسم الجبّار ويُذكر في الخلوة وغيرها لإعادة الهيبة إلى من غلب عليه البسط وأحكامه ظاهرة في العالم ومرجعها إليه تعالى لأنّ الكبرياء له لا لغيره فظهورها به منه في شهود الوحدانيّة. ١،١٣٢

ولذلك يظهر من أهل الله تعالى في بعض الأحايين تعظيم المتكبّرين من أهل الجاه في الدنيا وليس ذلك منهم طمعاً ولا خوفاً بل لملاحظتهم معنى الكبرياء الإلٰهيّ الذي جعله على من ظهر به فأهل الله تعالى لا يرون سواه فيعاملون الموجودات معاملتهم للموجد الحقّ فإذا ظهر التكبّر ظهر لهم المتكبّر الحقّ فلا يلحظون الباطل أصلاً لاستيلاء الحقّ تعالى على نظرهم وأمّا من عامل الملوك في الدنيا بالتكبّر عليهم فهو أيضاً من ملاحظة المتكبّر تعالى من جانب تعظيم الشرع الشريف وحضرة العلم المنيف ولا يحجبون في ذلك عن العرفان. ٢،١٣٢

اسمه الخالق تعالى

اتّفق على إيراده الأئمّة الثلاثة وشاهده في سورة الحشر قوله تعالى ﴿هُوَ ٱللَّهُ ٱلْخَٰلِقُ﴾ ومعناه التقدير فإنّه تعالى قدّر كلّ شيء فهو ﴿خَٰلِقُ كُلِّ شَيْءٍ﴾ بمعنى ظهوره من باطن غيبه إلى ظاهر شهادته والتقدير بعلمه المحيط فهو ﴿عَٰلِمُ ٱلْغَيْبِ ١،١٣٣

Al-Mutakabbir: The Proud

This name is mentioned by al-Bayhaqī and al-Ghazālī, but not by Ibn Barrajān. Its occurrence in the Surah of the Gathering is well known, and it corresponds to the All-Dominating. It is invoked in the retreat and elsewhere in order to restore a sense of awe to those overcome by expansion. Its properties are manifest in the cosmos, and they return to Him. For pride belongs to none other than Him, and its manifestation is by Him and from Him in the witnessing of divine oneness. **132.1**

It is for this reason that God's folk sometimes appear to glorify the arrogance of men of worldly status. They do not do this out of worldly craving or fear, but because they observe the meaning of divine greatness that He places in those who display it. Indeed, God's folk see none other than Him, and they interact with existents just as they would interact with the Real Existentiator. When they see a display of arrogance, they see the truly Proud. They do not behold falsehood at all, because the Real has total control over what they see. Those who display pride toward the kings of this world do so because of their regard for the Proud, by way of showing reverence for God's noble Law and the lofty presence of knowledge. This does not veil them from direct recognition. **132.2**

Al-Khāliq: The Creator

The three eminent scholars agree that it is a divine name. It occurs in the Surah of the Gathering in the verse: «He is God, the Creator».[575] It means determination, for God determines all things. He is thus «Creator of all things»[576] in the sense that they emerge from His nonmanifest realm of invisibility to His manifest realm of visibility. Determination is through His all-encompassing knowledge, and He is thus the «Knower of the invisible and the visible».[577] The determination among these two is the manifestation of **133.1**

﴿وَٱلشَّهَٰدَةِ﴾ والتقدير بينهما ظهوراته بالتجلّيات الكماليّة واستناده إلى الاسم الله بالمراتب الاعتباريّة.

وهو من أذكار أهل مقام العبادة بمقتضى العلم النافع المطابق للعمل الصالح ٢،١٣٣
ولا يصلح أن يلقّن لأهل الاستعداد الوجدانيّ فإنّه يبعدهم من العرفان ويقرّبهم إلى الفقد العلميّ.

اسمه البارئ عزّ وجلّ

لم يذكره أبو الحكم وذكره الغزاليّ والبيهقيّ وشاهده في سورة الحشر قوله تعالى ﴿هُوَ ٱللَّهُ ١،١٣٤
ٱلْخَٰلِقُ ٱلْبَارِئُ﴾ ومعناه الخالق لأنّ البرء الخلق ويختلف اعتباره في مضمون الآية ليتحقّق معنى التعدّد.

اسمه المصوّر سبحانه وتعالى

اتّفق على إيراده الأئمّة الثلاثة وشاهده في سورة الحشر قوله تعالى ﴿هُوَ ٱللَّهُ ٱلْخَٰلِقُ ١،١٣٥
ٱلْبَارِئُ ٱلْمُصَوِّرُ﴾ ومعناه قريب من معنى الخالق لأنّ الصور تخليق والصور تكون في الأجسام وفي المعاني غيبها وشهادتها فالمصوّر محيط الاعتبار.

وهو من أذكار العبّاد وأهل العرفان يشهدونه بعد ظهور تجلّي الاسم الظاهر فلا ٢،١٣٥
يستوحشون من الكثرة ولا يتنكّر عليهم الوحدانيّة.

His disclosures of perfection. Moreover, determination depends upon Allāh in the perspectival levels.

This is one of the invocations of those who worship according to the dictates of beneficial knowledge that coincides with righteous deeds. It is not suitable to prescribe it to those who are prepared for inward finding, for it will prevent them from attaining recognition and will bring them closer to discursive knowledge. 133.2

Al-Bāri': The Maker

It is not mentioned by Ibn Barrajān, whereas al-Ghazālī and al-Bayhaqī do mention it. It occurs in the Surah of the Gathering in the verse: «He is God, the Creator, the Maker».[578] It means the Creator, because making is creating. Its consideration differs within the verse so that the meaning of plurality becomes realized. 134.1

Al-Muṣawwir: The Form-Giver

The three eminent scholars agree that it is a divine name. It occurs in the Surah of the Gathering in the verse: «He is God, the Creator, the Maker, the Form-Giver».[579] Its meaning is close to the meaning of the Creator, since forms are creations that are fashioned. These are found in corporeal bodies, as well as in supersensory realities, both those that are invisible and those that are visible. Thus, the Form-Giver encompasses creation in every respect. 135.1

This is one of the invocations of the worshippers. The recognizers, for their part, witness it after the manifest disclosure of the Manifest. They therefore do not feel alienated by multiplicity, nor do they lose sight of divine unity. 135.2

سورة الجمعة

وفيها اسم واحد

اسمه الرازق

أورده البيهقيّ وأبو الحكم ولم يذكره الغزاليّ وشاهده من سورة الجمعة قوله تعالى ١،١٣٦
﴿وَٱللَّهُ خَيْرُ ٱلرَّٰزِقِينَ﴾ ومعناه المعطي.

The Surah of the Congregational Prayer

The Surah of the Congregational Prayer has one name.

Al-Rāziq: The Provider

136.1 It is mentioned by al-Bayhaqī and Ibn Barrajān, but not by al-Ghazālī. It occurs in the Surah of the Congregational Prayer in the verse: «God is the best of providers».[580] It means the giver.

سورة تبارك

وفيها اسم واحد

اسمه الذارئ

انفرد بإيراده أبو الحكم وشاهده من سورة تبارك قوله تعالى ﴿هُوَ ٱلَّذِى ذَرَأَكُمْ فِى ٱلْأَرْضِ﴾. ١،١٣٧

The Surah of the Kingdom

The Surah of the Kingdom has one name.

Al-Dhāri': The Multiplier

Only Ibn Barrajān considers it to be divine. It occurs in the Surah of the Kingdom in the verse: «It is He who multiplied you on earth».[581] 137.1

سورة المعـارج

وفيها اسم واحد

اسمه ذو المعـارج

انفـرد بإيراده أبو الحكم وشاهده معروف من قوله ﴿ذِى ٱلْمَعَارِجِ تَعْرُجُ ٱلْمَلَٰٓئِكَةُ ١٠١٣٨
وَٱلرُّوحُ إِلَيْهِ﴾ والمعارج المراقي وهي اعتبارات القرب لا في الجهة بل في الحكم
ومعراجه صلّى الله عليه وسلّم هو كما أخبر عن نفسـه.

The Surah of the Ascending Pathways

The Surah of the Ascending Pathways has one name.

Dhū l-Maʿārij: The Lord of the Ascending Pathways

Only Ibn Barrajān mentions it as a divine name. It occurs in the well-known verse: «Lord of the Ascending Pathways, the angels and the spirit ascend to Him».[582] The ascending pathways are the steps that are expressions of proximity, not in terms of spatial direction, but in terms of their property. Moreover, the blessed Prophet's ascension is as he described it himself.[583] 138.1

سورة قل أوحي

وفيها اسمان

اسمه العالم

١،١٣٩ انفرد به البيهقيّ وشاهده قوله تعالى ﴿عَـٰلِمُ ٱلْغَيْبِ فَلَا يُظْهِرُ عَلَىٰ غَيْبِهِۦٓ أَحَدًا﴾
وهو من أذكار العبّاد ويصلح للمبتدئين من أهل السلوك ففيه تنبيه للمراقبة ويحصل
به الخوف والرجاء.

اسمه المحصي

١،١٤٠ اتّفق على إيراده الأئمّة الثلاثة وشاهده قوله تعالى ﴿وَأَحْصَىٰ كُلَّ شَىْءٍ عَدَدًا﴾ وفيه
معنى العالم والخالق بطريق التقدير ﴿أَلَا يَعْلَمُ مَنْ خَلَقَ﴾ وهو من أذكار العبّاد.

The Surah of the Jinn

The Surah of the Jinn has two names.

Al-ʿĀlim: The Knower

Only al-Bayhaqī mentions it as a divine name. It occurs in the verse: «Knower of the unseen, and He does not manifest His unseen to anyone».[584] It is one of the invocations of the worshippers, and it is suitable for the novice wayfarers, for it alerts one to self-examination, and inspires fear and hope. 139.1

Al-Muḥṣī: The Enumerator

The three eminent scholars agree that it is a divine name. It occurs in the verse: «He enumerates all things in number».[585] It contains the meaning of the Knower and the Creator by way of determination. «Does the One Who created not know?»[586] It is one of the invocations of the worshippers. 140.1

سورة البروج

فيها اسم واحد

اسمه الشديد البطش

انفرد بإيراده أبو الحكم الأندلسيّ وشاهده قوله تعالى ﴿إِنَّ بَطْشَ رَبِّكَ لَشَدِيدٌ﴾ ١،١٤١ وتدخل فيه أسماء النقمة كلّها باستناده إلى الاسم الله وفيه نسبة الاسم الرحمٰن من بعد.

The Surah of the Constellations

The Surah of the Constellations has one name.

Al-Shadīd al-Baṭsh: The Severe in Assault

141.1 Only Ibn Barrajān mentions it as a divine name. It occurs in the verse: «Truly the assault of your Lord is severe».[587] All the names of vengeance pertain to it by virtue of its dependence upon Allāh. It is also distantly related to the All-Merciful.

سورة الإخلاص

وفيها اسمان

اسمه الأحد تعالى

انفرد بإيراده أبو الحكم وشاهده ﴿قُلۡ هُوَ ٱللَّهُ أَحَدٌ﴾ والأحديّة حضرة جمع الجمع ١،١٤٢
وهي معروفة عند أهل السفر الثاني الذي آخره القطبيّة وله حيطة على الأسماء كلّها وشهوده عزيز ومقامه أشرف مقامات الأسماء.

اسمه الصمد عزّ وجلّ

أجمع على إيراده الأئمّة الثلاثة وشاهده معروف والصمد في اللغة الذي لا جوف ١،١٤٣
له فيكون معناه قريب من معنى الأحد. وقد يقال الصمد الذي يصمد إليه في الحوائج فيظهر فيه معنى المغني والمحسن.

انتهى.

The Surah of Sincerity

The Surah of Sincerity has two names.

Al-Aḥad: The Only

Ibn Barrajān alone mentions it as a divine name. It occurs in: «Say, He is God, the Only».[588] Only-ness is the presence of the All-Comprehensive Totality, and it is recognized by those who are on the second journey, which ends at the station of the axial saint. It surrounds all the names in its scope. Witnessing it is difficult to access, and its station is the most eminent station of the divine names. 142.1

Al-Ṣamad: The Self-Sufficient

The three eminent scholars agree that it is a divine name, and its citation is well known.[589] Linguistically, *ṣamad* can mean that which has no hollow interior. In this sense, its meaning comes close to the Only. It could also be said that *ṣamad* is the one to whom one turns in need. Thus, the meanings of the Enricher and the Benevolent appear in it. 143.1

﴿وَٱللَّهُ يَقُولُ ٱلْحَقَّ وَهُوَ يَهْدِى ٱلسَّبِيلَ﴾ و ﴿ٱلْحَمْدُ لِلَّهِ رَبِّ ٱلْعَٰلَمِينَ﴾ ١،١٤٤

وصلّى الله على سيّدنا محمّد وعلى آله وصحبه.

آمين.

Concluding Prayer

«God speaks the truth, and He guides the way».[590] «Praise be to God, Lord of the worlds».[591] May God send His blessings upon our master Muḥammad, and upon his Family and his Companions. 144.1

Amen.

Notes

1 Q Fātiḥah 1:1–3. Whether or not the formulaic *basmalah* is considered to be part of the Qur'an's Opening Surah is a longstanding debate among Muslim scholars. Although al-Tilimsānī does not explicitly stake out his position on this debate, he appears to adopt the mainstream Mālikī opinion that the *basmalah* is not a part of the Qur'an.

2 This seems to be a miscalculation on the author's part, for in fact the total number of names commented upon in this work is 143.

3 This sequence is the usual way to refer to a word that illustrates the primary meaning of a trilateral root in Arabic.

4 Direct witnessing—*mushāhadah*, *shuhūd*, and *ʿiyān*—are key terms in Sufism that generally imply direct knowing through visionary experience of the light of a divine name. The author describes the spiritual traveler as journeying through unveilings of the divine names until he attains the ultimate mystical experience; namely, passing away in the full disclosure of the Holy Essence.

5 When the Holy Essence discloses Itself to the wayfarer, It obliterates everything other than God, including His signs, names, qualities, and acts, and the essences of separative entities.

6 Al-Tilimsānī's point is that, unlike other divine names, such as the Generous, which can be ascribed to both the servant and God, the name Allāh is exclusive to Him alone. God's exclusive claim to the name Allāh is itself a miracle, since one could suppose that a parent, for example, could name their child Allāh just as they name their children by other divine names such as the Generous or the Glorious.

7 Q Isrāʾ 17:110.

8 Al-Bukhārī, *Ṣaḥīḥ*, "al-Tawḥīd," #7511.

9 An allusion to the Holy Saying: "My mercy takes precedence over My wrath." See al-Bukhārī, *Ṣaḥīḥ*, "al-Tawḥīd," #7511.

10 For a discussion of the perfect human being in the school of Ibn al-ʿArabī, see Todd, *The Sufi Doctrine of Man*, 83–108.

11 The aeon is the all-comprehensive reality of time. In other words, the aeon derives its principle from the humanness that embraces all the cosmic and divine names, just as time derives its principle from the aeon. See references to Ibn al-ʿArabī's discussions of *dahr* in Chittick, *The Self-Disclosure of God: Principles of Ibn al-ʿArabī's Cosmology*, 128–31.

12 Q Fātiḥah 1:1–2.

13 A Prophetic saying mentions the "Breath of the All-Merciful" and can be found in al-Bukhārī, *al-Tārīkh al-kabīr*, 4:71. The Breath of the All-Merciful is an important cosmological doctrine of manifestation developed in the Ibn al-ʿArabī tradition that describes the universe as an articulation of God's breath. See Chittick, *The Sufi Path of Knowledge*, 127–30.

14 Q Shūrā 42:53.

15 Preparedness (*istiʿdād*) is an individual's readiness and receptivity for disclosures of the divine names.

16 The names of servanthood denote human characteristics and imperfections inasmuch as they stand in contrast to the perfections of the Lord. For instance, the servant is weak and the Lord is strong. Thus, "the weak" is a name of servanthood, whereas "the strong" is a name of lordship.

17 The pronoun here is most likely in reference to God, not the servant, since al-Tilimsānī's point is to demonstrate how the names of servanthood enable the actualization of certain divine names.

18 Q Fātiḥah 1:1.

19 Q Baqarah 2:165.

20 Q Fātiḥah 1:1.

21 Q Fātiḥah 1:1.

22 Q Baqarah 2:247.

23 Q Fātiḥah 1:1–2.

24 Q Fātiḥah 1:3. Both this reading (with *malik*, king) and that which follows (*mālik*, owner) are traced back to the Prophet and are used in standard Qur'anic recitations.

25 Q Ḥashr 59:23.

26 This may refer to Abū Jaʿfar Aḥmad ibn Manīʿ al-Baghawī (d. 244/859), author of a lost *Musnad*. See al-Dhahabī, *Siyar aʿlām al-nubalāʾ*, 11:483–84.

27 Q Ghāfir 40:16.

28 Q Furqān 25:26.

29 Q Furqān 25:26.

30 A grammatically modified quotation of Q Baqarah 2:3.

31 Q Qāf 50:37.

32 Al-Bukhārī, *Ṣaḥīḥ*, "al-Īmān," #508.

33 Q Baqarah 2:3.

34 Al-Niffarī, *al-Mawāqif wa-l-mukhāṭabāt*, "Mawqif al-maḥḍar wa-l-ḥarf," 121.

35 A grammatically modified quotation of Q Sabaʾ 34:7.

36 This is a reference to the Prophetic Tradition of Transformation (*Ḥadīth al-taḥawwul*), which plays an important role in the works of Ibn al-ʿArabī and his students. The tradition describes God disclosing Himself to different groups in a variety of forms on the Day of Judgment (al-Bukhārī, *Ṣaḥīḥ*, "al-Riqāq," #6653). Some groups will deny Him until He "transforms Himself into the form in which they saw Him the first time and He says, 'I am your Lord.' They answer, 'Indeed, You are our Lord.'" According to Ibn al-ʿArabī, the forms that God assumes are in keeping with the receptivities of the individuals to whom He is disclosing Himself. As our author explains, bliss and torment are reactions to the experience of God's self-disclosure on the Day of Judgment, which are a result of individual receptivities, for the divine reality that discloses itself is none other than God's essential mercy, kingship, and oneness. Those who seek refuge from God are unprepared for the disclosure and are seeking refuge in their false god-of-belief. See Chittick, *The Sufi Path of Knowledge*, 99–103.

37 This is a reference to a prophetic tradition that describes the ultimate triumph of God's mercy. According to the tradition, nearly all inhabitants of the Fire are eventually released from hell after being purified, and anyone with as little as a "mustard seed's worth of good in them" is eventually admitted into the Garden. However, there remains within the Fire a group who are made for hell. Muslim, *Ṣaḥīḥ*, "al-Īmān," #477.

38 Q Isrāʾ 17:110.

39 Q Baqarah 2:19.

40 Ibn Ḥajar al-ʿAsqalānī narrates this prophetic tradition of ʿAbd al-ʿAzīz ibn Ḥuṣayn through a chain of transmission to al-Ṭabarānī. See al-ʿAsqalānī, *Takhrīj aḥādīth al-asmāʾ al-ḥusnā*, 15.

41 Q Ṭalāq 65:12.

42 In other words, although God's knowledge is a type of encompassing, His encompassing is not merely cognitive and cannot be reduced to knowledge.

43 Al-Bukhārī, *Ṣaḥīḥ*, "Badʾ al-khalq," #3230.

44 Al-Bukhārī, *Ṣaḥīḥ*, "al-Tawḥīd," #7511.

45 Q Baqarah 2:20.

46 The *muwalladāt* are cosmological "progeny" of the four elements, known as "pillars," *arkān*.

47 Matthew 5:39–41.

48 Al-Tilimsānī is referring to the standard distinction in Islamic theology between prophetic miracles (sing. *muʿjizah*) that substantiate the veracity of a Prophet and pose a challenge to the unbeliever, and saintly miracles (sing. *karāmah*) that may signal the sainthood of a holy person but are not divinely intended as a challenge to the unbeliever.

49 Q Baqarah 2:165.

50 Q Kahf 18:39.

51 For the sources of this saying, see ʿAyn al-Quḍāt, *The Essence of Reality*, §29.1.

52 Q Baqarah 2:32.

53 Q Ṭā Hā 20:50.

54 Q Mulk 67:3–4.

55 Al-Tilimsānī, *Dīwān*, 69 (Daḥw edition cited henceforth).

56 Q Baqarah 2:29.

57 Al-Bukhārī, *Ṣaḥīḥ*, "Bad' al-khalq," #3227, with slightly different wording.

58 Q Aḥzāb 33:4.

59 Q Baqarah 2:32. The Arabic text includes two words from Baqarah 2:33 for context.

60 I have not been able to trace the source of this statement.

61 In other words, beholding a powerful person as being a locus for the name the Powerful, or a wise person as having receptivity for the divine name the Wise, presumes the independent existence of an essence of the powerful or wise person. It is thus a relationship that posits a dualist separation between God on the one hand, and the created essence or locus of preparedness on the other. Hence, the discussion pertains to the "realm of separation" (*ʿālam al-farq*). However, from the perspective of "union" in which the loci of divine names in creation are not viewed as independent or separative entities, and God's exclusive oneness is taken into account, the nature of these purported relationships is altogether different.

62 Q Fāṭir 35:41.

63 Q Baqarah 2:37.

64 Al-Tilimsānī divides the spiritual path into four journeys. The first is the journey of the recognizer (sing. *ʿārif*) who advances toward annihilation through disclosures of the divine names. The second is that of the one who has arrived at the station of halting (*wāqif*), where he experiences annihilation and journeys in God toward subsistence. The third is that of the axial saint (*quṭb*) who descends back to the world, and the fourth is the mystic's second journey back to God, which according to al-Tilimsānī usually occurs after the physical death of the body.

65 For a detailed discussion of the concept of repentance in Sufism, see Khalil, *Repentance and the Return to God: Tawba in Early Sufism*.

66 Citing the famous prophetic tradition "God was, and there was nothing with Him" (al-Bukhārī, *Ṣaḥīḥ*, "al-Tawḥīd," #7507), the Sufi al-Junayd and others are quoted as replying, "And He is now as He ever was"; see Chittick, *Self-Disclosure of God*, 70, 180, and 182; and al-Iskandarī's aphorism 37 (al-Iskandarī and al-Harawī, *The Book of Wisdom*, trans. Danner and Thackston, 55).

67 According to the early-tenth-century Sufi al-Niffarī, the journey to God culminates when the seeker attains annihilation in God. He thus comes to a halt (*waqfah*) before the divine presence at a station beyond stations. See Sells, *Early Islamic Mysticism: Sufi, Qur'an, Mi'raj, Poetic and Theological Writings*, 281–301. Al-Tilimsānī adopts al-Niffarī's notion of halting, or arrival, and equates it with the state of annihilation in God, which is the end of the first journey "to God" and the beginning of the second journey of subsistence "in God."

68 Q Baqarah 2:47.

69 Q Yūnus 10:44.

70 Q Yūnus 10:64.

71 Q Rūm 30:30.

72 Q Naba' 78:26.

73 A frequently recurring phrase in the Qur'an—for example, Yā Sīn 36:4.

74 All the Qur'an quotations in this paragraph come fromQ Mā'idah 5:3.

75 Q Hūd 11:118–19.

76 The verse is ascribed to Abū Madyan. See Farghānī, *Muntahā al-madārik fī sharḥ Tā'iyyat Ibn al-Fāriḍ*, 63.

77 Ibn al-'Arabī's *The Servants of God* (*Kitāb al-'abādilah*) discusses the spiritual typology of human beings in relation to an array of divine names, human virtues, and proper names that have correspondences to the inner "community" of the human self. This work left a deep impression on al-Tilimsānī and is cited repeatedly in his writings.

78 A reference to Ibn al- 'Arabī. Al-Tilimsānī refers to al-Qūnawī as "our shaykh, the heir," whereas he refers to Ibn al-'Arabī as "the axis of reality," "the shaykh," "my shaykh," and "our shaykh, the Seal of Saints."

79 Ibn al-'Arabī, *Futūḥāt*, 1:2. The term *mukallaf* in Islamic law denotes a sane individual of the age of maturity, or a person who is religiously accountable.

80 Q Qāf 50:37.

81 Q Baqarah 2:96. The phrase recurs frequently in the Qur'ān.

82 Q Baqarah 2:117.

83 The Ẓāhiriyyah was a literalist school of law established by Dāwūd ibn Khalaf (d. 884) in Iraq. Ibn Ḥazm (d. 1064) of Cordoba codified its doctrines and is known for his rejection of independent judgment (*ra'y*) and analogical reasoning (*qiyās*) in the legal process. The "Anthropomorphists" are theologians who reject metaphorical reading of scripture in favor of a literal approach and ultimately project imperfect attributes of created things onto God.

84 Ibn al-'Arabī, *Futūḥāt*, 3:132.

85 Al-Tilimsānī cites these verses in his commentary on al-Niffarī's "Mawqif al-qurb." See *Sharḥ Mawāqif al-Niffarī*, 76.

86 Q Baqarah 2:78.

87 Q An'ām 6:116.

88 Q Yūnus 10:36.

89 Q Baqarah 2:118.

90 Q Āl 'Imrān 3:15.

91 Here, al-Tilimsānī discusses how the name Seeing (*baṣīr*) manifests at each cosmic level. He employs a standard cosmological scheme in carrying out his explanation. Following the Essence, the cosmic hierarchy begins with the First Intellect, and is followed by the Universal Soul, Hyle, and finally the Universal Body. The First Intellect is the first descent from the Godhead and is equated with the Pen in religious symbolism. The Pen/First Intellect writes out God's knowledge of all things until the Day of Resurrection upon the Preserved Tablet, which symbolizes the Universal Soul. Hyle is still "above" manifestation since it is the receptive principle for all matter. The Universal Body is the material of the entire cosmos that can be perceived by the senses. It is the world of dominion and the visible (*'ālam al-mulk wa-l-shahādah*) in religious terms, but also encompasses the world of the Imagination (*'ālam al-khayāl*). For a discussion of the cosmological significance of the Pen and the Tablet, see Murata, *The Tao of Islam*, 153.

92 In philosophical terminology, Hyle refers to the pure potentiality of Prime Matter, which underlies all manifestation.

93 The "presence of Writing" is the locus where writing exercises its influence.

94 Namely, the four elements: fire, air, earth, water.

95 In this discussion (§§12.10–13), al-Tilimsānī explains how the Hyle's four non-sensory and simple elements of fire, air, water, and earth, which correspond respectively to God's four essential attributes of Life, Knowledge, Power, and Will, become manifest in the sensory world through the qualities of heat, wetness, cold, and dryness. While the elements themselves remain imperceptible, they are perceived by the senses through various sensory forms and qualities. The element fire manifests in the form of heat, which gives rise to living things characterized by motion; the element air manifests in the form of wetness, which gives rise to knowing things characterized by receptivity for intelligible forms; the element water manifests in the form of cold, which gives rise to willing things characterized by the willful propensity to freeze; and finally the element earth manifests in the form of dryness, which gives rise to powerful things as characterized by the dryness that freezes liquids. The properties of the four non-sensory elements thus interact in the sensory world to produce the mineral, vegetal, animal, and human

kingdoms, which are elemental mixtures, each dominated by one element. The human being is dominated by fire, animals by air, plants by water, and minerals by earth.

96 Q Raḥmān 55:15.

97 Q Baqarah 2:105.

98 This report is a gloss, not a verbatim report. In his commentary on al-Bukhārī's *Ṣaḥīḥ* collection entitled *Fatḥ al-bārī bi-sharḥ Ṣaḥīh al-Bukhārī,* al-'Asqalānī relates a similar but not identical report with a different chain, which includes Dhū l-Faḍl, in a different order (cf. *Fatḥ al-bārī*, #6047).

99 The realm of God's creative command (*ʿālam al-amr*) and the realm of creation (*ʿālam al-khalq*) are important correlative terms in Islamic thought. Ibn al-ʿArabī frequently reflects on how the objects of divine knowledge are brought into existence through God's will from the realm of the Qur'anic command *Be!* (Q Baqarah 2:117). For a discussion of "the creation and the command" (*al-khalq wa-l-amr*) in the writings of Ibn al-ʿArabī, see Chittick, *The Self-Disclosure of God*, 250–53.

100 Al-Tilimsānī is describing how the name the Ever-Creating bestows existence, or createdness, upon things at every level of creation in a descending manner until it finally reaches its end in the perfect human being, who stands at the lowest point of the arc of descent and the beginning of the arc of ascent back to God. There, the Ever-Creating begins its journey back to the divine Essence by displaying effects on wayfarers who are journeying back to God in the form of spiritual experiences. These wayfarers attract the properties of the name the Ever-Creating by virtue of their invocations, not thoughts.

101 Al-Bukhārī, *Ṣaḥīḥ*, "al-Īmān," #477.

102 Al-Tilimsānī is alluding to Prophetic sayings that describe believers, men and women, prostrating themselves before God on the Day of Judgment. "But there will remain those who used to prostrate in the world in order to be seen and heard. They will attempt to prostrate themselves, but their backs will become so stiff that it is as though they had one vertebra." Al-Bukhārī, *Ṣaḥīḥ*, "al-Tawḥīd," #7529; Muslim, *Ṣaḥīḥ*, "al-Īmān," #472.

103 According to Ibn al-ʿArabī and his students, the torment of hell purifies its inhabitants and restores them to a state of equilibrium. Moreover, the properties of the name the All-Merciful ultimately manifest themselves after all the names of vengeance are actualized. However, the inhabitants of the Fire who are decreed to remain in it forever shall remain in the Fire. But they too experience bliss in the Fire itself because they find it to be agreeable to their nature. For a discussion of Ibn al-ʿArabī's eschatological teachings, see Chittick, "Ibn al-ʿArabī's Hermeneutics of Mercy," 153–68; Khalil, *Islam and the Fate of Others*, 54–73; and Rustom, *The Triumph of Mercy: Philosophy and Scripture in Mullā Ṣadrā*, Chapters 6 and 7.

104 Q Sajdah 32:4. The author has mistakenly included it in place of the similarly-worded Baqarah 2:107.

105 According to Islamic law, a marriage between a man and a woman generally requires the consent of not only the bride and the groom but also of the bride's male matrimonial guardian (*walī*).

106 A reference to the hadith of Gabriel, in which archangel Gabriel asks Muḥammad to define the three levels of religion—namely, submission (*islām*), belief (*īmān*), and spiritual excellence (*iḥsān*). See al-Bukhārī, *Ṣaḥīḥ*, "al-Īmān," #50; Muslim, *Ṣaḥīḥ*, "al-Īmān," #102.

107 Muslim, *Ṣaḥīḥ*, "al-Īmān," #102.

108 The pillars of the Muslim canonical prayer (*arkān al-ṣalāt*) refer to steps and conditions that are to be observed in order to ensure the prayer's validity. These include intention, ritual purification, standing upright, recitation of the Opening Surah, bowing, prostrating, and sitting between prostrations. For a Sufi reading of the prayer movements, see Chittick, "The Bodily Gestures of the *Ṣalāt*," 23–26.

109 Al-Tilimsānī describes a hierarchy and variety of waking visions and spiritual voices that wayfarers experience on their journey to annihilation in God. Prayer, invocation, solitude, and ascetic discipline heighten the wayfarers' faculties of perception and make them receptive to visual or auditory disclosures. Visual disclosures appear to the witnesser as clearly as the letters on a page, just as auditory disclosures are heard as clearly as speech in the sensory domain. Al-Tilimsānī uses words like "lightning," "gleams," and "flashes" to describe visions as disclosures of the light of names. Here, he describes hearing spiritual voices (sing. *hātif*) in his ear as "imaginal discourses" that take on the image, or form, of uttered letters and verbal human speech, though in fact they come from within the self and not from the external sensory domain (for more on this, see below, §§19.6–7). These types of visions stand in contrast to direct communion with God that transcends imaginal forms.

110 The axial saint or the Pole is the highest saint in the Sufi spiritual hierarchy.

111 While the recognizer (*ʿārif*) gradually passes away from his lower self, the one who attains (*wāqif*) reaches a standstill, which is the end of the journey through the divine names. He is absorbed in the divine Essence, and experiences subsistence (*baqāʾ*) after annihilation (*fanāʾ*). The one who attains is thus beyond the recognizer-recognition-recognized dynamic, and his journey ends at the station of the axial saint.

112 Muslim, *Ṣaḥīḥ*, "al-Birr," #6721.

113 That is, the Pole sees each name manifested in its opposite on his way back down from the nondual divine presence.

114 Muslim, *Ṣaḥīḥ*, "al-Ḥajj," #3339. This is a traditional prayer that is recited when commencing a journey.

115 Unidentified. The name Sulaymā is frequently used to designate the beloved in Arabic love poetry. The poet, moreover, seems to intentionally employ the verbs *istilām* and *taqbīl*, which are found in hadiths that describe the rite of circumambulating the Kaaba during pilgrimage. This is why I translate *ḥajar* as Black Stone.

116 Q Baqarah 2:107–8.

117 Al-Bukhārī, *Ṣaḥīḥ*, "al-Jihād," #3002.

118 Q Āl ʿImrān 3:126.

119 Q Baqarah 2:115.

120 Unidentified.

121 Al-Tilimsānī uses the term *Tāsiʿ*, "ninth," in his writings to denote the highest sphere of the stars directly below the Footstool (*kursī*). For a detailed study of classical Islamic cosmologies, see Nasr, *An Introduction to Islamic Cosmological Doctrines*.

122 Al-Tilimsānī is describing what Ibn al-ʿArabī calls the "station of no station" in which the perfect human being is qualified neither by gender nor by the properties of a specific divine name or attribute and thus stands as an analogue to God's nondelimited Essence, embracing all stations, states, standpoints, and names. For a study of male-female complementarity in the context of Islamic cosmology, see Murata, *The Tao of Islam*.

123 Q Baqarah 2:117.

124 Q Shūrā 42:11.

125 That is, man is only God's like from the perspective of His lordship over man, not from the perspective of God's exclusive, unqualified oneness. In this sense, al-Tilimsānī reads the verse «nothing is as His like» to mean "nothing is as man, the representative of the Lord."

126 Q Shūrā 42:11.

127 That is, the perfect human being, embodied by the prophets and friends of God, whose reality contains everything in the cosmos by inwardly combining the visible and invisible cosmic hierarchy. See Chittick, "Jāmī on the Perfect Man," 143–52.

128 Unidentified.

129 Q Baqarah 2:30.

130 Al-Ṭabarānī, *al-Muʿjam al-ṣaghīr*, 1:48.

131 Q Mulk 67:4.

132 Q Baqarah 2:124.

133 Q Muḥammad 47:31.

134 Q Aḥzāb 33:4.

135 Q Baqarah 2:127.

136 Ibn Maʿdīkarib, *Dīwān*, 136.

137 Moses is often referred to by his title *Kalīm Allāh*, meaning the one who spoke to God.

138 This is an allusion to Qurʾanic verses that categorically reject the idea of God "wronging" others, such as «And your Lord does not wrong His servants», Q Fuṣṣilat 41:46.

139 Q Mulk 67:3–4.

140 Q Baqarah 2:117 and elsewhere.

141 Q Yūnus 10:64.

142 Al-Dhahabī ascribes this verse to Abū ʿAbd Allāh al-Shūdhī al-Ḥalwī. See al-Dhahabī, *Siyar*, 23:316.

143 For a relevant discussion of animals and the nature of life in Ibn al-ʿArabī, see Chittick's "The Wisdom of Animals."

144 Q Baqarah 2:129.

145 See al-Niffarī, *al-Mawāqif wa-l-mukhāṭabāt*, "Mawqif al-ʿizz," 1–2.

146 The passage from al-Niffarī's *al-Mawāqif wa-l-mukhāṭabāt* is written in the divine voice: "God said to me: My friends who attain Me are of three types. One who attains Me with worship, to whom I make Myself known through grace; another who attains Me with knowledge, to whom I make Myself known through might; and one who attains Me with recognition, to whom I make Myself known through dominance" (*al-Mawāqif wa-l-mukhāṭabāt*, "Mawqif al-kibriyāʾ," 3–4; modified translation).

147 Q Anʿām 6:103.

148 A reference to Q Baqarah 2:217.

149 Q Aʿrāf 7:143.

150 Q Baqarah 2:137.

151 Q Tawbah 9:129.

152 Q Baqarah 2:143.

153 Q Baqarah 2:163.

154 *Samāʿ*, or "audition," refers to a Sufi musical ceremony of remembrance that typically involves chanting, musical instruments, poetry recitation, and dance.

155 The author is quoting a popular saying that is sometimes ascribed to the ninth-century Baghdad Sufi Abū Saʿīd al-Kharrāz.

156 These verses do not appear to be included in al-Tilimsānī's *Dīwān*.

157 Q Baqarah 2:165.

158 Al-Ḥākim, *al-Mustadrak*, 1:85.

159 The author is alluding to a divine saying found in several canonical sources including al-Bukhārī, *Ṣaḥīḥ*, "al-Tawḥīd," #7511.

160 The author here is contrasting the attributes' essential relationship to the Divine Essence with their differentiated aspects in creation, which causes the aforementioned continuous aversion.

161 A reference to Q Maryam 19:85.

162 Q Baqarah 2:173.

163 The name *al-Ghafūr* would conventionally be rendered as "Forgiving," but "Concealing" has been chosen in order to better bring out the author's perspective.

164 Q Zumar 39:53.

165 Q Ḥadīd 57:13.

166 Al-Mutanabbī, *Dīwān*, 483.

167 As described in the prophetic tradition narrated in al-Bukhārī, *Ṣaḥīḥ*, "al-Īmān," #22.

168 Al-Bukhārī, *Ṣaḥīḥ*, "al-Īmān," #22.

169 Q Furqān 25:70.

170 Matthew 3:13–17.

171 Q Humazah 104:7.

172 Q Anbiyā' 21:69.

173 A slight rephrasing of Q Rūm 30:40.

174 Q Baqarah 2:186.

175 Unidentified.

176 Al-ʿAjlūnī, *Kashf al-khafā'*, 2:159.

177 Ibn al-Fāriḍ, *Dīwān*, 55.

178 Al-Tilimsānī is alluding to the prophetic tradition "God was, and there was nothing with Him" discussed in §10.4.

179 Al-Tilimsānī, *Sharḥ Mawāqif*, 74–75.

180 Al-Niffarī, *al-Mawāqif wa-l-mukhāṭabāt*, "Mawqif al-qurb," 2.

181 Al-Niffarī, *al-Mawāqif wa-l-mukhāṭabāt*, "Mawqif al-ʿizz," 1.

182 Al-Tilimsānī, *Dīwān*, 241.

183 Al-Niffarī, *al-Mawāqif wa-l-mukhāṭabāt*, "Mawqif al-qurb," 3.

184 Q Baqarah 2:186.

185 Q Baqarah 2:186.

186 Al-Mutanabbī, *Dīwān*, 373.

187 Some classical sources attribute these sayings to the Prophet's companions Abū Bakr or ʿAlī; others to early Sufis such as al-Junayd and al-Tustarī.

188 Unidentified.

189 This verse is attributed to Ibn ʿAbbād, *Dīwān*, 176.

190 Al-Hujwīrī, *Kashf al-maḥjūb*, 2:573.

191 Al-Niffarī, *al-Mawāqif wa-l-mukhāṭabāt*, *mukhāṭabah* #13, 162.

192 Q Anbiyā' 21:87–88.

193 Q Baqarah 2:202–3.

194 A reference to Q ʿAnkabūt 29:20.

195 Al-Mutanabbī, *Dīwān*, 232.

196 Q Baqarah 2:225.

197 Q Fuṣṣilat 41:46.

198 There is no such single verse in the Qur'an. Al-Tilimsānī is probably citing the verse from memory and combines parts of various verses, such as Q Baqarah 2:194 and Baqarah 2:234.

199 The two quotations together form Q Mulk 67:14.

200 Q Ṭalāq 65:12.

201 Al-Tilimsānī, *Dīwān*, 244.

202 Q Baqarah 2:245.

203 Q Mulk 67:19.

204 Q Baqarah 2:245.

205 Q Raʿd 13:26.

206 Q Baqarah 2:54.

207 Matthew 5:39. This biblical passage occurs above in §7.5.

208 Q Mā'idah 5:54.

209 Al-Bukhārī, *Ṣaḥīḥ*, "al-Manāqib," #3600.

210 Q Raʿd 13:26.

211 Q Dhāriyāt 51:22.

212 Q Raʿd 13:38.

213 Here, al-Tilimsānī discusses the four seasons in relation to properties of God's names. For a discussion of the symbolic significance of the seasons and their correspondences with stages of life and the doctrine of the Breath of the All-Merciful, see Rustom, "Islam and the Density of Man," 62–66.

214 Q Baqarah 2:255.

215 This is a formula from the canonical prayer.

216 See n. 142.

217 The isthmus (*barzakh*) is a term in the Qur'an (Q Raḥmān 55:20) denoting a line that separates two things, levels, or realms. It is "liminal" in the sense that it serves as a boundary that faces two directions at the same time without becoming them.

218 Al-Tilimsānī, *Sharḥ Mawāqif*, 521.

219 Q Baqarah 2:255.

220 A grammatically modified quotation of Q Raʿd 13:33.

221 Q Qāf 50:15.

222 This verse is ascribed to Shihāb al-Dīn al-Suhrawardī but is not found in his *Dīwān*.

223 Q Ikhlāṣ 112:1–2.

224 Q Baqarah 2:255. By "them," the heavens and the earth are meant.

225 Q Ṭā Hā 20:5.

226 This verse is cited by al-Tilimsānī in *Sharḥ Manāzil*, 1:524.

227 These verses are cited by the author in *Sharḥ Manāzil*, 1:524.

228 Unidentified.

229 Q Yūsuf 12:21.

230 Al-Niffarī, *al-Mawāqif wa-l-mukhāṭabāt*, "Mawqif al-kibriyā'," 4.

231 Q Baqarah 2:255.

232 A reference to Q Yūsuf 12:21.

233 Q Najm 53:8.

234 Q Baqarah 2:267.

235 Ascribed to al-Shāfiʿī, *Dīwān*, 157.

236 Q Āl ʿImrān 3:97.

237 Q Tawbah 9:104.

238 I have been unable to trace this statement in Ibn al-ʿArabi's best-known works, the *Futūḥāt* and the *Fuṣūṣ*.

239 This is a reference to the extra-Qur'anic divine saying "I was a hidden treasure, and I loved to be known, so I created creation and they came to know Me through Me." Al-ʿAjlūnī, *Kashf al-khafā'*, 2:155–56.

240 Q Baqarah 2:267.

241 Q Fātiḥah 1:1.

242 Q Āl ʿImrān 3:4.

243 Q Āl ʿImrān 3:8.

244 A reference to Q Yūsuf 12:21.

245 Muslim, *Ṣaḥīḥ*, "Ṣalāt al-Musāfirīn wa-qaṣruhā," #1848.

246 Q Nisā' 4:78.

247 Q Āl ʿImrān 3:9.

248 Q Āl ʿImrān 3:9.

249 Q Taghābun 64:9.

250 An allusion to Q Shūrā 42:47.

251 For a detailed discussion of the bridge over one of the valleys of hell, see Hamza Yusuf's "Death, Dying, and the Afterlife in the Quran" in *The Study Quran*, 1819–55.

252 For this and the quotation later in the paragraph see n. 36.

253 A well-known Arabic proverb.

254 Ibn al-ʿArabī ascribes this verse to al-Basṭāmī. See Ibn al-ʿArabī, *Futūḥāt*, 1:745–46.

255 Q Nisāʾ 4:145.

256 Muslim, *Ṣaḥīḥ*, "al-Īmān," #477.

257 Al-Bukhārī, *Ṣaḥīḥ*, "al-Tawḥīd," #7511.

258 Q Āl ʿImrān 3:18.

259 Q Māʾidah 5:42.

260 Q Jinn 72:15.

261 Al-Tilimsānī cites this verse in *Sharḥ Mawāqif*, 378–79; *Sharḥ Manāzil*, 2:252.

262 Q Hūd 11:123.

263 Q Burūj 85:20.

264 Q Āl ʿImrān 3:26.

265 Q Fātiḥah 1:3.

266 Q Fātiḥah 1:3. Both variants (*mālik*, owner, and *malik*, king) are traced back to the Prophet and are used in standard Qurʾanic recitations.

267 Al-Bukhārī, *Ṣaḥīḥ*, "al-Wikālah," #2349.

268 The Prophet said this to his Companions who sought to retaliate against an uncouth Bedouin who rudely requested the blessed Prophet to repay his loan. In response, the Prophet said, "Let him be, for the one who has a rightful due has the right to speak."

269 The one who "arrives" is probably an allusion to the axial saint who, after his first journey "toward" the Essence in which he witnesses the disclosures of the names, gazes at the disclosing names *in divinis* and journeys back to the realm of forms. When the axial saint sets out on the third journey, which is his descent to the stages of those beneath him, he is free from states, aspirations, and ignorance of any kind, including the ignorance of the recognizers who are overcome by states or who deny a name that is contrary to the one they are witnessing.

270 This is probably an allusion to wayfarers on the first journey who experience the luminous disclosures of divine names as they travel toward annihilation in the Essence.

271 Q Aḥzāb 33:4.

272 Q Āl ʿImrān 3:26.

273 Al-Niffarī, *al-Mawāqif wa-l-mukhāṭabāt*, "Mawqif al-ʿizz," 1.

274 Q Āl ʿImrān 3:26.

275 Q Nabaʾ 78:26.

276 Al-Qushayrī attributes this statement to al-Shiblī. See al-Qushayrī, *Risālah*, 280.

277 Al-Qushayrī, *Risālah*, 444.

278 A grammatically modified quotation of Q Mulk 67:15.

279 Ibn al-Abbār ascribes this verse to al-Ḥasan ibn Muḥammad al-Ṣabbāḥ al-Zaʿfarānī. See Ibn al-Abbār, *Muʿjam aṣḥāb al-qāḍī Abī ʿAlī l-Ṣafadī*, 84.

280 The phrase is worded differently in the *Mawāqif*; see al-Niffarī, *al-Mawāqif wa-l-mukhāṭabāt*, "Mawqif al-fiqh wa-qalb al-ʿayn," 71.

281 Q Insān 76:1.

282 In Abbasid love poetry, the name ʿAlwah often denoted the beloved or was used as a symbol of love.

283 Al-Tilimsānī, *Dīwān*, 215.

284 Q Āl ʿImrān 3:55.

285 Q Anʿām 6:57 and elsewhere.

286 Q Mumtaḥana 60:10.

287 This saying is based on a prophetic tradition cited in al-Bukhārī, *Ṣaḥīḥ*, "al-Iʿtiṣām bi-l-kitāb wa-l-sunnah," #7438. This saying was frequently quoted in legal discussions over demarcating the boundaries of Islamic legal pluralism. For a succinct discussion, see Rabb, "Ijtihād."

288 Q Zumar 39:3.

289 In this context, "God's folk" refers to the gnostics or recognizers who affirm the multiple expressions of truth as disclosures of divine names.

290 Human actions are categorized into five distinct legal categories in Islamic law: obligatory, recommended, permitted, discouraged, and forbidden.

291 Q Anʿām 6:139.

292 Q Shūrā 42:40.

293 Q Raʿd 13:27.

294 Q Āl ʿImrān 3:150.

295 Q ʿAbasa 80:4.

296 Al-Bukhārī, *Ṣaḥīḥ*, "al-Jihād," #3063.

297 Q Āl ʿImrān 3:126.

298 Al-Munāwī, *al-Kawākib al-durriyyah fi tarājim al-sādah al-ṣūfiyyah*, 2:46–47.

299 The litany is a daily devotion that is individually and collectively practiced by Sufis at specific times. The Sufi disciple is instructed by their master to practice the litany in the same way as a doctor may prescribe a daily medication to their patient.

300 Al-Tirmidhī, *Sunan*, "Tafsīr al-Qurʾan," #3256.

301 Q Āl ʿImrān 3:156.

302 See n. 91.

303 A reference to Q Ḥijr 15:29.

304 Q Āl ʿImrān 3:156.

305 The author seems to suggest here that illusory life could be from the Death-Giver because it is not life at all, while successive deaths could be from the Life-Giver because they are successive and have motion, which are characteristics of life.

306 Q Āl ʿImrān 3:173. See Khalil's "Ibn al-ʿArabī on the Circle of Trusteeship and the Divine Name *al-Wakīl*," and "Ibn al-ʿArabī and the Sufis on the Virtue of *Tawakkul* (Trust in God)."

307 Q Muzzammil 73:9.

308 In al-Tilimsānī's spiritual hierarchy, the axial saint is above the one who arrives at the station of halting. While the latter experiences annihilation (*fanāʾ*) and thereby completes the first journey to God, the former experiences subsistence (*baqāʾ*) and thereby completes the second journey in God.

309 The "world of means" denotes workaday life where one interacts with God indirectly through causes instead of relying purely on Him for direct sustenance. For example, a person may seek to earn a livelihood by means of a job. The job itself is not the true source of one's livelihood. Rather, the job is a secondary cause through which one interacts with God's name the Provider.

310 An allusion to Q Aḥzāb 33:4.

311 Q Nisāʾ 4:1.

312 Q Ṭā Hā 20:7.

313 Q Mujādilah 58:7.

314 Q Sabaʾ 34:3.

315 Al-Bukhārī, *Ṣaḥīḥ*, "al-Īmān," #540; Muslim, *Ṣaḥīḥ*, "al-Īmān," #102.

316 Al-Niffarī, *al-Mawāqif wa-l-mukhāṭabāt*, "Mawqif al-qurb," 2.

317 Al-Muḥāsibī, *al-Riʿāyah li-ḥuqūq Allāh*, 45–55.

318 Al-Qushāyrī, *Risālah*, 57–85.

319 Observing courtesy or proper conduct (*adab*) with God is a major theme in Sufi moral psychology. It involves both outward manners of the body, such as posture in sitting, and inward inclinations of the heart, such as controlling one's base thoughts.

320 Al-Tilimsānī presumably means responsibilities toward God, society, family, and oneself.

321 See n. 111; also n. 67.

322 Q Nisāʾ 4:6.

323 Q Nisāʾ 4:86.

324 Q Nisāʾ 4:6.

325 Q Anʿām 6:96.

326 Muslim theologians generally hold that the main purpose of a prophetic miracle is to prove the veracity and divine origin of the prophet's revelation. In contrast to such supernatural feats that pose a challenge to those who reject the prophets, saintly miracles are gifts from God (lit. karāmah), and their function is not necessarily to prove the sainthood of a holy person.

327 The Arabic text has a double negative and literally reads: "If my hand does not go into the fire and if I do not feel pain, then I am not a Friend of God."

328 Also cited by author in *Sharḥ Manāzil al-sā'irīn*, 517; *Sharḥ Fuṣūṣ al-ḥikam*, 235.

329 Q Nisā' 4:33.

330 Q Āl 'Imrān 3:18.

331 Q Āl 'Imrān 3:18.

332 Q Baqarah 2:165.

333 Al-Bukhārī, *Ṣaḥīḥ*, "al-Janā'iz," #1382.

334 In al-Tilimsānī's spiritual hierarchy, the Pole, or axial saint, is one who attains not only the end of the first journey of annihilation in God, but also the second journey of subsistence in God. The supreme axial saint (lit. "Pole of Poles") here is thus the fully realized saint who completes the third journey back to this world of forms through the stages and stations of descent of those beneath him. See §§14.9–10.

335 Q Nisā' 4:64.

336 For a relevant discussion, see Chittick, "The Metaphysical Roots of War and Peace," 277–90.

337 Q Ra'd 13:27.

338 Al-Bukhārī, *Ṣaḥīḥ*, "al-Jihād," #3002.

339 Q Hūd 11:118, with an interjection from Yūsuf 12:21.

340 Q Hūd 11:119.

341 Q Yūsuf 12:108.

342 Q Shūrā 42:53.

343 Ibn al-'Arabī, *al-'Abādilah*, 43.

344 Ibn al-'Arabī, *Laṭā'if al-asrār*, 49.

345 Q Nisā' 4:85.

346 In Qur'anic imagery, God inscribes His knowledge of all things from the beginning of creation to the Day of Judgment on the Preserved Tablet. For more on the cosmological significance of the Pen and the Preserved Tablet, see n. 91.

347 Al-Tilimsānī cites this in *Sharḥ Manāzil al-sā'irīn*, 288.

348 Q Nisā' 4:87.

349 See n. 142.

350 Al-Tilimsānī, *Dīwān*, 69.

351 Q Nisā' 4:147.

352 For studies on gratitude in Islamic ethics and Sufi moral psychology, see Khalil, "The Embodiment of Gratitude (*Shukr*) in Sufi Ethics," "The Dialectic of Gratitude (*Shukr*) in the Non-Dualism of Ibn al-'Arabī," and "On Cultivating Gratitude (*Shukr*) in Sufi Virtue Ethics."

353 The spiritual retreat (*khulwah*) is a Sufi practice of seclusion in which the disciple withdraws temporarily from the world for a period of solitude and invocation of God. The retreat typically lasts three to forty days, under the supervision of a master. According to his biographers, al-Tilimsānī performed forty forty-day retreats in the mountains of Anatolia during his period of training under Ṣadr al-Dīn al-Qūnawī in Konya.

354 Q Nisā' 4:149.

355 Q Nisā' 4:48.

356 Unidentified.

357 Al-Niffarī, *al-Mawāqif wa-l-mukhāṭabāt, mukhāṭabah* #15, 166.

358 Q An'ām 6:14.

359 Q Anbiyā' 21:30.

360 Unidentified reference to Ibn al-ʿArabī. This passage is also quoted in al-Tilimsānī, *Sharḥ Fuṣūṣ*, 69.

361 Q Nūr 24:35.

362 Q Ḥadīd 57:3.

363 Ibn al-ʿArabī, *Futūḥāt*, 1:305.

364 Q Anʿām 6:18.

365 Al-Bukhārī, *Ṣaḥīḥ*, "Bad' al-khalq," #3230.

366 Q Baqarah 2:279.

367 Q Mā'idah 5:56.

368 Al-Tirmidhī, *Sunan*, "Tafsīr al-Qur'an," #3256.

369 Q Anʿām 6:65.

370 Q Mā'idah 5:120.

371 Al-Bukhārī, *Ṣaḥīḥ*, "al-Riqāq," #6615.

372 In Islamic law, the act of ritual ablution is normally performed with the intention of removing *ḥadath*, or impurity, in order to perform the canonical prayer. Here, al-Tilimsānī is playing on the double meaning of the word *ḥadath*, which also means temporal origination, to suggest that the real intention of the act of ritual ablution is to purify the heart from its attachment to the ephemeral realm of other-than-God.

373 Q Baqarah 2:117.

374 Al-Tirmidhī, *Jāmi*ʿ, "Tafsīr al-Qur'ān," #1372.

375 This verse is Q Ghāfir 40:20, and is not in Surah 6, al-Anʿām, as the author states in the Arabic text.

376 Q Naml 27:78. The phrase also occurs at Yūnus 10:93 and Jāthiyah 45:17.

377 Al-Tirmidhī, *Jāmi*ʿ, "al-Aḥkām ʿan rasūl Allāh," #1322.

378 Q Anʿām 6:139.

379 Al-Munāwī, *Fayḍ al-Qadīr*, 3:189.

380 Proverbs 21:1–9.

381 Q Anbiyā' 21:47.

382 Aḥmad, *Musnad*, #18289.

383 Q An'ām 6:95.

384 Q An'ām 6:96.

385 Q An'ām 6:95.

386 Q Dhāriyāt 51:22.

387 Q An'ām 6:103.

388 Q A'rāf 7:29–30.

389 Q Qāf 50:15.

390 Al-Bukhārī, *Ṣaḥīḥ*, "Bad' al-khalq," #3227, with slightly different wording.

391 The author here is playing on the Arabic grammatical terms for subject and predicate, *mubtada'* and *khabar*. The latter also literally means "report."

392 Q A'rāf 7:178.

393 Q Fātiḥah 1:5.

394 Q Hūd 11:112.

395 Al-Bukhārī, *Ṣaḥīḥ*, "al-Riqāq," #6581.

396 Ibn Kathīr, *al-Bidāyah wa-l-nihāyah*, 3:31.

397 Muslim, *Ṣaḥīḥ*, al-Ṣalāt, #1118.

398 Q A'rāf 7:178.

399 Q A'rāf 7:54; Mu'minūn 23:14.

400 The *lām* (ل) and the *alif* (ا) are distinct letters. However, when brought together they merge to become a single orthographic entity (لا). The author uses this image to illustrate how knowledge of God renders "all opposites compatible" because it enables the knower to recognize divine unity behind the veil of multiplicity. I cannot find these verses in al-Tilimsānī's *Dīwān*.

401 Q Mu'minūn 23:53.

402 I cannot find these verses in al-Tilimsānī's *Dīwān*.

403 Q Anfāl 8:9.

404 Q Āl 'Imrān 3:126.

405 Q Yūnus 10:107.

406 A reference to Q Yūnus 10:26.

407 Q Baqarah 2:212.

408 See n. 254.

409 Q Yūnus 10:107.

410 Q Hūd 11:123.

411 Abū Nuwās, *Dīwān*, 383.

412 Q Hūd 11:66.

413 Al-Ghazālī, *Iḥyāʾ ʿulūm al-dīn*, "al-Tawḥīd wa-l-Tawakkul," 8:244. See Ormsby, *Ghazālī: The Revival of Islam*, 73, 132.

414 Q Hūd 11:57.

415 Q Anʿām 6:104.

416 It should be noted here that al-Tilimsānī is stating that God in Himself is existence pure and simple. His immutable self-subsistence necessitates the outward manifestation of the cosmos, or the existence of other-than-God.

417 Q Hūd 11:73.

418 It is unclear based on the available manuscripts whether the verse should be read as *fāzin bi-ifnāʾihi* or *fānin bi-afnāʾihi*. I cannot confirm if the scribes corrupted the text by changing the *nūn* of *fānin* to *zayn*, *fāzin*. The first reading, *fāzin bi-ifnāʾihi* gives the awkward meaning of "Immutable, yet obtaining his surroundings" or "achieving an ability to cause annihilation." My translation is based on the reading of *fānin bi-afnāʾihi*.

419 These lines are ascribed to the early Sufi al-Ḥakīm al-Tirmidhī.

420 Words reported by the Prophet on the Day of the Pledge, when the companions swore allegiance to the Prophet prior to signing the Treaty of Ḥudaybiyyah. The "hand of God" is also mentioned in Q Fatḥ 48:10 and may be read as an allusion to the Prophet's hand becoming God's. See Nasāʾī, *Sunan*, "al-Ihbās," #3624.

421 Q Fatḥ 48:10.

422 Q Nisāʾ 4:80.

423 These verses are not found in al-Tilimsānī's *Dīwān*.

424 Q Hūd 11:90.

425 Q Māʾidah 5:54.

426 Al-ʿAjlūnī cites a tradition with similar wording in *Kashf al-khafāʾ*, 2:156. This divine saying serves as a foundation for Sufi metaphysical discussions on cosmogony.

427 Q Hūd 11:102.

428 Ibn Maʿdīkarib, *Dīwān*, 136.

429 Al-Bukhārī, *Ṣaḥīḥ*, "Tafsīr al-Qurʾan," #4732.

430 See n. 254.

431 Q Hūd 11:107.

432 Q Yūsuf 12:64.

433 The author here is referring to the influential teachings of the third/ninth- or fourth/tenth-century group of anonymous Basran Muslim philosophers known as the Brethren of Purity (*Ikhwān al-ṣafāʾ*). For an introduction to their teachings on substance and accident, see Netton, *Muslim Neoplatonists: An Introduction to the Thought of the Brethren of Purity*, 22–27.

434 Q Yūsuf 12:76.

435 Al-Bukhārī, *Ṣaḥīḥ*, "al-Riqāq," #6580.

436 In Ibn al-ʿArabī and al-Tilimsānī's spiritual hierarchy of the friends of God, the axial saint or Pole is the supreme saint at the spiritual center of the universe. He has two Leaders, or Imams, beneath him, whose function is to ensure the world's equilibrium. The latter each have two Pegs beneath them, who in turn each have two Chiefs beneath them. See Chodkiewicz, *Seal of the Saints: Prophethood and Sainthood in the Doctrine of Ibn ʿArabī*, 93–96.

437 Q Raʿd 13:2.

438 Q Aʿrāf 7:54.

439 See n. 99.

440 Q Fātiḥah 1:1.

441 Al-Tilimsānī is referring to Surah 167 of Ibn al-ʿArabī's *Futūḥāt*. For an annotated translation, see Ibn al-ʿArabī, *The Alchemy of Human Happiness*, trans. Hirtenstein.

442 For an excellent study on selfhood in Islamic thought, see Faruque, *Sculpting the Self: Islam, Selfhood, and Human Flourishing*.

443 Q Raʿd 13:16.

444 Q Hūd 11:119.

445 Q Anʿām 6:18.

446 Q Raʿd 13:9.

447 The traces (sing. *athar*) are marks, properties, or signs of divine names.

448 Q Raʿd 13:9.

449 Q Anʿām 6:103.

450 Al-Tilimsānī, *Dīwān*, 77.

451 Q Ṭūr 52:43.

452 See n. 156.

453 Q Raʿd 13:34.

454 Q Insān 76:11.

455 Q Naḥl 16:81.

456 Q Baqarah 2:165.

457 Al-Ḥākim, *al-Mustadrak*, 2:154.

458 Muslim, *Ṣaḥīḥ*, "al-Ṣalāt," #1118.

459 I have not found a biographical reference to this figure.

460 Q Ibrāhīm 14:11.

461 Q Baqarah 2:245.

462 This quote is not found in the *Futūḥāt* or the *Fuṣūṣ*.

463 Q Ṭā Hā 20:50.

464 Q Ṭā Hā 20:50.

465 Q Naḥl 16:91.

466 Q Ḥadīd 57:28.

467 Q Baqarah 2:261.

468 Q Isrā' 17:70.

469 According to Ibn al-ʿArabī and his students, Adam is God's representative on earth and the angels' teacher because he reflects His all-comprehensive name Allāh and knows "all the names" (Q Baqarah 2:31). The true child of Adam, moreover, is the axial saint who acts as God's representative by inheriting Adam's knowledge of all the names and reflecting the all-comprehensive name Allāh.

470 Q Yā Sīn 36:38.

471 For a discussion of the distortion of scriptures, see commentary on Q Baqarah 2:75 in *The Study Quran.*

472 Q Najm 53:3–4.

473 These three quotations are from Q Nisā' 4:65; the last grammatically modified.

474 Q Kahf 18:45.

475 Q Insān 76:1.

476 Q Maryam 19:67.

477 Q Fuṣṣilat 41:11–12.

478 Q Maryam 19:13.

479 Al-Bukhārī, *Ṣaḥīḥ*, "al-Adab," #6066.

480 Al-Bukhārī, *Ṣaḥīḥ*, "al-Adab," #6055.

481 Al-Haythamī, *Majmaʿ al-zawāʾid wa-manbaʿ al-fawāʾid*, 8:21.

482 Q Naba' 78:26.

483 Q Maryam 19:40.

484 Q Ḥadīd 57:7.

485 See n. 66.

486 Q Ṭā Hā 20:73.

487 Muslim, *Ṣaḥīḥ*, "Alfāz min al-adab," #6003.

488 In other words, the intended meaning of this prophetic tradition is "Do not cure the everlasting aeon! For God is the aeon's everlastingness."

489 Q Tawbah 9:42.

490 Q Fāṭir 35:22.

491 There seems to be a scribal error in all the manuscripts. The people of unveiling or direct tasting is likely what is meant.

492 See n. 142.

493 Q Ṭā Hā 20:50.

494 Sections §§91.3–4 illustrate God's all-encompassing giving because He not only gives, but also gives things their ability to receive. God's giving is also reflected in the human act of giving names to things. This is equated with the Clear Book, which the Qur'an describes as a registry that stores God's knowledge of all things in the heavens and earth (Q Hūd 11:6, Q Yūnus 10:61, and elsewhere). By equating human beings with the Clear Book, al-Ṭilmsānī drives home the point that part of God's all-pervasive giving is the human act of giving things their names.

495 Q Ṭā Hā 20:82.

496 Q Muddaththir 74:56.

497 Q Muddaththir 74:56.

498 A grammatically modified quotation of Q Ṭā Hā 20:82.

499 Abū Nuwās, *Dīwān*, 469.

500 Q Anbiyā' 21:30.

501 For a similarly worded report, see al-Bukhārī, *Ṣaḥīḥ*, "Bad' al-khalq," #3227.

502 "He is now as He ever was" is a Sufi proclamation in response to the Prophetic Saying "God was, and there was nothing with Him." See n. 66.

503 Q Zumar 39:68.

504 Q Anbiyā' 21:30.

505 Q Ḥajj 22:7.

506 Al-Bukhārī, *Ṣaḥīḥ*, "al-Tahajjud," #1153.

507 In Islam, sleep is often described as the "sister of death." This is based on a saying ascribed to the Prophet: "Sleep is the sister of death, and the inhabitants of the Garden do not sleep." Ibn 'Adī, *al-Kāmil fī ḍuʿafāʾ al-rijāl*, 5:363.

508 Q Ḥajj 22:6.

509 Al-Bukhārī, *Ṣaḥīḥ*, "Manāqib al-Anṣār," #3889.

510 Q Ḥadīd 57:3.

511 For a survey of the problem of natural universals in Islamic philosophy, see Izutsu, "The Problem of Quiddity and Natural Universal in Islamic Metaphysics"; see also Faruque, "Mullā Ṣadrā on the Problem of Natural Universals."

512 This verse is in fact Q Anfāl 8:40; the author has confused it with Ḥajj 22:78, which contains a similar passage.

513 Q Jāthiyah 45:19.

514 Q Nūr 24:21.

515 Q Najm 53:32.

516 Q Nūr 24:25.

517 Q Nūr 24:39.

518 Q Āl 'Imrān 3:57.

519 Q Nūr 24:35.

520 Q Nūr 24:25.

521 Q Furqān 25:2.

522 Q Yūsuf 12:21.

523 Q Shuʿarāʾ 26:80.

524 Q Naml 27:40.

525 Q Ḥajj 22:18.

526 A grammatically modified quotation of Q Isrāʾ 17:70.

527 The recognizer's journey through the disclosures of divine names gradually causes him to pass away in the divine Essence, at which point he realizes that only God is real. He no longer ascribes any deeds or agency to himself, and thus his "deeds come to a halt." Moreover, his "hope is cut off" since only God's existence is real and necessary and there is thus nothing to hope for. His unitive vision of things is nondelimited and cannot be compared to anything since God has no opposite.

528 Al-Jīlānī, *Dīwān*, 79.

529 Q Qaṣaṣ 28:77.

530 Al-Bukhārī, *Ṣaḥīḥ*, "Badʾ al-khalq," #3230.

531 Q Rūm 30:27.

532 Q Nūr 24:40.

533 Q Rūm 30:27.

534 Q Jāthiyah 45:13.

535 Q Aʿrāf 7:29.

536 Q Aḥzāb 33:33.

537 Q Sabaʾ 34:26.

538 Q Sabaʾ 34:48.

539 The naturalists (*ṭabīʿiyyūn*) are deistic philosophers who hold that bodies are what they are by virtue of their natural constituents, which are the four humors.

540 Q Fāṭir 35:30.

541 Q Ghāfir 40:3.

542 The "faculty of perception" is a reference to the human heart.

543 Q Ghāfir 40:3.

544 Q Ḥadīd 57:21.

545 Q Ghāfir 40:15.

546 Q Anʿām 6:18.

547 For the recognizers, lordship and servanthood are correlative levels. While lowliness and abasement are qualities of servanthood, they also allow for the Lord's qualities of exaltedness and elevation to manifest. Given the interdependence of lordship and

servanthood, the recognizer sees both within each other. The Lord thus descends to the level of servanthood and proclaims, "I was sick, but you did not visit Me," while the servant ascends to the level of lordship by becoming the "hearing with which the Lord hears."

548 Q Ghāfir 40:15.

549 Q Ḥujurāt 49:3.

550 Q Dhāriyāt 51:58.

551 Q Dhāriyāt 51:58.

552 Q Anʿām 6:18.

553 Q Anʿām 6:149.

554 Unidentified.

555 Aḥmad, *Musnad*, #13252.

556 Q Ṭūr 52:28.

557 Q Najm 53:48.

558 Q Raḥmān 55:27.

559 Sufis often divide the names of God into the realm of majesty, which includes names of rigor and transcendence, and the realm of beauty, which includes names of mercy and proximity. The realm of perfection denotes the combination of both names of majesty and beauty.

560 Q Raḥmān 55:27.

561 Q Ḥadīd 57:3.

562 Q Ḥadīd 57:3.

563 Q Ḥadīd 57:3.

564 Q Anʿām 6:103.

565 Q Ḥadīd 57:3.

566 Al-Tilimsānī does not directly cite the verse that contains this name here. It is Q Ḥashr 59:23 . The same verse provides the next five names; the relevant section for this chapter is cited at §128.1.

567 Q Ḥashr 59:23.

568 Q Ḥashr 59:23.

569 Q Zukhruf 43:68.

570 Q Aḥzāb 33:23.

571 Q Ḥashr 59:23.

572 Q Ḥashr 59:23.

573 A reference to Jesus.

574 The name appears in Q Ḥashr 59:23 again, immediately after «The Mighty, the All-Dominating», as cited in §131.1.

575 Q Ḥashr 59:24.

576 Q An'ām 6:102.

577 Q An'ām 6:73.

578 Q Ḥashr 59:24.

579 Q Ḥashr 59:24.

580 Q Jumu'ah 62:11.

581 Q Mulk 67:24.

582 Q Ma'ārij 70:3–4.

583 A reference to the Prophet's *mi'rāj*, or ascension through the seven heavens to the divine presence.

584 Q Jinn 72:26.

585 Q Jinn 72:28.

586 Q Mulk 67:14.

587 Q Burūj 85:12.

588 Q Ikhlāṣ 112:1.

589 It is Q Ikhlāṣ 112:2.

590 Q Aḥzāb 33:4.

591 Q Fātiḥah 1:1.

Glossary

Abū Madyan Shuʿayb (d. 594/1198) influential renunciant saint and forerunner of Sufism in North Africa.

Abū Yazīd al-Basṭāmī (d. ca. 235/849) prominent ecstatic Persian Sufi and expositor of the Sufi notion of annihilation in God.

Ahl al-Ḥadīth an early network of Sunni Hadith transmitters that first appeared in the second/eighth century, who largely rejected rationalistic forms of Islamic theology and Ibn al-ʿArabī's mystical teachings, and emphasized a tradition-based approach to law and creed.

Akbarī Sufism an influential school of medieval Sufism inspired by the teachings of the "greatest shaykh" (*al-shaykh al-akbar*), Muḥyī l-Dīn ibn al-ʿArabī (d. 638/1240).

ʿAmr ibn Maʿdīkarib (d. 21/642) famous early Arab poet.

al-Bayhaqī, Abū Bakr (d. 458/1066) Shāfiʿī jurist, Ashʿarī theologian, and Hadith scholar from Khorasan.

Brethren of Purity an anonymous group of fourth-/tenth-century authors from Basra who wrote a collection of medieval epistles on the sciences, cosmology, philosophy, and mysticism.

al-Ḍaḥḥāk ibn Muzāḥim (d. 105/723) a famous early Qur'an exegete among the generation of Followers of the Companions.

Dajjāl a false Messiah who, according to Islamic eschatology, appears at the end of time and wreaks havoc on earth until he is finally killed by Jesus. In Muslim belief, Jesus was not crucified but taken up to heaven, and will return to live out his life and defeat Dajjāl.

al-Farghānī, Saʿīd al-dīn (d. 699/1300) a close friend and fellow classmate of al-Tilimsānī and a fellow pupil of Ṣadr al-Dīn al-Qūnawī who authored an important commentary on Ibn al-Fāriḍ's *Poem on Wayfaring*.

al-Ghazālī, Abū Ḥāmid (d. 505/1111) one of the most prominent theologians, philosophers, and Sufis in the Islamic tradition.

Ibn ʿAbbās, ʿAbd Allāh (d. ca. 68/687) early scholar of the Qurʾan and a cousin of the Prophet Muḥammad.

Ibn al-Aʿrābī (d. 231/845) early philologist, grammarian, genealogist, and compiler of Arabic poetry from Kufa.

Ibn al-Fāriḍ, ʿUmar (d. 632/1234) famous Arab Sufi poet whose *Poem on Wayfaring* was taught by al-Qūnawī and commented upon by al-Tilimsānī and al-Farghānī.

Ibn al-ʿArabī, Muḥyī l-Dīn (d. 638/1240) highly influential and controversial Sufi from Murcia known as the "greatest shaykh."

Ibn Barrajān, Abū l-Ḥakam (d. 536/1141) Sufi, Qurʾan commentator, Hadith scholar, and theologian from Seville.

Ibn Hūd (d. 699/1300) an Andalusī disciple of the nondualist Sufi philosopher Ibn Sabʿīn.

Ibn Sabʿīn (d. 669/1270) an Andalusī nondualist Sufi who wrote a number of Sufi and philosophical works and became the master of the famous Sufi poet al-Shushtarī (d. 668/1269).

al-Junayd, Abū l-Qāsim (d. 298/910) a central figure of early Baghdad Sufism who is celebrated as a master of the exoteric and esoteric sciences.

al-Kāmil Muḥammad ibn Ayyūb (d. 635/1237) fifth Ayyubid sultan, who reigned and died in Damascus.

Labīd (d. 41/661) early Arab poet who converted to Islam and authored one of the celebrated "suspended odes" that were hung at the Kaaba in Mecca.

Melissus (d. 430) an important representative of the ancient Eleatic school of philosophy. Zeno and Parmenides were also members of this school.

al-Muḥāsibī, Ḥārith (d. 243/857) a major Sufi moral psychologist whose work was very influential for the Sufi ethical tradition.

Musaylimah al-Kadhdhāb Musaylimah the Liar. A false prophet who claimed prophethood in first-/seventh-century Arabia.

al-Mutanabbī, Abū l-Ṭayyib (d. 354/965) Abbasid poet who is often regarded as the greatest poet of the Arabic language.

al-Niffarī, Muḥammad ibn ʿAbd al-Jabbār (d. ca. 354/965) early Iraqi Sufi who authored *The Book of Haltings*, which was influential to al-Tilimsānī.

Parmenides (d. ca. 450) major pre-Socratic philosopher from Elea.

al-Qūnawī, Ṣadr al-Dīn Muḥammad ibn Isḥāq (d. 673/1274) the foremost disciple of Ibn al-ʿArabī, who philosophically systematized the thought of his master and trained a number of leading Akbarī Sufis, including al-Tilimsānī.

al-Rabīʿ ibn Anas (d. 139/757) a Follower (a member of the second generation of Muslims), Qur'an exegete, and Hadith scholar from Basra.

Zayn al-ʿĀbidīn (d. 95/713) son of al-Ḥusayn ibn ʿAlī and great-grandson of the Prophet Muḥammad.

Bibliography

Abū Nuwās al-Ḥakamī. *Dīwān*. Edited by Aḥmad ʿAbd al-Majīd al-Ghazzālī. Cairo: Maṭbaʿat Miṣr, 1953.

Addas, Claude. *Quest for the Red Sulphur: The Life of Ibn ʿArabī*. Translated by Peter Kingsley. Cambridge: The Islamic Texts Society, 1993.

Aḥmad ibn Ḥanbal. *Al-Musnad*. 12 vols. Vaduz, Lichtenstein: Thesaurus Islamicus Foundation, 2006.

Al-ʿAjlūnī, Ismāʿīl ibn Muḥammad. *Kashf al-khafāʾ*. Edited by ʿAbd al-Ḥamīd Hindāwī. 2 vols. Cairo: al-Maktabah al-ʿAṣriyyah, 2000.

Al-ʿAsqalānī, Ibn Ḥajar. *Takhrīj aḥādīth al-asmāʾ al-ḥusnā*. Edited by Abī ʿUbaydah. Medina: Maktabat al-Ghurabāʾ, 1992.

———. *Fatḥ al-bārī bi-sharḥ Ṣaḥīh al-Bukhārī*. Edited by Muḥibb al-Dīn Khaṭīb, Muḥammad Fuʾād ʿAbd al-Bāqī, and Quṣayy Muḥibb al-Dīn Khaṭīb. 13 vols. Cairo: Dār al-Rayyān li-l-Turāth, 1986.

ʿAyn al-Quḍāt al-Hamadānī. *The Essence of Reality: A Defense of Philosophical Sufism*. Edited and translated by Mohammed Rustom. New York: New York University Press, 2022.

Al-Bayhaqī, Abū Bakr. *Al-Asmāʾ wa-l-ṣifāt*. Edited by ʿAbd Allāh ibn Muḥammad al-Ḥashidī. Jeddah: Maktabat al-Sawādī, 1993.

Al-Bukhārī, Muḥammad ibn Ismāʿīl. *Ṣaḥīḥ*. 3 vols. Vaduz, Lichtenstein: Thesaurus Islamicus Foundation, 2000.

———. *Al-Tārīkh al-kabīr*. Edited by Muḥammad ʿAbd al-Muʿīd Khān. 8 vols. Hyderabad, India: Dāʾirat al-Maʿārif al-ʿUthmāniyyah, 1941–58.

Casewit, Yousef. *The Mystics of al-Andalus: Ibn Barrajān and Islamic Thought in the Twelfth Century*. Cambridge: Cambridge University Press, 2017.

———. "Al-Ghazālī's Virtue Ethical Theory of the Divine Names: The Theological Underpinnings of the Doctrine of *Takhalluq* in *al-Maqṣad al-Asnā*." *Journal of Islamic Ethics* 4, nos. 1–2 (2020): 155–200.

———. "Shushtarī's Treatise *On the Limits of Theology and Sufism*: Discursive Knowledge (*ʿilm*), Direct Recognition (*maʿrifa*), and Mystical Realization (*taḥqīq*) in *al-Risāla al-Quṣāriyya*." *Religions* 11, no. 5 (2020): 1–32.

———. "The Treatise on the Ascension (*al-Risāla al-miʿrājiyya*): Cosmology and Time in the Writings of Abū l-Ḥasan al-Shushtarī (d. 668/1269)." In *Light upon Light: Essays in*

Islamic Thought and History in Honor of Gerhard Bowering, edited by Jamal Elias and Bilal Orfali, 182–238. Leiden, Netherlands: Brill, 2020.

Chittick, William. "The Last Will and Testament of Ibn 'Arabī's Foremost Disciple and Some Notes on Its Author." *Sophia Perennis* 4, no. 1 (1978): 43–58.

———. *The Sufi Path of Knowledge: Ibn al-'Arabī's Metaphysics of Imagination*. Albany: State University of New York Press, 1989.

———. *The Self-Disclosure of God: Principles of Ibn al-'Arabī's Cosmology*. Albany: State University of New York Press, 1998.

———. "Ibn al-'Arabi's Hermeneutics of Mercy." In *Mysticism and Sacred Scripture*, edited by Steven Katz. Oxford: Oxford University Press, 2000.

———. "The Wisdom of Animals." *Journal of Muhyiddin Ibn Arabi Society* 46 (2009): 27–37.

———. "The Bodily Gestures of the *Ṣalāt*." In *In Search of the Lost Heart: Explorations in Islamic Thought*, edited by Mohammed Rustom, Atif Khalil, and Kazuyo Murata, 23–26. Albany: State University of New York Press, 2012.

———. "Jāmī on the Perfect Man." In *In Search of the Lost Heart: Explorations in Islamic Thought*, edited by Mohammed Rustom, Atif Khalil, and Kazuyo Murata, 143–52. Albany: State University of New York Press, 2012.

———. "The Metaphysical Roots of War and Peace." In *In Search of the Lost Heart: Explorations in Islamic Thought*, edited by Mohammed Rustom, Atif Khalil, and Kazuyo Murata, 277–90. Albany: State University of New York Press, 2012.

Chodkiewicz, Michel. *Seal of the Saints: Prophethood and Sainthood in the Doctrine of Ibn 'Arabī*. Translated by Liadain Sherrard. Cambridge: The Islamic Texts Society, 1993.

———. "Le procès posthume d'Ibn 'Arabī." In *Islamic Mysticism Contested: Thirteen Centuries of Controversies and Polemics*, edited by Frederick de Jong and Bernd Radtke, 93–123. Leiden, Netherlands: Brill, 1999.

Dagli, Caner. *Ibn al-'Arabī and Islamic Intellectual Culture: From Mysticism to Philosophy*. New York: Routledge, 2016.

Al-Dhahabī, Shams al-Dīn. *Al-'Ibar fī khabar man ghabar*. Edited by Abū Hājir Zaghlūl. 4 vols. Beirut: Dār al-Kutub al-'Ilmiyyah, 1985.

———. *Tārīkh al-Islām wa-wafayāt al-mashāhīr wa-l-a'lām*. Edited by 'Umar 'Abd al-Salām Tadmurī. 53 vols. Beirut: Dār al-Kitāb al-'Arabī, 1990–2000.

———. *Siyar a'lām al-nubalā'*. Edited by Shu'ayb al-Arnā'ūṭ. 25 vols. Beirut: Mu'assasat al-Risālah, 1985.

Al-Dimashqī, Ibn Nāṣir al-Dīn. *Tawḍīḥ al-mushtabih*. Edited by Muḥammad Na'īm al-'Arsūqī. 10 vols. Beirut: Mu'assasat al-Risālah, 1993.

Al-Farghānī, Sa'd al-Dīn. *Muntahā al-madārik fī sharḥ Tā'iyyat Ibn al-Fāriḍ*. Edited by Ibrāhīm 'Āṣim al-Kayyālī. 2 vols. Beirut: Dār al-Kutub al-'Ilmiyyah, 2007.

Faruque, Muhammad. "Mullā Ṣadrā on the Problem of Natural Universals." *Arabic Sciences and Philosophy* 27, no. 2 (2017): 269–302.

———. *Sculpting the Self: Islam, Selfhood, and Human Flourishing*. Ann Arbor: University of Michigan Press, 2021.

Fernandes, Leonor. *The Evolution of a Sufi Institution in Mamluk Egypt: The Khanqat*. Berlin: Klaus Schwarz Verlag, 1988.

Geoffroy, Éric. *Le soufisme: Histoire, pratiques, et spiritualité*. Paris: Édition Eyrolles, 2019.

———. "Les milieux de la mystique musulmane à Alexandrie aux XIIIe et XIVe siècles." In *Alexandrie médiévale* 2, edited by Christian Décobert, 169–80. Cairo: Institut français d'archéologie orientale, 2002.

Al-Ghazālī, Abū Ḥāmid. *Iḥyā' ʻulūm al-dīn*. 10 vols. Jeddah: Dār al-Minhāj li-l-Nashr wa-l-Tawzīʻ, 2011.

Al-Hujwīrī, Abū l-Ḥasan ʻAlī. *Kashf al-maḥjūb*. Edited by Isʻād ʻAbd al-Hādī Qindīl. 2 vols. Cairo: al-Majlis al-Aʻlā li-l-Thaqāfah, 2007.

Al-Ḥākim al-Nīsābūrī, Muḥammad ibn ʻAbd Allāh. *Al-Mustadrak*. Edited by Muṣṭafā ʻAbd al-Qādir ʻAṭā. 5 vols. Beirut: Dār al-Kutub al-ʻIlmiyyah, 1990.

Halim, Fachrizal. *Legal Authority in Premodern Islam: Yaḥyā ibn Sharaf al-Nawawī in the Shāfiʻī School of Law*. New York: Routledge, 2015.

Al-Haythamī, Abū l-Ḥasan Nūr al-Dīn. *Majmaʻ al-zawā'id wa-manbaʻ al-fawā'id*. Edited by Ḥusām al-Dīn al-Qudsī. 10 vols. Cairo: Maktabat al-Qudsī, 1994.

Hofer, Nathan. *The Popularisation of Sufism in Ayyubid and Mamluk Egypt, 1173–1325*. Edinburgh: Edinburgh University Press, 2015.

Homerin, Thomas Emil. "Sufis and Their Detractors in Mamluk Egypt." In *Islamic Mysticism Contested: Thirteen Centuries of Controversies and Polemics*, edited by Frederick de Jong and Bernd Radtke, 225–48. Leiden, Netherlands: Brill, 1999.

Ibn ʻAbbād, al-Ṣāḥib. *Dīwān*. Edited by Muḥammad Ḥasan Āl Yāsīn. Beirut: Dār al-Qalam, 1974.

Ibn al-Abbār, Muḥammad ibn ʻAbd Allāh. *Muʻjam aṣḥāb al-qāḍī Abī ʻAlī l-Ṣafadī*. Cairo: Maktabat al-Thaqāfah al-Dīniyyah, 2000.

Ibn ʻAdī, al-Jurjānī Abū Aḥmad. *Al-Kāmil fī ḍuʻafā' al-rijāl*. 9 vols. Beirut: Dār al-Fikr, 1984.

Ibn al-ʻArabī, Muḥyī l-Dīn. *The Alchemy of Human Happiness*. Translated by Stephen Hirtenstein. Chicago: Anqa Publishing, 2019.

———, Muḥyī al-Dīn. *Al-Futūḥāt al-Makkiyyah*. 4 vols. Cairo: Bulāq, 1911.

———, Muḥyī al-Dīn. *Al-ʻAbādilah*. Edited by ʻAbd al-Qādir Aḥmad al-ʻAṭā. Cairo: Maktabat al-Qāhirah, 1969.

———, Muḥyī al-Dīn. *Laṭā'if al-asrār*. Edited by Aḥmad Zakī and Ṭaha ʻAbd al-Bāqī Surūr. Cairo: Dār al-Fikr, 1961.

Ibn al-ʿArīf, Aḥmad ibn Muḥammad. *Maḥāsin al-majālis*. Edited by Miguel Asín Palacios. Paris: Geuthner, 1933.

Ibn al-Fāriḍ, Sharaf al-Dīn ʿUmar. *Dīwān*. Beirut: Dār Ṣādir, 2011.

Ibn al-ʿImād, Shihāb al-Dīn. *Shadharāt al-dhahab fī akhbār man dhahab*. Edited by Mahmūd al-Arnāʾūt. 10 vols. Damascus: Dār Ibn Kathīr, 1986.

Ibn Kathīr, ʿImād al-Dīn. *Al-Bidāyah wa-l-nihāyah*. Edited by ʿAbd Allāh al-Muḥsin al-Turkī. 21 vols. Cairo: Dar Hijr, 1997–99.

Ibn Maʿdīkarib, ʿAmr. *Dīwān ʿAmr ibn Maʿdīkarib al-Zubaydī*. Edited by Hishām al-Ṭaʿʿān. Baghdad: Maktabat Wizārat al-Thaqāfah wa-l-Iʿlām, 1970.

Ibn Taymiyyah, Taqī al-Dīn. *Majmūʿat al-rasāʾil wa-l-masāʾil*. Edited by Muḥammad Rashīd Riḍā. 5 vols. Cairo: Lajnat al-Turāth al-ʿArabī, 1976.

Al-Iskandarī, Ibn ʿAṭāʾ Allāh, and ʿAbd Allāh al-Harawī. *The Book of Wisdom*. Translated by Victor Danner and Wheeler McIntosh Thackston. New York: Paulist Press, 1978.

Izutsu, Toshihiko. "The Problem of Quiddity and Natural Universal in Islamic Metaphysics." In *Études philosophiques offertes au Dr. Ibrahim Madkur*, edited by Osman Amin, 131–77. Cairo: al-Hayʾah al-Miṣriyyah al-ʿĀmmah li-l-Kitāb, 1974.

Jāmī, ʿAbd al-Raḥmān. *Nafaḥāt al-uns min ḥaḍarāt al-quds*. Edited by Maḥmūd ʿĀbidī. Tehran: Iṭṭilāʿāt, 1991.

Al-Jazarī, Muḥammad ibn Ibrāhīm. *Tārīkh ḥawādith al-zamān wa-anbāʾih wa-wafayāt al-akābir wa-l-aʿyān min abnāʾih*. Edited by ʿUmar ʿAbd al-Salām Tadmurī. 3 vols. Beirut: Dār al-Kitāb al-ʿArabī, 1998.

Al-Jīlānī, ʿAbd al-Qādir. *Al-Dīwān*. Edited by Yūsuf Zaydān. Beirut: Dār al-Jīl, 1998.

Khalīfah, Ḥājjī. *Kashf al-ẓunūn*. 2 vols. Beirut: Dār Iḥyāʾ al-Turāth al-ʿArabī, 1966.

Khalil, Atif. "On Cultivating Gratitude (*Shukr*) in Sufi Virtue Ethics." *Journal of Sufi Studies* 4, nos. 1–2 (2015): 1–26.

———. "The Embodiment of Gratitude (*Shukr*) in Sufi Ethics." *Studia Islamica* 111, no. 2 (2016): 159–78.

———. "The Dialectic of Gratitude (*Shukr*) in the Non-Dualism of Ibn al-ʿArabī." *Journal of the Muhyiddin Ibn Arabi Society* 64 (2018): 27–51.

———. *Repentance and the Return to God: Tawba in Early Sufism*. Albany: State University of New York Press, 2019.

———. "Ibn al-ʿArabī and the Sufis on the Virtue of *Tawakkul* (Trust in God)." *Journal of Muhyiddin Ibn Arabi Society* 71 (2022): 87–106.

———. "Ibn ʿArabī on the Circle of Trusteeship and the Divine Name *al-Wakīl*." *Journal of Sufi Studies*, forthcoming.

Khalil, Mohammad Hassan. *Islam and the Fate of Others: The Salvation Question*. Oxford: Oxford University Press, 2012.

Knysh, Alexander. *Ibn ʿArabi in the Later Islamic Tradition: The Making of a Polemical Image in Medieval Islam*. Albany: State University of New York Press, 1999.

———. *Islamic Mysticism: A Short History*. Leiden, Netherlands: Brill, 2000.

Al-Kutubī, Ibn Shākir. Fawāt al-wafayāt. Edited by Iḥsān ʿAbbās. 2 vols. Beirut: Dār Ṣādir, 1974.

Meisami, Sayeh. *Naṣīr al-Dīn Ṭūsī: A Philosopher for All Seasons*. Cambridge: Islamic Texts Society, 2019.

Al-Muḥāsibī, al-Ḥārith ibn Asad. *Al-Riʿāyah li-ḥuqūq Allāh*. Edited by Aḥmad ʿAbd al-Qādir ʿAṭā. Beirut: Dār al-Kutub al-ʿIlmiyyah, 2009.

Al-Munāwī, Zayn al-Dīn Muḥammad ʿAbd al-Raʾūf. *Fayḍ al-Qadīr: Sharḥ al-Jāmiʿ al-ṣaghīr*. Cairo: al-Maktabah al-Tijāriyyah al-Kubrā, 1356/1937.

Al-Munāwī, Zayn al-Dīn Muḥammad ʿAbd al-Raʾūf. *Al-Kawākib al-durriyyah fi tarājim al-sādah al-ṣūfiyyah*. Edited by Aḥmad Farīd al-Mazyadī. 2 vols. Beirut: Dār al-Kutub al-ʿIlmiyyah, 2008.

Murata, Sachiko. *The Tao of Islam: A Sourcebook on Gender Relationships in Islamic Thought*. Albany: State University of New York Press, 1992.

Muslim ibn al-Ḥajjāj. *Ṣaḥīḥ*. 2 vols. Vaduz, Lichtenstein: Thesaurus Islamicus Foundation, 2001.

Al-Mutanabbī, Abū al-Ṭayyib. *Al-Dīwān*. Beirut: Dār Bayrūt, 1983.

Al-Nasāʾī, Abū ʿAbd al-Raḥmān. *Sunan*. 2 vols. Vaduz, Lichtenstein: Thesaurus Islamicus Foundation, 2000.

Nasr, Seyyed Hossein. *An Introduction to Islamic Cosmological Doctrines: Conceptions of Nature and Methods Used for Its Study by the Ikhwān al-Ṣafāʾ, al-Bīrūnī, and Ibn Sīnā*. Albany: State University of New York Press, 1993.

Netton, Ian Richard. *Muslim Neoplatonists: An Introduction to the Thought of the Brethren of Purity (Ikhwān al-Ṣafāʾ)*. London: Routledge, 2016.

Al-Niffarī, Muḥammad ʿAbd al-Jabbār. *Al-Mawāqif wa-l-mukhāṭabāt*. Edited with English translations by Arthur Arberry. Cairo: Maktabat al-Mutanabbī, 1985.

Ormsby, Eric. *Ghazali: The Revival of Islam*. New York: Oneworld, 2012.

Post, Arjan. *The Journeys of a Taymiyyan Sufi: Sufism through the Eyes of ʿImād al-Dīn Aḥmad al-Wāsiṭī (d. 711/1311)*. Leiden, Netherlands: Brill, 2020.

Al-Qushāyrī, ʿAbd al-Karīm. *Al-Risālah*. Edited by ʿAbd al-Ḥalīm Maḥmūd and Maḥmūd ibn al-Sharīf. Cairo: Dār al-Maʿārif, 1989.

Rabb, Intisar. "Ijtihād [Islamic Jurisprudence]." In *Oxford Encyclopedia of the Islamic World*, vol. 2, edited by John Esposito, 522. New York: Oxford University Press, 2009.

Rustom, Mohammed. *The Triumph of Mercy: Philosophy and Scripture in Mullā Ṣadrā*. Albany, New York: State University of New York Press, 2012.

———. "Islam and the Density of Man." *Sacred Web* 46 (2020): 56–76.

Al-Suhrawardī, Shihāb al-Dīn. *Dīwān al-Suhrawardī al-maqtūl.* Edited by Kāmil Muṣṭafā al-Shaybī. Baghdad: al-Maktabah al-ʿAṣriyyah, 2005.

Al-Ṣafadī, Khalīl ibn Aybak. *al-Wāfī bi-l-wafayāt.* Edited by Aḥmad al-Arnāʾūṭ, Turkī Muṣṭafā. 29 vols. Beirut: Dār Iḥyāʾ al-Turāth al-ʿArabī, 2000.

Al-Sakhāwī, Muḥammad ibn ʿAbd al-Raḥmān. *Al-Qawl al-munbī ʿan tarjamat Ibn al-ʿArabī.* 3 vols. Edited by Khālid ibn al-ʿArabī Mudrik. Mecca: Jāmiʿat Umm al-Qurā, 2001.

Sells, Michael. *Early Islamic Mysticism: Sufi, Qur'an, Miʿraj, Poetic and Theological Writings.* New York: Paulist Press, 1996.

Al-Shāfiʿī, Muḥammad ibn Idrīs. *Al-Dīwān.* Edited by Muḥammad Ibrāhīm Salīm. Cairo: Maktabat Ibn Sīnā, 2009.

Shihadeh, Ayman, and Jan Thiele, eds. *Philosophical Theology in Islam: Later Ashʿarism East and West.* Leiden, Netherlands: Brill, 2020.

Sirriyeh, Elizabeth. *Sufi Visionary of Ottoman Damascus: ʿAbd al-Ghani al-Nabulusi, 1641–1731.* New York: Routledge, 2005.

The Study Quran: A New Translation with Notes and Commentary. Edited by Seyyed Hossein Nasr, Caner K. Dagli, Maria Massi Dakake, Joseph E. B. Lumbard, and Mohammed Rustom. New York: HarperCollins, 2015.

Al-Ṭabarānī, Sulaymān ibn Aḥmad. *Al-Muʿjam al-ṣaghīr.* Edited by Muḥammad Shakūr Maḥmūd al-Ḥājj Amīr. 2 vols. Amman: Dār ʿAmmār, 1985.

Al-Tilimsānī, ʿAfīf al-Dīn. *Dīwān al-ʿārif bi-llāh taʿālā al-Shaykh ʿAfīf al-Dīn Sulaymān ibn ʿAlī al-Tilimsānī.* Edited by ʿĀṣim Ibrāhīm al-Kayyālī. Beirut: Kitāb Nāshirūn, 2013.

———. *Dīwān Abī l-Rabīʿ ʿAfīf al-Dīn al-Tilimsānī al-Ṣūfī.* Edited by ʿArbī Daḥw. Algiers: Dīwān al-Maṭbūʿāt al-Jāmiʿiyyah, 1994.

———. *Dīwān ʿAfīf al-Dīn al-Tilimsānī.* Edited by Yūsuf Zaydān. Cairo: Idārat al-Kutub wa-l-Maktabāt, 1989.

———. *Maʿānī al-asmāʾ al-ilāhiyyah.* Edited by Orkhan Musakhanov. Istanbul: İSAM Center for Islamic Studies, 2018.

———. *Sharḥ al-Fātiḥah wa-baʿḍ sūrat al-Baqarah.* Edited by Orkhan Musakhanov. Istanbul: İSAM Center for Islamic Studies, 2018.

———. *Sharḥ al-Tāʾiyyah al-kubrā li-Ibn al-Fāriḍ.* Edited by Giuseppe Scattolin, Muṣṭafā ʿAbd al-Samīʿ Salāmah, and Ayman Fuʾād Sayyid. Cairo: Dār al-Kutub wa-l-Wathāʾiq al-Qawmiyyah, 2016.

———. *Sharḥ Fuṣūṣ al-ḥikam.* Edited by Akbar Rāshidī Niyā. Tehran: Intishārāt-i Sukhan, 2013.

———. *Sharḥ Manāzil al-sāʾirīn ilā l-ḥaqq al-mubīn.* Edited by ʿĀṣim Ibrāhīm al-Kayyālī. Beirut: Kitāb Nāshirūn, 2013.

———. *Sharḥ Manāzil al-sā'irīn ilā l-ḥaqq al-mubīn*. Tunis: Dār al-Turkī li-l-Nashr, 1989.

———. *Sharḥ Mawāqif al-Niffarī Muḥammad ibn 'Abd al-Jabbār ibn al-Ḥasan*. Beirut: Dār al-Kutub al-'Ilmiyyah, 2007.

———. *Sharḥ Mawāqif al-Niffarī*. Edited by Jamāl al-Marzūqī. Cairo: al-Hay'ah al-Miṣriyyah al-'Āmmah li-l-Kitāb, 2000.

Al-Tirmidhī, Abū 'Īsā Muḥammad. *Sunan*. 2 vols. Vaduz, Lichtenstein: Thesaurus Islamicus Foundation, 2000.

Todd, Richard. *The Sufi Doctrine of Man: Ṣadr al-Dīn al-Qūnawī's Metaphysical Anthropology*. Leiden, Netherlands: Brill, 2014.

Yaḥyā, 'Uthmān. *Mu'allafāt Ibn 'Arabī: tārīkhihā wa-taṣnīfihā*. Edited by Aḥmad Muḥammad al-Ṭayyib. Cairo: al-Hay'ah al-Miṣriyyah al-'Āmmah li-l-Kitāb, 2001.

Further Reading

Ali, Mukhtar H. *Philosophical Sufism: An Introduction to the School of Ibn al-ʿArabī*. New York: Routledge, 2022.

Cornell, Vincent. *Realm of the Saint: Power and Authority in Moroccan Sufism*. Austin: University of Texas Press, 1998.

Dagli, Caner. *Ibn al-ʿArabī and Islamic Intellectual Culture: From Mysticism to Philosophy*. New York: Routledge, 2016.

Al-Ghazālī, Abū Ḥāmid. *Moderation in Belief*. Translated by Aladdin Yaqub. Chicago: University of Chicago Press, 2017.

———. *Al-Maqṣad al-Asnā fī Sharḥ Asmāʾ Allāh al-Ḥusnā*. Translated by David Burrell and Nazih Daher. Cambridge: Islamic Texts Society, 1995.

Gimaret, Daniel. *Les noms divins en Islam: Exégèse lexicographique et théologique*. Paris: Cerf, 1990.

Ibn al-ʿArabī, Muḥyī l-Dīn. *Le secret des noms de Dieu*. Edited and translated by Pablo Beneito and Nassim Motebassem. Beirut: Dār al-Fikr, 2010.

Lala, Ismail. *Knowing God: Ibn ʿArabī and ʿAbd al-Razzāq al-Qāshānī's Metaphysics of the Divine*. Leiden, Netherlands: Brill, 2020.

Ridgeon, Lloyd, ed. *Routledge Handbook on Sufism*. London: Routledge, 2020.

Al-Samʿānī, Aḥmad. *The Repose of the Spirits: A Sufi Commentary on the Divine Names*. Translated by William C. Chittick. Albany: State University of New York Press, 2019.

Schmidtke, Sabine, ed. *The Oxford Handbook of Islamic Theology*. Oxford: Oxford University Press, 2018.

Index of Qur'anic Verses

Section numbers marked with * indicate the reference is a paraphrase or allusion rather than a literal quotaion.

Surah	Verse	Section(s)
4 Nisā'	1	§51.1
	6	§52.1, §52.3
	33	§53.1
	48	§58.2
	64	§54.1
	65	§86.4
	78	§40.4
	80	§73.4
	85	§55.1
	86	§52.1
	87	§56.1
	145	§41.7
	147	§57.1
	149	§58.1
	173	§99.2
5 Mā'idah	3	§11.6
	42	§42.1
	54	§32.6, §74.2, §74.3
	56	§60.3
	120	§61.3
6 Anʿām	14	§59.1
	18	§60.1, §80.2, §114.1, §118.1
	57	§46.1
	65	§61.1
	73	§133.1
	95	§63.1, §63.2, §63.4
	96	§52.4, §63.1
	102	§133.1
	103	§20.6, §64.1, §82.2, §125.1
	104	§72.1
	116	§12.2
	139	§46.3, §62.2
	149	§118.1
7 Aʿrāf	29	§65.2, §107.1
	29–30	§65.1
	54	§67.2, §79.2
	143	§20.9
	178	§66.1, §67.1
8 Anfāl	9	§68.1
	40	§97.1
9 Tawbah	42	§90.3
	104	§37.2
	129	§21.1
10 Yūnus	26	§69.5*
	36	§12.2
	44	§11.3
	64	§11.3, §19.4
	93	§62.1
	107	§69.1, §70.1
11 Hūd	57	§72.1
	66	§71.1
	73	§73.1
	90	§74.1
	102	§75.1
	107	§76.1
	112	§66.2
	118–19	§11.7, §54.3
	119	§80.2
	123	§42.4, §70.5
12 Yūsuf	21	§35.6, §36.2*, §40.3*, §54.3, §102.3
	64	§77.1
	76	§78.1
	108	§54.4
13 Raʿd	2	§79.1, §79.2
	9	§81.1, §82.1
	16	§80.1
	26	§32.1, §32.9
	27	§46.4, §54.2
	33	§34.1*
	34	§83.1
	38	§32.12
14 Ibrāhīm	11	§84.1
15 Ḥijr	29	§48.7*
16 Naḥl	81	§83.2
	91	§85.1
17 Isrā'	70	§86.1, §104.3*
	110	§1.5, §5.9

Surah	Verse	Section(s)
18 Kahf	39	§7.6
	45	§87.1
19 Maryam	13	§88.1
	40	§89.1, §89.3
	67	§87.2
	85	§24.5*
20 Ṭā Hā	5	§35.1
	7	§51.1
	50	§8.6, §84.3, §91.1
	73	§90.1
	82	§92.1, §92.3*
21 Anbiyā'	30	§59.1, §93.1, §94.1
	47	§62.4
	69	§25.8
	87–88	§27.7
22 Ḥajj	6	§96.1
	7	§95.1
	18	§104.2
23 Mu'minūn	14	§67.2
	53	§67.5
24 Nūr	21	§98.1
	25	§99.1, §101.1
	35	§59.3, §100.1
	39	§99.2
	40	§106.2
25 Furqān	2	§102.1
	26	§5.3
	70	§25.5
26 Shu'arā'	80	§103.1
27 Naml	40	§104.1
	78	§62.1
28 Qaṣaṣ	77	§105.1
29 'Ankabūt	20	§28.1
30 Rūm	27	§106.1, §107.1
	30	§11.3
	40	§25.9*
32 Sajdah	4	§14.1
33 Aḥzāb	4	§8.8, §18.7, §43.10, §50.10*, §144.1
	23	§129.1
	33	§108.1
34 Saba'	3	§51.1
	7	§5.8*
	26	§109.1
	48	§110.1
35 Fāṭir	30	§111.1
	41	§9.7
36 Yā Sīn	4	§11.6
	38	§86.3
39 Zumar	3	§46.2
	53	§25.1
	68	§93.6
40 Ghāfir	3	§112.1, §113.1
	15	§114.1, §115.1
	16	§5.1
	20	§62.1
41 Fuṣṣilat	11–12	§87.3
	46	§29.2
42 Shūrā	11	§17.3, §17.4, §17.7, §17.8, §17.9
	40	§46.3
	47	§41.2*
	53	§2.3, §54.4
43 Zukhruf	68	§129.1
45 Jāthiyah	13	§107.1
	17	§62.1
	19	§97.2
47 Muḥammad	31	§18.3, §18.6, §18.7
48 Fatḥ	10	§73.4
49 Ḥujurāt	3	§116.1
50 Qāf	15	§34.2, §65.2
	37	§5.5, §11.9
51 Dhāriyāt	22	§32.9, §63.3
	58	§117.1, §118.1
52 Ṭūr	28	§119.1
	43	§82.4
53 Najm	3–4	§86.4
	8	§36.3
	32	§98.1
	48	§120.1
55 Raḥmān	15	§12.15
	27	§121.1, §122.1

Index of Arabic Poetry

Section	Poet	Lines	Meter	Rhyme
§8.7	al-Tilimsānī	3	*basīṭ*	ظُهُورَاتِهِ
§11.7	attributed to Abū Madyan	1	*mukhalla' al-basīṭ*	وَاقِفْ
§11.8	Ibn al-ʿArabī	1	*makhbūn al-basīṭ*	ٱلْمُكَلَّفُ
§12.1	Ibn al-ʿArabī	1	*kamāl*	ٱعْتَقَدُوهُ
§12.2	al-Tilimsānī	2	*rajaz*	أَصَابَا
§14.10	unidentified	1	*kamāl*	مَكَامِنِهِ
§16.1	unidentified	2	*sarīʿ*	عَالَمِ
§17.8	unidentified	1	*basīṭ*	عَدَدِ
§17.8	unidentified	1	*basīṭ*	عَدَدِ
§19.1	ʿAmr ibn Maʿdīkarib	1	*wāfir*	هُجُوعُ
§19.5	Ibn al-ʿArabī	1	*wāfir*	ٱلْوُجُودِ
§23.5	al-Tilimsānī	3	*mutaqārib*	غَيْرِهِ
§25.4	al-Mutanabbī	1	*wāfir*	ٱلتَّمَامِ
§26.2	Ibn al-Fāriḍ	1	*ṭawīl*	صُورَتِي
§26.5	al-Tilimsānī	1	*khafīf*	يَفْنَى
§27.3	al-Mutanabbī	1	*ṭawīl*	ٱلصَّدَى
§27.3	unidentified	1	*kamāl*	ٱلْأَمْرُ
§27.3	attributed to al-Ṣāḥib ibn ʿAbbād	1	*basīṭ*	خَمْرُ
§28.3	al-Mutanabbī	1	*wāfir*	ٱلسَّقِيمِ
§30.2	al-Tilimsānī	1	*ṭawīl*	عُيُونِي
§33.3	Ibn al-ʿArabī	1	*wāfir*	ٱلْوُجُودِ
§33.6	al-Tilimsānī	11	*basīṭ*	فِيهِ
§34.7	attributed to Shihāb al-Dīn al-Suhrawardī	1	*ramal*	فَشَيْئًا
§35.3	al-Tilimsānī	4	*basīṭ*	إِطْرَاقَا
§35.4	al-Tilimsānī	3	*kamāl*	وَاطَرَبَا
§37.1	attributed to al-Shāfiʿī	1	*ṭawīl*	تَغَانِيَا
§41.6	attributed to al-Basṭāmī	2	*wāfir*	لِلْعِقَابِ
§42.2	unidentified	1	*ṭawīl*	مُخَالِفُ

Section	Poet	Lines	Meter	Rhyme
§45.7	attributed to al-Ḥasan ibn Muḥammad al-Ṣabbāḥ al-Zaʿfarānī	1	*ṭawīl*	بِٱلذُّلِّ
§45.9	al-Tilimsānī	2	*ṭawīl*	بِٱسْمِي
§54.5	Ibn al-ʿArabī	1	*mutaqārib*	ٱلرَّسُولِ
§56.5	Ibn al-ʿArabī	1	*wāfir*	ٱلْوُجُودِ
§56.5	al-Tilimsānī	3	*basīṭ*	ظُهُورَاتِهِ
§59.4	Ibn al-ʿArabī	2	*muḍāriʿ*	أَرَاهُ
§67.3	al-Tilimsānī	2	unidentified	ٱلْمُخْتَلِفُ
§67.5	al-Tilimsānī	3	*basīṭ*	فِرَقُ
§69.7	attributed to al-Basṭāmī	1	*wāfir*	لِلْعِقَابِ
§70.6	Abū Nuwās	1	*wāfir*	ذَاكَا
§73.3	attributed to al-Ḥakīm al-Tirmidhī	5	*sarīʿ*	لِأَبْنَائِهِ
§73.4	unidentified	4	*sarīʿ*	بَعْضِهِ
§75.1	ʿAmr ibn Maʿdīkarib	1	*wāfir*	ٱلسَّمِيعِ
§75.5	attributed to al-Basṭāmī	2	*wāfir*	لِلْعِقَابِ
§82.3	al-Tilimsānī	2	*ṭawīl*	مُقَيَّدُ
§82.6	al-Tilimsānī	2	*mutaqārib*	غَيْرِهِ
§90.5	Ibn al-ʿArabī	1	*wāfir*	ٱلْوُجُودِ
§92.5	Abū Nuwās	2	*ṭawīl*	يَـرَانِي
§104.3	ʿAbd al-Qādir al-Jīlānī	1	*kamāl*	أَتَـرَقَّبُ
§118.2	unidentified	1	*ṭawīl*	بَاشِعُ

Index of the Names

the Creator (*al-Khāliq*) (cont.), §135.1, §140.1
the Death-Giver (*al-Mumīt*), §1.7, §13.9, §35.5, §41.2, §48.8, §§49.1–7, §52.2, §63.2, §70.3, §93.5, 533n305
the Deliverer (*al-Mughīth*), §1.8, §§68.1–6, §69.5
the Determiner (*al-Muqaddir*), §§102.1–4
the Encompassing (*al-Muḥīṭ*), §1.8, §§6.1–6, §7.2, §35.6, §36.3, §42.2, §42.4, §42.5, §46.7, §51.7, §52.5, §52.6, §56.5, §80.3, §130.1
the Ennobler (*al-Mukarrim*), §1.8, §§86.1–5, §104.1, §104.2
the Enricher (*al-Mughnī*), §1.8, §68.3, §§120.1–2, §143.1
the Enumerator (*al-Muḥṣī*), §140.1
the Equitable (*al-Muqsiṭ*), §§42.1–9
the Ever-Knowing (*al-ʿAllām*), §1.8, §§110.1–3
the Ever-Merciful (*al-Raḥīm*), §0.0, §1.0, §1.8, §§4.1–2, §6.4, §10.1, §22.1, §25.1, §31.2, §74.3, §119.1, §129.2
the Ever-Turning (*al-Tawwāb*), §1.8, §§10.1–7, §25.4
the Everlasting (*al-Bāqī*), §1.8, §§90.1–7, §92.7, §100.3, §124.1
the Exalter (*al-Muʿizz*), §1.8, §§44.1–9, §45.1, §45.9, §68.3, §83.3
the Faithful (*al-Muʾmin*), §§129.1–4, §130.1
the Firm (*al-Matīn*), §1.8, §§118.1–4
the First (*al-Awwal*), §5.2, §10.3, §12.4, §12.5, §12.6, §12.19, §14.9, §59.4, §79.3, §96.1, §§123.1–2, §124.1, §125.1, §126.1
the Forbearing (*al-Ḥalīm*), §§29.1–5, §129.2
the Forgiver (*al-ʿAfū*), §1.7, §§58.1–5
the Form-Giver (*al-Muṣawwir*), §1.8, §56.3, §64.2, §64.3, §77.2, §77.3, §77.4, §§135.1–2
the Fulfiller (*al-Wafī*), §1.8, §§99.1–3
the Fully Active (*al-Faʿʿāl*), §1.8, §§76.1–5
the Gatherer (*al-Jāmiʿ*), §1.8, §§41.1–9, §67.5
the Giver (*al-Muʿṭī*), §1.8, §3.4, §10.3, §14.5, §24.4, §25.6, §25.8, §25.9, §31.4, §37.1, §37.2, §38.2, §38.5, §39.3, §40.1, §43.10, §83.3, §84.1, §84.4, §§91.1–6, §106.2, §117.1
the Glorious (*al-Majīd*), §1.8, §§73.1–5, 519n6
the Governing (*al-Mudabbir*), §1.8, §§79.1–5
the Gracious (*al-Mannān*), §1.8, §§84.1–6
the Grateful (*al-Shākir*), §1.8, §§57.1–6
the Great (*al-Kabīr*), §1.7, §§81.1–7, §82.1, §82.5, §82.7, §84.4
the Guarantor (*al-Kafīl*), §§85.1–4
the Guardian (*al-Walī*), §1.8, §§14.1–10, §25.9
the Guide (*al-Hādī*), §0.1, §1.8, §13.8, §13.9, §13.10, §15.2, §15.5, §18.7, §24.6, §25.2, §25.3, §25.6, §28.2, §28.3, §43.6, §46.5, §47.5, §47.6, §47.7, §47.8, §54.1, §54.2, §54.3, §54.4, §54.5, §64.2, §64.4, §§66.1–5, §67.2, §67.4, §68.4, §74.4, §79.4, §92.3
the Harmer (*al-Ḍārr*), §1.8, §10.3, §24.6, §§69.1–7, §70.2
the Healer (*al-Shāfī*), §1.8, §83.3, §§103.1–4
the Hearing (*al-Samīʿ*), §1.7, §4.2, §12.3, §§19.1–8, §104.1
the Helper (*al-Naṣīr*), §1.8, §§15.1–5, §68.1, §97.1, §97.2, §97.3

the One Who Favors (*al-Mufḍil*), §1.8, §§11.1–9
the One Who Originates (*al-Bādiʾ*), §1.8, §§65.1–5
the Only (*al-Aḥad*), §1.7, §13.10, §20.1, §20.2, §20.6, §26.4, §34.8, §130.1, §142.1, §143.1
the Opener (*al-Fattāḥ*), §1.8, §14.4, §§109.1–2
the Originator (*al-Mubdiʾ*), §1.8, §§106.1–3
the Overseer (*al-Muhaymin*), §1.8, §32.4, §51.7, §130.1
the Owner of the Kingdom (*Mālik al-Mulk*), §1.8, §37.3, §§43.1–10
the Painful in Retribution (*al-Alīm al-Akhdh*), §§75.1–6
the Patron (*al-Mawlā*), §1.8, §§97.1–6
the Peace (*al-Salām*), §§128.1–2, §129.1
the Possessor of Majesty (*Dhū l-Jalāl*), §1.7, §1.8, §§121.1–2, §122.1
the Possessor of the Throne (*Dhū l-ʿArsh*), §1.7, §§115.1–3
the Potent (*al-Muqtadir*), §1.8, §§87.1–5
the Powerful (*al-Qadīr*), §1.8, §3.5, §4.2, §§7.1–9, §8.2, §8.8, §9.3, §12.5, §12.9, §12.14, §12.17, §12.18, §14.9, §18.4, §19.1, §31.3, §31.4, §32.2, §52.1, §52.3, §52.5, §52.11, §55.1, §71.1, §114.1, 522n61
the Praiseworthy (*al-Ḥamīd*), §1.8, §§38.1–5
the Preserver (*al-Ḥāfiẓ*), §55.1, §72.1, §72.2, §72.3, §§77.1–6, §83.1
the Preserving (*al-Ḥafīẓ*), §1.8, §§72.1–5, §77.1
the Protector (*al-Wāqī*), §1.7, §1.8, §69.5, §75.3, §§83.1–6, §85.1, §129.2
the Proud (*al-Mutakabbir*), §1.7, §25.9, §36.2, §82.4, §84.4, §§132.1–2
the Provider (*al-Rāziq*), §2.4, §21.2, §52.2, §52.3, §63.3, §68.3, §69.5, §83.3, §85.1, §91.4, §122.1, §136.1, 534n309
the Pure (*al-Ṭāhir*), §1.8, §§108.1–2
the Purifier (*al-Muzakkī*), §1.8, §§98.1–2, §108.1
the Real (*al-Ḥaqq*), §1.8, §1.10, §2.4, §8.4, §11.2, §11.4, §11.6, §11.7, §12.2, §12.6, §12.8, §12.9, §12.19, §13.9, §14.2, §14.5, §14.6, §14.9, §15.5, §16.3, §17.10, §18.2, §19.5, §20.9, §23.2, §24.4, §25.3, §25.10, §26.1, §26.2, §26.3, §27.4, §27.5, §27.7, §29.2, §29.5, §30.1, §34.2, §34.3, §34.4, §34.5, §34.6, §34.7, §34.9, §41.5, §41.9, §42.2, §43.8, §46.2, §46.3, §47.4, §50.2, §50.5, §50.7, §50.10, §51.4, §51.5, §51.6, §51.9, §54.3, §56.5, §57.4, §58.2, §61.4, §62.3, §62.4, §62.5, §65.3, §65.4, §70.3, §70.4, §72.1, §72.2, §73.1, §73.2, §73.5, §74.3, §75.2, §76.4, §79.1, §79.2, §79.4, §80.5, §84.2, §90.2, §91.4, §95.4, §§96.1–6, §97.1, §97.3, §101.2, §101.3, §102.2, §104.1, §105.1, §106.3, §112.1, §115.2, §118.1, §127.2, §130.1, §132.2
the Reckoner (*al-Ḥasīb*), §§52.1–12
the Responder (*al-Mujīb*), §1.8, §§27.1–7
the Restorer (*al-Muʿīd*), §§107.1–2
the Resurrector (*al-Bāʿith*), §1.8, §§95.1–5
the Ruler (*al-Ḥakam*), §1.8, §9.1, §9.4, §§46.1–7
the Seeing (*al-Baṣīr*), §1.8, §4.2, §§12.1–19, §82.2
the Self-Subsisting (*al-Qayyūm*), §1.8, §3.5, §6.2, §9.7, §14.1, §25.8, §33.1, §§34.1–9, §63.6, §92.5, §92.6
the Self-Sufficient (*al-Ṣamad*), §1.7, §26.4, §34.8, §37.5, §91.4, §143.1

Index

This subject index features references to sections where substantial information about certain divine names can be found. Readers who are looking for the full index of all the divine names should refer to the Index of the Names on pages 562–66.

fire: and associationism, §41.6; and the Concealing, §§25.8–9; and the Death-Giver, §49.3; and elemental mixtures, §§12.14–16; and the Form-Giver, §§77.3–4; and Hyle, §12.10, §12.12; Ibn Hūd on, §52.9; and incineration of creation, §43.8; and knowledge, §8.6; and opposites, §24.6; and preservation, §72.3; and tasting, §24.3

the Fire: and bliss, §5.7, §5.9, §13.10, §§24.4–5, §25.5, §41.8, §49.3, §75.4, §105.2, 524n103; and deviance, §42.2; and the Gatherer, §§41.7–8; judges in, §62.1; and the Originator, §106.3; People of the Fire, §5.9, §13.10, §§24.4–5, §25.5, §41.8, §105.2, 521n37; saving from, §13.10, §25.8, 521n37. *See also* the Garden

firmness, §118.1, §118.3. *See also* strength

First Intellect, §12.4, §§12.5–6, §12.19, §79.3, 524n91. *See also* intellect; Supreme Pen

fixity, §47.2

food, §6.6. *See also* nourishment

Footstool, §16.1

forbearance, §§29.1–5

forbidding, §11.6

forgiveness, §§29.2–5, §§58.1–3. *See also* pardoning

forms: and the Cleaver, §59.1, §59.3, §59.5; and the Death-Giver, §§49.2–3; and determination, §§87.2–3, §89.5; and the Form-Giver, §§77.2–4, §135.1; and Hyle, §§12.7–8, §12.11; and the Inheritor, §§89.5–6; and the Life-Giver, §48.3; and nonexistence, §§33.4–5; and the Opener, §109.1; and the Potent, §§87.2–3; and the Preserver, §§77.2–5; and provision, §117.2; and the stitched mass, §93.1, §93.5, §93.6; and the Subtle, §64.3; unstitching of, §§94.2–3. *See also* creation; determination

freedom, §37.1, §97.3, §97.4, §127.1

freezing, §§12.12–13

friendship. *See* guardians and guardianship

Friends of God, §52.9, §70.5, 539n436

fruit, §10.7

fulfilment, §§99.1–2

Gabriel, 525n106

the Garden: and the Benefiter, §70.4; and the Benevolent, §105.2; and bliss, §5.7, §5.9, §13.10, §§24.4–5, §25.5, §105.2, §106.3; judges in, §62.1; and mercy, §5.9, 521n37; and the Misguider, §67.4; and sleep, 541n507; and tasting, §6.6; worshippers, fruit for, §23.2. *See also* the Fire

gender, §16.3, 527n122

genera, §§96.2–5, §124.1

gentleness, §64.4

al-Ghazālī, Abū Ḥāmid: about, xxv, xxvi; on the Abaser, §45.1; on the All-Concealing, §92.1; on the All-Dominating, §131.1; on the All-Embracing, §16.1; on the All-Provider, §117.1; on the All-Subjugating, §80.1; on the Avenger, §39.1; on the Aware, §30.1; on the Benefiter, §70.1; on the Bestower, §40.1; on the Clement, §119.1; on the Concealing, §25.1; on the Creator, §133.1; on the Death-Giver, §49.1; on the Deliverer, §68.1; on the Encompassing, §6.1; on the Enricher, §120.1;

movement and motion: and actions/abstentions, §23.3; of the All-Merciful, §§2.2–3; and the Equitable, §42.4, §42.9; and exaltedness, §44.3, §44.6; and existence, §15.5, §42.8; health and illness, §103.3; of plants, §12.16; rotation, §§87.3–4, §90.2; of spheres, §57.2, §§87.3–4, §90.2, §94.3, §103.3, §117.2; as (un)stitching, §94.3
Muḥammad (Prophet): on accountability, §62.4; on actions, §61.5; allegiance, swearing of, 538n420; and angels, §60.4, §72.1; ascension of, §138.1, 544n583; on the Bountiful, §13.1; and chastisement, §28.3; on elevation, §78.2; on the Encompassing, §6.1; on firmness, §118.3; on forgiveness, §95.2; generations following, §14.7; glory of, §73.2, §73.4; on help, §15.4, §54.2; and Jews, §86.4; on judges, §62.1; on mercy, §1.6, §60.2; and the Near, §26.1; in prayer, concluding, §144.1; in prayer, opening, §0.1; and the Protector, §83.4; on the Real, §96.1; on right to speak, §43.7, 532n268; on sleep, 541n507; on tenderness, §88.4; three levels of religion, 525n106; translating, xxxv; and vengeance, §32.6; on the Witness, §53.3
Muḥammad ibn Ibrāhīm, §6.1, §13.1
Muḥammad ibn Sīrīn, §6.1, §13.1
Muḥammad ibn al-Walīd, §5.1
Muḥammad ibn Yazīd, §5.1
Muḥammad ibn Yūsuf ibn Ibrāhīm al-Maghlūṭī, xxxiii
al-Muḥāsibī, §51.9
Mujāhid, §34.1
multiplication, §19.4, §20.9, §33.6, §137.1
multiplicity, §34.3, §88.3, §96.3, §135.2. *See also* unity
al-Munāwī, Zayn al-Dīn Muḥammad ʿAbd al-Raʾū, xxi
munificence, §36.5, §39.5, §50.3, §69.5, §85.2
Muqayyad ibn ʿAbd Allāh, xxxiv
Musakhanov, Orkhan, xxxiv
Musaylimah al-Kadhdhāb, §2.1
music, devotional, §23.2, §64.4, 528n154
al-Mutanabbī, Abū l-Ṭayyib, §25.4, §27.3, §28.3

al-Nābulusī, ʿAbd al-Ghanī, xxiii
al-Naḥḥās, §6.1
Named Essence. *See* Essence
names, divine: about, xxv–xxvii, xxviii–xxxi; actualization of, §2.4, 520n17, 524n103; beauty of, §1.5, §5.9, §17.6, §35.1, §57.5, §66.2, §114.2, §127.3; benefits of specific, xxviii–xxix, §50.7, §50.9; characteristics, §50.8; cosmic, §1.10, 519n11; counterparts, §§1.10–11, §7.3, §§10.3–4, §11.8, §32.1, §49.1, §49.5, §129.2; emphatic forms, §1.1, §§4.1–2, §8.1, §§10.1–2, §38.5, §58.1, §84.1, §117.1; etymology of, §1.1, §3.1, §8.1, §25.1; of existence, §§1.8–9, §3.2, §10.6, §22.1; healing powers of, xxviii, §105.3, §114.3, §127.3, §131.3; interpenetrative, §§1.5–7, §3.4, §§7.2–3, §7.8, §9.5, §12.6, §40.2; order of appearance, §0.2; of rank, §1.7, §1.9, §5.2, §11.8, §14.5, §20.5, §35.5, §45.1, §49.1, §76.2, §81.2; and recognizers, §35.5; root names, §1.1, §1.5, §12.18, §20.5, §70.2; subordination of, §13.2, §51.1, §80.3, §93.5, §117.1;

oneness: of acts, divine, §3.5, §10.2, §29.4, §58.3, §92.4, §111.1; and the Assister, §47.8; and axial saints, §14.10; and the Bestower, §2.4; and bliss, §5.4, §13.10; and the Cleaver, §§59.5–6; and the Clement, §119.2; and creation, realm of, §13.5; and Day of Judgement, §§5.3–4, §5.7, §§41.3–7, §41.9, 521n36; and the elite, §20.9; and the Encompassing, §6.3, §6.5; and the Ennobler, §86.4; and the Equitable, §42.3, §42.5; and the Ever-Turning, §10.2, §10.5; of existence, xxii–xxiii, §19.3; and forgiveness, §58.3; and the Forgiver, §58.3; and the Gatherer, §§41.3–7, §41.9; and the Harmer, §69.6; and the Hearing, §§19.2–3; and ignorance, §14.7; and the Independent, §37.3; and the Loving, §74.3; and Messengers, §45.3; and the Misguider, §67.5; and the Owner of the Kingdom, §43.8; passing away in, §14.2; and the Potent, §87.5; and the Powerful, §7.4; and pride, §36.2; and the Proud, §36.2, §132.1; of qualities, §92.6; and representatives, 527n125; and the Ruler, §46.7; and the Self-Subsisting, §34.3, §§34.6–7; and the Stitcher, §93.1, §93.6; and substrates, material, §75.2; and the Tender, §88.1, §88.3; and the Tester, §18.3; and the Thankful, §111.1; and the Transcendent, §82.5; and the Triumphant, §60.7; and union, 522n61; and witnessing, §41.5, §41.9, §93.6, §132.1. *See also* only-ness; unity

only-ness, §13.10, §20.1, §20.6, §34.8, §37.2, §46.7, §130.1, §142.1. *See also* oneness; unity

opposition, §4.1, §6.4, §7.3, §11.4, §32.3, §40.2, §§67.3–5, §76.2, §§104.1–2, 537n400. *See also* compatibility and incompatibility

ordinary believers, xxii, §3.7, §§20.8–9, §23.5, §55.4, §58.5, §88.5, §105.3, §112.2. *See also* believers

origination, §§65.2–5, §106.1, §107.1

orthography, xxxiv

other-than-God: and the Assister, §47.3, §47.8; and the Concealing, §25.9; and the Exalter, §§44.1–2; and existence, §23.5, §82.6; and the Magnificent, §36.4; and ownership, §43.4; perception of, §37.4; and the Purifier, §98.2; and recognizers, §12.3; and right and wrong, §29.5; and ritual ablution, 536n372; and self-subsistence, 537n416; and the Tender, §88.1; and wayfarers, §27.6, §47.3; witnessing of nonexistence of, §43.8. *See also* alterity; separative entities

ownership, §§43.1–6, §§43.8–9, §91.2, §91.3, §97.1. *See also* possessions

pain, §§39.4–5, §75.1, §75.3

pardoning, §25.1. *See also* forgiveness

Parmenides, §96.4

particular(s): and the Giver, §91.4; and knowledge, §8.3, §18.7; and the Loving, §74.3; and manifestation, §12.4; nobility, §86.3; and praise, §0.1; and the Seeing, §12.4, §12.19; and the universal, §8.3, §96.5

partnership, §19.5, §29.5, §41.6, §41.7, §58.2, §73.2, §82.6, §127.1

partridges, §53.2

shaykhs (cont.): *shaykh al-shuyūkh* (chief shaykh), xvii, xx; as spiritual masters, xxvii–xxviii, xxix–xxxi; and the Stitcher, §93.7; al-Tilimsānī's encounters with, xxi; and the Trustee, §50.9; and the Uplifter, §114.3; and the Watchful, §51.10. *See also* Ibn al-ʿArabī

al-Shushtarī, Abū l-Ḥasan, xxi, xxxvii n21, xxxvii n22

sight, §7.1, §8.7, §12.1, §12.4, §§12.6–7, §12.9, §12.13, §19.3, §20.6, §51.6, §§82.2–3, §125.1. *See also* perception; vision

signs, §§79.1–2, §79.4

singularity, exclusive, §34.6, §91.4, §106.2

sins, §§25.1–2, §§58.1–3, §58.5, §112.2

sleep, §23.4, §27.6, §94.3, §§95.1–2, §95.4, 541n507

souls: and the Assister, §47.7; and the Concealing, §25.3; and the Death-Giver, §49.4; and the Deliverer, §68.5; exaltedness, §45.7; and fire, §12.16; and the Guarantor, §§85.2–3; health and illness, xxviii, §103.2; inrushes, §§55.3–4; and invocations, xxxi; and the Judge, §§62.3–4; and knowledge, §12.5; and the Life-Giver, §§48.3–4, §49.4; and the Nourisher, §55.3; and the Preserving, §§72.3–4; provision of, §117.2; and reckoning, §28.4, §52.4, §52.7, §62.4; resurrecting of, §95.1; and Sufis, §23.2, §25.3; Universal Soul, §12.5, §§12.7–8, §12.11, 524n91; and the Unstitcher, §94.2; and the Watchful, §51.9; and the Withholder, §2.3

spatial distance, §89.4

speech: and actions, §61.5; and the All-Embracing, §16.3; and chastisement, §28.3; and the Deliverer, §68.4; of existence, §19.5, §33.3, §56.5, §90.5; and the Faithful, §129.3; and the Fully Active, §76.4; and the Gatherer, §41.4; and the Giver, §91.3; and gratitude, §57.2; and the Hearing, §19.1, §§19.4–8; imaginal, §14.4, 525n109; and the Innovative, §17.12; and knowledge, §110.2; and the Life-Giver, §48.4, §49.5; and the Magnificent, §36.4; and the Preserving, §72.4; and the Seeing, §12.3; and the Supreme Pen, §12.19; and the Truthful, §56.1, §56.5. *See also* language

spheres: and the All-Merciful, §2.3; and the Everlasting, §90.2, §90.5; and the Exalter, §44.3; and existence, §17.12; and the Great, §81.6; health and illness, §103.3; and the Life-Giver, §48.6; movement of, §57.2, §§87.3–4, §90.2, §94.3, §103.3, §117.2; ninth sphere, §2.3, §16.2, §93.3, 526–27n121; provision of, §52.4, §117.2

spirit, inblowing of, §48.3, §48.7, §49.1

spiritual: and the All-Merciful, §2.2; allusion, §52.7; brothers, §50.8; elite, §§20.8–10, 78.3; excellence, §§5.5–6, §14.1, §14.2, §§51.2–3, §66.2, §113.1, 525n106; experiences, 524n100; forms, §12.7; guidance, §11.6; guides, xxvii; hierarchy, 525n110, 534n308, 535n334, 539n436; homeland, §88.3; intimacy, §86.5; language, §§19.6–7, §69.5, §95.3; masters, xxvii–xxviii, §13.9, §14.4, §50.7, §69.6; and modalities, §42.7; openings, xxx, §63.6, §91.6, §100.4, §105.3, §109.2, §113.2, §119.2, §122.2, §127.3;

spiritual (cont.): path, §35.5, §43.4, 522n64; and the Powerful, §7.4; practice, §48.8; and qualities, §16.1; resolve, lack of spiritual, §47.6; speech, §68.4; states, §§19.6–7, §23.2, §38.3, §41.4, §§47.7–8, §55.3, §68.5, §72.5, §77.6; stations, xx–xxi; struggle, §61.4; and tenderness, §88.3; training, xxvii–xxxi, §78.4; travelers, xxvii, xxviii, xxxi, §10.4, §34.4, 519n4; typology, 523n77; voices, 525n109; wayfaring, §80.5. *See also* retreats, spiritual

splitting, §63.1

sponsors, §85.1

spring of divine witnessing, §35.2

stars, §103.3. *See also* spheres

station of halting. *See* halting

station of no station, §16.3, 527n122

stitching and stitched masses, §59.1, §93.1, §§93.5–6

Stone, Black, §14.10, 526n115

strength, §7.7, §58.3, §71.1, §§71.3–6, §118.1, §118.3. *See also* power

subjugation, §§80.1–3, §118.2. *See also* domination/dominance

subsistence: and the Able, §61.2; and the aeon, §1.11; after annihilation, §14.7, §20.10, §27.7, §78.4, 525n111, 534n308, 535n334; and the All-Concealing, §92.6; and the Bestower, §40.1; and the Cleaver, §59.5; and the Gracious, §84.3; and the Inheritor, §89.2, §89.6, §90.3; and journey, second, xxxi, 522n64, 523n67, 534n308, 535n334; and the Last, §124.1; and the Life-Giver, §48.5, §49.1, §49.3; and the Light, §100.3; and the Living, §33.1, §33.4, §33.7; and the Magnificent, §36.3; and the Noble, §104.3; and nurturing, §3.6; and the Originator, §106.3; of possibility, §71.3; and preparedness, §2.3; and the Preserver, §77.2, §77.4; and the Preserving, §72.4; of spherical rotations, §90.2. *See also* annihilation

subsistence, self-: and the All-Concealing, §92.5; and awareness, §§30.1–3; and the Encompassing, §6.2; and existence, §7.7, 537n416; and the Knowing, §8.7; and the Nonmanifest, §126.1; and nurturing, §3.5; and provisions, §32.1; and the Self-Subsisting, §§34.4–6, §§34.8–9; and servanthood, §91.4; and the Wise, §9.7

substrates, material: and the Cleaver, §§59.1–3; and determination, §§87.2–3; and existence, §17.2, §42.6, §75.2; and the Fully Active, §76.1; health and illness, §103.2; and the Inheritor, §§89.4–5; and letters, §86.2; and the Life-Giver, §48.3; and light, §59.3, §94.2, §96.2; and the Living, §33.4; and the Preserver, §§77.2–5; and the Subtle, §64.3; and tenderness, §88.3; unstitching of, §94.2; and the Withholder, §31.2

subtleness, §30.1

suffering, §75.1

sufficiency, §§52.1–2, §§52.3–4

sufficiency, self-, §7.9, §13.5, §17.12, §34.8

Sufism: about, xv–xvii; and the Abundant, §113.1; Akbarī tradition, xxii–xxiii, xxiv, xxvi, xxvii; in Alexandria, xxii; auditions, 528n154; and beauty, §§32.6–7, §50.3, §51.4, §66.2, 543n559;

جامعة نيويورك أبوظبي

NYU ABU DHABI

About the NYUAD Research Institute

The Library of Arabic Literature is a research center affiliated with NYU Abu Dhabi and is supported by a grant from the NYU Abu Dhabi Research Institute.

The NYU Abu Dhabi Research Institute is a world-class center of cutting-edge and innovative research, scholarship, and cultural activity. It supports centers that address questions of global significance and local relevance and allows leading faculty members from across the disciplines to carry out creative scholarship and high-level research on a range of complex issues with depth, scale, and longevity that otherwise would not be possible.

From genomics and climate science to the humanities and Arabic literature, Research Institute centers make significant contributions to scholarship, scientific understanding, and artistic creativity. Centers strengthen cross-disciplinary engagement and innovation among the faculty, build critical mass in infrastructure and research talent at NYU Abu Dhabi, and have helped make the university a magnet for outstanding faculty, scholars, students, and international collaborations.

About the Typefaces

The Arabic body text is set in DecoType Naskh, designed by Thomas Milo and Mirjam Somers, based on an analysis of five centuries of Ottoman manuscript practice. The exceptionally legible result is the first and only typeface in a style that fully implements the principles of script grammar (*qawāʿid al-khaṭṭ*).

The Arabic footnote text is set in DecoType Emiri, drawn by Mirjam Somers, based on the metal typeface in the naskh style that was cut for the 1924 Cairo edition of the Qur'an.

Both Arabic typefaces in this series are controlled by a dedicated font layout engine. ACE, the Arabic Calligraphic Engine, invented by Peter Somers, Thomas Milo, and Mirjam Somers of DecoType, first operational in 1985, pioneered the principle followed by later smart font layout technologies such as OpenType, which is used for all other typefaces in this series.

The Arabic text was set with WinSoft Tasmeem, a sophisticated user interface for DecoType ACE inside Adobe InDesign. Tasmeem was conceived and created by Thomas Milo (DecoType) and Pascal Rubini (WinSoft) in 2005.

The English text is set in Adobe Text, a new and versatile text typeface family designed by Robert Slimbach for Western (Latin, Greek, Cyrillic) typesetting. Its workhorse qualities make it perfect for a wide variety of applications, especially for longer passages of text where legibility and economy are important. Adobe Text bridges the gap between calligraphic Renaissance types of the 15th and 16th centuries and high-contrast Modern styles of the 18th century, taking many of its design cues from early post-Renaissance Baroque transitional types cut by designers such as Christoffel van Dijck, Nicolaus Kis, and William Caslon. While grounded in classical form, Adobe Text is also a statement of contemporary utilitarian design, well suited to a wide variety of print and on-screen applications.

Titles Published by the Library of Arabic Literature

For more details on individual titles, visit www.libraryofarabicliterature.org

Classical Arabic Literature: A Library of Arabic Literature Anthology
Selected and translated by Geert Jan van Gelder (2012)

A Treasury of Virtues: Sayings, Sermons, and Teachings of ʿAlī, by al-Qāḍī al-Quḍāʿī, with the **One Hundred Proverbs** attributed to al-Jāḥiẓ
Edited and translated by Tahera Qutbuddin (2013)

The Epistle on Legal Theory, by al-Shāfiʿī
Edited and translated by Joseph E. Lowry (2013)

Leg over Leg, by Aḥmad Fāris al-Shidyāq
Edited and translated by Humphrey Davies (**4 volumes; 2013–14**)

Virtues of the Imām Aḥmad ibn Ḥanbal, by Ibn al-Jawzī
Edited and translated by Michael Cooperson (**2 volumes; 2013–15**)

The Epistle of Forgiveness, by Abū l-ʿAlāʾ al-Maʿarrī
Edited and translated by Geert Jan van Gelder and Gregor Schoeler (**2 volumes; 2013–14**)

The Principles of Sufism, by ʿĀʾishah al-Bāʿūniyyah
Edited and translated by Th. Emil Homerin (2014)

The Expeditions: An Early Biography of Muḥammad, by Maʿmar ibn Rāshid
Edited and translated by Sean W. Anthony (2014)

Two Arabic Travel Books
Accounts of China and India, by Abū Zayd al-Sīrāfī
Edited and translated by Tim Mackintosh-Smith (2014)
Mission to the Volga, by Aḥmad ibn Faḍlān
Edited and translated by James Montgomery (2014)

Disagreements of the Jurists: A Manual of Islamic Legal Theory, by al-Qāḍī al-Nuʿmān
Edited and translated by Devin J. Stewart (2015)

Consorts of the Caliphs: Women and the Court of Baghdad, by Ibn al-Sāʿī
Edited by Shawkat M. Toorawa and translated by the Editors of the Library of Arabic Literature (2015)

What ʿĪsā ibn Hishām Told Us, by Muḥammad al-Muwayliḥī
Edited and translated by Roger Allen (2 volumes; 2015)

The Life and Times of Abū Tammām, by Abū Bakr Muḥammad ibn Yaḥyā al-Ṣūlī
Edited and translated by Beatrice Gruendler (2015)

The Sword of Ambition: Bureaucratic Rivalry in Medieval Egypt, by ʿUthmān ibn Ibrāhīm al-Nābulusī
Edited and translated by Luke Yarbrough (2016)

Brains Confounded by the Ode of Abū Shādūf Expounded, by Yūsuf al-Shirbīnī
Edited and translated by Humphrey Davies (2 volumes; 2016)

Light in the Heavens: Sayings of the Prophet Muḥammad, by al-Qāḍī al-Quḍāʿī
Edited and translated by Tahera Qutbuddin (2016)

Risible Rhymes, by Muḥammad ibn Maḥfūẓ al-Sanhūrī
Edited and translated by Humphrey Davies (2016)

A Hundred and One Nights
Edited and translated by Bruce Fudge (2016)

The Excellence of the Arabs, by Ibn Qutaybah
Edited by James E. Montgomery and Peter Webb
Translated by Sarah Bowen Savant and Peter Webb (2017)

Scents and Flavors: A Syrian Cookbook
Edited and translated by Charles Perry (2017)

Arabian Satire: Poetry from 18th-Century Najd, by Ḥmēdān al-Shwēʿir
Edited and translated by Marcel Kurpershoek (2017)

In Darfur: An Account of the Sultanate and Its People, by Muḥammad ibn ʿUmar al-Tūnisī
Edited and translated by Humphrey Davies (2 volumes; 2018)

War Songs, by ʿAntarah ibn Shaddād
Edited by James E. Montgomery
Translated by James E. Montgomery with Richard Sieburth (2018)

Arabian Romantic: Poems on Bedouin Life and Love, by ʿAbdallāh ibn Sbayyil
Edited and translated by Marcel Kurpershoek (2018)

Dīwān ʿAntarah ibn Shaddād: A Literary-Historical Study
By James E. Montgomery (2018)

Stories of Piety and Prayer: Deliverance Follows Adversity, by al-Muḥassin ibn ʿAlī al-Tanūkhī
Edited and translated by Julia Bray (2019)

The Philosopher Responds: An Intellectual Correspondence from the Tenth Century, by Abū Ḥayyān al-Tawḥīdī and Abū ʿAlī Miskawayh
Edited by Bilal Orfali and Maurice A. Pomerantz
Translated by Sophia Vasalou and James E. Montgomery (2 volumes; 2019)

Tajrīd sayf al-himmah li-stikhrāj mā fī dhimmat al-dhimmah: A Scholarly Edition of ʿUthmān ibn Ibrāhīm al-Nābulusī's Text
By Luke Yarbrough (2020)

The Discourses: Reflections on History, Sufism, Theology, and Literature—Volume One, by al-Ḥasan al-Yūsī
Edited and translated by Justin Stearns (2020)

Impostures, by al-Ḥarīrī
Translated by Michael Cooperson (2020)

Maqāmāt Abī Zayd al-Sarūjī, by al-Ḥarīrī
Edited by Michael Cooperson (2020)

The Yoga Sutras of Patañjali, by Abū Rayḥān al-Bīrūnī
Edited and translated by Mario Kozah (2020)

The Book of Charlatans, by Jamāl al-Dīn ʿAbd al-Raḥīm al-Jawbarī
Edited by Manuela Dengler
Translated by Humphrey Davies (2020)

A Physician on the Nile: A Description of Egypt and Journal of the Famine Years, by ʿAbd al-Laṭīf al-Baghdādī
Edited and translated by Tim Mackintosh-Smith **(2021)**

The Book of Travels, by Ḥannā Diyāb
Edited by Johannes Stephan
Translated by Elias Muhanna **(2 volumes; 2021)**

Kalīlah and Dimnah: Fables of Virtue and Vice, by Ibn al-Muqaffaʿ
Edited by Michael Fishbein
Translated by Michael Fishbein and James E. Montgomery **(2021)**

Love, Death, Fame: Poetry and Lore from the Emirati Oral Tradition, by al-Māyidī ibn Ẓāhir
Edited and translated by Marcel Kurpershoek **(2022)**

The Essence of Reality: A Defense of Philosophical Sufism, by ʿAyn al-Quḍāt
Edited and translated by Mohammed Rustom **(2022)**

The Requirements of the Sufi Path: A Defense of the Mystical Tradition, by Ibn Khaldūn
Edited and translated by Carolyn Baugh **(2022)**

The Doctors' Dinner Party, by Ibn Buṭlān
Edited and translated by Philip F. Kennedy and Jeremy Farrell **(2023)**

Fate the Hunter: Early Arabic Hunting Poems
Edited and translated by James E. Montgomery **(2023)**

The Book of Monasteries, by al-Shābushtī
Edited and translated by Hilary Kilpatrick **(2023)**

In Deadly Embrace: Arabic Hunting Poems, by Ibn al-Muʿtazz
Edited and translated by James E. Montgomery **(2023)**

The Divine Names: A Mystical Theology of the Names of God in the Qur'an, by ʿAfīf al-Dīn al-Tilimsānī
Edited and translated by Yousef Casewit **(2023)**

English-only Paperbacks

Leg over Leg, by Aḥmad Fāris al-Shidyāq (**2 volumes; 2015**)
The Expeditions: An Early Biography of Muḥammad, by Maʿmar ibn Rāshid (2015)
The Epistle on Legal Theory: A Translation of al-Shāfiʿī's *Risālah*, by al-Shāfiʿī (2015)
The Epistle of Forgiveness, by Abū l-ʿAlāʾ al-Maʿarrī (2016)
The Principles of Sufism, by ʿĀʾishah al-Bāʿūniyyah (2016)
A Treasury of Virtues: Sayings, Sermons, and Teachings of ʿAlī, by al-Qāḍī al-Quḍāʿī, with the **One Hundred Proverbs** attributed to al-Jāḥiẓ (2016)
The Life of Ibn Ḥanbal, by Ibn al-Jawzī (2016)
Mission to the Volga, by Ibn Faḍlān (2017)
Accounts of China and India, by Abū Zayd al-Sīrāfī (2017)
A Hundred and One Nights (2017)
Consorts of the Caliphs: Women and the Court of Baghdad, by Ibn al-Sāʿī (2017)
Disagreements of the Jurists: A Manual of Islamic Legal Theory, by al-Qāḍī al-Nuʿmān (2017)
What ʿĪsā ibn Hishām Told Us, by Muḥammad al-Muwayliḥī (2018)
War Songs, by ʿAntarah ibn Shaddād (2018)
The Life and Times of Abū Tammām, by Abū Bakr Muḥammad ibn Yaḥyā al-Ṣūlī (2018)
The Sword of Ambition, by ʿUthmān ibn Ibrāhīm al-Nābulusī (2019)
Brains Confounded by the Ode of Abū Shādūf Expounded: Volume One, by Yūsuf al-Shirbīnī (2019)
Brains Confounded by the Ode of Abū Shādūf Expounded: Volume Two, by Yūsuf al-Shirbīnī and **Risible Rhymes**, by Muḥammad ibn Maḥfūẓ al-Sanhūrī (2019)
The Excellence of the Arabs, by Ibn Qutaybah (2019)
Light in the Heavens: Sayings of the Prophet Muḥammad, by al-Qāḍī al-Quḍāʿī (2019)
Scents and Flavors: A Syrian Cookbook (2020)
Arabian Satire: Poetry from 18th-Century Najd, by Ḥmēdān al-Shwēʿir (2020)
In Darfur: An Account of the Sultanate and Its People, by Muḥammad al-Tūnisī (2020)

Arabian Romantic: Poems on Bedouin Life and Love, by ʿAbdallāh ibn Sbayyil (2020)

The Philosopher Responds, by Abū Ḥayyān al-Tawḥīdī and Abū ʿAlī Miskawayh (2021)

Impostures, by al-Ḥarīrī (2021)

The Discourses: Reflections on History, Sufism, Theology, and Literature—Volume One, by al-Ḥasan al-Yūsī (2021)

The Book of Charlatans, by Jamāl al-Dīn ʿAbd al-Raḥīm al-Jawbarī (2022)

The Yoga Sutras of Patañjali, by Abū Rayḥān al-Bīrūnī (2022)

The Book of Travels, by Ḥannā Diyāb (2022)

A Physician on the Nile: A Description of Egypt and Journal of the Famine Years, by ʿAbd al-Laṭīf al-Baghdādī (2022)

Kalīlah and Dimnah: Fables of Virtue and Vice, by Ibn al-Muqaffaʿ (2023)

Love, Death, Fame: Poetry and Lore from the Emirati Oral Tradition, by al-Māyidī ibn Ẓāhir (2023)

The Essence of Reality: A Defense of Philosophical Sufism, by ʿAyn al-Quḍāt (2023)

About the Editor–Translator

Yousef Casewit is Associate Professor and Chair of Islamic Studies at the University of Chicago Divinity School, where he specializes in Qur'anic Studies, Islamic intellectual history, Muslim perceptions of the Bible, Sufism, and Islamic theology. He had previously served as a Humanities Research Fellow at New York University Abu Dhabi, where he completed his award-winning book, *The Mystics of al-Andalus* (2017). Born in Egypt and raised in Morocco, Professor Casewit obtained a PhD in Islamic Studies at Yale in 2014, and has also spent many years studying with Muslim scholars in Morocco, Syria, and Mauritania.

www.ingramcontent.com/pod-product-compliance
Ingram Content Group UK Ltd.
Pitfield, Milton Keynes, MK11 3LW, UK
UKHW031331260525
458860UK00016B/106/J

9 781479 826124